From the
BIBLE to SHAKESPEARE

PANTELEJMON KULIŠ (1819–1897) AND
THE FORMATION OF LITERARY UKRAINIAN

Ukrainian Studies

Series Editor
Vitaly Chernetsky (University of Kansas)

From the
BIBLE to SHAKESPEARE

PANTELEJMON KULIŠ (1819–1897) AND THE FORMATION OF LITERARY UKRAINIAN

ANDRII DANYLENKO

Boston
2016

This publication was made possible by the financial support of Pace University and the Shevchenko Scientific Society, USA, from the John and Elisabeth Chlopecky Fund.

Library of Congress Cataloging-in-Publication Data:
A bibliographic record for this title is available
from the Library of Congress.

Copyright © 2016 Academic Studies Press
All rights reserved.
ISBN 978-1-64469-135-9
ISBN 978-1-61811-471-6 (electronic)

Cover design by Ivan Grave
Book design by Kryon Publishing
www.kryonpublishing.com

Published by Academic Studies Press in 2016
28 Montfern Avenue
Brighton, MA 02135, USA
press@academicstudiespress.com
www.academicstudiespress.com

*In Memory of My Parents,
Ivan and Svitlana Danylenko*

Contents

Acknowledgements... viii
Abbreviations.. x
Introduction: Writing a Linguistic Biography of a Ukrainian Maverick.....xi

PART I THE BIBLE... 1

CHAPTER 1 Exploring Psalmody 3
          The Book of Psalms 3
          Alexandrine Verse or Trochaic Foot? 6
          Invoking Gavrila Deržavin 13
          Church Slavonicisms 19
          "Kulišisms".. 21
          Xarkiv Chimes In 27
          The 1897 Poetic Crowning.............................. 32

CHAPTER 2 The Makings of the Rusian Bible 37
          A *Pentatevx* Prolusion................................. 37
          Gearing Up for New Challenges......................... 38
          "Poison and Ruin for the Rusian People"................ 41
          "The Labor Pangs of a Unified Ukrainian Literary Language" .. 43
          Reception of the Translation........................... 53
          The Sloboda Bulwark 60
          The Archangel *Havrylo*................................ 65
          Who Else Bears a Grudge?.............................. 90
          The Creation of the New Biblical Style 95
          Means of Archaization 96
          Means of Vernacularization 102

CHAPTER 3 Galicia "Writes Back"................................... 109
          The West or the East?................................. 109
          Fostering the "Rusian Church Vernacular"............... 124
          Any Palliative Solution? 131
          Lost in Diacritics 139
          To "Secularize" or "Synthesize"?....................... 151

CHAPTER 4 Here Comes the Bible!................................... 153
          The Holy Writ Doesn't Burn 153
          Tobit and Job... 156

	At the Crossroads of Poetry and Prose	172
	Ivan Nečuj-Levyc′kyj Takes It Personally	176
	The Pranks of Ivan Franko	193
	Ivan Puljuj Makes His Riposte	196
	How Should It Sound?	202
	How to String Words?	208
	How to Choose Words?	214
	How to Spell Words?	221
	Ivan Nečuj-Levyc′kyj Is Shuffled Backstage	242
	Interpreting Hebrew Poetry	249
	The Book of Job	253
	Lamentations	261
	The Song of Songs	265
	The Versified Bible	270

Summary ... 275

PART II SHAKESPEARE ... 280

CHAPTER 5 "Oh, Shakespeare, Our Father, Native to All Peoples" ... 281
    Ethics *Avant la Lettre*! ... 281
    Bringing Forth the "Ukrainian Shakespeare" ... 289
    The First (Over) Reaction ... 293
    Kuliš's translation ... 299
    The Language of the "Ukrainian Shakespeare" ... 300
    On the Threshold of a New Secular High Style ... 311

CHAPTER 6 Expanding the Literary Canon of the "Ukrainian Shakespeare" ... 315
    The First Step Is the Hardest? ... 315
    "*Huculia* Did Not Appear; Rather Shakespeare Was Merely Hidden" ... 320
    Hamlet or *Hamljet*? That Is the Question ... 331
    Hamlet in Peasant Leather Shoes ... 337
    The Younger Generation Steps to the Fore ... 354
    "We Are All Peasants Today" ... 359
    One or Multiple Homesteads? ... 367

Conclusion: Detours Offered But Never Taken ... 374
Bibliography ... 386
Indices ... 427
    Geographical and Personal Names ... 427
    Subjects, Names of Periodicals, Titles of Literary Works and Translations ... 431
    Word-Forms ... 438

Acknowledgements

The idea of writing this book came to me while I was embarking on a major project to write a history of modern literary Ukrainian during a stay at Harvard University in the spring of 2008. It became clear that the personality and literary work of Pantelejmon Kuliš (1819–1897) could hardly fit into a single chapter. But to write such a history without giving special credit to Kuliš, one of the founders and long-time leaders of the national movement in both Russian- and Austrian-ruled Ukraine in the nineteenth century, would be unrealistic.

As I amassed material about Kuliš and his language, it became apparent how little we know about him as a normalizer and a synthesizer of different traditions and styles in literary Ukrainian. My research persuaded me that his role in the formation of a new literary language seems to surpass in some ways that of Taras Ševčenko (1814–1861), another towering figure in the cultural landscape of Ukraine in the nineteenth century, and a man commonly viewed as the founder of modern literary Ukrainian. While Kuliš's contribution to the development of literary Ukrainian was no less significant—particularly in the diversification of stylistic devices—his vision of literary Ukrainian proved even more grandiose.

My work on this project was particularly rewarding while visiting different places in Ukraine and beyond. Working at the libraries of Harvard and Cambridge (UK) Universities, the V. I. Vernads′kyj National Library of Ukraine, and the Černihiv State Literary-Memorial Museum of Myxajlo Kocjubyns′kyj (Ukraine), where the bulk of Kuliš's protographs are preserved, was more pleasure than business.

I would like to extend my gratitude to the staff of the Bible Society's Library housed at the Cambridge University Library for assistance in this research and kind permission to obtain copies of the following publications: *Jevanhèlije Lukỳ* (Lviv, 1874) (*Luka-U*), *Evanhèlïe Luki* (Lviv, 1874) (*Luka-L*), and *Pys′mo Svęte. Jevanhelije Ioana* (Lviv, 1881), call numbers BSS 257 E74, BSS 257 E74.2, and BSS 257 E81 respectively. A special note of thanks is due to the Harvard Ukrainian Research Institute for honoring me, in 2008, with a Eugene and Daymel Shklar Research Fellowship in Ukrainian Studies that allowed me to concentrate on this project during the spring semester. Research on this project would not be possible without the collegial and professional support of many people with whom I have met over the last eight years. I am particularly grateful to Pavlo Hrycenko, director of the Institute of Ukrainian Language, who shared with me his expertise and helped me gain access to many rare manuscripts and protographs of Kuliš; Ksenya Kiebuzinski, head of the Petro Jacyk Central and East European Resource Centre and coordinator of Slavic Resources at the University of Toronto Libraries, who offered advice on locating some hard-to-find publications in North America; Olha Aleksic, Petro Jacyk archivist and bibliographer at the Harvard Ukrainian Research Institute; and Oleh Kupčyns´kyj, the former president of the Ševčenko Scientific Society in Lviv. Research on this book was also generously supported by grants from the Dyson College at Pace University in 2009, 2011, and 2015.

Finally, I am indebted to many colleagues who made this book possible, including Jan Fellerer (Oxford University), Michael S. Flier (Harvard University), Ljudmyla Hnatenko (V. I. Vernads´kyj National Library of Ukraine), Vasyl´ Nimčuk (Institute of Ukrainian Language of the National Academy of Sciences of Ukraine), Leonid Uškalov and Serhii Vakulenko (Kharkiv Pedagogical University), and Eleonora Solovej (T. H. Ševčenko Institute of Ukrainian Literature of the National Academy of Sciences of Ukraine).

My special thanks go to Meghan Vicks and Eddie McCaffray for their help with the editing of the manuscript.

However, without the support and understanding of my wife, Iryna, this project could never have come to life.

Abbreviations

Languages and Dialects		Grammatical Terms	
Bojk.	Bojkian	acc.	accusative
ChSl.	Church Slavonic	coll.	collective
ESl.	East Slavic	dat.	dative
EUkr.	East Ukrainian	derog.	derogative
Fr.	French	dim.	diminutive
Gk.	Greek	du.	dual
Gr.	German	f.	feminine
Huc.	Hucul	fut.	future
It.	Italian	gen.	genitive
Lat.	Latin	imper.	imperative
Latv.	Latvian	infml.	informal
Lemk.	Lemkian	instr.	instrumental
Lith.	Lithuanian	loc.	locative
MHGr.	Middle High German	m.	masculine
MoUkr.	Modern Ukrainian	n.	neuter
MUkr.	Middle Ukrainian	nom.	nominative
NUkr.	North Ukrainian	pl.	plural
OChSl.	Old Church Slavonic	PrAP.	present active participle
ORu.	Old Rusian		
ORum.	Old Rumanian	pres.	present
Pol.	Polish	pret.	preterit
RChSl.	Russian Church Slavonic	sg.	singular
Rum.	Rumanian	voc.	vocative
Rus.	Russian		
SWUkr.	Southwest Ukrainian	1	first person
Transc.	Transcarpathian	2	second person
Ukr.	Ukrainian	3	third person
WUkr.	West Ukrainian		

Introduction

Writing a Linguistic Biography of a Ukrainian Maverick

Pantelejmon Kuliš (1819–1897), a true Ukrainian maverick, is arguably one of the most controversial figures in the national revival of Ukraine. He is also a crucial early figure in the development of the modern understanding of Ukrainian literature and language. A prominent writer, historian, ethnographer, and translator, Kuliš came from an ancient, though impoverished, Cossack family in the Černihiv province in Russian-ruled (Dnieper) Ukraine. Certainly, the Cossack stereotype of an independent spirit with a large dose of stubbornness and a somewhat temperamental vitality could be applied to his personality (Luckyj 1983, 1). His emphasis on the development of a separate Ukrainian high culture, including a full-fledged literary language and a truly national literature, along with his support for the idea of political union with Russia, was heavily criticized by Ukrainian populists. Although his first historical novel, *Mixail Čarnyšenko, ili Malorossija vosem'desjat let nazad* (Mixail Čarnyšenko, or Little Russia Eighty Years Ago, 1843), was written in Russian, Kuliš became the first professional Ukrainian writer and journalist, as well as an innovative normalizer of written Ukrainian. Remaining a leading figure in the national Ukrainian movement, Kuliš debunked the myth of the Cossack past of Ukraine, expressed admiration for the Russian tsar Peter I and tsarina Catherine II, and made some humiliating remarks about the national bard and prophet Taras Ševčenko in his three-volume historiographic work, entitled *Istorija vossoedinenija Rusi* (The History of the Reunification of Rus´, 1874–1877).

In the years 1864–1867, Kuliš served in the Russian governmental office of spiritual affairs in Warsaw, where he blamed Polish nationalism for having caused the uprising of 1863–1864 that sought social reforms and independence for Poland. Yet as early as 1882 he authored a reconciliatory pamphlet appealing to Ukrainian-Polish understanding, *Krašanka rusynam i poljakam na Velykden' 1882 roku* (An Easter Egg for the Rusyns and the Poles for Easter 1882), that appeared in Lviv. In the same year, Kuliš even submitted his renunciation of Russian citizenship in order to remain in Austria-Hungary and found a printing house; however, government policies there changed his mind and he withdrew his renunciation. As a result, in April 1891, the writer was issued a new certificate of Russian citizenship, though only after he took an oath of allegiance (Luckyj 1983, 179; Naxlik 2007, 1:372).

Disillusioned with the populist movement in Austria-Hungary, Kuliš returned in 1882 to Russian-ruled Ukraine, where he lost no time in severing his relationships with organized Ukrainian community life. No Ukrainian intellectuals of Kuliš's time turned to Islam for answers to Ukrainian problems. An idealist Christian, he was the first modern Ukrainian poet to write several major poetic works on Islamic themes, for instance, "Mahomet i Xadyza" (Muhammad and Khadijah, 1883). Having settled on his farmstead (*xutir*) Motronivka, Kuliš worked on translations of the Bible and the works of William Shakespeare, George Gordon Byron, Wolfgang Johann von Goethe, and other European authors until his death in 1897. Even after his death, he remained an important force for national cultural awakening, demonstrating his unflagging devotion to his people who, in the end, recognized his unique legacy in literature and language.

There are two seminal dates—1983 and 2007—in the modern study of Kuliš's creative life and literary output. In 1983, George Luckyj published a pioneering book about the life and times of Kuliš. This English-language monograph was the first one to appear outside Ukraine, where, from the early 1930s onward, Kuliš had been perceived as inconsistent in action and a true egotist who came to reject some basic assumptions of the very Ukrainian movement he helped to found (Luckyj 1983, vii). This life of Kuliš, as Luckyj admitted, was incomplete, since it was retold in its principle phases without the detail to be expected in a full biography. In fact, the author could hardly produce a voluminous work because access to most of the archival material necessary for a study of such a caliber was proscribed at that time. Despite this major hindrance, the aforementioned book proved exemplary in many aspects. Its author managed not only to outline major events in the life and times of Kuliš but also to put him in the wider context of Ukrainian intellectual history and of the dilemmas of national culture found throughout the world. Read at its final stage by Ralph Lindheim and George Y. Shevelov, Luckyj's book has, until recently, remained the only serious study of Kuliš and his role in the Ukrainian national revival available in the West.

In 2007, a two-volume study of the personal and creative life of Kuliš appeared in Ukraine. Its author, Jevhen Naxlik, offered a sweeping view of Kuliš as a national awakener, writer, and thinker whose contribution to the formation of a new nation and its culture, in the form of literature, language, philosophy, and historiography, was meticulously recorded and projected onto the Ukrainian cultural and literary landscape. In all respects, Naxlik's study will remain the most exhaustive for many years to come, likely until serious incursions are made into Kuliš's literary works and language. Luckily, in many ways, Naxlik traced possible vectors for future research and outlined new vistas for both Ukrainian literature and language, progressively revealing their national past and future through the lens of Kuliš's literary output.

The aforementioned monographs of 1983 and 2007 will, no doubt, serve as beacons in the study of Kuliš and his voluminous output, including his language, largely neglected after Hordyns´kyj's (1928) analysis of his translations of Shakespeare. In recent years, however, Kuliš's personality and his oeuvre have begun to receive increased interest from literary scholars, bibliographers, and historians (Grabowicz 1981, 1992; Fedoruk 1998, 2000a, 2000b, 2000c, 2004; Zelens´ka 2000; Hončaruk 2006), although his language program has faded into oblivion. As a rare exception, one should mention, however, an insightful—though brief—analysis of Kuliš's incorporation of Galician elements into his language standard offered by George Y. Shevelov in 1966 (Shevelov 1966, 37–77; Ševel´ov 1996, 24–67). Apart from Shevelov, a mere handful of twentieth-century scholars have discussed the role of Kuliš in the formation of literary Ukrainian—especially its biblical style (Ohijenko 1949, 220–221; Horbač 1988; Muromceva and Muromcev 1995; Dzjubyšyna-Mel´nyk 1998, 279).

A true breakthrough in the study of Kuliš's language happened after Ukraine had gained its independence in 1991. Viewed today as a prophetic figure in the modern Ukrainian revival and, in addition to Ševčenko, a major founder of new literary Ukrainian, his language has become a focus of scholarly interest. With rare exceptions (e.g., Matvijas 2008), however, most of the recent publications demonstrate a fragmentary approach toward Kuliš's language and offer, instead, somewhat sketchy appraisals of his literary output and linguistic idiosyncrasies. Deserving of attention, nevertheless, are a number of recent studies examining the writer's language and its stylistic diversity in both his original works and translations (Jermolenko 2010; Solohub 2010; Dolžykova 2010; Kumeda 2010). Remarkably, all the aforementioned studies appeared in a special issue of the Ukrainian journal *Kul'tura slova* (The Culture of Word), published on the occasion of the 190th anniversary of Kuliš's birth. Of utmost interest is a probing insight into the recesses of the linguistic personality of Kuliš offered by Dolžykova (2004). In addition to poetic devices, she also analyzed dialectal features of Kuliš's language as well as the stylistic resources of its vocabulary, reserving a special place for his translations.

It should be noted that in almost all of the works investigating the language of Kuliš (Tymošyk 2000a; Dolžykova 2001; Tkač and Moroz 2003; Moroz and Tkač 2006; Danylenko 2010a; Jurkowski 2001), his translations of the Bible are consistently compared with other biblical translations into modern Ukrainian. Although a full study of Kuliš's language, premised on a comprehensive analysis of both his original works and translations in the context of the formation of literary Ukrainian in the nineteenth century, is still in the offing, some authors have already proposed some models for future research that were partly implemented in this book (e.g., Dzjubyšyna-Mel'nyk 1998). Thus, as early as 1995, following in the footsteps of Shevelov, two linguists, Muromceva and Muromcev, wrote a comprehensive article on Kuliš as an "innovator" and "creator of the Ukrainian literary language." Having criticized a hackneyed treatment of Kuliš as an extreme archaizer of the Ukrainian language, the authors emphasized the twofold nature of his normalization efforts. On the one hand, Kuliš was deeply interested in the history of Ukrainian, especially in those periods that antedated the appearance of Ivan

Kotljarevs´kyj's *Enejida* (1798), which is commonly viewed as the beginning of new literary Ukrainian, and in the works of Kotljarevs´kyj's epigones. On the other hand, Kuliš constantly experimented with Ukrainian dialectal and vernacular elements. All in all, according to Muromceva and Muromcev (1995, 13), Kuliš saw the future of Ukrainian in synthesizing the older literary tradition(s) with the vernacular-based one, whence the introduction of Church Slavonic, bookish, and loan forms into his vernacular standard.

Muromceva and Muromcev (1995, 16) came to the conclusion that Kuliš was the first to advance the "intellectualization" of literary Ukrainian through "the introduction of a large amount of abstract words and the enrichment of semantics of known words." One of his major achievements was the borrowing of numerous "Europeanisms," which elevated the overall cultural level of his native language (ibid.). That was a pioneering conclusion, especially if compared with their predecessors' ideologically biased treatment of Kuliš's language (Pljušč 1971, 331).

Viewed as a staunch innovator, Kuliš was given credit by Rusanivs´kyj (2001, 233–234) for his work on the diversification of genres and styles in the new literary standard of Ukrainian. Kuliš's main source of inspiration was arguably folklore, although he also employed Church Slavonic forms, whose number constantly increased in his literary works. Yet the creation of special devices for a new biblical style was, as Rusanivs´kyj (ibid.) pointed out, one of the biggest achievements of this writer, who cooperated with Ivan Puljuj in his translation of the Bible. Unlike in the work of Muromceva and Muromcev, who discussed the Europeanizing trend in Kuliš's language and especially in his translations, Kuliš's rendition of the Holy Scriptures was merely touched upon by Rusanivs´kyj (who nevertheless praised its quality). Yet, as Rusanivs´kyj argued (ibid.), the most significant contribution of Kuliš to the formation of literary Ukrainian was his historical novel *Čorna rada* (The Black Council, 1857), inasmuch as Kuliš succeeded in introducing lexical elements capable of creating a true historical coloring into written Ukrainian.

In contrast, a negative opinion of Kuliš's translations, including of some plays of Shakespeare, was expressed by Macjuk (1996), who placed the language of the writer in the context of the vicissitudes of literary

Ukrainian in Galicia. Unabashedly, the author argued that the phonetic, morphological, derivational, lexical, and syntactic features of Kuliš's translations vulgarized the lofty language of Shakespeare (ibid., 122). According to Macjuk, the innovations of Kuliš were prone to endow words with "negative aesthetics"; this is why neither Church Slavonicisms, nor Ukrainianized Slavonic forms together with coined forms, could enrich the nominative resources of the "Galician-Rusian language" (ibid.). Moreover, Kuliš was blamed for developing a peculiar "language doctrine" that could hardly appeal to Galician Ukrainians. A synthesis of Old Rusian with vernacular Ukrainian in Kuliš's language appeared, as Macjuk surmised, to be in dissonance with the period of "Europeanization of Ukrainian translations" in Austria-Hungary. This is why Kuliš's translations ostensibly looked obsolete the very moment they went to press (ibid., 123).

The aforementioned judgment is quite remarkable. Tentatively, being of Galician stock may have influenced Macjuk's judgment, as she was clearly at odds with the opinion formulated by the Kharkiv-based linguists Muromceva and Murovcev. Natives of Sloboda Ukraine, they extolled, for their part, the role of Kuliš in preserving the old tradition of literary Ukrainian through the re-introduction of bookish and especially Church Slavonic forms. As I argued elsewhere (Danylenko 2008b), the mix of such forms may well have been quite natural in the speech of Dnieper Ukrainians. In fact, a century ago the transition from the Meletian version of Church Slavonic (from the name of Meletij Smotryc′kyj, one of the codifiers of the language) to Russian Slavonic in these lands seemed to have taken place smoothly due to the long tradition of bilingualism: Church Slavonic (*slavenorosskij iazyk″*) and Ruthenian (*prostaja mova*). For most Little Russians (Ukrainians) in the eighteenth century, this process might have appeared as a natural stage in the development of the *slavenorosskij iazyk″*, although with a number of non-Russian elements reduced to little more than symbolic presence. The same attitude toward Church Slavonic was still observed in Dnieper Ukraine in the mid-nineteenth century. Suffice it to recall here the consistent use of Slavonic forms by Taras Ševčenko (Shevelov 1966, 43). Kuliš used them perhaps on an even greater scale, since he was prepared to view some Russian borrowings as Slavonic proper, thus belonging to the high-style stock of written Ukrainian as compared with its vernacular elements (Hnatjuk 2010). Needless to say, such a synthesis of Slavonic and vernacular elements could hardly satisfy the Galician populists in the second part of the nineteenth century, a stance uncritically transplanted by Macjuk into the linguistic paradigm maintained in today's Ukraine.

The dissonance in the appraisal of Kuliš's language by Muromceva and Muromcev, on the one hand, and Macjuk, on the other, becomes ever more pronounced in the case of his translations. The two eastern Ukrainian linguists discuss the intellectualization of the language in Kuliš's translations, while the Galician scholar considers his translations vulgar and void of any European flavor. Such conflicting views of Kuliš's language are reminiscent of those expressed in Austria-Hungary and tsarist Russia after the appearance of his translation of the Bible: in its own day, it was chastised in Galicia and highly praised in Dnieper Ukraine!

In the nineteenth century, the representatives of the two parts of Ukraine were unanimous in acknowledging the importance of translations for the formation of new literary Ukrainian and the creation of a new literary tradition capable of introducing differentiation and new vitality. According to Grabowicz (1992, 234), the period from the early 1860s to the early 1890s, taken as a whole, contained a literature that was neither fully provincial nor yet fully national, whence the use of Russian in some writings produced in Dnieper Ukraine or of German (e.g., Jurij Osyp Fed′kovyč) and Polish (e.g., Ivan Franko) in Galicia (ibid.). Kuliš believed that, for Ukrainian to become a full-fledged literary and national language, one had to make it not only variegated dialectally (the horizontal dimension) but also historically (the vertical dimension). His ambitious language program was premised on the positivist model that was perceived by the romanticists in Dnieper Ukraine and the younger generation of Galician populists as artificial and vulgar. It is not an exaggeration to say that, in this respect, Kuliš was ahead of many of his contemporaries, including Mykola Kostomarov (1817–1885), Jurij Osyp Fed′kovyč (1834–1888), Ivan Nečuj-Levyc′kyj (1838–1918), and even Ivan Franko (1856–1916), in emphasizing universal culture and literary values, the world, and attitudes of learning and Enlightenment. All this can explain Kuliš's receptiveness to literary influences and models, be they Russian or European, as well as the range of his translations from the Bible to Shakespeare, and his fundamental concern for a rational and structured, not metaphysical and nativist, vision of Ukrainian culture, especially in his later views (Grabowicz 1992, 237; Danylenko 2009b, 2010b, 16–21).

In a sense, the transcendental values of the Bible and Shakespeare became exemplary in the language program of Kuliš, with the Bible being a source of the biblical high style and Shakespeare a source of the secular high style. In the eyes of Kuliš, the universalism of these works was likely to reveal their twofold nature. They could not only enlighten his compatriots but also help create a full-fledged literary language capable of faithfully rendering the intricacies of reasoning and feeling in Ukrainian. Using such a literary language as a learning tool, the Ukrainians would be able to appropriate elements of universal culture and literature through translations of classical works. According to Kuliš and his advocates, such translations were ultimately destined to become an integral part of Ukrainian culture. And indeed, they are still of paramount importance today when, as in Kuliš's time, it is necessary to demonstrate the identity of endangered culture and language (Luckyj 1983, 182).

This is why Kuliš's translations are not analyzed in this book from the point of view of their faithfulness or aesthetic quality. The book concentrates, instead, on his translations as language products that reflect the vagaries of the formation and codification of written Ukrainian in the nineteenth century. These products are of particular importance since, back in Kuliš's time, they would delineate the functional range of both biblical and secular varieties of the high style in new literary Ukrainian. In other words, questions of textual reliability and faithfulness, in particular how the latter is reflected in rhythm and meter in poetic translations, are addressed in this book only sporadically. The major emphasis in this book is placed, instead, on the systematic description of language forms and the level of their codification by Kuliš in his translations.

This book may be viewed as a linguistic biography of Kuliš only in part. It is also concerned with a comparative study of a wide array of other Ukrainian authors who were engaged in translating the Bible and Shakespeare. Since this book deals primarily with the internal history of new literary Ukrainian through the material of specific translation products, comparison with parallel translations in other neighboring (e.g., Bohemian, Polish, or Russian) cultures will be minimal. Only cases of direct cultural and ideological impact, especially in the case of some western European and Russian translations and their discussion in biblical studies, will be taken into consideration. A thorough study of the Ukrainian translations of the Bible and Shakespeare in their connections with the translations made into other, first of all Slavic languages, is yet to be written. In sum, the approach chosen in this book is hardly more than a springboard for the integral history of the new Ukrainian literary language one can only dream of today.

The choice of the Bible and Shakespeare by Kuliš was not random at all. Neither was it random in the case of this book. The language used by Kuliš is quintessentially exemplary and consistent with his vision of the role of Ukrainian and its codification, including of orthography, in the national movement. Overall, the language of Kuliš's translations is likely to reflect quandaries he faced in the process of creating a new type of literary Ukrainian that, in his plans, was likely to strengthen an affirmation of national identity and function as a strategy to ensure acculturation of the Ukrainian people. Needless to say, a study of the language of Kuliš's translations can hardly substitute for an exhaustive description of his contribution to the formation of literary Ukrainian in the nineteenth century. However, a perusal of the linguistic dimension both of Kuliš's scriptural and secular translations, supplemented by a discussion of the time and people engaged in their assessment, may prove crucial to tracing the contours of a full and complete picture of the development of literary Ukrainian from the mid-nineteenth century onward.

A special comment is due here about the terminological challenges faced by those who are interested in the history of literary Ukrainian. The history of literary languages, the Ukrainian language among them, is not a new discipline. Its study usually focuses on the written language in works of literature, including translations, less often in journalism, and quite rarely in other genres. Though due to different reasons, literary Ukrainian in both Austria-Hungary and tsarist Russia in the late nineteenth century was a standardized language in the making. That is, it was a written language utilized in only a limited number of functional domains, particularly in Dnieper Ukraine. This is why, even for the written language used in Russian-ruled Ukraine, which theoretically was the standard language of the entire country, the designation of "standardized language" can be made only with great reservation. There was a certain norm of usage, but it was not codified, nor even exhaustively described, and there was no authority to prescribe it (Shevelov 1989, 18). In this book, therefore, a more traditional and less "prescriptive" term (i.e., "literary language") will be used in reference to a written language undergoing multiple changes dependent on subjective and objective (socio-political) factors (Danylenko 2015a, 230–237; Wingender 2013).

Additionally, a terminological distinction between "Rusian" and "Ruthenian" is maintained throughout this book. The Latin-based term "Ruthenian" is reserved for both the *rus´kyj jazykʺ* (Rusian language) and the *prostaja mova* (plain language) employed in the Grand Duchy of Lithuania and, later, in the Polish-Lithuanian Commonwealth from the fourteenth through the seventeenth centuries (Danylenko 2006a). Leaving aside discussion of these terms in the context of the linguistic and cultural patrimony of pre-modern Ukrainian and Belarusian peoples, I will resort to the term *prostaja mova* in order to refer to the vernacular standard that antedated the appearance of a new vernacular-based literary language in the early nineteenth century in Dnieper Ukraine and, though with some reservations, in Austrian-ruled Ukraine (Danylenko 2008a, 2008b). Using this term will allow me to emphasize the genetic continuity of the vernacularizing tendency first observed in the *prostaja mova* and later fully developed in new literary Ukrainian as early as the eighteenth century (Danylenko 2008b, 66, 2011b, 245–246; Peredrijenko 1979).

For the nineteenth century, the learned form "Ruthenian" is used in those contexts which deal with results of regional language mixing (commonly labeled *jazyčije*), including bookish elements extant from the Middle Ukrainian period, as used in Galicia, Transcarpathia, and Bukovyna. In these lands in the early eighteenth century, the Greek Catholic clergy who found themselves the only defenders of a separate Ruthenian regional identity advanced the idea of one literary language, based on Church Slavonic, though with a wide range of admixtures

(Danylenko 2008a, 111, 2009a, 225–226). No wonder, then, that the official name of the Ukrainian language in Austria-Hungary was "Ruthenian" (Gr. *Ruthenisch*). One implication of the name "Ruthenian" was a certain degree of non-identification of Austrian Ukrainians with Russian Ukrainians. In the literary language this provided some authorization for the preservation of local linguistic peculiarities and for the development of a regional variety of Ukrainian within Austria (Shevelov 1989, 24). Instead of the learned form "Ruthenian," the indigenous term "Rusian" is used in all possible ethno-linguistic and socio-political contexts, covering the regional (western Ukrainian) language and their speakers viewed in the pan-Ukrainian perspective. The use of this designation makes it also possible to distinguish the Rusians, i.e., the Galician Ukrainians, from the Rusyns, or the local population of Ukrainian origin in Transcarpathia and Bukovyna (Danylenko 2009a, 2009d).

Terminologically, another special case is "Little Russian," occurring in scholarly literature sometimes in conjunction with such terms as Hetmanate (Cossack Ukraine) and Sloboda Ukraine (Plokhy 2006, 329–333). The term "Cossack Ukraine" is employed in this book in reference to the population of the Hetmanate, who were often called "Little Russians" in official documents from the seventeenth century onward. Along similar lines, their language was referred to as "Little Russian," in opposition to "Great Russian," used by Russian speakers in Muscovy and, subsequently, in the Russian Empire. It should be recalled, however, that Ukrainian metropolitan Jov Borec′kyj (†1631) seems to have established the tradition of viewing the Little Russians and the Great Russians as brothers who together constitute a family. Only later did Muscovite Rus′, rooted in its dynastic and patrimonial way of thinking, accept such a vision of unity (ibid., 290–291), which subsequently became reflected in the opposition of Great Russian and Little Russian as describing, in particular, the socio-linguistic distribution of the Russian and Ukrainian languages as used in the Russian Empire.

Interestingly, still honored by the populists in nineteenth-century Ukraine, this distinction was also endorsed by Kuliš at the beginning of his literary career. Somewhat later, however, he came up with another opposition, Old Rusian (*staroruščyna*) versus New Rusian (*novoruščyna*), that is, literary Ukrainian whose tradition is traced back to the period of Kyivan Rus´ versus literary Russian, a newly created language with a younger (Muscovite) tradition (Kuliš 1914). Accordingly, in harmony with Kuliš's conception, the term "Old Rusian" is employed, in this book, to label the language and culture of Kyivan Rus´ (Shevelov 1979, 55–77). As far as the name "Ukrainian" is concerned, it is used throughout the text as an umbrella term *avant la lettre*, overlapping semantically with the modern understanding of this romantic concept wholly embraced by Kuliš in his conception of new literary Ukrainian.

As this book will show, the language of Kuliš is a unique aggregate of various elements belonging to different style registers and periods in the history of Ukrainian. In addition to bookish (Ruthenian) and Church Slavonic elements, as well as numerous borrowings, Kuliš's language is comprised of both vernacular and dialectal forms and constructions. In our book, the term "vernacular" is reserved for the description of colloquial (plain) phenomena in general, thus largely referring to urban speech patterns of the cultivated class (intelligentsia). All things "dialectal" are generally viewed in the light of dialectal geography, thus dealing primarily with products of rural speech patterns.

Finally, a word on textual sources and linguistic examples is warranted at this point. In a work of this nature, representation of some textual sources is determined by linguistic precision and typographic style. Major quotations appear as a rule in their original spelling. The modernized orthography is reproduced only as rendered in the source being quoted. In the interest of space, some short titles, especially in translations of biblical books, include elisions that are not indicated. In the case of direct correspondences, all English quotations from the Bible are supplied from the Authorized King James Version of the Holy Bible (Thomas Nelson Bibles, 1977). Unless noted, all other translations accompanied by grammatical annotation are my own, including examples excerpted from Kuliš's translations of both the Bible and Shakespeare. Direct correspondences in the latter case are provided from *The Complete Plays and Poems of William Shakespeare. A New Text Edited With Introduction and Notes By William Allan Neilson and Charles Jarvis Hill* (Houghton Mifflin Company, 1970). If no direct equivalent of a Ukrainian form is found in the English original, the former word is glossed accordingly and a page number or folio (recto or verso) is provided only for the corresponding Ukrainian translation.

All transliterations are made in accordance with the publisher's preferred style, with only a few exceptions reflecting primarily different sound patterns behind some similar characters. For all linguistic examples, the author distinguishes between the *jers* before their loss (shift) in the late twelfth to early thirteenth centuries and after. For the former case, one makes use of the signs ъ (back *jer*) and ь (front *jer*), while for the latter case, the corresponding Cyrillic letters are rendered by prime acutes (i.e., ″ and ′ respectively). In Middle Ukrainian, the letters "і," "и," and "ы" are transliterated as follows: *i, y,* and *ÿ*. If necessary, phonetic representations appear between square brackets ([]) or, in rare cases, in italics. Throughout the book the scholarly transliteration system is used to cite separate examples, while excerpts from literary texts are rendered in the original. Most of the personal, geographical, and ethnic names are given according to the official form or tradition used in the country where they are currently located, hence "Kyiv" instead of "Kiev" or "Rusian" instead of "Ruthenian," although "Gogol" instead of "Hohol′."

It is my hope that this book, addressing different audiences, lays one of the first bricks in the Western scholarship not only in the study of Kuliš's language but also in the history of literary Ukrainian in the nineteenth century. Introducing Kuliš's translations to Western readership will stimulate scholarly interest in the language and literature of Ukrainians as well as provide a model for the direction of future scholarship in Ukrainian language and literature.

PART I

THE BIBLE

CHAPTER 1

Exploring Psalmody

THE BOOK OF PSALMS

From 1869 to 1871, during his travels to Austria, Italy, and Germany, Kuliš was already working on a translation of the Holy Scriptures. There is some evidence that he began his translation project during his government service in conquered Poland, between 1864 and 1867 (Kuliš to Xil´čevskij, 90–92), or even earlier, in the late 1850s when he was preparing a second edition of a collection of sermons composed in Little Russian by Vasyl´ Hrečulevyč (1791–1870) (Makar 2006, 362). The inducement to serve in Warsaw after the defeat of the Polish uprising in 1863 was provided by the Russian government and by Kuliš's friends who had close ties to it. Condemned by some of his compatriots, who treated his service in Warsaw as springing from a servile desire to please his Russian masters, his government career was, from certain points of view, very fast-paced and productive (Luckyj 1983, 142–143). A year after his appointment on 23 December 1864, he rose to the rank of clerk of special assignments, fifth class, and a few months later he was appointed acting director of the Office of Spiritual Affairs. A good salary and a great deal of spare time enabled him to work in local libraries and archives, peering over Polish historical accounts of the Cossack wars. These he would later, though somewhat uncritically, use in his journalistic scholarship and in his historical writings, such as *Istorija vossoedinenija Rusi* (History of the Reunification of Rus´), published in three volumes in 1874 and 1877 (ibid.).

Indeed, from the late 1860s onward, Kuliš was almost completely engaged in the translation of the Holy Scriptures. He viewed this project primarily as an enlightening, rather than religious, mission. In a letter of

4 September 1872 to Oleksa Hatcuk (1832–1891), he wrote, "I have in mind not religion but philology [*slovesnist'*]" (Kuliš to Hatcuk, 49). As early as 4 August 1868, in a letter to Oleksander Kistjakivs'kyj (1833–1885), he informed his correspondent that he had already finished a translation of the Pentateuch (Kuliš to Kistjakovskij, 2:303). Deeply involved in the translation and boldly experimenting with stylistic devices, Kuliš confirmed the fast pace of his work three months later, in another letter of 29 November 1868 to Ivan Xyl'čevs'kyj (1819–1899), an old friend and a countryman from Nižyn (Xil'čevskij, Nekrolog). Excited by his translation project, Kuliš boasted that he was learning Hebrew and had "translated the fourth part of the Bible from the best translations, and in addition almost the entire book of Psalms in verse (already 107 psalms)" (Kuliš to Xil'čevskij, 90–91). Kuliš also wrote that Psalm 1 had by that time appeared in the Lviv periodical *Pravda*, founded with his financial assistance, in which the first fifty psalms of the Psalter, and Moses's two songs, were to be published soon. "Let our enemies have hard times!," he exclaimed, and added that he had finished translating the Song of Songs and "explained it, following Herder, whom I have been scrutinizing, as well as much else pertinent to the Bible" (ibid.).

From the outset, Kuliš intended to offer poetic paraphrases of the Hebrew Scriptures in Ukrainian, in particular of the book of Psalms, which would reflect his vision of the high style in the new Ukrainian literary language. He was working passionately and assiduously, while producing translation after translation, thus laying the groundwork for the creation of the Ukrainian Bible. In 1868, in the periodical *Pravda*, Kuliš published anonymously Psalm 1 (*Psal'ma* 1) and Psalm 13 (*Psal'ma* 13). As he added in the aforementioned letter to Ivan Xyl'čevs'kyj, he published in the same year, again anonymously and in the same newspaper, two of Moses's songs, *Musijeva pisnja* (Moses's Song) and *Peredsmertnja pisnja Musijeva* (Dying Moses's Song) (*Pisni*), which also appeared as a book, *Dvi Musijevi pisni* (Two of Moses's Songs).

In the next year, 1869, in addition to the paraphrases of Psalms 15 (*Psal'ma* 15) and 16 (*Psal'ma* 16), Kuliš published *Yov* (the book of Job) (*Yov*, *Pravda*; *Yov*, 1869; *Yov*)[1] and *Pentatevx Musijevyj* (Pentateuch) as a

---

1   The word-initial *y* in the name *Yov* (Ukr. Иов) was pronounced as *i* and not the glide *j*. The iambic pentameter of the syllabic structure proves that the syllable-initial vowel

supplement to the Lviv periodical *Pravda* (issues 1–24). All these works, except Psalm 15, appeared under the pseudonym Pavlo Rataj. In the same year, *Pentatevx Musijevyj* was reprinted under the somewhat pretentious title, *Svjate Pys′mo, abo vsja Byblyja staroho y novoho Zavitu, rus′ko-ukrajins′koju movoju pereložena* (The Holy Scripture, or the Complete Bible of the Old and New Testaments, Translated into the Rusian-Ukrainian Language; *Pentatevx*), under the auspices of the editorial board of the Galician newspaper *Pravda* (Studyns′kyj 1930, xxiii–xxiv, xxvii–xxviii). Finally, as early as 1871, Kuliš completed his versified translation of the Psalter, *Psaltyr abo knyha xvaly Božoji* (The Psalms or the Book of God's Praise), which appeared under the same pen name in Lviv (Levyckij 1888, 165). Kuliš was particularly proud of his *Psaltyr*, which was subsequently reprinted several times in different publications and collections of his works (Kyryljuk 1929a, 43–45), in particular in the third volume of the *Prosvita* edition of 1909 (*Psaltyr*, Rataj).

Doubtlessly, this was a series of groundbreaking publications heralding a new era in scriptural translation in the Ukrainian lands. It is not at all curious that, long before these publications, Kuliš included in his elementary primer *Hramatka* (1857, 2nd ed. 1861) anonymous paraphrases of Psalms 12, 53, and 132 (Kuliš 1857, 40–43, also 8–10, 15–25). In fact, they were excerpted from one of the closing pieces of the collection *Try lita* (Three Years) of Taras Ševčenko, comprising ten psalms translated by the author in 1843–1845 but published only in the first full edition of the poet's *Kobzar* in 1860.

Even a cursory look into the language of Ševčenko's paraphrases and the abovementioned translations of Kuliš seems to speak to a strong

---

was stressed, as evidenced from the following line: *Počav tohdï Iov i reče*, as opposed to *Počav znov Iov i reče*, "Moreover, Job continued his parable, and said" (*Yov*, 72–73; Job 29:1), where word-initially one can pronounce a glide (Naxlik 2007, 2:271, fn. 271). No doubt, this syllabic structure was originally set forth by Kuliš (*Yov*, 79). Incidentally, while working on the second (poetic) translation of this book, Kuliš introduced another transliteration, with the prothetic *h*, whence *Hyjob* (Kuliš to Biloborodov, 90; *Hyjob*). The latter transliteration was clearly patterned on *Hiob*, used in the German Bible at least since the time of Martin Luther's translation. Not surprisingly, the same transliteration is found in the Bible translated by Eduard Reuß, *Das Alte Testament: übersetzt, eingeleitet und erläutert*, which came off the press in Braunschweig in 1892–1894 (Reuß), and was most likely consulted by Kuliš.

vernacularizing tendency in Kuliš's stylistics. Nevertheless, despite a distinct limitation of Church Slavonicisms in his translations in comparison with Ševčenko's paraphrases, Kuliš's language program was much more complex. To take Ševčenko's Psalm 12, first published in *Hramatka* (Kuliš 1857, 41), as an example, I counted therein only four obvious Church Slavonicisms: *spasy* (2 sg. imp.) "to save" (4x), *vospoju* (1 sg. non-past) "to sing unto" (*Biblija* 1862, 278v), *blaha* "bounties," and *zlyi* (pl.) "vicious," that is, "those that trouble me" (Ps 13) as a substitute for the more morphologically complex *stužajuščiÿ* (pl.) with the same meaning in the Church Slavonic translation (*Biblija* 1862, 278v). By contrast, in addition to changes in its rhetoric and poetic devices, Kuliš's translation of the same psalm appears to be written predominantly in the vernacular stylistic key. The Church Slavonic undercurrent is fed by the lexeme *dokoli*, transferred from the Church Slavonic translation with the question word *dokolě* "how long" used in the first line (*Biblija* 1862, 278v; Ps 13). Instead of *zlyi*, as in Ševčenko, Kuliš turned to *zljušči ljude* "vicious people," with a long naturalized (vernacularized) intensive form in -*ušč*- (Kurylo 1960, 18), and instead of *blaho*, we find *dobro* "bounty." In one case, however, Kuliš resorted to the reflexive verb *spastysja* "to save, survive" (*spasus'* 1 sg. non-past) in a biblical context, a word commonly used at that time in the vernacular (Hrinč., 2:682–683). A similar distribution is observed in the language of Psalms 53 and 132.

Yet a more nuanced picture is gleaned from Kuliš's early paraphrases when compared with translations made by his predecessors, in particular by Petro Hulak-Artemovs'kyj (1790–1865) and Myxajlo Maksymovyč (1804–1873), and especially Taras Ševčenko (1814–1861), one of the founders of modern Ukrainian literature and language (Bilenky 2012, 299).

ALEXANDRINE VERSE OR TROCHAIC FOOT?

In the years 1857 and 1858, a fabulist, scholar, and translator of classical literature, Petro Hulak-Artemovs'kyj paraphrased Psalms 91, 123, 133, 139, and 140 (Hulak, 420–425, 437). Having gained massive critical acclaim after their publication in the early twentieth century, these paraphrases were dubbed "[as if] forged" (Jefremov 1924, 1:407) and "succinct, often clearly carved" (Zerov 1960, 156). With a colloquial style used to render the lofty poetic texture of the Church Slavonic *Vorlage*, these translations were laconic and aphoristic. "Full of deep internal energy and expression, exquisitely worked-up" (M. Moskalenko 2006 1/2, 181), Hulak-Artemovs'kyj's psalms were written in the Alexandrine verse form that was the most popular measure in French dramatic and narrative poetry during the seventeenth century, reaching its highest development in the tragedies of Pierre Corneille and Jean Racine. Zerov (1960, 157) concluded rightly that Hulak-Artemovs'kyj had produced the best Alexandrine verse in Ukrainian poetry, and cited specifically the final lines from his version of Psalm 91.

Hulak-Artemovs´kyj's Translation	Kuliš's Translation
[. . .] Він на мене сподївав ся;	Він на мене *уповає*,
Я слобоню його, зо мною він спізнав ся.	я за-те його *ізбавлю*,
Попросить він чого, послухаю його,	і *спасу* його од *муки*,
В пригодї буду з ним; зажурить ся чого,	бо імя моє він любить,
Я розведу журбу і од *печали збавлю*,	*призове* мене—почую,
Прославлю днї його і днї до днїв прибавлю;	озовусь до його в *тузї*,
І двір його житья я раєм обсажу,	довгий вік йому дарую,
І всїм моє над ним *спасїньня* покажу.	і пішлю йому *спасеннє*.
(Hulak, 421)	(*Psaltyr*, Rataj, 259)

[14. Because he hath set his love upon me, therefore will I deliver him: I will set him on high, because he hath known my name.

15. I will be with him in trouble; I will deliver him, and honor him.

16. With long life will I satisfy him, and shew him my salvation.] (Ps 91)

The extract from Hulak-Artemovs'kyj's translation looks particularly classicist from the metric point of view and in its stylistic coloring. What is striking, however, is that Church Slavonicisms are hardly used by Hulak-Artemovs'kyj. He resorts, instead, to vernacular devices as his chief technique in designing the high style of new literary Ukrainian. Overall, the verbal means of his psalm are unusually modest: there are no borrowings, no vulgarisms, no patent Church Slavonicisms, apart from a few bookish (Church Slavonic by origin) forms like *spasïn'nja* "salvation," *pečal'* "grief," and *zbavyty* "to deliver, save." The lexical material is clearly appropriate for the biblical narration, folding into a philosophical generalization about spiritual salvation. Yet the loftiness of the style is accomplished exclusively by a formal technique that was highly appreciated, as pointed out by Mykola Zerov and Serhii Jefremov, in the early twentieth century.

At first blush, Kuliš's lexical make-up is very similar to that in the translation made by Hulak-Artemovs'kyj, although the ratio of bookish, in particular Church Slavonic, elements is somewhat larger in Kuliš's paraphrase. All this is hardly accidental, since Kuliš was more experimental in new linguistic forms. His metric foot is different, however. To begin with, Kuliš's paraphrase reads somewhat lighter, closer to the spirit of a folk song; however, it is also written in regular trochees, a metric foot with a long formal tradition. Suffice it to say that trochaic meters were extensively used in Ancient Greek and Latin tragedy and comedy in a form that was particularly favored by Plautus and Terence, known as trochaic catalectic tetrameter.

With regard to rhetorical and linguistic devices, Hulak-Artemovs'kyj's translations are marked by an obvious vernacularizing tendency applied in tandem with the nascent indigenous classicist tradition. By contrast, Kuliš's paraphrases were largely oriented toward the blending of heterogeneous elements. To illustrate the stylistically uniform elements of Hulak-Artemovs'kyj's language, one can mention such vernacular lexemes as *pryhoda* "occasion," *najmyt* (m.), *najmyčka* (f.) "farm-hand," *pani* "mistress," *pan'skyj* "manorial," *neboha* "poor woman," *doškuljaty* "to annoy" (Hulak, 421–422). Among representative morphological forms, deserving of attention are diminutives like *nuždočka* "want" and *čvan'ko* "arrogant person" (ibid.). No wonder that all these lexemes, with the exception of WUkr. and NUkr. *doškuljaty* with the š ~ s fluctuation shared by West Slavic (Shevelov 1979, 740), are found in the burlesque *Enejida* of the founding father of modern Ukrainian literature, Ivan Kotljarevs'kyj (1769–1838) (*Enejida*, Index, 101, 106, 109, 119, 142, 196). These lexemes are also attested in Hryhorij Kvitka-Osnov'janenko's language (Kvitka, 1:408; 2:192, 233, 284–285), save for *čvan'ko* (m./f. sg.) next to the Russianism *čvannyj* (adj.)

"arrogant" (ibid., 3:597); also Kvitka-Osnov'janenko's regionalisms *nan'myt, nan'myčka* "farm-hand" (ibid., 2:201–202) derived most likely from the verb *nanjaty* "to hire" (Hrinč., 1:1041) (Rus. *nanjat'*).

Additionally, a conspicuous lack of the relative pronoun *kotryj* in Hulak-Artemovs'kyj's paraphrases is particularly noteworthy. Instead, he used the relativizer *ščo*, as found in the relative clause *ščo tam žyveš na nebi* "that dwellest in the heavens" (Ps 123), in place of the active present participle used in the Church Slavonic version *žyvuščemu* (m. dat.) *na nebesy* "dwelling in the heavens" (Hulak, 421). Kuliš deemed it necessary in this case to employ agentive nouns, appearing more neutral and less colloquial, in the stylistic framework of his translation: *nebesnyj žytel' i car* "celestial dweller and tsar." Apparently, he viewed the nouns as more appropriate for the biblical context than the relative clause found commonly in the southeastern Ukrainian vernacular.

Hulak-Artemovs'kyj's translation of Psalm 133 is even more revealing (Hulak, 422). Riddled with colloquial expressions that are hard to find in the paraphrases made by Kuliš and especially Ševčenko, this translation is one of the clearest examples of a vernacular standard that was cultivated in Sloboda Ukraine and in the former Hetmanate in the nineteenth century (Danylenko 2008a; Matvijas 1996). One should bear in mind, however, that, as early as 1861, this language variety was not yet unanimously treated as a unifying factor. Moreover, the concept of standard language was still vague among the literati. Identified as a "Perejaslav-Čyhyryn dialect" in the written output of Ševčenko, this variety, according to most of the Dnieper intellectuals, was purportedly flourishing as compared with the "artificiality" and "lifelessness" of the Galician language. Yet, as Kuliš surmised in 1861, it was not clear whether the Dnieper variety would ultimately serve as the literary language of all Ukrainians since talented new writers could easily begin writing in their local dialects (*Otvět'*, 258–259).

In Hulak-Artemovs'kyj's translation, one finds typical southeastern Ukrainian lexical forms. For instance, there is an excessive use of diminutives like *vkupci* "together" and *bratiky* "brothers." In this respect, deserving of attention is a colloquial and somewhat "old-fashioned" idiomatic expression, *skazat' prymirom k slovu*, that means "for example, by the way," which creates the authoritative yet cordial atmosphere of biblical narration

(Strixa 2006, 56). The same vernacular-based stylistic framework is discerned in the morphology. Even in such a short translation, one discovers a fluctuation of 3 sg. present tense forms in first conjugation, as attested in the bulk of southeastern dialects (Matvijas 2006, 63) (e.g., *stikaje* "to run down" next to *kapa* "to descend" and *pada* "to go down"). Surprisingly, there is but one uncontracted adjectival form in Hulak-Artemovs´kyj's paraphrase: *ščaslyveje* (sg. n.) "happy" (Hulak, 422).[2]

The approaches that Kuliš and Ševčenko use in the translation of this psalm are different. Ševčenko's paraphrase was first published, as has been mentioned, in Kuliš's primer *Hramatka*, while Kuliš included his own paraphrase in the complete translation of the Psalter published in 1871 under the pen name Pavlo Rataj. Ševčenko's translation is replete with numerous bookish and Church Slavonic elements such as *myro dobrovonnje* "odorous ointment," *ryzy dorohyi* "precious garments," *tvarjam″ zemnorodnym″* (dat.) "reptiles," *vocarytcja* (3 sg. non-past) "to rule, govern," and especially *omety* "skirts" (Kuliš 1857, 43; LLP, 2:541). Among morphological forms, it is worth citing a series of pronominal (uncontracted) plural adjectives: *šytyi* "embroidered," *dorohyi* "precious," *Ermons´kyi* "of Her´-mon," *svjatyi* "holy," *vysokyi* "high," and *Syons´kyi* "of Zi´-on." The use of such forms is one of the most characteristic features of the poet's language. In

---

2 Most of the above observations can be easily applied to a translation or, rather, a paraphrase of Psalm 136 made by Stepan Rudans´kyj (1834–1873), one of the most typical representatives of the populist trend in the Ukrainian literature of the nineteenth century (Rudans´kyj 1908). Skillfully crafted, his paraphrase appeared in 1858, that is, almost simultaneously with Hulak-Artemovs´kyj's translations. Some similarities between Rudans´kyj's translation and paraphrases made by Hulak-Artemovs´kyj jump out. To name just a few, the languages of the two authors are premised on the same southeastern dialects coupled with pronounced folkloric and vernacular admixtures, which seem to prevail especially in Rudans´kyj's very short text. In the vocabulary, suffice it to mention *husli i cymbaly* "psaltery and cymbals" (ibid., 299). In the morphology, the poet uses uncontracted forms like *tiji* "those" or *tjažkiji* [*vorohy*] "powerful enemies" (ibid., 299–300). Finally, one should cite the pair *Jerusalym ~ Rusalym* (ibid.) used in tune with the so-called euphonic processes and triggering alternations like *ihra ~ hra* "play" and the like in the fourteenth century (Shevelov 1979, 283, 294–301; Žovtobrjux et al. 1979, 198–200). What is unusual about Rudans´kyj's paraphrase is that it is written in iambic tetrameter with alternating female and male rhyme, a metrical foot also employed, with a classicist coloring, by Kuliš in his paraphrase of Psalm 13.

comparison with other Ukrainian writers of that period, the ratio of uncontracted forms in Ševčenko's works was particularly high as a result of the historical influence of Church Slavonic and Old Ukrainian. What is more remarkable is that the presence of such forms became even more tangible in his later writings, a fact that, according to Tymošenko (1971, 199), speaks for their normalized status in the poet's idiom.

Hulak-Artemovs′kyj's Translation
Нема вже красчої людської в сьвіті долї,
Як вкупцї братїки живуть по божій волї.
Так *миро* дороге лиснить на голові,
По Аароновій стїкає бородї
І капа на його одежу саєтову;
Так аєрмонськая, *сказать*
    примїром к слову,
Роса *пада* в горах сіонських з
    мокрих хмар;
Так і на їх росить із неба божий дар,
А з ним щасливеє житьтя й
    благословеньня,
І буде вік в чести їх у людей іменьня.
    (Hulak, 422)

Ševčenko's Translation
Чи є що краще, лучче в світі,
Як укупі жити,
З братом добрим добро певне
Познать, не ділити?
Яко *миро добровонне*
З голови честної
На бороду Аароню
Спадає росою
І на шитиї *омети*
Ризи дорогії;
Або роси *Ермонськиі*
На *святиі* гори
Високиі, Сионськиі
Спадають и творять
Добро *тварям земнородним*
И землі, и людям:
Оттак братів благих Своіх
Господь не забуде!
Воцаритця в дому тихих
В семъї тій великій
І пошле ім добру долю
Од віка до віка. (Kuliš 1857,
43; Ševčenko 1963, 1:344–345)

Kuliš's version, on the other hand, is shorter and seems to be modeled on the Church Slavonic version.

Kuliš's Translation	**Church Slavonic Translation**
Що за добре, що за любо всїм братам укупі жити! мов Ароновим пахущим миром голову мастити. любо пахощі стікають на браду, браду Ароню: так Єрмонські роси кроплять гору тучную Сіоню. кроплять зтиха, и не сякнуть благодатнї Божі ріки: у благих братів достатки не поменшають во віки. (*Psaltyr*, Rataj, 320)	Сѐ что̀ добро̀, и҆лѝ что̀ красно̀, но є҆́же жи́ти бра́тїи вкꙋ́пѣ; Ꙗ҆́кѡ мѵ́ро на главѣ̀, сходѧ́щее на брадꙋ̀, брадꙋ̀ а҆арѡ́ню, сходѧ́щее на ѡ҆мє́ты ѻ҆де́жды є҆гѡ̀: Ꙗ҆́кѡ роса̀ а҆ермѡ́нскаѧ сходѧ́щаѧ на го́ры сїѡ̑нскїѧ: ꙗ҆́кѡ та́мѡ заповѣ́да гдⷭ҇ь бл҃гослове́нїе и҆ живо́тъ до вѣ́ка. (*Biblija* 1862, 304)

[1. Behold, how good and how pleasant it is for brethren to dwell together in unity!

2. It is like the precious ointment upon the head, that ran down upon the beard, even Aa´-ron's beard:
that went down to the skirts of his garments;

3. As the dew of Her´-mon, and as the dew that descended upon the mountains of Zi´-on: for there the Lord commanded the blessing, even life for evermore.] (Ps 133)

Permeated though with Church Slavonicisms, Kuliš's paraphrase can easily compete with Hulak-Artemovs'kyj's translation, which contains only two lexical transfers from the Church Slavonic text of this psalm: *myro* "ointment" and *blahosloven'nja* "blessing" (*Biblija* 1862, 304r, Ps 133). Kuliš's leaning on the Church Slavonic translation can be illustrated by lexical and morphonological transfers from the Church Slavonic text that, most likely, was consulted by the writer. It is not therefore surprising to find the whole line *na bradu, bradu Aronju* "upon the beard, [even]

Aa´-ron's beard" with the soft stem in the name Aaron´ borrowed from the Church Slavonic (*Biblija* 1862, 304r).

There are a few more Church Slavonicisms in Kuliš's translation, such as *tučnuju* (acc. sg. f.) "fertile," *blahodatnï* (pl.) "blest" and *blahyx* (gen. pl.) "blessed," the expression *vo viky* "for evermore" (ChSl. *do věka*), and a long naturalized (vernacularized) adverb, *ukupi* "together," from ChSl. *vkupě* (*Biblija* 1862, 304r). Generally, these Church Slavonicisms have little effect on the biblical poem in the Ukrainian language (see Gillingham 1994, 190–206). Thus, showing a minimum of obsolete features, Kuliš's language looks moderately vernacularized and, in fact, exemplary in the context of the formation of new literary Ukrainian, especially of its high style.

In sum, the language of Kuliš is at variance with that of Hulak-Artemovs´kyj's translation, and shows a contrasting tendency. The latter's language is premised on the southeastern Ukrainian vernacular with a minimum of Church Slavonic elements sometimes Ukrainianized beyond recognition, such as the diminutive *nuždočka* "want" (Hulak, 422) without a new affricate in place of the dental *d* (Shevelov 1979, 629). Kuliš seems more fastidious and traditional and, at the same time, oriented toward the vernacular, while Hulak-Artemovs´kyj's texts show a homogenously woven high style, based exclusively on the vernacular and designed for both religious and secular genres.

INVOKING GAVRILA DERŽAVIN

A somewhat different picture arises in a comparison of Hulak-Artemovs´kyj's and especially Kuliš's language with Maksymovyč's translations of twenty-nine psalms that appeared in the 1859 issue of his almanac *Ukraynec"* (A Ukrainian), that is, almost ten years before Kuliš published his translations.[3] They demonstrate a variety of metrical values

---

3 The translation of these psalms was based most likely on the Church Slavonic Bible and the Russian translation of the Psalter published in 1822 under the supervision of the Saint Petersburg Ecclesiastical Academy's rector, subsequently metropolitan of Moscow, Filaret (Drozdov) (Danylenko 2010b, 10). Maksymovyč, who believed

comparable with different folkloric measures. Thus, Psalms 1, 11–14, 38, 41–42, 51, 54, 64, 78, 83, 114, 124–125, 128, 136, 141, 143, and 150 were translated in a fourteen-syllable meter. Apart from Psalm 81, written in a popular metric foot, the rest of the psalms were translated in a variety of chorei. Taken as a whole, these psalms were translated, according to Myxajlo Moskalenko (2006 3/4, 157), into "a robust language, which, generally, corresponds to the fundamentals of the literary language." In discussing the type of literary language used by Maksymovyč, one should concur with Moskalenko (ibid.) that Maksymovyč's paraphrases are characterized by "exquisite vocabulary, stylistic skill," and the use of folkloric devices coupled with the translator's familiarity with old poetry, chants, and church *koljadas*. All this allowed Moskalenko to juxtapose Maksymovyč's paraphrases with Ševčenko's masterly translations of some psalms, though leaving aside Kuliš's paraphrases allegedly marked by "some freshness of expression" and "in some cases, innovation . . . in formal approaches" (ibid.).

Still, the level of Kuliš's innovation in his first paraphrases remains unappreciated, with the exception, perhaps, of Horbač's appraisal of salient linguistic features in Kuliš's *Psaltyr* (Horbač 1988, 60–64). It is not our goal here to undertake an exhaustive linguistic analysis of Kuliš's psalmodic paraphrases, which appear rather as prolegomena to his future biblical translations, especially in the 1890s. Yet to gauge the innovative value of his early translations in the context of the formation of literary Ukrainian in the mid-nineteenth century, it would be profitable to compare some of Kuliš's paraphrases with the translations made by Maksymovyč.

Psalm 15 comes here first into consideration:

---

that his translations of the psalms were more faithful to the original than those made by Ševčenko, continued translating the psalms. Thus, in his letter of 18 March 1869 to Pëtr Vjazemskij (1792–1878), Maksymovyč wrote about the publication of Psalms 29, 35, 89, 93, and 101 in 1867 in *Halyčanyn*, then a literary supplement to the Galician periodical *Slovo*; in addition, he appended a draft of his translation of Psalm 103 to the same letter, which brought the total number of the psalms translated by Maksymovyč to thirty-five (Holovaščenko 2006, 58).

Exploring Psalmody

Kuliš's Translation

Господи, хто буде жити
У Твоєму домі?
Хто осяде на Твоєму
Сіоні святому?
Той, хто ходить *непороченъ*,
Робить щиру правду;
Хто добро у серці мислить
Убогому брату;
Хто нікому, підлестившись,
Зла не замишляє;
Хто сусідові докоромъ
Серця не вражає
Хто ледачихъ ненавидить
Добрихъ поважає;
Обіцявши, забожившись,
Слова не ламає
Хто грошима запомігши,
Лишку не приймає
Оттакий ніколи въ світі
Смутку не дознає.
(*Psal′ma* 15)

Maksymovyč's Translation

Хто-жъ, о Господи, тамъ буде
Въ дому Твоємъ жити?
Хто въ твою святую гору
Може доступити?
Той, хто чесно пробуває:
Все по правдѣ робить,
И святую правду людямъ
Зъ щирымъ серцемъ мовить;
Языкомъ своимъ не сѣе
Клеветы лихой;
Своимъ ближнимъ *зла* не коитъ
И ихъ не злословить;
Хто одъ всѣхъ богопротивныхъ
Очи одвертає,
А людей *благочестивихъ*
Добре поважає;
Хто, поклявшись свому другу,
Єго не зражає;
Сребла въ *ростъ* не позычає;
Взятокъ не приймає.
Хто такъ дѣяти пойметься,
Повѣкъ не звихнеться.
(Maksimovič 1859, 8)

 1. Lord, who shall abide in thy tabernacle? Who shall dwell in thy holy hill?
 2. He that walketh uprightly, and worketh righteousness, and speaketh the truth in his heart.
 3. He that backbiteth not with his tongue, nor doeth evil to his neighbour, nor taketh up a reproach against his neighbour.
 4. In whose eyes a vile person is contemned; but he honoureth them that fear the Lord. He that sweareth to his own hurt, and changeth not.

5. He that putteth not out his money to usury, nor taketh reward against the innocent. He that doeth these things shall never be moved.] (Ps 15)

These translations demonstrate a similar consequentiality and command of vernacular means, strengthened by a perfect trochaic foot. The overall impression of the two texts is that their authors intensely polished the material, eliminating possible stylistic contrasts and introducing instead semantic ones. Like Ševčenko's writing in 1857–1859, the effect is meant to invite the reader to deep thinking, not to deal him a blow that will throw him off balance (Shevelov 1962, 75).

Yet, on closer inspection, Maksymovyč's work looks simplistic. He ends up with excessive emulation of folkloric means piled one on top of another, while Kuliš, though oriented toward common linguistic devices, digresses deliberately from his southeastern dialectal basis. Kuliš remains open even to ecclesiastic influence. All this may explain his use of the nominal form *neporočen"* "upright," directly transferred from the synodal Church Slavonic translation (*xodęj* [m. sg. PrAP] *neporočen"* "he that walketh uprightly" [*Biblija* 1862, 279r]). At the same time, Kuliš was more intimately familiar with the system of his mother tongue—at least his language appears more complex. With an eye to filling in terminological gaps in a new literary language, he used, for instance, *lyška* (Hrinč., 1:902) in place of ChSl. *mzda* "reward" (*Biblija* 1862, 279r). Interestingly, in the *Prosvita* edition of 1909, the word *lyška* was replaced by a western Ukrainian counterpart, *lyxva* (Žel., 1:405; see Tymč. and Nimčuk, 1:405), influenced by the Church Slavonic lexeme *lyxva* "usura" (Sr., 2:25; *Lexicon*, 338) and the Polish equivalent *lichwa* (Vytv., 122). Obviously, the editors meant to avoid semantic confusion with Pol. *liszka* "fox" (ibid., 123), used at that time in what can be called "Galician koiné" (Shevelov 1989, 19–20; Macjuk 2001, 269), thus appearing homonymous to the indigenous *lyška* (Žel., 1:407). Maksymovyč, however, resorted to another lexeme, *rost"* "profit" (OChSl. *rastъ*) with a Great Russian coloring, since it had been commonly used in Middle Russian texts (Sr., 3:173). The lexeme *vzjatka* "bribe" might also have been viewed as a Great Russian element in, otherwise, the Little Russian translation, *vzjatok"* "what must be taken" (Tymč., 244; Sr., 1:374).

In his paraphrases of psalms, Kuliš tried to make a decisive break with the folkloric stylistics that are still observable in his translation of the two songs of Moses, thus contrasting with the 1903 prose version, polished largely by Puljuj after the death of his long-time friend and co-translator:

Kuliš's Translation of 1868	Kuliš's Translation of 1903
Ото жъ знайте й розумійте:	Подивітесь тепер, що я, се я, що
Я въ світі єдиний;	стою, і нема Бога крімі мене! Я
Нема Бога опрічъ мене,	вбиваю і оживляю, я задаю рани
Ні святої сили.	і сціляю; нема нікого, хто б спас
Я вбиваю й оживляю,	із руки моєї! (*SP*, 205)
Раню и сціляю;	
Мойму гніву нема впину,	
Милосердю—краю....	
(*Pisni*, 501)	

[See now that I, even I, am he, and there is no god with me: I kill, I make alive; I wound, and I heal: neither is there any that can deliver out my hand.] (Deut 32:39)

As evidenced above, as early as 1868 Kuliš was deliberately experimenting with vernacular means, which he apparently viewed as foundations for a future biblical (high) style in new literary Ukrainian. For this reason, perhaps, undersigned as "the editorial board," Kuliš wrote in a footnote that the translation of the two songs was published in anticipation of a possible reaction from the clergy (*Pisni*, 498). The anonymous translator (that is, Kuliš himself) was curious as to whether the clergy would approve the poetic version or insist on a prose translation of the two biblical fragments (ibid.). Despite this invocation, no one was particularly surprised to learn of a negative reaction from the conservative Greek Catholic clergy, who historically were not interested in promoting vernacular translations of the Holy Scriptures (Naxlik 2007, 2:273; Danylenko 2008a, 109–110).

At the outset of his work on the translation of the Psalms, Kuliš opted deliberately for another, non-populist creative strategy. He aimed at synthesizing a new high style, which would differ from the high style envisioned by most of the contemporary Ukrainophiles, including Petro Hulak-Artemovs´kyj. Rooted in the vernacular, Kuliš's language tended to blend various linguistic elements, including Church Slavonic and other bookish forms. This was not, however, a mechanistic amalgamation of dissimilar elements but rather an attempt to fuse them in one stylistic key. To give an example of the "classicist adaptation" of vernacular elements, it is worth citing the beginning of Kuliš's paraphrase of Psalm 13:

Доколі, Господи, забудешъ Мене въ напасті до кінця, И одвертатимешъ відъ мене Святу красу Твого лиця? Доколі сумною душею И серцемъ хирявимъ моімъ, На радість ворогу, я буду Молитися стінамъ німимъ? (*Psal´ma* 13)	[1. How long wilt thou forget me, O Lord? For ever? How long wilt thou hide thy face from me? 2. How long shall I take counsel in my soul, having sorrow in my heart daily? How long shall mine enemy be exalted over me?] (Ps 13)

The whole paraphrase is written in iambic tetrameter with alternating female and male rhyme, as if imitating the style and form of the Russian poet Gavrila Deržavin (1743–1816) in order to establish a perceptual framework for the introduction of one of the most intimate pieces of Hebrew poetry. The classicist coloring of this paraphrase is not surprising. Having pioneered first-rate classicist samples in the biblical genre, Kuliš seems to have unwittingly given credit to his father, who loved Pan´ko passionately but bored him with his readings from a leather-bound volume of Deržavin and with arithmetical exercises (Luckyj 1983, 3). It is therefore not surprising that in Kuliš's autobiographical story *Istorija Ul´jany Terent´evny* (The Story of Ul´jana Terent´evna), first published in Russian in 1852, the principal character recalls his father, who indulged in reciting Deržavin, especially the elegy on the death of his friend Field Marshal Aleksandr Suvorov (1729–1800) (Kuliš 1931, 149, 170): "The father, who knew four arithmetic rules and, by heart, all Deržavin's works, was treated by his neighbors as Aristotle" (Nikolaj M. 1852, 139, also 147–148, 161, 178, 193).

CHURCH SLAVONICISMS

In general, Kuliš excelled in the late 1860s as a spontaneous and avid experimenter. In fact, in the "psalmody period" of his creative life, Kuliš proved to be a master of linguistic ingenuity, not constrained by populist predilections and norms. It would be most instructive to compare his normalization endeavors of that period with the language employed by Taras Ševčenko in his biblical writings.

The "psalmody period" of Ševčenko's life falls tentatively into two rounds. During the first round, in the early 1840s, Ševčenko translated eleven psalms of David, conceiving them as stylistic and linguistic replicas of the canonical Church Slavonic translation (M. Moskalenko 2006 1/2, 155). The second round is circumscribed within the years 1857–1859 in the life of the poet. Here we find works of different genres and with different stylistic tours de force. But what gives this period its imprint, according to Shevelov (1962, 69), is Ševčenko's typical "imitations" of biblical prophets and psalms (Psalm 11; Isaiah, chapter 35; Ezekiel, chapter 19; Hosea, chapter 14) (Ševčenko 1963, 2:321–322, 324, 375–376, 378–379) and two poems from the time of the emergence of Christianity: "Neofity" (The Neophytes) and "Marija" (Holy Virgin Mary) (ibid., 279–295). Moreover, the particular style and mood of these poems characterized the majority of the other works of those years as well.

Obviously, there is an undeniable continuity in Ševčenko's turning to the religious themes, motives, images, and ideas that he had already tested out, for instance, in his translations of psalms during the first round. Yet one should bear in mind that the cyclical quality of his literary imaginary was paralleled in a particular set of linguistic means, including Church Slavonicisms commonly used by Ukrainian writers, including Kuliš. Hence the incorporation of many Church Slavonicisms in the poetic language of Ševčenko, whose paraphrases of David's psalms were in no way translations from a foreign language (M. Moskalenko 2006 3/4, 155). This is why, among numerous Church Slavonic forms in the poet's works, one encounters primarily those lexemes that had long ago been appropriated by the lower clergy, gentrified Cossacks, and the common people, all members of an egalitarian and democratic community. For this reason, such Church Slavonic lexemes as *drevo* "tree," *muž* "man," *vospoju* (1 sg. non-past) "to sing, hail," *blahaja* (f.) "good," *vosxvalili* (pl. pret.) "to praise," *izbavy* (2 sg. imper.) "save!," *bezzakonije* "lawlessness," *tvorjaščij* (m. sg. PrAP) "creating," *dokoli* "how long," and many other forms pertaining to both rounds, have never been treated as alien (Rusanivs′kyj 2002, 92). Moreover, many Church Slavonicisms were aptly adapted by Ševčenko to the system of his literary idiom (e.g., *okradenyj* and *obikradenyj* "robbed," *dovhoterpelyvyj* versus *dolhoterpelyvyj* "very patient," and the like) (ibid.).

As far as Church Slavonicisms are concerned, Kuliš and Ševčenko demonstrated different linguistic orientations based not only on their particular *Sprachgefühl* but also on their training and family milieu. As has been suggested, Kuliš was deliberately experimenting with Church Slavonic elements in his translations of the psalms. Ševčenko, instead, used them spontaneously in congruence with the old literary practice still cultivated in the Ukrainian lands. His stance was not unique under contemporary circumstances. Long before, laymen had become familiar with numerous lives of saints and characters of the Bible, Christian legends (many apocryphal), and moralizing works, as well as satiric and facetious verses, including verses of the Christmas and Easter cycles. Their authors and transmitters were vagabond students and teachers who applied the tradition of essentially religious and Church Slavonic baroque poetry to sometimes low subjects and dialects (Shevelov 1979, 710).

All these works Ševčenko imbibed at his mother's knee. As a "consul" in the local primary school, Ševčenko diligently studied Church Slavonic grammar and the *Horologion*. He apparently memorized the Psalter (Uškalov 2006, 194–196). As a boy, Ševčenko learned many holy songs and was familiar with the well-known song "Vsjakomu horodu nrav″ y prava" (Each City Has Its Customs and Its Laws), from Hryhorij Skovoroda's *Garden of Divine Songs*. Later, in his writings, Ševčenko consistently mentioned Christian martyrs and saints, such as Anthony the Great, Saint Catherine, Mary Magdalene, Saint Mark, Saint Nicholas, and especially

Saint Barbara, the most revered literary character in the Baroque Age. Ševčenko was also versed in the intricacies of Dymitrij Tuptalo's *Menaion*, a major Ukrainian collection of the lives of saints. These examples explain and evidence the poet's versatile knowledge of Church Slavonic, at least of its fundamentals as commonly taught and used by the clergy and laymen and found in religious literature from the Baroque Age onward.

Although Kuliš came from an old yet gentrified Cossack family, he missed much of Ševčenko's milieu, having spent his childhood in relative seclusion on a *xutir* (farmstead) on the outskirts of the small town of Voroniž. Life on the *xutir* was not exactly a peasant existence, though all the members of the Kuliš clan worked on the farm and in the apiary, along with a few servants (Luckyj 1983, 3; Naxlik 2007, 1:12–15). In such circumstances, he could hardly establish the steady contact with peasants and their vernacular that might have otherwise exerted some influence on his mastering of the language of the countryside and becoming a proponent of radical Ukrainianness, in social terms, as the nationality of commoners in the spirit of Ševčenko. The influence of his mother, who was all the closer to the Ukrainian language and folk culture, seemed to be minimal, since she died when he was five or six (Kuliš 1868, 21). She managed, however, to instill a love for the Ukrainian language and folk culture in her delicate son—whence came Kuliš's constant quest for an ideal vernacular standard, however open to various admixtures, to be used as a literary language. Not surprisingly, all his life he consistently studied folkloric records and the literary works of his predecessors, such as the Xarkovite Hryhorij Kvitka-Osnov'janenko (1778–1843) (Naxlik 2007, 2:87).

"KULIŠISMS"

Overall, Kuliš's first paraphrases proved successful and no less impressive than translations made by other literati, including Oleksander Navroc´kyj (1823–1892), Volodymyr Aleksandrov (1825–1894), Pylyp Moračevs´kyj (1806–1879), and a handful of anonymous Galician translators (M. Moskalenko 2006 3/4, 161, 163; 5/6, 175). In order to test more consistently the benefits of Kuliš's contribution to the vernacular translation of Hebrew poetry, it will be a productive exercise to discuss the most representative paraphrases made by some of Kuliš's contemporaries.

One should begin with Navroc´kyj, a member of the Cyril and Methodius Society (1845–1847), who, after his imprisonment in 1847 and subsequent exile, was banned from returning to Ukraine (M. Moskalenko 2006 3/4, 161). This latter fact could have instigated his keen interest in different literatures and translation from various languages. Unfortunately, his major translations of Homer's epics, *The Iliad* and *The Odyssey*, and of Šota Rustaveli's *The Knight in the Panther's Skin*, as well as the bulk of his original literary output, have never been published. For our discussion, however, of particular interest are his paraphrases from Hebrew poetry, *Pisn´ pisen´* (The Song of Songs; *Pisn´*, Navroc´kyj) and *Knyha Psal´miv Proroka Davyda* (A Book of Psalms; *Psal´my*, Navroc´kyj), which show some minimal degree of linguistic creativity. This is why, being notoriously exigent in his demands for literary perfection, Kuliš called Navroc´kyj, rather deprecatingly, "a nice guy without any talent" (Barvins´kyj 2004, 146). For instance, to illustrate his heavy dependency on Kuliš's paraphrases, suffice it to mention the form, found in Navroc´kyj's translations of the psalms, *zlorečč̌ja* (*Psal´my*, Navroc´kyj, 1), which was obviously derived from Kuliš's neologism *zlorikyj* and used in his translation of the same psalm (*Psal´ma* 1) (*zlorika* "a scornful person" [*Psaltyr*, Rataj, 107] and *zloričyty* "to backbite" [Hrinč. 1:696]). This verb is also attested in the writings of Kornylo Ustyjanovyč (1839–1903), a Galician artist and writer (Žel., 1:304), who as a contributor to the periodical *Pravda* might have borrowed it from Kuliš's language, which was very popular at that time among the western Ukrainian populists.

Among similar "Kulišisms" in the language of Navroc´kyj, one should also cite the noun *pravycja* "the right hand," a word coined by Kuliš (see, e.g., *Pentatevx*, 146) and used by Navroc´kyj (*Psal´my*, Navroc´kyj, 25v) in his translation of the same Psalm 16 (according to the Hebrew numbering) (*Psal´ma* 16), and similarly *pravaja ruka* (*Psal´my*, Navroc´kyj, 32v). One should add also *tverža* "support, foundation" (*Psal´my*, Navroc´kyj, 28v), an apparent neologism used by Kuliš in his paraphrase of the same Psalm 18 (according to the Hebrew numbering) (*Psaltyr*, Rataj, 130), although not attested in the dictionary of Borys

Hrinčenko (Žel., 2:952). Another apparent Kulišism is *zapomoha* "help" (*Psal'my*, Navroc'kyj, 36), that is, "saving strength" (Ps 20:6), which occurs in Kuliš's translation of the Psaltyr (e.g., *Psaltyr*, Rataj, 118).

Of particular interest is the diminutive *levčuk* "young lion" (*Psal'my*, Navroc'kyj, 28), a lexeme used by Kuliš in his paraphrase of Psalm 17 (according to the Hebrew numbering) (*Psaltyr*, Rataj, 129; *SP*, 511; Horbač 1988, 62). Remarkably, this word became popular among both Greek Catholic and Orthodox translators of the Hebrew Scriptures. Suffice it to say that in his translation of the same psalm (*Psaltyr'*, Bačyn'skij, 30; Haluščynskyj 1925, 317–318), the Greek Catholic priest Aleksander Bačyn'skij preferred Kuliš's neologism to the local diminutive form *levyk* (Žel., 1:399). It is noteworthy that the same Kulišism occurs in the same psalm translated by Ivan Ohijenko (*SP*, Ohijenko, 547), while Ivan Xomenko-Pljuta opted for another diminutive, *levenja* "young lion" (*SP*, Xomenko, 626). The latter form might have been also derived, or at least introduced into the written language, by Kuliš (Hrinč., 1:886; Žel., 1:399). It is therefore not surprising that in his poetic translation of the book of Job, Kuliš employed the two diminutives, *levuk* and *levenja*, in the same verse (*Yov*, 1869, 10).

One cannot omit the verb *jasuvaty* "to explain, speak for" (*Psal'my*, Navroc'kyj, 34v), a form consistently used (and apparently coined) by Kuliš (e.g., *Psaltyr*, Rataj, 119). The imperfective infinitive *jasyty* is attested in the dictionaries of Borys Hrinčenko and Jevhen Želexivs'kyj. The latter dictionary (Žel., 2:1116) also has another imperfective form, *jasuvaty*, excerpted from the written output of Myxajlo Staryc'kyj (1840–1904). Nevertheless, the chronological priority should be given to Kuliš, who used this verb very consistently long before Navroc'kyj and Staryc'kyj.

Among other obvious lexical Kulišisms in Navroc'kyj's translation are *tisnjava* "tightness, denseness" (*Psal'my*, Navroc'kyj, 29), also introduced into the written language by Kuliš (Hrinč., 2:776; Žel., 2:967), *potuha* "power" (*Psal'my*, Navroc'kyj, 22), one of Kuliš's favorite Galicianisms of Polish origin (Shevelov 1966, 42), *plid* "fruit," used by Navroc'kyj in the paraphrase of Psalm 1 (*Psal'my*, Navroc'kyj, 1), where Kuliš employed a bookish counterpart, without *ikavism* (*Psal'ma* 1; Horbač 1988, 60), perhaps *tamečky* "over there" (*Psal'my*, Navroc'kyj,

2v), a colloquial and dialectal form influenced by Kuliš's vernacular diminutives of the type *tamen'ky* (*SP*, 14; Gen 12:10). Here also belongs *vysokist'*, which is found in Navroc'kyj's translation of Psalm 18 (according to the Hebrew numbering) (*Psal'my*, Navroc'kyj, 30v) and attested also in Kuliš's paraphrase of the same psalm (*Psaltyr*, Rataj, 132).

The list of lexical transfers, which we call Kulišisms, and parallels (regular lexemes found in parallel translations of the two writers) could be expanded. This speaks for Navroc'kyj's slavish leaning on Kuliš; however, such borrowing seems to have been a common practice among the Ukrainian translators of that and subsequent times. For instance, despite its original archaic and folkloric embellishments, Ivan Ohijenko's translation of the Bible (*SP*, Ohijenko) was heavily modeled on Moračevs'kyj's translation of the New Testament made in the early 1860s (Horbač 1988, 78). From this point of view, Kuliš was more independent, although he might have also consulted (a copy of) Moračevs'kyj's translation.

In this respect, Navroc'kyj's case is most revealing. In combining Church Slavonic and folkloric (vernacular) forms, he merely mimicked Kuliš's style and poetic idiom. Thus, among the Church Slavonic forms used by Navroc'kyj one can cite the following: *vosxvalyty* "to praise," *blahyj* "feeble," *blahannja* "entreaty," *blahoslovennja* "blessing," *blažennyj* "blissful" (*Psal'my*, Navroc'kyj, 33v, 4v, 25, 26v), *drevo* "tree," and *premudryj* "sage" (ibid., 1). Also present are active present participles like *žyvuščyj* "he that lives" and *tvorjaščyj* "he that creates" (ibid., 2v, 22v), as are some Russian Church Slavonic forms such as *Vladўka* "Lord," *vyšni čertohy* "celestial palace, heaven," and, perhaps, *vsue* "in vain" (ibid., 29, 34). The problem for Navroc'kyj lay rather in the ratio of such forms. After all, they were routinely used not only by Kuliš but also by other Ukrainian authors, especially Ševčenko. Yet, unlike Kuliš, the number of Church Slavonicisms in Navroc'kyj's translation was conspicuously smaller. He used folkloric and vernacular elements in abundance, such as long (uncontracted) adjectives in cases like *narodnjaja syla* "people's power," *ljuds'kyi suddi* "people's judges," *ledačyi ljude* "ungodly people," *velykee blaho* "great good," *tjažkyi muky* "great sufferings" (2x), and *mury vysokyi* "high walls" next to regular (contracted) forms like *premudra sprava* "intricate question," that is, "the law of God" (ibid., 1v, 3, 4v, 22v, 31, 31v; Ps 1, 18), and also set expressions such as *brexnju hovoryty* "to tell lies" or intensifying constructions comprising two entities (e.g., *potuha-syla* "extreme power," *isty-požyraty* "to devour," *hynuty-pohybaty* "to perish," *ranen'ko-rano* "very early," and *t'ma t'mušča* "darkness") (*Psal'my*, Navroc'kyj, 22, 2, 23, 4v). Finally, the vocabulary of Navroc'kyj's translation was permeated with numerous vernacular lexemes, such as *nyškom* "imperceptibly," *oselja* "homestead," *lyxva* "profit, usury," *movljaty* "to say," *lynuty* "to rush, flow," and *šuhaty* "to hover" (ibid., 28, 15, 24v, 27v, 24, 25). In some places, one encounters in Navroc'kyj's translation synonyms occurring ostentatiously side by side, yet without the generation of semantic nuances that are so characteristic of Kuliš's stylistically variegated language (e.g., *pidmoha* and *pidpora* occurring on one page [*Psal'my*, Navroc'kyj, 30v], with the synonymous *zastupa* and *zaslona* "defense, protection" on another page [ibid., 32] in Psalm 18).

Some phonological and morphological dialecticisms are particularly characteristic of Navroc'kyj's language. To begin with phonology, it is worth mentioning a lack of neutralization of obstruent voicing across morpheme and word boundary (Danylenko 2006c, 189–190) (e.g., *zkaraty* "to punish," *zkepkuvaty* "to scoff," *z šljaxu* "off the way [of the righteous]," *z xaty* "from the house" [*Psal'my*, Navroc'kyj, 23v, 24v, 25v]). One could also point to some distinctive *sandhi* positions of the type *pido mnoju* "under me," *peredo mnoju* "in front of me" (ibid., 31, 33), where the secondary *o* shows no analogical change into *i* before clusters of consonants (Žovtobrjux et al. 1979, 283); see also *pered Bohom* "in front of God," *pered nym* "in front of him" (*Psal'my*, Navroc'kyj, 31, 34). Sporadically, one happens on the retention (reintroduction) of the etymological *o* in place of the new *i*, such as *vojny* (gen.) "war" (ibid., 32), which may be stylistically marked or simply reflect an areal phenomenon transitional from Southwest to Northeast Ukrainian (Varčenko 1954, 57).[4]

---

4 As a matter of fact, the alternation *o* : *i* is also absent in some dialectal (northern Ukrainian) forms like *vuhollja* "coil" (*Psal'my*, Navroc'kyj, 30; *AUM*, 1, map 164) with an anaptyctic vowel *o* in contrast to *e* attested mainly in the southwestern Ukrainian dialects (Flier 1993, 258). As far as the later form *vuhillja* with *ikavism* is concerned, one can explain it, following Shevelov (1979, 592), as a blend of dialectal *vuhil'* "coal" and *hillja* "twigs" (from which charcoal was made). For our case, the northern Ukrainian form *vuhollja* in Navroc'kyj is particularly interesting inasmuch as the translator's native dialect was located in the Čerkasy region, that is, in the same

In terms of morphology, one should mention vernacular adjectives of the type *paljučyj* and *harjučyj* "hot" (*Psal'my*, Navroc'kyj, 30; Danylenko 2006c, 78–86), third-person singular present tense forms, typically employed by southeastern Ukrainian authors, such as *oberta* "to turn," *obhorta ljakom* "to strike fear," *ljaha* "to lie down" (*Psal'my*, Navroc'kyj, 2v), numerous dative case forms in *-ovi/-evi*, including vernacular (folkloric) *sercevi* "heart" (ibid., 25v; Matvijas 2006, 55–56), and instrumental case forms with the hard-stem ending *-oju*, such as *dušoju* "soul." Attested cross-dialectally (Bevzenko et al. 1978, 79), the latter forms were also used by Ševčenko as a result of the generalization of the hard-stem conjugational paradigm (Tymošenko 1968, 137, 151). Finally, it is interesting to note two competing endings, *-e* and *-a*, used by Navroc'kyj for second declension neuter nouns with the assimilated *j* and resulting gemination. In fact, the translator employed three types of such nouns. The first one is modeled on Church Slavonic forms (e.g., *stohnanie* "groaning") (*Psal'my*, Navroc'kyj, 9), while the two other types are likely to reflect two competing dialectal inflections. One of them is the predominantly northern inflectional type in *-e* (e.g., *svidčennje* "evidence," *bezzakonnje* "unlawfulness") (ibid., 35, 9), and the second is the southeastern type in *-a* (e.g., *bezzakonnja*, *oblyččja* "face" [ibid., 6v, 21v]). The latter type prevails, thereby tentatively speaking for the transitional nature of Navroc'kyj's native dialect.

Leaving aside certain intricacies of its poetics, Navroc'kyj's language appeared to be fully in congruence with the written standard cultivated by Ševčenko and his populist followers. Navroc'kyj based his language on vernacular and folkloric foundations, although with an admixture of Church Slavonicisms and few Polonisms. For this reason, his paraphrases were sometimes cast in a solid folkloric form, although with some seemingly hackneyed rhythms and poetic clichés. However, and one should emphasize this fact again, the influence of Kuliš's paraphrases on Navroc'kyj's language was so massive that he could not help but borrow some elements from Kuliš's written standard, including numerous Kulišisms, which stood in contrast with the populist paradigm at that time.

---

transitional dialectal area where Ševčenko's dialect belonged (Danylenko 2006c, 358, 369–370, 2001, 272–273, 282–283; Rusanivs'kyj 2002, 41–44).

XARKIV CHIMES IN

A somewhat different approach toward the translation of the Holy Scriptures was taken by the Xarkovite poet Volodymyr Aleksandrov, a famous translator of Latin, German, Russian, and Polish (M. Moskalenko 2006 3/4, 161). Purportedly impressed by Kuliš's translations, he committed himself to translating the psalms using a completely revised poetic medium. With an eye to producing a most faithful translation of the Psalter into the Ukrainian vernacular, he assiduously studied Hebrew. This certainly helped him to offer a poetic rendering less dependent on the Church Slavonic version.

In a preface to the "Ukrainian Psalter," entitled *Tÿxomovni spivÿ na svjati motivÿ* (Quiet Songs on Sacred Motifs), on which he worked during 1882 and 1883, Aleksandrov outlined a new programmatic view of scriptural translation into Ukrainian, totally different from that of Kuliš at that time. Having opted for a poetic form with a syllabic-tonic structure, he decided to offer a radically new translation that would differ from the Church Slavonic version. First of all, he warned his readers that, while using a poetic medium, it was impossible to translate word for word; this would explain, he argued, the resulting dissonance between his translation and the Church Slavonic version (*Spivÿ*, 4–14). Aleksandrov based his work, instead, on the Great Russian translation of the entire Psalter, *Psalmÿ: Bukval'nÿj perevod"* (Psalms: A Literal Translation), made by Leon Mandel'štam and published in Berlin in 1871. The latter, according to Aleksandrov, could serve as a model for the reconstruction of "the true message of the Hebrew text" as well as for the true meanings of the words employed by the psalmists. In fact, Aleksandrov used Mandel'štam's translation critically, working out his own interpretation of some *loci classici*. To adduce just one example, he retained the Church Slavonic beginning in Psalm 1, *blažen" toj čolovik"* (*Spivÿ*, Ps 1; *Biblija* 1862, 277r), in contrast to Mandel'štam's *slava čelověku* that, as Aleksandrov believed, was poorly grounded in the original.

As a result, Aleksandrov maintained that, having followed the "exact lexical meanings of the words," he translated truthfully (*po ščyrij pravdi*). Even though the psalms were presented in verse form, Aleksandrov argued that his work did not deviate from their true message; rather, it shed light on some vague places in the Church Slavonic translation. In conclusion, he expressed his hope to see other biblical texts translated into the mother tongue in the same manner, that is, within a framework of reference to the poetry of the Old Testament (*Spivŷ*).

Unlike Navroc′kyj, Aleksandrov's translation reads easily and is, in fact, very close to the local variety of literary Ukrainian conceived in the ferment of the first half of the nineteenth century by the Xarkiv Romanticists. Largely reminiscent of Hulak-Artemovs′kyj's vernacularizing tendency in the poetic presentation of conventional biblical themes, Aleksandrov's attempt to adhere to the same tradition is especially noticeable in vocabulary, grammar, and metrical system. Nevertheless, his translations could hardly compete with those made by Hulak-Artemovs′kyj and even Maksymovyč, whose originality was demonstrated in their choice of poetic forms. Aleksandrov's uncertainty in applying poetic technique to the structuring of the language is more than evident in his translation of Psalm 1:

Aleksandrov's Translation	**Maksymovyč's Translation**
Блаженъ той чоловікъ, що по совіту	Блаженъ мужъ той, що не ввойде
Людей безпутныхъ не ходывъ	Въ раду нечестивыхъ,
И не стоявъ на іхъ дорозі	И не стане на дорозѣ
И въ раді зъ нымы не сыдівъ;	Грѣшныхъ, неправдивыхъ,
А все до Божого Закону	И не сяде у беседѣ
Душею й серцемъ припадавъ,	Людей израдливыхъ;
Про той законъ Законъ щодня, щоночі	А въ Господнёму законѣ
	Свою держить волю,
И помышлявъ и розсуждавъ.	День и нôчъ себе навчає
Вінъ буде мовъ плодове древо,	Закону Господню.
Посажене біля воды:	И якъ древо, надъ потокомъ
На ёму листя не повьяне	Посажене чистымъ,
И въ пору дасть воно плоды.	Плодъ приносить въ свою пору
(*Spivŷ*, Ps 1)	И не вьяне листомъ.
	(Maksimovič 1859, 3)

Maksymovyč's translation looks like a typical paraphrase made in the spirit of Hulak-Artemovs´kyj, while Aleksandrov's text shows tension between the author's adherence to the folkloric tradition and a modicum of originality. Yet his originality is regionally limited, hence the use of Church Slavonic and Russian forms (e.g., *rozsuždav"* [m. sg. pret.] "to meditate" and *sovsim"* "altogether, completely") (*Spivỹ*, Ps 1), in addition to those Church Slavonicisms that also occur in Maksymovyč and even Kuliš: *plod"* (Maksimovič 1859, 3; *Psal´ma* 1); also compare *plodove drevo, posažene bilja vodỹ* in Aleksandrov (*Spivỹ*, Ps 1) to the vernacular rendering in Kuliš—*dobre drevo, posadžene kolo krynyci*, "a tree planted by the rivers of water" (*Psal´ma* 1).

Generally, Aleksandrov's language contains some lexemes which, belonging to the older literary tradition, are also attested in the works of Kuliš and other contemporaries (e.g., *od"* "from," *lyce* "face," *mini* [dat.] "I," old aorists *proreče* and *reče* [3 sg. pret.] "to declare," *šatro* "tent" [*Spivỹ*, 31] referring to "tabernacle" [Ps 15:1], *žurba* as a substitute for the original *pečal´* [*Psalom"* 20], Church Slavonicisms like *hlas"* "voice," *honỹtel´* "persecutor," *blahodijstvo* "bounty," *spasenie* next to *spasennja* "salvation," and some other forms). Yet, what is remarkable about Aleksandrov's language is its local (southeastern Ukrainian) coloring, especially evident in its grammar (e.g., *v" očyx"* "in the eyes" [*Spivỹ*, 32] with the ending -*ix* [< -ьхъ], typical of the Sloboda dialect [Bevzenko et al. 1978, 112]), and third-person singular present tense verb forms of the type *zminja* "to change" and *robe* "to do" (*Spivỹ*, 32), as found in works of eastern Ukrainian authors in the nineteenth century (Bevzenko et al. 1978, 317–318).

To show the regional limitations of Aleksandrov's poetic approach as compared with Kuliš's attempt to create a synthetic poetic rendering of the entire Psalter, it is instructive to compare parallel fragments from the two translations of Psalm 16:

Aleksandrov's Translation
Сохрани мене, мій Боже!
Я на тебе уповаю,
На единого на Тебе
Всю надію покладаю.

Kuliš's Translation
Сохрани мене[,] мій Боже,
На Тебе моя надія.
Ти не требуєш від мене,
Щоб тобі добро я діяв,

Ти, душе моя благая, Пророкла еси до себе: Ти Господь мій и Владыка И ніхто окроме Тебе. . . . Боже! Ты міні покажешъ Всіхъ одрадъ незлічні ліки, Жизни путь и світлу радість Предъ лицемъ Твоімъ во віки. (*Spivŷ*, 33)	А щоб добрими ділами Ущедряв твоіх спасенних И кохав іх щирим серцем Серед грішників мизерних, . . . Ти покажеш міні, Боже, Стежку праведну на світі: Повно щастя коло тебе, Радість вічня—по правиці. (*Psal′ma* 16)

[1. Preserve me, O God: for in thee do I put my trust.

2. O my soul, thou hast said unto the lord. Thou art my Lord: my goodness extendeth not to thee.

3. But to the saints that are in the earth, and to the excellent, in whom is all my delight . . .

11. Thou will show me the path of life: in thy presence is fullness of joy; at thy right hand there are pleasures for evermore.] (Ps 16)

Remarkably, both translations have the same metrical foot—they are written entirely in trochees, thus revealing the same vernacularizing approach of the two translators. Moreover, the two translations have the same beginning, based most likely on the Church Slavonic text. However, Aleksandrov tries to follow the Hebrew original, although his translation contains many Church Slavonicisms as well (e.g., the obsolete perfect *prorekla esy* [2 sg. f.] "to say," non-pleophonic *blahaja* [f.] "good," *Vladŷka* "sovereign," *pred″* "before," the verb *soxrany* [2 sg. imper.] "preserve!," *upovaju* [1 sg. pres.] "to put trust," also *žyzny put′* in contrast to ChSl. *put′ žyvota* "path of life") (*Biblija* 1862, 279r).

Kuliš is more dependent on the poetics of the Church Slavonic translation. Suffice it to say that he uses his favorite neologism, *pravycja*, in reference to the Church Slavonic equivalent *desnyca* "right hand." However, the lexical and grammatical make-up of Kuliš's translation looks more uniform in comparison with the language of Aleksandrov. The latter's language is rather more contrastive, with a wide stylistic gap between the above-cited Church Slavonic devices and plain vernacular (folkloric) elements. The general impression is that Aleksandrov's creative ability had not yet achieved a functional apogee compatible with that of Kuliš's paraphrases.

All in all, there is an apparent contrast between Kuliš, on the one hand, and the translations of Aleksandrov and his populist predecessors, on the other, who, nevertheless, attempted to ground their language standard in a somewhat different cultural and ideological framework. Suffice it to mention here the poetic trend developed by Pylyp Moračevs´kyj in his translation of the Psalter in 1865. Although not published until 2015 (*Psaltyr"*, Moračevs´kyj), this translation had much in common with those of Aleksandrov and especially Maksymovyč. The translation of Psalm 1 by Moračevs´kyj speaks for itself: it shows solid vernacular foundations with numerous long naturalized Church Slavonicisms commonly used in Dnieper Ukraine, such as the nominal adjectival forms *blažen* "blessed" and *nečestyvyi* (pl.) "ungodly," *zakon Hospodny* "law of the Lord," *lyce* "face," and the like.

Moračevs´kyj's Translation of Psalm 1

1. *Блаженъ* той чоловікъ, хто не ходить на раду *нечестивихъ*, и на дорозі грішнихъ не *становитця*, и на лавці душогубцівъ не сідае;

2. А у *законі господнёму* уся воля ёго, и въ законі ёго навчаєтця день и ніч.

3. Вінъ, якъ древо посажене при потокахъ водъ, що овощъ свій дає у свій часъ, и *листъ* ёго не опадае, и усе, що тількі вінъ робить, буде гараздъ.

[1. Blessed is the man that walketh not in the counsel of the ungodly, nor standeth in the way of sinners, nor sitteth in the seat of the scornful.

2. But his delight is in the law of the Lord; and in his law doth he meditate day and night.

3. And he shall be like a tree planted by the rivers of water, that bringeth forth his fruit in his season; his leaf also shall not wither, and whatsoever he doeth shall prosper.

4. Не такъ *нечестивіи*, не такъ, але якъ та курява пилу, що вітеръ зъ *лиця* землі підоймае.	4. The ungodly are not so: but are like the chaff which the wind driveth away.
5. Такъ, не встоять *нечестивіи* на суді, и грішники на раді *праведнихъ*.	5. Therefore the ungodly shall not stand in the judgement, nor sinners in the congregation of the righteous.
6. Бо знає Господь дорогу *праведнихъ*, а дорога *нечестивихъ* загине. (*Psaltyr″*, Moračevs′kyj, 33; *Psaltyr*, Moračevs′kyj, 3r)	6. For the Lord knoweth the way of the righteous: but the way of the ungodly shall perish.] (Ps 1)

The question remains as to what Kuliš could offer instead of this amalgam of the southeastern Ukrainian vernacular and Church Slavonic. What is evidenced in his early translations of Hebrew poetry is that he was prepared to synthesize elements excerpted from various dialects, though primarily Southeast Ukrainian, and previous literary traditions. Kuliš's language program tended to transgress the Little Russian cultural space and time, frozen as it was within the confines of the Russian Empire. His original vision of the future of the Ukrainian language became ever more obvious in his later translations of the Holy Scriptures, and in particular of the Psalter.

THE 1897 POETIC CROWNING

Kuliš's indefatigable stamina in elaborating on the interpretation of psalmody in the Ukrainian language led him, in 1897, to undertake a poetic translation of the lyrical pearls of Hebrew poetry (Voznjak 1928a, 216). His intent was to set out the entire Psalter in syllabic-tonic patterns on vernacular foundations. This was a revolutionary plan that resulted in a series of pioneering translations, never equaled before (or after) in Ukrainian literature.

To take again Psalm 1 as an example, one notes first of all a new beginning in the translation of 1897, deviating not only from the Church

Slavonic but also from almost all other translations or paraphrases made in the nineteenth century. There is no place for the traditional Church Slavonic form *blažen"*!

> Благо тому, хто не ходить у раду ледачу
> И не стоить зупинившись на грішний дорозі,
> И не сідае в громаді злорік язикатих.
> Ніж до *закону Господнёго* хилитьця серцем
> И про *Господень закон* уночі й удень дбае.
> Мов над криницею дерево, буде рости він,
> Те, що *плоди* свои родить щоліта, роскішне,
> И ёго лисьтє не жовкне, не сиплецьцья марно. . . . (*Psaltyr'* 1897)

The most significant feature of the new poetic translation is the use of a limited number of Church Slavonic and other bookish forms. Indeed, the 1897 translation was designed by Kuliš so as to meet the aesthetic needs of the common people, who were accustomed to listening to biblical accounts transmitted through the art of performance, either through the popular activities of folk religion or within the more formal liturgy of the church community. Yet, his was not a total ban on the use of Church Slavonic forms. On the contrary, Kuliš easily resorted to those forms, which were familiar to the Ukrainian clergy and laymen almost from the cradle. They are *Hospoden' zakon* "the law of the Lord," referring to a concept indispensable in the biblical Psalms, and the lexeme *plod"* "fruit," belonging to the older literary tradition. This may explain why this lexeme is attested in Ivan Kotljarevs´kyj's *Enejida* (*Enejida*, Index, 128), too. Interestingly enough, Kuliš retained in the translation of 1897 his favorite neologism, *zlorika*, first used as *zlorikyj* "a scornful person" in the 1868 paraphrase of the same psalm (*Psal'ma* 1). In the 1897 translation, the word *zlorika* is enhanced by a descriptive adjective, *jazykatyj* "talkative."

The orthography used in this translation also speaks for the distinctiveness of Kuliš's approach in 1897. But this distinctiveness does not diminish the contrast between Kuliš, as a translator of the late 1860s, and other contemporary translators of the poems and psalms of the

Hebrew Bible. We certainly have to mention here the "most radical phonetics" of Ukrainian spelling propagated by Kuliš from 1881 onward (Barvins´kyj 2004, 201) and applied consistently in his new translation of the Psalter in 1897. For instance, leaving aside the Russian letter "ё," which was commonly used at that time in Russian-ruled Ukraine, Kuliš employed the letter "є," denoting palatalized consonants only, as in *lys´tje* "leafage." He also marked assimilation (assibilation) of consonants at the morpheme boundary before the reflexive particle in verb forms of the type *xylyc´cja* (3 sg. pres.) "to be inclined toward" and *syplec´cja* (3 sg. pres.) "to pour forth," as compared with "less radically" phonetic spellings of the type *xovajutcja* (3 pl. pres.) "to hide" in his earlier spelling practice (*Kobzar*).

Finally, one should note another peculiar spelling in Kuliš's autograph of 1897, reminiscent of the orthographic rule implemented by Jevhen Želexivs´kyj in his *Malorusko-nimeckyj slovar* (Little Russian-German Dictionary, 1884–1886), revised after his death by Sofron Nedil´s´kyj (1857–1917) (Žel., 1:viii). Unlike *želexivka*, where all sibilants before the letter *v* were marked as palatalized, Kuliš denoted assimilative palatalization of these sounds in the position before all kinds of obstruents (e.g., *lys´tje* with palatalization of a sibilant before the dental *t* and so forth) (Danylenko 2012b).

In contrast to the author's first poetic paraphrases, the 1897 rendering of the entire Psalter proved unexpectedly "less poetic," despite the fact that it followed rather straightforwardly the biblical narration in terms of style, form, and even structure (Gillingham 1994, 18–21). Kuliš demonstrated a more sophisticated distinction between prose and poetry in his translation of 1897, with its stronger evocative power and his intention to distance himself from obvious folkloric structures. One of the best examples is Kuliš's translation of Psalm 14 (according to the Greek numbering), especially if compared with the trochaic meter used in the corresponding translation made by Aleksandrov. The lack of this metric foot in Kuliš's translation is surprising since he was famous for introducing the trochaic verse into Ukrainian poetry, as attested, for instance, in Rataj's 1868 translation of the same psalm (*Psal´ma* 15).

Kuliš's Translation of 1897	Aleksandrov's Translation of 1882–1883
Господи! Хто у наметі мойму по заслузі госьтиме? Хто по заслузі живе на с[ь]вятій горі в тебе? Той хто по праведьній ходить дорозі, все робить по правді И в свойму серьці говорить одну щиру правду. . . . Хто в сьвіті ходить сим робом, Хитатись ніколи не буде. (*Psaltyr'* 1897, Ps 14)	Господи! Хто зможе жыты У твоім шатрі? Хто поселитця у Тебе На святій горі? Той, хто ходе непорочно, Крывды не творыть; Той, хто звыкъ въ незлобстві серця Правду говорыть. . . . Хто так робе,—той по кривді Честный чоловікъ, Той нігде не похытнетьця, Не змылыть во вікъ! (*Spivy̆*, 31–32)

In addition to changes in the poetic form, Kuliš also introduced new vocabulary. The most arresting example is the expression *hrišmy procentuvaty* "to take reward (by usury)" (*Psaltyr'* 1897, Ps 14). Deserving of attention is also *lyšku* (acc. sg. f.) *pryjmaty* in 1868 (*Psal'ma* 15), which was replaced, as has been mentioned, by the western Ukrainian form *lyxva* (f.) "profit, reward" in the *Prosvita* edition of 1909 (Kuliš 1909, 3:127). No less surprising is the fact that Aleksandrov also used a similar, "modernized" expression, *v˝ procenty̆ hroši davaty* (*Spivy̆*, 32). Yet again, in this case, Kuliš remained faithful to himself by offering a neologism, *procentuvaty*, rather than resorting to the aforementioned Russian calque found in Aleksandrov (Ukr. *procent pravyty* [Hrinč., 2:493]).

Already in his early paraphrases of the psalms, one can discern the magisterial individuality of Kuliš's approach toward the development of new literary Ukrainian. Unlike the confluence between vernacular and colloquial devices found in the work of Petro Hulak-Artemovs'kyj, Volodymyr Aleksandrov, and Oleksander Navroc'kyj, or the style of folklore in Myxajlo Maksymovyč, Kuliš favored more heterogeneous means in creating a new high style. Marked by obvious talent, some of his paraphrases could look experimental, while others were exemplary from the point of view of their stylistically multifarious nature. This is why the vernacular translations of Aleksandrov and especially of Navroc´kyj could hardly compete with Kuliš's paraphrases, and even less so with his poetic translation of 1897.

However, the baroque architectonics of Ševčenko's translations speak to the poet's strong footing in a vernacular permeated with long-naturalized (vernacularized) Church Slavonicisms. Obviously, vernacularization of the Church Slavonic legacy was at variance with Kuliš's programmatic views. For this reason, he tried to break the linguistic confines of the burlesque modality of the vernacular paradigm (*kotljarevščyna*), set up by the epigones of Ivan Kotljarevs´kyj (Ajzenštok 1928), by freely resorting to Church Slavonic and other dialectal elements, and ultimately by revealing the vista of a new language standard. Kuliš's first translations were only the beginning of his life-long work on the translation of the Holy Scriptures, which, in the long run, demonstrated a pioneering fusion of linguistic devices pertaining to different style registers and dialects.

CHAPTER 2
The Makings of the Rusian Bible

A *PENTATEVX* PROLUSION

In 1869, after the publication of Kuliš's book of Psalms and the *Pentatevx Musijevyj* (Pentateuch), Natal´ Vaxnjanin (Vaxnjanyn, 1841–1908), a young confidant of the translator and the editor of the periodical *Pravda*, suggested that Kuliš submit his translation for publication by the British and Foreign Bible Society in Vienna. Having received Kuliš's consent, Vaxnjanin contacted a representative of the society, Edward Millard (1822–1906), who in turn expressed his wish to have the manuscript of the Ukrainian Pentateuch first reviewed by the priests and writers Ivan Naumovyč and Hryhorij Hnylevyč, as well as by some other local intellectuals—even though none were specialists in linguistics (Studyns´kyj 1930, xxxii–xxxiii). Miller chose Franz Miklosich (Franjo Miklošić, 1813–1891), a prominent Slovenian-Austrian Slavist who had previously approached the society asking to be informed about any Ukrainian translation of the Bible already existing or in preparation, as a reviewer.

A famous ethnographer and public figure in Galicia, Meliton Bučyns´kyj (1847–1903), wrote in a letter of 12 April 1872 to his Dnieper correspondent Ivan Rudčenko (1845–1905) that Millard had secretly passed Kuliš's translation of the Holy Scriptures to some Galician and Bukovynian literati, including prominent Russophiles, such as Ivan Naumovyč, Antin Petruševyč, and Ivan Branik from Černivci. All of them heavily criticized the phonetic orthography introduced by Kuliš, although their understanding of linguistic phenomena in general was minimal to say the least (Studyns´kyj 1930, xxxii–xxxiii). For instance, in 1868 in Kolomyja, Branik published an amateurish treatise entitled *Pryčyna tvorenija sja narěčej* (A Reason for the Formation of Languages). Full of fallacious etymologies and far-reaching hypotheses, the book was strongly criticized, and rightly so, by Omeljan Partyc'kyj (1840–1895) in *Pravda*. In particular, the reviewer brought to the attention of the readership Branik's deficient argumentation about the advantages of etymological orthography in Ukrainian. In effect, as Partyc'kyj (1868, 250) noted, Branik adduced "semi-etymological information" about three vowels, *o*, *ě*, and *ў*, only with an eye to proving the inevitability of the adoption of the etymological principle in spelling.

Considering the biased criticism of his work by the aforementioned Galician and Bukovynian literati, Kuliš did not accept their verdict and asked Millard to approach Miklosich about a possible review. On 2 February 1871, Kuliš sent to Ivan Puljuj (1845–1918), whom he had befriended in 1869 in Vienna, "all those parts of the Holy Scripture [The New Testament]" in which Millard might have been most interested. Kuliš assured him that he "had translated word for word in accordance with Greek," and in murky places consulted the English version, disregarding all other translators, including Martin Luther (Studyns'kyj 1930, 8).

According to Puljuj (1905, 23), Millard received some samples of Kuliš's translation and expedited them right away to Miklosich. The latter concluded that Kuliš's translation was a mere paraphrase rather than a close translation of the original Greek text. Millard then informed Kuliš that the Bible Society was ready to buy a Ukrainian translation of the Holy Scriptures, provided it was an exact copy of the Greek original (Studyns'kyj 1930, xxvii–xxviii). Disappointed but not entirely disillusioned, Kuliš accepted, understanding Miklosich's critique, taken as a whole, as fair and well-balanced. Kuliš truly believed in the future of the Bible in Ukrainian. This is why, in a letter of 8 October 1871 written to Puljuj from Dnieper Ukraine, he prophesied that "the Rusian Bible [*Rusyns'ka Byblyja*] will follow its own way without his [Millard's] mercy, though not so fast" (ibid., 11).

GEARING UP FOR NEW CHALLENGES

Arguably, Kuliš's first translations of the Holy Scriptures were largely poetic paraphrases. In the late 1860s, while working on the translation of a series of psalms, Kuliš had in fact only a vague idea as to how to translate the Bible into vernacular Ukrainian. Should such a translation be poetic (loose) or prosaic (faithful)? Yet what he knew for sure was the importance of the Bible in the everyday life of all Ukrainian laymen. Moreover, the Ukrainian Bible would be of paramount importance from a wider, international point of view. Having received a Ukrainian translation of the Bible, Europe would be able to recognize the uniqueness of the Ukrainian people, their culture, and their language. In a letter of 6 July 1871 to Oleksander Barvinsʹkyj (1847–1927), a prominent cultural figure in Galicia at that time, Kuliš expanded on the power of the Ukrainian Bible, which, he firmly believed, could guarantee the political equality of the Austrian Rusyns with their Polish neighbors (Barvinsʹkyj 2004, 167). Conversely, in order to persuade the Great Russians of the ethno-cultural distinctiveness of Ukraine, the Ukrainians had, first, to make Europe turn her face to Ukraine (Naxlik 2007, 1:247).

However, before embarking on a translation of the Bible, Kuliš had to address several critical questions. To begin with, how could one reconcile folk culture with the enlightenment of the Ukrainian people? Could one translate the Bible into vernacular Ukrainian without resorting to the common Church Slavonic legacy claimed largely by the Great Russians? To what extent was one supposed to incorporate into such a translation previous literary tradition(s), especially the baroque style that flourished during the Cossack period? Would creating an exclusively vernacular translation diminish the authority of the Ukrainian nobility (*šljaxta*) and elevate instead the peasantry together with the "barbarous Cossacks" who demonstrated, however, general asceticism and extreme loyalty to Orthodox Christianity? And how to deal, in this case, with their "features of the Varangian Rusʹ and even of the Greek Argonauts" (Kuliš 1874, 2:371–373)? If they did show, in fact, an elitist tendency, based on the Polish model, did that mean the translator with obvious elitist inclinations should account for the foundation of such a Polish model? And if these Cossacks did show, in fact, an elitist tendency of the Polish type, should a translator with obvious elitist inclinations account for the existence of such a Polish type?

Since Kuliš had to answer numerous questions of this type during the late 1860s, his conception of the translation of the Holy Scriptures underwent a series of transformations. At the outset, Kuliš deliberately chose to offer a free adaptation of the Bible, which he considered primarily as a monument of Hebrew poetry, into a *poetic framework*. Hence, he chose an archaic pen name, Pavlo Rataj (literally, Paul the Plower), being inspired by various narratives and legendary characters. Gradually, however, Kuliš came up with another, parallel vision of the Holy Scriptures in vernacular Ukrainian. Having realized that, for church use, the Bible had to reflect strictly the text accepted at that time as the authoritative *Vorlage*, Kuliš might have embarked on a *scholarly translation* in the late 1860s. Step by step, he was conceptualizing the art of translation with an eye to creating a new type of the high style in nineteenth-century literary Ukrainian. For this reason and despite the negative review by Miklosich, Kuliš did not abandon his idea to publish a complete text of the Ukrainian Bible. On the contrary, Miklosich's criticism could have only spurred Kuliš to accomplish his mission of translation.

What is remarkable is that both the *poetic adaptation* and *scholarly translation* of the Bible never ceased to interest him, and they sometimes overlapped in the narrative model, as demonstrated in some of his subsequent publications. As late as 4 January 1895, Kuliš wrote to his old friend, Stepan Nis (1829–1900) (Kuliš to Nos, 24), that he was working intensely at that time on a second translation of the Old Testament, the so-called *ustyxotvorena Byblija* (the Versified Bible) (Zelens´ka 2000, 361), which was conceived in the vein of the translation made in the time of the Old Britons (Kuliš to Tymčenko, 99). For Kuliš, this was a new type of translation synthesizing two approaches divorced somewhat artificially in the literary tradition. Regrettably, only a few samples of Kuliš's synthetic translation came off the press. Yet what is clear from them is that Kuliš worked his entire life on his own translation conception that was modeled, in some of its elements, on contemporary western European vernacular translations of the Holy Scriptures.

While in Vienna in the spring of 1869, Kuliš met for the first time Ivan Puljuj, who had just completed his theological and philosophical studies at the University of Vienna, and invited him to collaborate on a translation of the Bible. As Puljuj recalled later, their first meeting was not conventional but rather cordial. They feverishly discussed much of mutual interest, from the literary activity in Galicia, with which Kuliš was intimately familiar, to national relationships in the two historical parts of Ukraine and the academic communities in Vienna and Lviv. At the end of their meeting, Puljuj expressed his sincere enthusiasm about Kuliš's proposal to collaborate on a new translation of the Holy Scriptures; he also spoke of the urgent need to publish a prayer book in vernacular Ukrainian, which he was preparing at that time (Studyns´kyj 1930, xxvi).

"POISON AND RUIN FOR THE RUSIAN PEOPLE"

Kuliš found in Puljuj a true comrade-in-arms, steeled by previous battles. By the time of their first meeting in 1869, Puljuj had already prepared some translations of religious texts into Ukrainian. Shortly afterwards he published *Molytvoslov˝ y korotka nauka o xrystijans´ko-katolyckôj věrě* (A Prayer Book and A Short Course on the Christian-Catholic Faith), written with the help of Myxajlo Osadca's orthography specifically for Rusian conscripts. As early as 1870, Puljuj prepared a second, revised edition of the prayer book, this time written in the phonetic orthography invented earlier by Kuliš. At a meeting with Josyf Sembratovyč, Greek Catholic archbishop of Lviv in the years 1870–1882, at the University of Vienna, Puljuj petitioned for church approval of the revised edition of his prayer book.

At the request of Sembratovyč, Puljuj's *Molytvoslov˝* was reviewed by the eparchial consultor Myxajlo Malynovs´kyj. Malynovs´kyj called Puljuj's translation, because of its vernacular and phonetic orthography (*ukrainščina i kulišôvka*), "poison and ruin for the Rusian people." A conservative cleric, Malynovs´kyj argued that the introduction of the *ukrainščina* and *kulišôvka*, "innovations without any grounds," was likely to destroy the intimate relationship between "Little Russian literature" and "our church books" (Puljuj 1871, 3; Studyns´kyj 1930, xv). Malynovs´kyj denounced, in particular, the vernacular spelling *Isus* (which was subsequently employed by Puljuj and Kuliš in their translation of the Bible), for it recalled a similar spelling employed by the Russian Old Believers. Hence, the so-called *ukrainščina* and *kulišôvka* could never be cultivated in the local theological seminary where the students had to work on "literary Church Slavonic and Little Russian as bequeathed ages ago" (ibid., xvi).

Malynovs´kyj also proposed corrections in the translation of some mainstream religious terms. For instance, he argued that the word *nasuščnyj* could not be translated *ščodennyj* "everyday" (Puljuj 1871, 4). Generally, Malynovs´kyj suggested that the manuscript of the revised version of Puljuj's *Molytvoslov"* be immediately destroyed in accordance with canon law (Studyns´kyj 1930, xiv).

Puljuj took up the cudgel. In his extensive reply to Malynovs´kyj's recommendations, entitled "Lyst bez koverty jako odpovid´ Vpr. Krylošanynu Malynovs´komu na referat molytovnyka" (A Letter Without an Envelope, As a Reply to Eparchial Consultor Malynovs´kyj in Reference to the Prayer Book) (Vienna, 1871) (see Levyckij 1888, 165), Puljuj criticized shortcomings in the argumentation of the conservative cleric, reproaching him for parochialism, regionalism, and particularism. Puljuj also defended the phonetic system of spelling (*kulišôvka*) on the grounds that it could serve as a bridge between fifteen million Ukrainian speakers in the two parts of Ukraine (Puljuj 1871, 7–8). Puljuj also did not accept the thesis about the Russian Old Believers, since the Serbs had long been using *Isus* and nobody had ever accused them of schism; moreover, he continued, the above spelling was quite common in many orthodox medieval records. While defending the use of *ščodennyj*, Puljuj (ibid., 11–13) cited the vast literature in support of his choice. Among other scholarly and narrative sources and traditions of various rites, the young translator deemed it necessary to mention Miklosich, who had offered a similar translation in his *Lexicon palaeoslovenico-graeco-latinum* (Vienna, 1862–1865) (*Lexicon*, 415).

This incident is, in fact, the first known interference of the Ukrainian church hierarchs into the normalization process of literary Ukrainian in the nineteenth century. In the long run, Puljuj won his fight, and the appearance of the prayer book under the title *Molytovnyk dlja rus´koho narodu* (A Prayer Book for the Rusian People) (*Molytovnyk*) in 1871 was hailed by the local intelligentsia since, as was noted in *Pravda*, Galician women and peasantry had long been using Polish prayer books (Studyns´kyj 1930, xxii). What is important about the preparation and publication of *Molytvoslov"/Molytovnyk* is that it not only influenced Kuliš's way of translating but also triggered a series of further translations into Ukrainian by a group of intellectuals, including Omeljan Ohonovs´kyj

(1833–1894), who was one of the founders of the *Prosvita* and the Shevchenko Scientific Society in 1893. Working under the guidance of Sylvester Sembratovyč, a future archbishop of Lviv from 1882 to 1898, this group ultimately prepared three popular prayer books using etymological orthography. The books were printed in Lviv in 1878 (ibid., xxiii).

"THE LABOR PANGS OF A UNIFIED UKRAINIAN LITERARY LANGUAGE"

Already an experienced translator and proponent of vernacular Ukrainian for use in the church, Puljuj avidly zeroed in on the translation of the New Testament from Greek, according to the strict rules set up by the British and Foreign Bible Society. Cooperation with Kuliš proved engaging and extremely challenging inasmuch as the two translators represented different regional varieties of written Ukrainian. The translation progressed steadily, not more than one page per day, but persistently; the translators were comparing their work with the Church Slavonic, Russian, Polish, Serbian, German, Latin, English, and French translations. The two strove to render the Greek original as faithfully as possible, although in harmony with the spirit of the native (Ukrainian) tongue. Proficient in Geek, Puljuj first made a kind of interlinear translation, which was then edited primarily by Kuliš in its stylistics. As a *locus classicus*, one can cite Puljuj's description of this creative process *in extenso*:

> From the very outset, our work proceeded very slowly; one small page per day! More often than not we would discuss, compete over certain expressions; we would end up by postponing our decision. Each one would ponder the problem, and in several days we would embark on a new debate leading to one mutual objective. . . .
>
> We divided the work between us so that Kuliš would first copy down everything that I translated from Greek, caring rather for the thoroughness than beauty of a word. Then we would compare this translation with the Church Slavonic, Russian, Polish, Serbian, German, Latin, English, and French. Having assured ourselves, in this way, of the correctness of our translation, we would edit it ultimately from the point of view of its beauty. . . . After lunch we

would rest not more than half an hour, while taking a stroll in the public garden, and then settle down again and work with a small break till eight at night. Kuliš would never get tired after this. In bed, he would read Shakespeare or Dickens for one or even two hours before falling asleep. (Studyns′kyj 1930, xxviii, 2)

By late May 1871, Kuliš and Puljuj had finished their translation of almost the entire New Testament, up to the first epistle of Peter. After Kuliš left for his *xutir* Motronivka in Russian-ruled Ukraine, Puljuj went to his parents' home, where he intended to translate the rest of the text of the New Testament. In August, the draft was finalized and mailed to Kuliš for his approval. Apparently, the latter found Puljuj's translation felicitous and invested his colleague with full power in making, if deemed necessary in the future, all arrangements with the British and Foreign Bible Society regarding the publication of the New Testament. Kuliš, however, expressed some reservations as to Puljuj's competence in the use of Ukrainian, which was still, according to him, quite laudable:

> You have already sufficiently studied our Ukrainian tongue and will not make any change for the sake of Polonisms that would be the worse for us. One had better resort to Church Slavonic [*cerkovščyna*] rather than to Polish [*ljads′ka mova*]. (Studyns′kyj 1930, xxix, 12)

Kuliš, however, remained consistent in his linguistic views, crystallized in the course of his long literary and translation activities. For this reason, Kuliš criticized some of Puljuj's innovations and suggestions and, despite his own orientation in some cases toward the Galician vocabulary, remained devoutly loyal to the old literary tradition and the linguistic legacy of the Xarkiv romanticists. In reply to Puljuj's proposal to replace some Central Dnieper forms less familiar to the Galicians, Kuliš, somewhat sharply, wrote on 26 September 1870 from Venice that "the Holy Scripture is being printed not so much for Galicia as for Ukraine; this is why I must limit myself to our taste" (Studyns′kyj 1930, 4). Interestingly enough, while providing feedback about the language of Puljuj's *Molytvoslov″/Molytovnyk*, Kuliš made a clean breast of his linguistic stance and its basis on the vernacular cast of Central Dnieper Ukrainian, although with a substantial admixture of Church Slavonicisms:

While you are afraid of repelling the people [from the prayer book] by innovations, I am afraid of maiming our mother tongue. We shall reach a compromise on the first day of our reunion. (Studyns′kyj 1930, 7)

In another letter, Kuliš's criticism of Puljuj's language became more caustic:

In Church Slavonic one finds: *Duše* [voc. sg.] *istyny* "soul of truth," but you wrote *Duxu* (*duchu* in Polish). For our language, we should rather have Old Bulgarian instead of Polish. Whenever you cannot come up with something, leave a Slavonic word (or form): this will never cause harm. In due course, it shall be substituted for by a common word. As far as Polish is concerned, you must avoid it as much as possible. (Studyns′kyj 1930, xxvii, 9)

Kuliš's ambivalent treatment of the Polish admixture in the regional (Galician) variety of Ukrainian was not accidental, this being a consequence of his deeply rooted and controversial attitude toward the Poles and their culture. On the one hand, he appreciated Polish literature and culture and had many Polish friends. On the other hand, he hated the Jesuits and Polish nationalism that might have instigated, according to him, the Polish uprising of 1863–1864 (Studyns′kyj 1930, 261). In a letter to Ostap Veresaj, written during his service in Warsaw, Kuliš expressed his views in a very emphatic manner that is worth citing:

It happened so, you know, that the Cossack offspring rule over the Polish lands, just as the Poles [*ljaxy*] used to rule in our Ukraine. Except that they governed us proudly and did not wish us well, but we behave in their land in a Christian manner. They enslaved the common people in our country, while we are now freeing the Polish dregs from the domination of the greedy landlords, and we do no injustice to the lords themselves except that we do not allow them to govern as the *szlachta* did, but require them to obey the law. (Kuliš to Veresaj, 224–225; Luckyj 1983, 144)

In this regard, one can pose a legitimate question as to whether, in view of the coercive Polish acculturation of the past, the Cossack offspring should drop their linguistic legacy, unassertive as it may appear in the face of the magnificence of Polish culture. Indeed, characterized by an exceptionally long history and rich literary tradition(s), Polish culture might have exerted a ruinous influence on Galicia, thus thwarting its indigenous progress. According to Kuliš (Kuliš to Veresaj, 225), one can hardly strike a political agreement or union with the Poles, who have been building their history on numerous lies, in either Galicia or in Dnieper Ukraine. Yet doesn't it stand to reason that, in order to create a viable literary standard, one should first promote indigenous Orthodox culture and language, with its salient features dating back to Kyivan Rus´, and only then get down to business with loan elements appropriated *volens-nolens*, in particular by the Galicians?

It is pertinent to state, however, that Kuliš's ambivalence toward the Poles could hardly be a consequence of his purportedly unsteady *Weltanschauung*, treated by Jefremov (1923) as a result of Kuliš's *lack of synthesis* even at the level of intra-personal relationships. Kuliš strongly believed that, under current conditions, any union with the Poles would endanger Ukrainophilism and aggravate the situation of Ukraine in the Russian Empire. For this reason, Kuliš advised Galicians against sympathy with the Polish anti-tsarist activities. It is worthwhile quoting here a poetic excerpt from a letter written by Kuliš to one of the Barvins´kyj brothers in 1870 or 1871:

> . . . з Ляхами в нас до суду
> Єднання не буде.
> Поки Рось зовецця Россю,
> Дніпро в море ллєцця,
> Поти серце Українське
> З лядським не зіллєцця.

[We shall never side with the Poles until the Judgment Day. / As long as the Ros´ River is called the Ros´, / [and] the Dnieper River discharges into the sea, / the Ukrainian heart will never merge with the Polish one.] (Franko 1898, 11–12)

A more belligerent note was taken by Kuliš in his address to the Poles published in 1868 in *Pravda*. However, as was pointed out by Naxlik (2007, 1:303–304), the writer protested not against Polish culture in general, but against the acculturation of a weaker people by a stronger neighbor. One can apply this explanation to linguistic matters, arguing that Kuliš wanted to shy away from only those Polish elements in the language of his translation of the Bible that were replacing indigenous forms, including Church Slavonicisms (of the East Slavic recension).

As Kuliš maintained in his "church epistle" to young Galicians, written presumably in the early 1870s (Franko 1898, 13–14), their "thoughts and feelings" were poisoned by the *ljads'kyj* (Polish) spirit, so they could hardly be of much help in fostering an all-Ukrainian culture. What they did achieve was a retention of the old words that came into oblivion in Left-Bank Ukraine. Unlike the Dnieper Ukrainians who created a full-fledged literature, the Galicians were only stretching their wings at that moment, while making use of an outdated tradition ("etymology") or "something mid-way between etymology and phonetics" (ibid., 14). Hence their rejection of the vernacular forms like *Musij* (Moses) and *Ovram* (Abraham) used by Kuliš in his translation of the Pentateuch. Kuliš believed that, while insisting on their particular forms, the Galicians, in a sense, revealed "the narrowness of their tendency." Moreover, the Galicians intended to write for Galicia only, and the Ukrainians, Kuliš argued, wanted their work to be read not only in Ukraine but also in Galicia (ibid.). As a result, in order to obtain a fully developed literature, Galicia had to abandon their "etymology" and even a combination of etymology and phonetics in their language. Instead, Galicia would do better to become spiritually united with Ukraine, thus working out mutual norms for a common literary language (ibid.). In this respect, Kuliš's own literary activity in Galicia in the late 1860s and early 1870s could serve as an example, particularly in producing what was somewhat awkwardly dubbed by Macjuk (1996, 123) samples of the "Ukrainian intellectual speech (translations of the Bible and works of the foreign classics)."

In a letter of 15 December 1892 to the Galician socialist and publicist Myxajlo Pavlyk (1853–1915), Kuliš largely reiterated his main arguments as first expressed in the "epistle" cited above, thus demonstrating consistency in his treatment of the Polish element in Ukrainian culture and language. He argued in particular that, during Polish rule, the "Old Rusians" (*starorusy*) had forgotten Old Rusian (*staroruščyna*) (Voznjak

1928a, 178). In the same vein, the Ukrainians forgot their language during the "New Rusian," or Muscovite, rule in Dnieper Ukraine. This is why Pavlyk had to publish pictures and excerpts from the older texts, for instance *The Igor' Tale*, together with elementary paraphrases that would be comprehensible to the average reader (ibid.).

Kuliš believed that Galicians' works would be read in Ukraine if they adopted the "Ukrainian taste" and got over all "the apery à la Holovac´kyj and Didyk" (*Holovaščyna, Didyščyna*) and "all the new Galician phenomena" (*halyčanščyna*) (Franko 1898, 14). In his poem "Hryc´ko Skovoroda" (Hryhorij Skovoroda), written in the early 1890s, Kuliš more often than not stressed his negative opinion of modern Galician writers who allegedly were not capable of authoring literary works comparable with the output of the writers in Dnieper Ukraine:

Так нам тепер поети-Львівці,
Мов у селі під вечір вівці,
Хрипливий голос подають:
Кастальську бо з калюжі п'ють.

[Nowadays the poets speak hoarsely to us from Lviv / like sheep in the evening / since they drink the Castalian water from a puddle.] (Kuliš 1909, 2:293–294)

As the above philippic shows, Kuliš's vision of literary Ukrainian was at odds not only with the Galician Muscophile theory, but also with the Galician populist cultural paradigm as a possible contributor to the development of literary Ukrainian. In other words, there was no place either for *halyčanščyna* (the Galician variety of Ukrainian) or *pol´ščyzna* (Polish) in Kuliš's language program. But how, then, despite his ambivalence toward all things Galician and Polish, did Kuliš happen to channel a sizable number of Galician and Polish elements into his language, including his translations of the Holy Scriptures? Was this a double standard or a natural, yet somewhat unexpected, consequence of the complex system of Kuliš's linguistic views, appearing in some ways self-contradictory? As the material discussed below shows, the second explanation looks more plausible.

Nevertheless, while translating the New Testament, Kuliš and Puljuj tried to compromise on the ratio of regional, bookish, and Church Slavonic forms and expressions in their text. Reconciling in this way different cultural, literary, and linguistic traditions, Kuliš and Puljuj were persistently searching for a verbal medium capable of uniting the two historical parts of Ukraine. The perseverance of the translators was finally rewarded in 1871, when *Jevanhelyji po sv. Matfejevi, Markovi, Luci i Ioanovi* (The Gospels according to Matthew, Mark, Luke, and John) appeared anonymously in Vienna.

The fact that the authors preferred to remain unknown to the general readership was not incidental. In the years 1868–1871, Kuliš published all his works in the Austro-Hungarian Empire (primarily in the periodical *Pravda* and under separate covers in Lviv and Vienna) either anonymously or under one of his pen names (Pavlo Rataj, Denys Fedorenko, Danylo Koval', Mykola Volovid, Opanas Prač) (Naxlik 2007, 1:252). In this way, Kuliš tried to avoid providing any pretext to Russian conservatives for launching attacks against the language of the translation of the New Testament in the periodical press or for possible persecution by the tsarist police. Kuliš remembered very well their previous charges directed against him and his publications in *Osnova*, which defended the distinctiveness of the Ukrainian language and literature, in the early 1860s. As early as 4 August 1868, during his government service in Warsaw, Kuliš confided in a letter to Oleksander Kistjakivs'kyj that he did not intend to publicize his civic and literary activities, in particular his translation of the Holy Scriptures, thereby thwarting the constant desire of Mixail Katkov and Ivan Aksakov to harass him through the tsarist administration (Kuliš to Kistjakovskij, 2:303).

Meanwhile, Kuliš wished to close a chapter in his relationship with Miklosich, the first serious critic of the Ukrainian Bible who, nevertheless, supported Ukrainian as a separate language in his scholarly works. Kuliš hastened to dispatch a copy of the Gospel according to Matthew to him. In a letter of 5 April 1871, Kuliš expressed his gratitude for fair comments that eventually persuaded him to undertake a word-for-word translation of the Holy Scriptures into Ukrainian. As if closing the circle, Kuliš suggested in the final sentence of his brief letter that Miklosich gauge the level of adequacy of the new translation compared to the original:

> Es macht mir viel Vergnügen Ihnen meinen herzlichen Dank auszudrücken für Ihre gerechten Bemerkungen, die Sie bei der Revision der russinischen Bibelübersetzung gemacht haben. Da ich so viele freie Übersetzungen in allen modernen Sprachen vor mir hatte, so glaube ich auch die russinische Übersetzung mit mehr Freiheit durchführen zu können. Das Resultat Ihrer Revision überzeugte mich indessen von der Notwendigkeit einer genauen, wörtlichen Übersetzung. Wie weit ich dieser Übersetzung treu geblieben bin, werden Sie, nach gütiger Einsichtnahme, aus dem Evangelisten Mat[thäus], den ich Ihnen zu verehren das Vergnügen habe, erfahren. (*Lystuvannja*, 234)

That was only a small step on the path to victory, since the prospect of having the whole Bible published in Ukrainian still looked vague. Despite unsuccessful negotiations with the British and Foreign Bible Society, Kuliš did not lose his self-confidence, writing in a letter to Puljuj that the Rusian Bible will go its way without Millard's good graces (Studyns´kyj 1930, 11). For this reason, while in Motronivka, he decided to publish the Bible in a Prussian town, Naumburg, where, as he described it in a letter to Ivan Xyl´čevs´kyj upon his arrival there, both living and book printing were much cheaper than in Leipzig and Berlin (Kuliš to Xil´čevskij, 117).

Before setting out for Prussia, Kuliš boasted in a letter dated 20 April 1872 to Vasyl´ Tarnovs´kyj, Jr. (1837–1899), that he had a manuscript of the entire Bible of the Old and New Testaments, including the book of Job and the book of Psalms translated in prose. His intention was to publish the whole Ukrainian Bible abroad (Kuliš to Tarnovskij, 85). While in Naumburg in the late summer of 1872, Kuliš informed Puljuj of his plans and asked his friend to send him copies of the Polish, Serbian, and German Bibles as well as the Big English Bible (*velyka anhlyc´ka Byblyja*) and the Russian New Testament (Studyns´kyj 1930, 13–14). Evidently, Kuliš was still feverishly brushing up on his translation of the Old Testament. He was so committed to his idea of having the Ukrainian Bible finally printed in its entirety that he was ready to cover immediately all publication costs out of his pocket through the sale of a parcel in his farmstead (Kuliš to Xil´čevskij, 113). Yet, he had to cancel all his plans and go back home because of his wife's sudden illness. Even more disconcerting in his situation were financial disputes with one of his wife's brothers, Ivan Bilozers´kyj (Kuliš to Xil´čevskij, 114; see Naxlik 2007, 1:308–309), who unexpectedly changed his mind about selling the farmstead Olenivka (Šamraj 1929).

The brief trip to Naumburg and the failed enterprise ushered in the finale of the entire creative period in Kuliš's life. The only serious achievement of that period seemed to be the publication of the four Gospels, which only partly met Kuliš's expectations. Only *en passant*, however, on 6 July 1873 he inquired of Barvins´kyj (2004, 167) whether there was anybody from "the honorable contingent" in Galicia available to undertake the publication of the Holy Scriptures at Kuliš's expense. Having spent so much time on translating the Bible, it would be unreasonable, he explained, to sojourn the whole year in Germany, waiting for the Germans to complete printing of the book. At the end of the letter, Kuliš rhetorically asked Barvins´kyj "if you, the Rusyns, will ever free yourselves from the Poles and their political dominance without the [Ukrainian] Bible?" (ibid.). But he tried to no avail. Somewhere between 1876 and 1878, in a fit of utmost disillusionment, caused by scathing critique of his latest historiographic works and, more plausibly, a lack of understanding by his compatriots of the significance of the Ukrainian Bible, Kuliš may have burnt his first prose translation of the Old Testament (Studyns´kyj 1930, 37).

Yet one can concur with Naxlik (2007, 1:307) that Kuliš did not waste the years 1867 through 1872 as a translator and a writer. Promoting different genres and experimenting with various styles, including the biblical one, Kuliš assiduously collected words and constructions able to faithfully render narratives in literary Ukrainian. He sifted through hundreds and hundreds of old and dialectal forms and expressions that, to his mind, would cohere into foundations for a new biblical style in literary Ukrainian. By any measure, this was a major preparatory period before the undertaking of a final translation of the Bible into vernacular Ukrainian. Moreover, as time revealed, the work on this translation became a true springboard for his future activities aimed at the creation of a new type of literary Ukrainian.

Only nine years later, in 1880, the whole text of the New Testament, *Svjate Pys'mo Novoho Zavitu* (The Holy Scripture of the New Testament), went to press in the Ševčenko Scientific Society in Lviv with the names of the two translators (Levyckij 1888, 352). With constant delays in fundraising, the process of printing (in fact, reprinting) the previous Vienna edition lasted several months, despite Puljuj's desperate appeals to the patriotism of the workers in his letters to Kornylo Suškevyč, head of the Ševčenko Scientific Society at that time (Studyns'kyj 1930, lxii–lxiii).

A true breakthrough in the process of the "Ukrainianization" of the Holy Scriptures happened in 1885 when Millard approached Puljuj with a proposal to buy the rest of the printed copies of the New Testament. Shortly after that, he made it clear that the British and Foreign Bible Society was ready to buy the copyright of the Ukrainian edition of the New Testament. As a result, in 1887 and 1893, the New Testament, entitled *Svjate Pys'mo Novoho Zavitu movoju rus'ko-ukrains'koju pereklaly vkupi P.A. Kuliš y dr. Y. Puljuj* (*NZ* 1887), appeared in its entirety as a publication of the Bible Society in Vienna and subsequently was reprinted several times (Kyryljuk 1929a, 45, 50, 54, 63). Trying not to lose the opportune moment, Puljuj pressed Kuliš to complete the translation of the Old Testament. The latter, however, wrote in 1878 that he had destroyed his translation because of the criticism of "Lviv wiseacres," wishing he had translated "simply from Luther, while looking a little at a time at the Orthodox [translation]" (Studyns'kyj 1930, 37, 40). As late as 25 April 1896, in a letter to Oleksij Biloborodov (Oleksa Tyxyj), Kuliš confirmed that, annoyed by his Galician compatriots, he had burnt his first translation (Voznjak 1928a, 90).

Despite some inconsistencies and shortcomings in the translation that went through several stages of preparation, the publication of the New Testament in Ukrainian became an epochal event. The leading role of Kuliš, who initiated the project and edited the whole text of the New Testament, can hardly be overestimated. Moreover, vis-à-vis the stylistic and dialect variance in the language of the translation, completed by the representatives of the two different literary traditions, culturally and dialectally, this translation may be aptly called, to use the words of Horbač (1988, 51), "the labor pangs of a unified Ukrainian literary language" (Nimčuk 2005, 30–38).

RECEPTION OF THE TRANSLATION

At first sight, paradoxically, the publication of the Ukrainian Bible did not satisfy either conservative clerics, headed by the all-powerful Malynovs´kyj, or the liberal intelligentsia in Galicia. Thus the translation was immediately denounced by Ivan Franko (1856–1916), whose ideological and political views were notoriously at odds with the Ukrainophile theory of Kuliš's "farmstead Ukraine" (*xutirna Ukrajina*) (Hrycak 2006, 413). However, particularly unappeasable and unfair was the critique of Meliton Bučyns´kyj, who, purportedly, could hardly stand either Kuliš or Puljuj. Apart from disparaging remarks about the activity of Kuliš in Galicia, Bučyns´kyj argued that, in the translation, "phonetics is distorted, older forms are neglected, and murky places are consciously retained [by the translators]: word is translated for word, without caring for the meaning" (Studyns´kyj 1930, xxxiii). According to him, Kuliš "misused the Holy Scriptures for the sake of his own linguistic vagaries." The extremum of his criticism could be well reduced to the hackneyed maxim that "on neither side of the border would anybody ever speak such a language" (ibid.).

What looked more disturbing in the context of the relationship of Kuliš with the Galician populists was Bučyns´kyj's assumption that Kuliš might have brought with him a translation of the Holy Scriptures made by someone in tsarist Russia. Studyns´kyj (1930, xxxiii) was inclined to take Bučyns´kyj's hypothesis into consideration. He was sure that Kuliš could have learnt something about a translation completed and sent over to the Holy Synod and then to the Imperial Academy of Sciences in Saint Petersburg by Pylyp Moračevs´kyj in the early 1860s. According to Studyns´kyj, Kuliš might have also known about a positive review of Moračevs´kyj's work by the Department of Russian Language and Philology at the Imperial Academy of Sciences in Russia. Moreover, Kuliš, as was hypothesized by Studyns´kyj (ibid., xxxiv), could allegedly have obtained a copy of Moračevs´kyj's translation. Fortunately, Studyns´kyj stopped short of accusing Kuliš and Puljuj of any plagiarism, admitting that it would be premature to speak about a direct connection of their translation with the work of Moračevs′kyj without a thorough comparison of the two texts. Nimčuk (2005, 31–32) contended recently that there were no solid grounds for propounding such a hypothesis at all. Even without comparing the two translations, Nimčuk's line of reasoning looks persuasive. The main argument of Nimčuk (ibid.) can be reduced to the following assumption. Moračevs′kyj was still alive at the time of the publication of Kuliš and Puljuj's translation of the New Testament. Had they somehow utilized his translation, Moračevs′kyj might have vociferously reacted to any kind of alleged plagiarism.

In 1898, a long-time nemesis of Kuliš, Franko, accused Kuliš of self-delusion and lack of perspicacity, casting serious doubt on the necessity of any translation in view of, to his mind, more serious lacunae in literary Ukrainian as cultivated in the entirety of Ukraine. In particular, he found Kuliš too naïve in claiming that the translation of the Holy Scriptures was the most important undertaking in the second part of the nineteenth century (Franko 1898, 15). Galicia experienced at that time, according to Franko, some more urgent needs and, contrary to Kuliš's presumption, this translation did not bear any fruit: the Galician priests and sextons were quite capable of making sense of the Church Slavonic version of the Holy Scriptures even without his translation. Sarcastically, he added that Kuliš did his job; however, the translator did not care how (ibid.).

Poorly grounded, this criticism was obviously tendentious and could hardly contribute to a serious discussion of Kuliš and Puljuj's translation from the historical and regional perspectives of the formation of literary Ukrainian (Danylenko 2008a). Not surprisingly, feeling hurt for his late friend, Puljuj came to his defense, stating that Franko had distorted or merely concocted some maxims and ascribing them to Kuliš (see Puljuj 1905, 107–108).

In the long run, if one takes into consideration ideological and other discords with the Galicians, for instance the use of Kuliš's phonetic orthography (*kulišivka*) for the purpose of enlightenment (Danylenko 2012b), the negative reaction of the Galician Ukrainians comes as no surprise. It was clear that, under current socio-political circumstances, members of the Greek Catholic church hierarchy were by default hostile to the idea of any vernacular translation of the Holy Scriptures. Instead of blessing such an endeavor, they would rather see it immediately destroyed, as was unabashedly recommended by Malynovs'kyj in 1870 with regard to Puljuj's revised manuscript of *Molytovnyk*. Speaking in linguistic terms, one should also bear in mind that most Galicians and Transcarpathian Rusyns were accustomed to the idea of *one* literary language, based on Church Slavonic, though with a wide range of admixtures (Danylenko 2008a, 109–111). In other words, most of the Galician speakers might not have been yet ready at that time to accept the Bible translated into the vernacular, let alone one that demonstrated Central Dnieper features, even if diluted with the Galician elements.

The reception of Kuliš's translation in Dnieper Ukraine was mostly influenced by the vagaries of imperial language policy in the aftermath of the Polish uprising of 1863–1864, as well as by the translation of the New Testament made by Moračevs'kyj in the early 1860s. Notoriously, the official reaction to the latter, enhanced by Saint Petersburg's mistrust of Ukrainophiles as allies of the Polish insurgents, was heavy-handed. A secret edict was issued, known as the Valuev Circular of 18 July 1863 (Danylenko 2010b). This limited the scope of Ukrainian language publications to belles lettres, while also banning all religious and educational literature in Ukrainian (Saunders 1993; Remy 2007). To be sure, translations of the Holy Scriptures into local vernaculars were of overriding importance in the education of common people, and Moračevs'kyj's translation could have contributed to the feverish atmosphere in which the anti-Ukrainian edict was implemented (Lotoc'kyj 1966, 2:390–392). But it is also possible that the translation of the Bible was never a pretext for launching repression against the Ukrainian language in 1863. In fact, the circular, as Miller (2003, 124) argued, might have been envisioned as a temporary measure for the time of the Polish uprising. Thus, the intention of Pëtr Valuev, Russia's minister of the interior at that time, was most likely to "hold back" the wave of Ukrainophile activity, including Moračevs'kyj's translation of the Gospels, in order to provide the government with time to prepare itself for a competition with the separatist intentions of the Ukrainophiles (ibid., 11–12). One can see here a personal factor in play. According to Remy (2007, 109), the Valuev Circular was not merely a reaction to the Polish uprising but reflected the author's fundamentally hostile, long-term stance toward Ukrainian as a literary language. Valuev's negative attitude toward publications in Yiddish indicates that the Ukrainian case was not completely unique. The minister was, in general, opposed to any vernacular developing into a full-fledged literary standard. His was an imperial rather than nationalistic attitude; but, nevertheless, it amounted to the promotion of ethnic attributes of the Great Russian nationality (ibid., 110).

Overall, the circular could therefore be a corollary of the complex bureaucratic process and nationalistic shift in public opinion, predetermined for the most part by the Polish uprising of 1863–1864 and, by extension, the Ukrainophile movement leading, in particular, to a vernacular translation of the Holy Scriptures. Suffice it to recall here an anonymous letter sent in March 1863 to Prince Vasilij Dolgorukov, the head of the Third Department and chief of gendarmes, about the political consequences of the publication of the Holy Scriptures in the "miserable Little Russian dialect" (Studyns′kyj 1930, xxxv–xxxvi). Written by someone of the upper clergy, the letter beseeched Dolgorukov to employ all means possible to protect the Orthodox faith from "profanation" and the fatherland from "a split and dangerous schism." The author(s) must have been extremely annoyed by the Third Department's sluggishness in dealing with the *xlopomany*'s escapades (Miller 2003, 99–100).

There was, however, a rare voice of dissent among the fiery supporters of the above circular in the tsarist government. Known for his liberal reforms within the universities, Aleksandr Golovnin, the minister of public education, expressed in a memorandum of 20 July 1863 definite reservations about Valuev's views, especially about the ban on the publication of Moračevs′kyj's translation of the New Testament. Among other counterarguments, Golovnin wrote that "the Little Russian translation of the Gospels into the local dialect, corrected by ecclesiastical censorship, is one of the most glorious endeavors that mark the present reign" (Lemke 1904, 306). He believed that the authors "strive to elaborate grammatically on every language or dialect and, for this reason, to write in it and publish is rather useful in view of public enlightenment and deserves full esteem." This was why, he argued, the Ministry of Public Education had an obligation to encourage these attempts and contribute to them, while the Holy Synod had the most sacred obligation to disseminate the New

Testament among all the citizens of the empire in all its languages, and that "it would be a true holiday of our church if every household had a copy of the Testament in a comprehensible language" (ibid., 295–309).

That was "the voice of one crying in the wilderness" (Mt 4: 3), which was not capable of changing the decision made by the government and approved by the tsar under the pressure of Mixail Katkov (1818–1887) and other conservative publicists (Tymošyk 2006, 9–11). Overall, the Valuev-Golovnin controversy epitomized an important moment in government policy. Some ministers were ready to think in categories of modern nationalism, while others, including Golovnin, remained stuck in the Enlightenment's imperial ideal, primarily represented by the pre-nationalistic Russia of the first half of the nineteenth century (Miller 2003, 118).

However, irrespective of the primary intention of its authors, the Valuev Circular must have been viewed as particularly damaging by Kuliš, who at that time was most likely thinking about embarking on the translation of the entire Bible into Ukrainian, a task which, for several reasons, he did not fulfill in 1867–1872 but accomplished much later, in the 1890s. Kuliš was most likely consulted by Mykola Kostomarov (1817–1885) and other Ukrainophiles protesting against the Valuev Circular. Although Kuliš was in agreement with their protests, his own reaction to the circular was rather cautious. And, indeed, what could one expect from a moderate Ukrainophile brooding at that time over a future translation of the Bible, a book devoid in Kuliš's eyes of any political connotation, in sharp contrast to the suspicions of the tsarist police (Petrov 1929, 278–305, especially 288–292; Naxlik 2007, 2:61)?

One should also bear in mind that in the early 1860s, finding the Ukrainophiles' pragmatism vulgar, Kuliš tried to reconcile populism with his conservatism. What was needed instead was a rational approach to the national idea that accounted for "the enlightened non-Ukrainian and even anti-Ukrainian societies in the cities" (Hruševs′kyj 1927, 17–18). This is why Kuliš was unwilling to support those Ukrainophiles who reacted to the tsarist policies by moving further to the left. He was determined not to be drawn into a conflict by either side, but to stand beyond any confrontation that was likely to damage his goal of the enlightenment of Ukrainians (see Luckyj 1983, 137–138). Accordingly, Kuliš considered his main task to be building the high culture, in particular through translations of the Bible (Šenrok 1901 74 (7/8), 81–82). And only to those for whom culture and politics were interconnected, whether in Austria-Hungary or tsarist Russia, might his translation appear to be inadequate.

Overall, Kuliš and Puljuj's translation of the New Testament gained critical acclaim in Russian-ruled Ukraine (*PSP*; see Nimčuk 2005, 37; Tymošyk 2006, 12–15), although the official reaction was shaped by repressive Russian policies, in particular by the anti-Ukrainian Ems Decree of 18 May 1876, a natural sequel to the Valuev Circular of 1863. Strange as it may appear, the reaction of local Ukrainophiles was not uniformly optimistic. Some of them, for instance Ivan Rudčenko, a brother of the writer Panas Myrnyj (1849–1920), expressed radical populist opinions. In his letter to Meliton Bučyns'kyj, Rudčenko, having praised the "exemplary translation" of the book of Job together with *Pentatevx Musijevyj* (Pentateuch), argued that the translator of the Gospel according to Matthew (which he had at his disposal)

> ... adapted to the high style, which does not beseem the vernacular language (*narodna mova*) that is always plain and serious about important matters. Having such an objective, the translator employed neither popular nor coined expressions, though the language would benefit greatly from a truly popular translation. And indeed, why are personal names not taken from the vernacular, while keeping largely Greek pronunciation? Why do we have *Matthej* instead of *Matvij*, *Thamara* instead of *Tamara*, *Ruf* in place of *Ruxva*, *Ioan* (which is hard to pronounce!) in place of *Ivan*, which has been used since time immemorial in *Ivan Xrestytel'*, *Ivan Blahovisnyk*. ... And if you have *Ioan* instead of *Ivan*, you should write *Iysus* and not *Ysus* for "Ysus" as is written throughout the text. On reading such things as: *propovidujučy xreščennje pokajanija na vidpuščennje hrixiv*, I was literally baffled by this translation! One does not use this syntax or speak this language in the countryside. ... As I noticed, there are too many nouns ending in *nnje* coined without any necessity in the text; one could easily dispense with a similar coinage. Yet if the

translator cannot do without it, he should adjust to the vernacular make-up and pronunciation of the coined words. (Studyns´kyj 1930, xxxi–xxxii)

The above criticism, though sketched rather impressionistically, was reiterated subsequently by other writers, especially Ivan Nečuj-Levyc´kyj (1838–1918) (Nečuj-Levic´kyj 1907, 1912), whose comments will be discussed below. But it should be noted here parenthetically that the stance of Rudčenko proved to some extent its tenacity, especially if observed from the vantage point of the later populist school that flourished in the early twentieth century and was represented by such linguists as Ahatanhel Kryms´kyj (1871–1942), Jevhen Tymčenko (1866–1948), Serhij Smerečyns´kyj (1891–?), Olena Kurylo (1890–1937) in her early writings and, outside Dnieper Ukraine, Vasyl´ Simovyč (1880–1948) in his *Na temy movy* (On the Subject of Language, 1924) (Danylenko 2003b, 89–91). Deeply rooted in ethnographic romanticism, their programmatic tenets are reminiscent of the opinion expressed by Rudčenko, particularly in the treatment of the deverbatives ending in *-nnje/-ttje*, ultimately *-nnja/-ttja*.[1]

Despite the criticism of the home-bred populists, the significance of Kuliš and Puljuj's translation for Russian-ruled Ukraine is hard to overestimate. Needless to say that after the Valuev Circular of 1863 and especially the Ems Decree of 1876, the development of literary Ukrainian was much hindered, although the process of ethnic and primarily cultural reaffirmation of identity in Dnieper Ukraine never ceased (Danylenko 2010a, 83–91). This is why, under the political conditions in Russian-ruled

---

1 As an example of the populist interpretation of the aforementioned deverbatives, one can recall the position of Kurylo (1960, 47–48) who, as early as 1923, noticed the abundance of deverbatives with the zero suffix in vernacular Ukrainian, unlike (literary) Russian (Ukr. *obereha* "defence," *osud[a]* [m. and f.] "condemnation" next to parallel Rus. *predoxranenie, osuždenie*). Quite in congruence with Rudčenko's criticism of Kuliš and Puljuj's predilection for nouns ending in *-nnje/-ttje*, Kurylo (ibid., 45–46) argued that "numerous forms ending in *-nnja* and *-ttja* in the literary [Ukrainian] language make the phrase cumbersome and introduce uniformity, thus providing a limited room for derivation of other deverbatives and, subsequently, obliterating semantic nuances so necessary for the richness of a literary language." Doesn't this argumentation resonate with the reasoning of Rudčenko and other contemporary critics of Kuliš and Puljuj's translation?

Ukraine, a remarkable role in the common revival of interest in popular language and its upgrade to a lofty level was played by the translation of the New Testament made by Kuliš and Puljuj. Yet what was more important for the progress of intellectual life in this part of Ukraine was that the work on the translation and its appearance in Galicia, as controversially as it could be discussed in some Galician periodicals, stirred, first of all, the minds of the Little Russian intelligentsia concerned with the national awakening through the development of literary Ukrainian.

THE SLOBODA BULWARK

Among the Little Russian intelligentsia supporting the idea of a national awakening through the development of national literature and language, one should mention again a group of Xarkovite authors who made a significant contribution to the national revival under the influence of Kuliš's literary and social activities. Their emphasis on the translation of the Bible as a framework for the creation of a new high style proved ultimately to be tenable and productive. Instigated by Kuliš's translation of the New Testament, their paraphrases of the books led to periodic outbursts of enthusiasm, although most of these works, as it became obvious later, were pastiches rather than true translations. However, Kuliš and Puljuj's work in the late 1870s and 1880s did spark the ideal of a new Ukrainian literary language, if only among the small number of educated Little Russians, who nevertheless tried to keep it alive through the following years of a subdued atmosphere under prohibitive measures against the Ukrainian language in Dnieper Ukraine and especially in its Sloboda provinces (Danylenko 2010b; Kohut 1988, 244).

From among a few translators of the Bible who followed in the steps of Kuliš, one should mention a prominent Xarkovite, Volodymyr Aleksandrov.[2] Under the influence of Kuliš and Puljuj's work, Aleksandrov

---

2   A graduate from the local university, Aleksandrov worked as a medical doctor almost all his life in Xarkiv, besides several years spent in Warsaw. In addition to Polish, he was versed in Hebrew, Greek, Latin, and French. In his time, Aleksandrov was a rather popular Little Russian author. Besides several poems published in the periodical *Osnova*, he also wrote two operettas, *Za Neman' idu* (I Am Going to the Neman),

translated the whole Psalter and several books from Hebrew and the book of Tobit from Greek (Studyns´kyj 1930, lvi). A seasoned translator, he vividly corresponded with Puljuj in the years 1874–1886 and was *au fait* with the translation project initiated by Kuliš and Puljuj in the early 1870s. His reaction to the publication of their work was exuberant. When presented with a copy of the translation of the New Testament together with Puljuj's *Molytovnyk*, he expressed his ultimate reverence for the language used by the translators, although with some "regional reservations." In his letter of 19 November 1877 to Puljuj, Aleksandrov wrote confidentially that the translation of Kuliš's *Pentatevx Musijevyj* (Pentateuch) had somewhat disappointed him (Studyns´kyj 1930, xxxix). However, as early as 1 October 1877, Aleksandrov, who most likely heard from Puljuj about Kuliš's work on the translation of the Old Testament, discussed his intention to translate the Bible on his own, using "a language familiar to all of us, not a mere regional dialect" (ibid.). Overall a devoted populist and an amateur poet, Aleksandrov became completely obsessed with his idea of translating the Bible into a pure (regional) vernacular. For this reason, as Aleksandrov confessed in a preface to his translation of Psalms (*Spivÿ*), he took several years of Hebrew lessons to prepare for this holy mission (Kovalenko 1908, 322).

In 1878, that is, precisely twenty-five years before the appearance of the first edition of the Bible in Vienna, Aleksandrov completed his translation of the books of Genesis, Exodus, Job, and Tobit, printed under the title *Byblija syrič´ Knyhy Svjatoho Pysanija. 1. Staroho Zapovitu* (The Bible, or the Books of Holy Scriptures. The Old Testament) in Xarkiv. As late as 1883, and also in his native city, he prepared his next translation from Hebrew, a collection of psalms, entitled *Tÿxomovni spivÿ na svjati motivÿ* (*Spivÿ*), which, as was already mentioned, is characterized by an original poetic rendering and a local southeastern (Sloboda) tinge to the written language.

---

which was successfully performed several times in the local drama theater, and *Ne xody, Hrycju* (Do Not Go, Hryc´). In particular, he excelled in translating the works of Mixail Lermontov and Adam Mickiewicz.

Equally illuminating was a translation of the New Testament made by another native of Xarkiv, Myxajlo Lobodovs′kyj (1874–1913).[3] A graduate from a theological seminary, he began his career as a teacher in the province but in a short while applied for a clerical position. Spurred on by the publication of folk songs and legends by Myxajlo Maksymovyč, Izmail Sreznevskij, Pantelejmon Kuliš, and others, Lobodovs′kyj followed in their steps and amassed huge ethnographic material that he subsequently donated to the Department of the Southwest of the Imperial Russian Geographical Society. His lexical records were later incorporated into *Slovar′ ukrajinskaho jazyka* (Dictionary of the Ukrainian Language, 1907–1909), prepared for publication by Borys Hrinčenko at the request of the editorial board of the journal *Kievskaja starina*. In the 1870s, Lobodovs′kyj suddenly emigrated and worked for some time in the Geneva print shop of the Ukrainian publicist and political thinker Myxajlo Drahomanov (1841–1895). After his return to Xarkiv, Lobodovs′kyj began translating little by little the Holy Scriptures into, to use the terms of Čaplenko (1955, 124), "hard-boiled vernacular Ukrainian," used also in his translation of Nikolaj Gogol's *Taras Bul′ba* (1873). As Žytec′kyj surmised in his survey of 1905, Lobodovs′kyj's translation of the Holy Scriptures, which he submitted in 1903 to the Imperial Academy of Sciences in Saint Petersburg for an expert review, was poorly executed and replete with numerous vulgar and dialectal forms.

Yet the figure of Lobodovs′kyj and his translation of the New Testament became invisibly intertwined with Kuliš and his plans to create the Rusian (Ukrainian) Bible. An abstemious Ukrainophile and a long

---

3   In 1905, Pavlo Žytec′kyj (1837–1911), a prominent philologist and ethnographer, wrote a comparative study of the language and stylistics of several Ukrainian translations of the New Testament, including those made by Kuliš and Puljuj, by Myxajlo Lobodovs′kyj (Loboda), and by Moračevs′kyj (Žiteckij 1905). Needless to say that Žytec′kyj, who did not seem to have much sympathy for Galicians and Rusyns, did not include in his study a single translation produced by that time in Galicia or Subcarpathian Rus′. Nevertheless, even with such lacunae, his work established the discursive framework for subsequent critics, in particular regarding the cultural significance and literary value of the translation made by Kuliš and Puljuj. What is most important in this respect is that the names of Lobodovs′kyj (Loboda) and Moračevs′kyj have appeared since Žytec′kyj's study to be intrinsically connected with the translation activity of Kuliš and Puljuj, although the logic of cultural life in the two historical parts of Ukraine was likely to ultimately generate concurrent programs of the development of the biblical style.

admirer of Kuliš's poetic and historiosophic oeuvre, Lobodovs′kyj visited Kuliš and his wife in their *xutir* Matronivka in 1884. In his memoir, Lobodovs′kyj (Lobodovskij 1897) reminisced that, among other things, he had discussed with the host his dealings with the Poles back in 1882 and the charge made against Kuliš that he had betrayed Ukrainian national interests. Kuliš explained to Lobodovs′kyj to what extent he had been naïve at that time to hope that some rich Poles, including Prince Adam Sapieha, a descendent of the Ukrainian nobility and a leading defender of Galician autonomy, would genuinely collaborate with the Ukrainians in Galicia. Moreover, while manipulating Kuliš for their own political purposes, they had hatched a scheme directed against the Ukrainian Uniate monasteries (ibid., 167–170).

In fact, in the early 1880s Kuliš accepted the Polish proposal to promote a united front with the Galicians who were more opposed to Russian than Polish influence (Luckyj 1983, 161; Naxlik 2007, 1:373). To expedite matters, Kuliš seriously considered becoming an Austrian subject. With an eye to submitting the necessary paperwork in Vienna, he first decided to obtain permission to renounce his Russian citizenship from the Russian government (Lobodovskij 1897, 167–168). He even asked Puljuj to make necessary enquiries at the Russian embassy in Vienna (Studyns′kyj 1930, 63). In the long run, Kuliš did file an application to Saint Petersburg, but official confirmation reached him on 1 July 1883, when he had already changed his mind due to an incident that occurred in Galicia one year earlier.[4]

The point is that in 1882, all Ukrainian Uniate monasteries were transferred to Polish Jesuit control. Disenchanted with the Poles who did not support his idealistic plans for Polish-Ukrainian reconciliation, as outlined in his famous pamphlet *Krašanka rusynam i poliakam na Velykden′ 1882 roku* (An Easter Egg for the Rusyns and the Poles for Easter 1882,

---

4 That was not a weakness of, to use Jefremov's (1923) formula, "a lack of synthesis." In his letters to Oleksander Barvins′kyj (2004, 185, 195, 206), Kuliš confided several times that, while changing his views, he always remembered Aleksandr Puškin, who had proclaimed that only fools would not change their views. Luckyj (1983, 163) rightly observed that, in order to explain such changes, one should consider what exactly might have prompted them. Unfortunately, Kuliš's objectivity and, in most cases, perspicacity was brushed aside by some of the leaders of the contemporary cultural movement in Galicia, including Franko (1898, 16).

Lviv, two editions, 1882), Kuliš wrote another pamphlet, in German, *Vergewaltigung der Basilianer in Galizien durch Jesuiten* (Levyckij 1888, 405–406; Naxlik 2007, 1:392). In this work, he denounced the Dobromyl reform of the Ruthenian Order of Saint Basil as outlined in a bull issued by Pope Leo XIII in 1882. It is no wonder that the whole printing of the pamphlet was promptly confiscated by the Austrian authorities. All this discouraged Kuliš from further cooperation with the Poles and Austrians in fostering the cultural autonomy of Galician Ukrainians (Fedoruk 2000b).

As is evidenced by the memoir of Lobodovs′kyj, Kuliš still felt upset by the whole affair, remembering the fierce criticism of the aforementioned pamphlets and other of his works that appeared in 1882. However, particularly deprecatory were anonymous reviews in the periodical *Zorja*, written by its editor, Omeljan Partyc′kyj. Partyc′kyj (1882, 17) criticized the lack of any program for collaboration between the Poles and the Ukrainians in Kuliš's attempt to reconcile the two sides. Yet especially biased was his review of Kuliš's translations of Shakespeare's plays (ibid., 1882, 21) where the reviewer tried not so much to find shortcomings in his translations as to discredit Kuliš's pioneering approach to rendering Shakespeare in Ukrainian (Kočur 1968, 30). For this reason, during his meeting with Lobodovs′kyj, Kuliš argued bitterly that a traitor would never believe in the future of Ukrainian literature and, moreover, spend time translating Shakespeare into Ukrainian (Lobodovskij 1897, 166).

Quite remarkably, neither Kuliš nor his guest mentioned any translation of the New Testament. Was it because Lobodovs′kyj had not yet begun his work on the translation of the Holy Scriptures? Apparently, Lobodovs′kyj knew about Kuliš's poetic versions of the texts, published as early as the late 1860s, although he could have been unaware of Kuliš's authorship of the New Testament that appeared in its entirety in 1880. It is therefore tempting to assume that subsequent publications of the Holy Scriptures by the British and Foreign Bible Society in 1887 and 1893 might have instigated Lobodovs′kyj's interest in experimenting with vernacular Ukrainian, much in the same vein as Aleksandrov did several years before him.

Overall, despite severe prohibitive measures against the Ukrainian language in the Russian Empire, there was a healthy reaction among the local intellectuals to the new impulse in the formation of a new literary standard based on the Central Dnieper vernacular, which proved appropriate and well suited for this religious goal. At this point, it is interesting to note that Kuliš and Puljuj found themselves unexpectedly, though quite predictably, caught between two opposite poles. On the one hand, they were attacked by the conservative clergy in Galicia along with the local discontented Ukrainophiles and, on the other, by "pure populists" like Volodymyr Aleksandrov and Myxajlo Lobodovs′kyj, who were oriented toward the strong vernacular cast of the written language ushered in by the Xarkiv Romanticists in the early 1830s. At any rate, the translation of Kuliš and Puljuj triggered the process of liberation of written Ukrainian from the Greek Catholic church in Galicia and from the Russian church in Ukraine, revealing a vista for the transformation of internal animosities among the representatives of different cultural and religious traditions into productive discourse.

THE ARCHANGEL *HAVRYLO*

The translation of the New Testament and some texts made by Pylyp Moračevs′kyj[5] stand out among all other translations extant from Dnieper Ukraine, in particular those made by Sloboda representatives. Indeed, Moračevs′kyj's translation does differ cardinally from the language program of Kuliš, the translator.

---

5 Inspector at the Nižyn Lyceum of Prince Bezborod′ko in the years 1849–1859, Moračevs′kyj authored a number of second-rate poems both in Russian and Ukrainian. A series of patriotic Ukrainian-language verses, compiled in the mode of *kotljarevščyna*, were published in a collection with the characteristic title *Do čumaka, abo vojna janhlo-xrancuzo-turec′ka u 1853 y 54 rokax* (To the *Čumak*, or the English-French-Turkish War in the Years 1853 and 1854) (Naumenko 1902, 177–178, 460). Regrettably, as Jefremov (1924, 1:374) pointed out, Moračevs′kyj as a writer proved an incidental phenomenon in Ukrainian literature and therefore his literary output can hardly warrant discussion in greater detail. Clearly, no one would ever have remembered this provincial literatus had he not showed a keen interest in Ukrainian, first in the compilation of *Slovar′ malorossijskaho jazỹka po poltavskomu narečiju* (Dictionary of the Little Russian Language Based on the Poltava Dialect), and his translation of the Holy Scriptures, which, with the parallel Church Slavonic text, appeared posthumously at the beginning of the twentieth century in Moscow (ibid., 466; Hnatenko and Kotenko 2007, 182–183; Kotenko 2013, 82–83).

To begin with, long before its publication in 1906–1911, Moračevs′kyj's translation of the New Testament became critically acclaimed in Russian-ruled Ukraine. The story of the publication of his work became a litmus paper in the creation of an indigenous biblical style and, ultimately, a new literary standard, despite the Russian government and the Holy Synod's hostile, long-term stance toward the Ukrainian language. What is more remarkable, however, is that one deals in the case of his translation with an undeclared contest for priority among vernacular translations of the Holy Scriptures made in Russian- and Austrian-ruled Ukraine. For this reason, a detailed survey of Moračevs′kyj's language in comparison with that used by Kuliš and Puljuj would be most instructive, since it may shed additional light on the role of their translations in the formation of new literary Ukrainian. Besides, it can help assess the objectivity of the commonly reiterated view of Moračevs′kyj's translation (and not that of Kuliš and Puljuj) as true to the spirit of vernacular Ukrainian (Nimčuk 2005, 29–30; Ohijenko 1927, 9).

Moračevs′kyj completed his translation of the Gospels according to John and Mark in 1860, that is, long before Kuliš initiated his work on the translation of the Bible. Chronologically, Moračevs′kyj was a pioneer in bringing holy texts within reach of the common people. Yet, as one can glean from Moračevs′kyj's language, he seemed to have a completely different vision of the lofty style of Ukrainian from that of Kuliš's language program. This comes as a surprise since, seemingly, both translators practiced a similar approach to the process of translation. On 1 August 1868, Kuliš wrote in his letter to Oleksander Kistjakivs′kyj that, while making use of practically all the European languages, he finally completed his translation of the Pentateuch (Kuliš to Kistjakovskij, 2:303). During his service in the governmental Office of Spiritual Affairs in Warsaw in 1864–1867, with an eye to producing a first-rate Ukrainian paraphrase of the Bible, Kuliš diligently studied Hebrew with the help of a local rabbi. Moreover, aware of multifarious linguistic pitfalls facing him in his work on the translation of the New Testament, Kuliš also took some lessons in ancient Greek with Jan Niecisław Baudouin de Courtenay (1845–1929), a precursor to structural linguistics, who from 1862 to 1866 studied at the newly opened Warsaw university (called *Szkoła główna* "main school") (Kuliš to Tymčenko, 104; Naxlik 2007, 1:247).[6] Later, as has been already mentioned, in their work on the translation of the New Testament Kuliš and Puljuj routinely consulted the Church Slavonic, Russian, Polish, Serbian, German, Latin, English, and French Bibles (Studyns′kyj 1930, xxviii–xxix).

Deeply rooted in the ethnographic culture of Dnieper Ukraine, Moračevs′kyj had objectively fewer chances of expanding his vision of the nature of the vernacular translation of the Holy Scriptures. It is not accidental that from the outset Moračevs′kyj's translation was largely anchored in the Church Slavonic Bible and its Russian translation. Only later, with the entire translation completed, did Moračevs′kyj decide to compare his text with the Latin, French, German, and Polish translations of the New Testament. While editing the final draft of his translation, Moračevs′kyj jotted down in the margins some parallel fragments in several languages, albeit no example in Hebrew or Greek (Sreznevskij 1902, 090–091). Arguably, the difference in Moračevs′kyj's approach was connected not so

---

6   In a letter to Jevhen Tymčenko, written on 2 November 1895, Kuliš recalled his lessons with Baudouin de Courtenay, while extolling his professionalism and scholarly achievements and highly recommending him to his young and inexperienced correspondent. Kuliš also mentioned Baudouin de Courtenay's promise made to Vasyl′ Bilozers′kyj to write a grammar of Ukrainian. In his reply of 31 December 1895 to Kuliš, Tymčenko expressed his view of the Polish linguist very trenchantly, dubbing the latter "a Russifier" (*obrusytel′*), allegedly for the introduction to his *Pieśni białorusko-polskie z powiatu Sokólskiego, gubernii Grodzieńskiej* (Belarusian-Polish Songs from the District Sokólski of the Hrodna Region) (Kuliš to Tymčenko, 104, 105). Yet Kuliš's praise of Baudouin de Courtenay proved perspicacious and intuitively well grounded. Though the renowned linguist did not publish a separate grammar of Ukrainian, he remained a true defender of all national minorities and their languages in the Russian Empire. After moving back to Poland, Baudouin de Courtenay authored a series of studies about the Ukrainian language and its speakers, such as *Uniwersytet ukraiński w państwie polskim* (A Ukrainian University in the Polish State, 1922), *Rosja, Białoruś i Ukraina* (Russia, Belarus′, and Ukraine, 1928), and *Z drobiazków folklorystycznych* (From the Folkloric Trifles, 1928) (Svjencic′kyj 1993, 38); some other articles on issues of national minorities and their languages are reprinted in volume 6 of Baudouin de Courtenay's collected works (1983). Yet, most interesting is a programmatic article, "Kilka ogólników objektywnej i subjektywnej odrębności "Ukrainy" pod względem językowym, plemiennym, narodowym i państwowym," published by the Ševčenko Scientific Society in 1925 (Baudouin de Courtenay 1925) and by the Xarkiv Historical and Philological Society in 2002 in a Ukrainian translation by Viktorija Piddubna (Boduèn de Kurtene [Baudouin de Courtenay] 2004).

much with his training and education as with the cultural and ideological foundations of his work. Unlike the "eurocentrism" of Kuliš and Puljuj, Moračevs′kyj was a true devotee of "homestead ethnographism," which could look, nevertheless, no less dangerous in the eyes of tsarist censors. One can only feel sorry for Moračevs′kyj's text, which, only due to restrictions imposed by the Russian government on Little Russian literature and the local language and the fear of the Russian Synod of religious separatism in the former Hetmanate, was not published in the nineteenth century, thus failing to contribute to the development of a new biblical style of literary Ukrainian.

At the very beginning, however, nothing seemed to predict oblivion for Moračevs′kyj's translation. Corrected and revised at the end of 1860, the manuscript was forwarded by the translator to Isidor, metropolitan of Saint Petersburg and Novgorod, for permission to publish the work in Ukrainian. However, quite in the spirit of the impending Valuev Circular of 1863, publication of Moračevs′kyj's translation was not allowed by the Holy Synod (Hnatenko and Kotenko 2007, 156). Shortly after that, Moračevs′kyj sent the entire translation of the New Testament to the Imperial Academy of Sciences in Saint Petersburg, asking for an evaluation by specialists and eventual recommendation for publication. Convened by the prominent Slavist Izmail Sreznevskij (1812–1880), a special commission consisting also of the academicians Aleksandr Vostokov (1781–1864) and Aleksandr Nikitenko (1804–1877) positively reviewed the translation, which, according to them, was an exceptional work from the religious and philological points of view. They wrote in particular that:

> From the first point of view, one can ask, first of all: is the Little Russian dialect, in the modern level of its literary development and formation, able to teach the divine and great truths which are found in the New Testament? The translation, we believe, answered this question more than compellingly. The Little Russian dialect in it, one can say, stood the test successfully and dismissed any doubt, shared by the majority, in its capability to express sublime ideas of reason, sublime feelings of the heart, without appearing vulgar, without making them rude, without

paralyzing them. The translation of Moračevs′kyj proves completely that both nature or character of the words, and the quality of Little Russian expressions have never failed either the dignity or meaning of thoughts rendered by them. ... There is no doubt that the translation of the New Testament by Moračevs′kyj will make an epoch in the literary education of the Little Russian dialect. (Naumenko 1902, 475–476)

In its resolution, the Department of Language and Philology of the Imperial Academy of Sciences stated that Moračevs′kyj coped with his translation brilliantly despite numerous pitfalls faced during his work. One of the major problems lay in a lack of special devices in Little Russian able to convey equally aptly everyday needs and abstract concepts and "ideas belonging to the loftiest intellectual sphere" (Naumenko 1902, 477). Highly versed in Little Russian, the translator, according to the resolution, found inspiration in "the simplicity of the greatness of the holy truths" and managed to extract from his native dialect such expressions and constructions that, despite their common character, most adequately accorded with the lofty meaning of the thoughts rendered by them (ibid.). Cognizant of the spiritual and religious significance of Moračevs′kyj's translation, the department asked the president of the Imperial Academy to appeal to the Holy Synod for permission to publish the translation. The manuscript was sent over to Archbishop Grigorij (Mykola Mytkevyč) of Kaluga who praised the translation. As one of the witnesses recalled, Archbishop Grigorij, a native of the Černihiv region, while reading Moračevs′kyj's translation, began crying and extolling the virtues of its language and vernacular stylistics (ibid., 472).

Yet the Holy Synod disregarded the recommendation of the Imperial Academy of Sciences and of its own experts and resolutely banned publication of the Ukrainian translation. In 1904, an attempt to reverse this decision was made by the board of directors of the Charitable Society of the Publication of Useful and Cheap Books, although to no avail (Lotoc′kyj 1966, 2:386–388). The Ukrainophiles based in Saint Petersburg decided to try some other means, approaching the president of the Imperial

Academy of Sciences and the Ministry of the Interior, headed at that time by Vjačeslav Pleve and, after his unexpected death on 15 July 1904, by Pëtr Svjatopolk-Mirskyj, who was subsequently credited with liberal reforms allowing more rights to national minorities. Due to the active support of the Imperial Academy of Sciences, in particular its academicians Aleksej Šaxmatov and Fëdor Korš, on 15 February 1905 the committee of ministers chaired by Count Sergej Vitte abrogated limitations on the publication of the Holy Scriptures in Ukrainian (Vul'pius 2005a, 214, 2005b, 157–169; also Vlasovs'kyj 1957, 297–300). As a result, two commissions were set up, one by the Holy Synod and the second by the Imperial Academy of Sciences, to prepare Moračevs'kyj's translation of the four Gospels for synodal publication, which eventually took place in 1907–1911 (Hnatenko and Kotenko 2007; Kotenko 2013).[7] However, the two commissions, headed by Bishop Parfenij Levyc'kyj of Kam'janec'-Podil's'kyj and Aleksej Šaxmatov respectively, worked in fact independently (Vlasovs'kyj 1957, 297–300; Pšepjurs'ka-Ovčarenko 1988, 212–214). Thus, almost all comments and emendations proposed by the academic group were routinely ignored by the synodal commission of experts. In the final stage, this commission consisted of two members only: Bishop Parfenij Levyc'kyj himself, sent at that time to Tula, and a certain Komarnickij, director of the local gymnasium (Lotoc'kyj 1966, 2:398). Overall, strengthened by the linguistic intervention of Bishop Parfenij Levyc'kyj, the editing of Moračevs'kyj's translation resulted in the neutralization of its most characteristic "lay features" as found in the protograph.

---

7 All the Gospels translated by Moračevs'kyj were published in 1907–1911 and reprinted, without the parallel Church Slavonic text, only once in 1921 in Lviv and Vinnycja, thus exerting a minimal influence on the development of the new Ukrainian biblical style. An amateurish reproduction of the Gospel according to John, a copy of which is held at the Vernads'kyj National Library of Ukraine in Kyiv, was made recently by a propagator of Moračevs'kyj's work, Myxajlo Maljuk (1995, also 1993; see Strixa 2006, 105–106). However, due to orthographic simplifications introduced by Maljuk, the text can hardly be used for scholarly purposes. Moračevs'kyj's literary works along with some letters and archival material pertaining to the translation of Holy Scriptures were published by Samojlenko (1999, 2006). Fortunately, the Institute of Ukrainian Language of the Academy of Sciences has finally published Moračevs'kyj's translation of the Psalter (*Psaltyr''*, Moračevs'kyj).

A patriotic stance was taken at that time by many Ukrainian intellectuals, who hailed the preparation of the manuscript for publication. Some of their positions, for instance, of Žytec´kyj, were expressly pro-Ukrainian, in conformity with the political momentum. Thus, in his survey of Ukrainian translations of the Holy Scriptures, Žytec´kyj (Žiteckij 1905, 29–30) noted that the translation made by Kuliš and Puljuj had not gained popularity among the Galicians. He admitted that the text was written somewhat awkwardly, while the overall style of the translation of the New Testament lacked consistency and uniformity, especially in its vocabulary. The main problem lay, as Žytec´kyj (ibid.) argued, in the different tasks taken on by the translators. That is, while Puljuj was preparing an interlinear translation, Kuliš was honing in on the final version of the text, whence allegedly an ostentatious artificiality of the language of their translation. Žytec´kyj maintained that the translation of the Bible into literary Little Russian, still connected intimately with the local vernacular, should be premised on solid dialectal and, what is more important, uniform stylistic foundations (ibid., 34).

Žytec´kyj (Žiteckij 1905, 34) advanced several recommendations for future translators of the Holy Scriptures. First, the translators, according to him, should be encouraged to resort to popular Slavonic words as found in sermons and religious set expressions or idiomatic clichés familiar to common speakers. Second, they should skip Ukrainianized forms of names like *Isus* for Jesus, *Havrylo* for the archangel Gabriel, and the like, inasmuch as the Bible is not a fairy tale where one can take liberties with its characters and their names. Third, Church Slavonic words should be preferred over native elements with a vulgar tinge in their meaning as, for instance, in the case of *iudej, iudejskij* in place of *žyd* "Jew," *žydivs´kyj* "Jewish," *svjaščennyk* instead of *pip* "priest," *ženo* (voc.) in place of *žinko* (voc.) (ibid.) (*Žydy* "Jews" [*SP/NZ*, 91, Jn 2:13], and *car Žydivs´kyj* "king of the Jews" [*SP/NZ*, 4, Mt 2:2]). Fourth, as Žytec´kyj (Žiteckij 1905, 34) stressed, it would be highly advisable to use Church Slavonicisms in place of native lexemes with a vulgar, even obscene connotation like *cyca* (infml.) in the translation of Lobodovs´kyj, *cyc´ky* (derog.) in the translation of Moračevs´kyj compared to *sosky, ščo ty ssav jesy* "the paps which thou hast sucked" in Kuliš and Puljuj (*SP/NZ*, 71, Lk 11:27), or *kurvy* (derog.)

(Lobodovs´kyj) and *nepotrebnyci* (infml.) (Moračevs´kyj), compared with *bludnyci* "harlots" in Kuliš and Puljuj (*SP/NZ*, 77, Lk 15:30).

Finally, Žytec´kyj (Žiteckij 1905, 35–36) dwelled on innovations in the translations made by Lobodovs´kyj, Moračevs´kyj, and Kuliš (together with Puljuj). Among all the other translators, Lobodovs´kyj purportedly coined the greatest number of "still-born" neologisms, while Kuliš, in spite of some awkwardly coined words, remained a reasonable innovator, even if juxtaposed with Moračevs´kyj's stylistically "exemplary" translation. Some of the examples cited by Žytec´kyj (ibid.) appear quite revealing in this respect (e.g., ChSl. *v″pakybỹtiy* "in the regeneration" [Mt 19:28] is translated *u znovožỹtti* by Lobodovs´kyj, *u novonastannju* by Kuliš, and *u novonaroždennju* by Moračevs´kyj; ChSl. *ne lžesvidětel´stvuj* "do not bear false witness" [Mk 10:19] is translated *ne brexnesvidkuj* by Lobodovs´kyj, *ne svidkuj kryvo* by Kuliš; also *ljudohubec´* in Lobodovs´kyj, *dušehubec´* in Kuliš, and *čolovikovbyvec´* in Moračevs´kyj for "murderer" [Jn 8:44]; *zlorob* in Lobodovs´kyj, *zločynec´* in Kuliš, and *lyxodij* in Moračevs´kyj for "malefactor" [Jn 18:30]). Overall, Kuliš avoided using patently vulgar and regional forms that would be unintelligible to speakers of different Ukrainian dialects (*zalỹčkovuvan´nja* "hypocrisy" [Lk 12:1] in Moračevs´kyj compared to *lycemirstvo* in Kuliš [Žiteckij 1905, 36]).

Žytec´kyj (1905, 42) concluded that the translation made by Moračevs´kyj, despite minor caveats, was the most impressive from the textological and linguistic points of view. Nevertheless, Žytec´kyj deemed it necessary to praise the language of Kuliš (and Puljuj) for "[their] adeptness in choosing words, which although popular, remain rarely utilized" (ibid., 31). Interestingly enough, this opinion was shared by Horbač (1988, 50–51) and most recently by Nimčuk (2005, 28). Nimčuk (ibid., 37) argued, and rightly so, that Žytec´kyj overstated possible blemishes in the translation made by Kuliš and Puljuj with an eye to raising the merits of Moračevs´kyj's work, which Žytec´kyj recommended for publication in Russia.

In view of the almost unanimous fascination with the language of Moračevs´kyj, it is intriguing to compare his language with that of the translation made by Kuliš and Puljuj. All this can help us ascertain the configuration of the most characteristic features in the language of

Kuliš, which appears heterogeneous in comparison with all the aforementioned translations. Most interesting in this respect is a fragment from Moračevs′kyj's translation of the Gospel according to Matthew (5:1–48) as reproduced by Vsevolod Sreznevskij (1902; also *Svedenija*) from the manuscript donated, together with a draft, by the family of the late translator to the Imperial Academy of Sciences in Saint Petersburg in 1902.[8] Yet emendations made by Moračevs′kyj, in comparison with the first draft, are of particular interest inasmuch as they are likely to demonstrate the course and logic of Moračevs′kyj's work. In this respect, juxtaposing Moračevs′kyj's "editing in progress" with the translation of the same verses in chapter 5 of the Gospel according to Matthew by Kuliš and Puljuj may reveal fundamental differences in the stylistics of the two translations and in the linguistic views of their authors. The ultimate question to answer would be whether Moračevs′kyj's translation is in fact the best, as taken by many students on faith, in comparison with the major work of Kuliš and Puljuj, or may be given credit exclusively within the vernacularizing trend that was prevailing in Central Dnieper Ukrainian.

---

8   In 1899, while conducting an inventory in the manuscript division of the Library of the Imperial Academy of Sciences in Saint Petersburg, the revised manuscript of the translation, borrowed in March 1864 and returned in January 1865 for safe-keeping by Moračevs′kyj, was not found. In addition to the aforementioned two manuscripts bequeathed from the family of Moračevs′kyj, Sreznevskij (1902, 085, 087, 090, 015) gave a thorough description of three other manuscripts authored by Moračevs′kyj, which are the following: (1) *Dijanyja svjatyx″ apostoliv″ pysannyi svjatym″ apostolom″ y jevanhelystom″ Lukoju* (The Acts of the Apostles), revised by Moračevs′kyj and donated to the library in 1865, (2) *Apokalypsys″ čy odkrovennje svjatoho apostola Yvana Bohoslova* (The Book of Revelation), handed over by Moračevs′kyj to Izmail Sreznevskij in February 1864 and passed to the library in 1899, and (3) *Psaltyr″ na malorossyjskim″ jazyci* (The Book of Psalms in Little Russian), donated by the author in May 1865 toward possible publication "for the popular consumption" (see *Psaltyr″*, Moračevs′kyj). All in all, based on Sreznevskij's description of the parts of the Holy Scriptures translated by Moračevs′kyj, it becomes clear that the years 1860–1865 were the most productive in his literary life, securing him the position of a true pioneer in the translation of the Bible into vernacular Ukrainian (Komarov 1913, 22); for the full description of the all the copies of Moračevs′kyj's translation of the New Testament, Acts, Psalms, and Revelation, which are held at different libraries in Ukraine and the Russian Federation today, see Hnatenko and Kotenko 2007, and also Esipova 2014.

Moračevsʹkyj's Translation
(amended forms are enclosed in parentheses)

1. Бачучи стільки народу, Исусъ изійшовъ (= зійшов) на гору; и (= а) якъ сівъ, то підойшли до ёго ученики ёго; 2. и (= а) вінъ одкривши уста свої, почавъ учити (= навчавъ) іхъ, кажучи: 3. Блаженні убогиі (= гі) духомъ: бо іхъ е царство небесне. 4. Блаженні плачущиі (= щі): бо вони втішатця. 5. Блаженні тихиі (= тихі): бо вони наслідять (= -слідують) землю ... 12. Радуйтесь и веселітесь: бо велика вамъ награда на небесахъ. Такъ гнали и пророковъ, що були ще до васъ ... 14. Ви світло світа: не може вкритися городъ, коли стоїть на горі. 15. И (= тай) засвітивши свічку, не ставять (= становлять) іі підъ посудину, а на лихтарі, и вона світить усімъ, хто тільки е у господі (= хаті). 16. Такъ нехай світить світло ваше передъ людьми, щобъ вони бачили добрі діла ваши, и (= та) прославляли Батька вашого небесного (= котрий на небесехъ). 17. Не думайте, що я пришовъ нарушити (= зруйновати) пришовъ я [omission], а виповнити. 20. Бо кажу вамъ: коли правда ваша не переважить (= важе) правди (= кривди) книжниківъ и хварисеівъ, то не увійдете у царство небесне.

Kuliš and Puljuj's Translation

1. Побачивши ж народ, зійшов на гору, і, як сїв, приступили до Него ученики Його; 2. і відкрив Він уста свої, і навчав їх, глаголючи: 3. Блаженні вбогі духом, бо їх царство небесне. 4. Блаженні сумні, бо такі втїшять ся. 5. Блаженні тихі, бо такі осягнуть землю ... 12. Радуйтесь і веселїтесь: бо велика нагорода ваша на небі; так бо гонили й пророків, що бували перше. 14. Ви сьвітло сьвіту. Не може город сховати ся, стоячи на горі; 15. і, засьвітивши сьвічку, не ставлять під посудину, а на сьвічнику; то й сьвітить вона всїм, хто в хатї, 16. так нехай сяє сьвітло ваше перед людьми, щоб вони бачили ваші добрі дїла, й прославляли Отця вашого, що на небі. 17. Не думайте, що я прийшов знївечити закон або пророків; не прийшов я знївечити, а сповнити. 20. Глаголю бо вам: Що коли

21. Ви чули, що сказано предкамъ: "не вбий; а хто убье, той повиненъ суду." ... 25. Еднайся хутчій зъ ворогомъ твоімъ, поки ти зъ нимъ (приб.: ще) на (= у) дорозі: щобъ ворогъ не оддавъ тебе судді, а суддя не оддав тебе слузі, и ти не бувъ би кинуть у темницю. 26. Запевне, кажу тобі: не вийдешъ звідтіля, поки не оддаси до останнёго шеляга (= поки останнего шеляга не оддаси). 27. Ви чули, що сказано предкамъ: "не любочинсьтвуй." 28. А я кажу вамъ: усякий, хто тількі погляне на молодицю (= жінку) зъ похотініемъ (= похотливимъ окомъ), той любочинсьтвовавъ уже зъ нею у своімъ серці ... 30. А коли права рука твоя доводить тебе до гріха (= искушае тебе), одотни іі. ...
(Sreznevskij 1902/4, 092–093; *Svedenija*, 96–98)

ваша правда не переважить письменників та Фарисеїв, то не ввійдете в царство небесне. 21. Чували ви, що сказано старосьвіцьким: Не вбивай, а хто вбє, на того буде суд ... 25. Мирись із твоїм противником хутко, доки ти ще в дорозі з ним, щоб не віддав тебе противник судді, а суддя не віддав тебе осавулі (слузі), і не вкинуто тебе в темницю. 26. Істино глаголю тобі: не вийдеш звідтіля, доки не віддаси й останнього шеляга. 27. Чували ви, що сказано старосьвіцьким: Не чини перелюбу. 28. Я ж вам глаголю: Хто спогляне на жінку жадібним оком, той уже вчинив перелюб із нею в серці своїм ... 30. І коли права рука твоя блазнить тебе, відотни її. ... (*SP/NZ*, 6)

To get a more comprehensive picture of the differences between the two translations, it would be useful to juxtapose them with the same verses as edited by the synodal commission under the guidance of Bishop Parfenij Levyc´kyj of Kam'janec´-Podil´s´kyj. Possible deviations in the version (M-Synod) that went to press in 1907 will shed light on Moračevs´kyj's creative logic, which was ultimately blurred by the corrections introduced by the synodal commission.

Here is a parallel fragment from chapter 5 in the Gospel according to Matthew as published in 1907:

Moračevs′kyj's Translation, edited by the Synodal Commission

1. Побачивши народ, Ісус зійшов на гору, і як сів, то підійшли до Нього ученики Його. 2. І він, одкривши уста Свої, учив їх, промовляючи: 3. Блаженні убогиї духом, бо їх є Царство Небесне. 4. Блаженні плачущиї: бо вони втішаться. 5. Блаженні тихиї, бо вони осягнуть землю. . . . 12. Радуйтесь і веселіться: бо велика вам награда на небесах. Так гнали й пророків, що були перше вас. . . . 14. Ви світ мирові, Не може заховатися город, коли стоїть на горі. 15. І засвітивши свічку, не ставлять її під посудину, а на свічнику, і вона світить усім, хто є въ [sic] хаті. 16. Так нехай світить світ ваш перед людьми, щоб вони бачили добрі діла ваші й прославляли Отця вашого Небесного. 17. Не думайте, що Я прийшов зламати закон, або пророків: не зламати стародавнім: не убий а хто вбьє, на того буде суд. . . . 20. Бо кажу вам: коли правда ваша не переважить правди книжників і фарисеїв, то не ввійдете в Царство Небесне.

[1. And seeing the multitudes, he went up onto a mountain: and when he was set, his disciples came upon him: 2. And he opened his mouth, and taught them, saying, 3. Blessed are the poor in spirit: for theirs is the kingdom of heaven. 4. Blessed are they that mourn: for they shall be comforted. 5. Blessed are the meek: for they shall inherit the earth. . . . 12. Rejoice, and be exceedingly glad: for great is your reward in heaven: for so persecuted they the prophets which were before you. . . . 14. You are the light of the world. A city that is set on the hill cannot be hid. 15. Neither do men light a candle and put it under a bushel, but on a candlestick; and it giveth light unto all that are in the house. 16. Let your light so shine before men, that they may see your good works, and glorify your Father which is in heaven. 17. Think not that I am come to destroy the law of the prophets: I am not come to destroy, but to fulfill. . . . 20. For I say unto you, That except your righteousness shall exceed the righteousness of thescribes and Phar′-i-sees, ye shall in no case enter into the kingdom of heaven.

21. Ви чули, що сказано стародавнім: не убий а хто вбьє, на того буде суд. . . . 25. Мирись хутко з супротивником своїм, поки ти в дорозі з ним, щоб супротивник не віддав тебе судді а суддя не віддав тебе слузі, і не засадили б тебе в темницю. 26. Истинно кажу тобі: не вийдеш звідтіля, поки віддаси до останнього шеляга. 27. Ви чули, що сказано стародавнім: не прелюбодійствуй. 28. А Я кажу вам: усякий, хто тільки спогляне на жінку, бажаючи її, той прелюбодійсвовав уже з нею у своїм серці. . . . 30. І коли права рука твоя вводить тебе в гріх, одітни її й кинь од себе. . . .
(M-Synod, 17–31)

21. Ye have heard that it was said by them of old time, Thou shalt not kill; and whosoever shall kill shall be in danger of the judgment. . . . 25. Agree with thine adversary quickly, whiles thou art in the way with him; lest at any time the adversary deliver thee to the judge, and the judge deliver thee to the officer, and thou be cast into prison. 26. Verily I say unto thee, Thou shalt by no means come out thence, till thou hast paid the uttermost farthing. 27. Ye have heard that it was said by them of old time, Thou shalt not commit adultery. 28. But I say unto you, That whosoever looketh on a woman to lust after her hath committed adultery with her already in his heart. . . . 30. And if thy right hand offend thee, cut it off. . . .] (Mt 5:1–30)

A cursory look at the synodal version (M-Synod) as compared with the original translation of Moračevs′kyj does not reveal, at first blush, substantial deviations in the vernacular-based language. However, there is a significant digression in the linguistic medium as conceived by the synodal commission. While trying to make the translation look loftier, the commission decided to reverse the vernacular nature of some forms and expressions proposed by Moračevs′kyj. For this reason, members of the commission resorted to Church Slavonic as the principle means of archaization. To adduce some obvious examples, they replaced a seemingly awkward expression *nakormleni j napoeni budut′* in Moračevs′kyj with the Church Slavonic verb *nasytjat´sja* (M-Synod, 18), the colloquial *do vas"* in verse 12 by a morphosyntactic calque, *perše vas* "before you," influenced by the Church Slavonic expression *prežde vas"* (ibid.); the expression *perše vas* is also attested in the translation of Kuliš and Puljuj (*SP/NZ*, 6). Most striking is the substitution of the Church Slavonic expression *svit myrovi* for its vernacular counterpart *svitlo svita* "light of the world" in verse 14. In verse 25 (M-Synod, 21), one finds *suprotyvnyk* instead of *voroh* in Moračevs´kyj's translation (Sreznevskij 1902, 93). In verses 27–28, one happens on *preljubodijstvovat´* as a substitute for Moračevs´kyj's individual neologism *ljubočyns´tvovat´* "to commit adultery" with the vernacular base *čyn-yty* "to do" in the second part of the compound. In verse 26, the commission introduced *istynno* (*istyno* in Kuliš and Puljuj) instead of Moračevs´kyj's wonderful vernacular equivalent *zapevne* "verily." The commission introduced *Otec´* throughout the entire text in place of *bat´ko* "Father." The commission also restored the sound *f* in the loan form *faryseji* "Phar´-i-sees" instead of the counter-etymological x^w in the vernacular (Shevelov 1979, 631–634).

Remarkably, the version prepared by the synodal commission demonstrated, in fact, a reverse trend in dealing with the target language. Thus, one happens on vernacular and western Ukrainian forms introduced instead of the bookish and northern Ukrainian elements found in Moračevs´kyj's translation. For instance, the Church Slavonic lexeme *predky*, used by Moračevs´kyj in verses 21 and 27, was replaced by *starodavni* "they of old time," and the Church Slavonicism *povynen" sudu* in verse 21 by a stylistically neutral expression *bude sud* "shall be [in danger of] the judgment." The preposition/prefix *od-* used by Moračevs´kyj was replaced in some cases by *vid-*, which was criticized at that time by Nečuj-Levyc´kyj as a true Galicianism (e.g., *viddaty* "to deliver" in verse 25). The commission re-introduced the vernacular *xata* instead of *hospoda* "house," offered among other emendations by Moračevs´kyj.

An old form, attested in the history and dialects of Ukrainian, is found in the expression *zlamaty zakon* (verse 17) (M-Synod, 19; see Tymč. and Nimčuk, 1:397) instead of *narušyty zakon"* "to destroy the law" as proposed by Moračevs´kyj in his original translation (*zlamač* "Eidbrüchiger" [Žel., 1:302]). Remarkably, aside from one example from the collections of Ukrainian proverbs and sayings prepared by Matvij Nomys (1823–1900), all other examples of the verb *(z)lamaty* "to violate (a law)" are cited in *Slovar' ukrainskaho jazyka* (The Dictionary of the Ukrainian Language) edited by Borys Hrinčenko (Hrinč., 1:878–879) from various works of Kuliš. Generally, it is possible to trace the origin of this meaning in the old, northern Ukrainian literary tradition. Not surprisingly, this verb is only once attested with the same meaning as in Kotljarevs'kyj's *Enejida* (*Enejida*, Index, 85; see Umanec'and Spilka, 497), which, otherwise, is replete with northeastern Ukrainian dialectisms (Danylenko 2008b, 66–71). In the late eighteenth century these were transitional north-to-south features, developed on a northern Ukrainian base later to be gradually replaced by Southeast Ukrainian (*AUM*, 3, maps 6–9). This is why the emendation made by the commission looks obsolete as compared with the variant of Moračevs'kyj. One can legitimately wonder at this stage why Kuliš, who widely used the verb *(z)lamaty* "to violate (the law)" in his writings (Hrinč., 1:878–879), did not insist on its use in the translation of the corresponding verse.

Returning to the excerpt from the translation authored by Moračevs'kyj (Sreznevskij 1902) and the corresponding fragment from the translation of Kuliš and Puljuj, their phonetics as reflected in the orthography seem to demonstrate a number of similar sound features. Both Moračevs'kyj and Kuliš (together with Puljuj) make use of the alternation *u-* : *v-* and of the cluster breaker *i* in congruence with the principles of the so-called euphony, typical primarily of Southeast (literary) Ukrainian as cultivated in Russian-ruled Ukraine in the second half of the nineteenth century (Shevelov 1979, 297–300), whence some inconsistencies in the translation of Kuliš and Puljuj (e.g., *uvijdete* in Moračevs'kyj next to *vvijdete* in Kuliš and Puljuj "ye shall in no case enter," *u hospodi* in Moračevs'kyj next to *v xati* "in the house" in Kuliš and Puljuj, *Ysus" yzijšov"* in Moračevs'kyj as compared with *zijšov* in Kuliš and Puljuj, preceded by a word-final consonant in *narod* "people," yet after a pause, "he [Jesus] went up") (Žovtobrjux et al. 1979, 206–207). Unexpectedly, some elements look more archaic in Moračevs'kyj, who combines some eastern and northern Ukrainian features under the influence of his formative years at Xarkiv University and his native dialect of the Černihiv region

(Naumenko 1902, 172; Maljuk 1993, 60). Suffice it to cite such forms as *pidojšly* (pl.) "came up" and *odkryvšy* "[having] opened" without *ikavism* of the secondary *-o-* in the prefix *pido-* (< *podo-* < *podъ*) and of the etymological *o* in the prefix *od-*, which is typical of North and Southeast Ukrainian (Žovtobrjux et al. 1979, 283–284). The form *pidijšly* is used throughout the synodal version. Kuliš and Puljuj resort in this case to forms like *vidkryv* (m. sg. pret.) "to open" with the prefix *vid-*, which is attested in Southwest and, in parallel use with *od-*, in Southeast Ukrainian (*oddasy* as used by Moračevs´kyj next to *viddasy* [2 sg. non-pres.] "to return" in Kuliš, *odotny* in Moračevs´kyj next to *vidotny* [2 sg. imper.] "to cut off" in Kuliš and Puljuj). An intermediate form, *oditny* "to cut off," is found in the synodal version. The form *zvidtilja* "from there" occurs in Moračevs´kyj as well as Kuliš and Puljuj.

By contrast, Moračevs´kyj uses the form *xvarysei* "Phar´-i-sees" with a labialized phoneme x^w instead of *f*, still alien in East Ukrainian at that time (Matvijas 2005a, 34). As in the synodal version, Kuliš and Puljuj employ the phoneme *f* in this word, whence *faryseji*, a form that looks quite normal in modern literary Ukrainian (Arpolenko 2003, 214). The only phonetic form deviating from new standard Ukrainian is *do Neho*, which occurs, by the way, repeatedly in all translations of the Holy Scriptures made by Kuliš and Puljuj. This form is attested in the bulk of southeastern Ukrainian dialects (Matvijas 2006, 59) and was commonplace in Galicia at that time.

In the morphosyntax, deserving of attention are uncontracted forms used by Moračevs´kyj in those cases where Kuliš and Puljuj prefer contracted forms that look quite standard from the point of view of modern literary Ukrainian. What is baffling in this case is that Moračevs´kyj in the final version of his translation replaced contracted forms with the uncontracted, which migrated later into the synodal version (e.g., *blaženni ubohyi* [as emended by Moračevs´kyj in place of *ubohi* in the first draft] compared to *blaženni vbohi* "blessed are the poor in the spirit" in Kuliš and Puljuj or *blaženni tyxyi* [instead of *tyxi* in the first draft] in Moračevs´kyj compared to *blaženni tyxi* "blessed are the meek" in Kuliš and Puljuj). It is difficult at first to understand the logic of Moračevs´kyj's emendations, especially in view of such forms in Ševčenko's writings imbued with "deep thoughts, feelings, and often tragedy" (Sulyma 1924, 219). Two scenarios seem to be possible here. First, Moračevs´kyj could have intentionally archaized his text, which appeared to him all of a sudden too vernacular to speak of holy things. Second, one can also assume that the translator was vernacularizing the text by introducing additional folkloric devices, in particular uncontracted forms commonly used in his native (northern Ukrainian) dialect (Horbač 1988, 61). Comparing these forms with the Church Slavonic (*Biblija* 1862, 514r), one can reasonably accept the first, archaizing scenario. Kuliš and Puljuj, however, are consistent in choosing contracted forms in both the nominal part of compound predicates and noun phrases, which appear in tune with the norms of literary Ukrainian at that time rather than in the native (northern) dialect of Kuliš (see Matvijas 2006, 62). Both positions are represented, for instance, in verses 2–5 as cited above (e.g., *blaženni sumni* "blessed are they that mourn" in Kuliš and Puljuj).

Of interest is another emendation made by Moračevs´kyj (*Bat´ko vaš" nebesnyj* instead of the relative clause introduced with the bookish [Ruthenian] conjunction and a new locative form *kotryj na nebesax"* "[your Father] who is in heaven" in verse 16, ChSl. *iže na nebesěxъ* [*Biblija* 1862, 514v]). Remarkably, Kuliš and Puljuj employ here the vernacular relativizer *ščo*, a construction that is primarily attested in Southeast and North Ukrainian and in modern literary Ukrainian (Matvijas 2007a, 46). Both Moračevs´kyj and Kuliš (together with Puljuj) resort to impersonal constructions with the forms ending in *-no* and *-to* and the accusative direct object as found in verse 29. Yet this construction occurs more often than not in the translation made by Kuliš and Puljuj. This shows its popularity in western Ukraine, especially Galicia, under the influence of Polish (Danylenko 2003a, 188–194). In such cases, Moračevs´kyj makes use, instead, of passive constructions (e.g., *y ty ne buv" by kynut" u temnycju* as opposed to *i ne vkynuto tebe u temnycju* "and thou be cast into prison" [Mt 5:25]). In the synodal version, they use the active type of construction (M-Synod, 21). Most telling here is the archaic nominal form of the past passive participle *kynut"* (m. sg.) "cast," obviously chosen by Moračevs´kyj under the influence of the Church Slavonic text: *vъ temnicu vverženъ budešy* (*Biblija* 1862, 514v; Horbač 1988, 61).

In verse 21, one happens on an interesting "covert Church Slavonicism," (i.e., *povynen″ sudu* [gen.] "shall be in danger of judgment" [literally, "should be judged"] borrowed from the Church Slavonic version: *povynen″ jest′ sudu*) (*Biblija* 1862, 514v). Kuliš and Puljuj do not follow the archaic governance, introducing instead a commonly used construction *na tebe bude sud* similar to that used in the synodal version (M-Synod, 20). Additionally, one should mention *osavulï* "officer" in verse 25, a dative form with the ending *-i*, which is sporadically attested for inanimates in North and Southeast Ukrainian (Matvijas 2006, 54). As far as the animate *osavul* is concerned, it could be associated by the translators with the above ending under the influence of the masculine locatives in *-ě* > *-i* (Bevzenko et al. 1978, 98–99). The unusual dative *osavulï* might have been specially designed to fit in with the overall vernacular morphosyntactic basis of the translation. Speaking about verbal morphology, Moračevs′kyj used *perevažyt′* (3 sg. non-past) "to exceed" in place of *perevaže* (modern second conjugation), commonly attested in the bulk of southeastern and easternmost Polissian dialects (Matvijas 2006, 63), as well as in the literary standard as cultivated in Russian-ruled Ukraine. Among grammatical forms compromised on by Kuliš and Puljuj, one can name a separate use of the reflexive particle in verbal forms like *vtišjat′ sja* (3 pl. non-past) "to cheer up," according to the Galician tradition, compared to *vtišatcja* (with a phonetic spelling that reflects assimilative changes at the morpheme boundary) in Moračevs′kyj. Needless to say that in the synodal version, the present tense verbal forms were retained with the etymological spelling as in Kuliš and Puljuj.

Of interest here is the palatalization of *š′* as reflected in *vtišjat′ sja*. This type of palatalization is primarily attested in the Left Bank southeastern Ukrainian dialects (*AUM*, 3, part 3, map 17). Yet this spelling (also with other hushing sounds) was most likely introduced into the translation of the New Testament by Kuliš, who employed this type of spelling in Ševčenko's *Kobzar* of 1860 (Tymošenko 1979, 121). Never used (without the editor's intervention) by Ševčenko, the verbal forms with palatalization were commonly employed not only by Kuliš but also by other writers representing different dialectal areas in Dnieper Ukraine, such as Leonid Hrebinka, Ivan Nečuj-Levyc′kyj, Lesja Ukrajinka, and Panas Myrnyj (ibid.; Hrycenko 2007, 25).

Most telling in Moračevs′kyj's translation, along with the strong vernacularizing undercurrent, is that its phonetics and morphosyntax look more archaic than the corresponding elements and patterns in the language of Kuliš and Puljuj. Strange as it may appear for their translation, permeated in some places with Galician forms (Nimčuk 2005, 35), its phonetic and major morphosyntactic features appear more normalized. Southeastern Ukrainian at their core, although with a northern Ukrainian admixture, these features contrast with the northern Ukrainian basis of Moračevs′kyj's language. Whether it is coincidental or not, the above excerpts from Moračevs′kyj's translation are riddled with those northern (Černihiv) features that, having played a significant role in the previous literary tradition, belong today to the periphery of modern Ukrainian (Shevelov 1966, 10–24): hence the impression of both archaic and folkloric foundations of Moračevs′kyj's language.

What is really at issue here is the vocabulary as used in the two translations. To begin with, the vocabulary of Moračevs′kyj is moderately archaic. In his translation, Moračevs′kyj limited himself to that level of archaization that was cultivated in folklore (or appropriately conventionalized belle lettres) and appealed to the commoners and educated populists. In a sense, one deals here with a kind of "vernacular archaization" or, to put it bluntly, "vernacular Slavonic," which was commonly taught by the lower clergy to gentrified Cossacks, peasants, or (former) serfs like Ševčenko (who is known to have indulged in religious themes since his adolescence) (see Rusanivs′kyj 2002, 86–96).

In view of a particular Slavonic canon as cultivated by the laymen, a close inspection of Moračevs′kyj's moderately archaic vocabulary does not bring about unexpected results. The majority of Church Slavonicisms as detected in the above fragment (and elsewhere in his translation) belong to a corpus of archaic forms and expressions used traditionally by local intelligentsia and peasantry in Russian-ruled Ukraine at that time. Meanwhile, the synodal version of his translation reflects more archaic features influenced seemingly by the parallel Church Slavonic text. This is why the nature of the Church Slavonicisms in Moračevs′kyj's original translation is somewhat different from the Church Slavonicisms introduced by the members of the synodal commission.

Church Slavonicisms were perceived by Moračevs´kyj as long naturalized lexemes, as reflected in their phonetic spelling, and thus belonging to the Orthodox legacy pertaining to all common and educated Little Russians. Among such plain or "vernacularized" Church Slavonicisms, one can name the following lexemes used both by a speaker of a transitional (northern Ukrainian) dialect, such as Moračevs´kyj, and a representative of Sloboda Ukraine, like Kvitka-Osnov'janenko: *usta* "mouth" (Kvitka, 3:506; see *Enejida*, Index, 188), *blažennyj* "blessed," *naslidjat´* (3 pl. non-past) "to inherit" (ChSl. *naslědętь*; *naslidovaty* in Kvitka, 2:217; see *Enejida*, Index, 103), *naslědjat´* in Bačyn´skij's translation of Psalm 36 (*Psaltyr´*, Bačyn´skij, 72), and *osjahnut´* in the synodal version (Arpolenko 2003, 216). I would add also *carstvo nebesne* "kingdom of heaven" (Kvitka, 3:579), *nebesa* "heaven" (ibid., 231–232; see *Enejida*, Index, 105), *Bat´ko nebesnyj* "Father who is in heaven," *knyžnyk* "scribe" (*knyžnyk* "bookseller" in Kvitka, 2:5), as used in the Poltava region with the meaning "a literate person" (Hrinč., 1:793), and *xvarysej* "Phar´-i-see" with the counter-etymological x^w. This sound seems to be a constituent part of Moračevs´kyj's phonetic system. It is not surprising to come across another *xv*-spelling, *porxvyru* (acc.) "[clothed] in purple" (Lk 16:19) as found in the translation of the parable of the rich man and Lazarus (Lk 16:19–31; see Žiteckij 1905, 59; Arpolenko 2003, 214).

The sound x^w seems to be of paramount importance for the vernacularization of the translation of the Holy Scriptures. Generally, this is an old substitute for a foreign *f* in Middle Ukrainian. For instance, the form *xvarysejska* "Phariseean" is first attested in the Gospels from Kam'janka-Buz´ka (Strumylova; north of Lviv) of 1411 (Shevelov 1979, 633). However, the fate of *f* and its substitute is different in various Ukrainian dialects. Thus, in Southwest (Lemkian) Ukrainian, the word *farysej* with the foreign *f* is attested in two meanings, the "Pharisäer" and lay "schlechter, falscher Mensch," to wit, "hypocrite," in Verxratskyj (1902, 477). Interestingly, there are more than forty words with the word-initial *f* in the glossary in Verxratskyj (ibid., 477–478), while in the entire literary output of the Xarkovite Kvitka-Osnov'janenko one encounters only four lexemes with the phoneme *f*, obviously alien in the Sloboda dialect at that time (i.e., an exclamation *fit´* with multiple connotations, its derivative *fit´fit´katy* "to whistle," and two French borrowings, *forbje* "very good" [Fr. *fort bien*] and [mediated by Russian] *furažka* "a type of military cap") (Kvitka, 3:514). In some cases, both *f* and its substitute are encountered side by side, as in one of Kvitka-Osnov'janenko's stories edited by Oleksander Potebnja (1835–1891) in 1887: *for"-bje* "very good" next to *xrancuz"* "Frenchman" (Osnovjanenko 1887, 24–25). In the religious context, Ševčenko used the form *farysej*, never resorting to the counter-etymological x^w (*SŠ* 2, 370; *Concordance* 4:2595). The latter phoneme is attested only in *Xvastov* and its derivatives (*SŠ* 2, 370–371; *Concordance* 4:2599).

In view of the aforementioned geographical distribution, the use of *f* by Kuliš and Puljuj may testify to their orientation toward a premodern treatment of *f* as reflected in the regional (Galician) appropriation of this sound.[9] However, it is most interesting to recall that in his first translation of the Bible, published under the title *Svjate pys'mo abo vsja Byblyja staroho y novoho zavitu* (The Holy Scripture, or the Entire Bible of the Old and New Testaments, 1869), Kuliš consistently followed the populist treatment of the alien *f*, using instead the vernacular x^w, whence multiple *xv*-spellings like *Xvaraon* "Pha´-raoh" (*Pentatevx*, 10, Gen 12:17–18, etc.), *Xvara* "Te´-rah" (*Pentatevx*, 10, Gen 11:26, etc.), *Vet-Xvehor* "Beth-pe´-or" (*Pentatevx*, 145, Deut 3:29), and so forth (*Faraon*, *Tara*, *Bet-Peor* in the second translation of the Bible published posthumously in 1903) (*SP*, 13, 14, 175).

In this respect, it is worth mentioning a similar substitution for *f*, employed with a comic connotation, in personal letters written by Kuliš in the year of publication of the *Pentatevx Musijevyj* in 1869 (*Pentatevx*). In a letter of 1 February 1869 addressed to Ivan Xyl´čevs´kyj from Florence, Kuliš used a popular form *koxve* "coffee" and seemingly mocked the name of the city of *Xlorencija* next to a regular form *Florencija* in the next letter of 14 April 1869 (Kuliš to Xil´čevskij, 93–94). Moreover, in 1869, while preparing the manuscript of Ivan Nečuj-Levyc´kyj's story

---

9 It is interesting to cite here the title of a song recorded in the late 1870s in Galicia, "Pro vojnu z Francuzom" (About a War with the French). In the text, one happens on *f* in loan forms such as *Franc* (the emperor's name) and *Francuz* "a Frenchman" (*Narodni Pisni*, 344). No wonder, the sound *f* is found in Galician translations of the Holy Scriptures, for instance, in the translations made by Markijan Šaškevyč (Šaškevyč, 110) and Antin (Antonij) Kobyljans´kyj (Luka-U, 52). The same translation of the Gospel according to Luke was published in Ukrainian script (Luka-U) and Latin-based script (Luka-L).

"Pryčepa" (The Cocklebur) for publication in the periodical *Pravda*, Kuliš consistently replaced the letter *f* with the digraph *xv* (e.g., the personal name *Xvedor* instead of *Fedor* or *xvylozoxvyja* for *fylosofija* "philosophy" in Nečuj-Levyc´kyj) (Voznjak 1928b, 5); however, in native or long naturalized borrowings he also used the digraph *xv* as in *akaxvyst* "acaphist" and *štraxv* "penalty, fine" next to *fortupljas* "piano" (Matvijas 2007b, 34, 36). Tentatively, one deals here with the results of two chronologically distinct approaches to the vernacular translation of the Bible. The first, *poetic* approach, supposedly elaborated by Kuliš before meeting Puljuj and receiving a critical review of his first translations by Miklosich, is employed in loose populist paraphrases of the texts. The second approach, applied by Kuliš in his later translation of the Bible, was premised on, strictly speaking, *scholarly* tenets. After his death, the scholarly approach was gradually replaced by the evangelical principle of faithful translation, as found in the first publication of the Ukrainian Bible by the British and Foreign Bible Society (Naxlik 2007, 2:284).

Among lexical items, one should recall *ljubočyns´tvovat´* "to commit adultery" as a semi-calque of *ljubodějstvovat´* (*Biblija* 1862, 514v) in the original translation of Moračevs´kyj (Sreznevskij 1902, 093), given as *preljubodijstvovat´* in the synodal version. No Polonisms or other modern borrowings are found in Moračevs´kyj's translation, which looks, from this point of view, synchronically homogeneous. For the sake of vernacular uniformity, he might have decided to substitute *hospoda* for the more ethnographic lexeme *xata* "house," reversed in the synodal version (*vytalnyc[a]: hospóda, xata ... , dom"* in the *Leksikon" slavenorosskij y ymen" tl"kovanije* of Pamvo Berynda) (Berynda, 15). Not surprisingly, the word *hospoda* was used by Moračevs´kyj elsewhere (Žiteckij 1905, 59). As far as the lexeme *xata* is concerned, it occurs, for instance, seventeen times in Kotljarevs´kyj (*Enejida*, Index, 191) and only once (!) in Potebnja's translation of the *Odyssey* (Danylenko 1999, 237). The word *šeljah* "farthing," used also by Kuliš and Puljuj, is a long naturalized German form (*DMU*, 2:555–556) attested already from the late Old Ukrainian period onward (see Tymč. and Nimčuk, 2:492; Šelud´ko 1931, 55). For this reason, this form does not affect the stylistic uniformity of Moračevs´kyj's translation or the multilayered lexical make-up of the translation of Kuliš and Puljuj.

The vocabulary in Kuliš and Puljuj is by contrast diachronically heterogeneous. To begin with, the translators easily employ vernacular lexemes with a wide range of connotation such as the aforementioned *xata* "house" (dropped by Moračevs´kyj), *nebo* instead of *nebesa* "heaven," a possible neologism *žertivnja* "altar" (Žel., 1:222; *oltar´* in Moračevs´kyj) as compared with MUkr. *žertovnyk"* (Berynda, 79; Tymč. and Nimčuk, 1:250), a possible neologism *s´vičnyk* "candlestick" (Hrinč., 2:620; Umanec´ and Spilka, 692), *staros´vickyj* "of old times" (Kvitka, 3:329), and even *osavul* "officer" with an obvious connotation of the Cossack past. On the other hand, the translators reduce a number of antiquated and outdated lexemes to a handful of Church Slavonicisms, some of which look "vernacularized" as in Moračevs´kyj: *usta* "mouth," *blažennyj* "blessed," *hlaholaty* "to say" used also in the "secular" context (Kvitka, 1:261), *farysej* "Phar´-i-see," *carstvo nebesne* "kingdom of heaven," *Otec´* "Father," and some bookish (East Slavic) forms like *istyno* "verily," attested also as *istynno* in Kvitka (1:625; *zapevne* in Moračevs´kyj), *pys´mennyk* "scribe" as a semantic neologism (Hrinč., 2:158; Kvitka, 2:243), and *horod* "city" (*Enejida*, Index, 38). All the above lexemes, though with some modified meanings, were attested in nineteenth-century written Ukrainian (ibid., 1:287–288) and folklore (Pšepjurs´ka-Ovčarenko 1988, 217).

To be sure, most interesting is the neologism *blaznyty* "to tempt," here "to offend" (e.g., SP/NZ, 7, Mt 5:30), used by Kuliš and Puljuj consistently throughout their entire translation. Sporadically one happens also on a regular *spokušuvaty* (SP/NZ, 99, Jn 8:6) (*spokušuvaty* in *Ukrajins´ko-nimec´kyj slovnyk* of Zenon Kuzelja and Jaroslav Rudnyc´kyj [Ukrainian-German Dictionary, 1943; see Kuzela and Rud., 1190] and *spokušaty* "to tempt" in Hrinčenko [Hrinč., 2:693]). The latter lexeme hardly fits in the holy narrative (Tymošyk 2000a, 243), a fact which might have prompted the translators to come up with a substitute: *blaznyty*. Interestingly, the neologism *blaznyty* also occurs in Moračevs´kyj, although in other derivational forms, thereby tentatively demonstrating a similar line of linguistic reasoning with regard to the Slavic stem *blaz(n)-* "temptation" (*EDU*, 1:204).

Following Ivan Ohijenko (Illarion), Pšepjurs´ka-Ovčarenko (1988, 220) viewed the form *blaznyty* as a tender spot in the language of Kuliš and Puljuj. According to her, this lexeme is likely to be associated in Ukrainian with the commonly used *blazen´* "Fratz, Bub; Narr" (Verxratskyj 1902, 392; see

Hrinč., 1:114), that is, "buffoon," whence allegedly *blaznyty* signifies "to make a fool of somebody." Nevertheless, disregarding the Middle Polish influence, the unusual derivational model *blaznyty* (Rus. *soblaznit'* "to tempt, seduce") can hardly resuscitate any vernacular (pejorative) associations and relates clearly to ChSl. *blazn"* "mistake, temptation" and *blaznyty* "to tempt" (*LLP*, 1:111; *EDU*, 1:204; see Tymč., 98). It is interesting that Pavlo Bilec´kyj-Nosenko in his *Slovar' malorossijskaho, ili juho-vostočnorusskaho jazýka* (A Dictionary of Little Russian or, Southeastern Russian Language, 1838–1843, first published in 1966) (Bil.-Nos., 57) deemed it necessary to cite in the entry for *blazen'* "greenhorn; fool" the Church Slavonic verb *blaznyty*, as used in a verse excerpted from the Gospel according to John (Jn 6:61). In other words, he was cognizant of two different meanings associated with the same stem in Southeast Ukrainian (Moroz and Tkač 2006, 23–24).

All in all, the vocabulary of Kuliš and Puljuj demonstrates a higher level of synthesis compared with that of Moračevs´kyj. The lexical make-up of their translation is comprised of several layers of Church Slavonic, bookish (Ruthenian), and Old Rusian elements, representing different literary traditions as practiced in the Middle Ukrainian period. Among the tendencies adjusted to the needs of their translation, Kuliš and Puljuj resorted to both archaic and vernacular forms extant from the late seventeenth century and even earlier. All things considered, two different conceptualizations of the vernacular rendition of the Holy Scriptures are represented in the two translations. Which one appealed to the average readership depended on a series of factors related *grosso toto* indirectly to the quality of the translation itself seen synchronically.[10]

---

10 Remarkably, Puljuj published his translation of practically the same excerpt from the Holy Scriptures much earlier in a revised edition of his *Molytvoslov"* under a changed title, *Molytovnyk dlja rus´koho narodu* (A Prayer Book for the Rusian People), which appeared in 1871 in Vienna (*Molytovnyk*, 151). Slight differences in the orthography aside, there are only a few deviations, primarily in the vocabulary, between the two translations of the fragment. Thus, in *Molytovnyk*, Puljuj used the form *pekel´nyj* (adj.) changed into *pekol´nyj* (adj.) "hellish" (Žel., 2:67) as well as the comparative form *vyhodnišč* changed into *bil´ša koryst'* "[more] profitable" in the translation of the New Testament. There is no *osavul* in *Molytovnyk*, though Puljuj already used the verb *blaznyt'* "to tempt," later incorporated by Kuliš into the translation of the Bible. Vis-à-vis the above parallelism, the contribution of Puljuj in the translation of the New Testament seems to have been more significant than it may appear at first glance.

The first dissenting opinion of Moračevs′kyj's translation was published anonymously in the journal *Ukraina* in 1907. Signed with the initials "V. N." (Volodymyr Navroc′kyj?), the review evaluated the vernacular translation of the Gospel according to Matthew that appeared, though without the name of the translator, in Moscow in 1906. To understand the nature of the criticism, viewed implicitly through the prism of Kuliš and Puljuj's translation, one should bear in mind that the preparation of the translation for publication was completed by two independent groups of experts. On the one hand, the Holy Synod appointed Archbishop Parfenij Levyc′kyj (a native of the Poltava region) of Kam'janec′-Podil′s′kyj chief editor and head of a special commission, comprised primarily of theologians from the Kyiv Theological Academy. This commission worked on the revision of Moračevs′kyj's translation in Kam'janec′-Podil′s′kyj, located in Podolia (West Ukraine). On the other hand, in Saint Petersburg, academicians Aleksej Šaxmatov and Fëdor Korš headed a lay commission set up by the Imperial Academy of Sciences with an eye to revising the language of the translation made almost fifty years ago. The idea was as follows: first, the latter commission would make corrections in the manuscript and come up with necessary suggestions, then sending them over to the theological commission for spiritual approval. Unfortunately, the synodal commission ignored most of the emendations proposed by the commission of the Imperial Academy of Sciences and submitted, instead, their own version for publication (Vlasovs′kyj 1957, 298–299). As a result, it can hardly be safely said which changes were offered by the linguists and which were introduced by the theologians.

Noting that "the translation reads easily and does not lose the significance of the style," the reviewer, however, sorted out several shortcomings and proposed some corrections that looked quite convincing, especially, with regard to the lexical make-up of the translation. For example, the reviewer rejected *na kryli (cerkovnim)* "a pinnacle of the temple" (Mt 4:5, M-Synod, 14), used in the official publication, as an incomprehensible expression, while blaming Moračevs′kyj for using a "right-bank word" *na hanku*. The reviewer preferred *na kryl′ci* (V. N. 1907, 110). He also criticized the choice of another lexeme, *obuv'ja* "shoes," attested in the translation of Kuliš and Puljuj as well. The reviewer did not accept the word *skipočka* (M-Synod, 30) or *spyčka* "mote" (in Moračevs′kyj's original) (Mt 7:3), offering instead *skalka* (V. N. 1907, 111). Neither did he like *kusok xliba* "a piece of bread" in Moračevs′kyj, which might be replaced with "a plain popular *šmatok* [*xliba*]" (ibid., 112). All things considered, in contravention of all existing evidence, the quality of Moračevs′kyj's translation as well as all other vernacular translations of the Holy Scriptures could be conceived, according to the reviewer, only aesthetically in view of the lack of any stable norms for the written Ukrainian language at that time (ibid.).

For this reason, if taken out of the populist aesthetic context, Kuliš and Puljuj's translation of the New Testament is based, as had been already hypothesized, on more variegated foundations of style and dialect. Strange as it may appear, it is the synodal version of Moračevs′kyj rather than the translator's original that can be juxtaposed with the translation of Kuliš and Puljuj. The point is that the synodal commission archaicized Moračevs′kyj's text with the help of Church Slavonicisms, thus unwittingly expanding the balanced presence of Slavonic elements in the vernacular-based translation of Moračevs′kyj. Due to this heterogeneity, the resulting linguistic texture of the synodal version was likely to resemble the multilayered structure of the narrative in Kuliš's translation. Tilting the balance toward the Church Slavonic admixture in the synodal version was likely to cause a disruption in the solid vernacular basis of the translation made by Moračevs′kyj. Luckily, this kind of disruption did not happen, and the commission should be given credit for trying to keep the vernacular tinge of Moračevs′kyj's original translation, especially in its vocabulary and syntax (see Arpolenko 2003, 220).

WHO ELSE BEARS A GRUDGE?

As evidenced from the foregoing analysis of Moračevs′kyj's translation, the language program of Kuliš looked unique under the socio-cultural circumstances of contemporary Russian-ruled Ukraine. Unlike a few Sloboda populists like Oleksander Navroc′kyj and Volodymyr Aleksandrov whose translations were inspired by Kuliš, the ideological disparity between his language and Moračevs′kyj's translation was quite obvious. This disparity can be illuminated by a discussion of the linguistic views of Ivan Nečuj-Levyc´kyj, as outlined in his famous study *S´ohočasna časopysna mova na Ukraini* (Modern Literary Language in Ukraine, 1907). I will disregard anecdotal evidence concerning his motivation for writing this study as not relevant for our discussion (Tarnawsky 2012). Aside from Nečuj-Levyc´kyj's personal grudges against some younger Ukrainophiles, including Serhij Jefremov (1876–1939), he remained a talented literary critic and political activist. Nevertheless, Nečuj-Levyc´kyj's study was obviously a biased work authored by an annoyed old master who could hardly accept new linguistic and literary modes, largely influenced by the Galician vogue. This style was notoriously at odds with his vision of a one-dialect basis for literary Ukrainian in the late nineteenth and early twentieth centuries. This work was followed in 1912 by another, much shorter exposé of Nečuj-Levyc´kyj's position in his fight against all sorts of Galician admixtures (Shevelov 1966, 78–116). Overall, Nečuj-Levyc´kyj's arguments, outdated and reactionary as they might look today, relate to an undeclared contest between the translation of Moračevs´kyj, on the one hand, and that of Kuliš and Puljuj, on the other, for the literary and cultural priority of the respective translation projects and language programs.

Nečuj-Levyc´kyj correctly criticized a discordance in the work of the two commissions revising the manuscript of Moračevs´kyj's translation for publication (Nečuj-Levic´kyj 1907, 323). Having praised the phonetic principle of orthography in Kuliš and Puljuj's translation, first published in 1871, he deplored the quality of Moračevs´kyj's new translation of the Gospel according to Matthew. It was printed with a help of a "new Galician orthography" channeled through some contemporary fashionable journals from Austria-Hungary. In particular, the writer castigated the use of Galician lexemes and expressions, citing, first of all, the "Galician preposition" *vid* "from" in contrast to a "Ukrainian *od*" in the synodal publication of the New Testament. According to him, the theologian editors of Moračevs´kyj's translation kept only sporadically the original preposition *od*, generally in those places where Kuliš and Puljuj also resorted to this form, but the ratio should have been different in view of the popular nature of *od*. The occurrence of *vid* in Kuliš and Puljuj was easy to understand inasmuch as the translators were purportedly preparing their work primarily for Galicia. Yet the translation of Moračevs´kyj was designed not for the Podolia region, where the synodal commission held its meetings, but for the entirety of Ukraine (ibid., 324).

Among other Galician forms used indiscriminately in contemporary journals and newspapers, as well as in the 1903 Bible of Kuliš and Puljuj, Nečuj-Levyc´kyj (Nečuj-Levic´kyj 1907, 327) mentioned "Galician-Polish genitives" of the type *do Jehyptu* (gen.) (instead of *Jehypta*) "to Egypt," *bahato narodu* (gen.) (instead of *naroda*) "many people," and *zavitu* (gen.) (in place of *zavita*) "testament," *korenju* (gen.) (instead of *korenja*) "root." The writer also did not accept locatives like *po morju* "on the sea" preferring instead the "correct" form *po mori* (ibid.). In the vocabulary, Nečuj-Levyc´kyj rejected *svidoctvo* "testimony" as a Polonism, proposing instead *svidčennja* (ibid.); this compared to *s´vidkuvannje* in Kuliš and Puljuj (*SP/NZ*, 89, Jn 1:7). Among other "unacceptable" lexemes, he cited *usumpylys´* (Pol. *sumienie* "conscience") instead of the indigenous *zavahalys´* (pl. pret.) "to doubt," *naruha* for *hlum* "jibe," *uljublenyj* in place of "Ukrainian" *ljubyj* "beloved," found in Kuliš and Puljuj (*SP/NZ*, 5, Mt 3:17), or "Polish-Ukrainian" *koxanyj* "beloved" (Nečuj-Levic´kyj 1907, 327).

Remarkably, some "Polish-Galician" forms, chastised by the reviewer, are also found in the translation of Kuliš and Puljuj, which might have been a corollary to Puljuj's later intervention in the language fabric of the Bible. For example, Nečuj-Levyc´kyj (Nečuj-Levic´kyj 1907, 327–328) insisted on *zahadav* or *zveliv* instead of "Polish-Galician" *prymusyv* (m. sg. pret.) "to constrain" (Mt 14:22), which, incidentally, occurs in Kuliš and Puljuj as well (*SP/NZ*, 17). The reviewer, however, was less critical of "Galician" comparatives like *zlijšyj* "more wicked" (Mt 12:44) and verbs of the type *prijty* "to come" (Nečuj-Levic´kyj 1907, 328), which, though of northern and southwestern origin, were more often than not used in nineteenth-century literary language in Russian-ruled Ukraine (Matvijas 2005a, 37). One encounters *zliščyj* and *pijšov* (m. sg. pret.) "to go" in Kuliš and Puljuj (*SP/NZ*, 15, 16, Mt 13:36). The former seems to have been influenced by Puljuj (Tymošenko 1971, 205), while the latter is sporadically attested in the writings of Panas Myrnyj, a native of the Poltava region (Hrycenko 2007, 26). Some of Nečuj-Levyc´kyj's recommendations look naïve today. However, if viewed monodialectally through the prism of the linguistic debates of the late nineteenth and early twentieth centuries, one can understand them to be reasonable. Suffice it to mention Nečuj-Levyc´kyj's proposal to use *udjahanka* (Nečuj-Levic´kyj 1907, 328) as an umbrella term to denote any outerwear with long sleeves (Hrinč., 2:831), in place of Moračevs´kyj's *svyta*, which was dubbed by the reviewer "very vulgar."

In the realm of phonetics, Nečuj-Levyc´kyj (Nečuj-Levic´kyj 1907, 329) praised popular verbal forms like *molyssja* (2 sg. pres.) "to pray" and *odrečessja* (2 sg. non-past) "to renounce," found in the first editions of Kuliš and Puljuj's translation, in contrast to Russianized *molyšsja* and *vidrečešsja*, without any assimilative change at the morpheme boundary, found in Moračevs´kyj's translation prepared for publication by the synodal commission. In the first several publications of Kuliš and Puljuj's translation by the British and Foreign Bible Society, one comes across a typical Galician spelling of reflexive particles like *molyš sja* (*SP/NZ*, 7, Mt 6:5), which, however, was subsequently changed to a solid spelling like *molyšsja*. The separate spelling of the particle *sja*, never employed by Kuliš himself (Tymošenko 1973, 171), could have been introduced by Puljuj or, more likely, by an old acquaintance of his, the Galician priest Oleksa Sljusarčuk, hired by the British and Foreign Bible Society to proofread the entire manuscript of the translation of the Bible (Studyns´kyj 1930, lxv–lxvi; Naxlik 2007, 2:284).[11]

Among all other critics of Kuliš and Puljuj's translation, Ivan Franko stands out. Due mostly to personal animosity, Franko's assessment of their work was absolutely negative (Danylenko 2009b). While recalling the early translations of the Holy Scriptures made by Kuliš in the late 1860s, Franko (1910, 176) wrote in his *Narys istoriji ukrajins´ko-rus´koji literatury do 1890 r.* (An Outline of Ukrainian-Rusian Literature up to 1890) that Kuliš's translation did not meet his expectations from the religious, literary, and linguistic

---

11 There is scant information about Oleksa Sljusarčuk in the Ukrainian-language *Encyclopedia of Ukraine*. The anonymous entry says that Oleksij (Oleksa) Sljusarčuk (1838–1912) authored prayers, sermons, and *Psaltyr´ rozšyrena* (*Sljusarčuk*), in fact, *Psaltyrja rozšyrena v˝ dusě xrystijan´skoj molytvў y cerkovnoho bohosluženja* (An Expanded Psalter in the Spirit of Christian Sermon and Church Service), published in Žovkva in 1904 (Horbač 1988, 31–32, fn. 9).

point of view. He argued that the entire translation proved very poor and full of "unpleasant linguistic eccentricities" inasmuch as Kuliš, who allegedly did not know any European language, save perhaps for Russian, failed to find the fine line between vernacular Ukrainian and Church Slavonic (ibid., 176). For this reason, Kuliš disproportionately employed such obsolete forms as the old aorist *reče* (3 sg.) "to say" along with other "incomprehensible" words. The Galician writer also criticized the "odd Ukrainianization" of personal names of the type *Musij* instead of *Mojsej* (Moses) (ibid.). Interestingly enough, Franko was reluctant to criticize the use of Galician dialectal forms like *bez Neho* "without Him" (*SP*, 89, Jo 1:1), which, as Nimčuk (2005, 35) hypothesized, might have been introduced into the text by Puljuj, who edited the text of the Bible after the death of Kuliš. One should add in this respect that, characteristic as they may appear, such corrections could hardly change the overall fabric of Kuliš's translation, based on Southeast Ukrainian.

Much later, after the publication of the whole Bible in 1903, Franko (1910, 177) proved particularly unfair in castigating Kuliš for allegedly construing an "arch-Ukrainian" expression *Xaj dufaje Srul'* [Is´-ra-el] *na pana*, without even mentioning Psalm 130 where this expression might have been used (Danylenko 2009b). According to Studyns´kyj (1930, lxxviii), the above phrase was cooked up by local Russophiles who despised the very idea of translating the Holy Bible into vernacular Ukrainian. Treating Kuliš as an ideological opponent of the Galician populists (see Naxlik 2007, 1:356–392, 453), Franko imprudently parroted the concoction of the Russophiles. Needless to say, as a highly educated writer with a profound knowledge of literary traditions and Ukrainian dialects, Kuliš would never use a form like *Srul'* "Is´-ra-el," thereby alluding to its double meaning through alliteration in the stem *sra-l'*- in *sral'nja*, *sratva* "latrine" (Hrinč., 2:703). In his paraphrase of Psalm 130, Kuliš wrote: ... *vpovaje / Na Hospoda blahyj Izrail'* (*Psaltyr*, Rataj, 317–318). In his translation of the same psalm Puljuj made use of a similar set of lexemes: *Vpovaj, Izrajilju, na Hospoda* "Let Is´-ra-el hope in the Lord" (*SP* 564, Ps 130:7).

Overall, while criticizing stylistic deficiencies in the language of Kuliš, Franko unabashedly concluded that the first translation of the Holy Scriptures did not meet the expectations of the Ukrainian readership;

it was, according to him, a complete disaster. And what, as Franko (1910, 175) argued, can the Ukrainian reader expect from a "true Russian" who is an inveterate doctrinaire in virtually everything?

Obviously, Franko's review of Kuliš's work was unfair and biased. By contrast, a balanced appraisal was offered by an anonymous reviewer in 1881 in *Vestnik Evropy* (V., 1881). In his survey of the history of vernacular translations of the Holy Scriptures in the Ukrainian lands, the author dwelled briefly on Kuliš's major scriptural translations, including the latest of the New Testament. According to the reviewer (ibid., 896–897), his translation stood out compared with the translations made by Markijan Šaškevyč and Antin (Antonij) Kobyljans'kyj, leaving aside several fragments from the Bible translated by Russophiles and published in the journal *Nauka*, edited by Ivan Naumovyč in Kolomyja (Levyckij 1888, 182, 198).

Among the linguistic achievements of Kuliš and Puljuj, the reviewer mentioned their more liberal use of Church Slavonic forms in contrast to the highly vernacularized language of Kuliš's *Pentatevx Musijevyj* of 1869. At the same time, however, the reviewer deemed it necessary to note some inconsistency in applying his phonetic orthography "as compared with that which is now being implemented in Austria and even reaches Russia" (V., 1881, 897–898). Overall, the translation of Kuliš and Puljuj, as the reviewer concluded, was "the most comprehensible translation of the Holy Scriptures," and "much closer to vernacular Ukrainian than, for instance, the well-known synodal publication of the New Testament . . . in the Great Russian language" (ibid.).

THE CREATION OF THE NEW BIBLICAL STYLE

The publication of the New Testament in Ukrainian in 1887 and 1893 triggered mixed reactions in the two historical parts of Ukraine. Perhaps with the exception of Nečuj-Levyc'kyj, who was notoriously ambivalent toward the Galician vogue that had, allegedly, much earlier corroded the language of Kuliš, the translation found more favor with the Ukrainophile intellectuals living in Dnieper Ukraine than with the Russophiles or even the populists active in Galicia, Bukovyna, and Transcarpathia. Conceivably, the contemporary assessments of Kuliš's translation(s), as discussed above, were dictated by deeper cultural and ideological differences in Austrian- and Russian-ruled Ukraine. These differences affected not only critical responses to the publication of the Gospels in Ukrainian but, in general, the respective language programs cultivated by the Russophiles and populists in Galicia, Bukovyna, and Transcarpathia, on the one hand, and by the Ukrainophiles in Dnieper Ukraine, on the other.

Apart from the biased and personal commentaries by Nečuj-Levyc′kyj and, especially, Franko, the main problem lay primarily in the choice of dialect to use as the foundation for the new (vernacular) literary Ukrainian. The fact that it was largely oriented towards Southeast Ukrainian was arguably at variance with the Russophiles' and some Ukrainophiles' inclinations in Galicia (Danylenko 2008a). In other words, balancing out archaic and vernacular linguistic means within a new biblical (high) style was of paramount importance for the normalization of written Ukrainian at that time (Horbač 1988, 47–51; Haluščyns′kyj 1925, 312–319). Some of these linguistic means were so salient that, based on the ratio of their use and, respectively, on their archaization and vernacularization, one can trace two major conceptualizations of the high style in new literary Ukrainian in the nineteenth century.

MEANS OF ARCHAIZATION

Means of archaization consisted primarily of Church Slavonic and some obsolete or bookish (Ruthenian) forms. In the phonetics, one should mention the form *jedynorodnyj* "[the only] begotten of the Farther" (*SP/NZ*, 90, Jn 1:14). In the Old Testament, for instance, two parallel forms, *drevo* (*SP*, 6, Gen 2:16) and a more regular *derevo* "tree" (*SP*, 5, Gen 1:12), are a good illustration in this regard. Contrary to all expectations, pleophonic forms like *derevo* predominate in Kuliš's translation of the Bible, especially if compared with the language of the translation of *Psaltyr* (Horbač 1988, 60). It is possible to add here also *žena* (*SP*, 18, Gen 17:15) and *žona* "wife" (*SP*, 6, Gen 2:24), although both these forms can be of southwestern Ukrainian origin (Žovtobrjux et al. 1979, 269); consider also EUkr. *žinka* "wife" in Kuliš and Puljuj (*SP/NZ*, 3, Mt 1:24; *SP*, 14, Gen 11:29) and *žinko* (voc.) "woman" (Jn 19:26) in Moračevs′kyj, a form hardly fitting the narrative (Žiteckij 1905, 36). A possible contrast is discerned in the pair of WUkr. *vid [Duxa]* and EUkr. *od [Duxa]* "of, through the Spirit" as used indiscriminately in passive constructions (*SP/NZ*, 92, Jn 3:6, 8).

In morphology, one happens on numerous outdated forms such as Church Slavonic present active participles like *hrjaduščyj* "[he] that comes [after me]" (*SP/NZ*, 90, Jn 1:15), *plodjušči* (pl.) "fruitful" (*SP*, 55, Ex 1:7), *rodjuščyj* "yielding" (*SP*, 6, Gen 1:29) next to *povzuču* (acc.n.) "[creature] that moveth" (*SP*, 5, Gen 1:21), and perhaps also *jdučyj* "as he walked" (*SP/NZ*, 90, Jn 1:36) and *virujučyj [v Neho]* "[whosoever] believeth in him" (*SP/NZ*, 92, Jn 3:15), despite their eastern Slavic suffix -*uč*-. Finally, one should add here numerous occurrences of the past active participle *poslavšyj* "that sent me" (e.g., *SP/NZ*, 98, Jn 7:16). However, one should be more cautious with present active participles of the type *poklykujučyj* "crying" (*SP/NZ*, 90, Jn 1:23) and *hlaholjučyj* "saying" (*SP/NZ*, 90, Jn 1:26). It is tempting to view them as regional forms, most likely influenced by Polish, although Macjuk (2001, 306) argued that such forms had been brought out by the older literary tradition. In this case, one can speak of a local practice maintained in Galicia under Polish influence long after it had *grosso modo* declined in Southeast Ukraine. It comes as no surprise that active participles were still used in Galician periodicals in the early twentieth century, though in the vernacular language they might look cumbersome for efficient communication (Hnatiuk 1982, 20–21).

Among other archaic verbal forms of interest are present tense forms commonly encountered in Kuliš and Puljuj: *jesy* (2 sg. pres.) "art" (*SP/NZ*, 90, Jn 1:19; *SP*, 7, Gen 3:9) and *jest'* (3 sg. pres.) (*SP/NZ*, 95, Jn 5:32; *SP*, 19, Gen 19:12) next to the vernacularized *je* "is" (*SP/NZ*, 95, Jn 1:45). The latter is used typically in the nominative predicate in Southwest Ukrainian, whence its presence in the translation of Moračevs´kyj (Sreznevskij 1902, 092–094). Although commonly attested in Kuliš and Puljuj, the aforementioned personal forms of the verb "to be" occur, nevertheless, less frequently than the obsolete aorist form *reče* (*SP/NZ*, 90, Jn 1:39); the latter was criticized vehemently by Franko (a neutral *kaže* "[he] saith" (*SP/NZ*, 90, Jn 1:45). One should add here the archaic verbal form *hlahole* (3 sg. pres.) "to talk" ("talked [with him]" in *SP*, 17, Gen 17:3), which was also criticized by Franko but liberally used, as has been discussed, by Kvitka-Osnov'janenko in both religious and non-religious narratives.

A most controversial domain, from the viewpoint of its eventual archaization, is, to be sure, morphosyntax. In order to illustrate this thesis, it is worth comparing here different types of passive constructions with various agentive prepositional phrases used by different translators as a means of archaization. Depending on the preposition in the agentive phrase, the following extracts are representative of Kuliš and Puljuj:

(1) ... так усякий народжений *од Духа* (*SP/NZ*, 93).
   [... so is every one that is born of the Spirit.] (Jn 3:8)
(2) Роджене *від тїла*—тїло, а роджене *від Духа*—дух. (*SP/NZ*, 93)
   [That which is born of the flesh is flesh; and that which is born of the Spirit is spirit.] (Jn 3:6)
(3) Бо закон *через Мойсея* даний був; благодать і правда *через Ісуса Христа* стала ся. (*SP/NZ*, 90)
   [For the law was given by Mo´-ses, but grace and truth came by Je´-sus Christ.] (Jn 1:17)

Example (1) appears most archaic since it retains a common prepositional phrase that emerged as early as late Common Slavic and Old Church Slavonic (*otъ* "from" + genitive), used to refer to the agent in a passive or impersonal sentence (Vondrák 1924, 337). The same morphosyntactic pattern is attested in example (2) where one finds, however, a new phonetic form *vid* (< *od* < *otъ*) "from." Sporadically attested in Middle Ukrainian, this form was infamously denounced in the late nineteenth century by Nečuj-Levyc´kyj as "Galician-Podolian" and not recommended for literary use (Žovtobrjux et al. 1979, 284–285; Movčun 1999, 69.) Quite remarkable is example (3) in which there is the agentive prepositional phrase *čerez* "through" + accusative, which was probably triggered by Polish interference in medieval Galicia (Bulaxovs´kyj 1977, 567); however, an indigenous development of its agentive meaning is not to be discarded (Danylenko 2003a, 310–311).

Overall, the three examples excerpted from Kuliš and Puljuj reflect a hierarchy of agenthood, as was postulated elsewhere (Danylenko 2006c, 233), thus presenting a discrete continuum of archaization, from the oldest, Common Slavic/Church Slavonic agentive phrase with the preposition *od* "from, of" via Middle Ukrainian to the southwestern Ukrainian construction with the preposition *čerez* "through."

By contrast, Moračevs´kyj preferred active (or impersonal) constructions rather than passive syntactic patterns, although he sporadically resorted to archaic constructions, most likely under the influence of Church Slavonic. One should mention here a rare case of the passive construction with a nominal form of the past passive participle and the auxiliary verb "to be" (though in a vernacularized form) in the following excerpt:

Moračevs´kyj's Translation	Kuliš and Puljuj's Translation
22. Померъ убогий, и *однесенъ бувъ* янголами на ліжко Авраамове. Померъ и багатий, и *похоронили* (*погребли*) ёго. (Žiteckij 1905, 59)	22. Стало ся же, що вмер убогий, і *перенесли* його янголи на лоно Авраамове; умер же й багатир і *поховали* його. (*SP/NZ*, 78)
Бысть же оумрѣти нищемү, и несенү быти а҃гг҃лы на лоно Авраамле: оумре же и богатый, и погребоша его. (*Biblija* 1862, 551r)	[And it came to pass that the beggar died, and was carried by the angels into A´-bra-ham's bosom: the rich man also died, and was buried.] (Lk 16:22)

At first glance, the grammar of Kuliš and Puljuj in the above excerpt seems more vernacularized as compared with the same constructions in Moračevs´kyj. Although in this excerpt Kuliš and Puljuj used only active constructions, in the vocabulary they factored in several diachronic layers. In addition to vernacular forms like *vmer/umer* "died," the translators did not stop short of introducing MUkr. *bahatyr* "a rich man" (Тумč., 110) alongside ChSl. *lono* "bosom," respectively *bahatyj* and *ližko* in Moračevs´kyj.

As is evident from the except published in the early 1900s by Vsevolod Sreznevskij (1902), corrections made by Moračevs´kyj in the final draft of his translation demonstrate his intention to use mostly active constructions in those places where the Church Slavonic version contained predominantly passive constructions (Pšepjurs´ka-Ovčarenko 1988, 225–227). Hence the following emendations introduced by Moračevs´kyj in the fragment prepared for publication by Sreznevskij in comparison with the Church Slavonic version and the translation made by Kuliš and Puljuj:

Moračevs´kyj's Translation

13. Ви сіль землі; а коли сіль вивітритця, то чимъ солона буде (= осоліє)? Вона вже ни нà що пригодна (= здатна) не буде, якъ тількі щобъ викинути іі (= викинута була) вонъ и (= та) топтати (= потоптана) ногами (= людьми). (Sreznevskij 1902, 092; *Svedenija*, 97)

Вы́ є́стѐ со́ль земли́: а҆ще же со́ль ѡ҆б{у}а́тъ, чи́мъ ѡ҆соли́тсѧ, ни вочто́же б{у}детъ ктом{у}, то́чїю да и҆зсы́пана б{у}детъ во́нъ, и҆ попира́ема чл҃вѣ́ки. (*Biblija* 1862, 514v)

Kuliš and Puljuj's Translation

13. Ви сіль землї; коли ж сіль звітріє, то чим солити? Нї-на-що не годить ся тодї вона, тільки щоб викинути геть і щоб топтали її люде. (*SP/NZ*, 6)

[13. Ye are the salt of the earth: but if the salt have lost its savour, wherewith shall it be salted? It is thenceforth good for nothing, but to be cast out, and to be trodden under foot of men.] (Mt 5:13)

The instrumental *nohamy* (feet) instead of *ljud´my* (people) is an exemplary use of the fuzzy subject as found in Ukrainian folklore, for instance, in the well-known folk song "Oj u poli žyto kopytamy zbyto" (The Rye Has Been Trodden by Hooves in the Field) (Danylenko 2003a, 286). Being faithful to the folkloric spirit, Moračevs´kyj deemed it necessary to downgrade possible agent-salient features of the initiator of the action, rendered in the first version by the instrumental form *ljud´my*. All in all, in offering *nohamy* instead of *ljud´my*, Moračevs´kyj delineated a paradoxically short way from archaization to vernacularization of a non-secular text.

More archaic elements are also found in the vocabulary of Kuliš and Puljuj. Most telling among them are *vlast´* "authority" (*SP/NZ*, 94, Jn 5:4), *bolest´* "disease" next to *neduha* "infirmity" (*SP/NZ*, 94, Jn

5:5), *hrjade* (3 sg. pres.) "cometh" (*SP/NZ*, 90, Jn 1:30), *prorok jesy* "thou art a prophet" (*SP/NZ*, 93, Jn 4:19), *lono* "bosom" (*SP/NZ*, 90, Jn 1:18), *čudesa* "miracles" (*SP/NZ*, 91, Jn 2:23), *voskresennje* "resurrection" (*SP/NZ*, 95, Jn 5:29), and *voskresyty* "to raise up" (*SP/NZ*, 96, Jn 6:39). The list may be expanded, although the number of Slavonicisms in contemporary translations extant in Galicia was still larger. Overall, while translating the Bible, characterized by a much more complicated, multilayered system of stylistic devices, Kuliš, the idealist and devout Christian (Naxlik 2007, 1:457), demonstrated the reach of his imagination and ability to synthesize elements belonging to different epochs and literary traditions into one system.

To exemplify the concept of linguistic multilayerism as a basis for a new Ukrainian biblical style and, conversely, a new standard of literary Ukrainian, one can cite, for instance, the following Church Slavonic and bookish elements appearing alongside vernacular forms: *vino* "dowry" (*SP*, 37, Gen 34:12; see Sr., 1:487), *rab* "servant" (*SP*, 18, Gen 18:5; see Sr., 3:5–6), *xljaby (vikna) nebesni* (glossed in parentheses by Kuliš himself) "the windows of heaven" (*SP*, 10, Gen 7:11; see Sr., 3:1376), and *povverhaty* "to throw" (*SP*, 69, Ex 15:1) next to *povkydaty* (*SP*, 70, Ex 15:21). The latter pair is particularly representative, with the first bookish element adjusted to the second vernacular form. The point is that the verb *po-vverhaty* is derived from the eastern Slavic form of the Church Slavonic lexeme *vrěšti* "iacere" (Sr., 1:322). Yet the most peculiar fact about this verb is the use of the prefix *po-* in combination with *v-* (< *vъ*) as a member of a new alternation *u-* : *v-* emerging after the loss of *jers* (Shevelov 1979, 296–297).

Other translators from Dnieper Ukraine did not shy away from archaisms. Still, it might have been very difficult for them to keep the ratio of archaisms proportionate to the vernacular basis of their translations, as was the case, for instance, of Lobodovs'kyj. Žytec'kyj saw the same problem in the translation of Kuliš and Puljuj. According to him, some archaic forms in their text were hardly suitable for the vernacular texture of the whole translation. To give random examples, Žytec'kyj cited *obrjaščete* (2 pl. non-past) "to find" (Mt 2:8) in Lobodovs'kyj next to *znajdete* in Kuliš (*SP/NZ*, 4). Žytec'kyj (Žiteckij 1905, 32–33) also critically assessed Kuliš's predilection for all kinds of derivatives from the "ill-fated verb" *hlaholaty* (substituted for by vernacular lexemes in Moračevs′kyj) (Pšepjurs′ka-Ovčarenko 1988, 235), including a verbal adverb in *promovyv* [*Jeremija prorok*], *hlaholjučy* "[which] was spoken [by Jer′-e-my the prophet] saying" (*SP/NZ*, 4, Mt 2:17). He criticized, though erroneously, the use of the obsolete form *vbozi* instead of *ubohi* "the poor [in spirit]" (Mt 5:3) in Kuliš and Puljuj. In fact, one finds *vbohi* in their text (*SP/NZ*, 6).

Tentatively, one can agree with Žytec′kyj that the abundance of Church Slavonicisms may hinder "a natural flow of the speech," thus failing to furnish it with "sublime splendor" akin to simplicity (Žiteckij 1905, 33). Nevertheless, the real issue in this argument is not to be found in the quantity of Church Slavonicisms, although their number is, to be sure, of paramount importance in the context of the development of a lofty style. Rather, one should look to the ratio of archaic and vernacular forms as employed in most representative biblical texts. Such a ratio remained a stumbling block in most of the translations of the Holy Scriptures made in the second half of the nineteenth century. The true problem lay therefore in what could be vernacularized, and to what extent, in a typical translation of the Bible in the nineteenth century.

MEANS OF VERNACULARIZATION

Means of vernacularization are either cross-dialectal or regional forms. The language of Kuliš and Puljuj tended to reflect primarily North and Southeast Ukrainian, although with a lot of admixtures, while most of the other translations were oriented toward local dialects. It might be problematic to reconstruct the individual input of each of the two translators, which indirectly bears witness to a certain synthesis of the two regional varieties of written Ukrainian as found in their work.

Interestingly, unlike Antin (Antonij) Kobyljans′kyj's translation of the Gospel according to Luke and the Gospel according to John, based exclusively on "a Pokuttja-Dniester-Hucul dialect" (Horbač 1988, 48), Lobodovs′kyj was criticized by Žytec′kyj for "a dialect mixture [which is] random and motivated by nothing" (Žiteckij 1905, 24), as evidenced in a combination of "Galicianisms" and "eastern Ukrainian particularities." Among the "Galician" (in fact, eastern Podolian) elements, Žytec′kyj (ibid., 23) mentioned preterits of the type *bačÿlÿ-s'mo* "we have seen" (Lk 5:26) or *mÿ-s'mÿ* "we are" (Jn 9:28) (*mÿ* "we" [without an auxiliary] in Kuliš and Puljuj [*SP/NZ*, 101]). Remarkably, such preterits occur in Lobodovs´kyj side by side with eastern Ukrainian present tense forms like *ne znaxodju* "I find [no fault]" (Jn 19:4) as opposed to *ne znaxodžu* in Kuliš and Puljuj (*SP/NZ*, 112), which is a new southwestern (and western Polissian) Ukrainian form (Matvijas 2006, 63). Such forms with the affricate rendered by a special character, "ц" (*rozraцaje* "[she] dissuades"), came gradually into vogue from the 1837 almanac *Rusalka Dněstrovaja* (The Nymph of the Dniester) onward (*RD*, 11).[12] If Lobodovs´kyj opted for bringing together various "Little Russian" dialects why, Žytec´kyj wondered, did the author stop short of introducing into his translation northern (Ukrainian) elements (Žiteckij 1905, 23)? Clearly, Žytec´kyj did not criticize mixing dialectal forms as such but rather its inconsistency in the work of Lobodovs´kyj.

In this respect, the language of Kuliš and Puljuj seems to demonstrate a similar random blending of Ukrainian dialects, although a closer inspection reveals a somewhat different picture of the dialect variance; this might reflect, to some extent, Puljuj's mark on the language of the translation. In the phonetics, in addition to the treatment of etymological *o* and *e*, one should mention a very old and cross-dialectal alternation *u-* : *v-* (Shevelov 1979, 294–301). For instance, we see *vves' dim* "[his] whole house" (*SP/NZ*, 94, Jn 4:53) next to *uves'* (*SP/NZ*, 101, Jn 9:34), *vvijšov* (m. sg. pret.) "to enter" (*SP*, 10, Gen 7:13), *ato vmreš* (2 sg. fut.) "thereof thou shalt [surely] die" (*SP*, 6, Gen 2:17), and the like. Similar to this change, Kuliš used the cluster breaker *i* (e.g., *iz temrjavoju* "from the darkness" [*SP*, 5, Gen 1:18], [*vas*] *izvidsi* "hence") (*SP*, 64, Ex 11:1), adjusted to the principles of euphony, especially in Southeast Ukrainian. This is why the above changes are common in other translations made in Russian-ruled Ukraine (e.g., *uvijty* "to

---

12 It is interesting to note that Ševčenko used in similar forms only *ž* or *š*, that is, *syžu* (1 sg. pres.) "to sit" or *prošu* (1 sg. pres.) "to ask" (Synjavs´kyj 1925). These spellings were attested at that time in the language of eastern Ukrainian authors, including Kuliš's writings with northern Ukrainian features (Hancov 1924, 108–109). Only after Ševčenko did the western Ukrainian *sydžu* and similar forms begin penetrating first the written and then the oral literary practice (Tymošenko 1979, 115–117).

go in," *uves´* "full of" [Lk 15:28, 16:20] in Moračevs´kyj, and *ustav"* "[and he] arose" [Lk 15:20] in Lobodovs´kyj) (Žiteckij 1905, 58, 59, 63).

Among other phonetic features, most telling is the use of a palatalized hushing sound in *bačjat´* (3 pl. pres.) "to see" (*SP/NZ*, 96, Jn 6:19) and, especially, apheresis as found in *odno 'dnoho* "one another" (*SP*, 65, Ex 10:23). It is no wonder that this phenomenon is primarily reflected in the language of Kuliš's translation of the Bible and his literary oeuvre. Apheresis is known to have developed in North Ukrainian, and especially in East Polissja. Remarkably, this type of change infiltrated, though to a limited extent, the written language as used also by Ševčenko (Shevelov 1979, 452).

One might consider at this point northern Ukrainian second person plural imperatives as used by Kuliš in his translation of the Bible (e.g., *čynite* "do!" [*SP*, 19, Gen 19:7] and *pokažite* "show!" [*SP*, 61, Ex 7:9] next to a new *hledit´* "look [to it]!" [*SP*, 64, Ex 10:10]) (Bevzenko et al. 1978, 331–332). A native of the Černihiv region, Moračevs´kyj also made use of imperatives ending in *-ite*, though these forms competed also with those ending in *-it´* (e.g., *prynesite* "bring forth!" next to *odjahnit´* "put it [on him]" [Lk 15:22], also *pryvedit´* "bring hither" [Lk 15:23]) (Žiteckij 1905, 58). Interestingly enough, a similar distribution of imperatives ending in *-ite* and *-it´* is attested in the writings of Ševčenko (Sulyma 1924, 219). Needless to say that in the joint translation of the New Testament by Kuliš and Puljuj, one encounters predominantly southern Ukrainian forms: *rozvjažit´ joho i pustit´* "loose him and let him go" (*SP/NZ*, 104, Jn 11:44), *xoronit´ zapovidi moji* "keep my commandments" (*SP/NZ*, 107, Jn 14:15), and many others. The latter form is likewise used by Lobodovs´kyj: *prÿnesyt´*, *odjahnyt´*, and *prÿvedyt´* (Žiteckij 1905, 63).

Of particular importance in the morphology is also the choice of contracted and non-contracted (pronominal) adjectives, especially in the translation of the Bible by Kuliš: *narody zemniji* "the nations of the earth" (*SP*, 19, Gen 18:18) with a pronominal form occurring commonly in (northern Ukrainian?) folklore, next to more regular contracted forms in *čudyšča velyki* "great whales" (*SP*, 5, Gen 1:21) or *žyttje vične* "eternal life" and *Žydivs´ke s´vjato kučok* "the Jews' feast of tabernacles" (*SP/NZ*, 97, Jn 6:54 and 7:2) (see the idiomatic expression *vid mala do velyka* "both small and great" [*SP*, 19, Gen 19:11] that is paralleled in *vid molodyka, taj do dida* "both old and young" [*SP*, 19, Gen 19:4; see Macjuk 2001, 280]).

Speaking of noun derivation, Kuliš indulged in diminutives like *xlopčyk* "son" (*SP/NZ*, 94, Jn 4:51), *xlop'jatko* (*SP*, 56, Ex 2:7), and *nemovljatočko* "child" (*SP*, 56, Ex 2:6). Remarkably, a similar stance is demonstrated by Lobodovs'kyj and Moračevs'kyj (see the series of vocatives *bat'ku ~ baten'ku ~ batečku Avraame* "Father A´-bra-ham" in Moračevs'kyj [Žiteckij 1905, 59–60; Lk 16:24, 27, 30], as compared with the Church Slavonic form in Lobodovs'kyj—*otče Avraame!* [Žiteckij 1905, 64]). In Kuliš's translation of the Bible, affective suffixes are also taken by other word classes, especially by such adverbs as *teperen'ki* "now" (*SP*, 9, Gen 14:3), *xuten'ko* "quickly" (*SP*, 18, Gen 18:6), *tamen'ky/tamen'ki* "there" (*SP*, 19, Gen 18:30; *SP*, 14, Gen 12:10). Such vernacular forms occur more often than not in the first translation of the Bible made by Kuliš in 1869 (*Pentatevx*).

In the syntax, one also encounters dialectal constructions, for example, the use of the nominative-accusative direct object for plural inactive entities (animals, children, etc.) in the environment after transitives (e.g., *ponapovaty vivci* [nom. pl.] "water [the father's] flock" [*SP*, 56, Ex 2:16], *odpustyty syny* [nom. pl.] "let the children go out") (*SP*, 60, Ex 8:11). Plural animates are also used by Kuliš sporadically in the nominative-accusative case (e.g., *sklykaty mudreci* [nom.-acc.] *ta čarivnyky* [nom.-acc.] "to call the wise men and sorcerers" [*SP*, 61, Ex 7:11]). This construction is attested cross-dialectally, although in Kuliš this pattern seems to be of eastern Ukrainian origin (*AUM*, 3, part 1, map 63) since it occurs in parallel use with the genitive-accusative direct object (e.g., *odpustyty ljudej* [gen.-acc.] [*SP*, 61, Ex 7:14] and *vidpustyty ljude* [nom.-acc.] "to let the people go" [*SP*, 61, Ex 7:16]).

Of particular interest is the use of the genitive-accusative in constructions of the type *pasty svynej* (acc.-gen. pl.) in Moračevs'kyj and, similarly, *svÿnej* (acc.-gen. pl.) *pastÿ* "to feed swine" in Lobodovs'kyj (Lk 15:15; Žiteckij 1905, 58, 63) as compared with the nominative-accusative in Kuliš and Puljuj's translation of the same sentence: *pasty svynï* (*SP/NZ*, 77). The latter rection is attested cross-dialectally, and may be considered archaic in accordance with the traditional philological view expressed as early as 1822 by the Bohemian philologist Josef Dobrovský in his comparative grammar of Slavic languages (Dobrowsky [Dobrovský] 1822, 615–618).

Here belongs also a consideration of the attributive use of nouns in paratactic constructions such as those employed in abundance, for example, by Potebnja in his translation of Homer's *Odyssey* (e.g., *služkamy divkamy* [Homer, Pot., 7:300] and *čara dvijka* "a two-bottom goblet" [Homer, Pot., 3:63], where the second noun transforms into an adjective) (Danylenko 1999, 241–244). Remarkably, for the simplest way of combining concrete images in the attributive construction, Kuliš introduces both the postposed (a) and preposed (b) use of the genus name with respect to the species name (either personal or common). The postposed (a) use is exemplified by collocations of the type *Syddyn-dolyna* "the vale of Sid´-dim" (*SP*, 15, Gen 14:3) and *Sejir-hory* "mount Se´-ir" (*SP*, 15, Gen 14:6), while the preposed (b) use is most adequately represented in *baby spovytuxy* "midwives" (*SP*, 56, Ex 1:21). As I argued elsewhere (Danylenko 1999, 246; 2006c, 333–334) for the case of Potebnja's translation, these syntactic structures were not so much "archaizingly folkloric" (Shevelov 1994), as "folkloric and archaic." Like Potebnja, Kuliš seemed to proceed from the Middle Ages to contemporary folklore as the point of synthesis between history and the present day, thus absorbing various historical layers in the development of the language.

Finally, in the vocabulary, Kuliš freely employs folkloric elements, which stand out conspicuously even in the vernacular-oriented discourse of his translation, e.g., *molodycja harna* "fair woman" (*SP*, 14, Gen 12:11) and *molodyci motorni* "lively women" (*SP*, 56, Ex 1:19). Like Lobodovs´kyj and Moračevs´kyj, Kuliš cannot resist coining, though on a lesser scale, new vernacular-inspired forms. One of these terms is *jasovaty* "to make known" (*SP*, 72, Ex 18:16), a lexeme also used by Kuliš in his translations of Shakespeare, although sometimes with a different semantic component as in *jasyty* "to be produc'd [...] against [the Moor]" (Šekspir, 16, WSh., 1098). It is no wonder that Hrinčenko glossed this verb, using an example from Kuliš's writings only, and did not see any connection with *jasnyty* "to polish, make shine" and "to explain" (Hrinč., 2:1054), which is morphologically and semantically reminiscent of Kuliš's neologism. Among other innovations, it is worth citing *hlynyšče* "mortar" (*SP*, 55, Ex 1:14), *holodneča* "famine" (*SP*, 55; Hrinč., 1:345), and *zavahonity* "to conceive" (*SP*, 21, Gen 21:2), the latter two used likewise in Rataj's *Psaltyr* (*Psaltyr*, Rataj, 115). Of particular interest is the lexeme *zajmanščyna* "a plot of free land taken over as private." This neologism was derived with the help of the suffix -*ščyn(a)*, which became very productive in the second half of the nineteenth century under the influence of contemporaneous Russian (Muromceva 1985, 22). Kuliš also preferred this suffix in coining designations for different languages such as *moskovščyna* "(Great) Russian," *nimeščyna* "German," *rumunščyna* "Rumanian," *ukrajinščyna* "Ukrainian," and *ruščyna* "Ukrainian used by the Rusians in Galicia, Transcarpathia, and Bukovyna" (Barvins′kyj 2004, 187–188).

The list of such innovations can be expanded, for example, with those excerpted by Horbač (1988, 62) from Rataj's *Psaltyr*. Yet some of the neologisms discussed by Horbač are, in fact, regular indigenous forms. Thus, the form *popojisty* "to eat [a little]" as cited by Horbač (*Psaltyr*, Rataj, 143; *SP*, 18, Gen 18:5) is, in fact, an eastern Slavic and Baltic iterative with a reduplication of the prefix *popo-* (Danylenko 2003a, 215–226).

The differences in innovation are perhaps best revealed in the nature of a given stylistic system's transitions, from the burlesque linguistic medium as discerned in the translation of Lobodovs′kyj to a more neutral and sometimes more standardized mode in the translation of Kuliš and Puljuj and to a stylistic (vernacular) uniformity of language offered by Moračevs′kyj. With his burlesque innovations and numerous dialectisms, Lobodovs′kyj stood out among all other translators (e.g., *pozyr lycja* "the fashion [of countenance]" [Lk 9:29] compared to *vyd lycja* in Kuliš and *oblyččja* in Moračevs′kyj, *obvynuvatar* "accusor" [Jn 8:44] to *vynuvatel′* in Kuliš, *žytelyšče* "mansion" [Jn 14:2], compared with *oselja* in Kuliš and *budynok* in Moračevs′kyj, *orudarstvo* "magistrates" [Lk 12:11] next to *urjadnyky* in Moračevs′kyj, *vidhet′katy* "make [the commandment of God] of none effect" [Mt 15:6], *popereky* "loins" [Lk 12:35] with *boky* [pl.] in Moračevs′kyj and *pojasnyci* [pl.] in Kuliš, and so forth) (Žiteckij 1905, 35–36). Interestingly, the lexeme *pojasnycja* occurs also in Rataj's paraphrase of Psalm 38 (*Psaltyr*, Rataj, 171), while Puljuj prefers *stehna* "loins" (Ps 38:7).

One gets the impression of random choices between stylistic devices made in different translations, and these likely demonstrate a macaronic discourse with split stylistic alternatives. Indeed, the foregoing survey showed that, arguably, the ratio of archaic and vernacular means is different in various translations prepared by different authors. But did they really resort to various means randomly, using devices from different style registers? Close textual scrutiny proves that the authors were largely consistent in employing specific means and their configurations. For example, Lobodovs´kyj and Moračevs´kyj tended clearly to the vernacular pole of the "biblical continuum," which could make their translations look "outdated" already in the 1920s (Ohijenko 1927, 9). Kuliš's translation strategy was different. The latter resorted to language hybridization as a norm, and asserted the authority of interwoven archaic and vernacular devices. His stylistic program, misrepresented in fact by the editors of the 1903 Bible, which appeared after his death, seemed to have broken through the confines of a two-pole continuum, thus cohering into a multi-layered system. Tentatively, Kuliš's multiform translation(s) could serve as an illustration of the virtual impossibility of linguistic purity in the high biblical style under the historical and geo-political conditions of Austrian- and Russian-ruled Ukraine. Demonstrating the different cultural and linguistic contours of the intellectual homeland, the two parts of Ukraine were likely to need a synthetic language program that rejected a linguistic non-compromise in favor of "all-inclusive adaptation," and which could result in a fitful and discontinuous evolution of the written language.

In this respect, no other translator with a comprable language program could match Kuliš in Dnieper Ukraine. Unlike Kuliš, by predominantly employing vernacular-oriented devices, the western Ukrainian translators seemed to have lost much of the mixed discourse from the fifteenth through seventeenth century, including the idea of bilingualism as the foundation of a new literary norm (Danylenko 2008a). What is left at this point is to determine if the translators of the Bible in Galicia and Bukovyna endorsed the language program propounded by Kuliš, or, if not, what they offered as a recompense.

CHAPTER 3

Galicia "Writes Back"

THE WEST OR THE EAST?

In Galicia the Bible was translated into Ukrainian earlier than in Dnieper Ukraine. As fate would have it, the translation of Kuliš and Puljuj was preceded by that of a Galician author, Markijan Šaškevyč (1811–1843), a famous member of the *Rus′ka trijcja* (Rusian Triad). Yet one can hardly speak of a contest between the Galician translator and Kuliš (along with Puljuj) as to priority in the creation of the Ukrainian Bible. Šaškevyč's translation of the Gospel according to John and fragments of the Gospel according to Matthew (chapters 1–5) was made in 1842, at least a quarter of century before Kuliš settled down to translate the Bible into vernacular Ukrainian. Šaškevyč's translation was not published until 1912 by Myxajlo Voznjak (Šaškevyč, 107–142)[1] and therefore failed to influence the work of Kuliš, who was always open to alternative views, especially in the area of creating "national Bibles" in the age of late Romanticism. In other words, neither Kuliš nor Puljuj suspected the existence of Šaškevyč's work; otherwise, they would have addressed his translation as they did for all other major vernacular and classical translations of the Bible. No doubt, Kuliš would have been interested in perusing Šaškevyč's text with an eye to mining its treasure trove of Galician forms. All in all, it becomes necessary to compare the linguistic make-up of Kuliš's translation with

---

1 Together with his other works, excerpts (Mt 5:1–30 and Jn 4:1–54) from Šaškevyč's translation were published in 1913 in the series *Rus′ka pys′mennist′* (along with the works of Jakiv Holovac′kyj) (Šaškevyč 1913). The orthography and the language, however, were extensively corrected so that it is rendered useless from a linguistic point of view.

the vernacular translation of the Holy Scriptures made by "the most zealous son of Rus´," as Šaškevyč was called in 1893 on the occasion of his reburial (Hrytsak 2003, 107).

Disregarded (along with other western Ukrainian translations of the Holy Scriptures) in the 1905 programmatic study of Žytec´kyj, Šaškevyč's translation demands the attention of modern readership. First of all, in terms of priority, this is the first translation of the Holy Scriptures ever made into "modern Ruthenian" (Ukrainian), predating the translation of Kuliš and Puljuj by some thirty years. Second, the Gospels were translated into a vernacular Ukrainian permeated, as was argued by Horbač (1988, 47), with dialectal features that were in some cases suppressed by Šaškevyč, himself a speaker of a southern Volhynian dialect (Brody). These features make this translation appear deeply regional, with a tinge of vernacularized Church Slavonic as was cultivated in Galicia and especially in Transcarpathia at that time (Danylenko 2008a, 2009a, 2009c).

To begin with, among the suppressed dialectal features, Šaškevyč tried to omit the change *'a* > *'e*, which, nevertheless, does appear sporadically in the text (e.g., *ščob požjedaў eё* "to lust after her" [Šaškevyč, 111:166, Mt 5:28], or the instrumental singular ending *-ov/-ev* [Horbač 1988, 47], whence *pered pasxoju* [f. sg. instr.] "before the passover" [Jn 12:1]). On the other hand, he liberally utilized dative and accusative enclitic forms of personal and demonstrative pronouns such as *ho* (acc.) "him" (Šaškevyč, 112:169), *mu* (dat.) "him," *ju* (acc.) "her" (ibid., 128:658), *mja* (acc.) "me" (ibid., 116:187), *tja* (acc.) "you" (ibid., 113:59), which occur sometimes in parallel use with corresponding full-forms like *tobě* (dat.) "you" (ibid., 113:62), *jemu* (dat.) "him," etc. (ibid., 116:163). Šaškevyč employed the dative singular of masculines and neuters ending in *-ovy/-evy* (Horbač 1988, 47) (e.g., *synovy svojemu* "to his son" [Šaškevyč, 116:150, Jn 4:5]). The same ending is attested in the locative singular (e.g., *v čolověkovy* "in man" [Šaškevyč, 114:96, Jn 2:25]). One also encounters in Šaškevyč's translation the hard present tense personal ending *-t* (3 sg.) (e.g., [*kotorij*] *movyt″* "saying" [Šaškevyč, 109:60, Mt 2:17]), obsolete perfect tense forms with auxiliaries treated as enclitics of the type *čuliste* "ye have heard" (Šaškevyč, 111:155, Mt 5:21) or *ja vyděў y svědčyў jem″* "[And] I saw, and bare record" (Šaškevyč, 113:39–40, Jn

1:34), and a sizable number of active present participles of the type *plačušča* (f. sg.) "weeping" (Šaškevyč, 128:658, Jn 11:33) and verbal adverbs like *ne xotjašče* "not willing" (Šaškevyč, 108:23, Mt 1:19), all influenced by Church Slavonic. In the morphology, deserving of attention is the ending *-y* taken by feminines with the former stem ending in *-ā/-jā* (modern first declension) in the locative case (Bevzenko et al. 1978, 81) (e.g., *po zemly* "on the ground" [Šaškevyč, 123:443, Jn 8:6] next to *po zemlï* in Kuliš and Puljuj [*SP/NZ*, 99]), and by feminines with the former stem ending in *-ū* (modern third declension) in the genitive case (Bevzenko et al. 1978, 112–113) (e.g., *krovy* [gen.] "blood" [Šaškevyč, 120:349, Jn 6:53]; see also *krovï* in Kuliš and Puljuj [*SP/NZ*, 97]).

Among other archaic or folkloric features of Šaškevyč's translation, Horbač (1988, 47) mentioned full (uncontracted) forms of adjectives, as in *dobroje vyno* "good wine" (Šaškevyč, 114:77–78, Jn 2:10), and especially passive constructions with an agentive phrase with the prepositions *od* "of, from" or *čerez* "through," (e.g., [*sil'*] *bula vysypana y od ljudej potoptana* "[the salt] to be cast out, and to be trodden under foot of men" [Šaškevyč, 111:145, Mt 5:13], *buÿ čolověk poslannÿj od Boha* "there was a man sent from God" [Šaškevyč, 112:5, Jn 1:6], and, as a Polish interference, *čerez" neho mir" buÿ spasennÿj* "the world through him might be saved" [Šaškevyč, 115:120, Jn 3:17; see also Danylenko 2003a, 296–314]). Quite naturally, Šaškevyč sporadically introduced Church Slavonicisms like *jedinorodnÿj od otca* "begotten of the father" (Šaškevyč, 112:13–14, Jn 1:14) with a word-initial *je-* in the adjective, which might have been conceived by him as natural for this kind of the text. Some western Slavic borrowings also occur in the text. A peculiar case, however, is represented by the bookish lexeme *nevěsta* (Šaškevyč, 116:4, Jn 4:7; Hrinč., 1:1076), an old Slavic form attested in the *Leksikon"* of Pamvo Berynda (Berynda, 37), next to the native (eastern Slavic) *žena* "woman" (Šaškevyč, 166, Jn 4:17). For the language of Šaškevyč, it is difficult to ascertain whether this is a result of a secondary western Slavic influence at the semantic level (Nimčuk 1992, 302) or an indigenous form retaining the peripheral archaic meaning "wife, spouse" derivative of the primary meaning "bride" (Skljarenko 2007).

But what is remarkable for the vernacular make-up of Šaškevyč's translation is, according to Horbač (1988, 47), a limited number of dialectal words (e.g., *syn pervenok* "firstborn son" [Šaškevyč, 108:32, Mt 1:25], *xyžyna* "house" [Šaškevyč, 111:147, Mt 5:15], *bač* "behold" [Šaškevyč, 115:132, Jn 3:26]). Upon more attentive examination, however, the number of words with a strong regional tinge increases substantially. Interspersed with Church Slavonicisms and some obsolete forms, these dialectisms occur throughout the entire text, thereby starkly contrasting with the biblical narrative. Some of them are quite striking, ranging from pan-Ukrainian to local (regional) dialectal status (Tymošyk 2000b, 102). To elaborate for this situation a kind of a stylistic and dialectal continuum, fuzzy as it may appear, one should cite such forms as *reměnec čerevyka* "shoe's latchet" (Šaškevyč, 112:30, Jn 1:27) compared to *remen' obuv'ja* in Kuliš and Puljuj (*SP/NZ*, 90), where *obuvje* (nom.) is an obvious Galician form (Žel., 1:550; Vytv., 176; Kuzela and Rud., 498), and *pit'ma* "darkness" (Šaškevyč, 112:4, Jn 1:5), which is attested cross-dialectally (Bil.-Nos., 282; Hrinč., 2:193) and, in particular, in Franko's translation of a small extract from the Old Testament (Franko 1982).

The following dialectal forms also come into consideration: *konov'* "waterpot" (Šaškevyč, 116:181, Jn 5:28), attested in both Right- and Left-Bank Ukraine (see Žel., 1:363; Bil.-Nos., 191; Kuzela and Rud., 345; Hrinč., 1:814) compared to *vedro* without *ikavism* in Kuliš and Puljuj (*SP/NZ*, 93) and *zvěduvaỳsja u nyx"* "[he] demanded of them" (Šaškevyč, 108:38, Mt 2:4; Žel., 1:288) as opposed to *dopytuvav sja v nyx* in Kuliš and Puljuj (*SP/NZ*, 4)—both lexemes are attested in the dictionary of Borys Hrinčenko (Hrinč., 1:465, 677). Additionally, one could mention *hamor* "murmuring" (Šaškevyč, 121:384, Jn 7:12; Žel., 1:136) compared to *hovirka* in Kuliš and Puljuj (*SP/NZ*, 98), *neum* "fool" (Šaškevyč, 111:159, Mt 5:22) compared to *duren'* in Kuliš and Puljuj (*SP/NZ*, 6), and especially WUkr. *xyža* "house" (Šaškevyč, 129:695, Jn 12:3; see Vytv., 45) and *žyhačka* "fever" (Šaškevyč, 117:213, Jn 4:52; Žel., 1:222) compared to *horjačka* in Kuliš and Puljuj (*SP/NZ*, 94), which is an obvious Polish borrowing (Vytv., 82), while *žyhačka* might have been influenced by ChSl. *žehavycja* (Berynda, 36) and Polish forms like *żegawka* "nettle" (see Vytv., 392). Finally, also of interest is the following sentence, *xto pyty bahne* (3 sg. pres.) *naj prijde* "if any man thirst, let him come [unto me]" (Šaškevyč, 122:418, Jn 7:37) with a dialectal imperative particle *naj* and the Polish borrowing *zvada* "division" (Šaškevyč, 122:425, Jn 7:43; Žel., 1:286, Vytv., 389), *s'kaly* (pl.) "sought [to kill]" (Šaškevyč, 121:373, Jn 7:1), and some others.

It is worthwhile noting here phonological dialectisms like *narid* and stylistically marked (diminutive) morphological forms of the type *malen'ko času* "little while" (Šaškevyč, 122:412, Jn 7:33) and *světlyčka* "house" (Šaškevyč, 108:48, Mt 2:11). This phenomenon is obviously influenced by a similar trend in folklore (see Tymošyk 2000b, 103), whence also such uncontracted forms as *doroha hospodnjaja* "the way of the Lord" (Šaškevyč, 109:74, Mt 3:3) or *zliy slova* "all matter of evil" (literally, "bad, evil words") as opposed to *dobri děla* "good works" (Šaškevyč, 111:140, 148, Mt 5:11, 16).

All in all, this list of representative features in Šaškevyč, in addition to those discussed by Horbač, looks unexpectedly controversial and, with a few felicitous exceptions, is at odds with Horbač's and Tymošyk's assessment of the writer's work. Suffice it to say that, while calling Šaškevyč an idealistic translator, Horbač (1988, 46–47) argued that the writer introduced into his translation traits of his native dialect without taking into account their possible intelligibility for all the Ukrainian speakers at whom, ideally, the translation was directed. With this in mind, one can question the actual status of the aforementioned features in the context of the formation of new literary Ukrainian. As a result, it becomes obvious why Žytec'kyj disregarded all the Galician translations of the Holy Scriptures in his study of 1905.

A solution to the above controversy was offered by Moser (2005, 233), according to whom all the above features are typically associated with Galician Ukrainian literary works before 1859. It is possible therefore to view them not as western Ukrainian dialectisms but as representative traits of the Galician variety of the new Ukrainian literary language, before this variety joined the mainstream linguistic process in Russian-ruled Ukraine (see Danylenko 2015a). This hypothesis appears convincing, but one wonders to what extent the vernacular features in Šaškevyč constituted the core of the new biblical style as compared with the translation of the New Testament made by Kuliš and Puljuj. Parallel excerpts from the two translations are likely to illuminate the differences between the language standards as viewed by Šaškevyč, on the one hand, and Kuliš and Puljuj, on the other.

Translation of Šaškevyč

Гл. г҃. Тыхже днів прійшоў Іоаннъ *Креститель, проповѣдующе* в пущѣ юдейскій и *мовлячи:* покайтесѧ, бо сѧ приблизило царство небесноє; той бо єсть, о якимъ повѣдає Исайя пророк, коли мовитъ: Голосъ *кличущого* в пустини, готовте дорогу господнюю, правими чинѣтъ стежки єго. А самъ Іоаннъ маў *одежу* из волоса вельблюдового и поясъ ремѣнный коло бедрів своихъ, а ѣдѧ єго була *шараньча* и мед лѣсовый. Тогда виходиў *ид* нему Ѥрусалимъ и вся Юдея и всѣ стороны Іорданьскіи; и *крестилисѧ від него* в Іордани, повѣдающе грѣхи свои. А видѣвше многих фаріссеѣв и саддукеѣв, идущих *до* него на *крещеніє*, рѣк до нихъ: Роде гадинячій, ктож сказаў вамъ утѣкати перед будущим гнѣвомъ? Творѣтже *плод*, годенъ покаяня, и не начинайте говорити сами в собѣ: Отця маємъ Авраама; бо я вамъ повѣдаю, же может Бог з того каменя піднести дѣти

Translation of Kuliš and Puljuj

1. Того часу прийшов *Йоан* Хреститель, проповідуючи в пустині Юдейській,
2. і глаголючи: Покайтесь: наближилось бо царство небесне.
3. Се ж бо той, про кого казав пророк Ісаїя, *глаголючи:* Приготовте дорогу Господню, правими робіть стежки Його.
4. Сам же Йоан мав одежу свою з верблюжого волосу, й шкуряний пояс на *попереці* своїй; а їдою його була сарана та дикий мед.
5. Тодї виходили до него Єрусалим, і вся Юдея, і вся околиця Йорданська,
6. і хрестились в Йорданї від него, сповідаючи гріхи свої.
7. Та, бачивши він, що багато Фарисеїв і Садукеїв приходило до хрещення його, сказав до них: *Кодло* гадюче, хто остеріг вас, *щоб утїкали* від *настигаючого* гнїва?
8. Принесіть же *овощ* достойний покаяння;
9. і не думайте казати в серці своєму: В нас батько Авраам; бо я вам кажу, що Бог зможе з сього каміння підняти дітей Авраамові.

Авраамови. Вжебо и сокира при корени дерева лежить; *веськоє* бо дерево, що нечинит доброго *плоду*, висѣчено буває и в огонь вмеченно.

Бо я крещу васъ водою на *покаяньє*, а той, що за мною иде, крѣ(п)шій єсть над мене, закоторымъ я негоденъ сапоги носити, той васъ крестить духом святим и огнем, которому лопата врудѣ єго, и вичистить *гумно* своє и збере пшеницю свою до *гумна* свого, а полову спалить *огнемъ невгасающимъ.*—Тогда приходить І͠с из Галлилеи на Іорданъ до Іоанна, креститисѧ від него; А Іоанъ звороняў му тоє и мовиў: я потребую *від тебе креститисѧ*, а тыж до мене приходишь? Отповѣў же Ісусъ и мовиў: зістаў нынѣ, такбо подоба намъ споўнити всяку правду. Тогда дозволиў *му*; а коли І͠с охрестився, вийшоў зараз изводы и отворилисѧ єму небеса и видѣў духа святого, зходящого голубомъ, идущого на него, и се голосъ из небесъ мовлящій: Сей єсть сын мій любезный, *которогомъ* собѣ умилуваў. (Šaškevyč, 109:71–95)

10. Вже ж і сокира коло кореня дерева лежить; тим кожне дерево, що не дає доброго *овощу*, зрубують, та й кидають *ув огонь*.

11. Я оце хрещу вас водою на покаяннє; а той, що йде за мною, потужніщий від мене; недостоєн я Йому й обувя носити; Він вас хреститиме Духом сьвятим та огнем.

12. У руці в Него лопата, й перечистить Він *тік* свій. і збере пшеницю свою в *клуню*, а полову спалить огнем невгасимим.

13. Приходить тоді Ісус із Галилеї на *Йордан* до Йоана, охреститись від него.

14. Та Йоан не допускав Його, говорячи: Мені самому треба в Тебе хреститись, а Ти прийшов до мене?

15. Відказуючи йому Ісус, *рече* до него: Допусти тепер, бо так годить ся нам чинити всяку правду. Тоді допустив Його.

16. І *охрестившись* Ісус, вийшов зараз із води; й ось відчинилось Йому небо, і побачив він Духа Божого, що спустивсь як голуб, і злинув на Него.

17. І ось голос із неба, глаголючи: Се мій Син любий, що я. *вподобав* Його. (*SP/NZ*, 4–5)

[1. In those days came John the Bap´-tist, preaching in the wilderness of Ju-dae´-a,

2. And saying, Repent ye: for the kingdom of heaven is at hand.

3. For this is he that was spoken of by the prophet E-sa´-ias, saying, The voice of one crying in the wilderness. Prepare ye the way of the Lord, make his paths straight.

4. And the same John had his raiment of camel's hair, and a leathern girdle about his loins; and his meat was locusts and wild honey.

5. Then went out to him Je-ru´-sa-lem, and all Judae´-a, and all the region round about Jor´-dan,

6. And were baptized of him in Jor´-dan, confessing their sins.

7. But when he saw many of the Phar´-I-sees and Sad´-du-cees come to his baptism, he said unto them, O generation of vipers, who hath warned you to flee from the wrath to come?

8. Bring forth therefore fruits meet for repentance:

9. And think not to say within yourselves, We have A´-bra-ham to our father: for I say unto you, that that God is able of these stones to raise up children unto A´-bra-ham.

10. And now also the axe is laid unto the roof of the trees: therefore every tree which bringeth not forth good fruit is hewn down, and cast into the fire.

11. I indeed baptize you with water unto repentance: but he that cometh after me is mightier than I, whose shoes I am not worthy to bear; he shall baptize you with the Holy Ghost, and with fire;

12. Whose fan is in his hand, and he will thoroughly purge his floor, and gather his wheat into the garner; but he will burn up the chaff with unquenchable fire.

13. Then cometh Je´-sus from Gal´-I-lee to Jor´-dan unto John, to be baptized of him.

14. But John forbad him, saying, I have need to be baptized of thee, and comes thou to me?

15. And Je´-sus answering said unto him, Suffer it to be so now: for thus it becometh us to fulfil all righteousness. Then he suffered him.

16. And Je´-sus, when he was baptized, went up straightway out of the water: and, lo, the heavens were opened unto him, and he

saw the Spirit of God descending like a dove, and lighting upon him:

17. And lo a voice from heaven, saying, This is my beloved Son, in whom I am well pleased.] (Mt 3:1–17)

The language of Šaškevyč's translation demonstrates a most peculiar amalgamation of varied features, in contrast to the translation made by Kuliš and Puljuj. First of all, Šaškevyč did not Ukrainianize biblical names, *Ioann"*, *Ioan"*, *Iordan"*, while Kuliš and Puljuj employed bookish (Ruthenian) forms like *Joan* and *Jordan*, which were criticized by Franko. In the phonetics, as reflected in the orthography, Šaškevyč retained sporadically the back *jer*, primarily in bookish lexemes (e.g., *ohnem"* [instr.] "fire," *holos"* "voice," next to *pered* "in front," *vid* "from," *zaraz* "now," and even *Boh* "God"). Needless to say, the back *jer* is not found in Kuliš and Puljuj. Yet, of utmost importance is the use by Šaškevyč of the grapheme *ў* for rendering a reflex of *l* in closed syllables (e.g., *prijšoў* [m. sg. pret.] "to come"). This grapheme was no innovation at all in this translation, inasmuch as this letter had been introduced as early as 1837 in the almanac *Rusalka Dněstrovaja* (The Nymph of the Dniester) published by Šaškevyč and two other members of the *Rus'ka trijcja* (Rusian Triad), Jakiv Holovac'kyj (1814–1888) and Ivan Vahylevyč (1811–1866).

The dropping of the back *jer* and the use of the grapheme *ў* by the representatives of the *Rus'ka trijcja* was largely triggered by the vernacularizing trend, feeble as it was at the very beginning of the epoch of Romanticism in Galicia, Transcarpathia, and Bukovyna. One should recall here first and foremost Ivan Fogarašij (Fogorossě, Fogarassy), the dean at the church of Saint Barbara in Vienna (1820–1834), who authored *Rus'ko uhors'ka ili maděrska hrammatika. Orosz Magyar Grammatika. Rutheno Ungarica Grammatica* (Rusyn-Hungarian Grammar, 1833) based on the same theoretical tenets as Myxajlo Lučkaj's (1789–1843) grammar of Church Slavonic, *Grammatica Slavo-Ruthena* (Budae, 1830) (Danylenko 2009a). In his 1827 programmatic letter to Ivan Orlaj (1771–1829), based at that time in Saint Petersburg, Fogarašij compared Carpatho-Rusyn with Church Slavonic and Great Russian. Yet he proved more vernacular-oriented than Lučkaj because he admitted for Carpatho-Rusyn the change of *l* into *v* [w] at the end of 3 m. sg. past tense forms like *molyv"* "to entreat" and *movyv"*, *hvaryv* "to speak," as well as in some nouns (e.g., *vovk* "wolf," *vovna* "cotton," and so forth) (Svěncyckij 1905, 49). On balance, following Josef Dobrovský, Lučkaj argued that the back *jer*, together with the front *jer*, may be dropped both in the word-medial and word-final position (Danylenko 2009a, 208). Thus, in the spirit of Lučkaj and Fogarašij, although unknowingly, Šaškevyč based his spelling primarily on phonetic principles, while Kuliš and Puljuj tended to combine both phonetic and etymological principles (e.g., correspondingly *vpodobav* [m. sg. pret.] "to love" and *oxrestyvšys'* "[when he was] baptized").

Šaškevyč's morphosyntax is replete with active present participles with typical Church Slavonic desinence such as *holos″ klyčuščoho*, "the voice of one crying" (Šaškevyč, 109:73–74, Mt 3:3), compared to the Ukrainianized *poklykujučoho* in Kuliš and Puljuj. Unlike verbal adverbs ending in -*čy* in Kuliš and Puljuj, Šaškevyč used the same obsolete Church Slavonic desinence as in *propovědujušče* "preaching" alongside a vernacular *movljače* "saying." Kuliš and Puljuj resorted to a vernacular morphological pattern as applied to a Church Slavonic word—*hlaholjučy* "saying." Šaškevyč showed the opposite tendency in this case since he used a vernacular lexeme archaicized with the help of Church Slavonic phonological and morphological means (e.g., *nevhasajuščym″* [sg. instr.] "unquenchable"). Šaškevyč did not stop short of combining in one excerpt three relativizers belonging, in fact, to different style registers. These include the western Slavic (Polish) borrowing, *kotoryj* "which, who," blended with a vernacular auxiliary of the perfect tense in *kotorohom″* (*umyluvaẏ*), literally, "whom have I beloved," with a back *jer* under Church Slavonic influence. Šaškevyč also made use of the relativizer *jakyj* "which" and the most representative absolutive relativizer *ščo* in Ukrainian (e.g., *toj, ščo za mnoju yde* next to *toj, ščo jde za mnoju* "he that cometh after me" in Kuliš and Puljuj). Šaškevyč also resorted to different prepositions such as *do* and Transc. (Hucul) *id* "(up) to."

Taken as a whole, the translation of Šaškevyč appears to be a peculiar combination of Church Slavonic and vernacular components so that even statistically it is difficult to say which of them prevail. According to Tymošyk (2000b, 102–103), however, Church Slavonicisms prevail across the translations of all the fragments. As pointed out by Tymošyk, Šaškevyč retained a sizable number of morphological and syntactical patterns typical of the Church Slavonic translation, which supposedly served him as a major text of reference. At any rate, leaving aside the possibility of translation from the Church Slavonic as postulated by Tymošyk, one can easily identify Church Slavonic constructions, not only distinct expressions, transferred into the translation of Šaškevyč (e.g., *najšla sja majuščaja v žyvotě od Duxa sviatoho* "She was found with child of the Holy Ghost" [Šaškevyč, 108:22, Mt 1:18], although, remarkably, this phrase uses the vernacular genitive ending *-oho* instead of ChSl. *-aho* in *svjatoho*).

Overall, Šaškevyč used Church Slavonic and dialectal (southwestern) Ukrainian forms side by side, blending them in some cases: *Krestytel'* "[John] the Bap'-tist," *krestytysę* "to be baptized" next to the vernacular *oxrestyvsja* "was baptized"; ChSl. *humno* "garner" (see Sr., 1:609; Berynda, 38) compared to *klunja* in Kuliš and Puljuj, which is a Ruthenian borrowing from Lith. *klúonas* (Latv. *kluõns*) (Urbutis 1969, 61–62). Consider also ChSl. *polova* "chaff," retained most likely from the Church Slavonic Bible used by Šaškevyč in his own translation (Pšepjurs'ka-Ovčarenko 1988, 240), and ChSl. *bedra* (pl.) "loins," found among other texts in the Homilary Gospel written down in 1670 by the priest Semion Timofěevič from Rešetylivka, a small village west of Poltava (Žiteckij 1905, 54; Tymč., 65). Regional and vernacular forms like *šaran'ča* "locus," *ves'koje* "any," and *zaraz* "straightaway" occur in the same chapter.

As evidenced in the excerpt cited above, in the agentive prepositional phrase, Šaškevyč resorts mainly to the vernacular *vid* (e.g., *vid neho* "of him," as compared to the Church Slavonic *od Duxa* "of the Spirit" with no *ikavism*). It should be noted that the preposition *od* was commonplace at that time in Southeast Ukrainian and some northern Ukrainian dialects (Shevelov 1979, 479; Žovtobrjux et al. 1979, 284), whence the use of the form *od* by such authors as Ivan Kotljarevs'kyj, Ivan Nekraševyč, Hryhorij Kvitka-Osnov'janenko, Taras Ševčenko, Lesja Ukrajinka, and Panas Myrnyj (Danylenko 1999, 233, 2006c, 317; Hrycenko 2007, 30–31). Moreover, some normalizers of Ukrainian in the nineteenth and early twentieth centuries viewed the form *vid-* as a Galician dialectism (Nečuj-Levic'kyj 1907, 19), although *vid-* was later incorporated into modern literary Ukrainian.

The most peculiar feature of Šaškevyč's language is that he glossed himself in language variance, using synonyms from different styles or (regional) dialects (e.g., *hovoryty* and *movyty* "to say"). For greater comprehension and emphasis, he employed series of forms, appearing sometimes in one and the same chapter or even verse (e.g., *svyty* and *rȳzy* [Šaškevyč, 140:1102, 1103, Jn 20:5, 6] next to *odežy* "[linen] clothes" [Šaškevyč, 140:1109, Jn 20:12]), which concurs with Tymošyk's (2000b, 101–102) conclusion that the "translator's innovations" demonstrated "certain achievements in the domain of stylistic variance of the Ukrainian language." However, in contrast to Kuliš, who always indulged in experimenting with various linguistic means and styles, Šaškevyč proved to be a less consistent innovator, slanted in favor of "ostentatiously" vernacular and dialectal elements. For this reason, perhaps, Tymošyk (ibid.) found only two personal neologisms in Šaškevyč (i.e., *verxovodnyk* "governor" [Šaškevyč, 108:41, Mt 2:6; see also Žel., 1:65], which seems to be more felicitous than *het′man* in Kuliš and Puljuj [*SP/NZ*, 4], and *zlebedyte* [2 pl. fut.] "[ye shall] lament" [Šaškevyč, 135:917, Jn 16:20]).

Vis-à-vis the above examples, Tymošyk (2000b, 102) asserted that the language of Šaškevyč's translation reflected a lack of general norms in the Ukrainian literary language of that period. All this, she argued, could have brought about some mistranslations, distorted "the adequate transformation of the dynamics of the original [text]," and caused the loss of "preaching tempo" (ibid.). It is tempting therefore to assume that Šaškevyč's language demonstrated not so much a lack of pan-Ukrainian norms as a blending, a real hybrid of Church Slavonic discourse with regional (Galician) forms. What is important in this respect is that this hybrid was conceived of by Šaškevyč as a basis for the biblical style and the written language standard. His stance did not differ from the local vision of literary Ukrainian propounded by the defenders of a separate ethnic and religious regional identity in Galicia, Transcarpathia, and Bukovyna, who, in the eighteenth century, had advanced the idea of one literary language, based on Church Slavonic, although with a wide range of regional admixtures (Danylenko 2008a, 111).

It is no wonder that the parallel translation of Kuliš and Puljuj shows a totally different approach to the literary and language standard, appropriate in particular for a new type of religious literature. Although this type was offered in the translation of the Bible by the two representatives of Galicia and Dnieper Ukraine, its make-up appears more unified and stylistically more innovative.

The archaization of their translation is achieved through the use of Church Slavonicisms and some regional traits, deviating sometimes from the Central Dnieper dialect. To name a few Church Slavonicisms and bookish lexemes, there is Kuliš's favorite aorist form *reče* "said," the verb *hlaholaty* "to say," the passive construction with a reflexive verb and the agentive phrase of the type *xrestylysja vid neho* "were baptized of him" as opposed to *v Tebe xrestytys´* "[I have need] to be baptized of thee," unusual collocations of the type *čynyty pravdu* "to fulfill all righteousness," and separate lexemes like *pojasnyci* "loins," which is a semantically modified ESl. *pojasьnica* "belt" (Sr., 2:1340). Viewed at some point as a possible Russianism (see Umanec´ and Spilka, 762), the latter lexeme infiltrated the western Ukrainian variety of new literary Ukrainian (Kuzela and Rud., 849).

Among the dialectal and vernacular forms, one should focus on those forms that differ from the corresponding words and constructions found in the translation of Šaškevyč. They include, for instance, present active participles like *nastyhajučyj* (m. sg.) *hniv* "the wrath to come," introduced in the text most likely under the influence of Puljuj, and vernacular lexemes like *odeža* "raiment" and *kodlo* "generation" as an old borrowing from Pol. *godło* "sign" with the derogatory meaning of the foreign suffix *-dł(o)* (Shevelov 1979, 80). It is worthwhile comparing ChSl. *plod* "fruit" in Šaškevyč with *ovošč*, a long-naturalized Church Slavonicism (Vasmer, 2:249–250) found in the translation of Kuliš and Puljuj (see the newly borrowed form *ovoc"* in Ruthenian [Berynda, 83]). The word *ovošč*, hailed as a true "popular form" by Nečuj-Levyc´kyj (Nečuj-Levic´kyj 1907, 329), might have been introduced by Kuliš since, as was noted above, Puljuj used in his translation of Psalm 1 the western Slavic borrowing *ovoč* (Kuzela and Rud., 500). In this context, it is remarkable that Kuliš and Puljuj differentiated Church Slavonic and Old Ukrainian *humno*, borrowed by Šaškevyč most likely from the Church Slavonic (*Biblija* 1862, 514r), from *tik* "floor" and *klunja* "garner" (Tymč. and Nimčuk, 2:394). In some verses, Kuliš and Puljuj vernacularized their language ostentatiously, offering lexemes that seem incongruous with the biblical narrative and the context in particular (e.g., *het'man* "governor" and *knjazi Judyny* "the princes of Ju'-da" [*SP/NZ*, 4, Mt 2:6], although the lexeme *knjaz'* also happens elsewhere in the Church Slavonic translation).

Kuliš and Puljuj widely used the alternation *u-* : *v-* as adapted to the principles of euphony in Southeast Ukrainian (and today's standard Ukrainian) (e.g., *ščob utïkaly vid* "to flee from" and *kydajut' uv ohon'* "[they] cast into the fire" in Šaškevyč [Žovtobrjux et al. 1979, 225–227]), dating back to the end of the Old Ukrainian period, around the late fourteenth century (Shevelov 1979, 40; Danylenko 2003a, 85–90). In the realm of morphology, Kuliš and Puljuj consistently employed deverbatives ending in *-nnje* such as *xreščennje* "baptism" and *pokajannje* "repentance." These forms are commonly attested in North Ukrainian. Šaškevyč, in this case, was still at a loss as to which form to adopt: a Church Slavonic deverbative ending in *-ie* or a vernacularized (southwestern Ukrainian) one ending in *-n'je* (without gemination), which was ultimately connected with vernacular forms ending in *-nnje* found in Kuliš and Puljuj. It is not, therefore, incidental to notice forms like *kreščenie* and *pokajan'je* in Šaškevyč's text.

The translation of Kuliš and Puljuj reveals a conspicuous decrease in passive constructions, especially those derived from reflexives. On the other hand, perhaps under the Galician influence channeled by Puljuj, their translation is riddled, more often than not, with impersonal constructions. Revealing the residual perfective meaning, they are comprised of forms ending in *-no* and *-to*, without an auxiliary, along with the direct object in the accusative case: *zaprošeno i Isusa* (acc.), *j učenykiv* (acc.) *Joho na vesillje* "and both Je'-sus was called, and his disciples to the marriage" (*SP/NZ*, 91, Jn 2:2), also *budovano cerkvu* (acc.) "[forty and six years] was this temple in building" (*SP/NZ*, 91, Jn 2:20). In Šaškevyč, I found only one instance of a similar construction without an auxiliary: *tuju nevěstu* (acc.) *zlapano nÿně na bludě* "this woman was taken in adultery [in the very act]" (Šaškevyč, 123:439–440, Jn 8:3). Overall, unlike Šaškevyč's orientation towards the vernacularization of Church Slavonic, the translation made by Kuliš and Puljuj shows, stylistically, a less heterogeneous texture with a more uniform flow of varying elements. Needless to say, Šaškevyč's level of language normalization can, therefore, hardly be compared with that found in Kuliš and Puljuj. For another illuminating glimpse of the curious mixture of lofty and vernacular elements in the Church Slavonic make-up of Šaškevyč's translation, it would be interesting to compare a representative sampling from the Gospel according to John as translated by Šaškevyč, on the one hand, and by Kuliš and Puljuj, on the other, against the Church Slavonic Bible of Hryhorij Tarkovyč published in 1804–1805 in Hungary:

Šaškevyč's Translation

Гл. д̃. . . . а жнец бере заплату и збирає плоды на животъ вѣчный, щоб радуваў са сѣющій вкупѣ и з жѣнцемъ; о тѣмбо истинна приповѣдь, що иншій єсть сѣющій, а иншій жнущій; Я васъ послаў жати там, де сте са не трудили, иншіи са трудили, а вы прійшлисте в их труд. (Šaškevyč, 117:190–194)

Kuliš and Puljuj's Translation

36. І приймає жнець плату, й збирає овощ у життє вічнє, щоб і хто сіє, радував ся, і хто жне.

37. Бо у сьому слово правдиве: що инший, хто сіє, а инший, хто жне.

38. Я післав вас жати, коло чого ви не працювали; инші люде працювали, а ви на працю їх увійшли. (*SP/NZ*, 93–94)

The Tarkovyč Bible

. . . И҆ жна́й, мзду̀ прїе́млетъ, и҆ собира́етъ пло́дъ въ живо́тъ вѣ́чный: да и҆ сѣ́ѧй вку́пѣ ра́дуетсѧ и҆ жна́й. ѡ҆ се́мъ бо сло́во є҆́сть и҆́стинное, ꙗ҆́кw и҆́нъ є҆́сть сѣ́ѧй, и҆ и҆́нъ є҆́сть жна́й. А҆́зъ посла́хъ вы жа́ти, и҆дѣ́же вы не тру̀ди́стесѧ: и҆ні́н труди́шасѧ, и҆ вы въ тру́дъ и҆́хъ внидо́сте. (Tarkovyč, 5:139)

[36. And he that reapeth receiveth wages, and gathereth fruit unto life eternal: that both he that soweth and he that reapeth may rejoice together.

37. And herein is that saying true, One soweth, and another reapeth.

38. I sent you to reap that whereon ye bestowed no labour: other men laboured, and ye are entered unto their labours.] (Jn 4:36–38)

As evidenced above, the language of Šaškevyč's translation is, at its core, Church Slavonic, while admitting some vernacular elements like *trud* "labor" and *trudyly* (2 pl. pret.) "to labor," as if transferred from the Tarkovyč Bible. Moreover, the vernacular component in his translation is tinged with *la couleur locale*, such as in the enclitic use of the auxiliary of the former perfect tense and the reflexive particle *sja* as in *ste sę ne trudyly* "ye bestowed no labor."

FOSTERING THE "RUSIAN CHURCH VERNACULAR"

Šaškevyč's translation could serve as a litmus test of the respective level of education in Galicia, Transcarpathia, and Bukovyna as well as the state of written Ukrainian as cultivated in the Hapsburg Empire since the late eighteenth century. A priest of the Ukrainian Greek Catholic church, Šaškevyč was a graduate of the Greek Catholic Theological Seminary at the University of Lviv, which continued educational traditions cultivated at the Studium Ruthenum (1787–1809). The latter was established at the University of Lviv at the behest of Emperor Joseph II in place of the Barbareum, disbanded in 1784, and the Greek Catholic seminary in Lviv (1783), in order to prepare the Uniate clergy for philosophical and theological departments, whose scholarly level was far from satisfactory (Fellerer 2005, 87). As in the primary schools, the language of instruction, according to the Austrian officials, had to be Ruthenian (*Ruthenisch*), which, in 1786, was declared "Landes-, Volks- und Nationalsprache" (Ohonovs′kyj 1889, 100), although it was not clear which *Ruthenisch* was meant (Magocsi 1984, 53).

In the early nineteenth century and beyond, local intellectuals were faced with the same problem. Suffice it to say that, as late as 1851, Ivan Harasevyč, an eyewitness to the events of this period, offered a triple definition of the language of instruction in the Studium Ruthenum— *narodnȳj cerkovno-russkij jazȳk″* "Rusian Church vernacular," *russkij jazȳk″* "Rusian language," and *rodnoj jazȳk″* "mother tongue" (Levyc′kyj 1902, 118). Closer to an understanding of the real nature of this language was Ohonovs′kyj (1889, 12, 50–58), according to whom the Galician professors, including Petro Lodij, Andrij Pavlovyč, Myxajlo Harasevyč, and others, began teaching "in the extinct Church Slavonic language" (*v″ mertvôm″ cerkovno-slavjan′skôm″ jazycě*) (Franko 1891a). Church Slavonic as the language of instruction, with "involuntary Ukrainianisms and Polonisms" as well as Russianisms (Moser 2004, 318), appeared to be less than suitable for this purpose. This is why the professors, sometimes prompted by their students who were, in general, poorly prepared for university studies, often resorted to straight Polish (Ohonovs′kyj 1889, 53; Strumins′kyj 1984, 36).

As argued elsewhere (Danylenko 2008a), unlike the Ukrainians in the Hetmanate state and Sloboda Ukraine, the Rusians in Galicia in the eighteenth century abandoned the linguistic achievements of the previous period, thus eliminating any chance of creating a new literary language on the basis of their vernacular (Ohonovs′kyj 1889, 53). That was one of many missed opportunities that could hardly be rectified by the activities of Varlaam Šeptyc′kyj in Lviv or Andrij Bačyns′kyj in Mukačeve and Užhorod who, after the disbandment of the Barbareum, resisted efforts to close the Užhorod seminary and opposed a government order that Rusyns from Transcarpathia were to attend the Hungarian seminary at Eger (Rusinko 2003, 68).

Despite the leading role of the Greek Catholic clergy in fostering regional self-identification and linguistic tradition, only a few translations of the Holy Scriptures were made in Galicia after Šaškevyč (whose work was published only in the early twentieth century). What is more remarkable is that these translations were undertaken by laypersons rather than clergymen. Among the earliest attempts is a translation of Psalm 103 published by Vasyl′ Voljan, a native of Bukovyna, in a primer, *Ruska čytanka dlja nyžšoji hymnaziy* (Rusian Primer for the Elementary Gymnasium, 1852) prepared by Vasyl′ Koval′s′kyj (Moser 2005, 228–231). According to Moser, this translation reveals nothing interesting or new from the point of view of linguistic normalization as compared with the work of Šaškevyč. In fact, this is the same hybrid of Church Slavonicisms, amassed under the second Church Slavonic influence, Great Russian, and regional forms (ibid., 228–229).

A similar vernacularization of the local (Galician) variety of Church Slavonic is observed in an anonymous translation of some fragments from the Holy Scriptures that appeared in 1853 in the literary supplement *Otečestvennyj Sbornyk″* of the Vienna periodical *Věstnyk″*. As in the aforementioned translation authored by Vasyl′ Koval′s′kyj, this text demonstrates inconsistent Rusian features (Moser 2005, 229), such as short imperative forms like *bud'* (3 sg.) "be!," the relativizer *kotoryj*, preterital masculine forms derived with the help of the participle ending in *-l*, the use of pleophonic forms of the type *xorony* (2 sg. imper.) "keep!," the occurrence of full adjectival forms in the predicate like *mudrÿj budeš'* "you will be wise," dative singular forms like *Hospodevy* "Lord" and *Bohovy* "God" with the Ukrainian *ŭ*-stem desinence, and so forth. According to Moser, all the aforementioned features were not used consistently in this translation. Therefore, one can hardly speak in this case about a translation into [Dnieper] Ukrainian or even Rusian (ibid., 230).

At first blush, a similar approach was applied by an anonymous translator of Psalm 40 (*Psalom"*). Published in 1855 in the Lviv periodical *Zorja Halycka*, this was in fact a mere paraphrase with obvious folkloric foundations, a genre commonly practiced at that time by many populists in Russian-ruled Ukraine, including Kuliš and Ševčenko, and, if less frequently, in Galicia. At this point one may recall reminiscent folkloric elements in *Psalmÿ Ruslanovy* (Psalms of Ruslan) written by Šaškevyč with a good deal of vernacular and dialectal admixtures (e.g., *sumna piÿnič* "sorrowful north" or *oko tvoje zablyščyt' zirnyčkoju* "your eye will shine like a little star" [*Psalmÿ*, 69–70]). Used by Šaškevyč as a member of the *Rus'ka trijcja* in the 1830s, the first name Ruslan might have been a poetic tribute by the Ukrainian school in Polish literature of the 1820s and 1830s, and was coined purportedly from the ancient ethnic name Roxolanus. Hrycak (2003, 99–100), however, argued that the choice of this name by Šaškevyč was plausibly influenced by the heroic ethos of Aleksandr Puškin's poem "Ruslan i Ljudmila" (Ruslan and Ljudmila, 1820), whence also the title of the almanac *Rusalka Dněstrovaja* (The Nymph of the Dniester) and the title *Psalmÿ Ruslanovy* (Psalms of Ruslan).

Also of interest is another important detail of the anonymous paraphrase of Psalm 40. According to the editor's note, the text was allegedly excerpted from a manuscript containing a translation of the book of Psalms by a certain priest "Pl. Dn." One can legitimately wonder why the name of the real translator was withheld and never revealed to the public. As a possible explanation, one can assume that, by publishing a secular paraphrase of a psalm made by an anonymous author, the editor was trying to avoid possible criticism from the

Galician Russophiles or conservative clerics who might object to a large number of vernacular elements in a common religious text written in *jazyčije* (Danylenko 2008a, 85–87). It would suffice to recall here one of these clerics, Myxajlo Malynovs´kyj, who negatively reviewed the manuscript of Puljuj's *Molytvoslov″* (A Prayer Book) revised for the second edition in 1870 (*Molytovnyk*).

In fact, the number of regional (vernacular and dialectal) elements in the paraphrase of Psalm 40 is larger than in Voljan's translation of Psalm 103. Remarkably, upon closer inspection, the regional elements in the anonymous translation tend to be, in their configuration if not their frequency, similar to the texture of the corresponding paraphrase made by Kuliš.

The Anonymous Paraphrase of Psalm 40

Щасливъ, кто бѣдныхъ въ *потребѣ*
Словомъ и *даткомъ ратуе*,
Тое му Господь, що въ небѣ,
Съ *лихвовъ* ôддати *гадуе*.
[...] Що на свѣтѣ сь и неснило,
Злое на мене складали,—
Правда! Колись ся грѣшило,
Они бôльше причиняли.
Съ ними разомъ, съ ними *споломъ*!
Человѣкъ надѣя моя.
Згодованъ за моимъ столомъ,
Недавалъ мнѣ супокоя.
Въ тôмъ *казалъемъ*: "Боже! Боже!
Согрѣшилъемъ, але прошу
Няй покину тое ложе,
Скоро врагôвъ роспорошу."
А той *датокъ*, *щомъ* убогимъ,
Бѣднымъ *давалъ го* въ потребѣ,

Kuliš's Paraphrase of Psalm 41

1. Блажен той чоловік, що *дбає* про убогих:
   в день лютий, в день *журби*
2. Господь його ізбавить,
   заступить він його і жизнь йому *дарує*,
   благословить його всїм добрим поки віку.
5. ... Про мене *вороги* кругом говорять злая:
   "Коли вже він умре і ймя його загине!"
6. Хто прийде до мене, сплітає *марні* речи,
   таїть у серці зло, а вийшовши говорить.
7. Всї ненавидники про мене потай шепчуть,
   видумують *гуртом*, як зло мені зробити:

Повернулся *статкомъ* многимъ,
Такъ *лихва* взрастае въ небѣ.
И *повсталъемъ*, якъ бувало,
Коль ся Боже на мя дивишъ!
Серце мое мнѣ шептало,
Що сь недолѣ мои противишъ.
За се хвалю имя Бога,
Хвлѣтъ же *го* добрѣ люде!
Памятайте на убога,
А Богъ съ вами *булъ* и *буде*. (*Psalom"*)

8. "Прийшов його кінець! топтати рясту годі!
Лежить він, помертвів, не встане, не воскресне."
9. І той, хто хліб мій їв, кому я довіряв ся,
приятель щирий мій підняв пяту на мене.
10. Ти ж, Господи, мене помилуй і возстави,
верни мою *снагу*, щоб я воздав запеклим.
11. З того я впевню ся, що ти мене не кинув,
як не даси моїм лихим *празникувати*.
12. Прийми печаль мою, незлобіє в напастях,
і утверди мене на вік перед тобою.
13. Благословен Господь од віка і до віка,
Господь Ізраілев во віки буди, буди! (Kuliš 1909, 176–177)

[1. Blessed is he that considereth the poor: the Lord will deliver him in time of trouble.
2. The Lord will preserve him, and keep him alive; and he shall be blessed upon the earth: and thou will not deliver him unto the will of his enemies. ...
5. Mine enemies speak evil of me, When shall he die, and his name perish?
6. And if come to see me, he speaketh vanity: his heart gathereth iniquity to itself; when he goeth abroad, he telleth it.
7. All that hate me whisper together against me: against me do they devise my hurt.
8. An evil disease, say they, cleaveth fast unto him: and now that he lieth he shall rise up no more.

9. Yes, mine own familiar friend, in whom I trusted, which did eat of my bread, hath lifted up his heel against me.
10. But thou, O Lord, be merciful unto me, and raise me up, that I may requite them.
11. By this I know that thou favorest me, because mine enemy doth not triumph over me.
12. And as for me, thou upholdest me in mine integrity, and settest me before they face for ever. 13. Blessed be the Lord God of Is'-ra-el from everlasting, and to everlasting. A'-men, and A'-men.] (Ps 41)

The language of Psalm 40 (*Psalom"*) indicates that this paraphrase might have been based on the Church Slavonic text of the Bible published in 1804–1805 in five volumes under Hryhorij Tarkovyč at the Royal Hungarian University print shop in Buda. Hence the older Greek numbering of Psalm 40 as found in the Septuagint and Vulgate. Initiated in 1794 by Bishop Andrij Bačyns'kyj (1732–1809), publication of the aforementioned Bible, premised on a Great Russian edition of the Elizabeth Bible,[2] had far-reaching consequences for the Greek Catholic church in the Austro-Hungarian Empire. The authority of this Bible proved so overwhelming that almost all local parishes in the late twentieth century had a copy (Udvari 1986, 70–72).[3] By contrast, Kuliš's paraphrase of Psalm 41 and Puljuj's translation of the same psalm from Hebrew both seem to have been based on one of the editions of the Holy Scriptures produced by the British and Foreign Bible Society (e.g., *SK*, 549). Hence a modified (primarily, Protestant and recent Catholic) numbering of Psalm 41 as found in the Hebrew (Masoretic) text.

---

[2] Confusing the date of publication, Magocsi (1987, 6) erroneously wrote that "in 1809, Bačyns'kyj published the complete Bible in Church Slavonic, the only translation of this influential text to originate from the region [Subcarpathian Rus']." Magocsi, however, ignored his predecessors, including Tichý (1938, 22) who, following Aleksej Petrov, argued that the Bible of 1804–1805 was "a reprinting of a Russian edition of the late eighteenth century" (Sabov 1893, v–viii, 17–48). Horbač (1988, 36–37) assumed that comparing fragments published by Sabov with the Počajiv Bible of 1798 would demonstrate a minimum of divergences, primarily in stressing and spelling. Unfortunately, so far no one has analyzed the complete texts of the two Bibles in order to corroborate this hypothesis.

[3] It is also quite plausible that the author of the anonymous paraphrase made use of the Russian Elizabeth Bible or even the Russian version of the psalms first published in 1822 and reprinted several times by the Russian Bible Society (Batalden 2013, 214–215); the psalm in question is numbered 40 in all these editions (*Psaltyr'* 1862, 42–43; *Biblija* 1907, 435).

Dialectal elements prevail in the entire anonymous translation of Psalm 40 (*Psalom"*). They can be reduced to several especially representative features such as the clitic forms *ho* (acc.) "him" and *mja* (acc.) "me," the relativizer *ščo* "which, who," and old perfect tense forms with clitic auxiliaries of the type *kazal"em"* "I (have) said" and especially *ščom" . . . daval"* "which I have given/gave." Of interest also are imperative forms ending in hard consonants like *xvalět"* (2 pl.) "to praise," the imperative particle *njaj* "let," the dative singular feminine *moj* "my," and, finally, the verbal forms *bul"* (m. sg. pret.) "to be," *buvalo* (n. sg. pret.) "used to be," and the form *serce* "heart" with *-rc-* in place of the cluster *-rdc-*. In the morphology, a peculiar case is the form *lyxvov´* (sg. instr.) emended by Moser (2005, 230) as *lyxvom"* (sg. instr.) "profit." In fact, the form *lyxvov"* is commonly attested in Southwest Ukrainian. It does exist in Galician, Transcarpathian, and Lemkian, as well as in some Dniester and Sjan dialects (Bevzenko et al. 1978, 80–81; Verxratskyj 1902, 120–121).

Most explicit, to be sure, is the paraphrase's western Ukrainian vocabulary (e.g., *potrebě* [sg. loc.] "destitution" [*DMU*, 1:213], *datok"* "charity" [Tymč., 670], *ratuje* [3 sg. pres.] "to save" with a dispalatalized reflex *r* influenced by Pol. *ratować*, *haduje* [3 sg. pres.] "to think" [see Pol. *gadać* "to chatter" and *gaduła* "chatterbox"] [Vytv., 77], a Polish personal form instead of *hadaje* [Tymč., 499], *spolom"* "together with" [Žel., 2:926], *lyxva* "profit" [ibid., 1:505; Kuzela and Rud., 364], and *statek* "property" [Žel., 2:917]). Remarkably, Church Slavonic forms are not numerous in this paraphrase, making the regional forms stand out. Among a few Church Slavonic or bookish lexemes, one can name the nominal form *ščaslyv"* "happy" as opposed to *ščaslyvyj* in Puljuj and ChSl. *blažen* in Kuliš, *lože* "bed," *čelověk"* "man," *ubohym"* (pl. dat.) "poor," *vrahôv"* (gen. pl.) "enemy," and *supokoja* (gen.) "peace" where the original prefix must have been *sъ* or *sъ + o* (Shevelov 1979, 533).

Leaving aside Puljuj's translation and its peculiar Galician stylistics, Kuliš seemed to apply the same vernacularizing approach as the anonymous Galician translator. True, one encounters in Kuliš both vernacular and Church Slavonic elements. However, his approach appears to be more synthetic, bridging the two poles of Church Slavonic and vernacular Ukrainian. On the one hand, there are the vernacular *dbaty* "to care for," *žurba* "sorrow," *darovaty* "to make a present" with a northern Ukrainian

-*ova*-, *marnyj* "vain," *vorohy* "enemies," *hurtom* "in a body, together," *pryjatel' ščyryj* "a faithful friend," *snaha* "vigor,'" *praznykuvaty* "to celebrate" (Žel., 2:733), and other lexemes attested cross-dialectally. On the other hand, one finds in Kuliš's work Church Slavonic or other archaic lexemes, such as *zlaja* (n. pl.) "bad things," *tajity* "to hide," *pečal'* "sorrow" (Berynda, 81), *vozstavyty* "to stand [something up]," and *vozdaty* "to take revenge" with a reflex of the prefix *vъz-* (Shevelov 1979, 295). Finally, there is *nezlobije* "mildness" and *lože* next to WUkr. *postïl'* "bed" (Danylenko 1999, 237; 2006c, 322), a pair also used by Puljuj (*SP*, 508); see also WUkr. *postel'* in the anonymous paraphrase of Psalm 40 (Žel., 2:718).

But what is more interesting in Kuliš's translation is that some of his Church Slavonicisms are directly influenced by the Slavonic version of the Elizabeth Bible (reprinted in Buda in 1804–1805) (see ChSl. *blažen"* and *v" den' ljut"* as compared to *blažen* and *v den' ljutyj* in Kuliš). Taken as a whole, Kuliš's paraphrase demonstrates anew a masterful combination of both Church Slavonic and vernacular forms, with a slight admixture of other elements such as Great Russianism *žyzn'* "life," a favorite form used lavishly by Kuliš in his translations of Shakespeare.

In sum, one should reiterate that Kuliš's translation of the psalms is a successful combination of biblical poetry with the vernacular standard as cultivated in the second half of the nineteenth century in Russian-ruled Ukraine. For this reason, there is found in his paraphrases only a handful of regionalisms that subsequently did not make their way through to modern literary Ukrainian. As compared with Kuliš's translation of the psalms, criticized subsequently only by biblical scholars (Levyc'kyj 1924), Puljuj's translation could be less appealing to the *Sprachgefühl* of contemporary speakers of Southeast Ukrainian. Nečuj-Levyc'kyj was one of those whose disparaging criticism of the Galician vogue in the early twentieth century was somewhat naïve and biased, although perhaps it reflected the opinion of the average Dnieper Ukrainian speaker.

ANY PALLIATIVE SOLUTION?

In the same year that the Bible translated by Kuliš and Puljuj in cooperation with Nečuj-Levyc'kyj came off the press in Vienna (1903), the print shop of the Lviv Stavropegia published Aleksander Bačyn′skij's (1844–1933) translation of the book of Psalms, *Psaltyr′ v″jazŷcě cerkovno-sloven′skôm″ s″ perevodom″ na jazŷk″ narodno-ruskij* (Psalter in the Church Slavonic Language with a Translation into the Vernacular Rusian Language, 1903) (*Psaltyr′*, Bačyn′skij). Officially approved, this publication was a kind of a belated reply by the Greek Catholic church, initiated and supported by its hierarchs, who had long tolerated the translations by Kuliš appearing regularly throughout the 1870s and 1880s (Haluščynskyj 1925, 318–319). Quite possibly, they also knew about the vernacular translation of the Old Testament being prepared by the British and Foreign Bible Society for publication since 1901, when the society bought the copyright from Puljuj and the widow of the late Kuliš (Studyns′kyj 1930, lxv; Nečuj-Levyc′kyj 1968, 376, 377). For this reason, laying claim to be the exclusive custodian of the ethno-cultural legacy of Ukrainians living in the Austro-Hungarian Empire, the Greek Catholic church was inclined to welcome domestic translations by those who would support their ecclesiastical approach toward the normalization of the written language. It is not, therefore, accidental that Bačyn′skij furnished the Psalter with comments elucidating murky places in the Church Slavonic, obscured by the "old faith" presentations of the biblical content (*Psaltyr′*, Bačyn′skij, 5).

In the same year, 1903, the Greek Catholic church published Bačyn′skij's translation of the New Testament, also with parallel Church Slavonic and vernacular texts. It is interesting to note that, while working on the two translations, Bačyn′skij made use of the Latin Vulgate and a German translation.[4] Referring to Bačyn′skij's translation of the psalms, Horbač (1988, 65, 78) argued that his language reflected all the oddities of the Galician orthography (*maksymovyčivka*) of that time. Moreover, a cursory look through the first pages of the translation shows that it was conceived of as a local church-canonical work, without any thought for

---

[4] One should also mention here a translation of the book of Psalms made by Oleksij (Oleksa) Sljusarčuk (*Sljusarčuk*) who knew Puljuj and helped him with the proofreading of the Bible in the early 1900s. Published in 1904 in Žovkva, Sljusarčuk's translation might have been printed even earlier since it was approved by Bishop Peleš in 1899 and by Bishop Šeptyc′kyj in 1900 (Horbač 1988, 31–32, fn. 9; Haluščynskyj 1925, 318).

the Dnieper Ukrainian readership, whence a sizable number of regional lexemes, including obvious Polonisms. Nimčuk (2005, 39) surmised that the whole translation was made in the local vernacular permeated with occasional Church Slavonicisms.

To ascertain the ratio of Church Slavonic and vernacular elements in Bačyn´skij's translation, it is worth considering Horbač's (1988, 78) hypothesis. Although not substantiated by concrete examples, he argued that, in addition to the parallel Church Slavonic version, Bačyn´skij had also used a translation made by Kuliš. To adduce the major counter argument here, it should be kept in mind that Kuliš created a versified paraphrase, not approved by the Greek Catholic church, rather than a scriptural translation such as that made by Puljuj for the 1903 Bible. Therefore, it would be tempting to assume that Bačyn´skij was familiar rather with the translation of Puljuj. However, this seems unlikely since the entire Bible, including the psalms, had just come off the press and Bačyn´skij could hardly have had enough time, if any at all, to become familiarized with the translation of Puljuj.

To investigate possible differences between the translations made, on the one hand, by Bačyn´skij and, on the other, by Kuliš and Puljuj, it is useful again to return to Psalm 40/41.

Bačyn´skij's Translation of Psalm 40	**Puljuj's Translation of Psalm 41**
На конецъ, Псаломъ Давиду	Проводиреві хора. Псальма Давидова [41]
Въ конέцъ, Ѱалόмъ Двдⷣ, м҃.	[To the chief musician, A Psalm of David.]
2. [1] Щасливий, кто знає бѣдного и убогого; въ лютый день выбавить єго Господь.	1. Щасливий, хто про вбогих дбає! В день нещастя спасе його Господь.
Бл҃жέнъ раз8мѣвάяй на нища и оу҆бόга, въ дέнь лютъ и҆збάвитъ є҆гὸ Гдⷣь:	[Blessed is he that considereth the poor: the Lord will deliver him in time of trouble.]

3. [2] Господь нехай єго захова́є и живитъ єго, най єго ущасливитъ на землѣ, и нехай не выдастъ єго въ руки вороговъ єго.

Гдь да сохрани́тъ е҆го̀, и҆ живи́тъ е҆го̀, и҆ да ѹ҆блажи́тъ е҆го̀ на землѝ, и҆ да не преда́стъ е҆го̀ въ рꙋки врагѡ́въ е҆гѡ̀.

4. [3] Господь най поможе єму на постелѣ єго хоробы, всю постѣль єго ты обертавъ въ хоробѣ єго.

Гдь да помо́жетъ е҆мꙋ на ѻ҆дрѣ болѣ́зни е҆гѡ̀: всѐ ло́же е҆гѡ̀ ѡ҆брати́лъ е҆сѝ въ болѣ́зни е҆гѡ̀.

5. [4] Я сказавъ: Господи змилуй ся надо мною, уздорови душу мою, бомъ згрѣшивъ передъ тобою.

А҆́зъ рѣ́хъ Гди поми́лꙋй мѧ̀, и҆сцѣли́ дꙋшꙋ мою̀, ꙗ҆́кѡ согрѣши́хъ тебѣ̀.

6. [5] Вороги мои говорили мнѣ злобно: колижь умре и загине имя єго?

Врази́ мои́ рѣ́ша мнѣ̀ ѕла̑ѧ: когда̀ ѹ҆́мретъ и҆ поги́бнетъ и҆́мѧ е҆гѡ̀? (*Psaltyr'*, Bačyn'skij, 80–81; Tarkovyč, 3:10; *Biblija* 1862, 284v)

2. Господь заступить його і сохранить життє його; він буде на землі щасливий, і ти не віддаси його в руки ворогам зажертим.

[The Lord will preserve him, and keep him alive; and he shall be blessed upon the earth: and thou will not deliver him unto the will of his enemies.]

3. Піддержить його Господь на смертному ложі; ціле ліговиско його переміняєш в недузі його.

[The Lord will strengthen him upon the bed of languishing: thou wilt make all his bed in his sickness.]

4. Я сказав: Господи, змилуйся надо мною! Сціли душу мою, бо согрішив я проти тебе.

[I said, Lord, be merciful unto me: heal my soul; for I have sinned against thee.]

5. Вороги мої росказують лихі речі проти мене: Коли згине він і пропаде імя його?

[Mine enemies speak evil of me, When shall he die, and his name perish?] (SP, 523, Ps 41)

What becomes clear from the above translations is that Bačyn´skij slavishly follows the Church Slavonic original, although elsewhere he digresses from the canonical version, while lapsing into contradictory poetic imagery and even factual incongruences. Suffice it to cite here verse 12 in Psalms 16–17 where Bačyn´skij connected ChSl. *skimen"* (*skimьnъ*) "catulus" (*Lexicon*, 845) with a hole more suitable for mice, foxes, and badgers (Horbač 1988, 65). The translation of the verse by Puljuj fits well into the narrative, although Kuliš's translation looks more poetic.

Bačyn´skij's Translation

12. Обняли мене якъ левъ готовый на нападъ, и *левчукъ* мешкаючый въ норѣ.

Ѡбъѧ́ша мѧ̀ ꙗ́кѡ ле́въ гото́въ на ло́въ, и̇ ꙗ́кѡ скѵ́менъ ѡ҆бита́ѧй въ та́йныхъ.
(*Psaltyr´*, Bačyn´skij, 30)

Puljuj's Translation

12. Вони, як лев той, що добичі шукає, і як *левчук*, що в закутку притаївся. (*SP*, 511)

Kuliš's Translation

... наче той лев із-за кручі, наче *левчук* із-за скелі, здобич нагледївши певну, жде не діждеть-ся поживи.
(*Psaltyr*, Rataj, 129–130)

[Like as a lion that is greedy of his prey, and as if it were a young lion lurking in secret places.] (Ps 17)

Getting back to Psalm 40/41, the language of Bačyn´skij is a mixture of Church Slavonic, vernacular, and dialectal forms, although the latter elements do prevail. Among the Church Slavonicisms, lexical transfers are commonplace and mostly morphonologically adjusted to the local vernacular: *ubohoho* (gen.) "poor," *v" ljutyj den´* "in time of trouble," *vybavyt"* "[he] will deliver," *ôt" věka y do věka* "from everlasting, and to everlasting" (*Psaltyr´*, Bačyn´skij, 82; Ps 41:1, 13), *sut´* (3 pl. pres.) "to be," and *žyzn´* "life" (*Psaltyr´*, Bačyn´skij, 27, 15, Ps 7:5), a favorite form of Rataj; there appears also a bookish *kto* "who" in Psalm 40/41. In other psalms, the following "Ukrainianized" Church Slavonicisms appear: *ssučyx"* "suckling" (gen.) as compared with the Church Slavonic counterpart *ssuščyx"* (*Psaltyr´*, Bačyn´skij, 16, Ps 8:2), *lev" rykajučyj* "roaring lion" (*Psaltyr´*,

Bačyn´skij, 42, Ps 22:13) next to *lev″ rȳkaę, stohnanje* "groaning" (*Psaltyr´*, Bačyn´skij, 75, Ps 38:9; Horbač 1988, 65), and so forth.

Sometimes, Bačyn´skij translated word for word, while transferring entire verses from the Church Slavonic into vernacular Rusian, as is the case of verse 6 in Psalm 2:

Азъ же поставленъ есмь царь   6. Я єсмь поставленый ôтъ него
ѿ негѡ надъ Сїѡномъ горою   царемъ надъ Сіономъ, горою
с͠тою єгѡ.   святою єго. (*Psaltyr´*, Bačyn´skij, 8)

[(literally: I am set a king by Him upon his holy hill of Zi´-on)
Yet have I set my king upon my holy hill of Zi´-on.] (Ps 2:6)

In most cases, however, the translator replaced obvious Church Slavonicisms with neutral (vernacular) forms like ChSl. *lože* ~ WUkr. *postěl´* "bed," ChSl. *bolězn´* ~ WUkr. *xoroba* "sickness," and ChSl. *skorb´* ~ *smutok″* "trouble" (*Psaltyr´* Bačyn´skij, 42, Ps 22:11). As compared with Church Slavonic forms, including morphosyntatic calques like passive sentences with the agentive phrase *ôt″* (< *otъ*) "from" + genitive, vernacular and dialectal forms, nevertheless, prevail. The following forms seem most representative: *stôl´cy* "seats" (*Psaltyr´*, Bačyn´skij, 7, Ps 1:1), *načynje* "porter's vessel" (*Psaltyr´*, Bačyn´skij, 7, Ps 1:1; Žel., 1:500), *spočyvaju* (1 sg. pres.) "to lay down in peace" (*Psaltyr´*, Bačyn´skij, 11, Ps 4:8), *movbȳ* "as" (*Psaltyr´*, Bačyn´skij, 13), *zmučenȳj* "exhausted" (*Psaltyr´*, Bačyn´skij, Ps 6:6), *zapamoročylo sja* (sg. n. pret.) "to become obscured" (*Psaltyr´*, Bačyn´skij, 14), *zavstydajut´ sia* (3 pl. fut.) "to be ashamed" (ibid., Ps 6:10), *obmanjuje* (3 sg. pres.) "to backbite" (*Psaltyr´*, Bačyn´skij, 26, Ps 14:3), and *žoludok″* "bowels" (*Psaltyr´*, Bačyn´skij, 42, Ps 22:14; Žel., 1:225), with a characteristic *o* after a postdental (Shevelov 1979, 147).

Some of the above lexemes are regionally tinged, like *zasypljaju* (1 sg. pres.) "to sleep" (*Psaltyr´*, Bačyn´skij, 11, Ps 4:8; Verxratskyj 1899, 38–39), *vpravljaje sja* "doth he meditate" (*Psaltyr´*, Bačyn´skij, 11), and *koždyj* "ever" ("each") (*Psaltyr´*, Bačyn´skij, 13, Ps 6:6), attested cross-dialectally since the late Middle Ukrainian period (Shevelov 1979, 516–517; Hrinč., 1:799). Many of these dialectisms are western Slavic, primarily

Polish borrowings, such as *pôrvaty* "to steal" (*Psaltyr'*, Bačyn'skij, 14; Pol. *porwać* in Tymč. and Nimčuk, 2:174), *zamješkaje* (3 sg. non-past) "to dwell," *lyxva* "profit, usury" (*Psaltyr'*, Bačyn'skij, 26, Ps 15:1, 5), *pokvapyty* "to hasten" (*Psaltyr'*, Bačyn'skij, 25, Ps 16:4; Berynda, 120; Pol. *kwapić się* in Tymč. and Nimčuk, 1:360), *robak* "worm" (ibid., 156), *topnějučij* (PrAP m. sg.) *vôsk"* "[melt] is like wax" (*Psaltyr'*, Bačyn'skij, 41, 42, Ps 22:6, 16; Tymč. and Nimčuk, 2:395), *uhrjazly* (3 pl. pret.) "[arrows] stick fast" (*Psaltyr'*, Bačyn'skij, 74, Ps 38:2), *ôtvyrav"* (sg. m. pret.) "to open" (*Psaltyr'*, Bačyn'skij, *Ps* 38:13; Pol. *otworzyć* in Tymč. and Nimčuk, 2:62), and many others.

In morphosyntax, of interest are imperative forms ending in hard consonants like *prijmět"* (2 pl.) "to accept" (*Psaltyr'*, Bačyn'skij, 9), the imperative particle *naj* (ibid., 81), present tense forms like *jes'* (2 sg.) "to be" (ibid., 9), former perfect tense forms with auxiliary clitics of the type *bom" zhrěšyv"* "[because] I have sinned," and future tense forms of the type *ne bude movčav"* "shall not keep silence" (ibid., 96, Ps 50:3), which are commonly attested in Dniester (Galician) and adjacent (Lemkian) dialects as well as in Podolja (*AUM*, 2, map 244) (*ne bude movčaty* in Kuliš and Puljuj [*SP*, 527]). However, unlike his predecessors, especially Šaškevyč, Bačyn'skij used the regional perfect and future tense forms sporadically. For instance, the following future forms occur regularly in his language: *budu klykaty* "I [will] call" (*Psaltyr'*, Bačyn'skij, 11, Ps 4:3) and *budu vÿznavaty Tebe* "I will praise Thee" (*Psaltyr'*, Bačyn'skij, 17, Ps 9:2), compared to *slavyty mu* in Kuliš and Puljuj (*SP*, 508), a form which is largely found in North and Southeast Ukrainian (*AUM*, 2, map 244; Danylenko 2011a, 172–174). One should also note here Bačyn'skij's obvious predilection for active present participles influenced, most likely, by Polish (e.g., *levčuk" meškajučij v" norě*, literally, "a young lion living in a hole" [*Psaltyr'*, Bačyn'skij, 30]). Remarkably, *levčuk"* belongs to the preferred vocabulary of Kuliš, who used it more often than not in his paraphrases of the psalms (Horbač 1988, 62). In some cases, instead of such participles, Bačyn'skij employs relative clauses like *toj, ščo meškaje na nebesax"* "he that sitteth in the heavens" (*Psaltyr'*, Bačyn'skij, 8, Ps 2:4) or *Boh", kotrÿj spasaje* "God, which saveth" (*Psaltyr'*, Bačyn'skij, 15, Ps 7:10) with the western Ukrainian relative pronoun *kotrÿj* "which, who."

All in all, the aforementioned features demonstrate that Bačyn′skij's language remained, at its core, the same "vernacular Church Slavonic language" that had been used over the course of one hundred years in Austria and Hungary, since the foundation of the Studium Ruthenum in 1787 in Vienna. Indeed, the progress achieved in the creation of the biblical style and the normalization of written Ukrainian in these lands was surprisingly minimal. The difference between "vernacular Church Slavonic" used in the late eighteenth century and the variety of "vernacular Church Slavonic" still in use in Austrian-ruled Ukraine in the late nineteenth century lay not in the nature of vernacular admixtures but rather in their number. This is why the developmental trend in the formation of literary Ukrainian in these lands between 1787 and 1903 did not change substantially, while the local nationally-minded cultural activists, including the translators of the Holy Scriptures, were always faced with similar linguistic problems. The translators and normalizers of Ukrainian were never sure as to how many vernacular elements they could use in their written language, although they were ready to vernacularize, or rather "secularize," Church Slavonic only to a certain degree. At any rate, they could hardly ignore the Church Slavonic legacy in Galicia, Bukovyna, and Transcarpathia, where this language by default had been regarded as the foundation of a new literary standard. Suffice it to mention here the 1830 codification of "Carpatho-Rusyn" by Myxajlo Lučkaj (1789–1843). Lučkaj believed in a similarity between Church Slavonic and his native (Transcarpathian) dialect, which, unlike other Slavic languages, supposedly resonated with the Slavonic of the Bible (Danylenko 2009a). For this reason, the translations of Šaškevyč and Bačyn′skij were crafted linguistically in the same vein, notwithstanding the fact that they were made sixty years apart. Their language, including the anonymous translation of Psalm 40/41, had a more or less strong vernacular cast to its otherwise solidly Slavonic basis. In the aforementioned translations, this is the traditional, local Church Slavonic mix distinguished, depending on the native dialect of the translator, by varying amounts of dialectisms and borrowings.

To take Šaškevyč's translation of the Gospels as the starting point in the process of secularization of Church Slavonic in Galicia, Transcarpathia, and Bukovyna, the ratio of dialectisms and loan forms in his language is not yet significant since the translator treated Church Slavonic as the most fitting medium for the translation of the New Testament. Not surprisingly, Bačyn´skij, who some sixty years later followed in the steps of Šaškevyč, offered nothing innovative in his translation of the Psalter and the New Testament, which, in addition to Church Slavonicisms, contained many Polish elements (Ohijenko 1927, 8). Moreover, featuring Dniester dialectisms and Galician (Polish) regionalisms, his work, according to Horbač (1988, 65), proved an outdated reaction to the populist trend cultivated, sometimes inconsistently, in the local religious literature from the late eighteenth century onward (Danylenko 2008a, 85–87).

All in all, neither the Russophiles nor Ukrainophiles seemed to be interested in changing the secularizing trend of the nineteenth century. Yet, in order to counterbalance the impact of Kuliš's work, the Russophiles published several translations from the Bible in the journal *Nauka*, edited by Ivan Naumovyč in Kolomyja (Levyckij 1888, 182, 198). But all of these translations were made within the confines of the local tradition, which was premised on the notion of what we tentatively call "vernacular Church Slavonic." Even local Ukrainophiles, including Antin (Antonij) Kobyljans´kyj, were not ready to reverse the historical trend in the normalization of literary Ukrainian in the western Ukrainian lands, especially in the formation of its biblical style.

LOST IN DIACRITICS

Antin Kobyljans´kyj's contribution to the translation of the Holy Scriptures was comparatively large. In total, he translated two Gospels (i.e., the Holy Gospel according to Luke, which appeared in 1874 in two separate editions—one using Cyrillic script [Luka-U] and the other Roman script [Luka-L]—and the Gospel according to John, also published originally in two script versions in the late 1870s [Danylenko 2010a]).[5] A native of

---

5   The translation of the Holy Gospel according to Luke (both its Cyrillic- and Latin-based versions) is cited in the comprehensive bibliography compiled by Levyckij (1888, 211). Yet he omitted the translation of the Gospel according to John that appeared in two versions somewhat later, in 1877. Premised on the *Historical Catalogue of the Printed Editions of Holy Scripture* (London, 1903–1911), Horbač (1988, 30, fn. 5) wrote that the former Gospel was reprinted several times in 1874–1876. A sample of the Latin-based edition of the Holy Gospel according to Luke of 1874 is found in *The Gospel in*

Bukovyna,[6] Kobyljans´kyj's translation seemed to fit into the trend initiated, as was mentioned, by Šaškevyč and elaborated much later by Bačyn´skij (Haluščynskyj 1925, 318). Kobyljans´kyj's work, however, stands out from the populist secularizing mainstream in Galicia. Suffice it to say that, according to Horbač (1988, 48), Kobyljans´kyj's dependency upon the local "Pokuttja-Dniester-Hucul" dialect (Kobyljans´kyj 1928) was much more conspicuous in comparison with the language of Šaškevyč.

Kobyljans´kyj's translations appeared in two parallel editions, utilizing Cyrillic- and Latin-based scripts. Simovyč (1981, 117–118) placed the latter script in the context of other attempts at creating Ukrainian *latinica* with the help of Slavic orthographic devices exclusively (Franz Miklosich, Josef Jireček, Teodot Halip, and partly Myxajlo Drahomanov). There seem to have been several reasons behind Kobyljans´kyj's early efforts in introducing his own system of Latin-based characters. At first sight, his system might be a belated response to the orthographic debates initiated in the 1830s by the grammarian and ethnographer Josyf Lozyns´kyj (1807–1889) (Lesjuk 2004).[7] Quite in the spirit of Lozyns´kyj's proposal to use Roman letters to render the local vernacular, Kobyljans´kyj could opt for *latinica* as a counterbalance

---

Many Tongues, first published by the British and Foreign Bible Society in 1954 (*Gospel*, 170). I am using here the first two editions of the Holy Gospel according to Luke (Luka-U and Luka-L) and the last Cyrillic-based edition of the Holy Gospel according to John (*Ioan*), which appeared in 1881 (Danylenko 2010a). The original scripts are retained in order to illustrate the benefits of each orthographic system.

6 There is scanty information about Kobyljans´kyj available today, save for an obituary authored by Tyt Revakovyč in 1910. In particular, Kobyljans´kyj was praised for two pamphlets aimed against "the literary dictator" Bohdan Didyc´kyj, a Russophile who edited the journal *Slovo* in the local *jazyčije* (Revakovyč 1910, 166–167). Kobyljans´kyj compiled these pamphlets in Latin script: *Slovo na slovo do Redaktora "Slova"* (A Word in Reply to a Word Addressed to the Editor; Černivci, 1861), supplemented with poems by the author and Jurij Osyp Fed´kovyč exemplifying the regional vernacular, and *Holos na holos dlia Halyčyny* (A Word in Reply to a Word for Galicia; Černivci, 1861), with an addendum of several poems written by the author.

7 In reply to his major opponents, Markijan Šaškevyč and Josyf Levyc´kyj, Lozyns´kyj adduced the following argument: in order to make Rusian a literary language, the speakers need a grammar based on vernacular pronunciation. The latter, however, could be aptly rendered only by Latin letters (Makovej 1903, 83). Kobyljans´kyj, who liberally used diacritics in his translations of the New Testament, seemed to have endorsed Lozyns´kyj's reasoning.

against the conventional etymological orthography employed by the Russophiles. In this case, however, his intent to prepare a parallel edition in Cyrillic script remains uncertain. One can hypothesize that he wished to retain the dignity of the Holy Gospel, though translated into the vernacular, through the help of Cyrillic letters. Incidentally, a similar explanation holds true for the publication of Kuliš's translation of Gospel books in 1887 and 1893 with the use of Cyrillic script under the auspices of the British and Foreign Bible Society. Only the edition of 1880, sponsored by the Ševčenko Scientific Society, utilized a typical civil script.

As an alternative explanation, Horbač (1988, 48) suggested that Kobyljans´kyj created his own *latinica* for the Rusyns living in Bukovyna and North America, or for the Carpatho-Rusyn immigrants who commonly used the Hungarian variety of the Latin alphabet in their overseas publications. All in all, Kobyljans´kyj's *latinica* was premised on elements borrowed from various western Slavic and even Rumanian orthographic systems, a mix dubbed subsequently "Latin Czech" (Revakovyč 1910, 166) and "Czech-Croatian-Polish-Rumanian" phonetic script (Horbač 1988, 48). In the parallel edition, the translator slightly modified the Cyrillic script with an eye to rendering vernacular pronunciation without infringing on the etymological principles of Church Slavonic spelling. That sort of compromise reveals itself in the following parallel excerpts:

Luka-U
5. Бȣв за чăсŏв Ìрода королã Ιȣдеї с‚віăченик на імніã Захарïас, з днèвного ріăдȣ̀ Авìевого; і жінка ієгò з донìòк Аàронових, а імнiè ієì Єлісавета. (1)

Luka-L
5. Buv za čăsŏv Ìroda koroḷã Iudeï şviăčenyk na imniè Zacharïas, z dnèvnoho riădù Avìevoho; i žinka iehò z donìòk Aàronovych, a imniè ieì Elisaveta. (1)

[5. There was in the days of Her´-od, the King of Ju-dae´-a, a certain priest named Zach-a-ri´-as, of the course of A-bi´-a: and his wife was of the daughters of Aa´-ron, and her name was E-lis´-a-beth.] (Lk 1:5)

In his Latin-based orthography, Kobyljans′kyj routinely employed a caron (*háček*) to render the fricatives š, ž, and the affricate (e.g., *ščo* "that" and *Bože* [n. sg.] "relating to God" [Luka-L, 8:11, 12]). In the Cyrillic version (Luka-U), the translator dropped the back *jer*, an innovation first proposed in the 1837 almanac *Rusalka Dněstrovaja* (The Nymph of the Dniester). Most representative in this version is a sizable number of diacritics borrowed from different Latin-based scripts and used in combination with Cyrillic letters.

Thus, in addition to traditional Church Slavonic accents, Kobyljans′kyj introduced from Rumanian the breve and the tilde. Hence ă with a breve is a character denoting a mid central vowel, commonly a reflex of the old ę as attested in some Dniester, Sjan, and Hucul dialects (*AUM*, 2, map 41): for example, in *ciă* (Luka-U) = *sie* (Luka-L, 1:3) as compared with a stressed reflex in *взіăло* (Luka-U) = *vziălo* (n. sg. pret.) "to take" (Luka-L, 1:1).[8] In cases like *кŏнцã* (Luka-U, 1:3) the ŏ letter with a breve stands for a narrow reflex of the etymological *o* (*AUM*, 2, map 53; MoUkr. *kincja*), while the ã letter with a tilde represents a narrow reflex in the environment after a palatalized consonant. Modeled on Polish and Rumanian orthography, a tail placed at the bottom of the *н* denoted palatalization of the corresponding consonant (see the ș or ņ in the Latin-based version). In *ḷos* "lot" (Luka-L, 1:9), the tail happens to denote a Polish clear *l*. Kobyljans′kyj regularly marked assimilative palatalization, for example in *șviătỳm* (m. instr.) "holy" (Luka-L, 1:15), as attested today in some Dniester dialects (*AUM*, 2, map 77).

While rendering assimilative palatalization, Kobyljans′kyj seemed to follow the phonetic principle even more consistently than the system of the *želexivka* designed by Želexivs′kyj in his *Malorusko-nimeckyj slovar* (Little Russian-German Dictionary, 1884–1886). It is not therefore surprising that Kobyljans′kyj preferred denoting "jotated" vowels with the help of two symbols like *i𝑦/iu* or *u* (with palatalization of the preceding consonant marked by a tail) for ю, *ia/ia* for я, *iă/iă* or *ie* for ѧ, and *ie/ie* for є. Conceivably, Kobyljans′kyj's system can be placed within the

---

8 For this paragraph, here and in all other examples excerpted from the Cyrillic-based translations made by Kobyljans′kyj (Luka-U, *Ioan*), in order to highlight their difference from the Latin-based translation, the original script is maintained.

confines of the "most radical phonetics" as propagated by Kuliš in the early 1880s for Ukrainian orthography (Barvins′kyj 2004, 201), in contrast to the orthography used in his translation of the Gospels in 1871.

In all other matters orthographic, Kobyljans′kyj remained very close to the etymological spelling. He offered a slightly modernized version that did not undergo substantial revision in subsequent publications of his translations, especially that of the Gospel according to John (*Ioan*, 1881). In the latter translation, Kobyljans′kyj's spelling proved more conservative as compared with his previous experimentation with different orthographic systems. On the one hand, he stopped short of using the tail below consonants to render both assimilative and positional palatalization (e.g., *свѧтыни* [loc.] "temple" or *житьє* "life" [*Ioan*, 11:56, 1:4]), keeping, however, the front *jer* (soft sign). Neither did he use any longer a breve to mark the narrow reflex of the etymological *o*, introducing instead a circumflex (used in some contemporary publications) for both its stressed and unstressed reflexes (e.g., *плôдъ* "fruit," *нôчȣ* [instr.] "night," and *ôдповѣли* [pl. pret.] "reply") (*Ioan*, 4:36, 7:50, 9:20). A similar reflex is marked in some analogous forms like *зôправды* "verily" (ibid., 3:5), with the *ô* from a preposition ending etymologically in a back *jer*. He dropped also a breve above *a* (*ă*), reintroducing instead the old Cyrillic letter ѧ, for instance, in the reflexive particle *сѧ* (*Ioan*, 1:3).

Unlike his 1874 publications of Luka-L and Luka-U, in the 1881 translation, Kobyljans′kyj began using the *jat′*, though at times he obviously struggled with his native dialectal phonetics (*з Галілеї* [Luka-U] = *z Galileï* "from Gal′-i-lee" [Luka-L, 2:4] next to *до Галілеѣ* and *до Галілеї* "to Gal′-i-lee" [*Ioan*, 1:44, 4:3]). Reflexes of the former *jat′* and similar sounds tended to be marked consistently by the *jat′*, as in the Polish borrowing *кобѣта* "woman" or dialectal forms of the type *горѣ* "upwards" and *долѣвъ* "downwards" (ibid., 4:25, 1:52). Generally, Kobyljans′kyj used the letter *jat′* in those cases where he previously employed the letter *i* or *ê*, with both reflecting narrow reflexes: *до міста* "unto a city," *на дворі* "outside" (loc.), *чоловік* "man," and *долів* "downwards" (Luka-U, 1:26, 10, 2:25, 51) as compared with *чоловѣкъ* "man," *хлѣбъ* "bread," and *долѣвъ* "downwards" (*Ioan*, 1:9, 44, 52). One comes, however, across the character *ê* instead of ѣ in words that might have been conceived of by Kobyljans′kyj as vernacular clichés undeserving of any *jat′*, whence *о нêмъ* (loc.) "about him" and *жêнко* (voc.) "wife," as well as the adjective *камêнныхъ* (gen.) "of stone" (ibid., 1:48, 2:5, 6) with an *ê* in place of the "new" *jat′*. Still, as if emphasizing the ecclesiastical significance of the translation, Kobyljans′kyj reinstated the front and back *jers* and *jery* (e.g., *близько* "close," *водовъ* [f. instr.] "water," and *котрый* "who" [ibid., 11:55, 1:26, 27]). Interestingly, Kuliš did not use these letters in the classical 1857–1862 period of *kulišivka* based entirely on the phonetic principle (Simovyč 1937; Danylenko 2012b).

Behind the ostentatiously religious façade of the Cyrillic-based edition of 1881, one encounters some representative dialectal features. Thus in addition to *ô* as in *радôсть* "joy" (*Ioan*, 3:29), the circumflex was placed by Kobyljans′kyj above *и* (*û*) and *ы* (*ŷ*), although exclusively in the prefix *вы̂-*. The former character was sounded as a high-mid front vowel reflex of *i* or *y* (see *AUM*, 2, map 22), which, in turn, might be of different origin (e.g., *роджені̂* [pl.] "born," *ôвцı̂* "sheep," *свої̂* [pl.] "my" [*Ioan*, 1:13, 2:25, 1:11], *божницı̂* [gen.] "synagogue" [ibid., 9:22] next to *ні̂* "no" [ibid., 1:21] as opposed to *межи* "among" [ibid., 1:14]). For instance, the form *ні̂* is a reflex of the old *нѣ* that in modern Ukrainian, including Kobyljans′kyj's native dialect, took over the function of the old *ни* "no" as opposed to "yes" (Shevelov 1979, 662–663). For this reason, *ні̂* (< *нѣ*) is also attested in negative pronouns like *ні̂хто* "nobody" (*Ioan*, 1:18). In the prefix *вы̂-*, however, one deals with a narrow reflex *i* (< *y*) as found in the Sjan and especially Hucul dialects (*AUM*, 2, map 18), which also know the *i*-reflex in place of the etymological *o* in newly closed syllables (Shevelov 1979, 666; Pan′kevyč 1938, 66, 74–75) (consider *ôдповѣвъ* [m. sg. pret.] "to reply," *жидôвска* [f.] "Jewish" [*Ioan*, 1:21, 2:13] alongside *вы̂старчитъ* [3 sg. fut.] "to be enough" with a dialectally representative ending *-тъ, вы̂знавъ* [m. sg. pret.] "to admit" [ibid., 1:20, 6:7], as compared with etymological spellings *ты* "you," *сынови* [dat.] "you" [ibid., 4:5, 4:19]).

Overall, in Kobyljans′kyj's phonetics, one can observe movement from the solid dialectal basis of the language of Luka-U and Luka-L of 1874 to the slightly moderate vernacular language of *Ioan* of 1881, with its orthography showing a bias toward the Church Slavonic tradition.

As far as Kuliš's translation of the New Testament of 1887 is concerned, a more balanced approach is evidenced in both orthography and phonetics (Danylenko 2010a, 2012b). First of all, Kuliš's orthography is void of almost all outdated Slavonic letters, with the exception of ę (а); thus, unlike Kobyljans′kyj's translation of 1881, it appears in this way more "democratic." If viewed from a broader perspective, Kuliš's spelling system looks more conservative as compared with the more democratic (phonetic) approach, applied by the translator in his poetic paraphrases of some biblical books in the 1860s. In the case of the 1868 protograph of the book of Job (*Yov*), there are, however, in the text numerous features that are shared with his translation of the New Testament. Among them, one can mention the use of *i* irrespective of its origin, as in *tilo* "body," *svij* "someone's own" (*Yov*, 19r, 7r) next to *vin* "he," *vsi* "all" (*NZ*, Lk 2:10, 21), the old letter ԑ rendering jotation of *e* at the beginning of a word and, in other environments, palatalization of the preceding consonant (e.g., *jedynyj* "common," *maješ* [2 sg. pres.] "to have" [*Yov*, 14v] next to *Jelyzaveta* "Elizabeth," and *vytannje* "greeting" [*NZ*, Lk 1:41]).

Although less phonetically ostentatious in comparison with the 1861–1862 *kulišivka*, Kuliš resorted in *Yov* to orthographic devices that did not make their way into his translation of the New Testament, for instance, rendering assimilative changes at the morpheme boundary like *boiccja* (3 sg. pres.) "to be afraid" and *podyvyssja* (2 sg. fut.) "to look" (*Yov*, 4r, 16r). Neither did such assimilation make its way into the orthography of Kobyljans′kyj's translation of 1874. In Kuliš's translation of the New Testament, one finds numerous features representing different dialect areas. To begin with the alternation *u-* : *v-* in congruence with the principles of euphony, this change is typical primarily of Southeast Ukrainian and literary Ukrainian as cultivated in Russian-ruled Ukraine in the second half of the nineteenth century (e.g., *y vves′ dim* "and [his] whole house" next to *povyhanęv usix* "he drove them all out" [*NZ*, Jn 4:53, 2:15]). Among western Ukrainian forms, deserving of attention is *neho* (gen.) "he" (ibid., Jn 3:3) (*без него* "without him" in Kobyljans′kyj [*Ioan*, 1:3]). Kuliš used both the form *vid*, which, according to Ivan Nečuj-Levyc′kyj, epitomized the spread of Galician defective norms in Dnieper Ukraine (Nečuj-Levic′kyj 1907, 19), and its Central Dnieper equivalent *od* "from." Overall, Kuliš would use dialectisms from different regions or choose primarily cross-dialectal forms (*kʹernyčyna* with the dialectal lowering of the *ir*-reflex as opposed to a parallel form widely spread in North and Southeast Ukrainian, *krynycja* "well" [*NZ*, Jn 4:6; *AUM*, 2, map 71]).

Kobyljansʹkyj's forms, in contrast, are largely of southwestern Ukrainian origin. In the morphology, it is worthwhile mentioning neuters of the type весѣлье "marriage," житье "life," and повстанье "resurrection" (*Ioan*, 1:4, 2:1, 5:29), also имнье next to an archaic-dialectal blending имнѧ (ibid., 1:12, 6; Kobyljansʹkyj 1928, 39). One should also mention a liberal use of active participles like стоѧчій и слухаючій "which standeth and heareth," маючій "that hath [the bride]" (*Ioan*, 3:29), with vernacular suffixes -ѧч- and -юч-, and оучинившій "he that made," and зказавшій "which said" (ibid., 5:11, 12), influenced by the local literary tradition. Of interest also are masculine and neuter dative forms ending in -*ovy*/-*evy* where *y* < *i*, such as голосови "voice," сынови "son" (ibid., 3:29, 5:22), and some other forms as compared with newer (southeastern Ukrainian) datives *synovi* and *otcevi* "father" in Kuliš (*NZ*, Jn 4:5, 21) where *i* < *ě* (Bevzenko et al. 1978, 95). Kuliš also employed neuters ending in -*(j)e*, partly influenced by the old literary tradition and therefore criticized by Nečuj-Levycʹkyj (Nečuj-Levicʹkyj 1907, 21–22) (e.g., *žyttje* "life" and *svidčennje* "record" [*NZ*, Jn 1:4, 19]). Most interesting is Kuliš's sporadic use of active participles. Thus, in chapter 1 of the Gospel according to John, Kuliš employed only four present active participle forms, pertaining directly to the narrative about Christ, though only one of them with a Church Slavonic suffix (i.e., *hręduščij* "[he] that comes" [*NZ*, Jn 1:15]). Past active participles are also scant. There are only two forms in the translation of chapter 1—*zlynuvšyj* "descending" and *poslavšyj* "[he] that sent" (*NZ*, Jn 1:32, 33).

While Kuliš was open to multidialectal borrowings with an eye to diversifying his language, Kobyljansʹkyj remained largely focused on obvious regionalisms, attested also more often than not in Šaškevyčʹs translation. Of interest are reduplicated demonstratives inherited from the Old Ukrainian period like *ocece* "this," *momo, omomo* "that" (*Ioan*, 1:19, 28, 2:16; Luka-U, 1:18, 20), and so on (Panʹkevyč 1938: 277–282; Bevzenko et al. 1978, 133). One should also mention the abundance of clitic forms of personal and demonstrative pronouns occurring sporadically in parallel use with the corresponding full forms (e.g., *каже му* next to *каже єму* "saith unto him" [*Ioan*, 1:44, 47] or *го питали* next to *питали его* "asked him" [ibid., 1:19, 21]). Another very representative regional feature is the use of numerous feminine instrumentals of the type *з нев* "with her," *неплоднов* "barren" (Luka-U, 1:58, 36), *лючбовъ* "number" (*Ioan*, 6:10), and other forms that were no exception in contemporary literary texts in Austro-Hungarian Ukraine (Macjuk 2001, 272–273).

Deserving of special attention are dialectal erstwhile perfect forms with auxiliary clitics (Pan´kevyč 1938, 313–314; Kobyljans´kyj 1928, 59–60) of the type *šukàlysmo* "[we] have sought," *šukàlyste* "ye sought" (Luka-L, 2:48, 49) next to *абы смо дали* "that we may give" (*Ioan*, 1:22), or *приобрілас* "has found" (Luka-U, 1:30) next to *не вірив іес* "thou believest not" (ibid., 1:20) and *с чув* "though hast been instructed," literally "you (have) heard" (ibid., 1:4). Kuliš tried to avoid such dialectal forms despite the fact that they were well attested in Middle Ukrainian (Bevzenko et al. 1978, 325–326), including the clitic reflexive particle, and even codified in contemporary regional grammars (Macjuk 2001, 304). Only sporadically did he resort to old perfects in order to archaicize Christ's or his disciples' language (e.g., *skazala jesy* "[Je´-sus said unto her] Thou hast [well] said" [*NZ*, Jn 4:17]).

Remarkably, in the syntax, there are no major differences between Kobyljans´kyj's and Kuliš's translations, with both largely leaning on archaic (Church Slavonic) patterns, although dialectal constructions do occur in Kobyljans´kyj (e.g., *вернÿли ж сіă тих сімдесіăт, з радостев* [Luka-U, 10:17], with the genitive subject of the Polish type, next to *i vernulys´ simdesjat´ nazad z radoščamy* "and the seventy returned again with joy" in Kuliš [*NZ*, Lk 10:17]). Thus, both translators used passive constructions where the agent-salient participant was marked by a preposition *vid* (*od*), denounced later, as was mentioned, by Nečuj-Levyc´kyj as Galician, or *čerez*. These prepositions were also commonplace in the translation of Šaškevyč: *ôдъ Бога родженû* (*Ioan*, 1:13) alongside *vid Boha rodylysę* (*NZ*, Jn 1:13) or syntactically synonymous *право було дане черезъ Мovсеѧ* (*Ioan*, 1:17) next to Kuliš's equivalent *zakon čerez Mojseę danyj buv* "[For] the law was given by Mo´-ses" (*NZ*, Jn 1:17).

I did not find in Kobyljans´kyj impersonal constructions with forms ending in -*no* and -*to* and the accusative direct object. Kuliš, however, employed them sporadically, although he could consider them too vernacular to be included in the lofty (biblical) narrative (e.g., *zaprošeno ž Ysusa, y učenykiv ioho* [*NZ*, Jn 2:2] as compared with запрошеный же бȣвъ Іисȣсъ и оученики его "and both Je´-sus was called, and his disciples" in Kobyljans´kyj's translation [*Ioan*, 2:2]). Unlike Kobyljans´kyj who, in relative clauses, liberally employed *kotrȳj* "which, who" in compliance with the Polish literary tradition, Kuliš resorted to native means. In his translation of chapter 1 of the Gospel according to John, Kuliš made use of the relativizer *ščo* "that, which" fourteen times and of *kotryj* only twice.

Vocabulary, to be sure, is most useful for the assessment of the linguistic programs of Kuliš and Kobyljans´kyj who, incidentally, knew each other, purportedly by correspondence, and seemed to share most Ukrainophile views.[9] To begin with, unlike Šaškevyč's translation (see Tymošyk 2000b), there is a paucity of Church Slavonicisms in Kobyljans´kyj's vocabulary. Leaving aside church terminology, one can adduce, in fact, just a handful of Church Slavonic forms: аминь "amen" (*Ioan*, 3:3; see *Biblija* 1862, 557v), paralleled by various vernacular derivatives like зôправды (*Ioan*, 5:19), на правду (ibid., 6:26), по правдѣ (ibid., 6:32), правдиво (ibid., 6:53), or the bookish equivalent истинно "verily" (ibid., 6:10), commonly attested in Kuliš; пустынѧ (ibid., 6:31; *Biblija* 1862, 556v), which is paralleled by пуща "desert" (*Ioan*, 1:23), most likely under Polish influence; єднородный "only begotten [Son]" (ibid., 3:16) as compared with its Church Slavonic equivalent единородный (*Biblija* 1862, 556v). One should add also personal and geographical names used, as a rule in their Church Slavonic forms, like Іоарданъ (Jor´-dan) and Іоанъ (John).

Kobyljans´kyj's translations are replete with vernacular and dialectal elements: всѧчино (n. sg.) "all" (*Ioan*, 1:3), ôдки "whence" and ôси "hence" (ibid., 1:49, 2:16), заки "before, til" (ibid., 5:7), борше "faster"

---

9   There is a unique piece of evidence of an interpersonal relationship between Kuliš and Kobyljans´kyj. In a letter of 9 May 1861 that was never mailed, Kuliš wrote to Kobyljans´kyj about his admiration for Jurij Fed´kovyč's poems published by Kobyljans´kyj in his *Slovo na slovo* (Kuliš 1899). Extolling Fed´kovyč's language as different from the *jazyčije* used by some Galician poets, Kuliš expressed pessimism about Kobyljans´kyj's Latin-based script. According to him, such a script was likely to scare off a potential readership in Dnieper Ukraine (ibid., 4).

(ibid., 6:21), *хороба* "disease" (ibid., 5:4), *голота* "[a great] multitude" (ibid., 6:2), *бесѣда* "words [of eternal life]" (ibid., 6:68; Luka-U, 2:50), *гармѣдеръ* "murmuring" (*Ioan*, 7:12), *варводѣти* "to murmur" (ibid., 6:52; see Žel., 1:56), *вадити сѧ* "to strive among themselves" (*Ioan*, 6:52; Žel., 1:53), *напудити сѧ* "to become afraid" (*Ioan*, 6:19), *хлопакъ* "lad" (ibid., 6:9), and the like. Polish borrowings are typically forms long appropriated into the local variety of Ukrainian such as *кревна* (Luka-U, 1:36) compared to *родичка* "cousin" in Kuliš (*NZ*, Lk 1:36), *моцар* (Luka-U, 1:52) compared to *потужний* "mighty" in Kuliš (*NZ*, Lk 1:52), *офіра* "sacrifice" (Luka-U, 2:24) compared to *жертва* "sacrifice" in Kuliš (*NZ*, Lk 2:24), *выкурованый* (*Ioan*, 5:10; see Žel., 1:77) compared to *сцілений* "cured" in Kuliš (*NZ*, Jn 5:10; see Hrinč., 1:725), *не въістарчитъ* (*Ioan*, 6:7) compared to *не стане* "it will not be sufficient" in Kuliš (*NZ*, Jn 6:7), *лу̑дка* (*Ioan*, 6:24) compared to *чoвен* "ship(ping)" in Kuliš (*NZ*, Jn 6:24), *королевство Боже* (*Ioan*, 3:3) compared to *царство Боже* "the Kingdom of God" in Kuliš (*NZ*, Jn 3:3), and finally *ufàv* (m. sg. pret.) (Luka-L, 11:22) compared to *вповав* "to trust" in Kuliš (*NZ*, Lk 11:22). This list of such pairs could be expanded. It becomes clear that Kuliš was loyal to the recommendation he had given to Puljuj, while working together on the translation of the Gospels. In most cases, "one had better resort to Church Slavonic rather than to Polish" since "the Old Bulgarian tradition, if there is no indigenous form, is more appropriate for Ukrainian" (Studyns′kyj 1930, xxvii, 9, 12).

In Kuliš's translation Church Slavonic forms intermingle with vernacular and explicitly regional elements. In contrast to Kobyljans′kyj (and Šaškevyč), such variegated elements, according to Kuliš, could serve as a verbal medium for uniting linguistically all Ukrainian speakers. It is useful to compare the following parallel excerpts from Kobyljans′kyj's and Kuliš's translations:[10]

---

10 Haluščynskyj (1925, 317) believed that Kobyljans′kyj's translations, influenced by German Protestantism, were made from the Greek original. Indeed, having obtained his theological education in Lviv and Černivci, Kobyljans′kyj served for several years as a preacher of "The Free German Religious Community" (Revakovyč 1910, 171). However, a cursory comparison of the translations made by Kobyljans′kyj and Kuliš prompts us to claim that the former author might have been intimately familiar with Kuliš's text. That comes as no surprise since Kobyljans′kyj designed his translations as a reply to Kuliš's translation of the New Testament of 1871.

Kobyljans´kyj's Translation

11. Каже ємȣ кобѣта: Пане, анû черпала немаєшъ, а стȣднᴀ є глȣбока; ôдки одже маешъ водȣ живȣ?

13. Ôдповѣвъ Іисȣсъ и каже ѣй пючій воды сеû єû прагнȣти бȣде зновъ.

15. Каже до него женщина: Пане, дай ми такоû воды, щобымъ не прагнȣла, анû не ходила сюды зачерати. (*Ioan*, 4)

Kuliš's Translation

11. Ка́же іому́ жі́нка: Добро́дію, и черпака́ не ма́єш, и коло́дазь глибо́кий; звідкіла ж маєш во́ду живу́?

13. Озва́всь Ису́с и рече́ ій: Всякий, хто пье во́ду сю забажа́є знов.

15. Ка́же до не́го жі́нка: Добро́дію, дай мени сіеї води́, щоб жа́ждувала, ані ходи́ла сюди́ че́рпати. (*NZ*, 4)

[11. The woman saith unto him, Sir, thou hast nothing to draw with, and the well is deep: from when then hast thou that living water?

13. Je´-sus answered and said unto her. Whosoever drinketh of this water shall thirst again

15. The woman saith unto him, Sir, give me this water, that I thirst not, neither come hither to draw.] (Jn 4:11–15)

Orthographic innovations aside, Kobyljans´kyj's language is riddled with regional forms like *кобѣта* and *женщина* "woman" along with *Пан* "Sir," *ôдки* "whence," and long naturalized Polish borrowings like *стȣднᴀ* "well" and *прагнȣти* "thirst" (Тymč., 2:209, 373), as well as the derivative *черпало* "scoop" with a dialectally productive suffix *-lo* (Verxratskyj 1899, 51) next to *зачерати* "to draw" (Žel., 1:281), the participial form *пючій* "drinking," influenced by both Polish and Church Slavonic, as well as the use of auxiliary clitics. Although vernacular at its core (*Ysus*), the excerpt from Kuliš contains an old aorist form *reče* (3 sg.) that was unfairly chastised by Franko (1910, 176). Moreover, Kuliš makes use of the western Ukrainian form *žažduvaty* "to quench one's thirst" (Žel., 1:216). The innovative use of the obsolete aorist form *rečé*, with the ultimate stress in the present tense meaning "says," was not incidental. Kuliš utilized Church Slavonicisms in order to emphasize, if needed contextually, the lofty style of the biblical narrative. To name just a few such forms, the following are quite representative from the morphophonological and lexical points of view: *blahodat'* "grace" (*NZ*, Jn 1:14), *hręduščij* "[he] that cometh" (ibid., 1:15), *jesy* "[thou] art" (ibid., 1:19), *hlaholaty* "to say" (ibid., 1:15), a nominal form, *nedostojen* (m. sg.) "not worthy" (ibid., 1:27), and the like. Statistically, such forms are not numerous, hardly exceeding fourteen percent (Tymošyk 2000a, 244). What is important, however, is not their number but their fusion with other elements in the make-up of the translation. In this respect, Kuliš's language is a true aggregate of various elements, including the aforementioned "Galician" *vid* "from" or *neho* "him," Church Slavonicisms like *voskresnuty* "to rise" (*NZ*, Mk 16:9), Russianisms of the type *trepet* "trembling" (ibid., 16:8; Hrinč., 2:791) and *bolest'* "disease" (*NZ*, Jn 5:4), Polonisms like *zmahannje* "question" (ibid., Jn 3:25; see Shevelov 1966, 138) (see *superečka* in Kobyljans'kyj [*Ioan*, 3:25]), and, finally, vernacular forms of primarily southeastern Ukrainian provenance like *barytysję* "to tarry" (*NZ*, Lk 1:21) as opposed to a western Ukrainian parallel form *(за)бавити ся* in Kobyljans'kyj (Luka-U, 1:21; see Tymč., 1:39, 43).

TO "SECULARIZE" OR "SYNTHESIZE"?

Overall, Kobyljans'kyj's translations marked a new round in the formation of a local variety of literary language aimed at bridging the rift between the educated clergy and common parishioners in Galicia, Transcarpathia, and Bukovyna. All things considered, his literary output can be juxtaposed with Šaškevyč's translation, which was largely premised on Church Slavonic literary norms and open already to vernacular and especially dialectal elements (Horbač 1988, 47). In his intention to explicate and enlighten in an intelligible manner, Kobyljans'kyj seemed to follow the same regional literary tradition cultivated already in the eighteenth-century Basilian monastery of Počajiv. The major quantitative difference lay in his introduction of a plethora of dialectal and non-native forms into the ecclesiastical text. This is why, despite an apparent minimum of Church Slavonicisms, Kobyljans'kyj's language can be placed within the same functional spectrum and, accordingly, conceived as a kind of "secular" Church Slavonic or *Church Slavonic-turned-vernacular*, and his translation of the Gospels as the first Ukrainian dialectal translation (Nimčuk 2001, 383). Clearly, there was a radical difference between Kobyljans′kyj's language and the language program of the creators of the Peresopnycja Gospel (1556–1561), Archimandrite Hryhorij and his amanuensis Myxajlo Vasylijevyč, who tried to combine Church Slavonic with the *prostaja mova* (Ruthenian) rather than with the local vulgar tongue (Danylenko 2008b, 59).

In contrast with Kobyljans′kyj and his predecessors, Kuliš opted for a *diametrically opposite* approach. Based on the southeastern Ukrainian vernacular as opposed to the Russian recension of Church Slavonic introduced by the Russian synod decrees in the 1720s, Kuliš strove for a synthesis of the intrinsically low-style vernacular with elements picked from other territorial and functional registers, including Church Slavonic, Russian, Polish, and Galician expressions. It is not, therefore, surprising that while working on the translation of the New Testament with Puljuj, Kuliš was routinely consulting the Church Slavonic, Russian, Polish, Serbian, German, Latin, English, and French versions of the Holy Scriptures (Studyns′kyj 1930, xxviii–xxix).

All in all, in his translation of the Gospels, Kuliš managed to introduce a new biblical style and, by extension, demonstrate the advantages of his vista of new literary Ukrainian. His vista differed not only from the program of the Galician Russophiles and populists, including Kobyljans′kyj, but also from those literati in Russian-ruled Ukraine who also translated the Gospels. The point is that Oleksander Navroc′kyj, Volodymyr Aleksandrov, Myxajlo Lobodovs′kyj (Loboda), and Pylyp Moračevs′kyj all propagated a kind of "homestead ethnographism" as the basis for a new language standard. Premised on the populist tenets of new literary Ukrainian, Kuliš managed, nevertheless, to work out a balanced use of vernacular and bookish, although not necessarily Church Slavonic, elements in the translation of the Holy Gospels. Although statistically underrepresented, Church Slavonicisms tend to occur in practically every verse of Kuliš's translation, thus creating a stylistically marked (elevated) atmosphere for the holy narrative. Yet his programmatic position never did become dominated by the Church Slavonic literary tradition, appropriated by the Greek Catholic clergy in Galicia, Transcarpathia, and Bukovyna as early as the eighteenth century.

CHAPTER 4

Here Comes the Bible!

THE HOLY WRIT DOESN'T BURN

Kuliš worked intermittently on the translation of the Holy Scriptures from the late 1860s until 1897. In the fall of 1872, Kuliš completed the translation of the entire Bible, including some of the Apocrypha that were not included in the first edition of 1903, sponsored by the British and Foreign Bible Society, or in the subsequent reprintings of 1908, 1909, 1912, and 1920 (Studyns′kyj 1930, lxx). The process of the publication of the 1903 Bible was rather convoluted. Given the year 1903 as the date of publication by the British and Foreign Bible Society, the Old Testament, bound together in one volume with the New Testament, actually appeared early in 1904. In a letter of 30 December 1903, Puljuj happily informed Kuliš's widow, Oleksandra Bilozers′ka-Kuliš (known by the literary pseudonym Hanna Barvinok), that the Holy Writ of the Old Testament was ready for printing (Zelens′ka 2001, 341). As late as 15 January 1904, he wrote to her that "the New Testament is in press, and the entire Bible is forthcoming" (ibid., 343).

Regrettably, all later efforts made by Kuliš's friends and family members to promote the Ukrainian Bible in tsarist Russia were to no avail. The Most Holy Governing Synod, which grudgingly permitted publication of Moračevs′kyj's translation of the New Testament, forbade outright both publication and dissemination of Kuliš's translation in the Russian Empire. As a last resort, in 1905, Hanna Barvinok sent a letter to the Russian empress, asking for special permission and arguing that in Russia the Bible was already available in forty languages (see Batalden 2013). The Holy Synod ultimately declined the widow's request (Studyns′kyj 1930, lxx).

As early as 1872, Kuliš intended to publish the Bible in Naumburg, Germany, where the printing costs were comparatively low. Though he changed his plan and postponed the publication project, supposedly due to family issues and financial problems, it is more likely that his enthusiasm was dampened by the negative reviews of his earlier translations with Puljuj, which had appeared by that time in the Austro-Hungarian Empire. Consequently, in 1873, he abandoned his work on the translation of the Bible and concentrated instead on researching the Cossack period in Ukrainian history (Naxlik 2007, 2:273–274). According to rumor, all this may have lead Kuliš to burn the complete text of his translation of the Holy Writ in the fireplace. According to other testimonies, the text of his translation, along with the bulk of his books, manuscripts, and vast correspondence, might have perished in the fire on his *xutir* Matronivka on 6 November 1885 (Šenrok 1901 75 (10), 21, 34; Dorošenko 1918, 202). The fire could have been set by some local peasants allegedly harassed by Kuliš (Kyryljuk 1929b, 35).

However, as evidenced by the pertinent documents, the whole story was much more nuanced and complicated (Naxlik 2006, 238–246). Kuliš's *xutir* might have been burnt down by a certain Apolinarij Zalens'kij (Załęski), a Pole from Minsk and a leaseholder, who, after a series of lawsuits, and perhaps in conspiracy with the local judge, decided to take revenge on Kuliš, his landlord (Studyns'kyj 1930, 74–75). In his letters to Oleksander Konys'kyj (1836–1900) and Myxajlo Balašenko, Kuliš, however, acknowledged that "not the *ljax* burnt down [the house] but our own people" (Naxlik 2006, 245, fn. 67). Yet shortly before his death, in a letter to Myxajlo Pavlyk, Kuliš again accused his leaseholder of the arson (Voznjak 1928a, 238).

Whoever the real culprit was, the chance that Kuliš burnt his translation of the Bible does not appear less than the chance that it was destroyed in the arson. Some testimonies and hints scattered in various letters from and to Kuliš seem to corroborate this theory. For instance, apart from the disclosure of his secret in a letter of 1878 to Puljuj (Studyns'kyj 1930, lxiv), Kuliš changed his story in 1895 in a letter to Myxajlo Drahomanov, justifying the alleged destruction of the manuscript by disillusionment and disappointment in his compatriots who failed to understand his work. Yet more revealing is Kuliš's explanation found in letters addressed to Oleksij

Biloborodov (Oleksa Tyxyj). As Kuliš wrote in February 1896, he was very upset by the changes introduced by Puljuj, "in the Rusian spirit" (*rusyns'kyj lad*) of their joint translation of the New Testament. These changes purportedly made him destroy, in a fit of self-deprecation and, especially, anger at his "aide" (*pidpomaha*), his translation of the Old Testament. He hastened, however, to add that his had been a correct decision inasmuch as "over the last twenty years biblical studies in France, Germany, and England have thrown light on many murky questions in the Holy Writ" (Kuliš to Biloborodov, 89). Most likely, Kuliš referred in this case to the four Gospels that appeared in Ukrainian in 1871 in Vienna. Interestingly, as early as 29 May 1871,[1] he entreated Puljuj not to publish, in the future, anything "like chapter XIV of [the epistle of] Paul the Apostle: it looks like mine, though the language is different" (Studyns'kyj 1930, 275).

There is, however, a more reliable argument to be found in a draft of *Pjat' knyh Mosejëvyx* (The Five Books of Moses, 1895), held today at the Myxajlo Kocjubyns'kyj Literary-Memorial Museum in Černihiv, Ukraine. On one of the pages of the manuscript, Kuliš jotted down the following remorseful comment:

> I wish I had not burnt my old translation: perhaps, there is a word [used] in it that I do not recall [now]. It was not worthwhile getting angry with my compatriots. (*Mosej, Biblija*, 7r; Zelens'ka 2000, 355)

After the fire of November 1885, Kuliš and his wife lived in a shack nearby, plowing and sowing the field like common farmers. As late as 1888, he was still ashamed and afraid of hosting his friends and colleagues in this shack. Thus, in a letter of 1 May 1888, sent to his old friend Stepan Nis from "the farmstead Hannÿna Pustyn' that had previously been Motronovka," Kuliš expressed his happiness to see him at his place. He was nevertheless dismayed by the dire straits in which he had been living with his wife since

---

1 Based on the contents of this letter, Naxlik (2007, 2:275) surmised that it might have been written, in fact, between 1872 and 1874. This correction does not change the essence of Kuliš's accusation. Though accepting a limited number of Galician borrowings in his original works and numerous translations, he seemed to be ever opposed to the introduction of a large number of Galician borrowings, which might bring an influx of Polish expressions into his new Ukrainian literary language.

the memorable fire (Kuliš to Nos, 12). There was literally no place to put a cot for a guest. Notwithstanding all the severe trials, Kuliš did not fall into despondency and despair and found time for writing and re-translating, in particular, parts of his latest adaptation of the Bible (either burnt by Kuliš himself or having perished in the fire). Recreating some minor works from memory, Kuliš began, in fact, to translate the Old Testament from scratch and only his death in 1897 brought this herculean work to a stop.

Only a fraction of Kuliš's translation of the Bible came off the press during his life. It was Myxajlo Pavlyk, a close confident of Myxajlo Drahomanov and an editor of the radical periodicals *Narod* and *Xliborob* (Lozyns´kyj 1917), who played a significant role in disseminating the scriptures translated into Ukrainian by Kuliš in the early 1890s. Having acquainted himself with Pavlyk through correspondence in 1892, Kuliš began cooperating with the aforementioned journals based in Kolomyja. In December 1892, Kuliš published in two installments in *Narod* an open letter to the editor, "P. Kuliš pro svoju spravu z Poljakamy" (P. Kuliš about His Affair with the Poles). In the first installment, he described, in detail, his conflict with the Galicians in 1882, provoked largely by his controversial pamphlet *Krašanka rusynam i poljakam na Velykden´ 1882 roku* (An Easter Egg for the Rusyns and the Poles for Easter 1882). In the second installment, Kuliš outlined a new vision of the current state of the Polish-Ukrainian relationship. As was typical of Kuliš, this was a highly polemical letter. Pavlyk wrote in the editor's preface to the publication that Kuliš's letter "blew like a severe cold wind," purifying "a stifling air" that amassed over time in Ukrainian history (Voznjak 1928a, 180). Giving credit to Kuliš as a patriarch of Ukrainophilism in the two parts of Ukraine, Pavlyk tried, although to no avail, to persuade Kuliš to write his memoirs (ibid., 173, 177–178).

Obviously, Kuliš laid his own plans.

TOBIT AND JOB

In July 1893, Kuliš sent Pavlyk his *Tovytovi slovesa* (The Book of Tobit), asking him to print three hundred copies of this work "in renowned Kolomyja on cheap paper" (Voznjak 1928a, 208, 227). Pavlyk highly praised *Tovytovi slovesa*, which, according to him, was "translated wonderfully." It came out anonymously in the same year (Kyryljuk 1929a, 56). Kuliš was more than happy with the publisher, who seemed to be sincerely interested in his literary work. As early as 1896, inspired by recent success, Kuliš finished another translation, *Holosin′nja j Pis′nja Pisen′* (Lamentations and the Song of Songs [the Song of Solomon]), and was ready to dispatch it to Pavlyk, but, due to unknown reasons, changed his mind and concentrated instead on another collection of his translations entitled *Pozyčena kobza* (The Borrowed Kobza). This collection, which ultimately appeared in the year of his death (Studyns′kyj 1930, lxiv), proved no less successful than his translation(s) and poetic adaptations of the Holy Scriptures. Suffice it to say that the collection contained translations of sixty-three poems by Friedrich Schiller, Johann Wolfgang von Goethe, Heinrich Heine, and Lord Byron that even today ring with poetic beauty (Luckyj 1988, 181).

Still, it is difficult now to prove that Kuliš abandoned his initial publication plan because of his work on the aforementioned collection. This would seem strange since almost all his translations, furnished with brief prefaces in the spirit of the famous Protestant biblical scholar Eduard Reuß (1804–1891), were meticulously crafted for eventual publication already in 1896. Kuliš even wrote calligraphically on the title page of each of the manuscripts "printed in Lviv in the year 1896 under the supervision of Myxajlo Pavlyk" (Zelens′ka 2000, 356–359). One of the possible explanations for the change in his creative plans is that Kuliš became by that time more preoccupied with the idea of propagating his socio-cultural views on the history of Ukraine. His intensive research work in this field might have distracted him from the magisterial translation of the Holy Scriptures, which required much time and assiduousness.

One only regrets that Kuliš shelved his plan to translate the whole Bible in verse, including the book of Job that had been first paraphrased and published as early as 1869 (*Yov*; *Yov, Pravda*; *Yov*, 1869). Unfortunately, after the writer's death, most of his poetic paraphrases of the Bible fell into oblivion. Yet it would be extremely profitable to know how his adaptation of the biblical books into a poetic framework, if published in the year 1896, could have influenced subsequent translations of the Bible into

Ukrainian, including the free paraphrases made later by Ivan Ohijenko and Ivan Xomenko-Pljuta (Naxlik 2007, 2:283).

A relatively small work, *Tovytovi slovesa* was the only biblical book published by Pavlyk during the life of Kuliš. Since it was a translation of one of the Apocrypha, it was not included in the 1903 Ukrainian edition of the Bible by the British and Foreign Bible Society, although this translation was reprinted in 1909 in the *Prosvita* collection of Kuliš's works (*Tovyt*). Conceptually and linguistically, *Tovytovi slovesa* could be juxtaposed with Kuliš's early translations of the biblical stories. This is why, envisioned as a paraphrase, this work demonstrated remarkable consistency in the vernacularizing principle as applied by the author in his poetic translations and paraphrases. In fact, this Ukrainian-language version of the book of Tobit was not a mere continuation of Kuliš's early paraphrases but rather a new stage in the vernacular interpretation of the Holy Writ driven by the writer's keen interest in the elaboration of a new biblical style of literary Ukrainian. What is also obvious is that all the vernacularizing efforts invested by Kuliš in his translation of the book of Tobit proved fully in harmony with the fictional and historical narrative of this and other biblical books. What was more important for the rendering of this biblical story was that the book of Tobit, related to key events in Jewish history, was a sample of popular Judaism in the third or early second century BC. Not surprisingly, it made respectful mention of the Law of Moses, but invoked it loosely with reference to traditional custom (Collins 2005, 39). In other words, it would be strange for Kuliš to apply in this case the principle of archaization in order to render a rather popular narrative of the Jewish story of Tobit.

The poetic framework of the "Ukrainian Tobit" (*Tovyt*) looks unusual. Prepared in the late 1890s, its versification was somewhat different from other poetic translations of the Holy Scriptures made by Kuliš some twenty years earlier. Unlike his translations of the book of Psalms (1871), with various syllabic-tonic patterns, and the book of Job (*Yov, Pravda* and *Yov,* 1869), with iambic pentameter, Kuliš used the popular *kolomyjka* syllabic structure throughout the entire text of *Tovytovi slovesa*. This folk structure consisted in Kuliš's versification of two variously rhyming lines with a set fourteen-syllable meter. To give a random example, one can cite the following two pairs of rhyming lines in the opening of chapter 6:

Тогді годі Ганна плакать, по сину тужити.
А ті в двох дойшли до річки, стали ноги мити.
Тигром річка прозивалась. Глянуть—пливле риба.
Уловили, спекли рибу, сїли пообідать. (*Tovyt*, 348)

In terms of genre attribution, the above excerpt appears at variance with the English translation in the King James Version, although the outer narrative frame remains the same, with the exception of some smaller details:

5.22. Then she made an end of weeping.
6.1. And as they went on their journey, they came in the evening to the river Tigris, and they lodged there.
6.2. And when the young man went down to wash himself, a fish leaped out of the river, and would have devoured him. (*Apocrypha*, 30)

Kuliš's translation of the book of Tobit is not the result of a mere vernacularization of the holy biblical story. Linguistically, this is an example of a new, synthetic, vernacular-based idiom with a number of contextual archaisms, including both native and Church Slavonic elements. For this reason, perhaps, Kuliš identified the language of his translation with *staroruščyna* (Old Rusian), thus projecting the inception of this language into the Old Rusian period in the history of Ukrainian, characterized by a *diglottic* distribution of local vernacular and Church Slavonic (Uspenskij 2002, 386–388). That said, it is worthwhile to examine the most representative traits of Kuliš's language in this translation.

In the domain of orthography (phonetics), where excessive regionalization or archaization would be out of place, Kuliš did not introduce any overtly deviant forms. Among "standardized" sounds one can cite, for instance, the alien *f* never rendered by the counter-etymological x^w that is characteristic of Moračevs'kyj's language. Only sporadically does one happen upon dialectal forms that were not commonly used in written language at that time in both parts of Ukraine. To name one of these rare forms, Kuliš rendered dissimilation in the two-consonantal cluster *čn* > *šn*, which historically affected individual words (e.g., *bidolašnyj* "poor, pitiful" and *neobašnyj* "heedless" [*Tovyt*, 345]) that might have reflected his native (northern Ukrainian) dialect (see Shevelov 1979, 491; Žovtobrjux et al. 1979, 218). Among other possible northern Ukrainian features, apheresis seems to be most representative in this translation. However, more often than not, Kuliš resorted to this phonetic device in order to maintain syllabic structures in the versification: *'ddaty* "to give back," *'dvernet'-sja* (3 sg. non-past) "to turn around," *'biznanyj jesy* (2 sg.) "to be familiar," *do 'cja-nen'ky* "to the parents" (*Tovyt*, 345, 346, 347, 350). There are also some features that can be viewed as both archaic and dialectal (e.g., the Old Rusian substitution of *e* for Church Slavonic *ě* in *rekly* [pl. pret.] "to say" [*Tovyt*, 344, 349] and *sedity* "to sit" [ibid., 343]; see also *žona* "wife," with a reflex of the etymological *e* after a palatal, next to a "neutral" *žena* or folkloric *podružžja* [ibid., 350, 346]). Of interest here is a morphonological variant of the dialectal preposition *id* used with the dative case (Nimčuk 1969, 74), which is discussed below.

In the field of morphology, the long (non-contracted) forms, typical of folkloric texts, were barely employed by Kuliš. A rare example is found in *bohy čužiji* "alien gods" (*Tovyt*, 341) next to *visty dobri, ljubi* (pl.) "kind, nice news" (ibid., 353). Diminutives like *dolen'ka* "fate" (ibid., 346) occur sporadically. In stylistically marked environments, for instance, in reference to the Law of Moses and some other settings, Kuliš made use of an obsolete perfect form in 2 sg. such as *xovav jesy* "to bury" and *ustav jesy* "to stand up" (ibid., 355). The future is rendered commonly with the help of an analytic form like *žyt' budeš* (2 sg. fut.) "to live" (ibid., 345). Future tense forms of the type *maty-meš* (2 sg. fut.) "to have" are particularly rare in this poetic translation, especially as compared with the prose translation of the Holy Bible prepared jointly by Kuliš and Puljuj, where the synthetic future prevails. As a true (northern Ukrainian) dialectal form, one should note 2 pl. imperatives ending in *-te* of the type *žyvite* "live!," *xvalïte* "praise!," and *obernites'* "turn around!" next to a rare *čynit'* "make!" (ibid., 356). In accordance with the western Ukrainian tradition, Kuliš makes use of present active participles, although morphonologically disguised as Church Slavonicisms through suffixes ending in *-šč-*, such as *vydjuščyj* "able to see," *jaduščyj-pyjuščyj* "the one who eats and drinks," and *alčuščyj* "wishing" (ibid., 356, 342) next to a rare *slipujučy* (m. sg.) "blind" (ibid., 354) derived, tentatively, from *slipuvaty* "to be blind, shortsighted" (Hrinč., 2:662) as used in Kuliš's 1869 paraphrase of the book of Job (*Yov, Pravda*, 66). The participial form did not make its way into the translation of the book of Tobit by accident. Yet it occurs in Kuliš's letters, for instance in the expression *Ukrajina, s'lipujuča kalika* "Ukraine, a blind invalid" (Voznjak 1928a, 91), with the dynamic meaning of "blindness" rather than the static meaning of the corresponding adjective *slipa* (f.) "blind."

With regard to *s'lipujučy* (m. sg.) "blind" and similar dialectal forms like *staren'ki* (m. sg.) "old" (*Tovyt*, 352) with a dropped syllable-final *j*, it is interesting to note that they were introduced in accord with the views of Ivan Nečuj-Levyc'kyj. The latter consistently used forms of the type *merši* "faster," *dali* "further," and *na kruti hori* (loc. sg.) "on a steep hill," all without a syllable-final *j* (Jefremov 1918, 163). At the same time he castigated "new" spellings like *meršij, na krutij hori* as Galician forms (Nečuj-Levyc'kyj 1968, 455). He argued that the forms without *j* were commonly attested in vast territories, in particular, in Right-Bank Ukraine, in Bukovyna, in some Galician territories, and in Central Ukraine, except for the Černihiv region, as well as in Sloboda Ukraine (Jefremov 1918, 163–164).

However, the authority of Kuliš in this case proved decisive. In a letter of 29 May 1907 to Myxajlo Lobodovs'kyj (Loboda), Nečuj-Levyc'kyj (1968, 471) wrote that Kuliš had explicitly advised him to write like they were speaking in the southern Kyiv region, that is, in the Kaniv, Čerkasy, and Čyhyryn districts due to the lack of any obvious Great Russian or Polish elements in the local dialects. Clearly, the loss of the syllable-final *j* was to be taken as one of those Ukrainian features proper, although Kuliš himself was seemingly reluctant to introduce it into his translation of Tobit.

Interestingly, Nečuj-Levyc'kyj enumerated in his letter the changes that are known to have taken place by stages in the loss of the syllable-final *j* (Nečuj-Levic'kyj 1907, 22; Matvijas 2007b, 37). To begin with, the emergence of the comparative form of adjectives without *j* might have occurred after the change of *ě* to *i* in South Ukrainian as early as the late fourteenth century. North Ukrainian could not share this change because *ě* did not evolve into *i* at that time (Shevelov 1979, 745–747). Dialects, which had more forms of the comparative originally ending in -*ěj*, might have had a larger repertoire of such forms without *j* (e.g., *xutči* "faster") in the late nineteenth and early twentieth centuries. As far as the ending of the dative-locative feminine in adjectives (*na kruti hori* "on a steep hill") is concerned, the loss of *j* became possible after the change of *o* into *i*, that is, after the mid-seventeenth century. In tune with Nečuj-Levyc´kyj's observations, this stage affected the southern Kyiv, Lubny (Lubni), Dniester, Bukovyna, Hucul, and Bojkian dialects, while North Ukrainian did not share the loss of *j*, with the exception of some transitional dialects.

In sum, the loss of the syllable-final *j* in the language of Nečuj-Levyc´kyj and Kuliš might have been triggered by the same, transitional status of their native dialects. Yet, unlike Nečuj-Levyc´kyj's orientation toward his native dialectal system, transitional, roughly, from Southwest to Northeast Ukrainian, Kuliš would resort to forms without *j* only sporadically, while experimenting with them as particular stylistic devices.

As regards possible archaization, there are not so many Church Slavonicisms or other obsolete (Old or Middle Ukrainian) forms in the translation. They all occur primarily in elevated, "spiritual" contexts typical, for instance, of address formulae. Suffice it to cite such clichés with short adjectival forms in the nominal predicate as *praveden jesy* "[O Lord,] thou are just" or *blahosloven jesy* "blessed are thou [O Lord my God]" (*Tovyt*, 344, 345; *Apocrypha*, 12, 16). Morphological Church Slavonicisms are represented, for instance, by such prefixed verbal forms as *nyzvodyty* "to lead down," *nyzposlaty* "to bring down," and *voznosyty* "to bring up" (*Tovyt*, 356; *Apocrypha*, 62). One can add here also preterits like *rekly* (pl.) "to say" (*Tovyt*, 344, 349, 345) and present tense forms of the verb "to be" like *jesy* (2 sg.) (*Tovyt*, 346). Among other archaic or archaizing forms are neuters with the assimilated *j* as in *blahosloven´nje* "blessing" and *xvalen´nje* "praise" (ibid., 346, 357). The use of the desinence -*e*, criticized by Nečuj-Levyc´kyj (Jefremov 1918, 160), is influenced in such nouns by the northern and southwestern literary tradition (see Bevzenko et al. 1978, 87–88). In the text, there is also a limited number of non-pleophonic forms of the type *vrah* "enemy" (*Tovyt*, 358) and *zlato* next to *zoloto* (ibid., 342, 356). Traditional Church Slavonic derivational patterns are also attested, for instance, in the use of the agentive suffix -*tel´* in *vozviščatel´* "herald, messenger" (ibid., 351).

The archaizing tendency is also observed in the vocabulary of *Tovyt*. For example, consider the following forms: *nyščyj* next to *ubohyj* "poor, destitute" (*Tovyt*, 346), *oven* "sheep" (ibid., 350), *slovesa* "words" (ibid., 351), *terzaty* "to torment" (ibid., 342), *hrjade* (3 sg. pres.) "to come" (ibid., 354), *jazyki* "peoples" (ibid., 346), *brašno* "food" (ibid., 350; see Tymč., 138), and also "lay" archaic forms like *pyr*, as opposed to the Middle Polish borrowing *benket* "banquet" (*Tovyt*, 351, 354; Danylenko 2006c, 322).

True to his linguistic practice, Kuliš employed in *Tovytovi slovesa* some of the neologisms that he had coined in his earlier translations of the Holy Scriptures. In particular, he employs the former aorist *reče* (3 sg. pres.) "to say," used in the present tense (*Tovyt*, 345, etc.); *jasuvaty* "to explain, speak for" (ibid., 342); *vidradošči* "delight, comfort" (ibid., 355) in place of *vidrada* or *vidrad(n)ist'* (Hrinč., 1:268); and, finally, *pravycja*, modeled on ChSl. *desnycja* "right arm," both of which are attested in his translation of Tobit (*Tovyt*, 346, 354).

In short, the list of vernacular elements and Church Slavonicisms employed may be expanded. All this, however, does not substantially change the linguistic make-up of this translation. Certain details aside, Kuliš chose for the translation the same type of language that he had elaborated in the late 1860s: a literary standard premised on moderate vernacularization with the use of comparatively few Church Slavonic and other archaic elements that did not infringe on the vernacular texture of the biblical narrative.

At first sight, a similar picture appears in a translation of the same biblical book made in 1881 by a Xarkovite poet, Volodymyr Aleksandrov, who intended to translate the whole Bible into a plain local vernacular comprehensible to all Ukrainians living in both Galicia and Dnieper Ukraine. According to Aleksandrov, his had to be an exemplary language that could compete with the language of Kuliš and Puljuj, elaborating at that same time a new stylistic means for written Ukrainian, particularly in its high stylistic register. In the preface to his translation, *Knyha Tovytova, na malorus'ku movu pereložena s" tekstu hreces'koho* (The Book of Tobit, Translated from the Greek Text into Little Russian), Aleksandrov decided not to dwell on the intricacies of his "plain Little Russian." Instead, he merely emphasized that his language had to be so standardized as to exceed, at least, that of the medieval Latin recension of this apocryphal book (*Knyha Tovyta*).

The overall impression of Aleksandrov's translation is its clear-cut vernacular basis, riddled sporadically with Church Slavonicisms that do not play a substantial role in the biblical narrative of the text. At first sight, at least in its programmatic tenets, Alexandrov's language tends to look similar to that of Kuliš. Yet on closer inspection, one can discern major differences between the two.

To begin with lexical make-up, Aleksandrov asserts his authority as a normalizer of the local vernacular based not only on Southeast Ukrainian but also on the older (Polissian) literary tradition (Danylenko 2008b). Taking just a few lexemes, they all look dialectally homogeneous, although they do happen to be attested cross-dialectally: *odsaxnutysja* "to recoil" (*Knyha Tovyta*, 1; Žel., 1:102), *krad′koma* "stealthily" (ibid., 4; also in Taras Ševčenko, Marko Vovčok, Hrinč., 1:833), *posobyty* "to assist" (*Knyha Tovyta*, 7), a possible Russianism (1x in Kotljarevs′kyj, *Enejida*, Index, 138) next to a homophonous West Slavic borrowing in Ivan Vahylevyč (Žel., 2:716), *barytysja* "to linger" (*Knyha Tovyta*, 17; also in Amvrosij Metlyns′kyj, Žel., 1:13; Hrinč., 1:72), *mennja* "name" (*Knyha Tovyta*, 11; Hrinč., 1:953), *skupatys′* "to take a bath" (*Knyha Tovyta*, 20; Hrinč., 2:656–657), and *majdan* "square, place" (*Knyha Tovyta*, 6), attested cross-dialectally (e.g., Lysenko, 120; Homer and Pot., 8:5, 7:44). Finally, one should mention the form *vp″jat′* (*Knyha Tovyta*, preface, 7) that occurs thirteen times in Ivan Kotljarevs′kyj's *Enejida* (*Enejida*, Index, 116) and nine times in the works of Hryhorij Kvitka-Osnov'janenko (Kvitka, 2:338). Remarkably, this form happens to be attested in the language of Klymentij Zinovijiv († ca. 1717) and Ivan Nekraševyč († ca. 1796), both speakers of North Ukrainian (Danylenko 2006c, 318, 2008b).

As evidenced from the autograph held today in the manuscript repository at the T. H. Ševčenko Institute of Ukrainian Literature of the National Academy of Sciences of Ukraine, Aleksandrov was assiduously brushing up on his language. He was searching, in particular, for the most fitting vernacular lexemes and dropping obvious Russianisms or Russian Church Slavonicisms. Thus, he substituted *skarbivnyčyj* for *kaznačej* (*Knyha

Tovyta, 5), which was likely to look too "Muscovite" at that time (see *Moskovs'ka kazna* in Kuliš [*ČR*, 185]). In another place, Aleksandrov dropped *jazÿčeskij* for the benefit of *pohans'kyj* "pagan," while enclosing in brackets an optional version, *busurmens'kyj* "Muslim, pagan" (*Knyha Tovyta*, 3; Tymč., 87). Some emendations were primarily stylistic and hardly influenced by purist criteria (e.g., *domovyna* "coffin, grave" used instead of *peklo* "hell" in the expression *zvesty v" domovynu* "to bring down to the grave" [*Knyha Tovyta*, 10]). Though randomly and uncertainly, the translator introduced a few neologisms like *rukopys'mo* "epistle" (ibid., 17).

The morphosyntax of Aleksandrov's language is largely based on Southeast Ukrainian. To take some examples in the noun morphology, the translator consistently used the dative case ending *-ovi/-evi* with masculine animates of the type *xazjainovi* "master," *najmytovi* "laborer," *panotcevi* and *bat'kovi* "father," *sÿnovi* "son," and *bohovi* "God" (*Knyha Tovyta*, 8, 15, 17, 19). He also sporadically employed locative forms like *na očix"* "in the eyes" and *po ljudix"* "[to work as a farm hand] at somebody's place" (ibid., 7; Bevzenko et al. 1978, 110–111). One should mention the use of neuters like *prorokuvannja* "prophecy" and *bohomillja* "pilgrimage" (*Knyha Tovyta*, 6, 19). Another salient feature is the occurrence of 3 sg. non-past tense forms of Class 3 and 4 verbs like *pam"jata* "to remember," *robe* "to do," and *posÿla* "to dispatch" (ibid., 6, 13, 15).

Yet distinctive in Aleksandrov's translation is his frequent use of constructions ending in *-no* and *-to* with the accusative direct object. What is more remarkable about this syntactic pattern is that, despite the general tendency in the works of eastern Ukrainian writers (Shevelov 1969, 182–183), he never made use of the auxiliary "to be" to refer to the future or the past. Moreover, the translator preferred the old agentive phrase with the "Galician" preposition *vid*, not *od* (e.g., *y šukano vid" carja tix" y ne znaxožuvano* "and the tsar has ordered to search for them and they have not been found" [*Knyha Tovyta*, 4]) where *vid" carja* denotes the source of an action rather than its performer (Danylenko 2006c, 232–233).

The following common examples of this construction are worth citing: *y rozhrabovano vsju moju xudobu* "and all my cattle have been stolen" (*Knyha Tovyta*, 5), *y mini oddano žinku* "and my wife has been returned to me" (ibid.), *nahotovleno bahato strav"* "many dishes have been prepared" (ibid., 6) with a noun phrase in the place of the direct object (Danylenko 2003a, 265), *odnoho z" našoho rodu zadušeno y kynuto na majdani* "one of our kinsmen has been strangled and thrown into the square" (*Knyha Tovyta*, 6), and *nas" roskydano* "one has dispersed us" (ibid., 9).

The question that arises here is this: why did Aleksandrov make use of a typical impersonal structure proper specifically to West Ukrainian, that is, without the use of any auxiliary? Was his predilection instigated by Polish fashion channeled through Galician literary texts that could sound lofty in this type of translation made in Sloboda Ukraine? One can hardly find a persuasive explanation for this, although the tinge of exoticism could have played its role in the translator's choice. Tentatively, however, since we deal here with the basically descriptive character of biblical narrative, I venture to assume that Aleksandrov found this western Ukrainian impersonal syntactic pattern most suitable for the recital of subsequent events. This construction was also likely to furnish the text with a kind of moderate loftiness of style.

In general, unlike Kuliš's paraphrase, Alexandrov's translation was characterized by a high degree of vernacularization achieved at the cost of eliminating older layers of morphonological and especially lexical elements in his written language. What is more remarkable is the fact that the dialectal basis of Alexandrov's language looks more homogeneous, consisting primarily of southeastern Ukrainian forms.

Four years earlier, although with a somewhat different religious and linguistic message in mind, Aleksandrov had also translated the book of Job. Entitled *Knyha Iova na Malorus'ku movu pereložena* ... (The Book of Job, Translated into Little Russian), the final draft was completed in 1877. Yet, after having taken private lessons in Hebrew for two years, Aleksandrov revised the text in accordance with the Hebrew original in 1879 (*Iov*, Preface). What is particularly interesting about Aleksandrov's autograph is that he copied it using the so-called Orthodox "Half-Ustav," a handwriting that looked much like print. The translator's primary concern at that time seemed to be with developing and recovering an appropriate relationship between the older East Slavic literary tradition and the new vernacular-based one. For that reason, perhaps, the language of this translation is much more anchored in Church Slavonic than its

Great Russian recension, although the Ukrainian vernacular element seems to prevail in the linguistic make-up. The combination of the two aforementioned components in Aleksandrov's translation looks particularly awkward in light of Kuliš's 1869 poetic paraphrase of the book (*Yov; Yov, Pravda*). Since the two translations are so different, it would be useful to compare their languages and thereby illuminate possible dissimilarities in the linguistic programs of the two normalizers of written Ukrainian.

To begin with phonetic phenomena, deserving of attention are numerous shifts in the alternation *o, e : i* typical of Aleksandrov's language. Although sporadically (but more frequently than Kuliš), Aleksandrov used forms without such alternations, which were provoked by several factors such as morphological leveling and the influence of the corresponding Polish and, especially, Russian lexemes (Varčenko 1954, 57–58). To name just a few typical forms with the alternation suppressed, most likely due to Russian interference, there are *premudrost'* "wisdom" with a characteristic Church Slavonic prefix, *spokojnyj* "quiet," *robotnyk"* "worker," *spor"* "argument," *veselost'* "merriment," and even the native *pevnost'* "confidence" (*Iov*, 1, 5, 13, 13v, 23, 25v). These are contrasted to the alternation pattern in local vernacular forms such as *rozlehlïst'* "spaciousness," *tverdïst'* "firmness," and especially such (Russian) Church Slavonic lexemes as *prespidnę* "inferno, abyss" and *posmišešče* "mockery" (ibid., 22, 26, 27) (see also *prespodnycja* and *posmixovyšče* [Hrinč., 2:368, 408] and RChSl. *pos'mišyšče* [Žel., 2:716]). In his translation of 1869, Kuliš showed consistency in using more regular forms, later integrated into literary Ukrainian, like *vysokist'* "height" and *preyspodnja* "inferno," although *premudrist'* does appear next to *premudrost'* on the same page (*Yov*, 1869, 16, 24) (see also *nepravdyvost'* "falsity" [ibid., 10] next to *yz"ęn"* "deficiency" in Aleksandrov's translation [*Iov*, 7]). In this respect, one should also cite the form *bezvidnyj* "arid" in Kuliš (*Yov*, 1869, 18), noted by Jevhen Želexivs'kyj (Žel., 1:16) and Borys Hrinčenko (Hrinč., 1:80), and attested cross-dialectally (e.g., in Hucul and southeastern Ukrainian dialects [Shevelov 1979, 725]). Remarkably, one finds this form also in Panas Myrnyj's autographs (Hrycenko 2007, 24).

However, of particular interest is the fluctuation *š ~ s* found in consonant clusters with *k*, as represented in at least two lexemes: *škelę* "cliff" and *škarb* "treasure" (*Iov*, 5v, 22v, 27v) next to the more regular *skelja* and *skarb* (Hrinč., 2:1009). Although particularly frequent in West Ukrainian, purportedly under the influence of West Slavic, the above switch in series is expressive and results from an affective factor in the rise of the (East) Slavic *š* from *s* (Shevelov 1979, 737, 740). Due to the limited scope of this change in literary Ukrainian, although this phenomenon is attested in some Central Dnieper dialects (Matvijas 2007b, 35), one of the readers of Aleksandrov's autograph deemed it necessary to emend the form *škarb* to *skarb*. Assimilation in place of articulation is poorly represented in Aleksandrov's language, especially in comparison with that of Kuliš, who tried to render all possible types of assimilation across morpheme and word boundaries. Leaving aside the spelling of *ščytaty* "to consider" (*Iov*, 29), Aleksandrov tried to eschew in most cases marking the assimilation of obstruents, whence *sčastę* "happiness" and *sčeznuty* "to disappear" (ibid., 30v, 31v). Surprisingly, Kuliš did not render in his spelling such assimilations as *ščezaty*, from *is-čezaty* "to disappear" (Shevelov 1979, 485). He employed instead another form *počeznuty* (*Yov*, 1869, 11; also *Psal'ma* 1), cited by Želexivs'kyj in Tymko Padura's writings (Žel., 2:1062). It is noteworthy that Aleksandrov used another form, *pozčeznut'* (*Iov*, 7v).

Overall, Kuliš proved to be one of the most versatile normalizers of Ukrainian orthography. For instance, he consistently rendered all kinds of assimilation, especially in morpheme boundary. His translation of the book of Job is permeated with forms like 3 sg. pres. *boiccja* "to be afraid" and 2 sg. non-past *podyvyssja* "to look" (*Yov*, 1869, 4, 16), at variance with the historical spelling of such verbal forms as found in Aleksandrov (2 sg. pres. *xovaešsę* "to hide" and 2 sg. non-past *posmiješsę* "to laugh" [*Iov*, 8v]). One can add here *s popelu* "from the ashes" (*Yov*, 1869, 11), with the neutralization of voicing in the original *iz* (in the environment before the voiceless consonant) after its coalescence with *sъ*. The form *s popelu* can be opposed to *zperšu* "at first" in Aleksandrov's translation (*Iov*, 12v) where *z-* is a voiced reflex of the preposition *sъ* (in the environment before the voiceless consonant) in compliance with a phonemic protensity system as postulated for the bulk of the eastern Ukrainian dialects (Danylenko 2006c, 189–190).

As far as morphology is concerned, Aleksandrov demonstrated a strong predilection for southeastern Ukrainian features, which are also found in the scriptural translations of Oleksander Navroc´kyj and Panas Myrnyj (Hrycenko 2007, 28). For instance, Aleksandrov tended to drop almost regularly the ending *-t´* in 3 sg. present tense forms of modern second conjugation verbs (e.g., *hovore* "to speak," *love* "to catch"; see also contracted forms of first conjugation verbs like *spasa* "to save," *umyra* "to die," and many others [*Iov*, 22, 23, 8, 8v], typically attested in Southeast Ukraine and elsewhere [see Vaščenko 1957, 222–225; Matvijas 2006, 63]). As in Kuliš's work (*Yov*, 1869, 5, 8, 12, 19) and most of the southeastern Ukrainian dialects (*AUM*, 2, map 235, 3, part 3, map 40), Aleksandrov lavishly used the non-alternating type *prosju* (1 sg. pres.) "to ask" and *zaprymitju* (1 sg. pres.) "to note" (*Iov*, 10v, 14), whence secondary (analogical) infinitives with palatalized stem consonants like *ouprosjuvaty* "to implore," *zaxvatjuvaty* "to seize," and the like (ibid., 29v, 31; Žylko 1966, 255). As parallel forms, Aleksandrov made use of synthetic and analytic future tense forms like *ljakatymut´* (3 pl. fut.) "to scare" and *xodyty bude* (3 sg. fut.) "to walk" (*Iov*, 27v, 28) respectively, although he seemed to prefer the synthetic form, a tendency also discerned in Kuliš.

In nominal morphology, Aleksandrov's language showed regular local features that were, in part, also paralleled in Kuliš's writings of that period. To name just a few of Aleksandrov's features, there is the dative case ending *-ovi/-evi* for masculine animates of the type *bohovi* "God" and *čolovikovi* "man," as well as the locative ending in *-ovi/-evi* (e.g., *v˝ praxovi* "in the dust" [*Iov*, 8, 11, 26, 27, 32]), and in *-ix* from *-ěxъ*, like *v˝ ïx˝ očix˝* "in their eyes" and *v˝ hrudïx˝* "in the breast" (ibid., 29, 30), the neuters ending in *-(j)a* like *xotinnę* "wish" and *dўxannę* "breath" (ibid., 9v, 26v), and so forth.

With regard to morphosyntax, both Aleksandrov and Kuliš conspicuously avoided using archaic constructions, although they demonstrated minor differences in the use of relative clauses. For this type of subordination, Aleksandrov preferred using the inflecting relativizer *kot(o)ryj* "which, that," which in the socio-linguistic situation of Sloboda Ukraine might have been encouraged by the Rus. *kotorўj* (Danylenko 2003a, 188–194, 2014a, 188–194). The "true relative subordination [in Ukrainian]," according to Oleksander Potebnja, was only sporadically rendered with the help of a native device, that is, the absolutive relativizer *ščo* "that" (e.g., *Iov*, 31). In this respect, Kuliš was clearly more oriented toward native morphosyntactic patterns. For that reason, he might have retained the older distributive meaning of the conjunction *kot(o)ryj* as found in the expression *kotore z nas* "which one among us?" (*Yov*, 1869, 15). At any rate, use of the inflecting relativizer *kot(o)ryj* is conspicuously less common in Kuliš's paraphrase than in Aleksandrov's translation, embellished as the latter is with a number of Russian Church Slavonicisms.

Interestingly enough, both Aleksandrov and Kuliš liberally employed impersonal constructions with the accusative direct object and the predicate form ending in *-no* and *-to*. What seems to distinguish them, in this particular case, is that Aleksandrov, unlike in his later translation of the book of Tobit as discussed above, would introduce in this type of construction an auxiliary referring either to the past or future (e.g., *otdano bulo zemlju* "the land has been given [to them]" [*Iov*, 24]). It is tempting to posit for this particular case influence from the Russian parallel passive construction, wherein an auxiliary designates either the past or future (Rus. *zemlja bÿla otdana* "the land was given [to them]"). In general, Kuliš seemed to follow in this case the Polish impersonal model, using no auxiliary (e.g., *ix byto* "they have been beaten" [*Yov*, 1869, 11]), with the referential context of the whole paragraph based on anteriority.

Among some unusual constructions, one can cite the independent accusative of time as projected by Popov (1881, 105–110) onto Slavic material in particular and discussed subsequently by Tymčenko (1928, 3) for the Ukrainian dialects and folklore. Remarkably, in some parallel places, both Kuliš and Aleksandrov used the same independent accusative of time, but with a characteristic morphological difference: *sim den' i sim nočej* in Kuliš (*Yov*, 1869, 7) next to *sim" den' y sim" nič"* "seven days and seven nights" in Aleksandrov (*Iov*, 4v, Job 2:13). While keeping the old genitive plural form of the noun *den'*, Kuliš resorted to the innovative form *nočej* with the desinence *-ej* as attested in most Ukrainian dialects and in contrast to the variant *-yj* typical of Southwest Ukrainian (Kernyc'kyj 1967, 95–96; Shevelov 1979, 279–280).[2] Aleksandrov

---

2 It would be out of place to discuss here the origin of these two desinences. I will limit myself to noting the fact that the vacillation in Ukrainian between the inherited desinence *-yj* and the innovative desinence *-ej* is commonly regarded as a matter of dialectal preference (Shevelov 1979, 279–280; Bevzenko et al. 1978, 105). Flier (1987), however, claimed that the emergence of the latter ending was motivated by the shape of the 3rd

resorted, in this case, to a zero ending, *nič"* (gen. pl.), influenced most likely by the appearance of such an ending in the masculine accusative of time in folkloric texts (Bevzenko et al. 1978, 105) (e.g., *sïm den'* "seven days," *sïm rik* and *sïm hod* "seven years" [Tymčenko 1928, 3]).

Yet what stands out most in Aleksandrov's language is its vocabulary. A cursory comparison of Aleksandrov's lexemes with their counterparts in Kuliš's paraphrase reveals significant differences between the two translations.

The following pairs (Alexandrov ~ Kuliš) are deserving of particular attention: *xlopci* (*Iov*, 2v) ~ *raby* "servants" (*Yov*, 1869, 5, Job 1:16), *kriposnÿj* "serf" (*Iov*, 5v) ~ *rab* "slave" (*Yov*, 1869, 8), *robotnyky* "laborers" (*Iov*, 1) ~ *čeljad'* "household" (*Yov*, 1869, 3, Job 1:3), *vïstovÿj* (*Iov*, 2) ~ *vistjanec'* "messenger" (*Yov*, 1869, 4, Job 1:4), *benket* (*Iov*, 1) ~ *obid* "feast" (*Yov*, 1869, 3, Job 1:4), *xoromÿ* (*Iov*, 5v) ~ *svitlyci* "houses" (*Yov*, 1869, 8, Job 3:15), *mučytel'* (*Iov*, 10v) ~ *rozbyšaka* "tormentor" (*Yov*, 1869, 15), *šater"* (*Iov*, 9) ~ *namet* "tabernacle" (*Yov*, 1869, 13, Job 5:24), *vsederžytel'* (*Iov*, 12v, 32, 35v) ~ *vsevyšnij* "The Almighty" (*Yov*, 1869, 11, Job 8:5), *veselost'* (*Iov*, 5) ~ *radošči* "joy" (*Iov*, 7), and, finally, the awkward *ščenęta vid" l'vyci* (*Iov*, 7) ~ *levčuk* and *levenja* "young lion" (*Yov*, 1869, 10). The latter two lexemes are well-known diminutive innovations of Kuliš, which are attested in both Borys Hrinčenko's (Hrinč., 1:886) and Jevhen Želexivs'kyj's (Žel., 1:399) dictionaries.

It is clear that Aleksandrov had a different vision of literary Ukrainian as compared with the language program of Kuliš. For greater comprehension of the biblical narrative, the Xarkovite author tried to base his stylistic language variance on the old East Slavic tradition that, in matters ecclesiastical, had by that time been largely supplanted by the Russian recension of Church Slavonic and, in matters secular, by literary Russian. Introducing vernacular elements could hardly help Alexandrov to "Ukrainianize" his text since their number had to be minimal in order to achieve the stylistic register appropriate, according to the author, for the lofty narration. For this reason, regional vernacular elements like *xlopotá* "vanity" (*Iov*, 24v, Job 15:31) were

---

declension loc. pl. *-ex*, the dat. pl. *-em*, and some other morphophonemic factors. Analogy was also purportedly at play, according to Žovtobrjux et al. (1979, 190), although projected onto the period before the loss of *jers*. Remarkably, Kuliš did not use the older (southwestern) Ukrainian desinence *-yj*, which might have sounded too regional to his ear.

likely to completely undermine the authority of the high style as initially envisaged by Alexandrov (consider *Vïn″ veštaetsę ousjudў za šmatkom″ xliba* "He wandereth abroad for bread" [*Iov*, 24, Job 15:23]). Despite all his efforts and literary talent, Aleksandrov did not manage to create what, as early as 1877, was conceived of as a language comprehensible for all Ukrainians, rather than a mere regional dialect (Studyns´kyj 1930, xxxix).

Remaining southeastern Ukrainian at its core, Kuliš's language was nevertheless comprised of variegated dialectal elements and loan forms that could turn its chaotic state to its advantage by encompassing more dialects and literary traditions (e.g., Russianisms *sud'ba* "fate," *grjaz'* "dirt" [*Yov*, 1869, 7, 8], the Polonism *potuha* "power," Church Slavonicisms *oblyk* "face" and *hlaholat'* [ibid., 6, 7, 8] compared to *homonity* "speak" in Aleksandrov [*Iov*, 25]). In addition to neologisms (e.g., *pryvyddja* and *pryvydky* "apparition" [*Yov*, 1869, 72, 16]), Kuliš glossed himself aptly in an idiomatic medium that, in general, was difficult for Aleksandrov to replicate (e.g., *xiba revut' voly, jak jasla povni?* [ibid., 13] as compared with Aleksandrov's *čy reve bўk″ pry svoïm″ pijlï?* "loweth the ox over his fodder?" [*Iov*, 9v, Job 6:5]).

As a result, Kuliš's discursive strategies proved more virtuoso than Aleksandrov's translation of the book of Job. Interestingly enough, this translation was completed in 1877, the same year Aleksandrov declared in a letter to Puljuj his plan to create a new high style capable of eclipsing Kuliš's literary standard.

AT THE CROSSROADS OF POETRY AND PROSE

In the early 1890s, Kuliš was still translating the Holy Scriptures, although the whole process differed from his early experience in translating the biblical texts. It should be recalled that his initial intention, as shaped in the late 1860s, was to create a vernacular translation of the Bible, thus making it more comprehensible for the common people. Yet this plan underwent substantial changes in the early 1890s. After the manuscript of his first translation of the Old Testament had perished in a fire on 6 November 1885, the writer settled down to translate it for the second time—from scratch! In a letter of 24 April 1895 to Oleksij Biloborodov, Kuliš clearly stated that, after the Old Testament, he would prefer to return to the translation of the New Testament because the language of his first translation had been largely distorted by his co-translator, Puljuj, in a Galician direction (Kuliš to Biloborodov, 89).

A new translation of the Old Testament was a twofold process. Kuliš began to work simultaneously on a prose translation (with poetic elements) and a poetic (versified) one. In a letter of 4 January 1895 to Stepan Nis, Kuliš confided in his friend that he had begun a new translation of the Bible "in place of that which burnt till the end of the Apocalypse," thus greeting him "from verse 21 in chapter 19 of Exodus" (Kuliš to Nos, 28). In this project, he was striving to translate "what was prose, in prose, [and] what was poetic, in verse" inasmuch as "a good quarter of the Old Testament was written in verse without rhyme" (Kuliš to Biloborodov, 89). As early as 10 October 1895, Kuliš claimed to have reached chapter 15 of the first book of Moses, while on 19 October, he purportedly completed the translation of twenty-four full chapters of, to use his words, "the versified Bible" (Voznjak 1928a, 230, 231). This was a totally new type of poetic paraphrase that was not, alas, completed, due to Kuliš's untimely death in 1897. In general, he managed to translate (exclusively in verse) the first book of Moses and the first four chapters of the second book of Moses (Zelens′ka 2000, 361; *UB*).

While working on "the versified Bible," Kuliš embarked on a prose translation of the Holy Scriptures with an eye to offering it subsequently to the British and Foreign Bible Society. In late December 1894, Kuliš wrote in a letter to Myxajlo Pavlyk that he had been busy lately working on "a prose [Ukrainian] Bible" and had already completed the first book of Moses. In order to receive feedback from specialists and regular readers, he asked Pavlyk to publish, as a start, one hundred copies of this translation (Voznjak 1928a, 213). A year later, in a cable to Stepan Nis, Kuliš confirmed his intention to publish the translation in small installments and in small numbers of copies, not more than one hundred pamphlets (Kuliš to Nos, 28–29). According to Kuliš, who was ready to change the order of the books in the Bible, as had been proposed by some scholars, it would be most natural to publish the poetic adaptations first, then follow with prose translations, inasmuch as "our language would not show its principle in prose as much as in verse" (Kuliš to Biloborodov, 91).

Due to unknown reasons, this publication project was not carried out. This, however, did not discourage Kuliš. In 1896, his perseverance seemed to have been rewarded by a complete new translation of the Bible, as one can glean from the writer's letter to Vasyl′ Bilozers′kyj (1825–1899). And indeed, as early as 6 August 1896, the Old Testament was translated both in prose and verse (Naxlik 2007, 2:278). Earlier, he had even inquired whether Jevhen Tymčenko could find for him a person to copy his translation of the Old Testament—not the poetic one, but sort of "our Oxford revised version" (Kuliš to Tymčenko, 101).

Overall, by April 1895, Kuliš had translated the bulk of the canonical and some of the deuterocanonical books, both in prose and verse, depending on the original as interpreted by Emil Friedrich Kautzsch (1841–1910) and his students, as well as the "poetics" of the individual biblical books. The following books were translated: Pentateuch (*Pjatoknyžže*), Joshua (*Iosuja Nunenko*), Judges (*Sud′di*), Samuel (*Samuel′*), Kings (*Cari*), Isaiah (*Iesaja*), Jeremiah (*Ieremija*), Ezekiel (*Ezekyjel′*), Hosea (*Hoseja*), Joel (*Ioel′*), Amos (*Amos*), Obadiah (*Obadyja*), Jonah (*Ioana*), Nahum (*Nahum*), Habakkuk (*Habakuka*), Haggai (*Hakhkheja*), Zechariah (*Zaxaryja*), Malachi (*Malejaxyj*), and, partially, Job (*Hýob*) (Kuliš to Biloborodov, 89; Zelens′ka 2000).

Kuliš was inclined to group the books in the spirit of some Protestant scholars, putting poetic translations first and, thus, reflecting the ancient layer of Hebrew poetry followed by prose translations. At its core, however, this division, as found in various contemporary translations, is blurred. The several variations of what counts as a poetic line form and what reads as prose demonstrates the uncertainty of scholarly opinion in this matter. Before going into the details of Kuliš's vision of poetry and prose in the Bible, it is expedient to cite the opinion of some biblical scholars (Kugel 1981, 302; Gillingham 1994, 19) that there are in fact no clear-cut distinctions between prose and poetry in Hebrew. As a matter of fact, between the eighth and tenth centuries, the Masoretes copied the ancient Hebrew texts (giving them their pointing, vocalization, and stress) with seemingly little regard for any consistent division of poetry and prose. Psalms, Proverbs, Song of Songs, Job, Lamentations, and some of the twelve minor prophets are presented in their entirety in poetic form. On the other hand, there is no specific literary category called "Poetic Books"; rather, the threefold division is that of Law, Prophets, and Writings.

Generally, a similar approach, without the rigid dichotomy of prose and poetry, was successfully applied in biblical scholarship and in particular by Eduard Reuß (1804–1891), whose division of the biblical books was into History, Prophets, Law, Chronicles, Hebrew Poetry, Religious and Moral Philosophy, and Political and Polemical Literature. His grouping of the books of the Bible, however, may look different from the "poetic" order elaborated by Kuliš in his translations of both the canonical and deuterocanonical books of the Bible (Zelens´ka 2000). Here it is helpful to include a chart that summarizes Reuß's "analytic" chronology and Kuliš's "poetic" order of the books in the Bible.

Reuß's "Analytic" Order	Kuliš's "Poetic" Order
Judges, 1 and 2 Samuel, 1 and 2 Kings	Psalter
Prophets	Lamentations, Song of Solomon
Pentateuch and Joshua	
1 and 2 Chronicles, Ezra, and Nehemiah	Job
	Proverbs
Psalms, Lamentations, Song of Solomon	Wisdom of Jesus Son of Sirach
	Amos, Hosea
Job, Proverbs, Ecclesiastes, Wisdom of Jesus Son of Sirach, Wisdom of Solomon, Jonah, Tobit, Susanna, Baruch, Prayer of Manasseh	Isaiah
	Micah, Zephaniah, Nahum, Habakkuk
	Jeremiah
Ruth, 1 and 2 Maccabees, Daniel, Esther, Judith, 3 Maccabees, Bel and the Dragon, Jeremiah	Ezekiel
	Prophet (unknown)
	Haggai, Zechariah, Obadiah

The grouping chosen by Kuliš is hardly corroborated in biblical studies. His is a classification intuitively construed by a poet, not a biblical scholar. Not surprisingly, Kuliš placed at the top of the list the book of Psalms that, in effect, represents as complex a genre as Hebrew poetry:

> The first part will be the Psalter, though not that one that has long ago been published, but the Psalter that is now being translated in the high light of German biblical scholarship. The second part will be again lyrics, that is, the Lamentations ascribed to Jeremiah and the Song of Songs, and the third part will be the book of Job, newly translated (so not the one

published in 1869), and then all that is versified in the Bible, and finally, prose books. (Zelens′ka 2000, 355)

Each psalm is a self-sufficient unit with a meaning not controlled by an editor's narrative commentary (Gillingham 1994, 189). As a highly creative individual, Kuliš was charmed by the spontaneity and responsiveness of Hebrew poetry to life. Using clear poetic conventions, in terms of form as well as style, the early poets—the psalmists included—were not constrained by the conventions that Kuliš himself maintained in his poetic writings.

One should bear in mind that there is, however, a handful of psalms (e.g., Psalms 87, 106, 103, and 136) where the dividing line between prose and poetry is not clearly delineated, so that they could be read as continuous prose (Gillingham 1994, 191). One can put up with the above special cases in the poetry of the Psalms. Yet, as has been mentioned above, it is practically impossible to find poetic books outside the Psalter, though the texts of Proverbs, Song, Job, and Lamentations are highly poetic as compared with the rest of the canonical and deuterocanonical books (Kugel 1981, 292–304). One can speak rather about poetry outside the book of Psalms, thus suggesting poetic pockets within such biblical categories as Law, Prophets, and Writings.

Viewed in hindsight, Kuliš's grouping might have been influenced by the contemporary classification of the discrete poetic books (*die poetischen Bücher*), comprised of Psalms, Lamentations, Song, Proverbs, and Job (Reuß; Kautzsch 1902). The Ukrainian writer intuitively transcended this traditional (analytic) theory by expanding the list of discrete poetic books. This is why Kuliš's grouping may be tentatively taken as a poetic/prose continuum of biblical categories, with the book of Psalms and the book of Obadiah situated on the opposite poles.

One wonders into what kind of poetic creation Kuliš's versified Bible could have ultimately transformed, had he finished his project.

IVAN NEČUJ-LEVYC′KYJ TAKES IT PERSONALLY

Unfortunately, in 1897 the death of Kuliš brought a halt to his work on the two different translations of the Holy Bible. Despite a severed relationship with Kuliš, Puljuj came to rescue the "more practical" (in his view) project after the death of his old friend. In continuation of their long cooperation with the British and Foreign Bible Society, Puljuj persuaded Henry Millard (a son of Edward Millard who had negotiated the publication of the New Testament after 1885) to buy the copyright on the prose translation of the Old Testament (Zelens′ka 2001, 317–318). On 31 July 1901, the representative of the British and Foreign Bible Society signed a publication contract notwithstanding the fact that the translation had not yet been completed in its entirety (Studyns′kyj 1930, lxv). The Bible Society promised to pay Kuliš's widow, Hanna Barvinok, 5,000 gulden, as well as a corresponding amount to Nečuj-Levyc′kyj, who, by that time, had finished translating the book of Ruth. Additionally, as Puljuj wrote to Hanna Barvinok on 7 May 1901, he had translated the bulk of the deuterocanonical books, to wit, 2 and 3 Esdras, Tobit, Judith, Wisdom of Solomon, Ecclesiastes, the epistle of Jeremiah, Baruch, and 1, 2, and 3 Maccabees. Unfortunately, as Puljuj added, the translation of these Apocrypha could not be bought by the British and Foreign Bible Society; moreover, they had not been approved by the Holy Synod either (Zelens′ka 2001, 317).

As Puljuj wrote in his autobiography, the manuscript of the whole Bible had not been edited and was not yet ready for publication since "there were in the text many omitted words and entire verses, there were also other shortcomings and drawbacks in the translation itself, and neither was the orthography uniform" (Studyns′kyj 1930, lxv). In a letter of 23 May 1902 to Kuliš's widow, Puljuj tried to reassure her that he had not changed the contents of her late husband's translation (Zelens′ka 2001, 338–339). However, he had to take on the revision of the whole text, while comparing it with other translations of the Bible in order to correct possible stylistic and factual shortcomings. Among them, he complained of missing sections and some murky places in the text. Puljuj cited several passages from a draft of Kuliš's translation, which, to his mind, warranted correction, in particular an excerpt from Numbers (4:15, 16) where he rightly suggested some changes:

Kuliš's Draft Translation of 1896

15. ... Се вагота про Кейатенків у *громадянському наметі*.

16. Догляд же Элейазарів Агароненка, жерьця, *олія*, про сьвітильник та кадильні пахощі и дари-приноси повсячасьні и помазальня-мастильня *олій*: та наглядати-ме и над усїм виталищем и що есьть у сьвятилищі й посуді-знарядді її. (*Mosej*, 315)

Puljuj's Emendations of 1902

15. ... Се ті речі із *громадянського намету*, що їх синове Кегата нести мають.

16. Єлеазар же син Арона священника матиме догляд над *олією* для сьвітильника, та над кадильними пахощами, та над повсякчасною жертвою хлїбною, та над миром і матиме догляд над усїм, що є в нїй, надсвятинею, як і над посудиною її. (Zelens'ka 2001, 338)

Almost all of the proposed corrections were retained in the final edition of the Bible that came out in 1903. There was, however, another change introduced into the revised version of the translation—the expression *hromadjans'kyj namet* was replaced by the more contextually appropriate *sobornyj namet* "the tabernacle of the congregation."

Much earlier, in the 1869 paraphrase, Kuliš tried to archaize this term without changing the vernacular texture of his work. If compared with his formulation of 1869, the version from 1903 looks more stylistically neutral, though oriented toward contemporary Galician literary practice as a result of Puljuj's intervention into the fabric of Kuliš's original translation:

Kuliš's Translation of 1869

15. ... Се буде тягар синїв Каатових у *скинї сьвідчення*.

16. А на послугу Єлеазара, сина жерця Орона, впадає *олива* на сьвітло, та пахуще кадило, та щоденна ідома жертва, та помазувальня *олива*, та догляд *скинї* и всього, що в їй, у святницї, и в надобах іі. (*Pentatevx*, 110)

Ukrainian Bible of 1903

15. Се ті із *соборного намет*у, що синове Кегата нести мають.

16. Елеазар же, син Арона сьвященника, мати ме догляд над *олією* для сьвітильника та над кадильними пахощами, та над повсякчасною жертвою хлїбною, та над *миром*, та догляд над усїєю *храминою* і над усїм, що є в нїй, над сьвятинею як і над посудиною її. (*SP*, 133)

[15. ... These things are the burden of the sons of Ko´-hath in the tabernacle of the congregation.

16. And to the office of El-e-a´-zar the son of Aa´-ron the priest pertaineth the oil for the light, and the sweet incense, and the daily meat offering, and the anointing oil, and the oversight of all the tabernacle, and of all that therein is, in the sanctuary, and in the vessels thereof.] (Num 4)

Instead of *namet*, Kuliš employed in this excerpt *skynja* (*svidčennja*) "tabernacle" as a possible version of *skynija* "tent" (Žel., 2:872). Unlike the draft translation and the wording proposed by Puljuj, Kuliš used in his *Pentatevx* (Pentateuch) the lexeme *olyva* "oil" commonly used in Southwest Ukrainian (Žel., 2:567; *EDU*, 4:181) as early as the sixteenth century. At that time, the Latin-Italian term *olyva* was borrowed to refer to the olive oil in parallel to the Old Rusian lexeme *maslyna* (Nimčuk 1992, 261). In the Ukrainian-Latin dictionary of Arsenij Korec´kyj-Satanovs´kyj and Jepifanij Slavynec´kyj, one happens on the following glosses: *maslyna drevo oliva* and *maslyčnyj olivarius* (Kor. and Slav., 113). Clearly, the lexeme *olyva*, used by Kuliš, might look obsolete in late nineteenth-century language when compared with *olija* "oil"— found, incidentally, in his prose translation of the Bible.

Obviously, Puljuj was doing his best to eliminate all possible shortcomings, including mere *lapsus calami* such as *I koly vmre mrec´ pry jomu*, literally, "and when the deceased dies by him" (Zelens´ka 2001, 338). Puljuj could not stop short of complaining of the excessive use of Church Slavonicisms in the translation of his friend, implying such forms as *az* "I," *slovesa* "words," and *hlaholymo* (1 pl. pres.) "to speak." Nevertheless, as Puljuj concluded, the situation with the manuscript was very precarious since he was making numerous emendations and even translating some paragraphs over from scratch (ibid., 339). Despite all the above, in order to meet the deadline as specified in the contract Puljuj deemed it necessary to ask Borys Hrinčenko (1863–1910) (together with his wife, Marija) for assistance. He also enlisted Ivan Nečuj-Levyc´kyj, a literary patriarch well-known in both Dnieper Ukraine and Galicia, and Oleksij Sljusarčuk, a long-time acquaintance of Puljuj's who was ultimately assigned the proofreading of the manuscript.

Hrinčenko, who at long last refused to participate in the publication project, wrote in his letter of 13 June 1901 to Hanna Barvinok that he could not collate the manuscript with the original held at that time in the Černihiv Museum of the late Vasyl' Tarnovs'kyj, Jr. (†1899). All in all, there were three reasons for his refusal to cooperate with Puljuj. First, Kuliš's draft was allegedly riddled with many synonyms left by the translator who, most likely, had intended to tackle them later. Second, the sequence of books was somewhat different in Kuliš's translation as compared with the synodal translation. Finally, the amanuensis assigned to make a copy for the museum was prone to spelling mistakes. If the Ukrainian proofreader was passing over mere typos, what could you expect, wondered Hrinčenko, from a foreign compositor preparing galley proofs from a copy with mistakes (Studyns'kyj 1930, lxvi)? Overall, he argued, in order to successfully carry out the project, the preparation of the manuscript for publication should be taken on by only one person (ibid.).

Nečuj-Levyc'kyj, who was very close with Kuliš in the late 1860s (Voznjak 1928b, 2), was seemingly ready to cooperate, albeit with some reservations. According to Fedoruk (2000a, 280), Nečuj-Levyc'kyj might have met Kuliš, his future mentor, for the first time in late 1867. Kuliš established cordial relations with Nečuj-Levyc'kyj, whose literary works devoted to the life of the peasantry seemed to have proved Kuliš's theory about the popular character of Ukrainian literature. In the late 1860s, having strengthened his influence on the editorial policy of the Lviv periodical *Pravda*, Kuliš cherished far-reaching plans about spurring literary activities in West Ukraine. These could then be connected with the mainstream literary process in Russian-ruled Ukraine, largely curtailed in the aftermath of the Valuev Circular of 18 July 1863. Kuliš rightly hoped that the periodical *Pravda* would be decisive in spreading his literary and socio-cultural views among Galician and Ukrainian intellectuals, including young authors like Nečuj-Levyc'kyj who happened to be teaching at that time in the local gymnasium in Siedlce (eastern Poland).

Already during their first meeting, Nečuj-Levyc'kyj was awestruck by the personality of Kuliš, who did much more for his young protégé than simply introduce him to the literary world. Their friendly relationship was known among the Galician populists whose ties with Kuliš were bitterly severed in the period of late 1869 through early 1870 (Studyns′kyj 1927). It is no wonder that in a letter of 17 October 1871, Meliton Bučyns′kyj wrote to Myxajlo Drahomanov that it would be a great pity if Nečuj-Levyc′kyj, "a good, polite fellow," kept contacts exclusively with Kuliš (Pavlyk 1910, 45). Quite in tune with his younger correspondent, Drahomanov argued in 1873 that Kuliš, who was purportedly a stubborn and pedantic person, "stuffed" Nečuj's head with a lot of prejudices so that the poor lad began mixing the truth with tendentiousness (ibid., 263).

Indeed, Kuliš was consciously mentoring and steering young Nečuj-Levyc′kyj in literary matters and beyond (Tarnawsky 2015, 33–34). When Nečuj-Levyc′kyj's story *Dvi moskovky* (Two Muscovites) appeared in *Pravda* in 1868 (Nečuj 1869), Kuliš gave credit to the writer's outstanding knowledge of vernacular Ukrainian. As early as 1869, in a letter to Oleksander Barvins′kyj (2004, 139, fn. 3) in which Kuliš disparagingly evaluated the contribution of contemporary Ukrainian writers to the formation of Ukrainian literature and language, he did praise Nečuj-Levyc′kyj. In several subsequent letters, Kuliš helped Barvins′kyj (ibid., 139–152) choose authors for his Ukrainian literature reader while offering many dogmatic judgments on the essence of the Ukrainian literary language (Luckyj 1983, 163). According to Kuliš, Nečuj-Levyc′kyj was one of the best Ukrainian writers and definitely had to be included in Barvins′kyj's reader since "much linguistic erudition reveals itself in Nečuj. He goes in the right direction! He knows all *dumys*, all songs, all folkloric works!" (Barvins′kyj 2004, 139, fn. 3). In this respect, it comes as no surprise that Nečuj-Levyc′kyj was much influenced by the authority of Kuliš, who was not only his literary mentor but also a demanding editor of his literary pieces. Kuliš is known, for instance, to have meticulously edited Nečuj-Levyc′kyj's novel *Pryčepa* (The Cocklebur), which was being published in installments in the periodical *Pravda* from February 1868 to December 1868, appearing in issues 12–26 and 28–46. Bučyns′kyj was astonished by the corrections that were made by Kuliš in the manuscript submitted by Nečuj-Levyc′kyj, noting that "it was a pity and a fear to look [at them]" (Pavlyk 1910, 106–107).

As a matter of fact, Kuliš did not correct only spelling and stylistic shortcomings. In some cases he crossed out entire sentences, adding instead his own sentences and even paragraphs. Kuliš also insisted on adding stress marks (lacking in the autograph) and using quotation marks to render dialogue (Voznjak 1928b, 3). Yet all this did not affect in any way Kuliš's high opinion of Nečuj-Levyc'kyj's talent and knowledge of vernacular Ukrainian. This is why, in the late 1860s, Kuliš sent a draft of his translation of the book of Psalms to Nečuj-Levyc'kyj, asking him to look into its language and make as many corrections as possible. Interestingly, Nečuj-Levyc'kyj offered in the manuscript numerous emendations that, however, did not make their way into the final version of the translation, although some of them were certainly correct. To illustrate Nečuj-Levyc'kyj's masterful use of Ukrainian, it suffices to cite here, according to Fedoruk (2000a, 282, fn. 19), his most revealing corrections. Instead of *vydumky lukavi* in Kuliš (*Psaltyr*, Rataj, 120), Nečuj-Levyc'kyj offered *vyhadky lukavi* "devices" (Ps 10:2). Instead of *v horni mene pereplavyv* (*Psaltyr*, Rataj, 129), he suggested *v horni mene peretopyv* "[thou] hast tried me" (Ps 17:3), where *(pere)topyty* seemed to him more Ukrainian (see Hrinč., 2:783) in comparison to *plavyty* (ibid., 194), with its Russian or Church Slavonic tinge. Also in *z odra mene ty dvyhnuv* "thou hast brought my soul from the grave" (*Psaltyr*, Rataj, 152, Ps 30:3), Nečuj-Levyc'kyj proposed the verb *zrušyty* instead of *dvyhnuty* "to move," which might have appeared to him as either a Polish or Church Slavonic form (Tymč. 675–676; Vasmer, 1:330). All in all, viewed through the prism of the vernacular and dialect uniformity of Nečuj-Levyc'kyj's language, Kuliš's translation demonstrated a wider array of linguistic elements, from Church Slavonic to western Ukrainian and Polish. Fedoruk (2000a, 282) wondered why Kuliš did not take into consideration Nečuj-Levyc'kyj's recommendations. Perhaps Kuliš could not accept Nečuj-Levyc'kyj's corrections because they looked to him "too uniformly vernacular" to be incorporated into his encoded language, open as it largely was to both internal structural innovations and external influences.

Weak as the relevant evidence can be, Kuliš may have personally invited Nečuj-Levyc'kyj to cooperate with him in the translation of the

Bible. In the late 1860s, while staying in Warsaw, Kuliš was taking lessons in Hebrew with a local rabbi and suggested that Nečuj-Levyc′kyj likewise take lessons. As written in a letter of 27 March 1905 to Puljuj, Nečuj-Levyc′kyj (1968, 443) declined Kuliš's offer, although he did not explain why. Be that as it may, one should bear in mind that Kuliš's work on the history of Ukraine was heavily criticized by populists, among them Nečuj-Levyc′kyj. This may be among the reasons Kuliš severed once and for all his relationship with his former protégé (Fedoruk 2000a, 286–287, fn. 37).

In a letter of 10 February 1902 to Puljuj, Nečuj-Levyc′kyj (1968, 393) dared to express some reservations about the quality of Kuliš's translation. By that time Nečuj-Levyc′kyj had completed his part of the translation, which, arguably, was not itself flawless. In Kuliš's translation, according to Nečuj-Levyc′kyj, there was, among other shortcomings, no consistency in the rendition of most biblical names. In some places, as he was informed by a copyist working with Kuliš's manuscripts, Kuliš left pairs of the type *Abraham* and *Abrajam* for A′-bra-ham (Gen 35:12) or *Jakob* and *Jakov* for Ja′-cob (Gen 42:1). Moreover, in Nečuj-Levyc′kyj's translation, the copyist also found no uniformity in the spelling of some ethnic names such as *fylystymljany* (Phil′-is-tines) as compared with *fylystymci* and the like. For this reason, Nečuj-Levyc′kyj (1968, 392) asked Puljuj to "correct the names, basing them on one form, which he would deem necessary," or simply to restore those forms that had been introduced in the translation of the New Testament.

Yet in the same letter Nečuj-Levyc′kyj hastened to add that he, personally, would prefer popular forms of ethnic designations as commonly used in Ukraine: *bohuslavci, korsunci, steblivci, dac′kivci, semyhorci,* all referring to the inhabitants of particular villages and towns. Nečuj-Levyc′kyj, who highly esteemed Kuliš's literary and language talent (Antonovyč 1969, 21; Nečuj-Levyc′kyj 1968, 471), singled out in his mentor's translation one allegedly inappropriate word form, *jehypci,* for E-gyp′-tians (e.g., Gen 43:32). To his mind, one had better use a form like *jehyptjany,* appearing congruent with, for example, *kyjany* and not *kyjanci* "inhabitants of Kyiv" (Nečuj-Levyc′kyj 1968, 392).

Puljuj (or rather Sljusarčuk, who edited Kuliš's translation) did not take into consideration Nečuj-Levyc′kyj's recommendations with regard to ethnic name forms. In the final version of the Bible that appeared in 1903, not only Kuliš's but also Nečuj-Levyc'kyj's forms were replaced by less appropriate, western-Ukrainian-styled designations like *jehyptiji* (*SP*, 69, Ex 14:27) and *fylystiji* (*SP*, 394, 1 Chr 10:1); these were not even attested in the dictionaries authored by Borys Hrinčenko, Teodor Vytvyc'kyj, and Jevhen Želexivs'kyj. The last of these, for instance, recorded only *ehypetnyk* or *ehyptjanyn* "Egyptian" (Žel., 1:213). Ironically, final substitutions as sanctioned by Puljuj prevailed, to use the biblical saying, against wisdom. As far as the ethnic designations were concerned, Nečuj-Levyc'kyj did not insist on the use of the older desinence *-e*, which, competing with a new desinence *-y* in such forms as *jehyptjany*, was gaining ground in nineteenth-century written Ukrainian. Most interesting in this respect is the fact that in his later writings Ševčenko was gradually expanding the use of the forms ending in *-e* at the cost of the forms in ending in *-y* (Tymošenko 1968, 152–158; Kernyc'kyj 1967, 53, 55–56). However, in the writings of Panas Myrnyj the desinence *-e* in the lexemes with the suffix *-yn-* in the singular was rather common (e.g., *ljude* "people," *ital'jane* "Italians," and so forth [Hrycenko 2007, 26]).

Despite his numerous teaching assignments and service outside his department, Puljuj translated the book of Psalms and edited all five books of Moses for the future Ukrainian Bible. He also proved very efficient in managing the publication project. Under his leadership, the entire Ukrainian-language text of the Old and New Testaments came out of press as early as 1903 and was subsequently reprinted in 1906, 1908, 1909, 1912 (Vienna), and 1920 (Berlin) (Kyryljuk 1929, 65, 73; Studyn'skyj 1930, lxx). To be sure, this was not only a long-awaited publication success, but also an epochal contribution to the development of literary Ukrainian, in both its upper registers and high style devices. All in all, the appearance of the Bible was the realization of Kuliš's dream to make the Holy Scriptures available in Ukrainian in libraries and study-rooms across all Ukraine (Kuliš to Hatcuk, 49).

Who would expect that the first critic of the Ukrainian Bible would be one of its co-translators, Nečuj-Levyc'kyj, whose linguistic views were notoriously arbitrary, inconsistent, and occasionally based on an erroneous understanding of the normalization of written Ukrainian from the beginning of the twentieth century until his death in 1918 (Tarnawsky 2012, 296)? In the case of the Ukrainian Bible, Nečuj-Levyc´kyj was offended by the intervention of Puljuj into the scriptorial standard set by Kuliš and himself. This intervention drove a wedge between the two regional varieties of literary Ukrainian as practiced in Russian-ruled and Austro-Hungarian Ukraine (Nimčuk 2005, 34). In order to understand the nature of Nečuj-Levyc´kyj's criticism, one should bear in mind that his contribution to the translation hardly compares with that of Kuliš. In fact, Nečuj-Levyc´kyj translated a quarter of the Old Testament from the Protestant German Bible, though largely referring, as he admitted, to the Russian synodal text (Nečuj-Levyc´kyj 1968, 373–374). Taken on the whole, Nečuj-Levyc´kyj translated the following canonical and deuterocanonical books: Ruth, 1 and 2 Chronicles, 1, 2, and 3 Ezra, Nehemiah, Judith, Tobit, Esther, Jeremiah, Baruch, Daniel, Proverbs, and 1, 2, and 3 Maccabees, as well as the last psalm in the book of Psalms (otherwise translated by Puljuj). With regard to the deuterocanonical books, Nečuj-Levyc´kyj quite reasonably noted in a letter to Puljuj that these books had to be translated since in Russia the Holy Synod would not even consider a translation lacking the Apocrypha (ibid., 374, 376). Therefore, in order to disseminate the Ukrainian Bible and help promote the book in the Russian Empire, the British and Foreign Bible Society would need to print both the canonical and apocryphal (deuterocanonical) books.

In a letter of 2 July 1901, as if having a premonition of future misunderstanding, Nečuj-Levyc´kyj (1968, 383) asked Puljuj to oblige the British and Foreign Bible Society to have the Bible printed in Kuliš's phonetic script (*kulišivka*). He explained that in Russia the etymological orthography of letters such as *ô* was banned, with the exception of phonetic orthography, even if such a scheme were different slightly from the system of *kulišivka*. Puljuj, however, allegedly changed not only the orthography but also replaced some lexemes and expressions in the translation made by Nečuj-Levyc´kyj and Kuliš with "obsolete and regional

Galician words." In addition to lexical substitutions, Puljuj indiscriminately used parallel forms like *cej ~ sej* "this," *se ~ otse ~ oce*, a confusion that, according to Nečuj-Levyc´kyj, was inexcusable (ibid., 467).

The main argument in Nečuj-Levyc´kyj's (1968, 451) logic was that his own standard represented "a spoken popular language of our time as used in all Central Ukraine, even the whole of Ukraine, save for the Černihiv region, Galicia, as well as a small zone of the eastern Polissian dialect." Forms like *cej* "this," *myni/mini* (dat.) "to me," and *davniše* "earlier" were commonplace in this language. For this reason, he was following the popular language of Ševčenko rather than of Kuliš, a native of the Černihiv region (ibid., 455), because the latter made use of forms not attested in Central Ukraine. This was a desperate, cantankerous revelation from an old writer who unexpectedly felt that he was losing ground in his fight against the presumed "Galician vogue" in the written language of his time.

Determined to fight to the last, Nečuj-Levyc´kyj (1968, 473–474) sent an official complaint to the British and Foreign Bible Society in October 1907 in which he accused Puljuj of willful intervention into "the pure Ukrainian language" of Kuliš and himself in the translation of the Bible. Puljuj, according to him, changed "not only some Ukrainian etymological forms of words into Galician forms, for us so provincial and strange, but even Ukrainian words with such provincial Galician words, as will be totally incomprehensible in Ukraine and look like foreign words" (ibid., 473). For this reason, Nečuj-Levyc´kyj (ibid., 474) asked the Bible Society to have the translation of the Bible reprinted not in the "Galician dialect" but in the Ukrainian language, while restoring the orthography of Kuliš as used primarily in the translation of the New Testament that appeared in 1871, 1880, and 1887 as a publication of the British and Foreign Bible Society (*NZ*).

Nečuj-Levyc´kyj was particularly upset by "the defective and very unpractical diacritic orthography of Želexivs´kyj" (Nečuj-Levic´kyj 1907, 326). Endorsing the regular phonetic rendition of the assimilation of consonants like *molyssja* (2 sg. pres.) "to pray" in Kuliš's authentic spelling, Nečuj-Levyc´kyj could hardly accept the *želexivka* that was designed by Jevhen Želexivs´kyj (along with Sofron Nedil´skyj) for *Malorusko-nimeckyj slovar* (The Little Russian-German Dictionary)

(Žel., 1:viii). Leaving aside cultural differences in spelling practice in Galicia and Dnieper Ukraine there was, to be sure, a linguistic reason behind Nečuj-Levyc´kyj's posture of angry defiance.

To understand the introduction, to use Nečuj-Levyc´kyj's words, of *dvojenije allyluja* ("doubling of Hallelujah"), that is, the use of two dots in the letter *ï* as practiced in Galicia (Nečuj-Levic´kyj 1912, 7), one should remember that the *želexivka* was premised on those Ukrainian dialects where the dentals *d, t, z, s*, and *c* and the sonorants *n, l*, and *r* are palatalized in the environment before *i* from *ě* and etymological *e*, while remaining plain in the environment before *i* from the etymological *o*, whence the opposition of *d'id* "grandfather," *t'itka* "aunt," ~ *dim* "house" (Žovtobrjux et al. 1979, 287). This model is attested in West Ukrainian (excluding its southern part), namely in much of the Dniester and southern and eastern Volhynian, as well as in Podolja dialects (Nazarova 1972, 18). Since Nečuj-Levyc´kyj's language standard, particularly its phonetics, was modeled primarily on Southeast Ukrainian, it becomes clear he did not endorse "doubling of Hallelujah" as represented in the *želexivka*, see *dïd* [дѣд-] "grandfather" (Žel., 1:184), with a reference to the etymological *jat'*, *tïtka* "aunt" (ibid., 2:967), as opposed to *dim* (*domu*) "house" (ibid., 1:186), with the etymological *o* in the genitive case form.

Generally, the use of the letter *ï* proved a stumbling block to the process of harmonization between the two spelling practices cultivated in Galicia, Transcarpathia, and Bukovyna on the one hand and in Dnieper Ukraine on the other. For instance, Borys Hrinčenko, whose dictionary was premised largely on southeastern Ukrainian orthoepy, adduced both practical and pedagogical arguments against the implementation of this letter in Russian-ruled Ukraine (Lesjuk 2003, 35). To reach a consensus, the Galicians, according to Hrinčenko, had to make use of the apostrophe to distinguish between *r'ja* and *rja*, write the reflexive particle *sja* together with the verbs, and drop the soft sign before *v* in words like *s'vit* "world" (Kryms´kyj 1929, 185). Exactly the opposite was done by Puljuj, who presumably followed the instructions of his friend Sljusarčuk.

In his criticism of Puljuj's voluntary editorship, Nečuj-Levyc´kyj (1968, 434, 398) was ready to accept Kuliš's excessive use of archaisms: for despite their occasional disagreements, Kuliš always remained an utmost authority for Nečuj-Levyc′kyj in language issues (Antonovyč 1969, 42). In this particular case Nečuj-Levyc′kyj made a considerable concession, since the issue of the archaization of Ukrainian was of primary significance in his linguistic system. He had long been protesting against excessive and "deep" archaization of the language. Over the last fifty years, written Ukrainian had changed so much in the Kyiv and Poltava regions that, according to Nečuj-Levyc′kyj, one had not simply to go but to run after the vernacular in order to keep up. Reminded in 1907 of his disparagement of publication of the Bible in Ukrainian, Nečuj-Levyc′kyj (1968, 468) put aside for a moment his disagreement with the archaizing principle of Kuliš and instead recalled, quite sympathetically in a letter to Lobodovs′kyj, the proposal of Kuliš to discard the Galician written language entirely.

From the modern point of view, it is rather difficult to determine to what extent Puljuj went beyond his editorial authority in finalizing the manuscript for publication. One should recall that Kuliš himself was unsatisfied with the orthography adopted in the first editions of the New Testament. As he wrote in a programmatic letter of 26 August 1881 to Oleksander Barvins′kyj on the principles of spelling, the orthography employed in the New Testament was not his but had been introduced by Puljuj (Barvins′kyj 2004, 202), whence a feeling of bitterness expressed by Kuliš in some other letters (Studyns′kyj 1930, xxxix–xl). Yet, despite Kuliš's remarks, Puljuj seemed to have always loyally followed his mentor who, during the years of their active cooperation, would often guide his younger Galician friend in language issues. One can only assume that, long after Kuliš's death, working frantically on the collation of the copies made in Černihiv and managing the entire publication project, Puljuj's pursuit of the all-Ukrainian message of the "Rusian Bible" might have been sidelined under pressure from the regional (Galician) paradigm of literary language and culture.

Quite revealing, in this respect, is Puljuj's letter to Kuliš's widow where, obviously hurt by the criticism of the "esteemed writer," he tried to explicate his stance and the real reasons behind the changes that were so vehemently renounced by Nečuj-Levyc′kyj. Puljuj began with the matter of some words that, according to Nečuj-Levyc′kyj, had been substituted for Kuliš's own lexemes, like *čambul* "detachment of Tatars or Cossacks" (Žel., 2:1060), *nadolužyty škodu* "to rectify a damage" (ibid., 1:475), *strebuvaty* "to demand," *blahyj* "good, virtuous" (ibid., 1:31), and *štukars´kyj* "skillful" (Zelens´ka 2001, 360). As was jotted down by Hanna Barvinok in the margins of this letter, Nečuj-Levyc´kyj would prefer *štučnyc´kyj* instead (ibid. fn. 1). The latter proposition was well grounded in the writer's view on language. Thus, among other neologisms derived with the help of the suffix *-ist´*, Nečuj-Levyc´kyj propagated the word *štučnist´* "art" that, however, did not make its way into modern literary Ukrainian, as well as other lexemes (e.g., *prosvitnist´* "enlightenment," *naxyl´nist´* "inclination," and *pryljubnist´* "predilection" compared to MoUkr. *prosvita* "enlightenment," *naxyl* "inclination" [Muromceva 1985, 15], and *pryljubljaty* "to like, love" [Hrinč., 2:428]).

Complaining of editorial hardships, Puljuj added that he himself edited only five books of Moses and Ruth. The rest was done by Sljusarčuk in conformity with norms established in advance by Puljuj. Since Nečuj-Levyc´kyj submitted a translation already proofread, Sljusarčuk was purportedly instructed to unify only the system of spelling (Zelens´ka 2001, 360). In conclusion, Puljuj contended that the language of the translation of the Holy Scriptures, including its phonetic script, belonged to Kuliš (ibid., 361). He reminded his interlocutors that, as early as 1870, while translating the New Testament, Puljuj and Kuliš had it in mind to set up foundations for a new literary language, comprehensible both in Galicia and Ukraine. For this reason, in their translation, they resorted not only to Ukrainian but also to Galician dialectal words, which Kuliš particularly appreciated (ibid.).

Nevertheless, Puljuj's alleged failure to remain loyal to Kuliš's legacy is only one side of the coin. The overall situation regarding the preparation of the manuscript will remain incomplete unless we mention also Nečuj-Levyc´kyj's participation in this project, however insignificant it may look in the light of Puljuj's corrections. Well informed about prerequisite conditions set by the British and Foreign Bible Society for vernacular translations of the Holy Scriptures, Puljuj tried to eliminate poetic passages in the translation of Kuliš, since retaining them would violate the principle of adequate translation as adopted by the Bible Society. He may have asked Nečuj-Levyc´kyj to help him edit Kuliš's translation to make it "less poetic," especially those books which were traditionally identified as poetic (Kautzsch 1902), namely, Psalms (which Puljuj volunteered to translate in prose), Song of Solomon, Job, Proverbs, Wisdom of Jesus Son of Sirach, and the prophetic writings (Gillingham 1994, 123).

As a result, Nečuj-Levyc´kyj tried to use prose in those parts of Kuliš's translation where the poetic rendering appeared too obvious, or simply to slightly change Kuliš's syllabotonic meter so that it would look less poetic overall. Yet his corrections were minimal and delicate. As Nečuj-Levyc´kyj (1968, 386) mentioned in one of his letters to Borys Hrinčenko, he had just persuaded the widow that "nobody even thinks about correcting the work of the late Kuliš as regards the contents, but only in what is pertinent to the form (of the prophet Isaiah)." Naxlik (2007, 2:281) argued that despite all the efforts of the editors, including Nečuj-Levyc´kyj, one sporadically encounters residual instances of poetic translation in the prose narration of the books of the Old Testament. To give an example of the editors' intervention, he cited Moses' prayer (Ex 15:1–8), compiled in fourteen-syllable meter without a rhythm scheme (*kolomyjka*), which, according to him, was intentionally printed in prose. In some other places, the original translation, after such an editing, gives an impression of incondite (in fact, distorted) versification.

Leaving aside for a moment the extent of the editors' intervention, one should not disregard prose that might be read, in fact, as poetry in the Bible. The genre of prose prayer, such as that of Moses in the book of Exodus, is a good example:

Kuliš's Translation of 1903

1. ... Ой сьпіваймо ж Господеві, славно бо прославивсь, і коня і їздця він повергав у море.
2. Господь, сила моя й велич, був моїм рятунком. Він мій Бог, і я споруджу дом йому преславний. Вознесу його, прославлю Бог-отця благого.

[1. ... I will sing unto the Lord, for he hath triumphed gloriously: the horse and his rider hath he thrown into the sea.
2. The Lord is my strength and song,
and he is become my salvation; he is my God, and I will prepare him an habitation; my father's God, and I will exalt him.

3. Господь—муж боїв страшенний, на імя Господь він.	3. The Lord is a man of war: the Lord is his name.
4. Колесниці в Фараона і полки-потуги Божа сила потопила, поввергала в море, і вибране отаманнє потонуло в морі; лицярі над лицарями згинули в Червонім.	4. Pha´-raoh's chariots and his host hath he cast into the sea: his chosen captains also are drowned in the Red sea.
5. Глибиня їх повкривала по всї вічни роки; ов каміннє потонули у морю глибокім.	5. The depths have covered them: they sank into the bottom as a stone.
6. Господе! Твоя правиця вславилась в потузї; Господе! Твоя десниця ворога згубила. (*SP*, 69)	6. Thy right hand, O Lord, is become glorious in power: thy right hand, O Lord, hath dashed in pieces the enemy.] (Ex 15:1–6)

Like the poetic material, prose prayers are cast sometimes in the form of petition and reproach and at other times in the form of thanksgiving or praise. In this way, they are conscious imitations of poetic prayer forms, though their literary context is unmistakably prose narrative: they form an intrinsic part of their story, and the poetic features include generally a terse style and figurative language, more specifically ellipses, changes in word order, word-pairing, word-plays, chiasmus, and repetition, all of which Kuliš strove to render in Ukrainian. Such prose prayers occur throughout the various literary sources of the Old Testament. They are found in the Yahwistic account of the Pentateuch, for instance in the books of Genesis and Exodus (Gillingham 1994, 29).

As a result, it is problematic to treat Kuliš's translation of Moses' prayer in the second book of Moses (Ex 15:1–18) as poetry supposedly twisted by the editors' changes in syllabic structure. Most likely one deals in this case with prose conceived as poetry. If the editors tried to make the prayer seem less or more poetic, they could hardly change the overall pattern of murky distinction between poetry and prose as accepted by Kuliš under the influence of contemporary biblical scholarship. If any attempt to classify poetry in Hebrew fails on account of the lack of clear boundaries, then any attempt to ascertain the borderline between poetry and prose in the Ukrainian translation of Kuliš would likewise be irrelevant. Concerning some tonic accent or rhythmic stress in Hebrew and, correspondingly, Ukrainian poetry, we face a similar phenomenon in prose. As the 3:3 meter, seen sometimes as six accents for each verse and therefore called hexameter, was undoubtedly a flexible poetic device used widely throughout the literature of ancient Israel (Gillingham 1994, 54, 58–59), so the iambic meter was the key criterion for determining Kuliš's biblical language.

This said, one can hardly concur with Naxlik (2007, 2:283), who hastily argued that the adaptation of the Bible with the help of syllabic or syllabotonic versification in Kuliš "was, to be sure, anachronism," or "inertia" of the outdated romantic cult of paraphrases that was replaced by *vers libre* in the modern translations of Ivan Ohijenko and Ivan Xomenko-Pljuta. It is true that biblical verse is elusive and reflects much original and creative freedom of its own. Yet, it is obvious that the essence of Hebrew poetry is hidden behind the metric model of "sung speech" (Gillingham 1994, 52), which Kuliš seemed to have grasped intuitively.

This is best illustrated by way of the same episode from the biblical text, rendered in prose, unlike the above account written in verse:

Kuliš's Translation of 1903

27. І просьтіг Мойсей руку свою понад морем, і почало вертатись море ранішньою добою до своєї потуги. Египтії ж метнулись навпроти його, і скидав Господь Египтії в безодню морську.

28. І вертались води, та й затопили колесниці, й комінника з усією потугою Фараоновою, що поввіходили за ними в море. (*SP*, 69)

[27. And Moʹ-ses stretched forth his hand over the sea, and the sea returned to his strength when the morning appeared; and the E-gypʹ-tians fled against it; and the Lord overthrew the E-gypʹ-tians in the midst of the sea.

28. And the waters returned, and covered the chariots, and the horsemen, and all the host of Phaʹ-raoh that came into the sea after them; there remained not so much as one of them. (Ex 14:27–29)

Comparing the two renditions of the same event, one can argue that Kuliš's approach was as appropriate for the Ukrainian translation as it was for Hebrew prose-in-poetry. Indeed, understanding the differences between prose and poetry had more to do with appreciation and less to do with knowledge. In other words, the distinction was so subtle that it required a more intuitive and aesthetic approach opted for by Kuliš in his later years.

Luckily, the intervention of Nečuj-Levyc′kyj, in his turn upset by changes introduced by his Galician collaborators and more so by Puljuj, could hardly change the aesthetic appreciation of the Ukrainian Bible of 1903 in years to come. It is also worth emphasizing that, despite the editorial emendations made by Puljuj and Sljusarčuk, Kuliš's translation did retain its characteristic features and remained attuned to his vision of the biblical style of new literary Ukrainian.

The criticism of Ivan Franko, which followed in 1904, can be seen as an exception that proves the rule.

THE PRANKS OF IVAN FRANKO

Unlike Nečuj-Levyc′kyj, who criticized Puljuj only for his distortion of the central Ukrainian literary standard, Franko published in 1904 a rather scurrilous review of the translation (Franko 1982; see also Danylenko 2009b). The reviewer contended that Kuliš's translation did not justify itself at all, despite giving full credit to the translator for his endeavor. According to Franko (1982, 275), an ideal translation of the Bible must be either popular (intelligible to the lay people) or scholarly, while conveying correctly the meaning of each sentence in the original.[3] Unfortunately, as Franko claimed, Kuliš was not versed in any foreign language, least of all Hebrew, whence his alleged total ignorance of scholarly publications dealing with existing translations of the Bible. This

---

3 Yet, extrapolating Žytec′kyj's (Žiteckij 1905, 29) opinion about the translation of the New Testament onto the 1903 Bible, it becomes apparent that Kuliš intended from the outset to sustain the spirit of the native tongue; moreover, he believed that the Ukrainian translation of the Bible had to be written in Dnieper Ukrainian (East Ukrainian) and not the Galician dialect. The latter fact might unwittingly be a stumbling block in the appropriation of Kuliš's language in Galicia.

is why in some places the translator moved slowly, as if testing the waters. Instead of setting forth his translation as a model of modern literary Ukrainian and using plain and intelligible language, Kuliš resorted, in Franko's opinion, to obsolete Church Slavonicisms like the old aorists *reče* and *hlahole* (3 sg.) "to say," nouns of the type *vojinstvo* "army," *hlasy* "voices," *pečali* "griefs," and so forth (ibid.).

As a result, Kuliš's translation, according to Franko, proved much less comprehensible for the common people. This made the critic offer his own "popular" translation of chapters 1 and 2 in the first book of Moses, premised on a critical reading of the Greek translation and the Hebrew original (Franko 1982, 276–277, 285–287). The Galician writer admitted that his translation was not perfect either, though he claimed it was much better than that made by Kuliš:

Franko's Translation	**Kuliš's Translation**
Глава 1	*Голова* 1
1. На початку, коли Бог *сотворив* небо і землю,	1. … У початку *сотворив* Бог небо та землю.
2. а земля була *видима* й *невпорядкована* і пітьма лежала на морі і дух Божий сидів на водах,	2. Земля ж була *пуста* і *пустошня*, і *темрява* лежала над *безоднею*; і дух Божий ширяв понад водами.
3. тоді сказав Бог: "Нехай буде світло!" І сталося світло. (Franko 1982, 276)	3. І *рече* Бог: Настань, світе! І настав світ. (*SP*, 5)

[1. In the beginning God created the heaven and the earth.
2. And the earth was without form, and void; and darkness was upon the face of the waters.
3. And God said. Let there be light: and there was light.] (Gen 1:1–3)

Apart from numerous textual and critical comments, it is easy to reduce Franko's criticism to alleging that a few lexemes employed by Kuliš were unsuitable. First, Franko (1982, 279) denounced the pair *pusta i pustošnja* "void and unpopulated," since one could hardly tell the difference between these two words. It should be noted that Franko did admit to the poor quality of his own version, *vydyma j nevporjadkovana* "visible and unformed," modeled on the Greek translation of the original Hebrew expression. Second, the meaning of the verb *šyrjav* (m. sg. pret.) "to hover" seemed to him especially murky (ibid., 281) in this context. But what is undoubtedly revealing for the "popular" character of the critic's translation is that Franko used side by side the dialectal (Bojk., Huc.) *pit´ma* "darkness" (Hrinč., 2:193; Onyškevyč, 2:76; Pipaš and Halas, 140; Bil.-Nos., 282) and several Church Slavonic and bookish elements such as the non-pleophonic *hlava* "chapter," the present passive participle *vydyma* "visible," and *sotvoryty* "to create" with a characteristic Church Slavonic prefix. To the contrary, Kuliš used in his translation only two Church Slavonicisms, *sotvoryty* and *reče*, together with two bookish (Ruthenian) words, *bezodnja* (Berynda, 6) and *pustošnij*, first attested in sixteenth-century Ukrainian (*khrunt pustošnij* "free ground, land [without settlers]" [1598] [Tymč. and Nimčuk, 2:259]). Yet no dialectism or patent regionalism is found in his translation!

In sum, Franko's critical appraisal looks narrow and provincial since even today Kuliš's translation reads in places like the sonorant King James Version (Luckyj 1983, 151; Lypa 1939, 51). Trying to reply to the main opponent of Kuliš's translation of the Old Testament, Puljuj offered apt counter arguments, which, if taken out of context, may look excessively biting today (Gajda and Pljacko 1998, 206). First of all, Puljuj waived off Franko's criticism of *pusta i pustošnja* in Kuliš (incidentally, not corrected by Puljuj in the final version of their translation) as insignificant and poorly grounded. He noted that Franko's emendation *vydyma j nevporjadkovana* resonated with two translations of the Old Testament, to wit, the Church Slavonic Elizabeth Bible reprinted by Myxajlo Dykovs´kyj in 1859 in Peremyšl´ (Pol. Przemyśl) (*Biblija* 1862, 1r) and, as was admitted by Franko, the Greek text of the Bible:

The Elizabeth Bible (Peremyšl´, 1859)	Vetus et novum testamentum (Romae, 1857)
Землѧ́ же бѣ невидима, и неустроена	Ἡ δὲ γῆ ἦν ἀόρατος καὶ ἀκατασκεύαστος

As Puljuj (1905, 112–115) further argued, in all other translations, especially those sponsored by the British and Foreign Bible Society, the translators used the same semantic collocation (*dumka*), although with slight linguistic differences (*mova*): *wüste und leer* (the German Elberfelder Bible of Carl Brockhaus, 1871), *wüst und wirre* (the Judeo-German Bible of Ludwig Phillipson, 1874), *nesličná a pustá* (the Czech Bible, 1899), *niekształtowna i próżna* (the Polish Bible, 1899), *bez obličja i pusta* (the Serbian Bible of Vuk Stefanović Karadžić, 1901), *sans forme et vide* (the French Bible, 1900), *una cosa deserta et vacua* (the Italian Bible, 1903), and, finally, Lat. *inanis et vacua*. In view of the parallelism in all the above translations, Puljuj concluded that Franko was too hasty to charge Kuliš with some inconsistency in translating the underlying Hebrew terms *tōhû wābōhû* "without form and empty," especially since the critic himself was not familiar with this language. Franko was right, perhaps, only in raising the problem of those terms since they are attested only in this verse and later biblical texts that are clearly alluding to this one (Green 2005). Having placed linguistic evidence in the context of the stories of creation, Franko, however, failed to persuasively substantiate his accusations of crude mistakes by Kuliš in his translation of the Bible (Danylenko 2009b). Moreover, he based his alternative translation on the Old Church Slavonic version that served as only one possible reference for Kuliš.

As one can glean from Franko's review of Kuliš's translations, the form *reče* was the main bone of contention in his line of criticism. Yet, surprisingly, this form was favored not only by Kuliš but also by other translators of the Holy Scriptures, in particular Volodymyr Aleksandrov, Oleksander Navroc´kyj, and Myxajlo Lobodovs´kyj. Paradoxically, Lobodovs´kyj used the old aorist form *reče* in the future tense meaning. Consequently, viewed through the prism of the vernacular make-up of the entire translation, this form together with *hlaholaty* "to say," also occurring in various contemporary translations, could serve in the lofty narrative as an archaizing embellishment (Žiteckij 1905, 32).

IVAN PULJUJ MAKES HIS RIPOSTE

On the whole, Puljuj tried to follow those principles of archaization that had been applied by Kuliš in his translation of the Old Testament as well as in his paraphrases of the Psalms (*Psaltyr'*, Rataj). The main difference between the two authors was likely to lie in the ratio of archaic, folkloric, and vernacular devices borrowed from Southwest or Southeast Ukrainian and their configuration in the corresponding portions of the translation. A cursory survey of these translations shows that Puljuj's was almost exclusively premised on his native dialect with an array of regional and antiquated elements, although Horbač (1988, 63) saw "a great resemblance, even identity" between Kuliš's paraphrases and Puljuj's translation of the Psalms. Among obvious western Slavic (Polish) borrowings and dialectisms in Puljuj's translation, one can cite the following lexemes: *ovoči* "fruits" (*SP*, 506, Ps 1:3), *bramy* "gates" (*SP*, 509, Ps 9:14), *hrib* "open sepulcher" (*SP*, 507, Ps 5:9; Žel., 1:159), *sxovysko* "lurking place" and *zapopasty* "to catch" (*SP*, 509, Ps 10:8, 9; Žel., 2:940), *postil'* "couch" next to ChSl. *lože* "bed" (*SP*, 508, Ps 6:6)—both attested in the dictionary of Jevhen Želexivs'kyj (Žel., 1:411; 2:718)—and *zeliznyj* "of iron" (*SP*, 506, Ps 2:9; Žel., 1:297) as a result of old distant assimilation of *zalizo* "iron." One can also observe a combination of lofty and low elements in the lexical series *usta* "mouth," *serce* "inward part," and *pel'ka* "throat" (*SP*, 508, Ps 5:9) (Lemk. *p'jalka* "Speiseröhre," that is, "gullet" [Verxrats'kyj 1902, 459]). Of interest is the sporadic *ikavism* in *narid* "people," *spimnuty* "to recall," *mid* "honey" (*SP*, 510, 511, 513), and other lexemes that are typical of Southwest Ukrainian. In other places, however, Puljuj used such forms without any *ikavism* (e.g., *narod* in Psalm 59 [*PS*, 530, Ps 59:11]). Horbač (1988, 64) assumed that Puljuj might have unwittingly overlooked this and some other similar forms when consulting the original translation made by Kuliš.

According to Horbač (1988, 60), the phraseology, vocabulary, and even some grammatical patterns are largely similar in Kuliš and Puljuj, an assumption that is open to doubt. To illuminate the factual state of this alleged similarity, it is expedient to compare translations of Psalm 1 in Rataj's *Psaltyr'*, originally published anonymously in 1868 in the periodical *Pravda* (*Psal'ma* 1), and in Puljuj's translation of the book of Psalms:

Rataj's Paraphrase

Блаженний, хто туди не ходить,
де раду радять *нечестиві*,
хто стежку грішників минає,
серед злоріків не сїдає;
а прихиляєть-ся до Бога,
всїм серцем, до його *закону*,
про заповідь його сьвяту
і день і ніч собу міркує.
І буде він—як добре *древо*,
посаджене коло криницї,
що в пору *плодом* процьвітає
і лист його не опадає:
Щó він нї робить, щó нї *творить*—
Господь йому допомагає.
Не так, не так ледачим буде:
почезнуть, як пилина в полї
як вітер пил з землї зметає,
так слїд їх марно погибає.
Ото-ж не встануть *нечестиві*
проти *благих* людей на судї,
і сила *грішних* панувати
у радї *праведних* не буде.
Господь бо *праведних* дорогу
із неба бачить-назирає,
а *путь* ледачий *нечестивих*
на віки вічні погибає.
(Kuliš 1909, 3:107–108)

Puljuj's Translation

1. *Блаженний* чоловік, що не ходить на раду безбожних і не ступає слїдом за грішниками, анї засїдає на зборах злоріків,
2. Но в *законї Господа* любується й розмишляє о *законї* його день і ніч!
3. І буде він як дерево посаджене над водистими потоками, що приносять овочі свої у пору свою, і которого лист не вяне; і що він творить, все удається йому.
4. Не так безбожні: вони, як полова, що вітер розносить.
5. Тому не встоять безбожні на суді, анї *грішні у* зборі *праведних*;
6. Знає бо *Господь* про дорогу *праведних*, а дорога безбожних щезне. (*SP*, 506)

[1. Blessed is the man that walketh not in the counsel of the ungodly, nor standeth in the way of sinners, nor sitteth in the seat of the scornful.
2. But his delight is in the law of the Lord; and in his law doth he mediate day and night.

3. And he shall be like a tree planted by the rivers of water, that bringeth forth his fruit in his season; his leaf also shall not wither; and whatsoever he doeth shall prosper.
4. The ungodly are not so: but are like the chaff which the wind driveth away.
5. Therefore the ungodly shall not stand in judgement, nor sinners in the congregation of the righteous. 6. For the Lord knoweth the way of the righteous: but the way of the ungodly shall perish.] (Ps 1)

Comparing the grammar and the vocabulary (with obvious Church Slavonicisms italicized) in the two versions shows an ever more convoluted picture of the creative interrelationship between the two translators. Chronologically, it is quite possible that Puljuj might have largely benefited from the work of his predecessor, thus retaining some of Kuliš's Church Slavonic and innovative forms (Horbač 1988, 60), although vectors of influences are hard to determine for other psalms and their paraphrases.

To take the first verse as an example, Puljuj kept ChSl. *blažennyj* "blessed" in collocation with the vernacular *čolovik* (consider Rataj's neologism *zlorika* "a scornful person"), while dropping another Church Slavonicism, *nečestyvi* (pl.) "ungodly" for the vernacular *bezbožni*, used also in all other verses of this psalm. Surprisingly, Puljuj introduced pleophonic *derevo* instead of ChSl. *drevo* "tree" and a vernacular form *ščezne*, with word-initial assimilation in place of articulation, instead of *pohybaje* (3 sg. pres.) "to perish," encountered in Rataj. Puljuj also changed *rada* "council," commonly attested in folklore and Middle Ukrainian texts, into *zbory* "congregation," a later derivative widely attested cross-dialectally and especially in Southwest Ukrainian, whence numerous derivatives *zbirannyk* "collector," *zbirnyčka* "focus," *zbirnyšče* "reservoir," and the like (Žel., 1:284). On the other hand, Rataj employed some Church Slavonicisms that are not attested in Puljuj's text (e.g., *blahi ljude* "the righteous" and *na viky vični* "forever"). Among vernacular and folkloric forms in Rataj's language, it is worthwhile mentioning *stežka* "path," *krynycja* "well," *kolo* "close to," *mirkuvaty* "to think," *počeznuty* "to disappear" (Žel., 2:728; Hrinč., 2:395), and *radu radyty* "to be in session."

Statistically, one can reveal another significant difference between the two versions of Psalm 1. To begin with, there are seventeen Church Slavonicisms in the paraphrase of Rataj and only six Slavonic forms in Puljuj's translation. At first glance, these figures look strange given the secular message of Rataj's paraphrase, and more Church Slavonic forms would seem more fitting for the literal translation made by Puljuj. It is tempting to assume that a limited number of Church Slavonicisms in Puljuj's text might have been censored by Kuliš (and eventually by Puljuj himself) because the Galician and Transcarpathian Russophiles commonly used such antiquated forms in their *jazyčije*. Unlike variegated folkloric, vernacular, bookish, and Church Slavonic lexical devices employed by Rataj, the translation of Puljuj appears more uniform. The presence of Church Slavonicisms, sometimes unobtrusively used by Puljuj, is enhanced by regionalisms serving as additional archaizing factors from the perspective of Central Dnieper speakers.

In Puljuj's translation, as was mentioned, there are entire Church Slavonic phrases excepted from or influenced by the Slavonic text (e.g., *Hospod', ščo sydyt' na nebesax*, "[the Lord] that sitteth in the heavens" [*SP*, 506, Ps 2:4]). But they are not numerous. Among non-Slavonic means of archaization in Psalm 1, one can easily discern western Slavic (Polish) borrowings like *ovoči* "fruits" and the inflecting relativizer *kotryj* "which." Quite remarkably, the former lexeme occurs only a few times in the translation made by Pylyp Moračevs'kyj, who instead resorted to the Central Dnieper lexeme *ovošč* inherited most likely from the Ukrainian recension of Church Slavonic (Pšepjurs'ka-Ovčarenko 1988, 239). The relativizer *kot(o)ryj* occurs, on balance, in parallel with the indigenous absolutive relativizer *ščo*, represented cross-dialectally. In other psalms translated by Puljuj, one notices a drastic increase in present active participles, often ending in ChSl. *-ščyj*, or their substantivized forms (e.g., *vsi dilajuči bezzakonnje* "all ye workers of iniquity" [*SP*, 508, Ps 6:8], *spasajuščyj* [m.] "savior," *strily paljašči* "burning arrows" [*SP*, 508, Ps 7:2, 13], and *bojaščyxsja* [gen. pl.] *joho* "[them] that fear him" [*SP*, 519, Ps 34:7]; here also belongs a substantivized past participle form *pomeršyj* [m.] "a dead man" [*SP*, 517, Ps 31:12]). The above participles compete more often than not with relative subordinate clauses introduced with the help of the relativizer *ščo* "that" (although without a resumptive pronoun), a construction attested cross-dialectally and especially in Kuliš's translation of the Old Testament (e.g., *polova, ščo viter roznosyt'* "the chaff which the wind driveth away" [*SP*, 506, Ps 1:4]).

Following Horbač (1988, 64), one should also take into consideration Russian forms attested sporadically in Puljuj's translation such as *šahy* "goings" (*SP*, 511, Ps 17:5)—literally "steps,"—*razvratylys'* (pl. pret.) "[they] are corrupt" (*SP*, 510, Ps 14:1), *šljatysja* "to wander up and down" (*SP*, 530, Ps 59:15), and *zaščyta* "defence" (*SP*, 530, Ps 59:16). Though outweighed by Church Slavonicisms proper, their archaizing effect is even more obvious in conjunction with native, southwestern Ukrainian forms (e.g., *lyčyt' s'pivaty* "[for praise] is comely for the upright" [*SP*, 518, Ps 33:1], *bramy* "gates" [*SP*, 515, Ps 24:7], *naxovstaty uzdoju* "to hold in with bit and bridle" [*SP*, 518, Ps 32:9; Verxratskyj 1902, 478], *xovzkyj* "slippery" [*SP*, 519, Ps 35:6; Žel., 2:1042], and *čekaty* "to wait" [*SP*, 519, Ps 33:20]).

In sum, the above means, varied as they may seem, make the translation of Puljuj less colorful in comparison with Rataj's paraphrases. Indeed, these paraphrases were primarily designed by Kuliš as non-ecclesiastical literary works. This is why the presence of Church Slavonicisms lends verisimilitude and authenticity to the popular narrative without, however, violating the discursive demands of the biblical text. In other words, if there were any residual resemblance between Rataj's *Psaltyr'* and the translation of Puljuj, as suggested by Horbač (1988, 64), it could be ascertained through the configuration of the corresponding stylistic devices, instead of mere statistics. At the time of his death, Kuliš had acquired undeniable authority in literary matters as well as in the codification of new literary Ukrainian encompassing different literary traditions and linguistic elements. As a follower of his friend's talent, Puljuj managed to synthesize in his translation, if somewhat mechanistically, two regional varieties of literary Ukrainian as cultivated in the late nineteenth century in Dnieper Ukraine, on the one hand, and in Galicia, Transcarpathia, and Bukovyna, on the other (Tkač 2007, 52–91). Unlike the vernacular-based language employed in Dnieper Ukraine, the latter variety was premised on the old (Ruthenian) literary tradition of the *prostaja mova*, diffused by the early eighteenth century in Church Slavonic (Danylenko 2008a, 2015a).

Franko's criticism of the supposedly excessive number of Church Slavonic forms in Kuliš's translation of the Bible appears, therefore, less than persuasive. Importantly, despite Puljuj's editing of Kuliš's translation, some of those forms made their way into the 1903 Bible and were used by the writer in stylistically neutral contexts. Such was the case with *reče* (3 sg. pres.) "to say" (Kuliš 1909, 2:203, 246, etc.).[4] It is true that Kuliš could not resist combining Church Slavonicisms with vernacular elements, sometimes rendering biblical personal and place names primarily under the southeastern Ukrainian guise. To adduce just one of the most representative examples, Kuliš (like Nečuj-Levyc′kyj) consistently used patronymics with a distinctive eastern Ukrainian suffix *-enk(o)* (for the sons) and, to a lesser extent, *-ivn(a)* (for the daughters) (e.g., *Syxem, syn Hemmora, Evejanena* or [*Syxem*] *Hemmorenko* [*SP*, 36, 37], that is, "She′-chem the son of Ha′-mor" [Gen 34:2, 4, 6]). Note also *Sejir Horijenko* (*SP*, 36, 39), that is, "Se′-ir the Ho′-rite" (Gen 36:20) or *Mylka Haranivna* "Mil′-cah, the daughter of Ha′-ran" (*SP*, 14, Gen 11:29) as compared to *Milka, dočka Harana*, a genitive possessive construction used also by Ivan Ohijenko and Ivan Xomenko-Pljuta in their translations of the Bible (Horbač 1988, 56).

One may wonder at this point if the aforementioned case of Ukrainianization could have been the main provocation for Franko's scathing criticism of the stylistic devices offered by Kuliš in his translation of the Bible.

HOW SHOULD IT SOUND?

In order to ascertain the most representative features of the 1903 Bible, it is expedient to juxtapose it with the poetic paraphrase of the Old Testament made by Kuliš in 1869 (*Pentatevx*). This paraphrase was criticized by the conservative Greek Catholic clergy (Studyns′kyj 1930, xxv–vi), despite Kuliš's efforts to substantiate, in most conciliatory terms, his programmatic views in the preface to the translation (*Pentatevx*, 2). As if anticipating the clergy's negative reaction to the vernacular basis of his

---

4 It is most interesting to note that, in his translation of Homer's *Odyssey*, Potebnja used more often than not the same reflex of the old sigmatic aorist *reče* with, however, the preterital meaning, along with a parallel form *rik* (Danylenko 1999, 246, fn. 21).

translation, Kuliš deemed it necessary to assure the clerics that his was not a perfect translation and that he viewed it as mere "galley proofs." Moreover, "every clever person," versed in the "Rusian-Ukrainian language" (*rus′ko-ukrajins′ka mova*), would be welcome "to correct these galley proofs at his discretion and send over his emendations to the editorial board of *Pravda*" (ibid.). The editorial board, as Kuliš promised, would collect all kinds of corrections and keep them for a subsequent revision of the translation. As he argued, the Galician-Rusian clerics would be most helpful in this endeavor inasmuch as with their support it would be possible to convene a "council of smart and knowledgeable devotees of the Rusian people" (ibid.). Neglected by the literati, the Rusian (Ukrainian) people retained their vernacular language, while imploring the intellectuals to share with them "a key to comprehension." Leaving aside political misunderstandings and personal rancor, it was time to meet their request (ibid.).

This preface was, in fact, a reprinting of the corresponding section in the editorial board's invitation to the subscription published in issue 46 on 22 December 1868 (Mykyta and Kuliš 1868, 541–542). At that time Ivan Mykyta was only nominally the editor of the periodical (Studyns′kyj 1927, 77), which means that this invitation was authored by Kuliš. He may have penned another editorial address entitled "Do čytateliv Svjatoho Pys′ma" (To the Readers of the Holy Scriptures) that appeared in issue 12 on 30 March 1869 when Natal′ Vaxnjanin had just filled the office of the editor. In this address, Kuliš shed additional light on his translation principles, while again stressing that the translation of the Holy Scriptures as published by *Pravda* was a mere blueprint for a future synthesis. For this reason, Kuliš added, "the translators" had been purposely resorting to various synonyms and different forms inasmuch as "they hoped to learn from the correctors which version they would love better" (Vaxnjanin and Kuliš 1869a, 112).

One can concur with Fedoruk (1998, 280) that the publication of the *Pentatevx* comprised a provocative double meaning. Among other things, it was aimed at instigating debates about the language of a future vernacular translation of the whole Bible. Unfortunately, what Kuliš achieved by undertaking this pioneering translation was the immediate animosity of the local clerics and a subdued optimism of the Ukrainophiles about his work.

However, the outburst of extremely contentious criticism, especially by Franko, was triggered by the appearance of the New Testament in 1871 and the complete text of the Bible in 1903, translated in a *scholarly* manner with a solid admixture of Church Slavonicisms. Despite Puljuj's intervention in the final draft of the posthumous publication of the Ukrainian Bible in 1903, this "authoritative version" crowned a long cooperation of several translators with different linguistic views and literary tastes that were influenced in one way or another by what had been achieved by their pioneering predecessor.

To look first into the phonetics, Kuliš sporadically, sometimes according to the eighteenth-century tradition, retained the etymological *o* and *e* in newly-closed syllables, although in separate words Puljuj might have later restored the old *i*, as in *narid* "people" (*SP*, 59, Ex 5:16) (e.g., *mylost'* "goodness," which looked bookish in comparison with *nespravedlyvist'* "iniquity" [*SP*, 89, Ex 34:6, 7] and *mid* "honey" [*SP*, 88, Ex 33:3], which is still attested today in many southwestern Ukrainian dialects, for instance, in Volhynja and Podolja [Žel., 1:441; *AUM*, 2, map 37]). Here also belongs the form *hod* (*SP*, 8, Gen 5:3, etc.), hardly borrowed, however, from the Xarkiv or Poltava region inasmuch as it is found in early Middle Ukrainian texts extant predominantly from western Ukraine (Danylenko 2006c, 317; *AUM*, 2, map 353; Žel., 1:147). One can add here some *sandhi* positions of the type *peredo* "in front of" and *zo mnoju* "with myself" (*SP*, 74, 7), where the secondary *o* shows no analogical change into *i* (Žovtobrjux et al. 1979, 283), which was regularly found in western Ukrainian grammars (Voznjak 1911, 117) (consider *zijde* [3 sg. fut.] "to come down" [*SP*, 73]). In Kuliš's *Pentatevx*, one finds more often than not a similar parallelism, e.g., *ziždav* next to *zoždav* "he stayed [yet]" (*Pentatevx*, 8, Gen 8:10, 12), although *ikavism* tends to prevail in positions of the secondary *o* as in *viz'my* (imper.) "take [her]!" (*Pentatevx*, 10, Gen 12:19).

In accordance primarily with the northern Ukrainian literary tradition, one finds in the 1903 Bible shifts in the distribution of *i* and *y* like *vmiraty* "to die," *zabiraty* "to take" (*SP*, 74, 66), and the *e*-reflex of the nasal *ę* in *vyhledity* "to provide out [of all the people able men]" (ibid., 72, Ex 18:21). Hyperistic spellings of the type *hrjad* "hail" (*SP*, 64), *hrjanycja* next to *hranycja* (ibid., 73, Ex 19:23, 24), are primarily retained in Southwest Ukrainian (Žel., 1:162). A typical late Middle Ukrainian spelling of voiced consonants before voiceless ones (Shevelov 1979, 478) is exemplified in such pairs as *mužs'kyj* "male" (*SP*, 67, Ex 12:48) and *muz'kyj* (*SP*, 128, Num 1:2). It is noteworthy that, in addition to the form *muz'kyj* found in the paraphrase of 1869 (*Pentatevx*, 109), Kuliš also employed a western Ukrainian form, *mužes'kyj* [*pohlav*] (ibid., 13; Žel., 1:457), arguably in order to archaize the narrative about the circumcision of "every male among the men of A´-bra-ham's house" (Gen 17:23).

In the Bible of 1903, of interest are instances of Old Ukrainian substitution of *e* for Church Slavonic *ě* like *narekannja* "murmurings" (*SP*, 70, Ex 16:7) and *rekly* "they said" (*SP*, 19, Gen 2:19; Žel., 1:489), with a more historically convoluted reflex of *jat'* in *sedity* "to sit" (*SP*, 19; Shevelov 1979, 200) as found already in the Laurentian codex of 1377 (e.g., *sedit'* [3 sg. pres.] "to sit" [Laur. 1377, 141, especially 695]). Žovtobrjux et al. (1979, 263) treated the latter form as a result of the confusion of *e* with *y*. Yet the latter confusion seems to be discernable in the spelling *mini* (dat.) "to me" as used throughout the text of the *Pentatevx* in contrast to *meni* in the translation of 1903. Deserving of special attention is another case of the aforementioned confusion, *zymlja* "earth" (*Pentatevx*, 8, Gen 8:22), as compared with the regular *zemlja* in the 1903 edition of the Ukrainian Bible (*SP*, 11).

In the authoritative version of 1903, one also encounters parallel forms with the "new *a*," which is likely intended to convey a semantic difference between *bohatyj* "rich" (*SP*, 14) and *bahac'ko* "some more" (ibid., 70, Ex 16:17) in some southwestern Ukrainian dialects (Shevelov 1979, 515). However, on closer inspection, there seems to be no clear-cut distinction between this type in most of the forms used by Kuliš (e.g., *bahatyj* "rich" and *bohato* "many [of them]" [*SP*, 85, 72, Ex 30:15, 19:21; Žel., 1:35, 8]). It is tempting to connect this phenomenon in the language of Kuliš with the generalization of many *a*-forms in Middle Ukrainian literary texts extant from different Ruthenian lands, including Volhynja, Polissja, and Sloboda Ukraine (Žovtobrjux et al. 1979, 288).

In examining the morphonology, one should note the preposition *id* (e.g., *id pivnoči* "northward" [*SP*, 15, Gen 13:14]), used sporadically in sharp contrast to the regular *do* "up to." This is clearly a Transcarpathian (Hucul) regionalism attested in the seventeenth-century Uglja *Ključ* and blended most likely of *yk"* ~ *k"*, commonly taking the dative, with *do* (Shevelov 1979, 689; Bevzenko et al. 1978, 425; *DUL*, 13:25). The preposition *id* was likely introduced by Kuliš himself since this form, sometimes in parallel spelling, also occurred in his *Pentatevx* (e.g., *yd pivnoči, yd poludnju* "northward[,] and southward" [*Pentatevx*, 11, Gen 13:14] or *id Sydym-dolyni* "in the vale of Sid'-dim" [ibid. 14:3]). In the paraphrase of 1869, Kuliš also used the dialectal preposition of direction *yk* (< *yk"*), attested in Middle Ukrainian from the fourteenth century onward (Bevzenko et al. 1978, 425) (e.g., *yk poludnju* "into the south" [*Pentatevx*, 11, Gen 13:1]). The same Transcarpathian (Lemkian?) provenance can be ascribed to another preposition *pro* "for" as found in the Bible of 1903 (e.g., *pro ščo* "why" [*SP*, 71]); the latter is semantically reminiscent of *pro* as attested, for instance, in the *Catechism* of Ioann (Ivan) Kutka (1801) (Danylenko 2008a, 91–92, fn. 11).

Of utmost interest are some other archaizing features in the 1903 Bible dating back to the Middle Ukrainian period, for instance, the use of *uz* (< *vъz-*) with a new optional *u-* and *v-* in *uz berih riky* "by the river's bank" (*SP*, 56, Ex 2:3) (see also *vozxodyty* "to ascend" [*SP*, 30, Gen 28:12] and *voz'my* [imper.] "take!" [*SP*, 89, Ex 34:9]). Such forms are conspicuously lacking in Kuliš's *Pentatevx*. Among obvious dialectal features in the edition of 1903, I will mention the change *j* > *l'* on morphemic boundaries (in Podolja, western Polissja, and Transcarpathia) as reflected in *zdorovlja* "welfare" (*SP*, 72, Ex 18:7), as well as the exchange of the dental *d'* with *j* in numerals ending in *-cjat'*, as attested in Southwest and North Ukrainian (e.g., *tryjdcjat'* "thirty" [*SP*, 8]). Such forms were already commonplace in the text of the *Pentatevx* and could reflect a sort of Galician norm in the making (Macjuk 2001, 297–298). One can add here partial generalization of *e* in the oblique forms of numerals like *po semy dnjax* (*SP*, 10) in the Bible of 1903. Among the pronouns, Kuliš consistently used the personal pronoun *vin* "he" without a word-initial *n-* in the environment after a preposition like *u jomu* "therein" and *na jomu* "thereon" (ibid., 71, Ex 16:24, 17:12). Generally, such forms are typical of the northern Ukrainian dialects, as well as of the bulk of southeastern and some northern Volhynian dialects (*AUM*, 2, map

208, 3, part 1, map 51). No wonder it was commonly used in the Central Dnieper variety of literary Ukrainian throughout the nineteenth century.

The demonstrative pronoun *sej* (m.), *sja* (f.), *se* (n.) as encountered in Kuliš's work belonged to the same literary standard, permeated with northern Ukrainian elements and cultivated by such writers as Ivan Kotljarevs´kyj, Hryhorij Kvitka-Osnov'janenko, and Leonid Hrebinka (Danylenko 2008b). Interestingly, parallelism of *sej* and *cej* is observed in the works of such Right-Bank Dnieper writers as Petro Hulak-Artemovs´kyj and Taras Ševčenko, thus reflecting a distribution of the two forms in North and Southeast Ukrainian as well as in Volhynja and Podolja (*AUM*, 2, map 210, 3, part 3, map 34). Explaining the predominant use of *sej* by Ševčenko in his private letters, especially after his return from exile, Tymošenko (1969, 109) assumed the influence of the poet's correspondents, including Myxajlo Maksymovyč and Myxajlo Ščepkin (1788–1863), all speakers of the transitional dialects developed on a northern Ukrainian basis. For the case of *sej* in Kuliš, however, it is possible to speak of his general orientation towards the previous literary tradition, while Southeast Ukrainian served as a primary basis for the grammatical make-up of his literary language. However, fluctuations of the type *se* ~ *oce* (n. sg.) were also attested in the language of the *Pentatevx* (e.g., 11, 46).

Finally, among neuters of the type *zillja* (coll.) "herb(s)," the translator (and the editor) employed only the northern Ukrainian ending *-e* after long palatalized consonants—*byllje* "grass," *nasinnje* "seed," *znattje* "knowledge," and so forth (*SP*, 5, 6, Gen 1:11, 2:17)—unlike the Galician-Bukovynian group of Southwest Ukrainian where there is no gemination before the ending *-e* (Žluktenko at el. 1979, 210). However, forms like *byllje* also belonged to the idiolect of Kuliš. It is no wonder that he used them in abundance in his personal letters. To take randomly his letters written to Stepan Nis, one comes across forms like *sÿlkuvanne* "effort(s)," *pečatanne* "publication, printing," *podružže* "(a married) couple," *rukopysanne* "manuscript" (Kuliš to Nos, 11, 31, 23). Only one form in *-a* is found in his letters to Nis (i.e., *pysannja svoje* [n. sg.] "one's own writing" [ibid., 23]), although it might have been a mere typographical mistake. Overall, neuters ending in -*e* and not -*a* were commonplace in the nineteenth century and beyond. Suffice it to mention that, in the twentieth century, neuters with long palatalized consonants ended by -*e* were still attested in the northern Poltava dialects (near Pryluky) and in the eastern Polissian dialects where they prevailed (*AUM*, 1, map 205; Hrycenko 2007, 27).

Yet a peculiar distribution of such neuters is observed in the *Pentatevx*. First of all, there are only a few reliable examples of such forms in this text (e.g., *znattja* [gen.] "knowledge" [*Pentatevx*, 4, Gen 2:17], although *oblyččja* [2x, *Pentatevx*, 5] as opposed to *oblyččje* "face" [ibid., 13, Gen 17:3], also *uzhranyččja*, literally "borderland" [*Pentatevx*, 145] and *uzberižžja* "coast" [ibid., Deut 3:17]). On balance, one encounters some neuters here, used with the collective meaning of the type *otamannja* (coll.) "princes" (*Pentatevx*, 10, Gen 12:15) and *brattja* (coll.) "brethren" (*Pentatevx*, 46, Gen 2:11). Yet what is more significant in this respect is that Kuliš apparently tried to avoid using deverbatives, introducing instead regular vernacular nouns. Their simple morphological forms seem to contrast with somewhat bookish neuters in the translation of 1903: *byllje travne* (*SP*, 5) ~ *trava, bylyna* [*zernjana*] "grass, the herb yielding fruit" (*Pentatevx*, 5, Gen 1:11), *nasinnje* (*SP*, 5) ~ *zerno* "seed" (*Pentatevx*, 5, Gen 1:12).

Altogether, the language of the 1903 authoritative edition is more bookish and less variegated in terms of its dialectal and vernacular features, while the paraphrase of 1869 appears to be, from this point of view, more democratic and diverse.

HOW TO STRING WORDS?

The morphosyntax of the 1903 Bible's language is largely southeastern Ukrainian. The following features look representative. For instance, there is a comparatively limited number of impersonal constructions with indeclinable forms ending in -*to* and -*no* in the predicate and the accusative of direct object such as *vzjato molodycju* (acc.) "the woman was taken" (*SP*, 14, Gen 12;15), and in the *Pentatevx* (10). Relative clauses are introduced with the help of the absolutive relativizer *ščo* "that" accompanied commonly by an oblique resumptive pronoun (e.g., *zemlja, ščo na jij ležyš* "the land whereon thou liest" [*SP*, 30, Gen 28:13], with the resumptive pronoun [*na*] *jij* [loc.], next to *žinka, ščo dav jesy buty zo mnoju* "the woman whom thou gavest to be with me" [*SP*, 7, Gen 3:12], without any resumption). This is one of the litmus tests testifying to the southeastern basis of the new literary language as shaped in the second half of the nineteenth century. The use of *kot(o)ryj* in relative clauses at that time was influenced by Polish in the west and by Russian in the east (Sulyma 1924, 220). It is therefore no wonder that Ševčenko did not use this conjunction a single time in his major collection of poems, *Kobzar*. Kuliš seems to follow here the mainstream trend to use the Ukrainian *ščo* in the relative function. To take the *Pentatevx* as an example, *kotryj* is not attested in this translation in a similar function. It comes therefore as no surprise that, as an editor, Kuliš replaced almost all cases of the inflecting relativizer *kotryj* "who, which" in Nečuj-Levyc´kyj's *Pryčepa* (The Cocklebur) with *ščo* together with the resumptive pronoun (e.g., *ščo z nym* for *z kotrym* "with whom/which" in Nečuj-Levyc´kyj [Voznjak 1928b, 9]).

In his scriptural translations, Kuliš used particularly often the so-called synthetic future tense form expressed by the imperfective infinitive and personal forms of the auxiliary *jati* "to take" treated, however, as clitics (Danylenko 2006c, 195–217; 2011a; 2012a, 21–26). To give a random example from the edition of 1903, they are formations like *jisty me* "shall he eat" (*SP*, 67, Ex 12:44) and *vykupovuvaty meš* "thou shalt redeem," used in the same verse alongside *vykupovuvaty musyš* "shalt thou redeem" (*SP*, 67, Ex 13:13) with the de-modal meaning. Although sporadically, future tense forms with the auxiliary *buty* "to be" and the imperfective infinitive occur in Kuliš's translations of both 1869 and 1903 (e.g., *budete posluxaty* "you will obey" [*SP*, 73, Ex 19:5]).[5]

The use of the future tense ending in -*mu* in the biblical translations is particularly noteworthy. The areal distribution of this form in Ukrainian speaks for its northern Ukrainian provenance in Kuliš's writing, although as has already been pointed out the synthetic future tense is also attested

---

5 Puljuj seems to demonstrate a similar distributional pattern of future tense forms in his part of the translation (e.g., *ščo robyty me pravednyj* "what can the righteous do?" [*SP*, 510, Ps 11:3] alongside *ne bude slidyty* "[the wicked] will not seek" [*SP*, 509, Ps 10:4]).

cross-dialectally, first and foremost in Southeast Ukrainian. Having embarked on a joint translation of the New Testament in the early 1870s, Puljuj might have accepted this form as one of the linguistic devices to be reserved for a new biblical style in the making. In fact, he could hardly seriously object to its introduction since he was cognizant of a seemingly identical form occurring in Bukovyna, Pokuttja, and Hucul dialects (*AUM*, 2, map 244). The major morphosyntactic difference of this western Ukrainian form lies in maintaining the auxiliary clitics, which can occur in clause second or verb-adjacent position (Macjuk 2001, 305), whence WUkr. *mu braty* or *braty mu* as opposed to southern/northern and standard Ukr. *bratymu* "I will take" (Danylenko 2011a, 172–174, 2010c). Described as synthetic, the latter form is usually juxtaposed to the analytic future tense with the auxiliary *buty* "to be" (*budu braty* "I will take") as allegedly synonymous (Vyxovanec´ and Horodens´ka 2004, 254; Matvijas 2006, 64).

Overall, due to the northern Ukrainian provenance of the synthetic future tense, it is not surprising that in the 1869 edition of the *Pentatevx* Kuliš made use of the corresponding form spelled as a single word (e.g., *sudytymu* "I will judge," *robytymut´* "they will work" [*Pentatevx*, 12, Gen 15:14]). Not surprisingly, similar formations were prevailing in the writer's idiolect. For instance, in most intimate and friendly letters written to Stepan Nis, Kuliš resorted more often than not to forms like *spomy̆naty̆mu* "I will recall," *perepolyrovuvaty̆mu* "I will polish again," *pečzzzzzzzzzzzzzzzzzzzzzzzz* — *pečataty̆mu* "I will print," and *čytaty̆mete* "you will read" next to a rare future tense form *roby̆ty̆ budu* "I will do" (Kuliš to Nos, 9, 10, 12, 14, 28). In Nečuj-Levyc´kyj's manuscript of *Pryčepa* (The Cocklebur), Kuliš largely replaced analytic future tense forms with the synthetic future ending in -*mu* (e.g., *huljatymy* instead of *ja budu huljaty* "I will walk" [Voznjak 1928b, 7]). A traditional Galician spelling of the auxiliary separate from the infinitive was introduced in the posthumous edition of the 1903 Bible by Puljuj who, according to Nečuj-Levyc´kyj (1968, 467, 473, 474; Jefremov 1918, 160), replaced a lot of Dnieper Ukrainian forms with their Galician counterparts. Hence such spellings as *tisnyty mut´* "they shall afflict [them]" (*SP*, 16, Gen 15:13), and *promovljaty meš* (*SP*, 58) as compared with *hovorytymeš* "thou shalt speak" in Kuliš's translation of 1869 (*Pentatevx*, 47, Ex 4:15), although see also *obrizuvaty metesja* (*SP*, 17) next to *poobrizujte v sebe* "ye shall circumcise" (*Pentatevx*, 13, Gen 17:11).

Yet more revealing from this point of view are similar corrections in the text of the New Testament, which was originally published with spelling reflecting the agglutination of the auxiliary clitic with the infinitive (Danylenko 2006c, 260–261, 2011a, 174–176), whence *žytyme* (*NZ*, 6) ~ *žyty me* "shall [not] live" (*SP/NZ*, 5, Mt 4:4), *klanętymessja* and *služytymeš* (*NZ*, 7) ~ *klanjaty meš sja* (sic) "thou shalt worship" and *služyty meš* "thou shalt serve" (*SP/NZ*, 5, Mt 4:10). Overall, the difference in the spelling of the future tense forms ending in *-mu*, and likewise of the reflexive particle, was determined by the corresponding system of orthography. Unlike the *kulišivka* alphabet, which allowed the combination of the auxiliaries together with the main lexemes, the system of Jevhen Želexivs´kyj as construed by him for *Malorusko-nimeckyj slovar* (The Little Russian-German Dictionary) and used officially in Galicia from 1893, did not accept any univerbation of the auxiliary with the infinitive (see Nimčuk 2004, 11).

Regrettably, the corresponding spelling in the 1903 publication of the Bible was not congruous with the original spelling and, therefore, with the meaning of the future tense form ending in *-mu* as used by Kuliš in his writings, including the biblical translations. Some clarification is necessary here. As early as 1874, Potebnja (1958, 358) posited for the future tense form ending in *-mu* (from the auxiliary *jati* "to take") an inceptive meaning that is not to be found in the analytic future tense with the auxiliary *buty* "to be." The same differentiation was substantiated later (Dem'jančuk 1928), and is still maintained today by some scholars (Danylenko 2011a, 2012a, 23–27). For instance, Bevzenko (1997, 216–217) claims that the future tense with the auxiliary "to be" denotes "a future event, [conceived] in general," without any nuance of inceptiveness, thus presenting an upcoming event as "prolonged and gradual," while the future tense in *-mu* with the auxiliary "to take," instead, focuses on the inceptiveness (inchoateness) of a particular event (Marčylo 1997, 23–24, 2001; Danylenko 2010c, 118). Consequently, one needs to distinguish between the westernmost Ukrainian future tense formation with the auxiliary clitics and the eastern Ukrainian with the auxiliary concatenated with the infinitive; the latter form began infiltrating the language of Galician speakers in the late nineteenth and early twentieth centuries (Tymošenko 1979, 126–127). If the westernmost Ukrainian future tense form with the auxiliary clitics demonstrates residual de-modal semantics, the eastern Ukrainian synthetic form brings attention to the beginning of a certain action rather than its duration, whence a stylistic differentiation of the future tense forms in modern Ukrainian. For this reason, Puljuj, while introducing the Galician spelling in such cases, obliterated inadvertently the original meaning of the synthetic future tense form as construed in the linguistic mentality of Kuliš.

Among southwestern Ukrainian features, one can also mention the comparative and superlative forms of the type *xytriščyj* "more subtle [than any beast]" (*SP*, 7, Gen 3:1). As for forms like *xytriščyj* with the dialectal suffix -*išč*- (Matvijas 1990, 73), they could have been introduced by Kuliš himself (Tymošenko 1971, 205). Note also that a similar form is found in the same verse in the *Pentatevx* (4, Gen 3:1). Among archaic (northern) forms, deserving of attention are the dual locative forms *v oču v mene* "in my sight" and *v ušu* "in the ears" (*SP*, 87, 88, Ex 32:2, 33:17), occurring in parallel use with new plural forms *v ušax* and *v očax* (*SP*, 87, 88, Ex 32:2, 33:16). The same dual locative *v oču* "in the sight" occurs in the *Pentatevx* (146, Deut 4:6). In addition to the noun phrase *pered očyma* (instr. du.) "in the sight" (*Pentatevx*, 50, Ex 7:20) with a regular instrumental dual form *očyma*, one happens on a peculiar noun phrase *pered viččju* (*Pentatevx*, 48, Ex 4:30), which is reminiscent of constructions like MUkr. (Lemk.) *spere(d) očiju* (gen. du.) (sixteenth century; see Kernyc´kyj 1967, 80). The genitive-locative form *viččju* is due to a methanalysis of the locative phrase (*u*) *vъ* + *očiju* (e.g., *PG* 1556–1561, 457v), also *viči* "eyes," with a secondary *i* arising from *o* in a position that did not require this change (Shevelov 1979, 606). It should be reminded that the locative dual form of *oko* is not attested in most sixteenth-century written records (Kernyc´kyj 1967, 80).

Kuliš also retains the auxiliary verb only in the compound preterit indicative 2 sg. form that sporadically competes with a regular preterit ending in -*v* (< *l*): *vdijav jesy* "thou hast done," *pro ščo pevnyv jesy* "why sadist thou" (*SP*, 14, Gen 12:18, 19), as opposed to a rare *ty vyviv nas* "thou hast brought us up" (*SP*, 71, Ex 17:3). In the *Pentatevx*, such former perfects are particularly representative and serve as archaizing devices, especially in "holy narratives," for instance, of God's law or the Wisdom Tradition. Speaking of other tense forms, the pluperfect forms of the type *ja buv učynyv* "I have done" (*Pentateuvx*, 8, Gen 8:21) also have an archaizing effect. Statistically, however, the archaizing morphosyntactic means are less numerous than expected in the *Pentatevx* of 1869.

In addition to the verbal forms, one can consider nominal adjectival forms, which are as a rule of Church Slavonic origin (e.g., *sotvoren* "made" and *prokljat* "cursed" [*Pentatevx*, 8, Gen 9:6, 25], *slaven* [*Pentatevx*, 9, Gen 9:26], *blahosloven* next to *blahoslovennyj* "blessed" [*Pentatevx* 12, Gen 14:19, 20]; consider also *nahi* [pl.] "naked" [*Pentatevx*, 4, Gen 3:7] without alternation of the stem-final consonant).

As in the prose translation of 1903, present active participles are used in the *Pentatevx* with the corresponding Church Slavonic suffix, whence *hrjaduščyj* "future" and *tekuščyj* "flowing [with milk and honey]" (*Pentatevx*, 46, Ex 3:8), *vydjuščyj* "seeing" (*Pentatevx*, 47, Ex 4:11), and *mohuščyj* "mighty" (*Pentatevx*, 6, Gen 6:4). Remarkably, all the aforementioned forms, save for the last one, are found in the dictionary of Jevhen Želexivs′kyj (Žel., 1:74, 162; 2:954). The lexeme *vydjuščyj* functions in this case as an active verbal derivative, unlike its eastern Ukrainian counterpart revealing primarily middle voice semantics, that is, "[which] is seen" (Kvitka, 1:132; Hrinč., 1:198, 200) (synonymous versions of one and the same saying *vydyma smert′ strašna* ~ *vydjušča smert′ strašna* "the obvious death is scary" [Nomys, 8295]). It is worth adding another interesting example: *dymušča nič* "smoking furnace" (*Pentatevx*, 12, Gen 15:17), a metaphor that gets murky in the prose translation, [*nič*] *nače pič zadymuvala* "[a night] started smoking like a furnace" (*SP*, 16). One can add here *paxušče kadylo* "sweet incense" (*Pentatevx*, 81, Lev 4:7), *ohon′ žeruščyj* "consuming fire" (*Pentatevx*, 146, Deut 4:24), *lazjuščyj* "[any thing] that creepeth" (*Pentatevx*, 146, Deut 4:18), and other similar forms, all supplied with the bookish (Church Slavonic) form of the corresponding suffix.

In sum, apart from possible corrections made by Puljuj, the language of the 1903 Bible is premised on a southeastern dialectal basis. Church Slavonic means in this translation are used sparingly, even if compared with the *Pentatevx* of 1869.

HOW TO CHOOSE WORDS?

A particular tendency is visible in the vocabulary of the 1903 edition. In this translation, while resorting to different style registers, Kuliš tended to provide neutral or vernacular alternatives to the Church Slavonic and bookish (Ruthenian) forms. Some of the bookish lexemes were adopted into Southwest Ukrainian and adjusted to the local morphological rules, while in Hetmanate and Sloboda Ukraine these lexemes tended to be replaced by their Great Russian counterparts. Yet borrowing scenarios could be extremely diversified through unique historical vicissitudes. For this reason, I will dwell only on some of the most telling examples, comparing them with the vocabulary of the paraphrase of 1869.

To adduce a random example, Kuliš opted for the lexeme *ljampa* "lamp" (*SP*, 85) instead of *lampa*, which could be viewed as a true Russianism inappropriate for the Ukrainian translation of the Holy Scriptures. In fact, demonstrating a "light" (Central European) *l'*, the form *ljampa* was likely to look exclusively Galician already by the time of Kuliš, and especially during the first "language debate" of 1891–1893 devoted to the future of literary Ukrainian (Shevelov 1966, 61–68). However, the case of *ljampa* is particularly instructive. To begin with, this form was also utilized by Ioanykij Galjatovs′kyj (1660) (Tymč. and Nimčuk, 1:416), whose language might have been open to the local (northern Ukrainian) dialect features. Second, in his *Leksikon″*, Berynda (112) did not distinguish between *ljampa* and *lampa*, glossing them in two consecutive entries. Thus, under ChSl. *světylnyk″*, Berynda provided Ruthenian *lampa* along with a Polonism, *poxodnę*, while under ChSl. *svěšča* he made use of Ruthenian *svěča* "candle" next to a Polonized form, *ljampa*.[6]

---

6   The controversy of this form becomes more obvious in the light of the normalization of Ukrainian spelling from the early twentieth century onward. Thus, in the first pan-Ukrainian Orthography of 1928/1929, the authors agreed upon two principal compromises concerning the rendering of foreign *l* and *g*: to use *l* and *h* in loan words of Greek origin or mediation, and to use *l'* and *g* (for foreign *g*) in loan words of Latin and modern origin or mediation. Contradictory as they appeared, these rules reflected the usages in Central Dnieper (Russian) and West (Polish) Ukraine. Accounting for the historical political frontier between the two parts of Ukraine, Shevelov (1989, 133) concluded that the choice of *l* or *l'* and of *h* or *g* was dictated only by Russian or Polish influence. Prescribing the unknown pronunciation in each part of the country in 1928

With regard to *ljampa* in Kuliš and parallel *ljampa* and *lampa* in Galjatovs′kyj, one can tentatively posit two waves of borrowing from Greek and Latin. There are grounds for assuming that *lampa* is a long-naturalized result of the East Slavic (Old Ukrainian) borrowing from Gr. λαμπάς (ChSl. *lampada* [Sr., 2:7] used by Ševčenko [Hrinč., 1:879]). Later, under Polish influence, the form *lampa(da)* might have been readapted to the Polish-Latin model, whence *ljampa*, but not **ljampada*; the old *lampada* was apparently treated as an Orthodox Church Slavonic lexeme and subsequently retained even in the Galician-Bukovynian koiné (Žel., 1:396, 420; Shevelov 1989, 58–59).

A less convoluted borrowing scenario is observed in the case of another purportedly Polish-mediated loan form, *cynamon* "cinnamon" (*SP*, 85, Ex 30:23). Utilized by Berynda in his *Leksikon″* to gloss ChSl. *koryca*, the lexeme *cynamon″* is reintroduced in the Uniate *Leksykon″ syrěč″ slovesnyk″ slavenskij* (A Lexicon, To Wit, A Church Slavonic Vocabulary, 1722) as Pol. *cynamon* (*Leksykon″*, 61) and subsequently made its way into the *Pryručnŷj slovar′ polsko-sloven′skij y narodno-ruskij* (A Handy Polish-Slavonic and Vernacular Rusian Dictionary, 1849) of Teodor Vytvyc′kyj (Vytv., 52) with penultimate stress (Žel., 2:1053). This lexeme became stylish in the eighteenth-century written language, in particular in the northern part of Russian-ruled Ukraine (e.g., *cynamon″* as attested in *Lečebnik* [A Book of Medical Charms, 1776] [*Lěč.*, 56] compiled, according to Oleksander Potebnja, not far from Romny [today's Sumy region]). Quite possibly, this could have ultimately triggered the choice of this word by Kuliš, despite the existence of the parallel lexeme *korycja* in Southwest Ukrainian (Umanec′ and Spilka, 369; Žel., 1:366), omitted incidentally by Borys Hrinčenko in his dictionary of the Ukrainian language.

---

and 1929 was a radical linguistic experiment since the phonetic system of the other part was unknown. Concurring with his conclusion about differences in the corresponding phonetic systems, elsewhere (Danylenko 2005) I adduced additional argumentation, supported by historical evidence, to demonstrate that the use of *g* or *h* in loan words was ultimately determined by a phonemic conflict between two different obstruent systems, operative in Southwest Ukrainian and East Ukrainian/Modern Ukrainian.

Generally, Kuliš's vocabulary in the 1903 edition of the Bible breaks down into numerous word clusters demonstrating moderate synonymy reminiscent of that in Oleksander Potebnja's translation of Homer's *Odyssey* (Danylenko 2006c, 318–326). Some lexemes denoting, in the King James Version, various types of domiciles come first into consideration (e.g., Gen 19:2, 3, 4, 10, 20:17). Apart from the neutral form *dom* and a peripheral lexeme *xata* "house" (*SP*, 19; Berynda, 15), Kuliš used ChSl. *palaty* "chamber(s)" (*SP*, 14; Berynda, 86), commonly attested throughout the seventeenth and eighteenth centuries (Vynnyk et al. 1983, 408), MUkr. *hospoda* "house" (ibid.; Berynda, 15), favored also by Pylyp Moračevs′kyj in his vernacular translation of the New Testament, *budivlja* "house, building" (*SP*, 19; Žel., 1:47), and *domivka* "house" (*SP*, 19; Žel., 1:196), which first spread in the (western) Ukrainian lands under Polish influence. This is why the latter lexeme appears neither in the *Enejida* of Ivan Kotljarevs′kyj nor in the works of Hryhorij Kvitka-Osnov'janenko and Taras Ševčenko, although it was used by Oleksander Potebnja to denote various ancient Greek domiciles (Danylenko 2006c, 321; Bil.-Nos., 121). More oriented in the 1860s toward the vernacular as used in Dnieper Ukraine, Kuliš stopped short of using the lexeme *domivka* "house" in his paraphrase of 1869 (*Pentatevx*, 51), although it might have been familiar to him.

Deserving of attention is a series of *verba dicendi* characterized by a moderate semantic variance. Thus, in addition to the neutral *hovoryty (do)*, *kazaty (do)* "to say unto" and *(pro)movljaty* "to speak unto" (*SP*, 19, 70), the translator often used only one Church Slavonic form *hlaholaty (do)*, which is paralleled in a Middle Ukrainian pleophonic form *holosyty (do)* "to speak unto" (ibid.). The latter verb was not yet attested in Ivan Kotljarevs′kyj's *Enejida*, although in West Ukrainian it retained two basic meanings, "to speak" and "to weep" (Žel., 1:150; Berynda, 24, 26); Pavlo Bilec′kyj-Nosenko glossed only the second meaning of this verb (Bil.-Nos., 102). All in all, this cluster looks like a Middle Ukrainian entry borrowed word for word from Berynda's *Leksikon˝* of 1627 (Berynda, 24; Tymč., 553). The above clustering of the *verba dicendi* is similarly reflected in the *Pentatevx*, for instance, in chapter 8 of *Vteky* (Exodus). Thus, both the obsolete form *reče* (3 sg. pres.) and the neutral *(s)kazaty* "to say" are attested five times each (*Pentatevx*, 50–51), while the verb *hlaholaty* occurs only one time in this chapter.

There are also minor clusters in the Bible of 1903, consisting of two or more lexemes that can be used concurrently regardless of their stylistic register: *pustynja* (ChSl. and ORu.) (*SP*, 15, Gen 14:6) next to *step* "wilderness" (*SP*, 70, Ex 16:2), *rat'* "war" (ChSl. and ORu.) (*SP*, 15, Gen 14:2) next to *svarka* "chiding" (*SP*, 71, Ex 17:7), *zvjaha* "strife" (*SP*, 15, Gen 13:7; Žel., 1:291), *nevolja* and *potala* "the [upper] hand" (*SP*, 71, Ex 18:9, 10), *horod* "city" (ORu.) next to *misto* "place" (ChSl.) (*SP*, 19, Gen 18:24)—that is "locus, spatium" (*LLP*, 2:260)—and *šolomje xovma* "top of the hill" next to *verx hory* "top of the mountain" (*SP*, 71, 73, Ex 17:10, 19:20) with ORu. *šolomje* (*za Šelomjanemъ* "behind *Šelomjanъ*" in *The Igor' Tale*) (Sr., 3:1587) probably related to ESl. *xolm* (Vasmer, 3:255, 388) or MUkr. (dial.) *xovm* not affected by the Middle Ukrainian loss of the labialization of *l*; see also WUkr. *xom*, *xomec'* (dim.) "hill" (*UDW*, 1402). Another possible example is *okolycja* next to *dubrovyna* "plain(s)" (*SP*, 15, 18, Gen 13:10, 18:1).

Many of these lexemes are frequently attested in the *Pentatevx* (e.g., *pustynja* [11], *step* [46], *horod* [144]), with the exception of some Galician forms. In some cases, Kuliš preferred central Dnieper lexemes such as *svara* (11) to WUkr. *zvjaha*. In some verses, one happens on simple nouns that were replaced in the 1903 edition by more complex derivatives (e.g., *dub* [*Pentatevx*, 13] next to *dubravyna* "oak" [*SP*, 18, Gen 18:1]). To mention another deviating form, the verb *vojuvaty* as found in the *Pentatevx* (11) was replaced by a somewhat cumbersome expression *včynyty rat'* "to wage war" (*SP*, 15, Gen 14:2), viewed by a Galician editor (either Puljuj or Sljusarčuk) as stylistically more suitable for this type of narrative.

Social terms are rendered in the 1903 edition of the Bible with the help of obsolete forms or largely parallel native or loan words, often with modified semantics. Some of the more interesting examples are as follows: ChSl. and ORu. *knjaz'* "ruler," used in the Church Slavonic Bible (Pšepjurs'ka-Ovčarenko 1988, 242) next to *het'man* "chief captain," *duka* "duke" (It. *duca* from Lat. *dux*), and *lycjari* "captains" (*SP*, 22, 39, 69, 71, Gen 21:32, Ex 16:22, 15:4), also used by Ševčenko, with the first *r* removed by dissimilation (compare Pol. *rycerz* glossed as *rycar'* and *lycar'* in the dictionary of Teodor Vytvyc'kyj [Vytv., 260]). Like ChSl. *rab* and MUkr. *kmet* (Pol. *kmieć*) (Tymč. and Nimčuk, 1:368), the word *dvorjanyn* (*SP*, 16, 18, 65) denotes "servant" (Gen 14:15, 18:1, Ex 11:3; Tymč., 683) (compare Pol. *dworzanin* [Vytv., 67]). A stylistic and semantic parallelism is evidenced in the pair MUkr. *komonnyk* (coll.) "horsemen" (*SP*, 69, Ex 14:23), a borrowing from West Slavic (Machek, 216), and *jizdec´* "rider" (*SP*, 70, Ex 15:21). In the 1903 edition of the Bible, one comes across a peculiar collective form *otomannje* "host" (*SP*, 69, Ex 15:4), clearly introduced by Kuliš since this word is also attested in his *Pentatevx* and Southwest Ukrainian (Žel., 1:583).

Not surprisingly, the *Pentatevx* contains few social terms extant from the Cossack period. For a new literary standard, Kuliš deemed it necessary to incorporate words from an older, eastern Slavic (Old Rusian) lexical layer. The following pairs are likely to exemplify differences between two programmatic visions of language standard as reflected in the two translations of the Bible of 1869 and 1903 respectively: *posluhač* (*Pentatevx*, 51) ~ *dvorjanyn* "servant" (*SP*, 63, Ex 9:14), *urjadovi ljude* (*Pentatevx*, 51) ~ *dvorjane* "servants" (*SP*, 63, Ex 9:20), *čeljad´* (*Pentatevx*, 51) ~ *raby* "servants" (*SP*, 63, Ex 9:20), *učeni do zbroji* (*Pentatevx*, 11) ~ *kmeti* "trained servants" (*SP*, 15, Gen 14:14), *čeljadija* (*Pentatevx*, 13) ~ *ljude* (*SP*, 18, Gen 17:23). By way of contrast, I will mention here *namet* "tent" (*EDU*, 4:35) used in both the *Pentatevx* (10) and the 1903 edition of the Bible (*SP*, 14, Gen 12:8). Yet in the paraphrase of 1869, this form is sporadically paralleled by the Church Slavonic and Old Rusian synonym *šater* "tent" (*Pentatevx*, 11, Gen 13:12; Sr., 3:1583–1584; Vasmer, 3:379), found in Ivan Kotljarevs´kyj's *Enejida* (*Enejida*, Index) and in the dictionary of Pavlo Bilec´kyj-Nosenko (Bil.-Nos., 396). Clearly, following the old literary tradition, Kuliš avoided the Ukrainianized version of this noun, *šatro*, which, along with the bookish *šater*, is attested in Jevhen Želexis´kyj (Žel., 2:1084; Umanec´ and Spilka, 621).

Overall, the paraphrase of 1869 is characterized by its solid vernacular, even folkloric, foundations, despite a few Church Slavonicisms that are mostly clichés or lexical transfers (e.g., *xljabi nebesni* [*Pentatevx*, 7] found also in the 1903 edition of the Bible [*SP*, 11]). The text of the *Pentatevx* is replete with colloquialisms like *volocjuha* "vagabond" (*Pentatevx*, 5, Gen 4:14), *babuvaty* "to perform the office of a midwife" (*Pentatevx*, 45, Ex 1:16), and *zbyraty do kupy* (*Pentatevx*, 47, Ex 3:16) next to *skupyty* "to gather together" (*Pentatevx*, 48, Ex 4:29), though inappropriate, according to Žytec′kyj, for a translation of the Holy Scriptures (Žiteckij 1905, 34–35). In some cases, such forms are difficult to distinguish from dialectal forms proper to the type *čom* "why" (*Pentatevx*, 46, Ex 3:3), *molodycja* "fair woman" (*Pentatevx*, 10; *SP*, 14), *mandrivka* "journey" (*Pentatevx*, 11; *SP*, 14), *natjahaty vody* (*Pentatevx*, 46) versus *načerpaty vody* "to draw water" (*SP*, 56, Ex 2:19), *popoisty* "to eat" (*Pentatevx*, 46, Ex 2:20), *zajistysja miž sebe* (*Pentatevx*, 46) versus *bytysja* "to strive [together]" (*SP*, 56), *baba* (*Pentatevx*, 45) versus *baba spovytuxa* "midwife" (*SP*, 55, Ex 1:15)—both treated by Jefymenko (Jefimenko 1862, 48) as indigenous—*mamka* "nurse" (*Pentatevx*, 45; *SP*, 56), *sjudy j tudy* "this way and that way" (*Pentatevx*, 46; *SP*, 56, Ex 2:12), *teren ta bodjaky* "thorns also and thistles" (*Pentatevx*, 5, Gen 3:18), *tel′buxy* "the inwards" (*Pentatevx*, 86, Lev 9:19), and *byty bojem* "to smite very hard" (*Pentatevx*, 143).

Of interest is *obuv'ja* (*Pentatevx*, 46) as opposed to *obuvje* "shoe" (*SP*, 57, Ex 3:5). The latter form might have been viewed by Kuliš as western Ukrainian (Žel., 1:550; Umanec′ and Spilka, 556), although it is found in the synodal version of Moračevs′kyj's translation. Finally, one happens on standard vernacular adverbs attested cross-dialectally, that is, *zavdovžky* "long," *zavšyršky* "wide," and *zavvyšky* "high" (*Pentatevx*, 7, Gen 6:15), which also made their way into the prose translation of the 1903 Bible (*SP*, 9).

Dialectal forms reinforced the vernacular discourse of the 1869 paraphrase. Being sandwiched between, on the one hand, a thin layer of Church Slavonicisms, and, on the other, a solid admixture of vernacular elements, dialectisms tended to serve as a link between the two opposites. To give several random examples, one can cite the following dialectal forms: *zuzdrity* "to see" (*Pentatevx*, 47, Ex 4:14), attested also in the language of Hryhorij Kvitka-Osnov'janenko and Ivan Franko (Kumeda 2010, 35; Kvitka, 1:609), *skotyna* and *xudoba* "cattle" (*Pentatevx*, 11, Gen 13:2; Kvitka, 3:243, 573), *okrome* "independently" (*Pentatevx*, 11; Kvitka, 2:331)—attested in Sloboda Ukraine—*zaky* "ere" (*Pentatevx*, 45, Ex 1:19; Žel., 1:248), *žakovyna* "spoil" (*Pentatevx*, 144, Deut 3:7; Žel., 1:217), *skoro* "shortly" and *sojužane* "confederates" (*Pentatevx*, 4, 11, Gen 14:13; Žel., 2:898) as found in West Ukrainian, and *u-pryvydky* "in a vision" (*Pentatevx*, 12, Gen 15:1), cited by Hrinčenko as *pryvydky* from *Yov* (*Yov*, 1869, 16; Hrinč., 2:412) (see also WUkr. *pryvydok* "specter" [Kuzela and Rud., 861]). One can add here the expressions *koza tretjačka* "a she-goat of three years" and *baran tretjak* "a ram of three years" (*Pentatevx*, 12, Gen 15:9) Yet such blatant dialectisms are rare in the *Pentatevx*.

Kuliš's translation of the Pentateuch also contains some interesting neologisms. Apart from the neologisms employed by the writer throughout his oeuvre (e.g., *pravycja* "arm" [*Pentatevx*, 146, Deut 4:34]), deserving of attention are the following innovative forms: *xarčivnycja* "inn" (*Pentatevx*, 47, Ex 4:24) as opposed to *xarčevnja*, possibly a Russianism, found in the works of Hryhorij Kvitka-Osnov'janenko (Kvitka, 3:521), *vydovyna jakoho bačyva* "a similitude of any figure" (*Pentatevx*, 146, Deut 4:16), and *ubyvač* "slayer" (*Pentatevx*, 146, Deut 4:42) with a non-productive agentive suffix *-(a)č* (Humec´ka 1958, 108–109) that nevertheless was revived in the second half of the nineteenth century (see *dijač* "public figure, statesman" and *perekladač* "translator," *nasliduvač* "follower," *dvyhač* "engine, mover," and so forth [Muromceva 1985, 40]). Interestingly, neither *bačyvo* with *vydovyna* nor *ubyvač* are found in the two regional dictionaries compiled by Jevhen Želexivs´kyj and Borys Hrinčenko.

In sum, the high style as elaborated by Kuliš in his prose translation of the 1903 Bible was largely oriented toward southeastern morphosyntactic and phonetic features, with an admixture of various dialectal and diachronic elements at all other functional levels. However fragmentary, the foregoing analysis demonstrates that the vocabulary tended to contain some archaic, primarily southwestern Ukrainian lexemes, although with a limited number of obvious regionalisms. In fact, the vocabulary does contain Church Slavonic and bookish forms, both native and borrowed from/mediated by Polish during the Middle Ukrainian (Ruthenian) period. All loan forms had been largely naturalized in the written language first cultivated in the western and subsequently the northern and eastern parts of Ukraine from the late seventeenth century onward (Danylenko 2008b).

Generally, it is possible to agree with Fedoruk's (1998, 279) conclusion that the translation of the *Pentatevx* was poetic, free, and included a liberal use of dialectal and vernacular vocabulary, thereby revealing Kuliš's intention to make his translation "entirely popular." One can hardly agree, however, that the poetic translation underwent "excessive

Ukrainianization," as reflected, primarily, in the translator's choice of vocabulary and the remodeling of personal names *à la moujik*. On the contrary, the popular basis of the language of the *Pentatevx* was well balanced as a result of the introduction of bookish elements, although with a minimum of Church Slavonicisms. Only later, after a revision of the translation as recommended by Franz Miklosich, did the Church Slavonic forms make their way *en masse* into the language of the New Testament that had first appeared in 1871.

Taken as a whole, the prose translation of the Bible, which went to press in 1903, was likely to be treated, both ecclesiastically and linguistically, as an achievement in comparison with the poetic paraphrase of 1869. True, the prose translation acquired a kind of photographic precision and closeness to the Hebrew original through constant reference to western European biblical scholarship and a meticulous editing of the text by Puljuj. The precision of the 1903 prose translation, which replaced the old prose translation possibly burnt by Kuliš in the late 1870s, was a quality that Miklosich would have rightly praised. However, the 1903 Bible irrevocably lost a good portion of the poetic charm so characteristic of the language of the paraphrase of 1869, first and foremost, in the vocabulary and even spelling. As we shall see, the latter held an important place in Kuliš's linguistic program.

HOW TO SPELL WORDS?

Since the language of the *Pentatevx* constituted a complex system, one can wonder to what extent this paraphrase epitomized the phonetic principle adopted by Kuliš for his innovative system of spelling, dubbed in Galicia *kulišivka* or, as Kuliš himself preferred, *kulešivka* (Simovyč 1937). It is no wonder that, due to its phonetic nature, Kuliš's spelling system was received in both Russia and in Galicia with hostility, especially by the Russophiles who were propagating instead the so-called etymological spelling used "by analogy with the other Slavic languages," first and foremost Great Russian (Holovac´kyj 1850).

Yet the position of the Russophiles and some other critics of the *kulišivka* system was not unique in this respect. A similar stance was taken in 1827 in the Russian Empire by Myxajlo Maksymovyč, who adopted the etymological principle for Little Russian spelling, which substantially differed from "the pronunciational method" (Maksimovič 1841, 173). In particular, he retained the bulk of traditional Russian/Church Slavonic letters, while introducing, however, one major innovation. He proposed to place a kind of *paerok"* above letters rendering "sharp" Little Russian pronunciation, such as *â, ê, ô, û, î* (Maksimovič 1859, 2). Under the conditions of the unstable orthographic rules for written Ukrainian at that time, Maksymovyč's suggestion may appear quite reasonable. And indeed, in this case, the Great Russian reader could easily identify the etymological *o* and *e* pronounced differently in various "Little Russian dialects." That device was subsequently borrowed by the Russophiles in Galicia, especially in the first Galician school grammar of Myxajlo Osadca (1862; 2nd edition, 1864; 3rd edition, 1876), who tried to synthesize the phonetic and etymological principles of orthography, as well as in Omeljan Partyc′kyj's grammar of the Ukrainian language designed for elementary schools (Skurzewska 2007). It comes as no surprise that the so-called *maksymovyčivka* survived in Galician schools until the appearance of the government's decree concerning the introduction of phonetic spelling in local education (Kysilevs′kyj 1956, 92, 95–96).

Before going into detail on the development of Kuliš's phonetic spelling, one should be reminded of a compromise orthographic system used by Amvrosij Metlyns′kyj (1814–1870) in his collection of folk songs, *Dumky y pěsny ta šče de-ščo* (Dumky and Songs and Something Else, 1839), as well as in later publications, especially in the almanac *Južnyj Russkyj Zbornyk"* (Southern Russian Collection) that appeared in Xarkiv in 1848. In fact, he was one of the first synthesizers of both etymological and phonetic principles in Ukrainian orthography. He strongly believed that "a middle way between the vagaries of pronunciation and excessive concern for the retention of roots" was the most suitable in matters of spelling (Metlinskij 1848, 13–14). The author proposed to use the letter "ъ" (″) only for split pronunciation (*m″jaso* "meat"), the letter "u" instead of *jat′*, and the old letter *i*; he also offered to substitute the letter "u" for "ы" and to use the old letter "є" to denote palatalization of the preceding consonant. The only diacritic sign in his system was associated with "u" used "in place of the root letter," such as "û" (ibid., 18).

In the 1850s and 1860s Kuliš could hardly accept any compromise system at odds with his far-reaching plans for translating the Bible and major literary works of famous western European writers such as William Shakespeare, George Gordon Byron, Johann Wolfgang von Goethe, Heinrich Heine, and so on into (vernacular) Ukrainian. The spelling of such translations had to reflect the nature of vernacular Ukrainian as closely as possible. While in Galicia, Kuliš enlisted the support of those who had been already long before him defending phonetic spelling as the most fitting for the local vernacular without such "dead letters" as "ы" (ÿ) and "ъ" (″) (Lozyns′kyj 1850; Lesjuk 2003, 35–36). It is to Kuliš's credit that, having joined the contest of the populists with the Russophiles, he consistently implemented the phonetic script in the periodical *Pravda* in the years 1867 and 1868, although the editorial board could not yet stop using the back *jer* word-finally. Only on 8 October 1869, due to his perseverance, was the letter "ъ" finally dropped in all publications of this periodical.

In 1882, Partyc′kyj (1882, 329), who by that time had severed his relationship with Kuliš, wrote in his review of Kuliš's translations of Shakespeare that Kuliš had neither invented nor introduced phonetic spelling. This spelling had existed, as Partyc′kyj argued, long before Kuliš, in Rus′ and Galicia, where "our Markian Šaškevyč" employed it most adroitly. Furthermore, Partyc′kyj concluded, due to the "chameleonic variability" and "a lack of philological knowledge" demonstrated recently by Kuliš, that any "stupid, heterogeneous, convoluted spelling" could be called *kulišivka* (ibid.). Leaving aside discussion of the true motivation behind this scathing critique (Studyns′kyj 1927), it is tempting nevertheless to adhere to one point in Partyc′kyj's argument. Strange as it may appear, Kuliš was indeed accustomed to use various spelling systems in almost every publication. It is easy to note his fluctuations in spelling principles, from the traditional (etymological) to the phonetic one, although this orientation did not work out in some cases. For instance, in his early works Kuliš resorted to *maksymovyčivka* or, in his own terms, *kotljarivka*, with the back *jer*, the circumflex accent (*paerok″*) above some letters, the letter *jery* "ы," and some other spelling features (Simovyč 1937, 58). Among early publications, most representative is the historiographic poem

Ukrayna (Ukraine, 1843). Suffice it to cite randomly the following lines in the original spelling characterized by the use of the traditional back *jer* and *jat'*, the *paerok"* over the etymological *o*, and the Russian letter *ë* to denote palatalization of the consonant before *o*.

> Мало було зъ князьковъ того, що кожному покойникъ панотець одказавъ, а всякому хотѣлось статки й маетки у братôвъ поодннимати, самому на Вкраинѣ пановати. Стали князьки воёватись . . . . (Kuliš 1843, 6)

[The princes found what they inherited from their late father very small, and everybody wanted to take away possessions and estates belonging to his brothers, and rule by himself in Ukraine. So the princes began waging wars.]

A similar mixture of different orthographic elements are found in three poems of 1890 that were reproduced in 1908 in a collection of Kuliš's works edited by Ivan Kamanin (1850–1921), namely "Posvjaščeno V. M. Bělozerskomu" (Dedicated to V. M. Bělozerskyj), "Do Hanny Barvěnok" (To Hanna Barvinok), and "Bojanovÿ Zamÿslÿ" (Boyan's Intents). Spelling in these poems is characterized by the retention of the letters "ы" and "и" (e.g., *ljud'my s'vjatÿmy* [instr.] "holy people"), the use of the Russian letter "э" at the beginning of words (e.g., *èntuziasm"* "enthusiasm"), and the traditional *jat'* along with the letter "ë" as in *drobně slëzÿ* "fine (small) tears" (Kuliš 1908, 428, 429, 427).

Most interesting, in this respect, is the fact that Kuliš employed some elements of the *maksymovyčivka* (*kotljarivka*) in his later works. Thus one can easily note synthesis of etymological and phonetic principles in Kuliš's manuscript of *Xutorni nedoharky* (Homestead Candle-Ends) that was initially prepared in the so-called *jarÿžka* (Simovyč 1937), a derogatory name (after the letter *jery* "ы") referring to the Russian alphabet as used in Ukrainian-language publications appearing in the Russian Empire after 1876 (Nimčuk 2004, 23–24, see fn. 7). What is more surprising is that Kuliš resorted to etymological spelling in such poems as "Mahomet i Xadyza" (Mohammad and Khadijah) and "Marusja Bohuslavka" (Marusja Bohuslavka), a phenomenon first commented on by the editor of his works, Ivan Kamanin. The latter cited two lines in the original spelling excerpted from the dedication of "Mahomet i Xadyza" to the author's wife, Hanna Barvinok:

Хадизо—свѣтъ очей Пророка Магомета,
Звізда Поэзіи, вінець ясный Поэта! (Kuliš 1908, 10, 15)

[Xadyza, a light of the prophet Mohammad's eyes
A star of poetry, a bright crown of the poet!]

This extract demonstrates retention of the grapheme "ы" along with "the new i," as well as the use of the Russian letter "э" after the vowel. The list of similar controversies or, in other words, orthographic fluctuations, observed throughout Kuliš's creative life could be easily expanded (Simovyč 1937).[7]

In this context, it is interesting to note the orthography of some of Kvitka-Osnov'janenko's stories prepared for publication by Potebnja in the late 1880s. For instance, based on the author's protograph held at that time in the library of the Kharkiv Imperial University, Potebnja carefully reproduced Kvitka-Osnov'janenko's spelling in the story "Božy dytŷ" (God's Children, 1887), while introducing slight emendations in the punctuation only in order to emphasize the unusual morphosyntactic patterns of the author's Sloboda idiolect. The Russian letters were skillfully used by the editor to render Ukrainian sounds with a minimum of assimilation changes. Thus the letter "ы" denoted the Ukrainian sound *y*, while the letter "и" referred to the vowel *i* irrespective of its origin; the letter "і" was used in compliance with the old tradition. As in Kuliš's system of the late 1850s, the Russian "ё" marked a palatalized consonant before the *o* in the initial or medial position, and the back *jer* was used at the word-final position or, marking split pronunciation, after the labials and *r* (e.g., *ljub'jazno* "kindly"). The Russian "э" was used at the

---

7 This orthography is reminiscent of the typical *jaryžka* as used already in the first half of the nineteenth century. According to Kryms'kyj (1929, 181), the term *jaryžka* (initially, *jeryžka*), although implying something official and forcefully introduced (by the Ems Decree of 18 May 1876), referred to a system of orthography that was not totally alien to the Ukrainian phonetic system. While rendering Ukrainian sounds "pretty well," writings in this orthography "could be easily read" by many Ukrainians (ibid.). It was not surprising, he argued, that such authors as Hryhorij Kvitka-Osnov'janenko, Jevhen Hrebinka, and Taras Ševčenko began using elements of the Russian alphabet (*jaryžka*) in the first half of the nineteenth century (ibid.; Nimčuk 2004, 23).

beginning of words. The above peculiarities that, as will be shown below, were incorporated into the early *kulišivka*, are represented in the following short fragment from a story authored by Kvitka-Osnov'janenko:

Щожъ Захарій зъ своимы дитьмы?—Эге! И сыротамъ Богъ пославъ такого чоловыка замысць батька, а жинку ёго замисць матеры; бо обое добри булы, такъ и ихъ Господь мылосердный, за ихъ добре дило, благословывъ у-во всимъ. (Osnov'janenko 1887, 6)

[And what Zaxarij with his children?—Well! And God gave the orphans such a man instead of a father, and his spouse instead of a mother, since both of them were kind, so they were blessed by the merciful God for their kind deed.]

Edited by Potebnja, Kvitka-Osnov'janenko's text reveals consistency in using Russian letters, which, if applied systematically, could quite satisfactorily render Ukrainian phonetics. Any systematic interference of Russian phonetics in this case could be removed from the orthographic context. This is what Potebnja demonstrated as an editor of Kvitka-Osnov'janenko's works and what Kuliš experimented with earlier.

As far as Ševčenko's orthography is concerned, it was also fully based on the letters that were employed in literary Russian, and he used them to mark roughly the same sounds as they denoted in Russian. In general, the poet used the letter "ы" to mark the Ukrainian vowel *i* that is written today as "и," while he employed "и" for what is today "i" (Remy 2005, 172–173). However, as evidenced from Ševčenko's autographs of the years 1847 to 1860, the poet's orthography was a much more complex system of correspondences than *kulišivka*. Unlike Kuliš, who was modernizing Ukrainian spelling throughout his life, the poet was singling out Russian letters rather randomly and, one must admit, intuitively, partly in accordance with the older literary tradition. To begin with, the vowel *i*, irrespective of its provenance, was rendered by Ševčenko with the help of the letters "и," "i" or "ы," although the letter "и" was used more often, with the letter "i" occurring in the environment before the following vowel and *j* or sometimes in the word-initial position. Moreover, this vowel could be traditionally marked by *jat'* as in *čolověk"* (Moskalenko 1968, 163–164). The vowel *y*, irrespective of its origin, tended to be marked either by the letters "ы" or "и" as in *Kẏev"* compared to *Kyev"* and, although exceptionally, *Kiev"* with an "i" (ibid., 164). Overall, since the poet employed letters found in literary Russian, it was easy for its speakers to read Ševčenko's writings.

For the above reason, perhaps, Borys Hrinčenko was sure that *jaryžka*, although "not very nice," accomplished its mission, while bringing printed books closer to the Ukrainian readership—mainly the peasantry. Being schooled with the help of Russian script, the broadest audiences of Ukrainian speakers were capable of grasping texts printed in *jaryžka*, with Cyrillic letters rendering Ukrainian speech purportedly as well as the Russian one. At the same time, the *kulišivka* spelling system, which was not commonly taught in schools, was likely to appear less intelligible to the common people (Kryms'kyj 1929, 181). This is why, certain reservations aside, one can agree with Ahatanhel Kryms'kyj that *jaryžka*, elaborated on by the literati in Russian-ruled Ukraine long before the official decree of 1876, was not entirely unfit for use in Ukrainian.

In view of the long-standing tradition of using the elements of *jaryžka* in tsarist Russia, one should give credit to Kuliš who, as an authoritative writer and public figure, initiated the spreading of phonetic spelling all over Ukraine, both in Galicia and Dnieper Ukraine (Naxlik 2007, 2:393). As early as 1856, he outlined his vision of Ukrainian orthography in a preface to his *Zapiski o Južnoj Rusi* (Notes on Southern Rus', 1856–1857). Among other suggestions, following from the orthographic practice of his predecessors, he proposed to drop the letter "ы" and to use instead "the soft southern *и*," while introducing the letter "і" in reference to "the sharp *и*" irrespective of its origin (Kuliš 1856–1857, vii–viii, 1857, 7). In addition, Kuliš continued to use the Russian letter "ё" to render a palatalized consonant before the vowel *o* either in the initial or medial position (e.g., *ëho* "his" and *po-svoëmu čytaty* "to read in his native language" [ibid., 3]). Moreover, he resumed using the back *jer* at the end of a word and employed it, though not consistently, after the labials and *r* in order to mark split pronunciation (Nimčuk 2004, 8–9). Initially, the letter "є" was used after palatalized consonants, for instance, in neuters of the type *zillje* "herb(s)," while the letter "e" occurred in all other positions, mostly after letters rendering consonants (Kuliš 1856–1857, viii; see Pivtorak 2000a, 263). Remarkably, this letter is encountered in the *Pentatevx* in the beginning of words and after vowels (e.g., *Jever* "E´-ber" [*Pentatevx*, 10, Gen 11:17], *svojeji* [f. gen.] "one's own" [*Pentatevx*, 10]).

During his life Kuliš continued to refine his spelling system relentlessly. The year 1862 became a turning point in the formation of a new Ukrainian orthography when some of his works were published with the help of phonetic spelling in the first major Ukrainian journal *Osnova*, edited by Vasyl´ Bilozers´kyj (a brother of Oleksandra Bilozers´ka-Kuliš) together with Kuliš, Mykola Kostomarov, and Oleksander Kistjakivs´kyj. Assisted by Kuliš, who remained its *spiritus movens* and main contributor (Luckyj 1983, 103), the journal opened a wholly new vista on the development of a vernacular-based Ukrainian literary language (Huzar 1992). In fact, *Osnova* served as a wide forum for representatives of different, primarily populist, theories about the formation of literary Ukrainian, including its script. To give just one telling example, Mykola Hatcuk, who created two versions of a highly sophisticated orthography (one based on the so-called *graždanka* and the other one on the Church Slavonic script) argued for the retention of the Church Slavonic system (supplemented by diacritics) instead of the phonetic spelling used by Amvrosij Metlyns´kyj, Levko Borovykovs´kyj (1808–1889), and Kuliš (Gaccuk 1862).

Despite Hatcuk's criticism, publications in *Osnova* may have triggered further experiments with phonetic spelling. In general, one can concur with Mykytyn's (2000) view that Kuliš's orthography in the journal *Osnova* was most suitable for vernacular Ukrainian since his language was characterized by northern and primarily southeastern Ukrainian dialectal features, including characteristic assimilation across morpheme and word boundaries. Among such features, it is worth mentioning a lack of neutralization of the obstruents at the end of words and across morpheme boundaries. For instance, there is the retention of the voiced *z* in the prefixes *bez-* and *roz-*, though the latter prefix occurs in Kuliš's language of that period in two variants, either with the voiced *-z-* or voiceless *-s-* in the environment before *k*, *p*, and *t* (e.g., *rospušču* [1 sg. fut.] "to loose" and *rosteklysja* [pl. pret.] "to spread" [*Osnova* 1861, 9:25; Mykytyn 2000, 154–155]). The prefix *z-* is realized as a voiceless *s-* before the voiceless obstruents *k, p,* and *x,* whereas *z-* happens before a voiceless *s,* as in *zsypaty* "to pour." At the same time, as has been mentioned, the voiced obstruents are not subject to neutralization at the end of words and before voiceless obstruents (e.g., *rid"* "family, kin," *tjažke* [n. sg.] "difficult," *sterehty* "to guard" [*Osnova* 1861, 9:25, 30, 96]). One finds a special case in the consistent spelling of a voiced obstruent in the prefix *od-,* commonly found in North and Southeast Ukrainian, in contrast with the Galician form *vid-.*

Assimilation is also attested in the journal *Osnova,* although not all of its types are represented evenly. Thus, Mykytyn did not find any example of dentals assimilating before hushing sibilants, a phenomenon which is attested in Kuliš's predecessors, Ivan Kotljarevs´kyj, Oleksij Pavlovs´kyj, and Pavlo Bilec´kyj-Nosenko. Mykytyn, however, found many examples of using sibilants in place of hushing sounds as in *zaporozci* "Cossacks" and *sxylyssja* (2 sg. fut.) "to bow" (*Osnova* 1861, 11–12:15, 31). Interestingly enough, the latter change, depending on what obstruent occurs in the environment before the sibilant, is poorly represented in works of Kuliš's predecessors.

In Sloboda orthography as practiced by Kuliš, assimilation across the boundary of the reflexive particle *-sja* with a preceding obstruent is attested abundantly inasmuch as, unlike Southwest Ukrainian, the southeastern dialects show deep fusion of the particle with the root (Zales´kyj 1969). Yet Kuliš marked only the corresponding change of the consonant in the particle, such as *vbyvaetcja* (3 sg. pres.) "to grieve," *yzdrihnetcja* (3 sg. non-past) "to tremble," and the like, as opposed to rare spellings with a soft sign of the type *rozmynat´cja* "to miss, come late" (*Osnova* 1861, 11–12:2, 9). All these examples prove that the phonetic principle outweighed the historical-etymological foundations of Kuliš's orthographic system.

The phonetic principle was appropriated and advanced by the editors of the Southwestern Branch of the Imperial Russian Geographic Society, who, for instance, dropped the letter "ъ" word-finally and began using the letter "ï," which had been absent from Kuliš's orthography, from 1873 onward. Meanwhile, in Galicia, Jevhen Želexivs´kyj (along with Sofron Nedil´skyj) offered in *Malorusko-nimeckyj slovar* (The Little Russian-German Dictionary) of 1884–1886 a revised version of phonetic spelling (Kryms´kyj

1929, 180; Nimčuk 2004, 10–11). Based largely on Southeast Ukrainian, phonetic spelling was also implemented by Borys Hrinčenko in *The Dictionary of the Ukrainian Language* of 1907–1909 (Kysilevs'kyj 1956, 98, 102, 105). Overall, according to Naxlik (2007, 2:394), the so-called *kulišivka* created solid foundations for modern phonetic orthography as practiced today in literary Ukrainian.

Yet Naxlik's conclusion is somewhat impressionistic and worth further discussion. With respect to modern Ukrainian spelling, one should remember that this orthography is based on two major principles. The first principle, that of phonetics, reaching back to the orthographic tradition developed in Old Rus', was successfully cultivated from the fourteenth to the sixteenth centuries. Thereafter this principle was replaced by the etymological (historical-etymological) one that flourished from the late sixteenth until the early nineteenth century (Pivtorak 2000b, 477). What is remarkable about this periodization is that, during the period from the sixteenth to the eighteenth centuries, a new trend of adjustment of traditional letters towards vernacular pronunciation took shape. As a result, modern Ukrainian orthography is premised on phonetic (e.g., the letter "о" rendering both etymology and the new sound *o*) and morphological principles (e.g., the use of uniform prefixes and suffixes irrespective of their position and possible assimilation or dissimilation). The latter principle is called sometimes phonematic, as it provides direct correspondences between phonemes and letters (Bilodid 1969, 416). The traditional-historical (etymological) principle (e.g., the use of the letters "я," "ю," "є," and "щ") is less influential in Ukrainian, as is the so-called differentiating principle, determining capitalization, hyphenation, and some other auxiliary rules in Ukrainian orthography (ibid., 413–417).

All in all, contrary to Naxlik, the contribution of Kuliš to the formation of new Ukrainian orthography appears minimal (Danylenko 2012b). One can also hardly agree with Tymošyk (1998) that "Kuliš's orthographic norms outstripped the rules that, beginning with *The Major Rules of Ukrainian Orthography* (1990), became normative in the Ukrainian language." What prevents giving him full credit as a precursor of modern orthography is that Kuliš utilized only the phonetic principle:

> Little Russian spelling must be premised on a most radical phonetics, to wit, on such [phonetics] that shows how the author

pronounced. Nobody can tell which pronunciation, either the Poltava-Černihiv or Galician-Rusian, the people's taste will adopt. Let it be even with such orthographic monuments as Kyivan spelling: *ŭiŭi* or *jiji*, or *iак*, *моiа* and so forth". (Barvins'kyj 2004, 201)

Although based on the phonetic principle as applied by some of the normalizers in Dnieper Ukraine and Galicia, Kuliš's claim seemed to be inherently innovative since his "vector of phonetization" was opposite to that of his predecessors. In order to ascertain this vector, it is useful to recall here the motto of the publishers of the almanac *Rusalka Dněstrovaja* (The Nymph of the Dniester) who, as early as 1837, posited in the preface the fundamental rule of spelling in Rusian (Ukrainian): "Write as you hear, and read as you see" (*RD*, v). In accordance with this motto, the publishers dropped the Slavonic letters "а," "ѫ," "ы," "ъ," and "ь," while introducing their phonetic correspondents; the *jat'* was, however, retained and used, replacing the etymological *o* and *e* or even the modern *ï* inconsistently (Poljuha 2004, 82). Influenced most likely by the orthographic principles of Vuk Karadžić (1787–1864), Šaškevyč devised a new grapheme, "ў," to denote a non-syllabic sound, marked in modern Ukrainian as *v*, and borrowed from Serbian a special sign for the Ukrainian affricate, rendered in modern Ukrainian as *dž* (Matvijas 1996, 27).

Kuliš's line of phonetic reasoning accounted for dialectal differences in various parts of Ukraine and his way of spelling was oriented not so much toward phonetic perception as toward the phonetics of articulation. To reframe the recommendation of the publishers of the almanac *Rusalka Dněstrovaja* (The Nymph of the Dniester), Kuliš's motto could be rephrased: "Write as you say, and read as you see," thus drawing the locus of phonetization from speaker to interlocutor. Consequently, the extent of phonetization knew in this case no constraint, a tendency that was exemplified by Kuliš from 1882 onward, especially in his collections *Dzvin* (The Bell, 1893), a first draft of which was finished in 1882 (Naxlik 2007, 2:285), and *Pozyčena kobza* (The Borrowed Kobza), published in the year of his death, 1897 (Simovyč 1937). However, as is evidenced from numerous spelling experiments undertaken by Kuliš especially during these six years, his orthographic system (*kulišivka*) was created *grosso modo* between 1856 and 1862. In fact, only the early system, as Simovyč (1937, 59) argued, contributed to the formation of modern Ukrainian orthography.

The morphological aspect of spelling was practically neglected by Kuliš, who based himself on naïve criteria for choosing a particular form:

> I heard some people who say *ulycja*, *vulycja*, *julycja* and other people who say *hulycja* ["street"]. The latter form appeals to me much better [since] I see that *hulycja* derived from *hul′nja* ["carousing, having a good time"], while I have no idea from what *ulycja* and the like might have derived. (Barvins′kyj 2004, 201)

As follows from the above, Kuliš's spelling was premised not on the morphonological structure of a particular word but on how this word was sounded by an individual speaker.

Kuliš devoted minimal attention to those linguistic criteria that he associated with the etymological principle. In his view, these were not particularly relevant for the codification of literary Ukrainian. With an eye to fostering its norms, different from all other Slavic languages including Russian, Kuliš could not help but strengthen the phonetic principle of spelling and thus distinguish written Ukrainian primarily from Russian. In a letter of 1881 to Barvins′kyj (2004, 199), he argued that, if one removes *tt* in the word *rosxottesja* (2 pl. imper.) "break up, disperse!" (MoUkr. *rosxod′tesja*), then there is no place for *dd* in *viddatysja* "to give oneself up" or *ss* in the word *smijessja* (2 sg. pres.) "to laugh" (MoUkr. *smiješsja*). Having designed such phonetic spelling, he continued, one could hardly please philology. Yet, he also added, it was worth reckoning with philology least of all (ibid.).

Strange as it may seem, the legacy of Kuliš in Ukrainian orthography looks less pioneering from the perspective of the current system of spelling rules, although one cannot deny his serious contribution, especially in work dating from 1856 through 1862, to the formation of modern orthography. To fully understand the innovative character of Kuliš's phonetic spelling and its implementation, it would be expedient to place his orthography in the cultural and historical context of Galicia in his time. In this respect, one should recall the first reaction of the clergy to the publication of the vernacular translation of the *Pentatevx* in 1869. The level of animosity of the church hierarchy toward the translation and orthography of Kuliš was high, to say the least. Suffice it to cite here a short note published on 15 March 1869 in *Pravda* by its editor, Natal´ Vaxnjanin, and most likely Kuliš (Vaxnjanin and Kuliš 1869b), who happily reported that a long-anticipated anathema against the translation of the Bible had been called off. Still the overall attitude of the Greek Catholic church to the translation did not change thereafter. In addition to the use of vernacular terminology, the conservative clerics and Russophiles accused the translator of using such names as *Musij* (Moses), *Xrat* (Eu-phra´-tes), *Oron* (Aa´-ron), *Ovram* (A´-bram), and other "allegedly voluntarily changed words" (ibid.). As one of the counterarguments, the members of the editorial board of *Pravda* brought to the attention of the critics the use of the form *Musij* in folk songs. They also cited the form *der Frat* as used in the book of Genesis (2:14) in Julius Fürst's *Illustrierte Pracht Bibel für Israeliten in dem masoretischen Text and neuer deutscher Übersetzung* (Leipzig, 1874) (Vaxnjanin and Kuliš 1869b): "und der vierte Strom ist der Frat (Eufrat)" (*Pracht Bibel*, 4) (see also *Xrat* [*Pentatevx*, 4] compared to *Evfrat* in the 1903 edition of the Bible [*SP*, 6; *Biblija* 1862, 1v]). Moreover, they encouraged their opponents to criticize, instead, the British who called Jesus "Džysee," or the others who called him "Žezju." If their phonetics allowed them to transform the name in this way, concluded Vaxnjanin and Kuliš (1869b), why does the "phonetics of our language have to produce *a*-forms in the case of the words *Oron*, *Ovram*, and the like?"

In effect, the introduction of *o* instead of the initial *a* in personal and geographical names might have looked like a radical vernacularization of Church Slavonic forms. However, this kind of change was deeply rooted in the transcription correspondences dating to the period of active contact between the East Slavs and Byzantium. Among other correspondences, the short Greek *a* was rendered by *o* in East Slavic (Vasmer 1941, 290). Also of paramount importance are regular correspondences as attested in Old Rusian and, especially, Middle Ukrainian texts, including *o-*, *je-* and the clusters *ia-, ie-, io-,* and *ioa-* in the word-initial position (Ostaš 2000). Similar correspondences found in the *Pentatevx* are likely therefore to testify to the archaic basis of the vernacular rendition of personal and geographical names. In general, the tradition of substituting *o-* for *a-* was operative through the entire Middle Ukrainian period, up to the sixteenth and seventeenth centuries. Despite the resistance of the church, which used Greek-based Church Slavonic forms of Christian names, variants with *o-* have been current throughout the aforementioned period (Shevelov 1979, 86) (e.g., *Ondrěj* [1392], *Semen" Oleksandrovyč"* [1457] next to *Semen" Aleksandrovyč"* [1459] [Rozov 1928, 47, 166, 171]). Remarkably, in their translation of the New Testament, Kuliš and Puljuj used as a rule Church Slavonic forms of Christian names like *Andrej* (*NZ*, 87).

There are many similar *o-*forms used in the translation in place of Church Slavonic variants beginning with *a-*. The following pairs, excerpted from the *Pentatevx* and the synodal Bible of 1862 (*Biblija* 1862), are highlighted by parallel forms in the 1903 edition of the Bible (*SP*): *Ovram* (10) ~ *Avram"* (5v), *Avram* (*SP*, 14), *Odam* (4) ~ *Adam"* (2r), *Adam* (7), *Omorij* (9) ~ *Amorrej* (5r), *Amorij* (*SP*, 12), *Orukij* (9) ~ *Arukij* (5r), *Arkej* (*SP*, 12), *Osur* (9) ~ *Assur"* (5r), *Assur* (*SP*, 13), *Orxaksad* (9) ~ *Arfaksad"* (5r), *Arfaksad* (*SP*, 13)—with a newly reintroduced *f*—*Ovymajlo* (9) ~ *Avïmayl"* (5r), *Abymavel'* (13), and finally, *Osyr* (45) ~ *Asyr"* (27r), *Asser* (55), *Oron* (85) ~ *Aaron"* (52r), *Aron* (103), and many others.

Changes involving the clusters *ia-, ie-,* and *io-* seemed to have been vernacularized less consistently. It is worth citing here only the most representative correspondences from the *Pentatevx* and the synodal Bible of 1862 (*Biblija* 1862) as compared with the 1903 edition of the Bible (*SP*), although some deviations are deserving of special attention: *Jektan* (9) ~ *Iektan"* (5r), *Joktan* (*SP*, 13), a change which is not discussed in Ostaš (2000), *Jevusij* (9) ~ *Ievusij* (5r), *Jevusij* (*SP*, 12), *Jarax* (9) ~ *Iarax"* (5r), *Jerax* (*SP*, 13), *Iovav* (9) ~ *Iovav"* (5r), *Jovav* (*SP*, 13), which is lacking in Ostaš (2000), *Jakov* (45) ~ *Iakov"* (27r), *Jakov* (*SP*, 55), and *Iosyp* (45) ~ *Iosyf"* (27r), *Josyf* (*SP*, 55), with a regular change of *io-* into *jo-* but no replacement of *f* by *p* as is the case in *Iosyp*, which retains the initial *io-*. All in all, and this is surprising, both the *Pentatevx* and the 1903 Bible reveal consistency in vernacularizing the above clusters. One can explain this, as was mentioned above, by the archaic basis of the vernacular rendition of personal and geographical names. Ohijenko (1939a, 3–4) argued, and rightly so, that the use of *j* in word-initial clusters like *ia-*, *ie-*, *io-*, and *ioa* in the scriptural translation was deeply rooted in the language of the Old Testament, which did not tolerate such clusters. In other words, the use of *i* in word-initial position in the biblical names was influenced by the Greek literary tradition (see Ohijenko 1927).

One needs, however, to add that, from the point of view of historical phonology, the treatment of *i* in word-initial syllables was dependent on various factors. In most of the examples, the treatment of *i* was a result of the loss of length in **(j)ī*, hence *ity ~ jty* "to walk," an alternation that encompassed some personal names introduced with Christianity (e.g., *Ivan ~ Jvan* [Shevelov 1979, 269]). However, the form *Josyp/Josyf* (< Ἰωσήφ) is another case where the initial *j* was lost as expected without any change in the vowel of the first syllable, as in *Osyp* (MUkr. *Josyp*, as attested in Kuliš's earlier translation, either has a prothesis or is a blend of the popular *Osyp* with the church-sanctioned *Josyf* as found in the 1903 Bible).

Some peculiar phonetic traits found in the language of the *Pentatevx* were ostensibly discontinued in the authoritative edition of 1903. I have already dwelt upon the counter-etymological x^w (also used by Moračevs′kyj) that was consistently applied in the *Pentatevx* but eliminated by Puljuj in the 1903 version of the Bible. In addition to the examples cited in previous sections, one should mention *Kaleb Jefunenko* (*SP*, 172) in place of *Xalev, syn Jexvunijev* "Ca′-leb the son of Je-phun′-neh" (*Pentatevx*, 143, Deut 1:36), *Jafet* (*SP*, 12) instead of *Jaxvet* (*Pentatevx*, 8, Gen 9:18), and *lystja smokovne* (*SP*, 7) as a substitution for *xvyhove lystja* "fig leaves" (*Pentatevx*, 4, Gen 3:7). In this case, it is difficult to determine what exactly influenced the replacement of the vernacular counter-etymological x^w by *f* inasmuch as the latter phoneme was operative in Church Slavonic, as used in Galicia and Russia at that time.

Speaking of the inventory of letters in the system of *kulišivka*, it is worth mentioning the Roman letter "g" introduced by Kuliš in *Zapiski o Južnoj Rusi* (Notes on Southern Rus′, 1856–1857) and explicated again in his *Hramatka* of 1857 (*Hramatka*, 7). He employed this letter consistently in most of his literary works, in particular in the novel *Čorna rada* (Black

Council, 1857). In this respect, one may wonder why the translators and editor(s) dropped the "g" in the 1903 edition despite its presence in the *Pentatevx*. Was this a result of the influence of Church Slavonic orthography, where no letter like "g" or "г," or the diagraph "кг," was found?

In the *Pentatevx*, the letter "г" (*g*) is attested in a few long-naturalized words as well as in forms originating in special phonetic environments. To give an example of the first group of lexemes, one can cite *graty* "bars" (*Pentatevx*, 144, Deut 3:5; Žel., 1:170), which is replaced by *zasuvy* in the 1903 edition of the Bible (*SP*, 174). Reflexes of specific phonetic environments are not numerous and can be reduced to the voiced reflex *g* of the voiceless phoneme/preposition *k*. Alongside the Polish borrowing *ku* and its phonetic continuation *gu* (Bevzenko et al. 1978, 425), the preposition *g* and its primary counterpart *k* are encountered in some western Ukrainian dialects (Verxratskyj 1902, 157). Behaving as stylistically marked devices, the *g*-forms occur in the language of the *Pentatevx* (e.g., *g Červonomu morju* "by the way of the Red Sea," *g pivnoči* "northward," and *g pustyni* "by the way of the wilderness" [*Pentatevx* 143, Deut 2:1, 3, 8]). The same preposition is also attested in the paraphrase of the book of Job (1869)—*g syrij zemli* "to the soggy ground" (*Yov, Pravda*, 43). No less interesting is the phonetic variant *yg* of *yk*, attested in records extant from the fourteenth century onward (Bevzenko et al. 1978, 425). Kuliš used *yg* in his introduction to the book of Job published under separate cover by the periodical *Pravda* (*Yov*, 1869, iii; Nimčuk 1969, 74).

Almost all other letters introduced in the *kulišivka* from 1856 through 1857 were retained in the *Pentatevx*, though with some innovations (Kryms´kyj 1929, 180–181). Thus, the translator dropped the back *jer* in the word-final position but kept using it in reference to the split pronunciation of hard and labial consonants of the type *ym"ja* "name" (*Pentatevx*, 4, Gen 2:14) and *z"javyvs´* (m. sg. pret.) "to appear" (*Pentatevx*, 46, Ex 3:2), although some inconsistencies are possible, such as *uzhir"ja* (sg.) "hills" (*Pentatevx*, 142, Deut 1:7) versus *uzhirrja* (*Pentatevx*, 143, Deut 1:41). Following Oleksij Pavlovs´kyj (*Grammatika*, 1–4), Kuliš used the letter "i" to render the corresponding vowel irrespective of its origin: *vin* "he" (*i < o*), *žinka* "wife" (*i < e*), *zmij* "serpent" (*i < ě*) (*Pentatvex*, 4). Instead of the letter "ы" (ÿ), attested with "ѣ" and "ъ" in the etymological orthography of Myxajlo Maksymovyč (Maksimovič 1827, 1841, 163–164, 167, 171), Kuliš resorted to the letter "и" to render a specific Ukrainian middle front sound distinct from the Russian ÿ (e.g., *xodytymeš* "thou shalt go" [*Pentatevx*, 4, Gen 3:14] next to *mini* "to me" [dat.] [*Pentatevx*, 4]). Kuliš borrowed the letter "ё" from Russian in order to mark the palatalization of a consonant (including *j*) before *o* as in *usého* (gen.) "all" (*Pentatevx*, 4, Gen 2:2), *ëho* (acc.) "him" (*Pentatevx*, 5, Gen 3:23), and the like. He much expanded the function of the letter "є," which was used not only after palatalized consonants as in *oblyččje* "face" (*Pentatevx*, 13, Gen 17:3) but also in all other positions where the so-called jotised vowels are attested in modern Ukrainian orthography (e.g., *jesy* [2 sg. pres.] "to be," *b'je* [3 sg. pres.] "to smite" [*Pentatevx*, 4, 46, Ex 2:11], and *tvoje* [n. sg.] "thy" [*Pentatevx*, 46, Ex 3:5]).

Needless to say, all the above peculiarities were eliminated by Puljuj in the 1903 edition of Kuliš's translation. Instead, he made several changes in phonetic spelling that were lambasted by Nečuj-Levyc'kyj after the appearance of the 1903 translation. Thus, in accordance with the *želexivka* system used in Galicia at that time, Puljuj introduced the letter "ï" for the reflexes of the etymological *e* and *ě* (e.g., *sïmdesjat'* "seventy" [*SP*, 137, Num 7:49] from ESl. and OChSl. *se[d]mь* "seven" [Vasmer, 3:608] and *nadïlyv* [m. sg. pret.] "set [the land before you]" [*SP*, 171, Deut 1:8; see also ChSl. *děliti* "to share" in Vasmer, 1:337]). The letter "і" was employed in order to mark reflexes of the etymological *o* as in *rid* "people" (*SP*, 11, Gen 11:6) from ESl. and OChSl. *rodъ* (Vasmer, 2:527). Instead of "ё" in the environment after a palatalized consonant, Puljuj introduced the digraph "ьо." In addition, Puljuj began marking the palatalized *z*, *c*, and *s* in the environment before *v*, as in *s'vit* "light" (*SP*, 5, Gen 1:3) and *z'vir* "beast" (*SP*, 5, Gen 1:24). Leaving aside some other innovations, Puljuj stopped short of marking the assimilation of consonants in morpheme and word boundaries, which was a signature feature of his *kulišivka*.

Indeed, there are numerous cases of assimilation of consonants as reflected in the orthography of the *Pentatevx*. Instead of suggesting a strict classification of such cases, it is worthwhile looking at the most representative, in place and manner of articulation and examples of assimilation, as well as at assimilation in voicing. In some cases, Kuliš's spelling is likely to render a combination of different types of assimilation. One can begin with the use of the prefixes *s* and *z*, which alternate depending on the following consonant. Thus, in congruence with his spelling practice in the journal *Osnova* (Mykytyn 2000, 154–156), the variant *s* occurred before voiceless *k*, *p*, and *x*, with *z* in the environment before a voiced consonant or *s* in the beginning of a root (in order to avoid gemination?). Some examples include the following: *spustyvs'* "I am come down" (*Pentatevx*, 46, Ex 3:8), *spalyt'* "[he] shall burn" (*Pentatevx*, 82, Lev 4:10), *sxamenuvs'* (sg. m. pret.) "to come to one's sense," *sxotily* (pl. pret.) "to want" (*Pentatevx*, 82, 143), *zrozumily* (pl. pret.) "to know" (ibid., 4, Gen 3:7), *zrobylas'* (f. sg. pret.) "to become" (*Pentatevx*, 47, Ex 4:3), and *zsyple* (3 sg. non-past) "to put" (*Pentatevx*, 83, Lev 6:10).

The same distribution is observed with the preposition *s* alternating with *z* as in *s xudoby* "of the cattle" (*Pentatevx*, 51, Ex 9:6), *zerno s povnoho kolossja* "corn [beaten] out of full ears" (*Pentatevx*, 81, Lev 2:14), and *s toho mista* "[get thee] out of thy country" (*Pentatevx*, 10, Gen 12:1), compared to *z skotu* "[offering] of the cattle" (*Pentatevx*, 80, Lev 1:2), *z slovamy* "with words" (*Pentatevx*, 144, Deut 2:26), and finally *z horodiv* "[the spoil] of the cities" (*Pentatevx*, 144, Deut 2:35). In the environment before a voiceless affricate, the preposition *s* is sounded (and accordingly written) as a voiceless fricative *š* (e.g., *š čeredy* "[offering even] of the herd" [*Pentatevx*, 80, Lev 1:2]). Yet this type of assimilation across word boundaries seemed to be unique.

The prefix *roz-* is realized in two variants depending on (the natural class of) the following obstruent. As in his writings published in *Osnova* (Mykytyn 2000, 155), Kuliš seemed to use the variant *ros-* before *k*, *p*, *t*, and, while the variant *roz-* was attested in all other environments, even before a voiceless consonant (e.g., *rozdobuvajte* [2 pl. imper.] "to get you [straw]" [*Pentatevx*, 48, Ex 5:11], *rozhledjat* [3 pl. non-past.] "to search out" [*Pentatevx*, 142, Deut 1:22], and *rozsypavs'* [m. sg. pret.], here "[the people] were scattered" [*Pentatevx*, 48, Ex 5:12] as compared to *a to vony rosplodjaccja* "lest they multiply" [*Pentatevx*, 45, Ex 1:10]).

Most characteristic was assimilation (in place and manner of articulation) of the consonants across suffix boundaries. Such assimilation regularly occurred in the personal forms of reflexive verbs (e.g., *dijdeccja* [3 sg. non-past] "[a war] falleth out," *zlučaccja* [3 pl. non-past] "to join"

[*Pentatevx*, 45, Ex 1:10], *staneccja* [3 sg. non-past] "it shall come to pass" [*Pentatevx*, 47, Ex 3:21], and *zrobyccja* [3 sg. non-past] "shall become" [*Pentatevx*, 49, Ex 7:9]). Expressing such assimilation was commonplace in late eighteenth and nineteenth century spelling in Dnieper Ukraine, in particular in the works of Ivan Kotljarevs′kyj, Oleksij Pavlovs′kyj, Amvrosij Metlyns′kyj, and most of the authors from Sloboda Ukraine (Moskalenko 1958, 15–23). Thus, there is no wonder that "radical phonetization" was also observed in nominal formations (e.g., *v ricci* [sg. loc.] "in the river" [2x] [*Pentatevx*, 50, Ex 7:20], a form that was also attested in Kuliš's writings in *Osnova* [Mykytyn 2000, 157], *occja* [gen.] "of thy father" [*Pentatevx*, 46, Ex 3:6]).

Unlike inconsistent assimilation across suffix boundaries as reflected in *Osnova* (Mykytyn 2000, 157–158), the language of the *Pentatevx* showed already significant progress in the "phonetization" of this position. I did not find not any example reminiscent of traditional spelling in *Osnova*'s publications (e.g., *zovetcja* [3 sg. pres.] "to be called" or *dobrat′cja* "to reach, get to"). Generally, lack of consistency in rendering assimilation in this position was typical of the writings generated at that time in Sloboda Ukraine (Moskalenko 1958, 23). Yet, seven years later Kuliš had already normalized this position from the point of view of phonetic spelling.

In view of the above peculiarities, one wonders again as to what extent Kuliš's "radical phonetics" proved pioneering in the history of Ukrainian orthography. Leaving certain deviations aside, Kuliš seemed to have followed a long-standing tradition of rendering vernacular *sandhi* phenomena, especially across word and suffix boundaries, in literary records. Taken diachronically, assimilation in place and manner of articulation was triggered in East Slavic by the fall of *jers*, although this might have developed differently in various dialects marked by distinctive voicing or distinctive protensity (Flier 1994, 146–148). Trying to synthesize elements pertaining to different dialects and literary traditions, Kuliš might have imitated some forms found in the Middle Ukrainian records that he studied, in particular, in private archives in Warsaw, peering over different historical accounts (Luckyj 1983, 143–146).

To explicate instances of complete assimilation in Kuliš's practice, for instance, *š čeredy* "[offering even] of the herd," it is expedient to dwell briefly on assimilation phenomena as attested from the late twelfth century onward in various Old Ukrainian texts extant from different dialectal areas (Žovtobrjux et al. 1979, 205–207). Despite scant material, one can trace a tendency toward complete neutralization (with a gradation of subtypes) before all obstruents, as opposed to other cases. Such a tendency is observed in most western Ukrainian dialects, including western Polissian, Volhynian, Dniester, Podolian, Bukovyna, and southwestern Ukrainian dialects (Flier 1994, 147). For instance, in the eighteenth-century copy of *Aleksandrija* made in Subcarpathian Rus´, one happens on regular neutralization like *prutko* "fast" (10) and *prozbÿ* (gen.) "request" (240), and cases of assimilation of the type *blyžže* "closer" (39) (Pan´kevyč 1922, 17). Remarkably, in the same record, the preposition *s˝* was used not only before voiceless consonants, but also in the position before the cluster *sv-* (ibid., 18), a case that reflects the environment in which Kuliš used the same morpheme. Similar assimilation in place and manner, though across prefix or word boundary, is observed in *žžyrajut´* (< *zžyrajut´* 3 pl. pres.) "to devour" (*PG* 1556–1561, 178v), *ny ščym˝* "with nothing" (Zinovijiv, 254) from *ny s˝čym˝*, and also *ščatkÿ* (1394) next to *sčadky* (1459) (Rozov 1928, 72, 154) (MoUkr. *naščadky* "descendants"). However, it is worthwhile mentioning another consistency in the language of *The Acts and Epistles of Krexiv*, written probably between 1563 and 1572 (Shevelov 1979, 403). Sharing largely Belarusian and northern Ukrainian features, this text reveals complete neutralization before all obstruents across prefix and word boundaries for the following morphemes: *s*, *z*, *ros*, and *roz*. In some cases, different variants occur side by side in the same sentence, such as *z˝ žydov* "from the Jews" alongside *s pohanov* "from the pagans" (271) (Ohijenko 1930, 1:289). Some exceptions occur, though they are quite rare (e.g., *rozsužaty ~ rossudyty* "to arbitrate" [ibid.]).

Deserving of attention are cases of assimilation in place and manner, reminiscent of the same type of assimilation in Kuliš's language. In addition to assimilation across prefix boundaries like *ž´ žydov˝* "from the Jews" (634) and *yš šalenstva* "because of insanity" (623) (Ohijenko 1930, 1:288, 2:36), there are numerous cases of assimilation across suffix boundaries of the type *perevÿššyly* (pl. pret.) "to exceed" (346) and *navÿššyj* "tallest" (24, 25, and so forth) (ibid., 1:291). What is also significant about this Ruthenian

(Polissian) text is that, despite the etymological principle in spelling, its translator could not help but reveal another feature of his native phonetics, that is, neutralization of the obstruents in syllable- and word-final position (e.g., *sjat* [2 sg. imper.] "sit down!" [ibid., 1:293]). In congruence with the classification of Flier (1994, 157), all the above features are typical of those Ukrainian, including Polissian, dialects that show the marks of a phonemic voicing system with complete neutralization.

Not surprisingly, a similar phenomenon is observed in eighteenth-century texts with northern Ukrainian features, for instance, in the writings of Ivan Nekraševyč: *occe* (voc.) "father" (9), *oččenku* (voc. dim.) "holy father" and *occja* (gen.) "father" (12), and the like. What is remarkable about all these forms is that they are found in stylistically marked, colloquial contexts, for instance, in the confession of a female peasant and the author's letter to a close friend. In all other contexts, such forms do not occur, since phonetic spelling might have looked too vernacular or stylistically low.

Overall, choosing the phonetic principle for his orthographic system was not random. Forms with neutralization and assimilation in place and manner seemed to be typical of non-lofty genres (charters, epistles, chronicles, even homilary gospels). All this was likely to fit well into Kuliš's language program, in which his vernacularizing practice was traceable to the written tradition as cultivated in the Middle Ukrainian period. One may wonder at this point what Ukrainian dialect(s) Kuliš decided to choose as a basis for pursuing this vernacularizing tendency. However, it is extremely difficult to ascertain with precision what dialectal types of assimilation are reflected in Kuliš's first translation of the Pentateuch. At first sight, to use the classification of Flier (1994, 147–148; Danylenko 2006c, 189–192), Kuliš's spelling signals his orientation toward East Ukrainian, as one encounters no *sandhi* evidence of neutralization of voiced consonants before voiceless consonants across suffix boundaries (Mykytyn 2000, 156). At the same time, the neutralization of voiced consonants in the position before voiceless obstruents across prefix boundaries (e.g., *z*- and *roz*-), as discussed above, likely reveals Kuliš's tendency to follow the southwestern Ukrainian pattern. All things considered, one seems to deal in the case of Kuliš's spelling practice with the crossbreeding of segmental sound features typical of different Ukrainian dialects. In other words, in matters of spelling, the writer deliberately tried to synthesize different sound patterns and their changes taken in synchrony and diachrony, as reflected in particular in the examples excerpted from Middle Ukrainian literary records.

If viewed in the wider historical perspective of positive efforts toward national self-definition and cultural assertion, the system of *kulišivka* was introduced because the phonetic principle was likely to differentiate literary Ukrainian from Russian. But its introduction was also the result of a historical coexistence between the older linguistic, democratic tradition in the normalization of local written language and a more conservative written tradition long practiced in the eastern Slavic lands (Danylenko 2006c, 140–141, 2012b). In a sense, Kuliš managed to offer a congenial vision of a new system of spelling accommodating the aforementioned tendencies.

IVAN NEČUJ-LEVYC′KYJ IS SHUFFLED BACKSTAGE

Ivan Nečuj-Levyc′kyj might have made his part of the translation of the 1903 Bible from the German translation authored by Emil Kautzsch. However, this fact could hardly explain the conspicuous differences between the language of his translation and the language used by Kuliš. The difference between the two vernacular-based written languages was first discussed by Antonovyč (1969) as being more of degree than of kind, though this difference, especially in vocabulary, was likely to appear rather striking in concrete cases. According to Antonovyč (1969, 42–43), Kuliš intentionally archaized his language (Nečuj-Levic′kyj 1907, 298) and Nečuj-Levyc′kyj, on the contrary, sometimes applied a more revolutionary approach, while trying to introduce newer, often incidental linguistic forms. Since a comparison of their languages might appear crucial for assessing the contribution made by Kuliš in the formation of a new literary language, it is worthwhile analyzing briefly the most representative features of Nečuj-Levyc′kyj's language.

To begin with, one finds in Nečuj-Levyc′kyj numerous examples of the cross-dialectal alternation *u-* : *v-* (e.g., *uv Aroeri* "in A-ro´-er" [*SP*, 388,

1 Chr 5:8], *do vvixodu* "unto the entering" [*SP*, 388, 1 Chr 5:9], and the like). Yet it is not clear if the corresponding principle of euphony was generally applied by Nečuj-Levyc'kyj, since his early writings do not reveal a consistency in the maintenance of the alternation *u-* : *v-*. Incidentally, one should mention here numerous corrections made by Kuliš in clusters of consonants in the original of Nečuj-Levyc'kyj's novel *Pryčepa* (The Cocklebur) (e.g., *vstupyv v xatu* changed by Kuliš into *vstupyv u xatu* "[he] entered the house" [Voznjak 1928b, 5–6]). Interestingly, Nečuj-Levyc'kyj shared with Kuliš the use of apharesis, which is a typical northern Ukrainian feature: *'d Davydovi* "to Da'-vid" (*SP*, 395, 1 Chr 11:15), *'k pivdnju i 'k sxodu* "toward the south, and toward the east" (*SP*, 778, Dan 8:9). *Ikavism* in Nečuj-Levyc'kyj's language is largely of southeastern Ukrainian origin, whence *narod* "people" (*SP*, 395, 1 Chr 11:15) with the limited change of *o* into *i* (Matvijas 2007b, 34). I would add here some *sandhi* positions of the type *nado mnoju* "above me" and *peredo mnoju* "before me" (*SP*, 772, 778, Dan 8:15) with no analogical change of the secondary *o* into *i*. Such forms are commonly attested in Middle Ukrainian records and are still found in some (primarily archaic) Ukrainian dialects (Žovtobrjux et al. 1979, 283; Nimčuk 1969, 78). It is therefore plausible that these forms were introduced into the translation by Nečuj-Levyc'kyj himself.

The sound *f* was already commonplace in the phonetic system of Nečuj-Levyc'kyj's idiom and likewise in vernacular Ukrainian. In addition to numerous personal and place names with this sound (e.g., *Jafet* for Ja'-pheth [*SP*, 383, 1 Chr 1:4]), I would name also an old borrowing *fylja* "flood" (*SP*, 782, Dan 11:22) (Pol. *fala*, Gr. *Welle*) (Žel., 2:1027; Shevelov 1979, 634), which is cited among other "deviating" forms by Nečuj-Levyc'kyj in his notorious polemical essay of 1907 on the state of contemporary written Ukrainian (Nečuj-Levic'kyj 1907, 317).

As one might predict, Puljuj, as a Galician speaker, might have inadvertently employed regional forms in the revised version of the Ukrainian Bible that were likely to be at odds with Nečuj-Levyc'kyj's *Sprachgefühl*. For instance, we see *dijament* "diamond" (*SP*, 782, Dan 11:38) next to *diament(")* (Berynda, 172; Vytv., 433) (*dijament* [Žel., 1:186]). Yet Nečuj-Levyc'kyj was particularly annoyed by inconsistencies in the spelling of the demonstrative pronoun *cej* (m.), *cja* (f.), *ce* (n.) "this" and its derivatives like *ocej* "this one" in the Ukrainian Bible of 1903, since he employed in his translation forms with -*c*- alone (Nečuj-Levic′kyj 1907, 22). Puljuj seemed to have opted for using the parallel forms *cej* (*SP*, 768), *si* "these," *se* (n.) "this" (ibid., 771, 394), and even a mixture of the two phonetic forms *otse* next to *oce* "this is" (ibid., 395), despite the fact that the two forms represented two distinct literary traditions and dialectal areas (Tymošenko 1969, 109–113). No doubt, this was a contentious decision by Puljuj (Nečuj-Levyc′kyj 1968, 467). Among other examples one can name the form *vid*, which was never used by Nečuj-Levyc′kyj (Nečuj-Levic′kyj 1907, 19). To look at several random pages from the novel *Čorna rada* (Black Council, 1857), one happens upon numerous examples of *od* in Kuliš (*ČR*, 108, 109–110). However, as early as 1869, Kuliš began gradually giving preference to the form *vid*, thus introducing this "Galician form" in place of Nečuj-Levyc′kyj's preposition *od* (Voznjak 1928b, 6).

In Nečuj-Levyc'kyj's translation, present active participles of the type *stojačyj* "[saw the angel of the Lord] stand" (*SP*, 403, 778, 1 Chr 21:16) are deserving of attention. Some of them are used concurrently with adjectives in similar expressions: *palajučyj ohon′* "fiery flame" (*SP*, 777, Dan 7:9) alongside *palajuča pič* (*SP*, 771, Dan 3:15) ~ *rozpalena pič* "burning fiery furnace" (*SP*, 771, Dan 3:11). One should emphasize those active participles that show a closer connection with their base verbs, thus presenting a static feature in a dynamic mode: *horijuči s′vičnyky* "lamps of fire" (*SP*, 782, Dan 10:6) (from *hority* "to be alight"), *streljajuči z luka* "archers" (*SP*, 392, 1 Chr 8:40) (from *streljaty* "to shoot"), *dobuvajuči meča* "[men] that drew sword" (*SP*, 403, 1 Chr 21:5) (from *dobuvaty* "to draw [a sword]"), that is, "men able to draw swords, if called to arms." A similar categorical meaning is rendered in some other places with the help of relative clauses introduced by the relativizer *ščo* (e.g., *muži, ščo nosyly ščyt i meč* "men able to bear buckler and sword" [*SP*, 388, 1 Chr 5:18]).

Interestingly, in his 1907 essay about the status of contemporary Ukrainian, Nečuj-Levyc′kyj stopped short of discussing the spread of present active participles in the "contemporary written language" in Ukraine (Nečuj-Levic′kyj 1907). As a matter of fact, participles of this type happened to occur in all genres of the author's writings, including polemical and philosophical works as well as belle lettres. To take his treatise *Svitohljad ukrajins'koho naroda* (World Outlook of the Ukrainian People, 1868) as an example, one finds here *panujučyj* "ruling," *stojačyj* "standing," *hrabljačyj* "robbing," and the like (Nečuj 1868, 415, 423). At first sight, his negative opinion of all Galician forms deviating eventually from vernacular Ukrainian prompts us to assume that the bulk of such participles in his translation of the Bible might have been introduced (or at least not replaced by a relative clause) by Puljuj. However, there are solid grounds for assuming that such forms were originally used by Nečuj-Levyc'kyj, who particularly indulged in them in his literary works. Suffice it to open Nečuj-Levyc'kyj's manuscript of *Pryčepa* (The Cocklebur), where Kuliš consistently replaced them with separate relative clauses or simply dropped them. Still, some participial forms did appear in the text of this novel (e.g. *vyxodjači ljudy* "people [who are] coming out" or, in the same sentence, *bystro tekuča voda* "water [that is] running fast" [Voznjak 1928b, 38]).

Despite a bookish (Church Slavonic) suffix, some such participles functioned as true adjectives (e.g., *nevsypuščyj* "watcher" next to *nevsypučyj* [*SP*, 772, 773, Dan 4:13, 23], that is, "that who always watches," where the latter lexeme is a typically vernacular adjective with a minimum of verbal features [Kurylo 1960, 16]). Sporadically, past active participles serve as an archaizing device in the vernacular-based text: *usta, hovorivši* (pl.) "a mouth that spake" (*SP*, 777, Dan 7:20), *vyvivšyj narod* "[our God] that hath brought thy people" (*SP*, 779, Dan 9:15), or *vystupavši na vijnu* "[those that] went out to the war" (*SP*, 388, 1 Chr 5:18).

One of the most representative features of Nečuj-Levyc'kyj's morphosyntax is the use of pluperfect tense forms irrespective of the narrative context (e.g., *buv vyris* "came up" [*SP*, 777, 1 Chr 7:20] and *pryjšov buv* "came" [*SP*, 777, 1 Chr 7:22]). In general, Nečuj-Levyc'kyj used more pluperfect tense forms than Kuliš, thus reflecting, presumably, a common trend in Dnieper Ukrainian in the last part of the nineteenth century (Tymošenko 1979, 125). It is interesting to note that obsolete perfect tense forms like *xvalyv jesy* "[thou] hast praised" (*SP*, 775, Dan 5:23) are barely attested in the translation of Nečuj-Levyc'kyj, thus demonstrating its peripheral status with a Church Slavonic tinge (Tymošenko 1979, 123–124). To give a rare example of a stylistically marked (Church Slavonic) form in Nečuj-Levyc'kyj, one can cite *slaven jesy* "blessed be thou" (*SP*, 411, 1 Chr 29:10). Likewise, quite a few

Church Slavonicisms are attested in the vocabulary of Nečuj-Levyc'kyj's translation (e.g., *nebesa* "heavens" [*SP*, 400, 1 Chr 16:26]). At any rate, in the scriptural translations of Kuliš there seem to be more Church Slavonicisms than in the translation made by Nečuj-Levyc'kyj. Clearly, this means that Nečuj-Levyc'kyj's language was more vernacular-oriented and purified of excessive admixtures of Church Slavonic and Polish.

In fact, the situation with Galician and Polish forms seems to be convoluted. Introduced supposedly by Puljuj and/or Sljusarčuk, they are attested in abundance in the morphosyntax (for example, the conjunction *pozajak* "inasmuch as" [*SP*, 771], castigated, and rightly so, by Nečuj-Levyc'kyj as artificial [Nečuj-Levic'kyj 1907, 18], and especially the so-called "Galician/Polish locative" as in *na hillju* "in the boughs" [*SP*, 772, Dan 4:12] instead of *na hilli*, also *v kraju* "in the land" [*SP*, 388, 1 Chr 5:11] in place of *v kraji* [Nečuj-Levic'kyj 1907, 14–15]). If not corrected by Kuliš, who used to edit his young protégé's language, a similar locative made its way even into Nečuj-Levyc'kyj's own language (e.g., *v" oburennju* "in indignation" [Nečuj 1868, 438]). Overall, the locative forms ending in *-u* might have been retained in Southwest Ukrainian since the Middle Ukrainian period (Verxratskyj 1902, 177).

Nouns ending in *-e* like *ljude* "people" and *lystje* "leaves" (*SP*, 780), including Church Slavonicisms *spasennje* "saving" and *vsespalennje* "burnt offering" (ibid., 399, 412, 1 Chr 29:21), were also at variance with Nečuj-Levyc'kyj's treatment of the corresponding forms in Ukrainian. In a letter of 21 September 1905 to Petro Stebnyc'kyj (1862–1923), he resolutely rejected the etymological spelling of neuters ending in *-e* (*nasinnje* "seeds") inasmuch as these forms were sounded as ending in *-a* (*nasinnja*) (Nečuj-Levyc'kyj 1968, 450, 454). It is worthwhile recalling that Kuliš consistently used the forms ending in *-e*, thus purportedly trying "to bring the language closer to old Ukrainian literature" (Nečuj-Levic'kyj 1907, 21–22). There is, however, a seemingly unique form in 1 Chronicles, *čerez prohnannja* "by driving out" (*SP*, 401, 1 Chr 17:21), instead of *čerez prohnannje*. One might surmise that the editors simply failed to adjust this form as used by Nečuj-Levyc'kyj to the aforementioned Galician model.

There are numerous constructions with forms ending in *-no* and *-to* in the predicate and the accusative direct object in Nečuj-Levyc'kyj (e.g.,

Tijeji ž noči Valtasara, carja Xaldejs'koho, vbyto "In that night was Bel-shaz'-zar the king of the Chal-de-'-ans slain" [*SP*, 775, Dan 5:30]). One may hypothesize that Puljuj could have added some of these constructions on his own, as two factors could interact in this case. First, there were numerous impersonal constructions with predicative forms in ending *-no* and *-to* in the text. Second, such constructions occurred without any auxiliary, though with a clear perfect meaning (Shevelov 1969; Danylenko 2003a, 314–326). All this might tentatively speak for their southwestern Ukrainian origin. However, the use of such constructions in the language of other eastern Ukrainian writers of that time, particularly of Panas Myrnyj (Hrycenko 2007, 28), is likely to prove their local provenance in the language of Nečuj-Levyc'kyj.

The vocabulary of his translation is particularly representative, especially as compared with Kuliš who was always open to borrowings and neologisms. Notoriously, Nečuj-Levyc'kyj could barely stand Galician and Polish borrowings in Ukrainian. This fact indirectly proves that some central Ukrainian lexemes as used by this writer might have been replaced in the final version by Galician counterparts like *rečenec'* "deadline" (*SP*, 777; Žel., 2:801) and *brama* (sg.) "gates" (*SP*, 404, 1 Chr 22:3; Žel., 1:42), as opposed to the indigenous *vorotar* "porter" (*SP*, 393, 1 Chr 9:21; Žel, 1:121), *dveri* "door" (ibid.), and *porohy* "gates" (*SP*, 393, 1 Chr 9:22). Despite the editorial intervention of Puljuj, the translation of Nečuj-Levyc'kyj reads in some places as a true folkloric text (e.g., *posud zolotyj, sribnyj ta midjanyj* "vessels of gold and silver and brass" [*SP*, 401, 1 Chr 18:10] and *bovvan z ščyroho zolota* "the image's head [was] of fine gold" [*SP*, 770, Dan 2:32] next to *zolotyj idol* "an image of gold" [*SP*, 770, Dan 3:1]). The following verse looks like an excerpt from a typical Cossack chronicle, with representative lexemes and patronymic names ending in *-enko*:

Йоаб Саруєнко гетьманував над військом, Йосафат же Ахилуденко списував дії. (*SP*, 402)	[And Jo'-ab the son of Ze-ru-i'-ah was over the host; and Je-hosh'-a-phat the son of A-hi'-lud, recorder.] (1 Chr 18:15)

Archaic lexemes do occur sporadically in Nečuj-Levyc´kyj's translation, though their number is very small. One can mention, first of all, the synonymous triad *narody, plemena j jazyky* "people, nations, and languages" (*SP*, 771, Dan 3:4, 7), where the latter lexeme is employed in one of the antiquated (Old Church Slavonic and Old Rusian) meanings "people" (Sr., 3:1647–1648). Other bookish lexemes of the type *het´man* "prince" (*SP*, 783, Dan 11:22), *benket* "feast," *vel´moža* "lord" (*SP*, 774, Dan 5:1), and *radnyky j otamany* "the counselors and the captains" (*SP*, 775, Dan 6:7) date back to the Middle Ukrainian period and are permeated by historical myths and allusions. Not surprisingly, almost all of these lexemes, or their derivatives, are attested in the language of the Xarkovite writer Hryhorij Kvitka-Osnov'janenko (Kvitka, 1:2, 26, 103, 258, 351) and in *Slovar´ malorossijskaho, ili juho-vostočnorusskaho jazyka* (The Dictionary of the Little Russian or, Southeastern Russian Language) of Pavlo Bilec´kyj-Nosenko (Bil.-Nos., 53, 71, 97, 266).

Taken as a whole, Nečuj-Levyc´kyj's vocabulary is southeastern Ukrainian at its core. Yet one comes across northern and southwestern lexemes in his translation, which, as was assumed, might have been added by the editor(s). This is why in most cases one deals with obvious regional alternatives: *pryključka* (Žel., 2:747), used also by Kuliš (*SP*, 58), ~ *pryčyna* "occasion" (Bil.-Nos., 301) as attested in one and the same verse (Dan 6:4), *postelja* (*SP*, 770, Dan 2:29; Žel., 2:718) ~ *ližko* "bed" (*SP*, 772, Dan 4:5; Kvitka, 2:76), or *xarč* "provision" ~ *strava* "portion of the king's meat" ~ *požyva* "meat" (*SP*, 768, Dan 1:5, 10, 13). The latter lexemes are found in the language of Kvitka-Osnov'janenko (Kvitka, 3:347, 525, 2:526), where *požyva* is glossed as "catch, profit" (Bil.-Nos., 288). In the translation of Nečuj-Levyc´kyj, *požyva* is clearly used as a western Ukrainian form (Žel., 2:679) and is also attested in Kuliš's paraphrase of the book of Job (1869). Among contrasting regional forms, it is worth citing WUkr. *kryži* "loins" (*SP*, 774, Dan 5:6; Žel., 1:379) as compared with *pojasnycja* in Kuliš's paraphrase of Psalm 38 (*Psaltyr*, Rataj, 171), *poperek* "loins" in Kvitka-Osnov'janenko (Kvitka, 2:583), and EUkr. *lučytysja* "to happen" (*SP*, 774; Kvitka, 2:83; Bil.-Nos., 214).

Overall, Nečuj-Levyc´kyj's language shows its primary orientation toward the vernacular as spoken, to use his words, in "the whole of Central Ukraine," whence a minimum of Church Slavonic, Galician, or Polish forms, introduced in his translation of the biblical books most likely by Puljuj (or Sljusarčuk). By contrast, Kuliš in his biblical translations created a multilayered system of heterogeneous elements pertaining to various dialects and even literary traditions. Thus, the language of Nečuj-Levyc´kyj tends to be homogeneous, both dialectally and diachronically. Its homogeneity seems to be even more solid when compared with the vernacular standard in Moračevs´kyj's translation of the New Testament. The question arising at this stage is whether Puljuj or somebody else responsible for the preparation of the manuscript for publication had the right to introduce corrections in the translation of Nečuj-Levyc´kyj. To answer this question, one needs to understand that the problem lay not so much in the unification or differentiation of regionalisms as in the choice of a stylistic framework for the whole Ukrainian Bible. The latter, according to Puljuj, had to be premised on the programmatic tenets adopted by Kuliš and Puljuj in their joint translation of the New Testament in the 1870s. This is why the translation of Nečuj-Levyc´kyj could hardly fit the biblical parameters of a new high style of new literary Ukrainian.

INTERPRETING HEBREW POETRY

Already in his *Tovytovi slovesa* (the book of Tobit) of 1893, Kuliš demonstrated his keen interest in a poetic (versified) adaptation of the Bible. Not surprisingly, in a letter of 8 July 1896, Kuliš hastened to outline for Pavlyk, in whom he confided most of his creative plans in the early 1890s, the overall idea of his future poetic translation, which would differ both structurally and creatively from the prose one. He believed that feelings would come first to the minds and hearts of the Ukrainian people despite the fact that remnants of primitive poetry were purportedly fossilized in the Hebrew Scriptures (Voznjak 1928a, 216). In fact, "the ancient Hebrew spirit and taste" were reflected in the books of the Hebrew Bible, in particular in the Psalms. For this reason, the translation of the Psalter came out in Galicia as the first part of Kuliš's translation project (ibid.).

In his letter of 8 July 1896 to Pavlyk (Voznjak 1928a, 217), Kuliš contended that the full title of the translation of the Holy Bible into Ukrainian should somehow reflect the aforementioned structure and run as follows:

Старорýський Перéклад
Сьвятóго Письма
Старóго й Новóго Заповíду
Переклада́в же ёгó
Кулíш Олéлькович Панькó
Частина друга: Голосíньня и Пíсьня Пíсень

[The Old Rusian Translation of the Holy Scripture of the Old and New Testament, translated by Kuliš Olel′kovyč Pan′ko. Part 2: Lamentations and The Song of Songs]

On the title page of the manuscript prepared by Kuliš for Pavlyk (who promised to have Lamentations and the Song of Songs published in Lviv in 1896 or 1897) the translator added:

Печатано ввí Львовí
р. Б. 1897
За доглядом Павлика Михайла (*Holosin′nja*, 2r)
[Printed in Lviv in God's year of 1897 under the supervision of Pavlyk Myxajlo]

In a separate note, which is attached to the protograph held today at the manuscript repository at the T. H. Ševčenko Institute of Ukrainian Literature of the National Academy of Sciences of Ukraine, Kuliš asked Pavlyk to also print on the half title page "the Old Rusian Translation of the Holy Scriptures."

The title, proposed by Kuliš, underscored his vision of the Holy Bible in Ukrainian. In addition to the vernacularized version of his first and patronymic names, Kuliš made use of a folk etymological form *zapovíd* "Testament" (compare *zápovid′*) (Hrinč., 1:618; *Enejida*, Index, 60), with stress on the final syllable, instead of the true etymological *-vetъ* as attested in Old Church Slavonic and East Slavic (Vasmer, 1:193) (Rus. *otvét* and Ukr.

[dial. and obsolete] *odvít* "answer"). Obviously, this was an attempt to revive the oldest lexical layer, as used in his translation in contrast with the Great Russian version.

However, most telling in this respect is the distinction of *starorus'ka mova* "Old Rusian" from *novorus'ka mova* "New Rusian [Great Russian]," as discussed by Kuliš in the aforementioned letter to Pavlyk. Having made several translations of the Bible, the Russians were purportedly incapable of producing a poetic interpretation of what had been written by the Jews in verse, since Russian was "fairly poor in grammar" (Voznjak 1928a, 218). Deprived of what could be bestowed upon them only by God, the Russians failed to create such a flexible language as "our Old Rusian." Kuliš himself could hardly translate the Bible in verse into *novourus'ka mova* (Russian) in the same way as he was doing with Ukrainian (*starorus'ka mova*) (ibid.). Although somewhat controversial, this thesis nevertheless illustrated the creative enthusiasm that Kuliš was experiencing at that time and his sincere expectations that a new version of the Ukrainian Bible, comprised of the poetic and prose parts, would be a truly innovative work among all other Slavic Bibles, especially in comparison with the conservative and somewhat rigid style of the Russian translation(s).

With the appearance of a six-volume study of the Bible by Eduard Reuß (published posthumously in 1892–1894) (Reuß) and of the translation of the Bible by Emil Kautzsch (1890–1894) (Kautzsch), Kuliš declared that he was ready to undertake "a poetic translation of the lyrical pearls" of the Old Testament, which would be a second part of the overall translation project of the Bible (Voznjak 1928a, 216). In a final part of his work on the Ukrainian Bible, Kuliš promised to concentrate on a translation of "the religious holy Hebrew philosophy." Pavlo Rataj's *Yov* (Job), published as early as 1869 in Lviv, was, as he explained, a first attempt at the poetic translation of Hebrew philosophy (ibid.).

Though sketched in broad strokes, the above plan ushered in a new period in scriptural translation in Ukraine and, what is more significant, a new conceptualization of the vernacular translation of the Bible. Transformed into a versified form, the poetic translation was conceived of by Kuliš as the most comprehensible and adequate medium of God's word for laymen, who are capable of grasping the main ideas when they are represented in a rhythmic way (Ohijenko 1939c, 359–360). This understanding and appreciation of the poetic rendition of the Bible echoes *The Idea of Biblical Poetry* by Kugel (1981), according to whom, if Hebrew prose can be read as poetry, the reverse should also be the case. In other words, the suggestion that Hebrew verse is simply a developed prose style with rhetorical tendencies is applicable to Kuliš's intention to adapt the Bible into a versified framework, rather than to his wish to follow closely the original (Naxlik 2007, 2:279). Otherwise, it is not clear which original Kuliš was supposed to follow.

Overall, one must give credit to Kuliš for his intention to offer a new, metric interpretation of prose as found in the Hebrew Bible through the medium of poetry. In fact, Kuliš was the first European writer to elaborate on a metrical vernacular as used to render the model of "sung speech," which was as appropriate for Hebrew poetry as it was for Ukrainian folklore. In this respect, his metrical vision of the Bible in Ukrainian looked much more congruent with the nature of Hebrew poetry than Ivan Ohijenko's provision for the so-called "preaching rhythm" (*rytm molytovnyj*), as first discussed by Lypa (1939, 55) with respect to the language of Ohijenko's translation of the Holy Scriptures. For instance, discussing "the rhythm of the heart" as discerned in Ohijenko's language, Jurij Lypa described his translation as "plain and solemn" at the same time. According to Lypa one could not find any unnatural "inversion" (change of word order) in Ohijenko's translation—everything was in its right place, while the use of the predicate at the end of sentences added additional emphasis to the narrative (ibid.). Ohijenko (1939b, 60–61) argued that the Bible was replete with poetic parts that one could render only with the help of a versified translation.

The point is that both Lypa and Ohijenko, who endorsed the latter's understanding of the preponderantly poetic disposition of the ancient Jews and Greeks, reduced Hebrew poetry to one of its vital components—rhythm. Yet Hebrew poetry is also marked by stress and sonority, being dependent simply on rhythm for its conventions. Moreover, neither of these is identical to rhythm or, more broadly, meter. Each can be found where there is no meter, although obviously the reverse cannot hold (Gillingham 1994, 51–52).

As a result, one can hardly agree with the modern appreciation of Ohijenko's translation by Jusyp-Jakymovyč (2000, 418), who hastily contended that "rhythmicity of the language [of Ohijenko] is an innovation in the translation of the entire Holy Scriptures into Ukrainian." Kuliš, rather, was a pioneer in this domain, as he was the first to have worked not simply on rhythmicity as postulated for Ohijenko's translation by Jusyp-Jakymovyč and her predecessors, including Ohijenko himself, but on meter comprising several vital components such as rhythm, stress, sonority, and the like.

THE BOOK OF JOB

The poetry of the book of Job is unique in its presentation and rhythmic stress. Like the Psalter, Lamentations, and the Song of Songs, this book is literary poetry at its best, though it comes as close as possible to poetry-as-story, thus contrasting with the erotic imagery of the Song and the communal lament in Lamentations (Gillingham 1994, 102). At the very outset of his translation project, Kuliš became much fascinated by the book of Job, one of three books presented throughout in poetic line-forms in the Hebrew, with its distinctive accentual system and dramatic unity. In 1869, he had a poetic paraphrase of this book published immediately after the appearance of the Pentateuch (*Pentatevx*) and before the whole Psalter in Ukrainian came off the press in 1871 (*Psaltyr*, Rataj). In the early 1890s, when he began a new translation of the Bible, Kuliš planned not simply to revise the 1869 paraphrase of Job but, in effect, to offer a new interpretation of the poetry of this book, inspired largely by the latest extensive studies of Jewish scripture, including contemporary critical scholarship by Emil Kautzsch and his students. In addition, at that time Kuliš had at his disposal the English Revised Version of the Bible, which was published in 1881–1884, with the Apocrypha appearing in 1894 (Kuliš to Biloborodov, 90). All in all, in order to make the Ukrainian Job look more appropriate to Jewish rhetoric and literary conventions, the writer deemed it necessary to translate Job one more time, although he personally liked his first paraphrase and, unlike other biblical books, left the draft of *Hyjob* (Job) aside for subsequent revision.

To illustrate rhetoric and linguistic differences between the first paraphrase and the 1896 version, suffice it to compare here an excerpt from the earlier text and the modified poetic translation dating of the mid-1890s:

Translation of 1869	**Translation of 1896**
Погибни день, що я на світ родився,	Проклятий день, що я на сьвіт родився!
И тиха ніч, що прорекла: "зачався!"	Проклята й ніч, що прорекла: Зачався!
О, щоб той день узявся *темнотою*,	*Нехай* той день вовіки темний буде!
Щоб не світив Господь на ёго зверху,	И Бог *нехай* про ёго не згадае,
И світ над ним не засияв во віки!	И сонечко *нехай* над нім не сьсяе!
Нехай ёго густий обійме *морок*,	*Нехай* ёго назад покличе *морок*,
Нехай ёго важка окриє хмара,	И *темрява* ёго повік обійме!
И *померки* исповнять ёго страхом! (*Yov*, 42)	И *страхітьте нехай* ёго лякае! (*Hyjob* 1327r; Kuliš to Biloborodov, 91)

> [3. Let the day perish wherein I was born, and the night in which it was said. There is a man child conceived.
> 4. Let that day be darkness; let not God regard it from above, neither let the light shine upon it.
> 5. Let darkness and the shadow of death stain it; let a cloud dwell upon it; let the blackness of the day terrify it.] (Job 3:3–5)

The two translations are characterized by a folkloric iambic pentameter and, at first sight, demonstrate a similar orientation toward the use of vernacular stylistic devices. Leaving aside theological issues, the translation of 1896 seems to be premised on slightly more rational tenets, whence a somewhat scanty pool of morphosyntactic patterns and lexical elements as compared with a more loose texture of the language of the 1869 translation. In the morphosyntax, it is worthwhile mentioning the uniform beginning of the first two lines, a more consistent use of the imperative particle *nexaj* "let" (4x compared to 2x in the first translation). In the vocabulary, the language of the 1869 translation looks more archaic and, at any rate, more bookish (e.g., *temnota, morok, pomerky* "darkness" [Žel., 2:956, 1:453, 695]) in comparison with the translation of 1896 where *morok* and *temrjava* are accompanied by a diminutive *sonečko* "sun" (also the bookish form *yspovnyt'* [*straxom*] [3 sg. non-past] in *Yov* compared to a vernacular form *ljakae* [3 sg. pres.] "to scare" in *Hyjob*). Arguably, Kuliš's later poetic translation of the Bible might have typified his search for a uniform vernacular standard that would be comprehensible to all the Ukrainian people.

To gauge the difference between the years 1869 and 1896, one should also remember Kuliš's early admiration for the French philosopher and writer Ernest Renan (1823–1892) as the ultimate authority in literary critical studies of biblical material in his time. This fact rationalizes Kuliš's choice of particular stylistic means in the paraphrase of 1869, heavily influenced by this scholar's critical works and translations of the Bible into French. Thus, in its separate publication in 1869 under the imprint of the newspaper *Pravda*, the first poetic translation of the book of Job was supplied with an extensive preface, "When the Book of Job Was Written," with a modest note saying that this study was based on "excerpts from the latest scholarship on this issue" (*Yov*, 1869, iii). On page xiii of the preface, Kuliš mentioned seven authors, with Renan listed last, who had all purportedly inspired his study. However, a closer inspection of Kuliš's preface and Renan's *Study on the Age and Character of the Book of Job* reveals striking parallels, not only in argumentation but also in stylistics. A selection of several random passages in Kuliš's preface demonstrate almost total dependence on Renan's text and look in some places very closely appropriated.

Renan's *Le livre de Job*	**Kuliš's Translation of 1869**
Au primier coup d'œil, en effet, ce poëme occupe dans la littérature hebraïque une position assez isolée. Les personages qui figurent ne sont pas Juifs; le lieu de la scène est hors de la Palestine. (Renan, xv)	На первий погляд, книга Иова здаєцця в Єврейській словесності геть одинокою. Діёві люде сієі поеми—не Євреї; сама дія — не в Палестині. (*Yov*, 1869, iii)
La langue du livre de Job est l'hébreu le plus limpide, le plus serré, le plus classique. On y trouve toutes les qualités du style ancien, la concision, la tendance à l'énigme, un tour énergique et comme frappé au marteau, cette largeur de sens, éloignée de toute sécheresse, qui laisse à notre esprit quelque chose à deviner, ce timbre charmant qui semble celui d'un métal ferme et pur. (ibid., xxxvii)	Мова книги Иова—найвиразніща Єврейщина, найсутужніща, взорова. Знаходимо в ій усі прикмети старосвіцького стилю, короткомовність, нахил до загадки, повороти енергишні, мов кованя молотом, ширину думок, без усякоі сухости,—таку, що зоставляє нам де-що відгадувати, и ту любу дзвінкість, яка була в металлі міцному и чистому. (ibid., ix)

Although a comparative study of the language of Renan remains beyond the scope of this study, one can find some identical means employed by the two translators. The overall impression of the two texts is their stylistic transparency, with a choice of predominantly low-key linguistic elements, interspersed with lofty forms, thus creating a distinctive poetic system.

This kind of stylistic similarity tends to stand out in comparison with Kuliš's poetic translation of 1896, which, as the writer pointed out, was largely inspired by Kautzsch's scholarship and translations. Not surprisingly, major stylistic differences in the language of the Ukrainian translation of 1896 in comparison with the language of Renan's French text are quite evident. Rather, one can easily discover parallelism between Kautzsch's language and Kuliš's translation of 1896. Leaving stylistic subtleties aside, suffice it to compare morphosyntactic patterns in the opening lines of the corresponding excerpts. Both Kautzsch and Kuliš use subjunctive forms of the verb "to be," correspondingly Gr. *sei* and Ukr. *bud´* ([*bud´*] *prokljatyj den´* "let the day be cursed"). Remarkably, in Reuß's German-language edition of the Old Testament, one happens on a slightly different construction *Fluch* ("curse," nom.) *dem Tag* ("day," dat.).

Finally, the Ukrainianized form of *Job* in the translation of 1896 is slavishly modeled on the German form *Hiob* (Kautzsch and Weizsäcker, 922), while the name *Yov* used in the late 1860s was most likely influenced by the French form as well as the native adaptation of this biblical name. Thus, contrasted formally with the major translations of Renan, Reuß, and Kautzsch, the translation of Kuliš was likely based on the text of this last scholar, who skillfully interpreted the liturgical poetry of Job as reflected in the use of the lament and the hymn.

It should be borne in mind that much of the book of Job consists of lengthy poems serving as an ongoing dialogue between Job and his friends. As in the Hebrew Scriptures, Kuliš is skilled in using linguistic means to distinguish between laments and hymns, in particular in his translation of 1896. The laments are placed in the mouth of Job, whereas the hymns are usually attributed to his friends. Correspondingly, the translator tries to make Job's laments look dark and full of despair, with the friends' false assurance allowing them only to increase the lack of resolution in Job's plight. One of the most obvious examples of the superficial hypocrisy of the friends is exposed in the hymn of E-li´-phaz (Job 5:9–16), who affirms blandly the creative power of the God who upholds the earth and the heavens. Trying to achieve a sense of unity within diversity, Kuliš aptly combines various stylistic devices appearing, nevertheless, anchored in a strong narrative content that tends to illustrate the glib traditionalism of E-li´-phaz's thinking (Gillingham 1994, 100). In Kuliš's translation of 1896, one feels that this is literary poetry of the caliber of the Hebrew original, thus evoking a response not only through its ideas, but also primarily through its form of expression.

Nevertheless, one can also agree with Kuliš that his 1869 paraphrase was "a nice translation" and perhaps no new translation was necessary in the late 1890s (Kuliš to Biloborodov, 90). The only excuse for a new translation, according to Kuliš, lay in the latest achievements in biblical studies and the need to incorporate them somehow in a new Ukrainian translation of the Bible: "I had previously only Renan as a translator, and now the whole of German-speaking Europe is at my disposal" (ibid.). A comparison of parallel excerpts from the 1869 and 1896 translations (see below) demonstrates their stylistic attunement to giving the liturgical poetry a familiar and conventional form. On the other hand, juxtaposing them with the translations made by Renan and Kautzsch prove Kuliš's dependence on these models in different periods of his creative life. Suffice it to cite, for instance, Renan's expression *la face de la terre* as emulated in 1869 by Kuliš in *lyce zemli* "the face of the earth" compared to *zemlja* "earth" in the 1896 translation, corresponding with Kautzsch's *Erde* "earth."

The issue is further illustrated in verses 9–16 from chapter 5 of Job as paraphrased by Kuliš in 1869 and 1896. Excerpts from the translations of Renan and Kautzsch are placed below corresponding paraphrases of Kuliš.

Translation of 1869

Велике він и несказанне
   творить,
Він безлічно дива свої являє.
Лице землі окроплює дощами,
И на поля пускає з неба воду.
Смиренного возносить на
   високість,
Мизерного из нужди визволяє.
Безбожникам псує ледачі ради,

И не дає рукам іх зла чинити.
Лукавого лукавством ёго ловить,
И хитрого у хитрощах
   туманить.
У день вони як серед ночі
   ходять,
И *полапки* шукають о полудні.
Тим бідного іх меч, *уста*, минає,
Безсильного не вхоплять сильні
   руки.

Вертаєцця нещасному
   надія,
И закрива неситу *пельку* злоба.
(*Yov*, 7v–8r)

Translation of 1896

9. Великі він діла и диви робить,
   И безліч их, и хто б же то
   збагнув их?
10. Дае дощі землі и воду *пашням*,
11. Принижених угору підіймає.
   Засмученим дае дознати
   шчасьтя.
12. Руйнуе він всі задуми *ехидних*,
   Щоб руки их не вкоили
   ехидства.
13. Премудрих він их хитрощами
   ловить,
   И хитрощі *лукавим* не
   вдаюцься.
14. Удень вони мов *поночі*
   блукають
   И *полапки* шукають ополудні.
15. Рятуе так він од меча, з их
   пельки
   Мизерного в *потужного* с
   потали.
16. Бессильному тоді *блишчить*
   надія,
   И в лютого затулюецьця
   пелька. (*Hyjob*, 1329v–1330r)

Renan's Translation	**Kautzsch's Translation**
[Dieu] qui fait de grandes choses qu'on ne saurait sonder.	9. [Gott] der große Dinge thut, die unerforschlich, und Wunder, die unzählbar sind:
Des merveilles qu'on ne saurait compter;	
Qui répand la pluie sur la face de la terre,	10. Der der Erde Regen schenkt und Wasser auf die Fluren sendet,
Et fait couler les eaux sur la face des champs;	11. der Niedrige hoch emporhebt, und Trauernde erfahren hohes Heil.
Qui relève les humbles,	12. Er vereitelt die Pläne der Listigen, daß ihre Hände nichts Beständiges schaffen.
Et sauve ceux qui sont dans le deuil;	
Qui dissipe les conseils des perfides,	
Et les empêche d'accomplir leurs projects;	13. Er fängt die Klugen in ihrer eignen List, und der Zerschlagenen Unschlag überstürzt sich.
Qui prend les habiles dans leurs propres ruses,	
Et fait manquer les desseins des hommes astucieux:	14. Am hellen Tage stoßen sie auf Finsternis und wie zur Nachtzeit tappen sie am Mittag.
De jour, ils vont se heurter contre les ténèbres;	
En plein midi, ils tâtonnent comme de nuit.	15. So rettet er vom Schwert, aus ihrem Rachen, und aus der Gewalt des Starken den Armen.
Ainsi Dieu préserve le pauvre du glaive de leur bouche;	
Ainsi Dieu sauve le faible des mains du puissant.	16. So geht dem Schwachen Hoffnung auf, und die Bosheit schließt ihr Maul.
Alors l'espérance revient au malheureux,	(Kautzsch and Weizsäcker, 926–927)
Et l'iniquité ferme la bouche.	
(Renan, 20–21)	

[9. [God] Which doeth great things and unsearchable; marvelous things without number:

10. Who giveth rain upon the earth, and sendeth waters upon the fields:

11. To set up on high those that be low; that those which mourn may be exalted to safety.

12. He disappointeth the devices of the crafty, so that their hands cannot perform their enterprise.

13. He taketh the wise in their own craftiness: and the counsel of the forward is carried headlong.

14. They meet with darkness in the daytime, and grope in the noonday as in the night.

15. But he saveth the poor from the sword, from their mouth, and from the hand of the mighty.

16. So the poor hath hope, and iniquity stoppeth her mouth.] (Job 5:9–16)

Granted the similar artistic values of the 1869 and 1896 translations, one is not surprised that in 1896 Kuliš employed the same forms as in the paraphrase of 1869 (e.g., *polapky* "gropingly" [Hrinč., 2:285], *pel'ka* "mouth," attested cross-dialectally [ibid., 110; Žel., 2:607], and a long-naturalized Church Slavonicism *lukavyj* "crafty," occurring also in Ševčenko [Hrinč., 1:916–917]). Thus, the difference between the two translations appears very elusive. In the vocabulary, the number of Church Slavonic or bookish elements is almost the same (e.g., *neskazannyj* "unsearchable," *smyrennyj* "low," *bezbožnyk* "ungodly," *lukavyj* "crafty," and *usta* "mouth," all found in the 1869 paraphrase, compared to *exydnyj* "spiteful," *exydstvo* "maliciousness," *premudryj* "wise," and *lukavyj* "crafty," used in the 1896 translation). In the two fragments, one finds a Latin borrowing, mediated by Polish and attested in East Slavic (Vasmer, 2:133), *myzernyj* "miserable" (Pol. *mizerny*; Vytv., 135; Bil.-Nos., 224). In 1896, Kuliš added one more of his favorite Polonisms, *potužnyj* "mighty." As a possible Russianism one can treat *pášnja* "field" with the penultimate stress, as is the case in East Ukrainian (Bil.-Nos., 274). It is not therefore accidental that *pášnja* is not attested in the dictionaries of Borys Hrinčenko and Jevhen Želexivs´kyj.

Despite statistical symmetry with *Yov* (Job) of 1869, especially in its lofty vocabulary, the paraphrase of 1896 reveals a broader range of stylistic devices. In addition to the aforementioned Church Slavonic and bookish forms, Kuliš used in 1896, for instance, *pel'ka* "mouth" (2x), *potala* "mistreatment, abuse," and the adverbs *ponoči* "in the night" and *polapky* "gropingly." This contrast is also strengthened by the phonetic spelling, rendering various types of assimilation of consonants, that was alpha and omega in the later period of Kuliš's linguistic creativity. Thus, assimilation in place and manner of articulation is observed in *ščast'tja* (gen.) "happiness," *blyščyt'* (3 sg. pres.) "to shine," and *vdajuc'cja* (3 pl. pres.) "to manage, succeed" (note also *s potaly* "from the hand of the mighty" with a neutralization in voicing of *z* in the environment before the voiceless *p*). Overall, a combination of contrasting forms in phonetics (spelling), vocabulary, and morphology brings about the effect of a masterfully-designed stylistic fabric overshadowing, in some places, nuances found in the paraphrase of 1869.

LAMENTATIONS

Deprived of the narrative content found in the book of Job, Lamentations and the Song of Songs were identified by Kuliš as primarily poetry, thus being assigned a second position (after Psalms) in the poetic hierarchy of the biblical books. Unlike his 1896 translation of Job, which left off without final editing, Kuliš honed his translations of Lamentations and the Song of Songs, preparing them for publication in Lviv in 1897. Unlike the Song of Songs, paraphrased in the late 1860s, the book of Lamentations was translated for the first time in 1897.

In a preface to the text of his translation of Lamentations (*Holosin'nja*), Kuliš wrote that, although associated in tradition with the prophet Jeremiah, the distinctive style and content of this book made Jeremianic authorship unlikely. The five "songs" were written for use as laments of mourning in memory of the conquest of Jerusalem by Neb-u-chad-rez'-zar and the devastation of the Temple by the Babylonians in the sixth century BC. Since they are genuine cultic songs, without any narrative framework, these laments, according to Kuliš, could be identified as "elegies" (*Holosin'nja*, 3r–3v). In Hebrew poetry, he continued, one could find traces of words that did not meet the standards of literary language, as is the case of vernacular Ukrainian in Galicia and Dnieper Ukraine. Having set the Psalter "as a tuning fork of Hebrew," along with Lamentations and the Song, at the poetic summit of the Bible, Kuliš addressed the book of Job, which, as he assured his readership, would be followed by both poetic and prose parts of the entire Old Testament (ibid., 4v–5r; Voznjak 1928a, 216–217).

With the above programmatic message of Kuliš in mind, the vernacular foundations of *Holosin'nja* stand out stylistically among other translations made by the writer in the 1890s. The language of this translation is replete with vernacular and, strictly speaking, folkloric elements that are less often attested in his translations of other biblical books. Among such expressions, deserving of attention is repetition or recurrence of synonymous predicates (verb serialization) and of some other features (e.g., *ženyxalys'-lycjalys'* [3 pl. pret.] "to woo" [*Hollosin'nja*, 6r], *bižjat'-utekajut'* [3 pl. pres.] "to go, flee" [ibid., 6v], *ženut'-pohanjajut'* [3 pl. pres.] "to pursue" [ibid., 7r]). Note also *v tisnoti-honyt'vi* (loc.) "in the days of [her] affliction" (ibid., Lam 1:7), *zlydniv-nedoly* (gen.) "miseries" (*Holosin'nja*, 7r), *slas'ni ta solodki* "delicate and sweet" (ibid., 16r), and many others. Very commonplace are tautological expressions of the type *movčky movčjat'* (3 pl. pres.) "to be afflicted by silence," *horem zažuryvsja* (3 sg. m. pret.) "to grieve, to be in bitterness" (ibid., 6v), *povybyvav* (3 sg. m. pret.) *boem* "hath trodden under foot" (ibid., 8r, Lam 1:15).

Many other forms are likewise modeled on the oral narrative style. Having long ago tempered his enthusiasm for the Cossacks, Kuliš resorted occasionally to ethnically tinged lexemes inherited from the Cossack times and widely retained in folklore, whence such words as *branka* "prisoner" (*Holosin'nja*, 6r), *jasyr* "booty, captives" (ibid., 6v), *otamany* "chieftains" (ibid.), and *čambul* "detachment of [Tatar or Cossack] cavalrymen" (ibid.; Hrinč., 2:954; Žel., 2:1060); one can add here *Judyna panna* "the daughter of Ju'-dah" and *panna Zyjons'ka* "the daughter of Zi'-on" (*Holosin'nja*, 8r, Lam 1:15, 17). In order to strengthen the vernacular foundations of his translation and make it more appealing to the common people, Kuliš introduced a few dialectal features that are strongly associated with northern Ukrainian folklore. I will mention only two morphological forms. First are neuters ending in *-(j)e*, influenced also by the old literary tradition and used by Kuliš in his earlier translation of the New Testament. Second are plurals with the desinence *-e*, attested in older folkloric texts extant from northern Ukraine (Tymošenko 1968, 152; Matvijas 2008, 98) (e.g., *nas´lid´dje* "legacy" [*Holosin´nja*, 6r], *oblyčče* "face" [ibid., 7r], *polom˝e* "flame" [ibid., 7v], *kamin´nje* [coll.] "stones" [ibid., 15v, Lam 4:1], *pročane* "pilgrims" [*Holosin´nja*, 6v], *ljude* "people" [ibid., 7v], and so forth).

The colloquial tinge of the translation is relatively moderate, without conspicuously vulgar forms that would appear out of place in a lament used to express genuine grief—especially in chapters 1, 2, and 4—and generally resembles a funeral dirge for the fallen city. However, some verses look intrinsically colloquial, thus presenting suffering and persecution as deeply personal and intimate:

Holosin´nja of 1897

Йуда покинув *отацьке наслідьдє*...	[3. Judah is gone into captivity because of affliction, and
Знуджений злиднями й рабством *важенним*,	because of great servitude: she dwelleth among the
Сьвіт за очима почав *сновидати*	heathen, she findeth no rest:
Проміж язиками, повен тревоги,	all her persecutors overtook
А вороги, позьбіравшись *докупи*,	her between the straits.]
У *заковулках* ёго здоганяли.	(Lam 1)
(*Holosin´nja*, 6v)	

The above fragment is very characteristic in its lexical make-up. Aside from the bookish *jazyk* "people" and *rabstvo* "slavery," the text is riddled with colloquial forms that were commonplace at that time in the two historical parts of Ukraine. The only exception seems to be *zakovulok*, which, as a possible Russianism, is not attested in either Jevhen Želexivs´kyj's or Borys Hrinčenko's dictionaries. Of interest also is the innovative form *važennyj* "very heavy, hard" cited in the above two dictionaries from Kuliš's literary works (Žel., 1:54; Hrinč., 1:163).

Occasionally, suffering is intensified with the help of unusual, bookish, or Church Slavonic elements serving as devices of stylistic embellishment typical of the baroque tradition. This becomes more obvious in comparison with the prose translation of 1903, edited by Puljuj:

Holosinʹnja of 1897	**Prose Translation of 1903**
Господе! Зглянься на мене в *печалі*:	Зглянься, Господи, бо я в *тіснечі*; *внутро* моє неспокійне, серце, неначе перевернулось у мені; Я бо упрямо противився тобі; в полі забрав меч діти мої, а дома—(голодова) смерть. (*SP*, 713)
Серце мое и *утроба* палає,	
Дух мій у грудіх тремтить, мре від горя:	
Згадую бунти мои *окаяньні*.	
В полі 'д меча полягло нас *премного*,	
Дома нас губить зараза голодна.	
(*Holosinʹnja*, 8v)	

[20. Behold, O Lord; for I am in distress; my bowels are troubled; mine heart is turned within me; for I have grievously rebelled: abroad the sword bereaveth, at home there is as death.] (Lam 1)

In this excerpt, stylistic effect is achieved through contrasting the bookish *pečalʹ* "grief," Church Slavonicisms *premnoho* "a lot of," *utroba* "womb," and *okajanʹni* (pl.) "cursed" with such dialectal forms as *hrudix* "breast," with the eastern Ukrainian locative ending -*ix* (also *Holosinʹnja*, 9r), and *ʹd meča* "from the sword," with a typical northern Ukrainian (eastern Polissian) type of apheresis. This kind of contrast also occurs in other verses where colloquial and dialectal forms occur alongside Church Slavonic or bookish lexemes: *stohnu-pobyvajusʹ* (1 sg. pres.) "to sigh, suffer" next to *vozveselylysʹ* (3 pl. pret.) "to rejoice" (ibid., 9r) and *pered viččju* "before thee"—literally, "before [your] eyes" (ibid., 9, Lam 1:21) and derived from the former genitive dual *očiju* "eyes"—next to *vozdavav* (3 sg. pret.) "to do unto someone," although similar lofty elements are much fewer than in other biblical translations. Finally, in spelling Kuliš adhered to what he dubbed in the early 1880s as a "most radical phonetics." The following phenomena come into consideration: anaptyxis in *ylʹljucʹcja* (3 pl. pres.) "to pour down" (*Holosinʹnja*, 6; Shevelov 1979, 461–467; Matvijas 2008, 96), neutralization in voicing (e.g., *peret*[d] *toboju* "before thee" [*Holosinʹnja*, 9r]), and assimilation in place and manner of articulation as found in *miz*[ž] *carstvamy* "among the provinces" (ibid., 6r, Lam 1:1) or at a word-internal boundary, *vic*[d]*curalysʹ* (3 pl. pret.) "to repudiate, forsake" (*Holosinʹnja*, 8v).

It becomes clear why Kuliš's translation included in the 1903 Ukrainian Bible differed from the original one he completed before his death in 1897.

Puljuj, let alone the British and Foreign Bible Society, could hardly accept the innovative character of Kuliš's work, which was at odds with the guidelines set up by the Bible Society. Comparing Kuliš's original translation with that resulting from heavy editing by Puljuj and Sljusarčuk, one can see to what extent Kuliš's initial plan was modified by the editors. This is why, both aesthetically and intellectually, the poetic translation of Kuliš outdoes the 1903 revised variant, which lost much of the writer's intention to versify what is versified in the Hebrew Bible: "And for what the Latin, German, and Slavic priests did to the Holy Scriptures, let them be judged at the court of righteous science" (Voznjak 1928a, 237).

In sum, with Church Slavonic, bookish, and Galician (or Polish) forms reduced almost to nothing, "the Old Rusian language" of Lamentations appears conspicuously vernacular-oriented. If somewhat reminiscent of Kuliš's poetic paraphrases of the late 1860s, the stylistics of this translation demonstrate a radical detour in the writer's understanding of literary Ukrainian as a belated reaction to what he called "[Puljuj's] Galician distortion of the New Testament" in the 1870s and 1880s (Kuliš to Biloborodov, 89).

THE SONG OF SONGS

This biblical book, comprising about twenty-five lyric poems and gathered together around the third century BC, was translated by Kuliš in the same fashion, that is, with a particular focus on poetic devices. In a preface to his translation Kuliš noted that, while following in the steps of Eduard Reuß, his main concern was "not so much biblical scholarship as the native tongue, employed throughout the Holy Scriptures with the help of biblical studies" (*Pis′nja*, 21v).

In fact, this was Kuliš's second translation of the Song. The first poetic paraphrase of this book, similar in stylistic design to his 1868 translations of Moses's songs, was likewise completed in 1868. On 29 November 1868 Kuliš informed his friend Ivan Xyl′čevs′kyj that he had also translated the Song of Songs, which, he expected, would be forthcoming along with his comments on this biblical book in 1869 (Kuliš to Xil′čevskij, 91). This translation, however, did not appear in 1869, and, because of a tenuous relationship with some local populists, including members of the editorial board of the periodical *Pravda*, neither did it appear later (Franko to Drahomanov, 95). Only ten years later did Kuliš have a chance to publish this translation, although with revisions resulting from new circumstances in imperial Russia. In order to elude censorship imposed by the Ems Decree of 18 May 1876, an early paraphrase of the book entitled *Xutorjanka* (A Farmstead Girl) was partly incorporated into his book *Xutorskaja filosofija* (Homestead Philosophy, 1879), which included large sections of poetry in Ukrainian. Since this biblical book could be stylized like a drama, being performative poetry of a literary nature, the text of *Xutorjanka* was presented as "a theatrical performance" allegedly compiled and staged by a certain blind priest Jakym who might have known the whole Bible by heart (Kuliš 1879, 33–34, 155–158; Naxlik 2007, 2:272).

In his intention to create a complete translation of the Bible from scratch, Kuliš offered a new interpretation of this composite work, full of sensuous and suggestive allusions to a couple enacting ancient myths of the love between a god and a goddess (Gillingham 1994, 111). Aware of the unashamed eroticism of these songs, the translator offered, nevertheless, a balanced perception of female love, with its sensual meaning not superseded by the spiritual message. In place of a thoroughly folkloric basis for *Xutorjanka*, one deals in the Song with a stylistically more complex texture, as observed in the following parallel verses:

Xutorjanka	**The Song of Songs**
Я смуглява та вродлива, доле моя нещаслива! гарна мов калина в лузі, мов на ниві колос повний. Не гордуйте, що я чорна: мене сонце осмалило. Не злюбили мене братья, сини матери моєї, стали в спеку посилати винограду доглядати; стерегла я, доглядала, свою воленьку втеряла. (Kuliš 1879, 30–31)	Я собі личком смуглява, та гарна. Гарна, паняночки Єрусалемські, Мов ті намети роскішні Кедарські, Мов килеми в Соломона в палатах. Ви не дивітеся, що я смуглява: Сонце в жару се мене осмалило. Рідні брати неприхильні до мене,— Мусила им стерегти виноград ник, Власний же був нестережен у мене. (*Pis´nja*, 22r–22v)

[6. Look not upon me, because I am black, because the sun hath looked upon me: my mother's children were angry with me; they made me the keeper of the vineyards; but mine own vineyard I have not kept.] (Song 1:6)

Written almost entirely in trochees, the text of *Xutorjanka* is heavily modeled on folkloric imagery and versification. Its language is the Central Dnieper vernacular with a few Church Slavonicisms like *lože* "bed" or *premudryj* "wise" (Kuliš 1879, 37, 41), despite the fact that the text is identified by the author as the libretto of an ancient folk performance. As is evidenced in the fragment of the Song quoted above, this book was translated by Kuliš in dactylic tetrameter, the verses having the rhythm of Greek elegiac poetry. The same dactylic meter was employed by Kuliš in other translations, in particular that of the "large and significant" book of Ecclesiastes, or the Wisdom of Jesus Son of Sirach, with the latter name Ukrainianized as *Jysus Syrašenko* (Voznjak 1928a, 237).[8]

In addition to a different rhythmic scheme, the language of the Song (*Pis′nja*) looks more complex than that of *Xutorjanka*. Leaving aside a few bookish morphological forms like *nesterežen* "[have I] not kept" (Song 1:6) in the above excerpt, the lexical make-up is thoroughly colloquial (e.g., *tovarystvo* "company [group of shepherds]," *kobylycja* "horse," *korali* "rows of jewelry" [*Pis′nja*, 22v, Song 1:10], *ližko* and *lihvo* "bed" [*Pis′nja*, 25r, 26r], *s′vitlycja* "room," *hospoda* "house," *kramnycja* "shop" [ibid., 25v], and many others). Borrowings are very rare in this text. I happened, for instance, on the Church Slavonic form *palaty* "chambers" (ibid., 23r), a long naturalized Polonism *benketuje* (3 sg. pres.) "to feast" (ibid.), and a possible Russianism *kryša* "rafter" (ibid., 23v, Song 1:17). Some neologisms also occur in the text, such as *nevmiraky* "valiant men" (*Pis′nja*, 25v, Song 3:7), *vynarnja* "banqueting house" (*Pis′nja*, 23v, Song 2:4; Žel., 1:80), and *stojalo* "leg" (*Pis′nja*, 30r). Unexpectedly, Kuliš introduces some archaic forms in morphology, including dual forms like *ruci* (du.) "hand" and *nozi* (du.) "leg" (ibid., 29v, 30 r).

In the second translation of the Song, one also finds representative forms borrowed from different dialects. To adduce a few examples, in the

---

8 In the manuscript prepared for publication by Myxajlo Pavlyk, Kuliš offered a slightly modified variant of the name *Jysus Syratenko* (Zelens′ka 2000, 357).

final revision of the manuscript, Kuliš changed *prošu* into *prosju* (1 sg.) "to ask" (*Pis′nja*, 23v), commonly attested in East Ukrainian, while using a rare southwestern Ukrainian form *xovm* "hill" (ibid., 26v) with [w] from *l* before *m* (Shevelov 1979, 417) and *hulycja* "street" (*Pis′nja*, 25r) instead of Polissian *julycja* (Matvijas 2008, 96). Generally, a focus on phonetics seems to predominate in the language of this translation. Two more interesting phenomena come into consideration. First, for the sake of stylistic ornamentation, Kuliš more consistently employed the digraph *kh* to denote the velar sound *g* in loan words of the type *khrona* "clusters" (*Pis′nja*, 23r), *khraty* "lattice" (ibid., 24r), *fikha* "fig" (ibid., 24v), *khazely* (gen.) "roe," and *piv-khranaty* "half a pomegranate" (ibid., 26v). Second, assimilative changes are rendered in accordance with the principle of "radical phonetics," ranging from conceivably simple cases like *ys*[z] *kizon′kamy* "with goats" via *uš*[z] *šatra* "beside a tent" (ibid., 22v) to *nac*[d] *carja* "[more] than a tsar" (ibid., 23r) and *š*[z] *ščyroho zolota* "of fine gold" (ibid., 30r, Song 5:15). Clearly, this is a vernacular-oriented language devised to appeal to common readers who care little about spelling rules.

The substance of Kuliš's poetry in this translation will look more convincing if compared to an unfinished translation of the Song of Songs made by Panas Myrnyj, who never excelled in poetic translations. With a fuzzy meter, his is a prose translation, which, however, can be read as poetry with a terse style using plain and dialectally homogeneous language, and, more specifically, word-pairing, wordplays, repetition, and a few other folkloric features. A cursory analysis of just a short excerpt from Panas Myrnyj's translation should illustrate this more clearly.

Kuliš's Translation of the Song	**Panas Myrnyj's Translation of the Song**
"Милий мій—мов кушчик мирри У мене на *грудіх*, Кипрового винограду *Кґрона*—мій коханий,— Винограду с того саду Славного в *Эн-Кґедах*." *Гарна* ти, моя кохана,	12 [13]. Милий мій—мов китиця мирри у мене на *грудях*. 13 [14]. Милий мій—мов *гроно* кипрове в виноградниках *Енгадських*. 14 [15]. Гарна ти, коханко моя, ой яка ти *пригарна*! Очі у тебе голубьячі.

О! яка ти гарна!
Очі в тебе голубині...
"И ти, мій коханий,
Прехороший, уродливий,
А постеля наша
Ряст мякий, трава зелена,—
Крашча над усяку."
В нас кедри замісь будинка,
Кипариси—криша. (*Pis′nja*, 23r–23v)

15 [16]. А ти, мій любий,
    прихороший та *вродливий*! і
    постіль наша, мов трава зелена;
16 [17]. Покрівля домів наших—
    кедри, сволоки над
    ними—кипариси.
    (*Solomon*, 2)

[13. A bundle of myrrh is my well-beloved unto me; he shall lie all night betwixt my breasts.
14. My beloved is unto me as a cluster of camphire in the vineyards of En-ge′-di.
15. Behold, thou art fair, my love, behold, thou art fair; thou hast doves' eyes;
16. Behold, thou art fair, my beloved, yea, pleasant: also our bed is green.
17. The beams of our house are cedar, and our rafters of fir.] (Song 1:13–17)

Stylistically, Panas Myrnyj's vocabulary is uniform, without patent dialectisms or western Ukrainian borrowings (e.g., the new locative form *hrudjax* as opposed to EUkr. *hrudix* in Kuliš). Despite Panas Myrnyj's interest in Ukrainian folklore, he tried to abstain from obvious folkloric constructions and forms in his translation, since in his view these were not suitable for the lofty style of the biblical content of the Song. There are practically no Church Slavonicisms, save for a few lexemes like *zaklynaju vas* "I charge you" (*Solomon* 2:7, Song 2:7) next to Kuliš's *prosju* (1 sg. pres.) "to ask" in the same verse (*Pis′nja*, 23v).

Spelling in Panas Myrnyj's translation exhibits his native southeastern Ukrainian phonetics. Deserving of attention, for instance, is a lack of the digraph *kh*, whence a lack of the velar sound *g* in the translator's Sloboda dialect and, by extension, in the literary variety as used in Dnieper Ukraine (Danylenko 2006c, 172–192) (e.g., *hrono* "cluster," *fyhovyna* "fig tree" [*Solomon* 2:13], or *hranatove jabluko* "pomegranate" [ibid., 4:3]). The form *zima* with *i* instead of *y* (ibid., 2:11) is typical of Panas Myrnyj's and Kuliš's phonetics (Hrycenko 2007, 24), thus reflecting southeastern (close to transitional) dialectal features in nineteenth-century written Ukrainian (Shevelov 1979, 667). Another southeastern Ukrainian feature in Panas Myrnyj's language is a characteristic confusion of *e* with *y* as, for instance, in *pryharna* (f.) "beautiful" and *pryxorošyj* (m.) "nice" in the cited passage, as well as in *vysnjankamy* (instr.) "spring songs" next to *vesna* "spring" (*Solomon* 2:12), though one consistently finds *meni* (dat.) "to me" in contrast to the vernacular form *mỹni*, attested in the writings of early Ševčenko and Kuliš (Tymošenko 1969, 104–106).

The overall impression of Panas Myrnyj's translation is its stylistically bleached substance that can barely be compared with Kuliš's interpretation of the Song of Songs. Stylistically varied and phonetically vernacularized throughout, Kuliš's translation advances a novel understanding of the biblical (high) style, apparently in tune with the vernacular basis of new literary Ukrainian. Premised on Southeast Ukrainian, Panas Myrnyj's translation appears, by contrast, excessively regional, thus paradoxically of a kind with the scriptural translations made in Galicia, including those penned by Markijan Šaškevyč and especially Antin Kobyljans'kyj.

THE VERSIFIED BIBLE

The true crown of Kuliš's life-long work on the translation of the Holy Scriptures is his "versified Bible," which was specifically designed for the common readership. However, his major concern in this case was not biblical poetry set within a prose form in the Hebrew original, or certain biblical books written in poetic line-forms such as Psalms, Proverbs, Ecclesiastes, the Song, or Job (apart from its prose prologue and epilogue). In the 1890s, in addition to a new prose translation that, heavily edited, appeared posthumously in 1903 (*SP*), Kuliš was working on a poetic translation of the Hebrew Scriptures, including the prose narrative and its poetic components. Concurring with the biblical scholars of his day, Kuliš believed that in the very first stages of cultural growth people would sing about rather than write down historical accounts. This is why the versified Bible, showing a distinct performative quality, must have antedated, in his opinion, the prose one.

For his "versified Bible" Kuliš had a chance to translate only the first book of Moses (Genesis) and some twenty-four chapters of Exodus.[9] Metrically, this was an innovative translation inasmuch as, in different chapters, Kuliš interspersed various poetic meters. To give the most telling examples, chapter 1 of Genesis was written in trochaic tetrameter. These are the opening lines of this chapter:

Chapter 1 of Genesis

Марно розум до початку
Світу хоче сягонути:
Бо й сам розум немовлятком
У ті давна мусив бути.
Як на слово ж став багатий,
На спасенний дар природи,
Став з Едему *вивожждати*
Всі коліна, всі народи.
Звався тихий рай Едемом,
Повен щастя *бес печали*:
Про сей рай діди давнезне
Слово нам переказали

Бо людський рід не на муку
Віковічно народився,
А щоб брав з біди науку
И до вічних *благ* добився.
Вічні ж *блага*—сьвіт, свобода
И *жаданьнє* духа правди.
Правоправницька природа
Без спокуси, без принади.
Так як в нетрях зьвір буяе,
Нам на сьвіті гірко жити:
Рід людський знай поривае
У Господень рай летіти. (*UB*, 2r–2v)

A more sophisticated meter is found in the following excerpt from chapter 2 of Genesis, which reads like ancient epic poetry. The impression of antiquity is conveyed through anapestic hexameter with the final syllable of the feminine rhyme, which, within Ukrainian conventions of poetry, is a rare poetic meter:

И вдихнув ёму жизни диханьнє в лице, вдихнув духа живого
И зробився *тогді* чоловік над всі тварі душею живою.
Насадив Господь Бог ёму рай у Едемі рукою благою,—

---

9 Two copies of the original draft dating back to the early 1890s are held today at the manuscript repository at the Myxajlo Kocjubyns´kyj Literary-Memorial Museum in Černihiv (Ukraine) (shelfmarks A-4540 and A-4541). There is also one more copy made most likely during the life of Kuliš, which is held at the Institute of Manuscripts in the V. I. Vernads´kyj National Library in Kyiv (Holding 3/37944).

На востоціх в Едемі, усяке там *древо* роскішне родило,
И на смак прехороше, и оку на нёго споглянути мило. (*UB*, 5v)

This more open-ended poetic adaptation contrasts with Oleksander Potebnja's archaizing translation of Homer's *Odyssey* (Danylenko 1999), thus making clear the pragmatic and didactic goal of the poetic translation of the Bible by Kuliš. Written in poetic meters appearing familiar to the common people, the translation treats broader themes and enlightens the readers in the spirit of Christian morality. According to Kuliš, the poetic interpretation of the Bible was the most appropriate form for the moral content of the Hebrew Scriptures (Naxlik 2007, 2:279).

The language of the versified Bible is largely reminiscent of that used in the translations of Job, Lamentations, and the Song. The latter books were conceived by Kuliš as an integral part of another, unversified translation of the Bible comprised of "prose-like elements" within the poetry and "poetic components" within the prose. With this observation in mind, we can argue now that the language of the versified Bible constituted a synthesis of vernacular foundations with Church Slavonic and dialectal features. Among the latter, of interest are northern Ukrainian neuters ending in *-(j)e* with gemination like *žadan'nje* "thirst, craving for" as cited above or *z'vir'rje* "animals" (*UB*, 4r) and *odrid'dje* "human beings," compared to *nas'lid'je* "heritage" without gemination (ibid., 2v). There are also southeastern Ukrainian locatives of the type *na vostocix* (pl.) "in the east," cross-dialectal *tohdi* "then," and so forth. I add here vernacular adjectival derivatives like *letjučyj* "able to fly," *povzjučyj* "able to creep," and *xodjučyj* "able to walk" (ibid., 4v; Kurylo 1960, 16).

Church Slavonicisms are not very numerous. Serving as stylistic ornamentation, they are all long naturalized in vernacular Ukrainian, thus appearing quite natural in Kuliš's versified paraphrase: *plidne drevo* and *drevo plodovyte* "fruit-bearing tree" next to *derevo* "tree" (*UB*, 3r, 4v, 5v), *blaha* "goods," *presvjatyj* "holy" (ibid., 2v), *tvar* "creature" (ibid., 4r), *vyvoždaty* (ibid., 2), and *roždaty* "to give birth" (ibid., 4r). Paradoxically, the language of the versified Bible has much in common with the language of Nečuj-Levyc'kyj's translation of 1 and 2 Chronicles, Ezra, Nehemiah,

Esther, and Daniel in the 1903 edition of the Bible, though it is much obscured by subsequent corrections made by Puljuj and most likely his friend Sljusarčuk. Both languages tend to be dialectally and diachronically homogeneous. The distinction is more quantitative than qualitative, more of degree than of kind.

It would be useful at this point to refer to Oleksander Potebnja's translation of Homer's *Odyssey*. This will accentuate Kuliš's conception of the biblical (high) style as used in a "secular," versified translation of the Bible. It should be reiterated that Potebnja's language, primarily its phonetics and morphology, was modeled on the eastern Ukrainian vernacular, while the translator tried to eschew dialectal and Church Slavonic forms. With an eye to creating a new high style in his literary experiment, Potebnja resorted, as was proven elsewhere (Danylenko 1999), to paratactic (archaic) syntax and lexical archaisms such as *komonnyk* "horseman," *sulycja* "arrow," and *suložnycja* "concubine." Trying to bring to the fore ancient Trojan and Achaean heroes, he occasionally employed conspicuously obsolete language patterns such as the attributive use of nouns of the type *Alkynoj knjaz'* "Prince Alkinoos" and some other paratactic constructions. Generally, Potebnja's language was folkloric and, by the same token, archaic, since the translator worked on the basis of the historical memory of the nation (Shevelov 1994, 115).

Compared to Potebnja's archaic and folkloric language, Kuliš's normalization project was premised on other grounds. As mentioned, he intended rather to vernacularize than to archaize the biblical narrative, thus making it comprehensible for everyone. Hence, in addition to simple poetic meters accompanied by "radical phonetics" in spelling (*kulišivka*), he made limited use of "popular" Church Slavonicisms together with dialectal forms borrowed primarily from Southeast Ukrainian. Syntactically, the language of the versified Bible is more vernacular than archaic or even folkloric. Indeed, there is no representative construction in the inventory of syntactic devices that, otherwise, would stylistically mark the language of Kuliš's translation. I found just a handful of examples of repetition or recurrence of synonymous predicates and other features, a construction copiously attested in the translation of Lamentations.

Leaving aside the question of the pertinence of syllabic-tonic versification for epic or biblical narratives in the Ukrainian literature of the late nineteenth-century (Naxlik 2007, 2:283), it becomes clear that the versified Bible heralded a new stage in the translation of the Holy Scriptures into Ukrainian. Created in accordance with contemporary vernacular norms, this type of translation seemed to have closed a circle of scriptural translations initiated by Kuliš in the late 1860s. In fact, in the 1890s, the author returned to his earlier idea of poetic paraphrases, though showing a higher degree of conceptualization of the Hebrew Scriptures and how, in compliance with the poetics of biblical narrative, the Bible had to be translated into vernacular Ukrainian.

Summary

With unflagging devotion to his people, Kuliš worked on translating the Holy Scriptures for more than forty years. Constantly modifying his conception of the Ukrainian Bible, he nevertheless demonstrated persistency in maintaining his programmatic vision of a full-fledged literary language. The years 1868–1871 and the 1890s should be viewed as two pivotal points in the process of the creation of the Ukrainian Bible. At the outset of his life-long translation *Odyssea*, Kuliš focused on the "poetic books" of the Hebrew Scriptures appearing to him most appropriate for the creation of a vernacular-based literary standard. Having chosen Psalms, the Song of Songs and the book of Job, Kuliš intended to paraphrase the Hebrew Bible in accordance with the populist nature of Ukrainian literature, and in particular with the folkloric patterns ushered in by Taras Ševčenko by that time. However, despite his obvious orientation toward Ukrainian folklore and Southeast Ukrainian as points of departure for the creation of the biblical style, Kuliš showed an innovative approach toward the translation of the Holy Writ.

First of all, he drew on what had been accomplished by his predecessors, though he never identified with the populist paradigm established by Ivan Kotljarevs´kyj and his epigones in particular. This is why Kuliš's earlier paraphrases, although so close to the spirit of Ukrainian folklore, could hardly be juxtaposed with Myxajlo Maksymovyč's folkloric paraphrases of the psalms. Nor did Kuliš mean to cultivate an homogenous idiom comparable with the language of Petro Hulak-Artemovs´kyj, who otherwise indulged in the idle fancy of classicism, or with Pylyp Moračevs´kyj's sterile vernacular translations. Kuliš's language showed a skillful blending of heterogeneous elements that was not paralleled either in Oleksander Navroc´kyj's or Volodymyr Aleksandrov's translations of the Psalter and some poetic biblical books. Neither author could help but imitate Kuliš's achievements in his biblical translations. In their paraphrases, they unwittingly and slavishly resorted to those stylistic devices that Kuliš aptly employed in his translation of the Holy Scriptures. Not surprisingly, cast in a solid folkloric form with hackneyed rhythm and poetic means, Navroc´kyj's translation of the psalms contained numerous lexical transfers ("Kulišisms") and parallels found in Kuliš.

Kuliš's biblical translations demonstrated a pioneering approach to borrowings, in particular Polish, Church Slavonic, and Russian forms. Unlike Ševčenko, whose influence was observable in Kuliš's early paraphrases, he expanded the functional possibilities of Church Slavonic and other admixtures in the biblical style of Ukrainian. Trying to break through the tenets of the Church Slavonic baroque tradition still imprinted in Ševčenko's poetry, Kuliš deliberately experimented with those Church Slavonic and other bookish elements that were not commonly found either in Ševčenko or the vernacular-based written language used in Dnieper Ukraine (Moroz and Tkač 2006, 35). It is no wonder, for instance, that Kuliš's *Yov* (Job) easily outshined Aleksandrov's translation of this poetic book, which was aimed at the precise interpretation of psalmody in the Jewish tradition. In matters linguistic, the Xarkovite poet wanted to translate this book into an exemplary language capable of competing with Kuliš's language in variance and heterogeneity. However, in order to make his translation of Job more understandable for all the Ukrainians, Aleksandrov based his purportedly exemplary idiom on the old eastern Slavic literary tradition. Since this tradition at that time was almost completely diluted with the Russian recension of Church Slavonic, Aleksandrov's idiom turned into a Russianized variety of the regional (Sloboda) vernacular, a metamorphosis totally unacceptable for Kuliš given his synthetic vision of the Ukrainian Bible.

As an original poet, not a mere competitor of Ševčenko, Kuliš was aware of his pivotal role in the national awakening, whence his assiduous work on the translation of the scriptures, primarily for the sake of the acculturation of the Ukrainian people. While contributing his literary talent and phenomenal erudition, Kuliš experimented with new forms of syllabic and syllabic-tonic versification not only in his original poetry (Naxlik 2007, 2:285–289) but also in his early paraphrases and later poetic translations of the Bible. To adduce a few random examples, in the 1869 translation of Job, the poet used iambic pentameter, while in *Tovytovi slovesa* (Tobit) of 1893, he employed the popular *kolomyjka* syllabic structure. Other metric feet are also found in Lamentations and the Song, translated in the late 1890s and both written in dactylic tetrameter in contrast to *Xutorjanka* (1868–1871), composed in trochees. As was pointed out, various feet are intermittently used in the versified Bible, with some chapters written in trochees and others compiled in anapestic hexameter. The above variety sheds light on Kuliš's intention to fully domesticate various ancient and canonical strophes employed sporadically by his predecessors (Ivan Kotljarevs'kyj, Petro Hulak-Artemovs'kyj, Leonid Hrebinka, Levko Borovykovs'kyj, Amvrosij Metlyns'kyj, and Taras Ševčenko). But what is most telling in our case is that Kuliš introduced various syllabic-tonic meters in both his original versification and his translations, thus much expanding the possibilities of poetic form in Ukrainian literature, especially in biblical translation.

Taken in the context of the formation of new literary Ukrainian, Kuliš's translation of the New Testament proved to be more innovative in comparison with those made in Austrian-ruled Ukraine. Despite the fact that, chronologically, the first vernacular translation of (some fragments from) the Holy Gospels was made in Galicia by Markijan Šaškevyč in 1842, the local trend cultivated by his followers, especially Antin Kobyljans'kyj, revealed nothing new from the viewpoint of the normalization of the written language as used in these lands over sixty years. As our analysis shows, most of the translations that appeared after Šaškevyč in Galicia and Bukovyna, including the outdated translation of the Psalter and the New Testament by Aleksander Bačyn'skij in 1903 (Horbač 1988, 65, 76), were made in *jazyčije*, a local hybrid of Church Slavonic, (local) Russian, and regional forms, primarily of Polish origin. Premised on the regional literary tradition reaching back to the late seventeenth century, this linguistic hybrid, although demonstrating a wide range of admixtures, remained Church Slavonic at its core (Danylenko 2008a, 109–111, 2015b). This is why, despite a few Church Slavonic forms, the language of Kobyljans'kyj's translations must be viewed not as vernacular proper but as Church-Slavonic-turned-vernacular.

Though striving for a synthesis of both regionally and stylistically heterogeneous elements, Kuliš's language never lost its ties with Southeast Ukrainian. One should not, therefore, overestimate the presence of Polish and Galician elements in his language, in particular in the biblical translations. Despite the presence of Polonisms in Kuliš's language, his ambivalent treatment of Polish forms in the regional (Galician) variety of Ukrainian was more than obvious. Yet this stance was not chosen by Kuliš on a mere whim. Already while serving in Warsaw, Kuliš was more than willing to sweep aside the influence of the Polish Catholic church, together with the Polish language, on the schooling of local Ukrainians in the Xolm (Pol. Chełm) region (Naxlik 2007, 1:230–231). In promoting education of Austrian Ukrainians (Ruthenians) in Russian, Kuliš aimed at erecting a reliable barrier against Polish acculturation. Moreover, he believed that the local *jazyčije* could hardly be used to fulfill educational roles effectively; in fact, this mixed language was a historical result of the long dominance of Polish culture and language in Austrian-ruled Ukraine (Danylenko 2008a, 109–111).

It becomes clear why, in the long run, Kuliš showed his frustration apropos Puljuj's editorial intervention at the final stage of the preparation of the translation of the New Testament for publication. Suffice it to mention his deprecating remarks about the role of "Puljuj and his compatriots" in introducing regional forms into this translation. Those forms, as he confessed in a letter of 26 April 1896 to Oleksij Biloborodov, appeared "loathsome" in the overall makeup of his early translation of the Holy Gospels (Kuliš to Biloborodov, 89, 90). Unfortunately, it is difficult today to ascertain the extent of the corrections made by Puljuj in the original translation handed over after Kuliš's death to the Vasyl´ Tarnovs´kyj Museum in Černihiv. As if having a presentiment, Kuliš's widow, Hanna Barvinok, cautioned Puljuj against substantial changes in her husband's manuscript(s) but, as it turned out, to no avail.

Overall, nobody before or after Kuliš was able to surpass his individual contribution to the creation of the biblical (high) style in new literary Ukrainian. His language program, as applied to the translation of the Ukrainian Bible, proved highly synthetic and original. He thus transgressed the inveterate Church Slavonic nature of Galician language practice and the "ethnographically bleached" language standard in composition at that time in Dnieper Ukraine. It is no wonder that his linguistic legacy, controversial as it may look through the vernacular prism of modern Ukrainian, exerted a long-lasting influence on future translations of the Holy Scriptures in the twentieth century, including those made by Ivan Ohijenko (*SP*, Ohijenko) and Ivan Xomenko-Pljuta (*SP*, Xomenko) (Ohijenko 1927; Nimčuk 2005, 40–44; Makar 2006, 365–368; Jurkowski 2001, 72).

PART II
SHAKESPEARE

CHAPTER 5
"Oh, Shakespeare, Our Father, Native to All Peoples"

ETHICS *AVANT LA LETTRE*!

Sometime in the late 1870s or, more likely, in the early 1880s, Kuliš experienced a series of setbacks in his translation of the Bible and his journalistic writings. Long before the appearance of the translation of the Gospels according to Mark, Luke, and John in Vienna in 1871, Galician Ukrainians who were not prepared to accept Kuliš's "artificial" language voiced strong criticism of his entire project. In addition, his three-volume historiographic treatise *Istorija vossoedinenija Rusi* (The History of the Reunification of Rus´, 1874–1877) proved rather controversial. The work met negative reception among most of the Ukrainophiles, who were taken aback by Kuliš's laudatory comments on Peter the Great and Catherine II and by his unfavorable assessment of Taras Ševčenko's view of the Cossacks as the pillar of the Ukrainian people throughout its history (Naxlik 2007, 1:319). Readers were particularly shocked by Kuliš's opinion of Ševčenko, namely, that the standing of the national bard and prophet was marred by his "semi-inebriated muse" (Kuliš 1874, 2:24). This reappraisal of Ševčenko was largely provoked by the poet's Bohemian lifestyle both before and after his exile, in Petersburg and Ukraine (Naxlik 2007, 1:320), although there were some other reasons behind what the populists regarded as a deliberate affront.

In his historiosophic studies of this period, Kuliš strove for the reevaluation of all sorts of misconceptions that had accreted to his fellow countrymen's understanding of their past. In the 1870s, as the aforementioned treatise revealed, the writer had come to see the Cossacks and even more so the *Hajdamaks* as unequivocally destructive, anarchic forces and as the creators of the "Great Ruin" into which Ukraine fell at the end of the seventeenth century (Grabowicz 1981, 191). In his debunking of the myth of the Cossack past of Ukraine, Kuliš went even further. In his collections *Xutorna poezija* (Homestead Poetry, 1882) and *Dzvin* (The Bell, 1893), his condemnation of Ševčenko was seen by many as nothing less than a treacherous and scurrilous attack on the national bard. Kuliš, in fact, charged Ševčenko with becoming a spokesman and an apologist for destruction and ruin.

In the late 1870s, deeply disillusioned but not without hope (Naxlik 2007, 1:360), Kuliš (1908, 255) turned again to translation, picking this time Shakespeare or the "Homer of the New Age," as he used to call him in his letters and studies. The choice, however, was not accidental. It rather resulted from his interest in the Homeric epos, along with contemporaneous advocates of enlightenment, as an ideal type and model for forming Ukrainian history, specifically in contrast to the mythologized Cossack past. As early as 15 April 1843, in a letter to Myxajlo Juzefovyč (1802–1889), acting deputy commissioner of the Kyiv school district at that time, Kuliš wrote in excitement about his purchase of twelve volumes of Shakespeare's collected works translated into Russian by Nikolaj Ketčer (Kuliš 2005, 1:16). Later in a letter to the same correspondent, Kuliš boasted that his literary taste had been shaped, among other factors, by studying assiduously the works of such authors as Homer, Dante, and Shakespeare (ibid., 65). Yet more revealing in this respect was his letter dated 30 March 1857 and addressed to a wealthy landowner, Hryhorij Galagan (1819–1888), who was providing at that time financial assistance for Kuliš's projects. Having translated Canto I from Lord Byron's *Childe Harold's Pilgrimage* into Ukrainian, Kuliš contended that "there was no Muscovite tongue in the entire world save for Ukrainian and English" (Kuliš to Galagan, 348–350). In order "to develop forms in our peasant vernacular (*zmužyčala naša reč'*) for the sake of all mankind's thought," he planned to translate William Shakespeare's *Hamlet*, Friedrich Schiller's *Wilhelm Tell*, Johann Wolfgang von Goethe's *Götz von Berlichingen*, and Walter Scott's *The Bride of Lammermoor* (ibid.).

Remarkably, some forty odd years later only the first two works from the above list were translated. However, unlike *Hamlet* (*Hamljet*-K/F), published posthumously in 1899, the translation of *Wilhelm Tell* has never appeared, although Kuliš regarded *Vyl'hel'm Tel'* as one of his best translations (Naxlik 2007, 2:269–270). In fact, *Vyl'hel'm Tel'* seemed to be doomed to misfortune. In 1894, Jevhen Tymčenko, a future linguist and lexicographer, came to visit the patriarch of Ukrainian literature and promised to assist him with the publication of the second volume of Kuliš's translations of Shakespeare, containing *King Lear*, *Coriolanus*, and *The Taming of the Shrew*, along with the manuscript of his translation of *Wilhelm Tell*. However, as soon as Kuliš learned that Tymčenko had arranged for the publication of Schiller's drama in the Lviv newspaper *Pravda*, he, because of his strained ties with Galicia (Franko 1898; Studyns'kyj 1928, 285–295), immediately backed out of his initial plan (Zaxarkin 1998, 94, 96, 98). When, in the long run, the manuscript of *Vyl'hel'm Tel'* made its way, via Oleksander Barvins'kyj, to Ivan Franko, the latter accepted the text but declined to have it published in the local periodical *Zorja*. First, as he explained, another translation of this drama by Volodymyr Kmicykevyč with a preface written by Franko himself had already appeared as early as 1887 and, second, the editorial board had already decided to publish yet another translation made by Borys Hrinčenko (which in fact appeared in *Zorja* in 1895) (Naxlik 2007, 1:449).

One is curious, however, as to whether Kuliš, back in 1857, was merely boasting of his translation projects so generously supported by Galagan, a liberal magnate who was the same age as Kuliš. Was he really planning to translate Shakespeare and Schiller, in particular? It is difficult to answer this question with certainty. What is possible, however, is that in the early 1860s Kuliš might have modified his initial plans. There is, for instance, some evidence of his understanding of the manifold problems faced by translators into Ukrainian at that time. One of his prominent Ukrainophile contemporaries, Oleksander Konys'kyj (1836–1900), recalled that Kuliš, during his meeting with the local young populists in Poltava in May 1860, declined to make the future journal *Osnova* exclusively a Ukrainian-language publication—the Ukrainian language, according to Kuliš, was not yet fully developed. When Konys'kyj, nevertheless, pressed further as to when Shakespeare would finally be translated into Ukrainian, Kuliš tittered and added that perhaps only their great-grandsons were destined to witness this (Šenrok 1901 74 (7/8), 53). However, in 1877, as if reversing their roles, Kostomarov questioned Kuliš's idea of translating Shakespeare into Ukrainian, claiming that all this would be of no use for educated bilingual Ukrainians, save perhaps the Galicians (ibid., 98). All this, as Hordyns´kyj (1928, 57) much later assumed, prompts us to posit the mid-1870s as the starting point of Kuliš's work on the translation of Shakespeare.

With the exception of several Western writers, Kuliš was in general opposed to translations, as these could hinder the development of belles lettres in Ukrainian. Any translation, as he pointed out in his letter to Barvins´kyj on 21 April 1876, was likely to obstruct the originality of the Ukrainian language; Ukrainian literature, therefore, would fall behind all other Slavic literatures (Barvins´kyj 2004, 188). In his letter of 27 March 1881, however, describing the charms of his rural life, Kuliš informed Puljuj of his work on the translation of *King Lear* and his intention to continue translating Shakespeare in the future (Studyns´kyj 1930, 54–55). At that time Kuliš came to believe that the role of Shakespeare in the process of the acculturation of the Ukrainian people was more significant than that of other translations. This is why, even while stressing the importance of original works, Kuliš allotted a unique place for Shakespeare in Ukrainian literature: a place that might be compared with that of the Ukrainian Bible. In other words, translation of both the Bible and Shakespeare was, among other things, a matter of moral and national awakening for the Ukrainians.

In another letter to Puljuj dated 30 May 1881, Kuliš wrote that he had already prepared for publication a volume of translations from Shakespeare that included *Romeo and Juliet* and *The Taming of the Shrew*, entitled *Prysmyrena kaverznycja* (Studyns´kyj 1930, 55). The latter was edited and published by Franko as late as 1900 under a changed title (*Pryborkona hostruxa*). On 18 June 1881 Kuliš confessed that he would rather first read the whole volume together with Puljuj, who would supply him with "more than one expression from the Galician language" (Studyns´kyj 1930, 56–57). However, as evidenced from Kuliš's letter dated 4 August 1881, he had, by that time, gotten in touch with Karol´ Bednars´kyj, director of the printing house of the Ševčenko Scientific Society, making arrangements for the publication of his translations of Shakespeare (Lučuk 1995).

Kuliš ultimately conferred the task of printing the translation of Shakespeare's dramas and comedies in Galicia on Oleksander Barvins´kyj. While planning a trip to Lviv with an eye to supervising the final stage of printing, Kuliš was actively discussing details of the project with his Galician lieutenant. In particular, in his letter of 26 August 1881, Kuliš disclosed to Barvins´kyj (2004, 202–203) his interpretation of the role of Shakespeare's oeuvre in the upbringing of the Ukrainian nation. He appended to the letter a "sermon to Shakespeare," which he wanted to be placed in the beginning of the volume of his translations. Published subsequently in the collection *Xutorna poezija* (Homestead Poetry) in 1882, the same year as his translations of Shakespeare, this "sermon" appeared a revisionary manifesto offered by a new, self-proclaimed *Kulturträger* (Kuliš 1908, 254–255; Zerov 1967, 38–39). Kuliš called Shakespeare "[our] father, native to all peoples" and "the greatest warrior from among the intellectuals," imploring him to take under his protection "the unworthy [Ukrainian] people who, lost in the steppes, were still praising the Cossack spirit," and help them thereby "to get rid of [their] Barbarism."

> Шекспіре, батьку наш, усім народам рідний!
> Чи чуєш, як зове тебе народ незгідний,
> Приблуда степовий, наслідник розбишацький,
> Що й досі чествує свій путь і дух козацький!

> [Oh, Shakespeare, our father, native to all peoples! / Do you hear how you are called by the unworthy people, / a stray in the steppes, a descendent of ruffians, / who are still praising their path and the Cossack spirit!] (Kuliš 1908, 255)

Concluding his letter to Barvins´kyj, Kuliš argued that those who were propagating the Cossack spirit (*kozaščyna*) "will achieve nothing in cultural affairs," thus connecting their future with "destruction rather than creativity" (Barvins´kyj 2004, 203). If Shakespeare became a favorite reading, he maintained, "it would sober our miserable literature and give it real wings. If Shakespeare's comedies and tragedies could draw our countrymen to the theater this would be a better school for them than all our writings and singing" (ibid.).

It is not surprising that Barvins'kyj found it difficult to publish the translations with a poetic introduction blaming the Cossacks for their lack of culture and their destructive role in the history of Ukraine, although, as he quickly added in his reply to Kuliš's letter, he would be happy to host Kuliš and his spouse in Ternopil' on their way to Lviv. On 23 September 1881, Kuliš ultimately backed away from his cooperation with Barvins'kyj. He asked, nevertheless, for forgiveness, realizing that he might have caused too much trouble without warning his correspondent in advance about his intent to publish such an introduction (Studyns'kyj 1930, 206).

The poetic introduction was not the only instance of bitterness, alienation, and critique directed at the people who, according to Kuliš, betrayed God and truth as both Christian and national attributes (Luckyj 1983, 161). In his collection *Xutorna poezija*, Kuliš (1908, 255–256) published the poem "Do ridnoho narodu" (To My Own People) on the occasion of "their introduction to Shakespeare's works." Calling Ukrainians "a people without any sense, honor, respect, or any truth in letters" who were formed by "heavy drinkers, chicaners, and great brigands," the author claimed that they had been saved from their ravaged national existence only by their ancestors' language (ibid.). Yet that language could help his people, "the miserable Asians," turn from their disunity and ignorance towards the "cultural path" indicated by Prince Volodymyr in the tenth century (ibid.). And Shakespeare as "the father of all peoples" could prove influential in changing the currently dim future of Ukrainians. This is why the appearance of his works in Ukrainian was a matter of utmost significance, thus reviving the "Old Rusian" (*starorus'ka*) identification of Ukrainians as a peaceful sedentary people and bringing them closer to educated Europe through the towering figure of Shakespeare (Naxlik 2007, 2:183).

In a poem published in another of his collections, *Dzvin* (The Bell), Kuliš returned to the role of Shakespeare in the acculturation of the Ukrainian people who, according to him, could overcome their spirit of barbarism by partaking of European culture. Nevertheless, in his programmatic poem "Homer i Šekspir" (Homer and Shakespeare), Kuliš, blaming the Ukrainian hetmans for helpless ruling, also distinguished culture from anti-culture, both represented in western Europe. Kuliš was prepared to see in the English revolution of the seventeenth century the apotheosis of destruction while juxtaposing its leader, Oliver Cromwell, with Bohdan Xmel´nyc´kyj:

Тоді Кромвель між Англами з'явив ся
В завзятьї рівня козакам сїпакам;
З Шекспіра глумом він гірким глумив ся.

[Among the English then, Cromwell appeared, similar in his vigor to Cossack brigands; he scoffed bitterly at Shakespeare.]
(Kuliš 1908, 344)

Kuliš's understanding of the role of Shakespeare in the process of national awakening among the Ukrainian people seems to have crystallized somewhat earlier, as a result of his study of the German literary and social historian Georg Gottfried Gervinus (1805–1871). This scholar was particularly famous for his four-volume critical work on Shakespeare that first appeared in 1849–1852 and was subsequently reprinted several times. Translated into Russian by Konstantin Timofeev in 1877, this study became a *sine qua non* socio-cultural study, which Kuliš employed while translating and propagating Shakespeare among his compatriots. Kuliš was fascinated by Gervinus's interpretation of Shakespeare who, according to the German historian, was a true genius standing above social prejudices and political parties, both a moral teacher and leader of mankind (Gervinus 1849, 1:i–xiv). Having borrowed the ethical nature of Gervinus's appraisal of Shakespeare, Kuliš stressed harmony and temperance as opposed to all kinds of extremism and libertarianism. This is why the ethical principle won priority of place in his translation of Shakespeare as well as in a series of poems dedicated to this author, viewed in the cultural and historical context of Ukraine.

In addition to the poetic preface to the first volume of his translations of Shakespeare, Kuliš also prepared an introduction entitled "How Much the Germans Appreciate Shakespeare," which in fact was a meticulous restatement of Gervinus's theory. Since Kuliš's introduction did not appear in the 1882 volume, the author offered it to the editorial board of the periodical *Svit*, headed by Ivan Franko and Ivan Belej (1856–1921). However, Franko rejected this text, arguing that Gervinus already looked outdated—the book, in fact, had first appeared more than thirty years before, and Kuliš himself was not familiar with the more recent publications in this field (Naxlik 2007, 1:364; Lučuk 1995, 375–376). In reality, however, Franko rejected Kuliš's article for a different reason: as a social democrat Franko could hardly accept the idea of social temperance and harmony as advocated by both Gervinus and Kuliš on behalf of Shakespeare.

Prepared for publication by Voznjak (1930), the article first appeared only as late as 1930. On closer inspection, Kuliš's study looks like a word-for-word translation of some fragments from Gervinus's preface and introduction to his magisterial study on Shakespeare (Gervinus 1849, 1:v–xiv, 1–56). What is more interesting in this respect is that Kuliš used the Russian translation of this work by Timofeev, in particular its second, revised edition of 1877, which was extremely popular at that time. Suffice it to compare the following excerpt from Kuliš with its parallel texts from the original and the Russian translation, used instead of Gervinus.

Kuliš's Translation	Timofeev's Translation
Нехай не думає хто небудь сліпуючи або туманіючи, що *такий* поэт и *такий* філософ проявились між *таким* народом через якийся простий случай. Той самий народний дух, той самий практичній, діловий, житейський розум, що создав и се государство и сю народню свободу, той же самий дух чи розум породив и сю премудру поэзію, и сю повну досвіду філософію. (Voznjak 1930, 170)	Да не подумаетъ кто-нибудь въ своемъ ослѣпленіи или тупоуміи, что простой случай забросилъ *такого* поэта и *такого* философа въ среду *такого* народа! Одинъ и тотъ же народный духъ, одинъ и тотъ же практическій, дѣловой житейскій смыслъ, который создалъ и это государство, и эту народную свободу, породилъ и эту житейски-мудрую поэзію и эту, исполненную опыта, философію. (Timofeev 1877, 14)

Gervinus's Original

Denn Niemand sei so voll Wahn und Thorheit zu glauben, daß jene so beschaffenen Dichter und Philosophen irgend ein Zufall in dies so beschaffene Volk hineingeworfen habe! Ein Volksgeist, derselbe praktische tüchtige Lebenssinn, der diesen Staat und diese Volksfreiheit geschaffen hat, hat auch jene lebensweise Dichtung und jene erfahrungsvolle Philosophie gestaltet. (Gervinus 1849, 1:xi)	[Let nobody be so blind and stupid as to think that such people get such a poet and philosopher by mere chance. A people's spirit, the same practical, everyday common sense that produced this state and this people's liberty, also brought about this wise poetry and this experienced philosophy.]

Comparing the Russian and Ukrainian translations prompts one to conclude that Kuliš slavishly followed Timofeev's text, while using similar lexical items and practically an identical word order in most of the sentences. Moreover, and this is the most compelling argument, Kuliš applied spacing to those lexemes that appeared in a cursive typeface in Timofeev's translation. What explains this mimicking on the part of Kuliš is, perhaps, his sincere fascination with Shakespeare and a wish to introduce Gervinus's work to his compatriots as soon as possible in conjunction with his preparation of the translations of this playwright.

To some extent, all this does justify Franko's decision to reject Kuliš's programmatic article on Shakespeare. In fact, one can agree that his article was based on a somewhat obsolete work. Moreover, it was a mere compilation of some theses excerpted randomly from Gervinus in tune with Kuliš's own historiosophic views and aesthetic predilections. He judged Shakespeare not only on his literary merits but also on the high level of morality typical of his works—a core element in Kuliš's opinion of Shakespeare as a bellman of social harmony and cultural progress in society (Voznjak 1930, 170). Especially significant is Kuliš's remarkable identification of the playwright's works as a "secular Bible" (ibid., 171), reverberating with his work on the translation of the Bible at that time. This is why Shakespeare, in Kuliš's system of views, stands above the ideological barriers of political parties, reaching well beyond the chronological confines of modernity and appearing perfectly attuned to the various demands of nineteenth-century society. Based on a rich culture amassed by his predecessors, Shakespeare transformed his own experience into a moral code to be closely followed by all people. The people of Ukraine must choose, Kuliš argued, Shakespeare as their spiritual leader and make his works accessible by translating his oeuvre into Ukrainian (ibid.).

Overall, with the help of the plays of Shakespeare, his was a program for the gradual rather than revolutionary acculturation of the Ukrainian people. It is no secret that the Galician periodicals run by populists and socialists were not interested in disseminating Kuliš's moderate views on social progress, to say the least of the strange language standard propounded in his translations of both the Bible and Shakespeare.

BRINGING FORTH THE "UKRAINIAN SHAKESPEARE"

Because of the aforementioned misunderstanding with Oleksander Barvins'kyj in the second part of 1881, Kuliš had to make changes in his publication plans and revise the contents of the first volume of his translations of Shakespeare. In a letter dated 30 December 1881, he informed Puljuj of his arrival in Lviv, where he took over supervision of the printing of his translations. On 24 February 1882, Kuliš wrote that the printing of the first volume was already underway (Studyns'kyj 1930, 58–59, 61). However, already in the summer, Kuliš faced financial and organizational problems and decided ultimately to postpone the printing of the second volume. Shortly thereafter he returned to his homestead Motronivka (Lučuk 1995, 374).

Kuliš's initial intention was to translate (from English, which he had picked up in the late 1840s while exiled in Tula) twenty-seven tragedies and comedies (out of thirty-seven plays that constitute today's Shakespearian canon) and publish them in nine volumes corresponding to the nine muses (Studyns´kyj 1930, 60). Although modeled, to some extent, on eighteen plays translated into prosaic Russian between 1841 and 1850 by Nikolaj Ketčer (Hordyns´kyj 1928, 92–93), Kuliš's translation of, in total, thirteen tragedies and comedies did demonstrate an independent approach toward the poetic rendition of Shakespeare's works. By the end of 1881, Kuliš had already translated six plays (ibid., 55, 60). Three of them, *Othello*, *Troilus and Cressida*, and *The Comedy of Errors*, were included in the first volume of the "Ukrainian Shakespeare" that appeared at the author's expense in 1882 under the auspices of the Shevchenko Scientific Society in Lviv. Kuliš translated the rest of the plays between 1883 and 1885 before the burning of his homestead Motronivka on 6 November 1885 destroyed much of his archive and most of the manuscripts. Yet in Kuliš's personal papers one finds evidence of his translation of two more plays of Shakespeare after *Hamlet* and before the fire (i.e., *The Merchant of Venice* and *Cymbeline*); Kuliš planned to include them in the fifth volume of Shakespeare's selected works (Hordyns´kyj 1928, 97; Šapovalova 1976, 69). On 21 April 1897, after the death of her spouse, Hanna Barvinok wrote to Puljuj that, because of her negligence, the text of *Venec´kyj kupec´* (*The Merchant of Venice*) was lost on its way to the Černihiv Museum of Vasyl´ Tarnovs´kyj, Jr. Puljuj (1905, 77) assumed that the same might have happened to the text of *Cymbelin* (*Cymbeline*), which Barvinok mentioned in a letter dated 18 May 1897; some scholars, however, do not take this for granted (Šapovalova 1976, 61).

The remaining translations, supplied with introductions and comments by Franko, who meticulously and perhaps captiously edited the language of each play, were published posthumously in Lviv at the turn of the twentieth century. The following is a list of the translations and the years of their publication (Kyryljuk 1929, 59–60, 61–64; Strixa 2006, 81–82):

Play	Year of Publication
Othello	1882
Troilus and Cressida	
The Comedy of Errors	
Hamlet	1899
The Taming of the Shrew	1900
Coriolanus	
Macbeth	
Julius Caesar	
Romeo and Juliet	1901
Antony and Cleopatra	
Much Ado About Nothing	
Measure for Measure	1902
King Lear	

In 1903, Vasyl´ Domanyc´kyj (1877–1910), a famous literary and public figure in Dnieper Ukraine, wrote in an editorial note in the journal *Kievskaja starina* (Kiev Antiquity) about an anonymous benefactor who, in 1881, had generously sponsored a future publication of the translations of Shakespeare undertaken by that time by Kuliš. It happened, however, that Kuliš spent part of this money on other literary projects and, therefore, could not complete his translation of Shakespeare's plays, especially after the rather cold reception of the three translations that appeared in 1882. While extolling the quality of Kuliš's translations, Domanyc´kyj (1903, 141–142) enthusiastically appealed to the public to contribute to the special Shakespeare Fund created by the Ukrainian-Rusian Publishing Union in Lviv, which had recently published ten volumes of Kuliš's translations edited by Franko. Domanyc´kyj believed that such a fund would help promote literary activities in both Austrian- and Russian-ruled Ukraine and contribute to the development of literary language through translations of major classical works in different European languages. It is difficult today to follow up on the outcome of this appeal, which otherwise predicted the lasting impact of Kuliš's work as a translator on the normalization of literary Ukrainian in the second part of the nineteenth century.

In sum, it is not too much to say that, taken even statistically, the contribution made by Kuliš in the creation of the Ukrainian canon of Shakespeare was quite remarkable. Yet some scholars have been too quick to disregard his legacy in this field from the perspective of modern translation studies, arguing that Kuliš "as a translator of Shakespeare does not exist for the modern readership" and his translations "belong to the historical-literary domain" alone (Lučuk, 1995, 372; Hordyns´kyj 1928, 164). To claim that his translations belong today to history is a blatant exaggeration, since his translations fell into oblivion primarily for non-literary reasons (Danylenko 2009b; M. Moskalenko 2006 5/6, 179). The preface written by Franko (1905, v–vi) to Kuliš's translation of *Childe Harold* serves as an example of his scathing critique of Kuliš's historiosophic and linguistic views. Among all the other "sins" committed by the translator, the Galician critic mentioned Kuliš's staunch opposition to the conventional understanding of the Cossacks and *Hajdamaks* and his treatment of them rather as destructive forces in the history of Ukraine. Franko could not accept that uncompromising position, which, as he argued, was fruitless and dangerous from the national point of view (ibid.). Furthermore, as far as the language norms were concerned, Kuliš, due to his negative assessment of the Ukrainian Cossacks and peasantry (*mužyctvo*), allegedly abandoned the vernacular and created a strange, "Old Rusian" Ukrainian with Church Slavonic and Muscovite admixtures. Admitting that, in this translation, Kuliš did leave a trace of his energetic personality, Franko dubbed his language to be "wooden-scholastic" (*dubovo-sxoljastyčna mova*) (ibid., vi). Overall, this judgment was ideologically biased and unfair.

Franko, nevertheless, had to admit the literary merits of many of Kuliš's translations in comparison with those made by his contemporaries (Naxlik 2007, 1:268). For instance, leaving aside issues of equivalence and faithfulness in translation, Franko (1901, xvi) regarded Kuliš's translation of *Romeo and Juliet* as "extremely successful and beautiful." The critic also extolled the translation of *Hamlet*, which, in his opinion, surpassed all other translations of this tragedy, including that made by Myxajlo Staryc´kyj (Franko 1899, xviii–xix). As he argued in the preface to this translation, "Kuliš is a first-rate star in our literature, a great expert in our vernacular, as well as a great expert in the languages and literatures of the European peoples" (ibid., xx). All in all, one can concur with Luckyj (1983, 169), who argued that Kuliš's translations are in many respects unsurpassed even today primarily because of his great linguistic virtuosity, especially in light of the translations made by his predecessors and contemporaries.

THE FIRST (OVER) REACTION

The first volume of Kuliš's translations of Shakespeare drew caustic criticism in Galicia as soon as it appeared in 1882. The Lviv periodical *Zorja* published, in November of 1882, an anonymous review authored most likely by its editor Omeljan Partyc′kyj. A former colleague of Kuliš's, he was best known for his *Hramatyka jazŷka ruskoho* (A Grammar of the Rusian Language) first published in 1873 and reprinted several times with corrections (last edition in 1889) (Skurzewska 2007, 572).

Partyc′kyj's review was full of scathing remarks and also largely unfair in its particulars (Lazurs′kyj 1929, 28). At the outset, the reviewer challenged the very idea of choosing Shakespeare on the grounds that not all of his plays were worthy of translation. Moreover, Kuliš, as Partyc′kyj (1882, 328) argued, was notorious for his numerous unfulfilled projects. Certain details aside, the reviewer's critique can be reduced to several theses covering major aspects of the translation under consideration.

To begin with, Partyc′kyj (1882, 328–329) blamed Kuliš for his "lofty style and unnatural language," while also criticizing what he considered blatant linguistic shortcomings. These included an excessive use of *vel′my* at the cost of *duže* "very," *fortuna* "destiny," *jexydnyj* "malicious," and *jasuvaty* "to explain, speak for," a form which is also found in abundance in Kuliš's translation of the Bible. The reviewer criticized "unbearable coined nouns" ending in *-nnje*, such as *svidkuvannje* "testifying." The author, as Partyc′kyj added, came up with his "own strange language and style," employed indiscriminately in all the translations.

Second, according to the reviewer, there were numerous inconsistencies and discrepancies in Kuliš's translations as compared with the original. Partyc′kyj argued that Kuliš misconstrued many formulations in Shakespeare's originals, although some of the reviewer's corrections, on closer inspection, do not appear stylistically grounded:

Kuliš's Translation	Partyc′kyj's Corrections	Shakespeare's Original
А розум слухае гайного часу. (Šekspir, 70)	А дотепъ (розумъ) полягае на выборѣ часу.	And wit depends on dilatory time. (Shakespeare, 1112)
Чи шваба чи вдача— се щастя військове. (Šekspir, 178)	Чи гараздъ чи лихо—це щастє воєнне.	Now good or bad—'tis but chance of war. (Shakespeare, 313)
О, обернимо в лад се пересердє! (Šekspir, 279)	Закôнчѣмъ по людски сю зваду.	[Nay] we must use expostulation kindly. (Shakespeare, 340)
Ні не одна ласота с такоі красоти на думці в мене. (Šekspir, 223)	Менѣ не тôлько роскоши на думцѣ, котрû приноситъ так велика краса.	I propose not merely to myself the pleasures, such a beauty brings with it. (Shakespeare, 326)

Third, the reviewer called into question the use of anachronistic terms of the type *amen* "amen" in the language of the Greeks at Troy or such Cossack jargon as *otamannja* (coll.) "atamans" (Partyc′kyj 1882, 328). Here also belong words like *očortity* "to bore," *karbovanec′* (local Ukrainian monetary unit), *neapol′ska kostoida* (*hostec′* in Partyc′kyj) "bone-ache," and, finally, *juxta* "cows' leather" (*juxt* m. and *juxta* f., "Juchten, Juften" in Žel., 2:1110). The reviewer cited several forms that looked unusual and artificial within the contexts where Kuliš used them (e.g., *dovoli koljoru* "sufficiently red, rosy," and *prystan′ voždelinna* "ports desired" [Partyc′kyj 1882, 329]). In particular, Partyc′kyj castigated numerous coined words like *brona* [cf. MUkr. *brona*] instead of *brama* "gate," *xvir* instead of *xvoroba* "sickness," and *počes′ki* instead of *česno* "honestly" (ibid., 329).

In addition, Partyc′kyj (1882, 329) reproached the translator for introducing unwarranted borrowings from Polish, German, and Church Slavonic such as *khaljantnÿj* "gallant, stylish," *vprejmost′* "kindness" (Pol. *uprzejmość* "courtesy"), *natxnennje* "inspiration" (Pol. *natchnienie*), ChSl. *alkannje* "wish," and so on.

Also, in Partyc′kyj's view, the translator violated rules of "the grammar of our language," while indiscriminately experimenting with unusual forms like *čari* (pl.) "charms" instead of *čarȳ*—a variance that might reflect a different dialectal distribution of the forms in question (Marvijas 2006, 57)—*dožu* "duke" (voc.) instead of the more usual *može* (voc.), *dosih* (m. sg. pret.) "to reach" with an excessive (analogous) *i* instead of regular *dosjah"* (Partyc′kyj 1882, 329) (m. sg. pret. *volik* "to drag" with an excessive *i* in the pleophonic sequence [Shevelov 1979, 608]).

The reviewer was particularly uncomfortable with variegated stress patterns introduced by Kuliš that, as Partyc′kyj (1882, 329) argued, were not rooted in any Ukrainian dialect. He noted, for example, numerous cases of unusual stressing of the type *fálšy* compared to *falšý* (gen.) "lie," *vospýtaly* (pl. pret.) "to bring up," *perevahá* "advantage," *druhé* "second," and so forth.

Finally, the reviewer could hardly accept the phonetic orthography (*kulišivka*), claiming that such spelling had never existed and would never exist in Ukrainian due to "the lack of the philological knowledge" of its inventor. So Partyc′kyj (1882, 329) concluded that, "for the sake of the healthy development of our literature, everybody has to stand against the inopportune experiments of Kuliš in the domain of orthography." At this point, the reviewer was right to criticize the motley character of the translator's orthography. In fact, in some of his works, Kuliš was accustomed to combining elements of different spelling systems (Danylenko 2012b).

No doubt, Kuliš's translations were not ideal and some of Partyc′kyj's remarks were valid, especially in regards to the equivalence and faithfulness of the translation. Still, Kuliš demonstrated an innovative approach to the translation of Shakespeare, trying to employ variegated, sometimes "extravagant" linguistic forms in order to capture the textual and cultural message of the original. All his remarks considered, Partyc′kyj was more interested in compromising this publication than in objectively assessing the quality of Kuliš's work (Šapovalova 1976, 65). In short, it was the political execution of a major opponent from Russian-ruled Ukraine (Kočur 1968, 30).

Seemingly less venomous was a review written in 1883 by the famous historian and Ukrainophile Mykola Kostomarov, who had severed his relationship with Kuliš by 1880. While treating Ukrainian literature as "a literature for homestead use," Kostomarov ostentatiously refused to consider the quality of Kuliš's translations of the New Testament and Shakespeare. In regards to the translation of the New Testament, he questioned to "what extent this translation suites its high subject and to what extent it may be utilized by the literate common people of southern Russian stock" (Kostomarov 1883, 221). Speaking of Shakespeare, he wondered why Kuliš had chosen second-rate plays (with the exception, perhaps, of *Othello*) and, for several reasons, refused point-blank to discuss the writer's translation of the English playwright (ibid., 222).

For starters, Kostomarov (1883, 222) reiterated his old thesis that "the current situation of the southern Russian [Ukrainian] dialect implies that one should create in this dialect rather than translate" because Russian had become a cultured language for all the Little Russian intellectuals. The all-Russian language (*obščerusskij jazyk*), he argued, had long since become a language of culture in the whole southern Russian region, since this language had been developed by the joint efforts of both Little and Great Russians. Since there is no other Little Russian society than a peasant one, Little Russian literature must therefore be vernacular in its subjects and ways of conveying ideas about such subjects (ibid.).

> It seems to us that there is no pressing necessity for a translation of Shakespeare into the southern Russian dialect inasmuch as any Little Russian who gained so much education as to be interested in reading Shakespeare is capable of reading him in the Russian translation, sometimes even with more pleasure than in southern Russian since one can hardly find a Little Russian who is not familiar with literary Russian to the same extent as his mother tongue; to render Shakespeare today in Russian is easier than in Little Russian, even for such a specialist as Kuliš. (Kostomarov 1883, 223)

By contrast, a totally different situation was observed in Galicia, where several million spoke a highly advanced southern Russian language, and the all-Russian literary language did not become that of the local intellectuals. Moreover, the latter language appeared alien to the Ukrainians in Galicia, compared with the German that was more familiar to them at least by virtue of its official status (Kostomarov 1883, 223). Yet they could not master German because of its genetic distance from their native tongue, while Polish reminded them of enforced Polonization. This is why they were striving "to develop their native tongue and transform it into a cultured language" (ibid., 224). In this respect, Kuliš's translations were doomed to be consumed in Galicia, where the native dialect was chosen as a cultured language, rather than in Russian-ruled Ukraine where Little Russian literature and language could be only vernacular-based. This is why much in the translation of Kuliš could appear to Little Russians, whose native dialect had not acquired by that time any "level of acculturation," as "unnatural, unpopular, artificial, forced, coined randomly," while the same would be treated differently by Galician readers (ibid., 224). Some fifty years later, Hordyns′kyj (1928, 108), who wrote an extensive study of Kuliš's translations of Shakespeare's plays, discerned surprisingly in Kostomarov's words "a slight critique of Kuliš's translations," although, no doubt, Kostomarov's argumentation fostered the official discriminatory language policy cultivated at that time by the tsarist administration.

Ukrainian patriotism, as one of Kostomarov's multiple loyalties, did not prevent him from being also Great Russian and all-Russian, sharing a common Russian (Rus′) culture (Bilenky 2012, 294). As evidenced in Kostomarov's programmatic work of 1883, he was not very clear about the relationship of the Ukrainian (Little Russian) nationality and language to (common) Russian. However, after the publication of Kostomarov's article, it became obvious that Kuliš's translations were at the center of debates that transcended the confines of literary issues (Šapovalova 1976, 65; Zerov 1967, 47–48).

Importantly, Kostomarov's ambiguity toward Ukrainian populism in general and Ukrainian literature in particular was not unique among Ukrainian intellectuals. In fact, elements of the all-Russian program were prevailing at that time among those Ukrainophiles who based their ethnic loyalty on the ethnolinguistic, Herderian concept of nationality (Bilenky 2012, 299). Suffice it to mention here Oleksander Potebnja, a towering figure in nineteenth-century eastern Slavic linguistics, who staunchly opposed the independence of the Little Russian language but also showed the utmost reluctance to support an all-Russian literary language (Danylenko

2006c, 335–355). In criticizing the independent development of Little Russian (Ukrainian), Potebnja apparently meant the then fashionable "school" of Myxajlo Staryc´kyj and his disciples, who were aptly called "wordsmiths" by their opponents. Like Kuliš, who rejected the views of extreme populism and Cossackophilism, Potebnja placed the inception of written Ukrainian in the time of Kyivan Rus´. In consonance with Kuliš, Potebnja also believed that the molding of written Ukrainian might have unfolded from Common East Slavic through the Middle Ukrainian period to the present, as manifested in archaic folklore (ibid., 353). It is worth recalling here Potebnja's translation of several rhapsodies from Homer's *Odyssey*, characterized by its archaic vocabulary and folkloric syntax (Danylenko 1999). Interestingly, it was exactly these features in Kuliš's translations of Shakespeare that were identified and heavily criticized by Partyc´kyj.

It is noteworthy that Kostomarov himself was the first translator of Shakespeare into Ukrainian. As early as 1849 he translated Desdemona's song from *Othello*. Entitled *Verba* (Willow), it was published posthumously in 1890. This was, in fact, a folkloric paraphrase that, without doubt, belongs today to the history of Ukrainian translation (M. Moskalenko 2006 1/2, 186).

Kostomarov's Translation

Ой вербице зеленая,
Вербонько моя!
Пидъ вербою зеленою
Дивочка сидила,
И бидную головоньку
Доли похилила.
Ой вербице зеленая,
Вербонько моя! (Kostomarov 1890, 229)

Shakespeare's Original

[The poor soul sat [sighing] by a sycamore tree,
   Sing all a green willow;
Her hand on her bosom, her head on her knee;
   Sing willow, willow, willow.
The fresh streams ran by her, and murmur'd her moans;
   Sing willow, willow, willow
Her salt tears fell from her, and soft'ned the stones;
   Sing willow, willow, willow.]
(Shakespeare, 1128)

Clearly, Kostomarov's translation is inspired by Ukrainian folklore songs, while offering nothing new from the point of view of its literary form and technique (M. Moskalenko 2006 1/2, 186). Among its folkloric features, one should name, first of all, diminutive forms: *verba* ~ *verbycja* (dim.) ~ *verbon'ka* (dim.) "willow," and *holovon'ka* (dim.) "head."

Kuliš's translation of the same fragment rings, however, with a true poetic beauty;

Сиді́ла небо́га під и́вовим дре́вом,
Співа́йте, співа́йте про и́ву зеле́ну
И руки зложи́ла й голо́вку схили́ла,
Співа́йте про и́ву, про и́ву, про и́ву.
Вода́ протека́ла, з не́ю розмовля́ла . . .
Співа́йте про и́ву, про и́ву, про и́ву,
А ви слёзи, ри́нте, камі́ннє мягчі́те . . . (Šekspir, 142)

Kuliš succeeded in infusing the translation with his own individual color, while creating a texture of masterly interwoven lexical elements, both neutral and stylistically marked, like the Church Slavonicism *drevo* "tree" or the diminutive *holovka* "head." The form *sljoza* is hardly a Russianism since it rather reveals a result of the phonetically conditioned replacement *e > o*, typical mostly of Southeast Ukrainian. In this respect, one can hardly agree with the critical assessment of Kuliš's translation of this and other separate songs as offered by Hordyns'kyj (1928, 88), who treated them as "mere paraphrases, rather awkward and free of poetic beauty." This verdict was based primarily on faithfulness of the translation to the original, rather than its use of stylistic alternatives available in the native language.

Luckily, this time Kuliš was not discouraged by the above reviews and continued translating Shakespeare. In 1884, when hosting Myxajlo Lobodovs'kyj on his homestead, the writer confirmed his deep interest in Shakespeare. Having placed his hand on a pile of manuscripts, Kuliš said: "This is a translation of Shakespeare into Little Russian . . . I am finishing already . . . I do believe in the future of Ukrainian literature" (Lobodovskij 1897, 166).

THE LANGUAGE OF THE "UKRAINIAN SHAKESPEARE"

The language of the first Ukrainian-language volume of Shakespeare, printed under Kuliš's supervision in 1882, is especially revealing as concerns the authenticity of the writer's language program, since all posthumous publications of his translations of Shakespeare were edited by Franko. One of the few serious studies of the language of Kuliš's translations of Shakespeare was made by Jaroslav Hordyns′kyj in 1928. Pioneering in many aspects, this study was deeply rooted in the local literary tradition still influenced by the towering figure of Franko and, what is more important, oriented toward the local variety of written Ukrainian. This is why, despite its pronounced scholarship, Hordyns′kyj's perspective should not be taken at face value, especially since the author stopped short of placing Kuliš's translations in the wider context of the normalization of new literary Ukrainian.

To begin with, even a very cursory survey of the language of the first volume of the "Ukrainian Shakespeare" exposes its resemblance to the vernacular standard elaborated by Kuliš in his translation of the Bible. For instance, some orthographic peculiarities aside, the most arresting feature in the phonetics (orthography) is consistent assimilation in voicing, as reflected in spellings like *ys kyšeni* "from the pocket" next to *yz rodu* "never," and *bes praktyky* "without practice" (Šekspir, 8, 10, Shakespeare, 1096). Hordyns′kyj (1928, 61) viewed this phenomenon as a mere "striving for phonetic spelling." However, it becomes clear that Kuliš was applying complete neutralization before all obstruents, as practiced in his own dialect and some other Ukrainian dialects, including West Polissian, Volhynian, Podolian, and Bukovynian, characterized by neutralization before a word boundary (Danylenko 2005, 49–51; Matvijas 2008) (see also *čeres knyharnyka pryxodo-rosxidnoho* "[because of] this counter-caster" [Šekspir, 10, Shakespeare, 1096], *ys početom* "in the conduct of" [Šekspir, 45, Shakespeare, 1105], and *yz nebom* "with the heavens" [Šekspir, 46, Shakespeare, 1105], all reflecting neutralization before a word boundary; note also *peret toboju* "before thee" next to *pered neju* "to her" [Šekspir, 246, Shakespeare, 332] and *peredo mnoju* "to me" [Šekspir, 45, Shakespeare, 1105]).

Neutralization before a morpheme boundary is exemplified in *besstydna kryvda* "bold and saucy wrongs" (Šekspir, 15, Shakespeare, 1098) and *oz'de* "here (is)" (Šekspir, 23, Shakespeare, 1099). With a more intricate place of articulation, regressive assimilation is represented by such spellings as *yž žinkoju* "with the wife" (Šekspir, 362) and *ščynylos* "[what] is the matter" (Šekspir, 12, 13, Shakespeare, 1097)—literally "happened"; such an assimilation is a common phenomenon in Middle Ukrainian texts extant from southwestern and northern Ukraine (Žovtobrjux et al. 1979, 205–208) (*ščezaty* < *is-čezati* or Lemk. *ščera* "yesterday" from *s'čera* < *s" v'čera* [Verxratskyj 1902, 487]). The assimilation looks routine with the postfix -*sja* (e.g., *pojavyccja* "[he] come[s]" [Šekspir, 338, Shakespeare, 3])—literally "he will appear"—*oddaduccja* "they shall obey" (Šekspir, 241, Shakespeare, 331), and especially *ščynyccja* "it will happen" (Šekspir, 349) with assimilation affecting both the prefix and postfix. Assimilation of the postfix is commonly attested in North Ukrainian, for instance, in the works of Ivan Nekraševyč (late eighteenth century) (Nekraševyč, 12, 14), a long-time priest in a village parish near Kyiv (Danylenko 2008b, 66–69). Remarkably, while preparing Kuliš's translations for publication, Franko did not correct spellings reflecting word boundaries of the type *is toboju* "with you" (*Makbet*-K/F, 15).

After the appearance of his *Pentatevx* in 1869, Kuliš changed, probably under the influence of the Galician literary practice, his attitude toward the "new g" in orthography and began rendering the "new g" indiscriminatingly in almost all loan words of western European origin or mediation. Yet, as a compromise, he kept using in his translations the traditional Middle Ukrainian digraph *kh*, as if distancing himself from the contemporary Galician practice, in particular in the translation of *Hamlet* by Pavlo Svij (Pavlyn Svjencic'kyj) published in Lviv in 1865 (*Hamljet*-S). Nevertheless, in harmony with the "overseas" coloring in most of Shakespeare's plays, the number of these words is exceptionally large in Kuliš's translations (e.g., *Jakho* [Iago] and *Rodrikho* [Roderigo], *khradacija* "gradation" [Šekspir, 10], *khondol'er* "gondolier" [ibid., 15], *rankh* "title" [ibid., 10], *makhnyfyka* [m.] "magnifico" [ibid., 19, Shakespeare, 1099], *khaleri* "galleys" [Šekspir, 20] and *khal'ony* "galleys" [ibid., 24], *khvaltom* "violently" [ibid., 38], *khlejtove pysannje* "charter" [ibid., 35,

Shakespeare, 1106], *panekhyryk* "eulogy" [Šekspir, 47] as compared to *proloh* "prologue" [ibid., 53], *fol'huem* [1 pl. pres.] "to weaken" [ibid., 285] with the spirant *h* as reflected in some Middle Ukrainian spellings [Tymč. and Nimčuk, 2:454–455; Ohijenko 1930, 2:139] next to WUkr. *fol'guvaty* "nachgeben, nachlassen, schonen" [Žel., 2:1029] under Polish [German] influence). Franko, the editor, reintroduced, instead, the letter "г" (*g*), sometimes adjusting particular lexemes to the local Polish-Latin pronunciation and orthographic model, whence *prol'og* "prologue" (*Makbet*-K/F, 12), *Tygr* "the Tiger" (ibid., 7), *Norveg* "Norway" (ibid., 11), *xirurg* "surgeon" (ibid., 5), *špig* "spy" (*Hamljet*-K/F, 70), and the like.

More often than not Kuliš retained etymological *o* and *e* in the newly closed syllables or similar alternation cases (Shevelov 1979, 721; Matvijas 2008, 96) (e.g., *nočnyx otamaniv* [gen. pl.] "officers [of night]" [Šekspir, 18, Shakespeare, 1098], *vvičlyvost'* "courtesy" [Šekspir, 53], *tyxost'* "stillness" [ibid., 63], *vol'nijše* "freer" [ibid., 74], *čestyvost'* "honesty" [ibid., 95], *pidlost'* "villainy" [ibid., 104] next to *molodist'* "youth," *ščedrist'* "generosity" [ibid., 194], *deriv* [gen. pl.] "tree," and *predmit* "subject" [ibid., 172, 229]). Sorting out similar examples, Hordyns'kyj (1928, 60–61) lumped together reflexes of etymological *e* and *jat'* (e.g., *lenyvyj* "lazy" [Šekspir, 283] next to ChSl. and ESl. *lěnь* "laziness," *dorekaty* "to rebuke" [Šekspir, 15] next to ChSl. and ESl. *rěčь* "word, speech"). While editing Kuliš's translations, Franko tended to introduce forms with *i*-reflexes at the expense of more archaic lexemes without *ikavism* (e.g., *voz'mite* next to *viz'mite* [2 pl. imper.] "take!" [*Hamljet*-K/F, 73], *rozpirka* "old end" [*Halas*, 12, Shakespeare, 184], and *nebiž* "cousin" [*Halas*, 12, Shakespeare 184]). The southeastern Ukrainian form *od* in the expression *od vostok do zapad* "from the east to the west" (Šekspir, 134, Shakespeare, 1126) stands out in comparison with Transc. (Hucul) *id* in Kuliš's translation of the Bible (*SP*, 15) next to a more regular *vid* (ibid., 19), castigated subsequently by Ivan Nečuj-Levyc'kyj as a Galician form.

As in Kuliš's biblical translations, one finds in the "Ukrainian Shakespeare" shifts in the distribution of *i* and *y* (*AUM*, 1, map 21) like *krivavyj* "bloody" (Šekspir, 63) or *trivohy* "concerns" (ibid., 349), also attested in abundance in the works of Ševčenko (Danylenko 2006c, 366–369). It is noteworthy that Franko did not emend such forms, thus leaving *skrivavlenyj* "bloody" (*Makbet*-K/F, 4), *zdrihnutysja* "to tremble" (ibid., 9), *strivaj* (2 sg. imper.) "wait!" (ibid., 7), and *ubijstvo* "murder" (*Hamljet*-K/F, 33) next to *umyraty* "to die" (ibid., 14). Additionally, in the "Ukrainian Shakespeare," Kuliš demonstrated more consistency in rendering the "new *a*" as found in such forms as *harazd* "well, fine" (Šekspir, 48), *bahata* (f.) "rich" (ibid., 49), *bahactvo* "wealth" (ibid., 338), and the like. Of particular interest is *karabel'* "ship" (ibid., 42), which is a dialectal form from Sl. *korablь* rather than Gk. καράβιον (Shevelov 1979, 511) (MUkr. *korablyk"* "women's hat" [Tymč. and Nimčuk, 1:378] and dial. *karablyk* "hood" [Bil.-Nos., 179; Žel., 1:335]). Among other means of archaization, one should name the western Ukrainian *h*-prothesis in *hulycja* "street" (Šekspir, 12; Žel., 1:164) and the dative form *mini* (dat.) "to me" (Šekspir, 14, 16) instead of *myni* as used throughout the *Pentatevx* (Pentateuch) and in the novel *Čorna rada* (The Black Council, 1857). Interestingly, although typical of the transitional dialects developed on a northern Ukrainian basis, the form *mini* is not found in Ševčenko (Tymošenko 1969, 107). Deserving of attention is the old form *fylja* "flood" (Šekspir, 41), which is paralleled by the vernacular counterpart *xvylja* (ibid., 340), with the counter-etymological x^w (Shevelov 1979, 634).

In the "Ukrainian Shakespeare," Kuliš consistently employed the northern Ukrainian ending *-e* after long palatalized consonants in neuters, including bookish and Church Slavonic lexemes, criticized, as was mentioned above, by Partyc'kyj (e.g., *zillje* "herbs" [Šekspir, 38, Shakespeare, 1103], *bdinnje* "watch" [Šekspir, 77], *roždennje* "birth," *alkannje* "wish" [ibid., 194], *poroždennje jexyden* "they are vipers" [ibid., 243, Shakespeare, 331], *zabvennje* "oblivion" [Šekspir, 252], *žyttje* "life" [ibid., 253], and *blahodijannje* "benefit" [ibid.], which is a blending of Church Slavonic and vernacular derivational models). This type of neuter was retained by Franko in later publications of Kuliš's translations (e.g., *volossje* "hair" [*Makbet*-K/F, 12] and *miždočassje* "the interim" [ibid., 13, Shakespeare 1187], *dyxannje* "breath" [*Makbet*-K/F, 10] as compared with WUkr. *volosje* and *dyxanje* without any gemination in the suffix [Žel., 1:119, 183]).

In terms of morphology, Kuliš used the old Ukrainian form of the demonstrative pronoun *sej* (m.), *sja* (f.), *se* (n.) "this," proper to the transitional dialects developed on the northern Ukrainian basis, although

EUkr. *cej, cja, ce* also occur sporadically (e.g., [*kljanus'*] *ocijeju rukoju* "by this hand" [Šekspir, 53]). As in the translation of the Bible, Kuliš indulged in the preterit indicative 2 sg. form with the auxiliary verb "to be" (*zbrexav jesy* [m.] "told a lie" [ibid., 163], *vbačav jesy* "didst thou see[?]" [ibid., 16, Shakespeare, 1098], *pociluvav jesy* "kissed" [Šekspir, 49]). The translator often resorted to old nominal forms of the nominative-accusative singular of masculine adjectives, which, taken in the context of the lofty narrative, could be treated as Church Slavonicisms (Horbač 1988, 61) (e.g., *prokljat* "cursed" [Šekspir, 9], *zakljat* "damn' d" [ibid., 10, Shakespeare, 1096], *peven* "sure" [Šekspir, 14], *povynen* "must" [ibid., 16], and *ne zdiben* "not able" [ibid., 77]). At the same time, pronominal forms of nominative-accusative adjectives might be viewed as folkloric or, rather, northern Ukrainian (Horbač 1988, 61) (e.g., *temnuju* [acc. sg. f.] "dark" [Šekspir, 15], *bilaja* [nom. sg. f.] "white" [ibid.] next to *harna* [nom. sg. f.] "fair" [ibid., Shakespeare, 1098], and *besstydnu kryvdu* [acc. sg. f.] "bold and saucy wrong" [ibid.]).

Among rare devices of archaization, of interest are dual forms of the type *dvi slovi* "in brief" (Šekspir, 338, Shakespeare, 3)—literally, "two words"—or *dvi hodyni* "two o'clock" (Šekspir, 347, Shakespeare 6). Dual forms were largely retained by Franko (e.g., *dvi pravdi* "two truths" [*Makbet*-K/F, 12] next to *uv uši* "in thine ear" [ibid., 17, Shakespeare, 1188]—literally, "in your [two] ears"; see also an obsolete form *v ušu* next to a new plural form *v ušax* "in the ears" in the 1903 Bible [*SP*, 87]).

In morphosyntax, Kuliš was reluctant to use the relative pronoun *kotryj* "which, that, who" as compared with the absolutive relativizer *ščo*, with the resumption looking more representative of his language, especially in his biblical translations. Without much exaggeration, one can infer that Franko, accustomed to the Galician relative pronoun *kotryj* (Pol. *który*), might have introduced in some cases this Polish-Ukrainian form instead of *ščo* with resumption (e.g., *Makbet*-K/F, 5, 15, 17). Sporadically, Kuliš made use of archaic syntactic patterns (e.g., *priobščus' tvoei žyzni* [gen.] "[...] makes me with thy strength communicate" [Šekspir, 359, Shakespeare, 9] with the genitive case [Danylenko 2006c, 213–214]).

For the secular variety of the high style designed by Kuliš for the "Ukrainian Shakespeare," of utmost importance is its lexical make-up.

Comprised of several layers, enhancing the overall archaization of the language, the vocabulary is largely premised on Church Slavonic lexemes occurring more often than not in their Ukrainianized version and sometimes with modified semantics. Interestingly, some of these Church Slavonic forms can be treated today as Russianisms: *žyzn'* "life" (Šekspir, 11; *DUL*, 9:163), *vertrohrad* "fertile climate" (Šekspir, 12, Shakespeare 1097; see also "garden" in *DUL*, 3:236), *blahočestie* "honesty" (Šekspir, 18; *DUL*, 2:108), *sokrovyščá* (pl.) "treasure" (Šekspir, 19) next to WUkr. *sokrovýšče* (Vytv., 39), *blahovolennje* "grace" (Šekspir, 33; *DUL*, 2:93), *vopie* (3 sg. pres.) "to yell" (Šekspir, 36; *DUL*, 4:228), *hrjaduščyj* "future" (Šekspir, 50; *DUL*, 7:110; Vytv., 245), *blaženstvo* "bliss" (Šekspir, 51; *DUL*, 2:110), *dobroditel'* "virtue" (Šekspir, 70; *DUL*, 8:55–56), *(prekrasne) suščestvo* "excellent wretch" (Šekspir, 80, Shakespeare, 1114) next to *súščestvo* "existence" (Vytv., 44), *preispodnij* "hollow" (Šekspir, 95, Shakespeare, 1118) next to *preyspodnŷj* "underground" (Vytv., 212), *sonmyščá* (pl.) (Šekspir, 324; Vytv., 379), *yskustvo* "cunning" (Šekspir, 325, Shakespeare, 351; Vytv., 37, 118), *vladyka* "master" (Šekspir, 352, Shakespeare, 7; *DUL*, 4:91), *exydztvo* "falsehood" (Šekspir, 352, Shakespeare, 7) with assimilation of the initial consonant in *-stv-* (*jexydna* "echidna" in Vytv., 392), and *lukavstvo* "corruption" (Šekspir, 352, Shakespeare, 7) next to WUkr. *lukavstvo* "craftiness" (Vytv., 49, 164).

In general, Kuliš used Church Slavonicisms as part of both the biblical and secular varieties of the high style in new literary Ukrainian. Contextually, Church Slavonicisms tend to be paralleled by lexemes belonging to other style registers as observed, for instance, in the case of *lyk* "visage" alongside WUkr. *lyce* "face" (Šekspir, 95, Shakespeare, 1118; Žel., 1:406) belonging to the middle style. Even if in some places Church Slavonicisms are seemingly less appropriate, for instance, in reference to certain "plain characters" like uncouth Ajax in *Troilus and Cressida*, one can hardly agree with Hordyns'kyj (1928, 63) that Kuliš was introducing Church Slavonicisms haphazardly, "without any plan." On the contrary, with an eye towards creating a full-fledged high style, Kuliš employed them consciously and, what is noteworthy, in complementary distribution with Russian (Church Slavonic) forms, thus enriching the lexical devices of vernacular Ukrainian, riddled as it was with many *lacunae* at that time.

Dubbed by Hordyns′kyj (1928, 64) "barbarianisms," Russian forms are quite numerous, in contrast to Polish borrowings, in the first volume of the "Ukrainian Shakespeare." The following examples are most revealing in this respect: *ob'jattja* "clasps," *nadežna straž* "good guard" (Šekspir, 15, 18, Shakespeare, 1098) next to *braty pid storožu* "to apprehend" (Šekspir, 22, Shakespeare, 1099) (*čata* and *storoža* "watch" in *Hamljet*-K/F [Šekspir, 4, 7, Shakespeare, 1047, 1048], edited by Franko). Note also *stydno* "it's my shame" (Šekspir, 38, Shakespeare, 1103), *doblest′* "valor" (Šekspir, 38), *nel′zja* "it is impossible" (ibid., 42, Shakespeare, 1104), *xvastannje* "bragging" (Šekspir, 52, Shakespeare, 1107), *plut* "knave" alongside the Polish loan form *ošust* "knave" on the same page (ibid.), *plutovstvo* "knavery" (Šekspir, 228, Shakespeare, 327), *pidozrytel′nyj* "curious" (Šekspir, 247, Shakespeare, 332), *zdravstvuj* "how now" (Šekspir, 255, Shakespeare, 334), *prostudytys′* "to catch a cold" (Šekspir, 271, Shakespeare, 338), *penjatymeš na mene* "you will curse me" (ibid.), *razlyčatys′* "to be distinguished" (Šekspir, 339, Shakespeare, 4), *prykažčyk* "factor" (Šekspir, 338, Shakespeare, 4), *ne ohorčajsja* "never fret" (Šekspir, 347, Shakespeare, 6)—literally, "do not get upset"—and *bišenstvo* "[fit of] madness" (Šekspir, 403, Shakespeare, 20).

Among apparent Russian forms, one can cite *parus* "sail" (Šekspir, 41, Shakespeare, 1104). The word, however, is rather an old East Slavic borrowing (mediated by Old Church Slavonic) from Gk. φᾶρος (Vasmer, 2:318). This lexeme was retained in Galicia (Žel., 2:603) and was commonplace in the nineteenth century in Southeast Ukrainian, in particular in the works of Taras Ševčenko (5x) (*SŠ*, 2:53) and Oleksander Potebnja's translation (of the fragments) of Homer's *Odyssey*. In his translation of *Othello*, Kuliš also made use of a parallel, Church Slavonic form *vitrylo* "tall ship" (Šekspir, 45, Shakespeare, 1105)—literally, "sail" (*větrilo*: *žagel′*, *parus″* [Berynda, 26], Lat. *acatium*, *větrilo* [Kor. and Slav., 64]). The form *vitrylo* is lacking in Potebnja's translation, which is explained by his vision of the high style (Danylenko 1999, 238, fn. 10), but is found only once in the writings of Ševčenko:

І попливе човен з широкими вітрилами. (*SŠ*, 1:103)

[And the boat with wide sails will glide.]

Sometimes, used as chancery clichés, Russian forms appear to be stylistically marked as, for instance, in the scene of Troilus and Cressida brought finally together by Pandarus:

Пандар: Словáми дóвгу не плáтять; давáй ій ділá. Та вонá знівечить тобí й ділá, як потрéбуе слýшної прáці. Як? Изнóв лизáтись? Оцé вонó, "во свидítельство чого, обідві стóрони взаімно."
Прóсимо до хáти. Пійдý принесý свíтло. (Šekspir, 246)

[PANDARUS: Words pay no debts, give her deeds; but she'll bereave you o'th'deeds too, if she call your activity in question. What billing again? Here's "In witness whereof the parties interchangeably"—
Come in, come in. I'll go get a fire.] (Shakespeare, 332)

The comic effect of the above fragment is comparable to that created by Hryhorij Kvitka-Osnov'janenko in his bilingual comedy *Šel'menko, volostnoj pysar* (Šel'menko, the District Scribe, 1831), which is characterized by a similar mix of languages and styles. The mixture of Church Slavonicisms, Russianisms, and vernacular diminutives is particularly arresting in the following extract from the aforementioned comedy:

Шельменко: Ось и я тутечка-здесєчка! А! здоровъ, здоровъ, благопрыятелю любезнійший [...],
Севастянъ Охримовичъ! Чыще жывенькы, здоровенькы хочъ трохы?—жиночка, діточкы?
Чаркодуєв: Вашими молитвами всѣ благоденствуемъ. (*Šel'menko*, 30)

[ŠEL'MENKO: Here I am! Oh! How are you doing, my venerable dear friend, Sevast'jan Oxrimovyč!
Are they still alive and somewhat healthy? Your wife, kids?
ČARKODUEV: We have been prospering by your prayers.]

However surprising it may appear in the translation of Shakespeare, Kuliš liberally used colloquial and vulgar forms, which, as Hordyns'kyj (1928, 65) argued, looked sometimes totally out of place and could be substituted for by "more meticulous, more literary [forms]." Yet, it is imperative to emphasize here that Kuliš was too experienced a writer to succumb so easily to what were called by Hordyns'kyj "vulgarisms" of the type *pleskaty* "to talk" (Šekspir, 14), *vlyznuty/ulyznuty* "to go out" or "to be gone" (ibid., 17, 246, Shakespeare, 1098, 332), *zuzdryty* "to find out" (Šekspir, 28, Shakespeare, 1101), *opec'ky* "fools" (Šekspir, 39, Shakespeare, 1106), *vtokmačyty* "to instruct" (Šekspir, 52), *vhonobljaty* "to compass [his salt and most hidden loose affection]" (ibid., 53, Shakespeare, 1107)—literally, "to appease"—(Žel., 1:59), *nahybaty* "to come across" (Šekspir, 53, Žel., 1:470), *cmulyty* "to drink" (Šekspir, 59, Shakespeare, 1109), *zveretenyvs'* "[became] dead drunk" (ibid.)—literally "to whirl or to twist"—(Hrinč., 1:664; Žel., 1:287), *rostryn'katy* "to squander" (Šekspir, 70), *zadljatys'* "to last so long" (ibid., 76, Shakespeare, 1113), *zaturkaty* "to talk someone out of patience" (Šekspir, 77, Shakespeare, 1113), *psity* "to pick bad" (Šekspir, 143, Shakespeare, 1129)—literally "to live like a dog"—(Žel., 2:786), *roščovpaty* "to comprehend" (Šekspir, 349; Žel., 2:837), *švendjaty* "to walk around" (Šekspir, 344), *toročyty* "to say, to repeat" (ibid., 350; Hrinč., 2:787; Žel., 2:977), *buxančyk* (dem.) "stroke," *vidduxopelyty* "to beat" (Šekspir, 353, 355), and many others.

In addition to Church Slavonicisms, Russianisms, and "vulgarisms," Hordyns'kyj (1928, 65–66) found among other of Kuliš's innovations the so-called voluntary liberties, criticized also by Jurij Fed'kovyč who translated *Hamlet* and *Macbeth* in the 1870s. No wonder, then, that, as a speaker of the southwestern variety of literary Ukrainian, Hordyns'kyj could hardly endorse most of the morphophonemic changes introduced by Kuliš (Lazurs'kyj 1929, 32). For instance, the writer often resorted to the alternation *u-* : *v-* in congruence with the principles of euphony, typical primarily of Southeast Ukrainian and modern Ukrainian (Shevelov 1979, 297–300), whence parallelism of *u vi sni* and *v vi sni* "in a dream" (Šekspir, 9, 16), also *vvixodyty* "to enter" (ibid., 9), *jak ty vpiznav jiji* "where didst thou see her?" (ibid., 17, Shakespeare, 1098), *ščo vhodno* "what would you [Desdemona]?" (Šekspir, 35, Shakespeare, 1116), *vves'* "all" (Šekspir, 42), *vpokij* "peace" (ibid., 55), *vpryvyleëvanyx* (gen. pl.) "prerogativ'd" (ibid., 90, Shakespeare, 1116), and so forth. According to Hordyns'kyj (1928, 66), the translator used more often than not the prefix *iz*- or added "too often *i*- word-initially" (e.g., *yssunuv* [*z hluzdu*] "turned your wit" [Šekspir, 134, Shakespeare, 1126], *yzmyloserdysja* "have mercy" [Šekspir, 156, Shakespeare, 1131]). In such cases Kuliš made use of the sound *i* as a cluster-breaker, which had emerged around the fourteenth century after the confusion of the two prepositions/prefixes *sъ* and *iz* due to the loss of the *jers* (Shevelov 1979, 270). The introduction of *i* was productive cross-dialectally during the Middle Ukrainian period, and as a result the alternation *u-: v-* has become adjusted to the principles of euphony in literary Ukrainian.

Hordyns'kyj also did not approve of "an arbitrary abbreviation of words" like *nedalečko 'd vas* "not far from you" (Šekspir, 53, Shakespeare, 1107) and *d' Otella* "[keep] from Othello's mind" (Šekspir, 108, Shakespeare, 1121); though Kuliš was clearly encouraged in this case by Shakespeare's language itself (*ja dam ëho tobi* compared to the original "I'll lay 't upon you," [ibid.]). Moreover, this kind of apheresis (of *o* in the vowel cluster) was a northern Ukrainian feature of Kuliš's native dialect as reflected also in his biblical translations (e.g., *ne 'dcurajsja* "don't shun" [Horbač 1988, 61]); remarkably, this type of change made its way, although in a limited fashion, into literary Ukrainian as found also in the writings of Ševčenko (Shevelov 1979, 452). No more persuasive was Hordyns'kyj's criticism of deverbatives ending in *-nnje*, which, although "beautiful and sonorous," were used, nevertheless, too often at the expense of more appropriate shorter forms (e.g., *ošukannje* "abusement [of the world]" [Šekspir, 22, Shakespeare, 1099], *koxannje* "love" [Šekspir, 30], *pryključénnja* [pl.] alongside *pryhody* "adventures" [ibid.]). It should be noted, however, that Kuliš easily introduced morphologically simple deverbatives of the type *rozvodu* (gen.) "divorce" (Šekspir, 19) or *perestup* "[love's] transgression" (*Romeo*, 12, Shakespeare, 979), not corrected by Franko. Interestingly enough, the use of neuters ending in *-nnja* (and *-ttja*) was subsequently criticized in the 1920s by representatives of the populist trend in Ukrainian linguistics (Jevhen Tymčenko, Serhij Smerečyns'kyj, and Olena Kurylo in her early writings).

As in his translation of the Bible, Kuliš masterfully adapted names of some ranks traditionally held by Ukrainian gentry long before the integration of the Hetmanate into the Russian Empire, such as *het'man* "lord" (Šekspir,

114, Shakespeare, 1122), *otaman* "officer" (Šekspir, 18, Shakespeare, 1098), *nakaznyj* "lieutenant," *xorunžyj* "ancient to the general" (Šekspir, 44, Shakespeare, 1105), and, finally *dvorjanyn* "gentleman" (Šekspir, 44, Shakespeare, 1105), a Russian imperial rank introduced in the late eighteenth century as a result of the cooptation of Ukrainian gentry after the abolition of the Hetmanate's institutions. However, Hordyns′kyj (1928, 65) noted that in some cases terms like *kozak* "Cossack" and *kiš* "palisade" seemed to be out of place, as in the phrase *kozače* (voc.) "Sirrah" (Šekspir, 244, Shakespeare, 331). One can add here another example with the Old Rusian rank *voivoda* and the Ukrainianized name *Stepan*:

Король Степан був ставний воівода. (Šekspir, 59)

[King Stephan was a worthy peer.] (Shakespeare, 1109)

Concluding the section dealing with the language of Kuliš's translations of 1882, Hordyns′kyj (1928, 67) stated despondently that the translator of Shakespeare was "very unselective in his language, he employed his own knowledge of the vernacular language very little and too often was receptive to alien influences or acted simply willfully." This is why, continued Hordyns′kyj (ibid.), Kuliš's language was not exemplary and could hardly be compared to the wonderful language of the original.

While disregarding the overall negative appraisal of Kuliš's contribution in Hordyns′kyj's study, one should take into consideration at least one of the critic's arguments, which explains tentatively the blending of vulgar, ethnographic, and lofty elements in Kuliš's high style. According to Hordyns′kyj (1928, 69), Kuliš was a first-rate expert in the Ukrainian language who had amassed a trove of forms and expressions excerpted from the writings of his predecessors. However, objectively speaking, Kuliš could not produce what was still missing or underdeveloped in written Ukrainian in the 1880s, to wit, "a reliable terminology of scientific phrases" (ibid.). This could explain why Kuliš introduced into his translations so many borrowings from "church jargon" (*cerkovščyna*) and forms created by representatives of the Russian terminological school, of which he was purportedly a loyal follower (ibid.).

One can wonder at this point why Hordyns′kyj's judgment was so uncompromisingly harsh. It is tempting to assume that the problem resulted from his regional *Sprachgefühl*, as reflected in the language practice of Franko and other populists who did not share Kuliš's socio-cultural and linguistic views. However, Kuliš was also partly responsible for the negative reaction of the young Galician writer and artist, who in 1928 had decided to analyze the language of Kuliš's translations of Shakespeare. It should also be borne in mind that, by that time, the vernacular-based paradigm of literary Ukrainian prevailed in the two parts of Ukraine. This is why the language of Kuliš could appear so "outlandish" in the late 1920s that Hordyns′kyj failed to see, in hindsight, its innovative character. This character, however, had attested to a totally different vision of literary Ukrainian when propounded by Kuliš some fifty years earlier.

ON THE THRESHOLD OF A NEW SECULAR HIGH STYLE

All in all, Hordyns′kyj's judgment was objectively unfair inasmuch as he tended inadvertently to push Kuliš's legacy to the periphery of the modern history of literary Ukrainian. In general, it was utterly fallacious to blame, in the critic's words, Kuliš's "haughty and pertinacious temper" for the "nationalization of Church Slavonic and Russian expressions, certain choice of sounds and forms, and unusual selection of words" as found in the language of his translations (Hordyns′kyj 1928, 70). In order to rationalize the mixture of so-called vulgarisms, archaic expressions (Church Slavonic and bookish forms), and "Great Russianisms," which in Russian-ruled Ukraine might have been treated at that time in complimentary distribution with "Little Russianisms" through the prism of the all-Russian language program (Danylenko 2008a, 104–109), one has to remember that Kuliš's endeavors were provoked by several factors. Shakespeare's own quest for linguistic synthesis might be viewed as an external factor that, together with the influence of Gervinus's conception of Shakespeare as a moral teacher and leader of the mankind, could impact Kuliš. Yet despite all his contradictions and inconsistencies, criticized in particular by Franko and Hordyns′kyj, Kuliš can be seen as a precursor of the later, essentially twentieth-century understanding of Ukrainian literature (Grabowicz 1992, 237). To prove this, suffice it to look at a brief programmatic preface written by Kuliš to the first volume of his translations of Shakespeare's plays, which foresaw possible criticism by the future readership, including Hordyns'kyj's appraisal of his language:

> In our translation, shocking blasphemes and rude jokes, employed by Shakespeare as the great master, to nuance the sublime and tender, are translated in the way they are observed in the British original.... They were prone to see in Shakespeare's mixture of the divine poetry of the human spirit with the loathsome prose of human callousness a moral helplessness of his time and a defect of his creativity. We see in it, by contrast, a force and merit of the depicting genius that are superior to all other poets." (Šekspir, Preface)

Overall, mixture and contrast of languages and cultural realities in Shakespeare were conceived of by Kuliš as intrinsic tenets of his own language variance stemming from his awareness of varied alternatives within literary traditions cultivated from pre-modern times onward in the Ukrainian lands. The variance inherent in the languages used in Ukraine since the period of Kyivan Rus' inspired the blending of idioms in time and space. What is significant in the case of Kuliš as a representative of Russian-ruled Ukraine is that he viewed the language and literature of Ukrainians in the greater East Slavic context. This explains, for instance, the introduction of numerous Great Russianisms along with Church Slavonicisms and borrowings from other languages, although with a minimum of Polish forms other than those long adopted in the Galician literary tradition. The historical dimension of Kuliš's language program is extended into the future as well, whence individual innovations based on traditional patterns found not only in Ukrainian but also in Great Russian as an "all-Russian partner" (Andriewsky 2003, 196–198).

At first sight, Kuliš's position could look perfidious in the eyes of the late nineteenth- and early twentieth-century populists or proponents of new nationalistic aesthetics, including Hordyns'kyj (1928) who, as if following in the steps of Partyc'kyj, criticized "uncommon" words and phrases forged, in his view, clumsily by Kuliš. Yet, on closer inspection, some of those coined forms prove to be either bookish (Slavonic) or vernacular Russianisms. If not found in the local *jazyčije*, they could appear unfamiliar to speakers of the Galician-Bukovynian koiné used in Austrian-ruled Ukraine at that time (Shevelov 1989, 19–20; Macjuk 2001, 269; Tkač 2007, 369–370; Danylenko 2009c): *voenščyna* "epithets of war" (Šekspir, 10, Shakespeare, 1096), *kljančyt'* (3 sg. pres.) "to beg" (Šekspir, 11), *pobudaražte* (2 pl. imper.) "to incense" (ibid., 12, Shakespeare, 1097), *žorstki* (pl.) "gross" (Šekspir, 15, Shakespeare, 1098), *provynnost'* "[my] offending" (Šekspir, 2, 8, Shakespeare, 1101), *prozirlyvost'* "providence" (Šekspir, 261, Shakespeare, 336). Strangely enough, Hordyns´kyj ascribed a similar "uncommonness" to some outdated lexemes like *provadyš* (2 sg. pres.) "to talk" (Šekspir, 181) or loan forms of the type *vkontentuvannja* "satisfaction" (ibid., 344). Interestingly, the former lexeme is not attested as a *verbum dicendi* in the dictionary of Jevhen Želexivs´kyj (Žel., 2:767), although it occurs in this meaning in the writings of Zaxarija Kopystens´kyj (†1627) (Tymč. and Nimčuk, 2:244) and in Ivan Kotljarevs´kyj's *Enejida* as well as in other contemporary works written in Dnieper Ukraine (Hrinč., 2:462). As far as the form *vkontentuvannja* is concerned, this lexeme seems to be of a Galician, ultimately Polish origin, which is not attested in the dictionary of Teodor Vytvyts´kyj, but is found in Jevhen Želexivs´kyj (Žel., 1:363). It is also a possibility that the choice of this word could have been influenced also by the English word "content" in Shakespeare, for instance, in the text of *The Comedy of Errors*:

КУПЕЦЬ: Бажáю вам *вконтентувáння*, пáне. (Šekspir, 344)

[1 MERCHANT: Sir, I commend you to your own content.] (Shakespeare, 5)

In sum, Kuliš, in his first translations of Shakespeare, proved to be a versatile normalizer who was apt at experimenting with various stylistic devices. In order to create a new high style proper for the "Ukrainian Shakespeare," he searched, sometimes too sweepingly, for a system of stylistically variegated elements. There were both native and loan devices borrowed from more structured languages like Russian and Polish. To draw a parallel with his historical views, rooted in the model, prospects, and demands of structured society, Kuliš offered in this case the first secular variety of the high style to be placed on par with its biblical variety, which he elaborated in his scriptural translations.

His was not the preeminent vision of the high style at that time. In fact, the language of the "Ukrainian Shakespeare" was competing with several other language programs outlined in some other translations of Shakespeare, which were made in the second part of the nineteenth and the early twentieth centuries by Pavlyn Svjencic´kyj, Jurij Ovsyp Fed´kovyč, Myxajlo Staryc´kyj, Panas Myrnyj, Lesja Ukrajinka, Ivan Franko, and Marko Kropyvnyc´kyj (Kočur 1968, 27–44; Šapovalova 1976, 32–157).

CHAPTER 6 Expanding the Literary Canon of the "Ukrainian Shakespeare"

THE FIRST STEP IS THE HARDEST?

Kuliš was not the first writer to translate Shakespeare into Ukrainian. Chronologically, full credit should be given to Pavlyn Svjencic′kyj (1841–1876) who, as early as 1865, published under the pen name Pavlo Svij his translation of Act I from *Hamljet". Dans′kyj korolevyč* (Hamlet. A Danish Prince) in the Lviv periodical *Nyva*. Translation of the rest of the tragedy did not follow, most likely, because of the cold reception of the first fragment by the subscribers. An ethnic Pole from the Ukrainian town Vynnycja, Svjencic′kyj studied at Kyiv University. Having taken part in the Polish uprising of 1863–1864, he had to leave Dnieper Ukraine for Lviv where he subsequently became a popular Ukrainian writer (M. Moskalenko 2006 3/4, 168). Rumor had it that Svjencic′kyj had also translated *Macbeth*, but the manuscript, as one of the local newspapers reported, had been stolen and never found by the translator.

Pavlo Svij's translation could hardly compete with the one prepared by Kuliš and published posthumously by Franko in 1899. As Pavlo Svij pointed out in his seven-line preface to the translation, his intent was to correctly "render the idea of the original," which made him choose prose instead of poetry. But, pressed by his friends, he ultimately switched to poetry (*Hamljet*-S, 36). This, however, did little for the quality of this translation. Rather critical, Franko wrote in his survey of Ukrainian translations of Shakespeare that Pavlo Svij's poetry was so unpoetical that prose would have been better, since one could hardly find therein either rhythm or poetry (Franko 1899, xviii; Terex 1964, 72). The translator, continued Franko (1899, xviii), was simply counting syllables and nothing more. Moreover, in view of such forms as *apel'* "summons" (*Hamljet*-S, 41, Shakespeare, 1049), *Norvegčyk"* "Norwegian," and *na vyžyni svojei potuhi* "at the height of its power" (*Hamljet*-S, 39–40), along with the characteristic Polish rhythm, Pavlo Svij might have translated *Hamlet* from the Polish. Almost one hundred years later, Šapovalova, although without going into details, argued that Pavlo Svij's translation did have a certain value for his time. What was positive about this translation, she argued, was its obvious tendency to disengage from the "traditions of travesty and Ukrainianization" (Šapovalova 1976, 34). Unfortunately, the first attempt at this supposed disengagement was a real flop due to the mediocrity of Pavlo Svij's translation, critically assessed by Franko and other specialists (Lazurs′kyj 1929, 22; Danylenko 2014b). To demonstrate numerous shortcomings in this translation, suffice it to survey the linguistic devices employed by Pavlo Svij, which will help us correctly ascertain the contribution made some twenty-five years later by Kuliš.

To begin with the orthography, the text of the translation demonstrates a series of regional features influenced by local dialects and the contemporary Polish literary tradition. Among others, the following examples are deserving of attention: *Kljavdij* (Claudius), *Hamljet"* (Hamlet), *Pol'onij* (Polonius), and *prol'og"* "prologue" (*Hamljet*-S, 40, Shakespeare, 1049), all with a characteristic spelling rendering *l'*, adopted in the borrowing from western European languages, through Polish mediation. Together with *g* in loan words, a typical regionalism (Danylenko 2005, 33–37) whence the use of the Roman letter "g" to denote the corresponding velar sound (e.g., *oryginal* "original," *norvegskyj* "Norwegian" [*Hamljet*-S, 36]). Other examples are *krivavyj* "bloody" (*Hamljet*-S, 40), *zadrižaty* "to tremble" (ibid., 41), *trivaty* "to persevere" (ibid., 55, Shakespeare, 1050), *trivoha* "fear" (*Hamljet*-S, 58, Shakespeare, 1048), and the like, with the anaptyctic *i* after the sonant *r* (Shevelov 1979, 463–465; *AUM*, 2, map 69), *detyna* "child" (*Hamljet*-S, 104) without disyllabic harmony as in *dytyna*, also *železnyj* "of iron" (ibid., 102), *Bih* "God" (ibid., 37).

From the point of view of its morphology, Pavlo Svij's language is replete with dialectal features typical of nineteenth-century Galician-Bukovynian koiné in the making (Shevelov 1989, 19–20, 58–59). Such dialectal features occurred together with many Polish forms appearing sometimes under the Ukrainian or Church Slavonic guise. For instance, the present active participles that, like their Polish counterparts, are encountered in abundance are mostly disguised as Church Slavonic, for example *vegetujuščoho* (gen. m.) "that rots itself" (literally "growing"), *v budujuščojsja* (gen. f.) *svjatyni* "at (this) temple [that] waxes" (*Hamljet*-S, 134, 101, Shakespeare, 1055, 1052)—that is, "in the temple that is under construction,"—*oznajmujuščyj* "the cock, that is the trumpet to the [morn]" (*Hamljet*-S, 41) (literally, "declaring"), and *vidbuvajušči vartu* "being on their watch" (*Hamljet*-S, 41, 71, Shakespeare, 1049, 1051); however, the vernacular suffix also occurs rarely (e.g., *spljučoho* [gen.] "sleeping" [*Hamljet*-S, 134, Shakespeare, 1055]).

One should also mention here preterits from the former perfect tense forms with auxiliary clitics concatenated with the participial form. Although patterned on local dialectal forms, they demonstrate Polish adaptation, most likely as a result of Pavlo Svij's slavish translation from the Polish original (e.g., *vhljenulys′mo* "we looked up" [*Hamljet*-S, 38], a Polish verb form with the characteristic *l′*). Of interest also are dialectal forms *pijaty* (imprfv.) and *zapijaty* (perfv.) (ibid., 40, 41) instead of *za(s) pivaty* (perfv.) "to sing" (Verxratskyj 1899, 76–77).

In the nominal morphology, one should begin with the use of (feminine) instrumentals ending in *-ov/-ev*, which were regularly attested in the Galician variety of the written language and the Dniester dialect (Macjuk 2001, 272–273; Verxratskyj 1899, 66), in particular in the translation of the New Testament made by Antin Kobyljans′kyj (Danylenko 2010a): *pryčynov″* (instr. f.) "reason" (*Hamljet*-S, 39), *sylov* (instr. f.) "force" (ibid., 40, 41), *zo mnov″* (instr.) "with me" (ibid., 37) alongside sporadic forms like *zo mnoju* (instr.) "with me" and *z″ pohodoju* (instr. f.) "with the weather" (ibid., 52). A peculiar combination of two parallel forms is found in *najbil′šov″* (instr. f.) *dozoju* (instr. f.) *rezygnaciji* (literally, "with the largest portion of resignation" [ibid., 137]).

Neuters with the assimilated *j* are particularly numerous in the language of this translation. Pavlo Svij uses predominantly the ending *-e*, influenced in such nouns by the northern and southwestern Ukrainian literary tradition (Bevzenko 1978, 87–88), as well as the ending *-a*. Interestingly, the translator resorts either to geminated or, more often than not, non-geminated forms (e.g., *žyttje* "life" [*Hamljet*-S, 119], *poxodžennja* "origin" [ibid., 117], *peredčuttja* "premonition" [ibid., 134] next to *ščastje* "happiness" [ibid., 102], *vydženje* "vision" [ibid., 71; Pol. *widzenie*], *blahoslovenje* "blessing" [ibid., 102], *skupovanje* "buying" [ibid., 39; Pol. *skupowanie*], *peresvidčenje* "avouch [of mine eyes]" [ibid., 38, Shakespeare, 1048]). Another Polish borrowing is *zadavanjesja* "giving words or talking" (*Hamljet*-S, 104, Shakespeare, 1054) with the reflexive particle concatenated with the preceding noun.

In general, Pavlo Svij's translation is brimming with numerous Polish or Polish-mediated forms, which proves, as was correctly suggested by Franko, that the translator was heavily reliant on the Polish original. To take the vocabulary, one can cite such typical Galician forms as *ovšem"* "certainly" (*Hamljet*-S, 137; Vytv., 195), *mord"* "slay" (*Hamljet*-S, 138; Vytv., 137), *potuha* "power" (*Hamljet*-S, 40; Pol. *potęga*), *vandrivka* "trip" (ibid., 40; Vytv., 322), *vontpyty* "to doubt" (*Hamljet*-S, 53; Vytv. 320), *konvencional'nyj* "conventional" (*Hamljet*-S, 54; Pol. *konwencjonalny*), *traktament" na učtu vesil'nju* "treatment for the marriage banquet" (ibid., 70; Gr. *Traktament* in Žel., 2:979), *vedlja skali* "in the gross and scope of my opinion" (*Hamljet*-S, 39, Shakespeare, 1048; Vytv., 267) (literally, "according to the scale"), *pugilares"* "wallet" (*Hamljet*-S, 135; Pol. *pugilares*), *posterunek"* "watch" (ibid., 39, Shakespeare, 1048), and many others. The latter two are not attested either in Jevhen Želexivs'kyj's or Teodor Vytvyc'kyj's dictionaries.

Another most arresting feature of Pavlo Svij's language is its solid colloquial texture, resistant in some places to bookish, primarily Church Slavonic elements. Forms like *otče* (2x; voc.) "my lord" (*Hamljet*-S, 103) are rare (usually instead *pane* [ibid., 8], *knjaze* [ibid., 9] "[my] lord," *vaša korolevs'ka mylost'* [ibid., 70] next to *vaša knjažs'ka mylost'* "my lord" [ibid., 71, 72, Shakespeare, 1051]). All in all, Pavlo Svij's work is reminiscent of Kobyljans'kyj's translation, especially its 1874 editions of Luka-L and Luka-U, moderately permeated with Church Slavonic elements (Danylenko 2010a). Thus, both translators are almost uniquely focused on obvious regionalisms. There is no wonder that, in harmony with the local tradition, Pavlo Svij indulges in vernacular forms like *teperky* or *nyn'ki* "now" (*Hamljet*-S, 38, 54), *tutky* "here" (ibid., 138), and *vsen'ka* (f.) "entire" (ibid., 134). Remarkably, such forms are attested in abundance in Kuliš's translation of the Bible of 1869.

To provide a fuller picture of Pavlo Svij's vision of written Ukrainian, suffice it to quote here an excerpt from Act 1, scene 1, which was also cited by Franko to demonstrate the low quality of Pavlo Svij's translation. In comparison with the parallel fragment from Kuliš's translation, it becomes clear why Franko criticized Pavlo Svij's poetic skills.

Pavlo Svij's Translation	**Kuliš's Translation**
Встріхнувсь якъ *преступникъ* на голосъ *апелю* Страшного. Чувавъ я, що півень, той трубачъ ранокъ *ознаймующій*, своімъ чутнимъ острашнимъ голосомъ, пробуджає бога дня и на цей знакъ кожний духъ, чи вінъ по землі блукається—въ воді, вогні, чи повітру—вертається звідки вийшовъ; а що це правда— *переконою* тому то, що ми тутъ самі побачили. (Hamljet-S, 41)	И затрусилося тогді, якъ злюка[1] Відъ призову страшного. Чувъ не разъ я, Що півень, сей трубайло ранній, будить Дневного бога, и по ёго гаслу Духъ *неприкаянный*, що *блудить* въ морі, Чи то въ огні, въ землі або въ повітрі, Втекае до свого притулку: правду жъ Намъ запевняе те, що мы вбачали. (*Hamlet*-K, 7r–7v)

[And then it started like a guilty thing Upon a fearful summons. I have heard The cock, that is the trumpet to the morn, Doth with his lofty and shrill-sounding throat Awake the god of day; and, at his warning, Whether in sea or fire, in earth or air, The extravagant and erring spirit hies. To his confine; and of the truth herein This present object made probation.] (Shakespeare, 1049)

---

1   While preparing the text of Kuliš's *Hamlet* for publication at the close of the nineteenth century, Franko surprisingly introduced only one change in these verses. Instead of *zljuka*, Franko used *hrišnyk* (*Hamlet*-K/F, 10), thus wiping out the historical connotation of one of the meanings of *zlyj* "bad, conscienceless, foul" (*DUL*, 12:37), skillfully revived by Kuliš in the original translation.

In contrast to the historical elevation of Kuliš's language by means of bookish and Church Slavonic elements such as *bludyty* "to go astray" (Sr., 1:115) and *(ne)prikajannyj* "unrepentful" (Shakespeare, 1202) respectively, Pavlo Svij's language is modeled on Polish, whence not only *apel'* "summons" (criticized by Franko) but also *oznajmujuščyj* "[that] which declares, herald," a Polish form (Pol. *oznajmujący*) furnished with the Church Slavonic suffix *-(j)ušč-*.

In sum, if compared with Kuliš's pioneering translations of the "Ukrainian Shakespeare," Pavlo Svij's contribution to the creation of a new literary standard was minimal due to its dependence on regional and, as is historically conceivable, Polish patterns. What was missing in Pavlo Svij's translation was a true talent and deep knowledge of the local dialect and vernacular, masterfully demonstrated by Jurij Osyp Fed´kovyč some ten years later.

"*HUCULIA* DID NOT APPEAR; RATHER SHAKESPEARE WAS MERELY HIDDEN"

Jurij Osyp Fed´kovyč (1834–1888), a prominent writer and a herald of the national revival in Bukovyna, began with a prose rendering of Shakespeare's *The Taming of the Shrew*, entitled *Jak kozam rohy vypravljajut'* (How the Goats Have Their Horns Straightened, 1872). Called *fraška* "a literary bagatelle" (Pol. *fraszka*), this translation had practically nothing to do with the comedy of Shakespeare, depicting instead the life of Bukovynian peasants (*Fraška*). Because of its farcical exuberances and slapstick elements, this rendering was negatively received by most Ukrainian intellectuals, including Myxajlo Drahomanov. Having learned in 1872 about Fed´kovyč's translation of *Macbeth*, Drahomanov expressed his concern about the language of the writer. Cognizant of Fed´kovyč's literary talent, he nevertheless emphasized the fact that his language was "very provincial, even for Galicia," let alone Dnieper Ukraine (Pavlyk 1910, 157). Reading Fed´kovyč's *fraška* completely disillusioned Drahomanov. He was upset by the very idea of paraphrasing, rather than translating, Shakespeare's works, in particular *Romeo and Juliette*, *Hamlet*, *Macbeth*, and *Richard III*, which, translated into vernacular Ukrainian, could appeal to the common people. Overall, Fed´kovyč showed a lack of literary taste in rendering *The Taming of the Shrew*. As a result, Drahomanov inferred, "*Huculia* did not appear; rather Shakespeare was merely hidden" (ibid., 183–184). It was clear to him that Kuliš's translations of Shakespeare and Byron alone proved successful because "only in those translations can one perceive a good literary schooling, in fact, a European one" (Drahomanov 1894, 115).

Thirty years after the publication of Fed´kovyč's *fraška*, Franko concurred with Drahomanov, reiterating that this farcical play demonstrated a complete lack of refined literary taste or any clear idea about either the original or its rendering (Šapovalova 1976, 49). All in all, Fed´kovyč remained within the confines of provincialism, evidenced in both the characters and local setting of his farce, and thus failed to create any link with the comedy of Shakespeare.

However, Fed´kovyč's translations of *Hamlet* and *Macbeth*, which followed in the late 1860s and early 1870s, showed his mastery of the literary material and subsequently were even compared with the translations authored by Kuliš. Unfortunately, Fed´kovyč's translations did not have any effect on the development of the regional variety of written Ukrainian, let alone on that of new literary Ukrainian as cultivated in Dnieper Ukraine. The point is that they remained unknown to the general public until 1902 when they were first published under the editorship of Franko. While working on the writer's manuscripts, Franko was surprised to learn about three independent versions of Fed´kovyč's translation of *Macbeth* that testified to the author's intentions to create, in the long run, a true literary adaptation of this famous tragedy. As for *Hamlet*, the translation was most likely made by Fed´kovyč during his stay in Lviv in 1874 (Lazurs´kyj 1929, 23). Although this translation did not undergo such substantial revisions as *Macbeth*, its quality was, no doubt, much better than that of Pavlo Svij's Polish-Ukrainian *Hamljet*.

Franko could not help but admit that the overall quality of Fed´kovyč's translations was nevertheless rather poor (Terex 1964, 74). As in the case of Pavlo Svij, the major problem lay in the fact that the writer did not know English. This is why Fed´kovyč had to rely slavishly on the German translation, which affected not only the faithfulness of his own translation but also its language. The result was a free translation of the text of *Macbeth* that tended to look in some places like a mere paraphrase. To illustrate this, Šapovalova (1976, 51) cited the last lines from Act 1, scene 5 from *Hamlet*, which Fed´kovyč interpreted so loosely that he deviated conspicuously from the original. Kuliš's translation in this case looks more restrained and faithful to the original:

Fed´kovyč's Translation	**Kuliš's Translation**
Світ ся повихнув,	Час вийшов із уторів. О проклята
Да як подумаю, що я 'го маю	
Назад направити, то аж мя сміх зберає!	Судьба, що я родивсь його наладить!
(*Hamljet*-F/F, 41)	(*Hamlet*-K/F, 40)

[The time is out of joint;—O cursed spite, That ever I was born to set it right!] (Shakespeare, 1057)

In Fed´kovyč's *Hamljet*, Franko (1902, ix) also noticed the excessive use of Germanisms and function words like the demonstratives *tse* or *otse* "this," employed merely to fill in some gaps in the syllabic structure of the translation. However, Franko believed that Fed´kovyč's translations also had some positive traits that could compete with the more refined translations made by Kuliš and even supersede them in terms of their lexical affluence. This is why Kuliš's translations, although made skillfully, looked, according to Franko (ibid., x), more clichéd in contrast to the less polished yet more colorful Hucul idiom of Fed´kovyč.

It should be noted, however, that the colorfulness of Fed´kovyč's language looked excessive outside "Huculia," in particular in Dnieper Ukraine (Lazurs´kyj 1929, 23). In other words, his translation was a literary experiment designed for regional consumption and completely void of any vision for a pan-Ukrainian literature and language. Unlike Kuliš, Fed´kovyč never tried to synthesize various dialectal elements into a unified system that could appeal to all Ukrainian speakers. This is why the language of Kuliš's translation is in fact replete with different regional variants, while Fed´kovyč's language appears stylistically and structurally homogeneous.

To begin with, Fed′kovyč's language demonstrates a minimum of phonetic variants. Among a few of these, deserving of attention are pairs like *norvec′kyj* next to *norvedz′kyj* (*Hamljet*-F/F, 7, 8) and *proz′bu* (acc.) next to *pris′bamy* (pl. instr.) "request" (ibid., 13). In the morphology, the translator consistently uses clitic forms *ho* (acc.) "him," *'mu* (dat.) "to him," *nju* (acc.) "her," *my* (dat.) next to *myni* (dat.) "to me," *tja* (acc.) "you" (ibid., 6, 7, 9, 11, 23, etc.), and the like (Matvijas 2006, 59). Most representative, however, are forms of the type *v'na* "she," *v'no* "it," and *v'ny* "they" (*vna, vno, vny* in the protograph; *Hemlet*-F) (Kobyljans′kyj 1928, 35) (see also forms *čo'* "what," [*bilš*] *ničo* next to *ničoho* [*bilš*] [*Hamljet*-F/F, 23]).

Among the morphological dialectal features, one comes across numerous feminine instrumentals of the type *z nev* "with her" (*Hamljet*-F/F, 4), *trunvov* "coffin" (ibid., 17), and *oxotojov* (*oxota* nom.) "wish" (ibid., 13); consider *z našov peršišnov sestrov, A teperišnov kralev, udovov dostojnov* "[Therefore] our sometimes sister, now our queen, The imperial jointress of this warlike state" (Shakespeare, 1049)—literally "with our previous sister, and now queen, an esteemed widow" (*Hamljet*-F/F, 11). Such instrumentals are commonplace in the Galician variety of literary Ukrainian (Macjuk 2001, 272–273).

Of interest are verbal formations that are attested outside the Hucul-speaking territories. One should begin with the status of the so-called synthetic future ending in *-mu*, called de-inceptive because of the originally inceptive semantics of the auxiliary "to take" (Danylenko 2011a). In the language of Fed′kovyč's *Hamlet* (*Hemlet*-F), this synthetic future tense form is very productive, even in comparison with a more regular eastern Slavic analytic form derived with the help of the auxiliary "to be" and the infinitive (Kobyljans′kyj 1928, 62) (e.g., *budu pidsluxaty sja* "I will eavesdrop" [*Hamljet*-F/F, 81]). Overall, the de-inceptive future tense forms in the language of Fed′kovyč fall into two groups depending on the positioning of auxiliary clitics. First, the clitic may occur before the infinitive (i.e., in clause-second [Wackernagel's] position). Second, it is used in verb-adjacent position (i.e., after the infinitive).

Clause-Second Position of Clitics	Verb-Adjacent Position of Clitics
меть вповідати "he/she will tell" (*Hamljet*-F/F, 5)	*говоритиме* "he will speak" (*Hamljet*-F/F, 11)
мете благословити "you will bless" (*Hamljet*-F/F, 25)	*сокотити му* (*Hamljet*-F/F, 22) vs. *сокотитиму* "I will watch" (*Hemlet*-F, s.p.)
меть сперати "he/she will stop" (*Hamljet*-F/F, 32)	*знатимете* "you will know" (*Hamljet*-F/F, 53)

Quite remarkably, the future auxiliary clitic in the verb-adjacent position is written, as a rule, together with the infinitive in the protograph of Fed´kovyč's *Hamlet*; however, it is consistently separated in Franko's redaction (see *sokotytymu* in Fed´kovyč's original translation compared to *sokotyty mu* as emended by Franko in the edition of 1902). No doubt, Fed´kovyč's spelling in this case is more idiosyncratic since it demonstrates that the de-inceptive future tense form in the writer's idiom turns into a synthetic formation with the auxiliary clitic concatenated with the infinitive (Danylenko 2012, 119). This is why Franko's corrections, which seem to be out of place in some instances, are likely to show to what extent the written language in Galicia at the turn of the twentieth century might have been influenced by local orthographic rules (Danylenko 2012a, 25–26, 2012b, 40).

Nevertheless, Franko's intervention in Fed´kovyč's language was minimal. Among a few emendations, one should mention his correction of some verbal forms, whose spelling, according to Franko, apparently reflected the author's dialectal pronunciation. These are inflected conditional auxiliary clitics like *byx* (1 sg.) and *by* (2 sg.) in place of *bex* and *be* in Fed´kovyč's protograph (*Hamljet*-F/F, 6, 34, fn. 1), where *e* is a regular reflex of (unstressed) *y* (Shevelov 1979, 537–538, 666). Not surprisingly, unlike this typical Hucul feature (Simovyč 1921, 256), Kuliš resorted only to "frozen" (uninflected) conditional clitics in his translation.

Fed´kovyč's Translation	Kuliš's Translation
Ніколи в світі був бих це не вірив,	Як перед Богом, не поняв би віри

Як був бих своїми очима це
Не видїв.
(*Hamljet*-F/F, 6)

Без осязного й вірного
сьвідоцтва
Моїх очей. (*Hamljet*-K/F, 6)

[Before my God, I might not this believe Without the sensible and true avouch Of mine own eyes.] (Shakespeare, 1048)

In the light of the consistent introduction of clitics like *byx* instead of *bex*, one wonders why Franko did not correct gerundial forms of the type *skazavše* "having said," *pomynuvše* "having disregarded," *spovnyvše* "having accomplished" (*Hamljet*-F/F, 12, 13), and the like. In such forms, the reflex *e* is a typical Hucul sound (Žylko 1966, 225).

"New preterits" retaining, in some cases, former auxiliary clitics are attested in particular environments. These forms tend to occur primarily in second person singular and plural, while no auxiliary is found in combination with the resultative participle ending in *-l* for first and third person singular and plural ([*vin*] *nosyv* "he carried," *mynav* "he passed," *my vydily* "we saw" next to *čoho-s'te zdrehly sja tak* "why did you become so scared" [*Hamljet*-F/F, 6], *jes poklav* "you put, hid" [ibid., 9], and *pryjšov jes'* "you came" [ibid., 18]).

All in all, in the verbal morphology as well as the phonetics, the language of Fed´kovyč's translation is typically Hucul (Simovyč 1921, 79, 256, 278, 348). Tentativley, as in the case of the aforementioned conditional auxiliaries, Fed´kovyč's dialectal idiom shows a transitional stage between the use of auxiliary clitics without concatenation and the resultative participle (for the "new preterit") or the infinitive (for the so-called synthetic or de-inceptive future tense) and their concatenation with the participle and infinitive. The latter testifies to a complete degrammation of the preterit auxiliaries (e.g., *-jes'* pret. aux. 2 sg.) and a complete grammation of the future auxiliaries (e.g., *-mu* fut. aux. 1 sg.) (Danylenko 2012a, 8–10, 23–26, also 2010c).

Fed´kovyč's translation is literally overflowing with lexical dialectisms and borrowings, especially from German, Rumanian, and Polish, all constituting a lexical core of what is called a Galician-Bukovynian koiné (Shevelov 1989, 19; Tkač 2007, 369–370). One should treat this concept, however, with reservations. As a matter of fact, it is not clear to what extent this koiné might have been "codified" in the 1870s when Fed´kovyč was completing his translations of *Macbeth* and *Hamlet*. What is evident, nevertheless, is that these translations, together with Fed´kovyč's major literary writings, were heavily influenced, on the one hand, by rural dialects and, on the other, by the German and Polish enjoying high social prestige in both Galicia and Bukovyna. This peculiarity becomes even more evident if juxtaposed with the varied means of vernacularization employed by Kuliš in his translations of Shakespeare (e.g., *car* next to *korol´* "king," *posol´stvo* "embassy," *tulumbasy* "kettle drums," and the like in his translation of *Hamlet* [*Hamljet*-K/F, 12, 13, 29]; see *posel´stvo* in the protograph [*Hamlet*-K, 8v; Tymč. and Nimčuk, 2:180]). To take Act 1 in Fed´kovyč's *Hamljet* as an example, one finds here only three lexemes that belong to the eastern Slavic stock and demonstrate some relevant historical connotation. They are *bojaryn* (*Hamljet*-F/F, 16, Shakespeare, 1051) "courtier," *božok Dažboh* (*Hamljet*-F/F, 10, Shakespeare, 1049) "the god of day," and *Vitynhrad* (*Hamljet*-F/F, 15) with a Church Slavonic stem *-hrad* and the pharyngeal *h* (*Wittenberg* in Shakespeare's original [Shakespeare, 1051]). These are, respectively, *caredvorec´*, *dnevnyj boh*, and *Vyttenberkh* in Kuliš's translation (*Hamljet*-K/F, 15, 10, *Hamlet*-K, 11r) compared to *Vittenberg* imposed by Franko (*Hamljet*-K/F, 15) in accordance with the Galician orthographic practice.

In Act 1 of Fed´kovyč's *Hamljet*, the following lexical dialectisms and regional colloquialisms are most indicative of the translator's vision of the future of literary Ukrainian:

краля (*Hamljet*-F/F, 2, etc.) "queen" (Žel., 1:375), a secondary derivative from Pol. *kralka* "queen (a card name)" (*EDU*, 3:74);

божкодайкати (*Hamljet*-F/F, 28) "to juggle; to cheat" (see also божкодайло = божкар "pharisee"). Another form, божкородіти, also found in Fed´kovyč's protograph, is attested in the dictionary of Jevhen Želexivs´kyj (Žel., 1:37); the latter is marked as Galician in the dictionary of Borys Hrinčenko (Hrinč., 1:124). The derivative model with the stem божко- has been productive in (Southwest) Ukrainian (*VUI*, 76–77);

борзо (*Hamljet*-F/F, 21) "fast" (Žel., 1:39), a common word in Ukrainian dialects, including North and Southeast Ukrainian (Hrinč., 1:128; Bil.-Nos., 59);

готло (*Hamljet*-F/F, 3) "watchword," not attested in major regional and dialectal dictionaries; an old borrowing from Pol. *godło*, MUkr. *khodlo* (*EDU*, 1:545);

димидіти (*Hamljet*-F/F, 6) "to vanish, disappear" (Žel., 1:182). The form is not attested in other major regional and dialectal dictionaries;

діськи (*Hamljet*-F/F, 14) "in reality, in fact." The form is attested, yet not appropriately glossed, in the dictionary of Jevhen Želexivs'kyj (Žel., 1:186);

дознаку (*Hamljet*-F/F, 5) "really." The form is not found in major regional and dialectal dictionaries;

дуфати (*Hamljet*-F/F, 36) "to hope" (Žel., 1:211). As an old borrowing from Pol. *dufać* (*EDU*, 2:149), this lexeme is commonplace in the Galician-Bukovynian koiné (*VUI*, 292); in the Hucul dialect, it is glossed, however, somewhat differently: "to take care; to esteem" (Pipaš and Halas, 53);

забресклити (*Hamljet*-F/F, 29) "to spoil," (see also *брескли* pl. "wet wood" [Žel., 1:43], *обресклий* "swollen" [Pipaš and Halas, 122]);

здуфалий (*Hamljet*-F/F, 8) "brave, courageous," a common Polish borrowing in the Galician-Bukovynian koiné (*VUI*, 576);

злюзувати (*Hamljet*-F/F, 4) "to relieve; to loose" (see also Pol. *loz* < Gr. *los* [Šelud'ko 1931, 38], also Pol. *luz* "relaxation"). The lexeme is not attested in major regional and dialectal dictionaries, although it might belong to the Galician-Bukovynian koiné;

змаза (*Hamljet*-F/F, 29) "stain," Gr. *Befleckung, Schandfleck* (Žel., 1:305). The lexeme is not attested in major regional and dialectal dictionaries, although it might belong to the Galician-Bukovynian koiné (see Pol. *zmaza* and *skaza*, glossed similarly by Vytvyc'kyj [Vytv. 268, 383]);

лоточити (*Hamljet*-F/F, 12) "to bother" (Žel., 1:414), an old borrowing from Pol. *łotoszyć, łatoszyć* "to beat, stripe" that belongs to the local koiné (*VUI*, 782) and is attested in the modern Hucul dialect (Zakrevs′ka 1997, 114);

непіт (*Hamljet*-F/F, 12) "nephew" (Žel., 1:518), a Rumanian borrowing used in the Galician-Bukovynian koiné (Tkač 2007, 172, 570) (see Hucul *непота* [m. and f.] [Pipaš and Halas, 115]);

облазунок (*Hamljet*-F/F, 3) "relief," a borrowing from German (see also Gr. *Ablösung* [Žel., 1:543]);

періже, переже (*Hamljet*-F/F, 21) "before, formerly" (see Žel., 2:628), ESl. *переже* "before, formerly" (Sr., 2:906);

перемотатись (*Hamljet*-F/F, 39) "to go over; to change places." The lexeme is not attested in major regional and dialectal dictionaries, although it might be an archaic (eastern Slavic) form (see Pol. *błąkać скитатися, премѣтатися, блукати* [Vytv., 38], ESl. *переметатисѧ* "to go, move over" [Sr., 2:910]);

першішний (*Hamljet*-F/F, 11) "previous, older." The form is not attested in major regional and dialectal dictionaries;

пленичитись (*Hamljet*-F/F, 10) "to enthuse" (see Žel., 2:658);

подуфалість (*Hamljet*-F/F, 7) "self-confidence, impudence." This is an old Polish borrowing in the local koiné (*VUI*, 1183);

претці (*Hamljet*-F/F, 6) "however, yet; at least" (see also *прецінь* [Pipaš and Halas, 153]); the two forms are not found in the dictionary of Jevhen Želexivs′kyj; *прецінь* is attested in the dictionary of Borys Hrinčenko (Hrinč., 2:409; see also Kuzela and Rud., 858);

просатарь (*Hamljet*-F/F, 28) "a person who invites to a wedding" (Žel., 2:777). This lexeme is also attested in Lemkian

(Verxratskyj 1902, 458); the final palatalized *r´* is typical of the Hucul dialect (Simovyč 1921, 48);

проява (*Hamljet*-F/F, 5) "ghost" (Pipaš and Halas, 159), see *прояв* "a strange person" (*VUI*, 1371);

раваш (*Hamljet*-F/F, 36) "sign; tablet." This is a borrowing from Rum. *răvaş* (Scheludko 1926, 141), which is not attested in major regional and dialectal dictionaries; yet it is found today in the Hucul dialect (Pipaš and Halas, 161);

самарати (*Hamljet*-F/F, 6) "to be like." This is a borrowing from Rum. *semără* (Scheludko 1926, 142), which is commonly attested in the Galician-Bukovynian koiné (*VUI*, 1456) and Southwest Ukrainian (Hrinč., 2:608), including the modern Hucul dialect (Pipaš and Halas, 170);

сокотити (*Hamljet*-F/F, 22) "to watch; to take care" (Žel., 2:894), a borrowing from ORum. *socoti* "to tend as a shepherd" (*EDU*, 5:346); this word is found in the Galician-Bukovynian koiné (Tkač 2007, 586);

спіжевий (*Hamljet*-F/F, 16) "of bronze," also *спижевий*; this is an old Polish borrowing (Pol. *śpiżowy*), attested in various Ukrainian dialects (Vytv., 276; *VUI*, 1509; Hrinč., 2:684);

сфантазоватіти (*Hamljet*-F/F, 32) "to become crazy," a form not attested in major regional and dialectal dictionaries, although it has been clearly influenced by Pol. *fantazować*;

тварь (*Hamljet*-F/F, 21) "face." This is a common Ukrainian lexeme (Bil.-Nos., 350; Žel., 2:952; Pipaš and Halas, 189) (see also ESl. *тварь* [Sr., 3:932]); during the Middle Ukrainian period, the word might have been influenced by Pol. *twarz* (Tymč. and Nimčuk, 2:386; Vytv., 122, 302);

тиму (*Hamljet*-F/F, 23) "this is why" (see also MoUkr. *тому*);

убій (*Hamljet*-F/F, `) "murder" (Žel., 2:999) (see also *убійник* "murderer" [Hrinč., 2:816]);

фрасунек (*Hamljet*-F/F, 14) "grief, worry." This is an old borrowing from Pol. *frasunek* (Vytv. 75) (see also MHGr. *Freise* "fear" and MUkr. *frasunok"* [Šelud′ko 1931, 51]);

штроль (*Hamljet*-F/F, 37) "good-for-nothing," most likely from Gr. *Strolch*. The lexeme is not attested in major regional and dialectal dictionaries.

At first blush, the list looks somewhat misleading, while the distribution of loan and native lexemes can hardly be projected onto the whole southwestern Ukrainian continuum. However, some figures deserve attention. To begin with, there are ten Polish, four Rumanian, and two German borrowings on the list. Remarkably, almost two thirds of all the borrowings are either long naturalized Polish forms or colloquialisms using Polish-derived models. Yet both long naturalized loan words and newly coined colloquialisms were used not only by rural speakers but also by the local intelligentsia as evidenced, in particular, in the translation of Fed′kovyč, whose vision of Rus′ (Ukraine) was notoriously "limited by the Dniester and Čeremoš rivers" (Ohonovs′kyj 1889, 635).

All this tentatively testifies to a special regional (Galician-Bukovynian) koiné in the making in late nineteenth-century Galicia and Bukovyna (Shevelov 1989, 19). This is why, perhaps, Franko's editorial intervention in the text of Fed′kovyč was minimal. Moreover, Franko's understanding of literary Ukrainian might, in principle, have been in accord with that of the Bukovynian writer, including in terms of vocabulary, morphosyntax, and, most likely, the orthography of a new local vernacular-based Ukrainian language. In any case, the foregoing survey of vocabulary in both the edition prepared by Franko and the protograph of Fed′kovyč's translation (*Hemlet*-F) has not revealed major differences between the two texts. In fact, this type of harmony between the two writers comes as no surprise. In

Austria-Hungary, where the dialects were more numerous and differentiated, speaking and writing in Ukrainian essentially meant using one's own dialect (Shevelov 1989, 18).

Unlike Kuliš's vernacular-based literary language, premised on Southeast Ukrainian with admixtures from other dialects, the conglomerate of local (indigenous and loan) forms in Fed´kovyč's language could appear to the Galician populists as a true way forward for the normalization of written Ukrainian. One wonders then as to what kind of literary standard the Ukrainian language could have evolved into, had this latter scenario, oriented primarily toward the Galician-Bukovynian koiné, prevailed in the late nineteenth and early twentieth centuries in all the Ukrainian-speaking territories. Needless to say, at that time Kuliš's standard of written Ukrainian seemed to be at odds with the language program of Fed´kovyč and especially Franko, who later had the nerve to rectify Kuliš's translations of Shakespeare according to his personal taste (Lazurs´kyj 1929, 30–31).

HAMLET OR *HAMLJET*? THAT IS THE QUESTION

Ivan Franko was notoriously picky about the language of Kuliš's translations of both the Bible and Shakespeare. In fact, Franko never considered himself to be an admirer of Kuliš's creative work (Hordyns´kyj 1928, 112; Danylenko 2009b). It is not surprising therefore that, while refraining from making any changes in the translations made by Fed´kovyč, Franko proved fastidiously critical of some shortcomings in Kuliš's texts. As an editor of his translations, Franko introduced so many corrections that Hordyns´kyj struggled to note all of them in the 1899 edition of Kuliš's *Hamlet* a quarter century later. To show the extent of Franko's intervention in the language of this translation and the nature of his corrections, it will be instructive to compare a fragment from Kuliš's protograph with the corresponding place in Act 1, scene 1 in *Hamlet* as edited by Franko and discussed by Hordyns´kyj in 1928. Leaving aside some orthographic peculiarities of the typical *jaryžka* as well as the use of the grave accent for stress in Kuliš's protograph, the major corrections made by Franko can be summarized as follows:

Kuliš's Protograph (*Hamlet*-K)	Franko's Edition (*Hamljet*-K/F)
*дванàццять (2r)	дванадцять (3)
*Марцèл (3r)	Марцель (4)
виходить Франційско (3r)	Франціско виходить (4)
*здаèцця (3r, also 6r)	здаєть ся (4, also 8)
*посвіччив (4r)	посьвідчив (5)
*не явицця воно̀ (4r)	не явить ся воно (5)
*освітѝла (4v)	осьвітила (5)
*тогдѝ (4v)	тоді (5)
обѝдилось (4v)	образилось (6)
тремтѝш поблѝдши [?] (5r)	тремтиш, поблїд? (6)
*свідòцтва (5r)	сьвідоцтва (6)
*Норвèга (5r)	Норвеґа (7)
Щò прòсто думати про се, не знàю;	Що саме думати про се, не знаю;
Міркуючи ж с первòгляду огулом,	Міркуючи ж загально, се віщує
Вонò вѝщує в нàшім государствѝ Якусь чудну хуртовину (5r–5v)	Якусь негоду в нашім государстві (7)
Ну, дòбре (5v)	[omitted]
Щò се встаè, що потовà поспішность	Чого ся потом скроплена поспішність
Зробѝла день и ніч рабàми праці?	Зробила день і ніч рабами праці?
Хто б міг се все менѝ ростовкувати? (5v)	Хто-б міг се все менї розтовкувати (7)
*Оччàював потòмству Фортінбраса (6r)	Одчаював потомству Фортінбраса (8)
*Гамлетовѝ (6r)	Гамлєтови (8)
за кусòк насущний хліба (6r)	за шматок насушний хліба (8)
як тѝлько 'двоювати (6r)	як лїш одвоювати (8)
*кòлоту-тревòги по вкраїні (6r)	і колоту-тріоги по вкраїнї (8)
*инше (6r)	иньше (8)
*войнѝ (6r)	війни (8)
*перет тим (6v)	перед тим (8)
*гулицях (6v)	по улицях (8)
світѝло вòгке (6v)	вогке сьвітило (8)

преттѐчі (6v)	*предтечі* (9)
прдлокги (6v)	*прологи* (9)
звичайни вістовці (6v)	*звичайні віщуни* (9)
У наших климатурах і в земляцтві (6v)	*У нашому підсоню і в народі* (9)
ілюзіе! (6v)	*привиде!* (9)
Ось, ось воно де! (7r)	*Ось, ось він де!* (9)
злюка (7r)	*грішник* (10)
*Втекае (7v)	*Втїкає* (10)
и ніякиі чари (7v)	*анї якії чари* (10)
и йму частину віри (7v)	*і йму по троха віри* (10)
*найлучче вранці (8r)	*найлучше в ранці* (11)

Among the above corrections, words marked with an asterisk (*) were not accounted for by Hordynsʹkyj (1928, 120–121), according to whom such cases could be viewed as minor or "common changes" as opposed to the "special changes." As evidenced above, the special changes, containing lexical, derivational, and morphosyntactic emendations, were introduced by Franko *en masse*.

However, on closer inspection, only a few of these changes look reasonable. The bulk of the emendations and substitutions seem to infringe on the language of the translation, taken as a system whose phonetic and morphosyntactic features are dialectally and stylistically balanced. Thus, when viewed as an isolated instance of "translation oddity," Kuliš's *potova pospišnost'* might in fact look awkward, especially if compared with the substitution proposed by Franko (i.e., *potom skroplena pospišnist'*). Yet, in this case, Kuliš seems to be closer to the "awkward original"—"sweaty haste" (Shakespeare, 1048). It is also tempting to question the validity of the expression *u našyx klymaturax i v zemljactvi*, and particularly the neologism *klymatura* (f.). Strange as it may appear though, the whole expression, including the aforementioned neologism, is more faithful to the original: "[demonstrated] unto our climatures and countrymen" (Shakespeare, 1049). On the other hand, Franko's correction *tremtyš, poblid* appears more appropriate since the past tense gerund in Kuliš's *tremtyš* [,] *poblidšy* slows down the narrative and is hard to pronounce. Perhaps the unexpected use by Kuliš of the loan word *iljuzija* (as a replica of the English "illusion" [Shakespeare, 1049]), not attested at that time in Ukrainian dictionaries, might also look too innovative in comparison with the more regular *pryvyd* offered by Franko.

While scrutinizing Franko's editorial changes, hailed by Hordyns'kyj (1928, 155) as most beneficial, it becomes obvious that something more significant in Kuliš's translations escaped the attention of his critics, to wit, his pioneering efforts in the normalization of literary Ukrainian. Premised on Southeast Ukrainian, Kuliš was inclined to tolerate not only multidialectal admixtures and liberal borrowing from other languages but also numerous derivatives. This said, some changes made by Franko likely look less persuasive. For instance, one can question such substitutions as *obrazylos'* for *obidylos'* and *viščuny* for *vistovci*. In the case of *obidylos'* "It is offended" (Shakespeare, 1048), the substitution was not well grounded, since this lexeme was commonplace in Dnieper Ukraine (Hrinč., 2:14) and could easily be left in Kuliš's translation. The form *vistovci* "messengers" was an innovative form aptly derived from a verb like *věstovati* "to inform, bring news" (eighteenth century) (Tymč., 490) with the help of the agentive suffix *-ec'*, known since early Middle Ukrainian (Humec'ka 1958, 80). By offering the lexeme *vistovci*, attested subsequently only in the dictionary of Borys Hrinčenko (Hrinč., 1:283), Kuliš proved quite creative, especially if one takes into account the Church Slavonicism *viščuny* suggested by Franko instead. Bringing forth a secondary meaning in the lexeme *xurtovyna* "snowstorm, storm, misfortune," quite commonplace in Southeast Ukrainian (Hrinč., 2:930), is, to be sure, another example of Kuliš's innovative use of the linguistic means available in his system.

Treated by Hordyns'kyj (1928, 120, 141) as negligible, the so-called common changes, including orthographic ones, are on the contrary most symptomatic. First of all, according to Hordyns'kyj, they are substitutions of the type *de* for *hde* "where," *todi* for *tohdi* "then," *pirja* for *pirr'ja* (coll.) "feathers," *oce* for *otse* "this," *vijny* for *vojny* (gen.) "war," including also some lexical substitutions like *poty poky* for *doty doky* "until" (ibid., 120) (see also *tohdi* "then," *pocilovaty* "to kiss," and *podvir'je* "yard" in the 1857 edition of Kuliš's *Čorna rada* [Black Council] [ČR, 99, 103, 104]). Leaving aside most lexical substitutions reflecting, in general, the lexical make-up of the Galician-Bukovynian koiné and some rural (Dniester) dialects, all other changes, particularly those in spelling, can be compared with the editorial intervention of Puljuj in the translation of several biblical books made by Nečuj-Levyc′kyj for the 1903 edition of the Bible. In other words, Franko aimed, though subconsciously, at making Kuliš's translation of *Hamlet* look more regional (Galician) and vernacular-oriented, thus stripping it of the pan-Ukrainian perspective discernable in Kuliš's creative interpretation of the Bible and Shakespeare (Ohijenko 1949, 224, 227).

The editor strove also to eliminate cases of phonetic spelling employed by Kuliš in order to render various types of assimilation of consonants. Instances like *ne javyccja* "[the ghost] will not appear" could hardly be tolerated in Galicia, where the Russophiles propagated etymological spelling and the populists defended the so-called *želexivka*, characterized according to Nečuj-Levyc′kyj (Nečuj-Levic′kyj 1912, 7) by "the doubling of Hallelujah" (the use of two dots in the letter *ï* as in Franko's substitution *menï* above) and other diagnostic features of the Dniester dialect and its phonetics. It is no wonder either that Franko meticulously eliminated all traces of apheresis as exemplified, for example, by *til′ko 'dvojuvaty* "but to recover [of us]" (Shakespeare, 1048)—literally, "only to recover." The latter phenomenon is known to have developed in avoiding the hiatus in North Ukrainian, and especially in East Polissja (Shevelov 1979, 452), where Kuliš was reared (Matvijas 2008, 95).

Kuliš consistently denoted the velar [g] in both new and long naturalized borrowings, employing either the Roman letter "g" as in his novel *Čorna rada* (Black Council), or the digraph "кг" as in his versified Bible. However, the use of this sound in conjunction with corresponding graphic devices is more typical of the Galician-Bukovynian koiné rather than North Ukrainian and, least of all, Southeast Ukrainian (Danylenko 2005). This is why Franko deemed it possible to introduce the corresponding spelling even in those forms, which, in accordance with Kuliš's native phonetics, would not tolerate such a sound (e.g., *Norvega* [gen.] "Norwegian"). What is also remarkable here is that Franko made use of the Roman letter "g" instead of the digraph "кг" found in Kuliš's protograph, whence *prology* offered by Franko instead of *prolokhy* (pl.) "prologue [to the omen]" in Kuliš (Shakespeare, 1049).

Franko also introduced palatalization of *z*, *c*, and *s* in the environment before *v* as, to give an example from the substitutions already cited, in *s′vidoctva* (gen.) "avouch" (Shakespeare, 1048). This spelling was controversial and could hardly satisfy speakers in Dnieper Ukraine. Even more controversial was the introduction by Franko of the palatalized *l'* in foreign words, first and foremost in personal names such as *Marcel'* instead of *Marcel* (Marcellus) and, most tellingly, *Hamljet* instead of *Hamlet* in Kuliš. Remarkably, the same spelling, *Hamljet*, was imposed by Franko in the edition of Fed´kovyč's *Hemlet Viljama Šekspira* (*Hemlet*-F). Dictated by Polish mediation rather than Franko's allegedly "better feel for the language" (Hordyns´kyj 1928, 155), this kind of spelling was alien to Kuliš and subsequently had little chance to gain the support of the bilingual intelligentsia and other social groups in Russian-ruled Ukraine (Shevelov 1989, 132–133). In fact, the problem lay not so much in the use of *l'* and *g* in foreign words as in the ratio and level of tradition of such instances in written Ukrainian. In Kuliš's language, the cases of *l'* and *g* were tested for their rootedness in the older literary tradition, as was the case of *ljampa*, occurring both in old and more recent borrowings. Such a distribution of these forms in the language of Kuliš reflected the eastern Ukrainian phonemic system, ultimately placed at the foundation of new literary Ukrainian (Danylenko 2005, 52).

The rest of Franko's substitutions were also intrinsically regional and, therefore, likely to distort the overall make-up of Kuliš's language, especially as they included a substantial admixture of western Ukrainian forms mediated in some cases by Polish. With this in mind, one wonders whether Franko's change of Polissian *hulycja* "street" in Kuliš's protograph into *ulycja* (without prosthesis), more typical of Lemkian and Central Transcarpathian, was well grounded. Perhaps Franko was inclined to treat this form as one of the recent loan words (Pol. *ulica*), which did not, in general, take any prothetic consonants (Shevelov 1979, 448, 454). One wonders whether Franko had the right to eliminate instances of the retention (reintroduction) of the etymological *o* in place of the new *i*, as in *vojny* (gen.) "war" and *pospišnost'* "haste." Interestingly enough, this was a practice implemented on a moderate scale by Puljuj and Sljusarčuk in the "canonical translation" of the 1903 Bible, which differed in its orthography and vocabulary from Kuliš's original translation. As in the Bible, cases of the retention of the etymological *o* in Kuliš's translations of Shakespeare could be stylistically marked, while reflecting an areal, northeastern or northern Ukrainian phenomenon, perceived by the translator as part of the norm (Matvijas 2008, 96).

To round out the list of Galician features hidden behind the substitutions offered by Franko, one should finally mention *u pidsonnju* (loc.) "climature" (Shakespeare, 1049) replacing *pidsonni* (loc.), which would otherwise fit into the language standard of Kuliš. Dubbed in the early twentieth century by Nečuj-Levyc´kyj (Nečuj-Levic´kyj 1907, 18) the "Galician/Polish locative," forms ending in *-u* had been retained, possibly under the influence of the Polish literary tradition, in Southwest Ukrainian since the Middle Ukrainian period (Kernyc´kyj 1967, 74). It is no surprise when one comes across such forms in the language of Franko and other normalizers of literary Ukrainian in Galicia, Bukovyna, and Transcarpathia from the beginning of the nineteenth century onward (Macjuk 2001, 277).

To sum up, if viewed through the prism of Kuliš's normalizing efforts, Franko's substitutions look regionally tainted. No doubt his editorial intrusion was at variance with Kuliš's language program. As in his translation of the Bible, Kuliš's ultimate ideal of literary Ukrainian aimed at its Europeanization through a synthesis of southeastern Ukrainian vernacular elements with various dialectal and stylistic admixtures. Among them one can name liberal borrowings from different languages, as well as some archaic and new derivatives following southwestern Ukrainian models (Shevelov 1966, 41–42). What Franko did was to pluck Kuliš's *Hamlet* out from the pan-Ukrainian context as construed by Kuliš in his literary works and place it within the confines of a regional cultural and linguistic paradigm. However, despite the Procrustean constraints, Kuliš's translation of Shakespeare proved more innovative linguistically than those made by his predecessors and could even compete with the translations made by his contemporaries (Myxajlo Staryc´kyj) and immediate followers (Panas Myrnyj, Lesja Ukrajinka, and Ivan Franko).

HAMLET IN PEASANT LEATHER SHOES

One of these contemporaries lived in Dnieper Ukraine and, almost simultaneously with Kuliš, set his heart on translating *Hamlet*. Ultimately his translation appeared in Kyiv in 1882, several months before the publication of Kuliš's "Ukrainian Shakespeare" in Lviv.

This was Myxajlo Staryc′kyj (1840–1904), a writer and theatrical and cultural activist who was known for his successful translations of the tales of Hans Christian Andersen (1873) and Serbian folk dumas and songs (1876), as well as his collection of poetry *Z davn′oho zšytku* (From an Old Notebook, two volumes, 1881, 1883) containing translations of George Gordon Byron, Heinrich Heine, Adam Mickiewicz, Mixail Lermontov, Nikolaj Nekrasov, and some other poets (Petrov 1884, 448). The publication of Staryc′kyj's translation of *Hamlet* became a seminal event in the cultural life of Dnieper Ukraine. His translation appeared despite draconian restrictions on Ukrainian-language publications in the Russian Empire following the enactment of the Valuev Circular (1863) and the Ems Decree (1876), which banned publication of "any original works or translations" in the "Little Russian dialect" (Miller 2003, 267). According to Lazurs′kyj (1929, 25), his translation crowned the so-called ethnographic-realistic period in the creation of the "Ukrainian Shakespeare."

What is particularly important about Staryc′kyj's translation is the fact that it was the first Ukrainian translation of a play by Shakespeare published with a commentary. The value of this publication was in no way diminished by the fact that most of Staryc′kyj's comments were naïve and superfluous, especially in respect to some linguistic forms found in Shakespeare. Let us take the beginning of Hamlet's famous monologue in Act 3, scene 1 as an illustration.

Staryc′kyj's Translation	**Shakespeare's Original**
Жити че не жити?	[To be, or not to be: that is
Ось в чімъ річъ. Бо що е	the question.
благороднішимъ.—	Whether 'tis nobler in the
Чи приймати і каміння й стріли	mind to suffer
Одъ лихоі-навісноі долі.	The slings and arrows of
Чи повстати на те море туги	outrageous fortune,
Й тимъ повстаннямъ покінчить	Or to take arms against a sea
все разомъ?	of troubles,
(*Hamlet*-S, 89–90)	And by opposing end them?]
	(Shakespeare, 1066)

In his comments, the translator explained his choice of the verb *žyty* "to live" by the fact that this expression would mean in English precisely "to exist, live." So he opted for the corresponding Ukrainian verb "since this is what is spoken about here" (*Hamlet*-S, 89). Some critics, including Daniil Mordovcev (Danylo Mordovec', 1830–1905), a Russian writer of Ukrainian origin, made a laughing stock out of the misconstrued line *žyty čy ne žyty— os' de zakavyka* (Pčilka 1904, 422). The last word, added by opponents of Ukrainian-language publications, was especially ridiculed, although, as was rightly noted by Franko (1955, 343), this form belonged to the Russian rather than the Ukrainian vocabulary. Nevertheless, Staryc'kyj's language, supposedly replete with incomprehensible and artificial (coined) forms, was long chastised in the local press, which mocked the very idea of translating Shakespeare into peasant parlance. The critique was rather shallow, to say the least. Some of the allegedly incomprehensible new words, as Staryc'kyj argued in his debates with these opponents, were subsequently incorporated into modern Ukrainian (e.g., *mrija* "hope, dream," *temrjava* "darkness," *pryvabnyj* "appealing," *znadlyvyj* "attractive," and the like [Pčilka 1904, 432]).

As if anticipating the future smear campaign of his critics, Staryc'kyj tried to explain in the introduction that his translation was aimed primarily at propagating Shakespeare and his major plays as well as advancing the development of the local idiom on the basis of classical examples. What inspired him in the case of Shakespeare was his "extremely vernacular, sometime even vulgar" language (Staryc'kyj 1882, i). Since the Ukrainian language at that time lacked adequate expressions for rendering high concepts of court etiquette, metaphors, and the embellishments of rhetoric, any phrase taken from Shakespeare could read in Ukrainian, as Staryc'kyj assumed, as "unnatural and forced" (ibid., ii). Trying to avoid such pitfalls, the translator decided to follow closely the original and resort therefore to those devices that had already been "approved in ethnography and literature" (ibid., iii). Among them were not only commonly accepted words like *terrasa* "terrace" or *scena* "scene" but also dialectal forms of the type *postoly* "a kind of peasant leather shoes" (for "sandals") and *paterycja* "staff, cane" (Hrinč., 2:374–375). Finally, the author deemed it necessary to praise Kuliš, a famous translator of the

Holy Scriptures into Ukrainian, who had launched the publication of "the whole of Shakespeare." Thus, the more translations appeared in Ukrainian, Staryc´kyj (1882, v) concluded, the more effective the work on the normalization of the literary language, which at that time was yet extremely underdeveloped, would be.

Although his achievements were more than obvious, Staryc´kyj failed to accomplish his plan (Šapovalova 1976, 79–80). For instance, the translator did his best to distinguish between prose and verse as in the original while stopping short of using rhymed couplets. Staryc´kyj also changed the iambic pentameter, a common meter in classical English literature including Shakespeare's canon, into the trochee foot, which was typically used in Ukrainian literature—in particular in the translator's own poetic oeuvre. Some deviations from the original resulted in an increased number of lines as compared with the original text. All this, according to Šapovalova (ibid., 79), made the end result somewhat monotonous and rather less dynamic, thus greatly diminishing the faithfulness of the translation in general. As a result, Staryc´kyj's translation turned out to be much longer than Shakespeare's *Hamlet* (Franko 1899, xix–xx). However, despite these shortcomings, Staryc´kyj's text read smoothly, thus demonstrating the work of a great master of the Ukrainian language (ibid.).

As has been mentioned, Staryc´kyj's translation received mostly unfavorable reviews. Yet even a cursory look at them suggests that the critique of his work was largely unfair and poorly grounded. The most biased review, entitled "Gamlet v postolax" (Hamlet in Peasant Leather Shoes), appeared in *Kievljanin*, a Russian chauvinist newspaper of Kyiv. Mocking the language of the translation, the anonymous author argued that there was no need for this kind of experiment in Ukrainian since the language simply did not exist in a literary form (Šapovalova 1976, 84). What was most frustrating for Staryc´kyj was that even some supporters of the Ukrainian literature and language failed to note positive aspects of his translation. Thus, a Ukrainian sympathizer, Nikolaj Petrov, in his *Očerki istorii ukrainskoj literatury XIX stoletija* (Notes on the History of Ukrainian Literature of the 19th Century, 1884), reiterated some most unscrupulous theses from reviews published by conservative and reactionary periodicals. Already, the first translations made by Staryc´kyj were called by Petrov "stillborn." He blatantly repeated, following one of the reviewers, that Staryc´kyj's translations could hardly find their readers since their language was uneven, fussy, and filled with ornament, provincialisms, Polish and German borrowings, and "inaptly coined words" (ibid., 448). This appraisal of Staryc´kyj's language was despicably unfair. Suffice it to add that Petrov failed to furnish any example or convincing argumentation.

Quite discouraging in this context was the critique of a Ukrainian literary critic and art scholar, Vasyl´ Horlenko (1853–1907). In his bibliographical survey of 1882 Ukrainian-language literary works he contrasted the language of Staryc´kyj's translations with the language of Leonid Hlibov (1827–1893), a populist writer and civic figure, to the detriment of the former. The critic's main concern was, purportedly, the artificial nature of Staryc´kyj's language. Hlibov also used some coined words. Yet, according to Horlenko, they could hardly be considered artificial since they were modeled, in contrast to Staryc´kyj's approach, on the true spirit of vernacular Ukrainian. In Staryc´kyj's translation, on the contrary, one stumbled upon such words, which, although semantically transparent, gave the impression that they had been prepared "somewhere in a special smithy" (Gorlenko 1883, 359). Among such allegedly artificial words, Horlenko cited *xvalij* "that who praises," lacking in vernacular Ukrainian (ibid., 360; Petrov 1884, 459). However, the word was coined in the very spirit of the Ukrainian language, whose derivational suffix -*ij* is used mainly in Volhynja, Podolja, and some Dniester dialects (Pokal´čuk 1969, 56; Matvijas 2005b, 6, 9). It is not therefore surprising that, as early as 1886, the word *xvalij* (see also *xval´nyk*, *xvalytel´*) made its way into the dictionary of Jevhen Želexivs´kyj (Žel., 2:1035) and subsequently into the dictionary of Borys Hrinčenko (Hrinč., 2:900).

Disappointingly, the tone for all of the negative reviews might have been set by Kostomarov in his programmatic article of 1882. In 1883, he also published an annihilating survey of the literary output of Kuliš, including his translations of the New Testament and Shakespeare (Kostomarov 1883). However, Staryc´kyj happened to be the first in a line of those who, allegedly, misled the Ukrainian people in matters cultural and literary. In particular, Kostomarov tried to explain the objectives of Ukrainophilism through the prism of the recent Ukrainian-language almanac *Luna* (Echo, 1881) in which Staryc′kyj published several of his translations.

Having sketched the historical and political underpinnings of modern Ukrainian society, Kostomarov (1882, 892) denounced efforts to keep developing the Ukrainian language through the creation of new words and expressions since, as he believed, they would simply "expose a pride often vain and inappropriate." Strangely, he doubted also that the younger generation of such ambitious Ukrainian writers would ever come up with neologisms that could be juxtaposed with those introduced by Russians (ibid.). From among the "ill-coined" words, he selected *bajdužist′* "indifference" derived, according to him, from the adverb *bajduže* "indifferently." He ridiculed the form *bajdužist′* by comparing it with the hypothetical Russian counterpart *vsenupočemnost′*, which would be treated by any Russian speaker as odd, to say the least (ibid., 893).

At the same time, Kostomarov praised a short story authored by Levyc′kyj, as he remained faithful to the realistic depiction of the Ukrainian peasantry. The point is that the critic believed that Ukrainian literature was designed exclusively for the peasantry as the basis of Ukrainian society. This is why it would be absurd to force literary status on Ukrainian, as if it were a language serving a full-fledged literature and science. In other words, the closer the writer was to the common people, the more successful he would be, as was the case, for instance, of Kvitka-Osnov'janenko in Sloboda Ukraine (Kostomarov 1882, 896). As a result, Kostomarov also expressed his deep skepticism as to whether the Ukrainians needed translations that were not comprehensible to the commoners. Among such inappropriate translations he mentioned first of all those made by Staryc′kyj and other contemporary literati from Shakespeare, Byron, Andersen, Mickiewicz, and the like (ibid., 897). In the aftermath of the 1876 pogrom of Ukrainian culture (see Danylenko 2010b), Kostomarov's logic seemed controversial, even harmful to the Ukrainian idea as propagated by Ukrainophiles—if the Ukrainian language was doomed to vanish, let it disappear without any pressure or enforcement from such writers as Staryc′kyj (Kostomarov 1882, 897). The Ukrainians, Kostomarov (1882, 900) believed, had to "leave all Byrons, Mickiewiczs, etc. in peace and not resort to the forcible coining of words and expressions that are not understandable to the commoners." As far as the Ukrainian intellectuals were concerned, they could read all those works in the original or with the help of Russian-language translations (ibid.).

The damage was done. It could not be rectified even by several positive reviews that praised translations made by Staryc´kyj for the benefit of literary Ukrainian (Šapovalova 1976, 86–87). Neither could an essay authored by Franko in 1902 (Franko 1955) or rather warm, if somewhat subjective, reminiscences written by the Ukrainian feminist writer, Olena Pčilka (Olha Kosač, 1849–1930), change the generally unfavorable reception of Staryc´kyj's translations. Pčilka recalled that, with an eye to producing a faithful translation of *Hamlet*, Staryc´kyj familiarized himself with the best French and German translations available, scrutinized the original with the assistance of a native speaker, and compared his translation with the original line by line; as a result, his translation turned out to be faithful and "very good" (Pčilka 1904, 421). In view of the underdog status of written Ukrainian, Pčilka inferred, this was a great translation deserving full credit (ibid., 422).

Interestingly enough, Pčilka did not discuss the possible influence of Kuliš on Staryc´kyj's translation of *Hamlet*. Franko filled in this blank in 1902. He mentioned Staryc´kyj's role in the development of literary Ukrainian in comparison with Kuliš, whose contribution was downgraded by Franko to the level of a mere epigone lacking much of Ševčenko's wit and style. The final verdict of Franko was disparaging. Unlike Staryc´kyj, whose original works and translations looked innovative despite some flaws in the form and language, Kuliš allegedly struggled all his life with the authority of Ševčenko, to no avail. Even in his translations of the Bible and Shakespeare, he purportedly failed to find an exit from the impasse into which he had worked himself (Franko 1902, 307). Clearly, this was another case of a biased appraisal that looked narrow and provincial (Luckyj 1983, 151).

An objective comparative perspective of the translations made by Staryc´kyj and Kuliš was offered as late as 1929 by Mykola Zerov, who convincingly refuted Franko's thesis about Kuliš's epigonism. Zerov (1960, 229–230) argued in particular that in his poems of the 1870s and 1880s Kuliš broke the confines of a literary and linguistic canon that had emerged during the Ševčenko period. In fact, Kuliš's translations and his theory of Old Rusian (*staroruščyna*) were aimed at the development of means to meet the demands of "pan-human thought." While introducing new stylistics, in particular in his translations, Kuliš differed from Staryc´kyj in that his innovative approach was deeply rooted in romantic and populist ideals, thus appearing more evolutionary and natural. By contrast, Staryc´kyj took a risk publishing his translation of *Hamlet* under the particularly unfavorable socio-cultural conditions existing in tsarist Russia (ibid., 231, 234, 237). This is why his normalizing efforts were largely viewed as inadequate and artificial by a cohort of biased critics and even some leading Ukrainophiles like Kostomarov and Horlenko.

As Zerov (1960, 240) rightly pointed out, Staryc´kyj's lexical neologisms were deliberately misconstrued and had never been catalogued by linguists. Paradoxically, Staryc´kyj's attitude toward linguistic innovation, in general, was quite temperate. Before introducing a particular form, he always checked it against existing vernacular and dialectal derivational patterns. In 1930, Pavlo Fylypovyč (1891–1937) demonstrated that many of the neologisms allegedly coined by Staryc´kyj were in fact attested in different Ukrainian dictionaries, first and foremost in the dictionary of Jevhen Želexivs´kyj. To give a few examples, Fylypovyč (1930, xxviii) mentioned such forms as *hordota* "pride," *lyxosliv'je* "swearing, cursing," and *nedijnis't'* "inactiveness" (Žel., 1:152, 406, 506).

However, as Shevelov (1966, 54) noted, some of the words cited by Fylypovyč had made their way into the dictionary of Jevhen Želexivs´kyj from the works of Staryc´kyj. Moreover, the bulk of the purportedly coined words were not even created by Staryc´kyj. They were borrowed from Right-Bank Ukraine, that is, Volhynja, Galicia, and even directly from the Polish language. However, Shevelov concluded against all odds that the author should be given credit for his innovative approach. While introducing forms of western Ukrainian and sometimes Polish origin, Staryc´kyj aimed at a synthesis of elements borrowed from different dialects and languages (ibid., 59). Indeed, Staryc´kyj's linguistic views were largely reminiscent of Kuliš's ideas. The difference lay perhaps in the conditions under which the two authors were trying to promote their programs and the milieus in which they were working. One should bear in mind also that Kuliš represented the older generation of Ukrainian writers while Staryc´kyj, more energetic and influential than most of his contemporaries, belonged to the younger generation. Different as they might appear in their programmatic views, Staryc´kyj and his advocates seemed to follow *in principle* the normalizing practice first introduced by Kuliš in his translations and original literary output.

Based on Southeast Ukrainian, the language of Staryc´kyj's translation of *Hamlet* does not contain so many coined words as one would expect. Neither has it any substantial amount of loan forms, especially if compared with the translation of Kuliš. Some interesting dialectal admixtures are found, nevertheless, in the phonetics. As in Kuliš's translations of the Bible, Staryc´kyj uses southwestern Ukrainian forms like *hrjanyčnyj* "(related to) border" (*Hamlet*-S, 11), *krivavyj* "bleeding (sword)" (ibid., 81, Shakespeare, 1064), and *rozxristana* "the mobled [queen]" (*Hamlet*-S, 82, Shakespeare, 1064) (see *čotyri* "four" [*Hamlet*-S, 65], attested mostly in Southeast Ukrainian [Shevelov 1979, 667]). Some of those forms are also found in Kuliš's translation of *Hamlet* such as *krivavyj* (*Hamlet*-K, 6v). Interestingly, unlike Kuliš, who used more or less consistently the velar [g] in loan words, Staryc´kyj was obviously reluctant to use this sound save for in the long naturalized lexemes of Southeast Ukrainian like *khvaltovnyj* "sudden" next to *norveh* "Norwegian," *proloh* "prologue," and *Vittenberh* (Gr. Wittenberg) (*Hamlet*-S, 10, 9, 23, 103). It should be recalled also that in the latter case Kuliš did not use the velar sound either (*Hamlet*-K, 5r), which was introduced by Franko in his translations in accordance with the regional (Galician) practice. Most revealing, however, are *nebezpešnyj* "dangerous" (*Hamlet*-S, 31) and *poštyvo* "in honorable fashion" (ibid., 35, Shakespeare, 1054) with a clearly Transcarpathian dialectal simplification of *č* to *š* (Shevelov 1979, 741).

A rare occurrence of *podobnyx"* (gen. pl.) "similar" without *ikavism* (MoUkr. *podibnyj*) might be dialectal as was usual, for example, in the eastern Polissian dialects as reflected in the language of Kuliš (Matvijas 2008, 96) (e.g., *pod"* "under" [*Hamlet*-K, 30r]). Yet, most likely, this use was influenced by the corresponding Russian Church Slavonic form. Here belongs also the consistent use of the preposition/prefix *od*-, typical of the language of Central Dnieper writers, including Nečuj-Levyc´kyj and Kuliš, in particular in their biblical translations, as well as Panas

Myrnyj (Hrycenko 2007, 30) (e.g., *od"* "from," *odpovid'* "answer," *oddjačyt'* "to thank" [*Hamlet*-S, 85, 94, 100], and the like). The "Galician" form *vid* is not attested in Staryc'kyj's translation of *Hamlet*. A rare case of assimilative changes in the morpheme boundary is found in *kljanessja* (2 sg. pres.) "to swear" (ibid., 106). In this regard, Staryc'kyj's spelling has nothing to do with the phonetic spelling invented and used by Kuliš, especially during the last creative period of his life (Luckyj 1983, 180–188). Needless to say that in Kuliš's translation of *Hamlet* the use of so-called radical phonetics prevailed (*beš" šapky* "without a hat" [*Hamlet*-K, 28v] with a place and manner assimilation in *bez" šapky*).

In the morphology, one finds several representative forms paralleled in the language of Kuliš. Among them, deserving of attention are plural locatives of the type *hrudix* "breast," *očix* "eyes," and *plečix* "shoulders" (*Hamlet*-S, 46, 65, 82) with the ending -*ix*, typical of the Central Dnieper and Sloboda dialects (Bevzenko 1978, 112; Hrycenko 2007, 27). Similar forms are attested in the biblical translations made by Kuliš and Alexandrov, whose language is likewise based on Southeast Ukrainian. Of interest are competing vocative case forms like *pryncju* and *prynce* "prince!" (*Hamlet*-S, 23). The regular ending -*e* for this class of masculines is paralleled in the form *pryncju* whose use was primarily influenced by nouns with the suffix -*ec'* with the palatalized *c'* (Bevzenko 1978, 101). Staryc'kyj derived superlative forms with the help of the dialectal suffix -*ijš*-, which was also characteristic of Kuliš's language (Matvijas 2008, 97) (e.g., *čystijšyj* "cleanest," *červonijšyj* "reddest [color]" [*Hamlet*-S, 45] next to *najljutišyj voroh"* "dearest foe" [ibid., 24, Shakespeare, 1051], see also *holovnijša* [f.] "most important" [*Hamlet*-K, 6r]). One should mention also the southeastern Ukrainian superlative form *radnišyj* (*Hamlet*-S, 91) from *radyj* "happy." It is no surprise that this form is attested in the language of Panas Myrnyj (Hrycenko 2007, 27). In this respect, it is worth citing unusual (dialectal) numeral forms ending in -*ijči* in the language of Kuliš such as *dvijči* "twice" and *trijči* "thrice, three times" (*Hamlet*-K, 4r, 5r, 29r) (compare *dvijčy* in North Ukrainian [Lysenko, 64]).

Among all other non-verbal forms found in Staryc'kyj's translation of *Hamlet*, of interest is the dative form *myni* "to me" used throughout the whole translation (e.g., *Hamlet*-S, 8). This old vernacular form was commonplace not only in Middle Ukrainian texts, especially those extant from the north of Ukraine (Kernyc´kyj 1967, 124), but also in the writings of early Ševčenko and Kuliš (Tymošenko 1969, 104–106).

The verb morphology in Staryc´kyj is consistently non-western Ukrainian. In this respect, the most representative examples are *vyxodjut´* "they exit" (*Hamlet*-S, 15) and, first and foremost, 3 sg. present forms of the type *maxa* next to *maxaje* "to wave," *promovlja* next to *promovljaje* "to speak," *znyka* "to disappear," *lama* "to break," *včašča* "to visit," and the like (ibid., 8, 9, 37, 40, 74). Such forms are attested today primarily in Southeast Ukrainian as well as in some eastern Polissian and Volhynian dialects (Vaščenko 1957, 223–225, 232; Matvijas 2006, 63). Remarkably, unlike Kuliš, Staryc´kyj almost neglected erstwhile perfect forms of the type *este davaly* "you have given" (*Hamlet*-S, 16). On the other hand, the use of pluperfect formations did not differ much from that found in Southeast Ukrainian, although there are only a few forms, such as *zhubyv buv* "he had lost" (*Hamlet*-S, 11), in the whole text of Staryc´kyj's *Hamlet*. Unlike their folkloric coloring in Staryc´kyj's translation, the pluperfect together with the obsolete perfect formation had rather an archaizing effect in Kuliš's translation. It is no wonder that the pluperfect formation was particularly preferred by Nečuj-Levyc´kyj in his part of the translation of the Bible.

Among other tense forms, one should mention the so-called synthetic future form ending in *-mu* used by Staryc´kyj throughout the translation. We do not have statistics but, tentatively, the use of this form might be very similar to that in Kuliš's translations. The only difference is dialectal. In the case of Kuliš, the provenance of the synthetic future was northern Ukrainian, while Staryc´kyj could rely on the southeastern Ukrainian dialectal usage of the future with the auxiliary clitic *-mu* concatenated with the infinitive (Danylenko 2011a, 173). In some cases, they do not reveal any inceptive semantics, thus competing with the more common analytic future tense with the auxiliary *budu* used across the Ukrainian speaking territories (e.g., *poky naležatyme myni* [*Hamlet*-S, 65] "while it will be belonging to me," compared with "whilst this machine is to him [Hamlet]" [Shakespeare, 1060], [*tijatr*] *mav, mae i matyme* [*Hamlet*-S,

97] "the theater had, has and will have," and *predstavljatymut'* "[they] will perform" [ibid., 103]).

To complete a survey of the representative morphosyntactic features in the language of Staryc´kyj, one may observe two more constructions.

First, one often encounters in Staryc´kyj, constructions such as *kynuty Vittenberha* (gen.) "to leave Wittenberg" (*Hamlet*-S, 23) and *zmaljuvaty partreta* (gen.) "to paint a portrait" (ibid., 57) with the so-called genitive-partitive case taken by the masculines. The latter is characteristic of Ukrainian, Belarusian, and some southern Russian dialects (Danylenko 2006c, 214). What is unusual about the aforementioned examples is that Staryc´kyj expanded the set of possible inanimate nouns that could take this type of genitive-partitive case, especially in contrast to the norms of modern Ukrainian (e.g., *prokažy-ž″ monoloha* [gen.] [*Hamlet*-S, 96] "speak the speech" [Shakespeare, 1068], that is, "[you will] deliver a monologue"). This feature is less pronounced in the language of Kuliš.

Second, as in the language of other central Ukrainian writers of that time, particularly Panas Myrnyj and Ivan Nečuj-Levyc´kyj, the translator routinely resorted to impersonal constructions with forms ending in *-no* and *-to* in the predicate and the accusative (genitive) direct object. No auxiliary is attested in such constructions, though they have, as a rule, the preterital meaning (Shevelov 1969) (e.g., *po vas posylano* "you were called for," *bat´ka moho vbyto* "my father was murdered," *mene vbyto* "I was murdered," *kazano jim″* "they were told," and so forth [*Hamlet*-S, 72, 88, 99, 100]). The fact that this type of construction was used by Kuliš less frequently testifies tentatively to its local provenance in the language of Staryc´kyj.

The critics' perception of Staryc´kyj's language as "alien" (Galician) was due to some lexical forms borrowed by the translator from different dialects or coined with the help of derivative means available in contemporary Ukrainian dialects. What is more remarkable about Staryc´kyj's translation of *Hamlet* is the presence of more Russian (Church Slavonic) than Galician (Polish) forms in this text. Among the former lexemes are *aktjer* "actor," *vozdux* "air," *buduščij xlib* "future bread," *postarajtes'* (imper.) "to try," *vetxyj* "old, ancient," and, perhaps, even a Ukrainianized *tijatr* "theater" (*Hamlet*-S, 16, 58, 75, 76, 81, 87). Here also belongs EUkr. *slučajem* "incidentally" (ibid., 59, 87) from *slučaj* "incident," attested cross-dialectally (Žel., 2:886; Hrinč., 2:664).

Kuliš was even more persistent in introducing such loan forms, whence the use of *vozdux"* "air," *hosudarstvo* "state" (*Hamlet*-K, 7r, 8r) compared to *panstvo* in Staryc´kyj (*Hamlet*-S, 15), as well as *movčuščyj* "silent," with the Church Slavonic suffix -*ušč*-, and *velyččje* "greatness," *dyxannje* "breath," and especially *spasennje* "salvation" together with *povedennje* "behavior" (*Hamlet*-K, 4v, 6v, 10v, 26v), also *preobrazytysja* "to change" and *yskustvo* "art" (ibid., 29v, 32r). In some cases, Kuliš used parallel—Ukrainian and Church Slavonic—forms, treating them as synonymous with slightly varying nuances in their meanings. One can mention here *džerelo* and *ystočnyk"* "source" found in the same sentence:

Він каже, дорога моя Гертрудо,
Що вже знайшовъ и джерело й источникъ
Турботы твого сына. (*Hamlet*-K, 31)

[He tells me, my sweet queen, that he hath found
The head and source of all your son's distemper.] (Shakespeare, 1059)

In Staryc´kyj's language, Galician forms are commonly found in parallel use with local forms: *zabijstvo* (Pol. *zabójstwo*; Vytv., 355) next to *dušohubstvo* "murder" (*Hamlet*-S, 86, 107), *zamir* (Pol. *zamiar*; Vytv., 362), *(po)žadane* (Pol. *żądanie*) next to *xit´*, *žaha* "wish, desire" (*Hamlet*-S, 31, 35, 37, 48; Vytv., 391).

There are, in fact, not so many neologisms proper in the language of Staryc´kyj. Some of them, as was pointed out by Shevelov (1966, 54), made their way to the dictionary of Jevhen Želexivs´kyj and not the other way around. These neologisms being attested in this dictionary, the public began treating them as Galician forms, sometimes ignoring the fact that the forms had been excerpted from Staryc´kyj's literary works. This was a trap into which some of the Ukrainian critiques fell while propounding the supposedly western Ukrainian origin of Staryc´kyj's coined words.

To show that the vector tended rather to work conversely, suffice it to cite randomly a few "Galician neologisms," derived in fact by Staryc′kyj:

дворовикъ "courtier" (*Hamlet*-S, 60), "attendant" (Shakespeare, 1049); SWUkr. *дворак* (Žel., 1:175); see *придворець* below;

здавання "look, pretending" (*Hamlet*-S, 19; Žel., 1:294);

зоружжя "weapon," *товариші по зоружжю* "comrades in arms" (*Hamlet*-S, 49; Žel., 1:313); EUkr. *зоружити* "to make, build" (Hrinč., 1:716);

кораблярня "shipyard" (*Hamlet*-S, 10; Žel., 1:365);

личкуватися "to feign, pretend" (*Hamlet*-S, 19; Žel., 1:407);

озбройний "armed" (*Hamlet*-S, 28; Žel., 1:562); SWUkr. *оружний* (ibid., 576);

певнякъ "a certain thing" (*Hamlet*-S, 92); "a self-confident person" in Southeast Ukrainian (Hrinč., 2:109) and "a laborer hired for a negotiated pay" in Southwest Ukrainian (Žel., 2:607);

постать "ghost" (*Hamlet*-S, 25), "behavior" in Kuliš (Žel., 2:718);

привідця "ghost" (*Hamlet*-S, 41), most likely borrowed from Kuliš (*привидця* in *Yov*, 1869, 72), SWUkr. *привидок* (Žel., 2:740); of interest is *страшна проява* (*Hamlet*-S, 7), "dreadful sight" (Shakespeare, 1048);

придворець "attendant" (*Hamlet*-S, 15, Shakespeare, 1049), attested as *придворці* (pl.) in Žel. (2:744); Kuliš's neologism *прибічник* (*Hamlet*-K, 30v) is found in Hrinč. (2:411) but not in the dictionary of Jevhen Želexivs′kyj;

причілля "visor" (*Hamlet*-S, 27) (see *забрало* in *Hamlet*-K, 20), "beaver" in Shakespeare (1052); SWUkr. *причіле* "forehead"

(Žel., 2:764), EUkr. *причіпок* "what is attached to something" (Hrinč., 2:457);

темритись "to darken" (*Hamlet*-S, 16; Žel., 2:956);

шаблёваний "armed with a sword" (*Hamlet*-S, 75; Žel., 2:1081).

It is noteworthy that the same tendency to introduce neologisms is observed in Kuliš's translation of *Hamlet*, although perhaps on a lesser scale. One of the curious examples is a re-interpretation of the word *korolycja* by Kuliš in the meaning "queen" (*Hamlet*-K; see "Matricaria chamomilla" in Žel., 1:368) and assiduously replaced with *koroleva* by Franko in 1899 (*Hamljet*-K/F).

Unlike Staryc´kyj, Kuliš was more consistent in introducing new borrowings from western European languages. In some cases he would simply transfer lexical elements without changing the source semantics and resort, in fact, to a kind of "interlingual homophony" (*yljuzija* "ghost" from "illusion" [*Hamlet*-K, 6v, Shakespeare, 1049], *brotel'* "brothel" from *brothel* [*Hamlet*-K, 28r, Shakespeare, 1058], *pasija* "sweetheart" from *passion* [*Hamlet*-K, 29r, Shakespeare, 1059]). An interesting experiment is the use of *partyzan"* (*Hamlet*-K, 7r) being a calque of "partisan" in Shakespeare's original (Shakespeare, 1049) and referring to a kind of spear or pike with two opposing axe blades or spikes (*kelep* "a big hammer" in Staryc´kyj's translation [*Hamlet*-S, 13; Hrinč., 1:770]). In sum, Kuliš is more open to western European forms than Staryc´kyj (*kuzyn, instrukcija* [*Hamlet*-K, 9v, 7r] compared to *nebiž* and *nakaz* in Staryc´kyj [*Hamlet*-S, 18, 17] for "cousin" and "message" in Shakespeare [Shakespeare, 1050]).

Dialectal, vernacular, and folkloric elements are markedly pronounced in Staryc´kyj's translation. Suffice it to cite the following deictic forms: *tepera* "now," *tuta* "here," and *nyn´ky* "nowadays" (*Hamlet*-S, 16, 21, 44, 88, etc.), also *povuz* "by, past" (ibid., 9, 25), modified most likely for syllabic-tonic purposes, in place of *povz* (Shevelov 1979, 479). Of interest is the vernacular onomatopoeic (predicative) particle *susil'* (*Hamlet*-S, 56), representing locomotion (a sudden appearance of the agent) and showing "semantic palatalization" of the final obstruent (Danylenko

2003, 218–222, 2015c, 532). Kuliš, in this respect, seems to be less vernacular-oriented, although he also sporadically makes use of some vernacular and dialectal forms like *tepera* "now" and *ottakol'ki* "that much" (*Hamlet*-K, 27r, 29r).

Staryc'kyj looks prepared to Ukrainianize other aspects of the narrative, whence, for instance, the use of folkloric clichés accompanied by diminutive forms: *moje serden'ko* "my dear" (*Hamlet*-S, 65) (MoUkr. *serce* "heart"), *zdoroven'ky* "hello" (ibid., 6, "welcome" in Shakespeare [Shakespeare, 1047]), *buvaj zdorov* in Kuliš's translation (*Hamlet*-K, 3v), *xlop'jata* "boys" (*Hamlet*-S, 70, "friends" in Shakespeare [Shakespeare, 1061]), *nyzen'ko* "low," *scenka* "stage" (*Hamlet*-S, 103), MoUkr. *nyz'ko*, *scena*, respectively. This trend is less obvious in Kuliš. Expressions like *kozače* (voc.) *mij* "my Cossack" (*Hamlet*-K, 29r) for "sir" in Shakespeare (1058) are relatively rare in his translation.

Quite commonplace in the language of Staryc'kyj are tautological constructions (Potebnja 1968, 216–247) of the type *pane-prynce* (voc.) "prince," *mandrivec'-hist'* "vagrant, travelling guest," *černec'-lukavec'* (*Hamlet*-S, 31, 48, 51, "ungracious pastor" [Shakespeare, 1053]), *vistun-poslanec'* "messenger" (*Hamlet*-S, 12), *dyvno-čudno* "[it is] surprising" (ibid., 84, "Is it not monstrous[?]" in Shakespeare [1065]), and *lyxa-navisna dolja* "outrageous fortune" from the famous "To be, or not to be . . ." soliloquy (*Hamlet*-S, 90, Shakespeare, 1066). Remarkably, Kuliš did not avoid using such constructions. However, viewed through the prism of the whole of his translation of *Hamlet*, these appear archaic rather than, strictly speaking, folkloric, as in the translation of Staryc'kyj. In other words, Kuliš's use of folkloric devices is reminiscent of that in the translation of the *Odyssey* by Potebnja, who seemed to proceed from medieval influences to folklore as the point of synthesis between history and the present (Danylenko 1999, 246–247, 2006c, 333–334). Remarkably, Kuliš in some cases modeled his constructions on seemingly repetitive expressions found in Shakespeare: *po tij rjadni-dohovory* (loc.) modeled on "by the same covenant and carriage of the [articled] design" (*Hamlet*-K, 6r, Shakespeare, 1048) and *kolotu-trevohy* (gen.) patterned on "[of] this post-haste and romage in the land" (*Hamlet*-K, 6r, Shakespeare, 1049) (compare *ta metušnja, ta klopit* in Staryc'kyj [*Hamlet*-S, 11]).

Thus Kuliš's translation appears to be a kind of replica of Shakespeare's *Hamlet* despite some cases of inappropriate Ukrainianization, as discussed above.

Finally, like Kuliš in his translation of *Hamlet*, Staryc´kyj glosses himself in lexical diversity and liberally employs parallel lexemes. The latter practice might have been influenced by the folkloric tradition and, what is more probable, the normalization-in-progress of literary Ukrainian at that time. It is worth citing such parallel forms as: *zabijstvo ~ dušohubstvo* "murder," *mara ~ postat´ ~ pryviddja* "ghost," *ozbrojnyj ~ oružnyj* "armed," *žadannja ~ xit´ ~ žaha ~ požadannja* "wish," *xutko ~ motorno ~ švydko* "fast," *družyna ~ žona* "wife," and *prydvorec´ ~ dvorovyk"* "attendant" (*Hamlet*-S, 15, 27, 28, 31, 34, 35, 36, 37, 48, 60, 86, 104, 106, 107, and so on). As a rule, these are interchangeable, although they are different by origin (e.g., *zabijstvo* from Polish compared to *dušohubstvo* from Church Slavonic, or the innovative derivation in *ozbrojnyj* "armed"). Here also belong cases of grammatical parallelism of the type *maxaje ~ maxa* (3 sg. pres.) "to wave" and *promovljaje ~ promovlja* (3 sg. pres.) "to speak" (ibid., 9, 10, 40, 41). Although both are attested in Southeast and North Ukrainian (with the exception of some eastern Polissian dialects) (Matvijas 2006, 63; *AUM*, 3, part 4, maps 216–217), the full form ending in *-aje* is clearly prevalent in the language of Staryc´kyj, as in the works of other Central Ukrainian writers of that period (Tymošenko 1969, 118–120).

As has been demonstrated, the two translators shared some linguistic predilections and translation procedures. Although belonging to different generations, both were pioneering normalizers of new literary Ukrainian in the making, especially during the second part of the nineteenth century. In particular, both believed that translations into Ukrainian would expand the functionality of literary Ukrainian and help crystalize its norms. Thus, there seems to be solid ground to claim that their language programs were almost identical, especially with regard to the coinage of new lexemes and introduction of words from different Ukrainian dialects and contacting languages. At the same time, however, there were also pronounced differences between their translations.

In general, Staryc´kyj's translation was simpler and less sophisticated compared with that made by Kuliš. Yet, however paradoxical it may be,

Staryc´kyj's text might be more easily comprehensible to contemporary readers. Kuliš was more sensitive to the historical dimension of the Ukrainian language, whence his wish to bring life back to the legendary Old Rusian language (*staroruščyna*) as the main literary variety of written Ukrainian. In a sense, he was more synthetic than Staryc´kyj, whose programmatic tenets were matters primarily of synchrony and space, thus including the southwestern dialectal area together with its neighboring languages, Polish and German. This is why his innovations were sometimes awkward and his syntax looked artificial. This is not observed to an equal extent in the language of Kuliš. Nevertheless, despite his innovative approach to the translation of Shakespeare, Kuliš was still anchored in the folkloric mode of poetic narrative. Hence his liberal use of folkloric devices, in particular diminutives, which would connect him with the first generation of Ukrainian translators such as Petro Hulak-Artemovs´kyj (Zerov 1967, 53).

It is hard to believe that only a few words created or borrowed by Staryc´kyj and Kuliš were subsequently integrated into modern literary Ukrainian (Shevelov 1966, 59). It is not, in fact, surprising, since the monodialectal ethnographic trend, which flourished from 1798 onward, ultimately prevailed in the development of literary Ukrainian during the late nineteenth and early twentieth centuries. This is why, though for different reasons, both Kuliš's and Staryc´kyj's translations of *Hamlet* belong today, according to some literary scholars (e.g., M. Moskalenko 2006 3/4, 171; 5/6, 180–181), to the history of literary culture and literary Ukrainian rather than its modern canon.

THE YOUNGER GENERATION STEPS TO THE FORE

Lesja Ukrajinka (the pseudonym of Larysa Kosač, 1871–1913), who belonged to the younger generation of Ukrainian writers, regarded both Kuliš and Staryc´kyj as her teachers in Ukrainian literature (Zerov 1960, 251). Indeed, the two authors were towering figures of the modern Ukrainian revival and, by that time, had made an extraordinary contribution to modern Ukrainian literature and the normalization of written Ukrainian. However different their language programs could be, the two strongly believed that Ukrainian translations of classic world literature were indispensable for the resurgence of Ukrainian culture and its promotion across Ukraine and beyond.

A founding member, along with her brother in 1888, of the literary circle *Plejada* (The Pleiades), Lesja Ukrajinka had no doubt that translations of the world's classics would benefit Ukrainian culture and literature. From among the plays of Shakespeare, Lesja Ukrajinka appreciated especially his tragedies *Hamlet, Othello, Macbeth, King Lear, Richard III*, and *Coriolanus* (Ukrajinka 1956, 201). Genuinely impressed by the translations of Kuliš and Staryc′kyj, Lesja Ukrajinka also decided to translate some plays of Shakespeare, prompting her at some point to begin studying English. As she wrote in one of her letters to her uncle, Myxajlo Drahomanov, dated 12 November 1893 (Ukrajinka 1956, 109), she was eager to read Shakespeare in the original (Minenko 2011). Most likely as late as 1894, when she stayed at Drahomanov's place in Sofia, Lesja Ukrajinka finally began reading Shakespeare in English; this ultimately expanded her vision of the English playwright and his oeuvre.

More often than not, Lesja Ukrajinka would speak of *Hamlet* and *King Lear*, as these were congenial to the views of the young poetess striving to project the universal values found in the works of Shakespeare onto her personal perception of the world. Shakespeare became a vital part of her creative tenets. Lesja Ukrajinka addressed the place and importance of Shakespeare in several articles devoted to various literary topics. She discussed, in particular, the place of Shakespeare as a playwright in the modern social drama of social groups in the nineteenth century. In another article, Lesja Ukrajinka offered a survey of "the women's question" in the European belles arts, arguing that one could hardly find a female character comparable to that of Cordelia, the youngest of King Lear's three daughters in Shakespeare's tragedy (Šapovalova 1976, 147–148). Shakespeare's themes are also easy to trace in some of Lesja Ukrajinka's literary works, in particular her "Adagio pensieroso" (1900), inspired by the tragic fate of Ophelia, whose death is presented in her work through the lens of Gertrude's views (ibid., 152–153).

Overall, Lesja Ukrajinka's highly personal interpretation of Shakespeare in her literary works and critical essays constitutes her major difference from Staryc'kyj and especially Kuliš, who considered translation of Shakespeare's works not so much a literary priority but a matter of moral and national instruction for Ukrainians. For Lesja Ukrajinka, Shakespeare was not important as an awakener of oppressed people but as a writer of unique caliber. All this might explain why Lesja Ukrajinka, who made a series of first-rate translations of such authors as Homer, Dante Alighieri, George Gordon Byron, Victor Hugo, and Adam Mickiewicz (Strixa 2006, 124–129), did not prepare a complete translation of any of Shakespeare's plays. Still, it is not clear why she did not undertake translating either *Hamlet* or *King Lear*, which are mentioned or incorporated one way or another into her literary and critical works as well as personal letters.

In March 1898, Lesja Ukrajinka wrote to her mother about her intent to translate the tragedy *Macbeth* (Ukrajinka 1956, 232). This ambition was not fulfilled. Lesja Ukrajinka translated only scenes 1, 2, and, partially, 3 from Act I (243 lines in total), first published in 1947 (Hozenpud 1947, 293–298), and never returned to this translation (*Makbet*-L). The fact that she did not complete her translation, which remained outside the mainstream of the "Ukrainian Shakespeare," was a true loss for the study of Shakespeare's works in Ukraine (Kočur 1968, 43). Nevertheless, fragmentary as it is, her translation demonstrates an essentially new understanding of both the tragedy and the Ukrainian language into which it should be creatively "transposed." Even a brief survey can prove that Lesja Ukrajinka's translation differed largely from Kuliš's translation, this latter oriented, as has been discussed, toward both historical and contemporaneous dimensions of new literary Ukrainian.

Lesja Ukrajinka modernized *Macbeth* in an accessible style that could attract primarily the younger generation to the play's audacity (Minenko 2011). To some extent, one can agree that by lowering the register of the narrative, the translator lost the figurative power of Shakespeare's text and thereby achieved lucidity in the translation without compromising the "naturalness of its language" (Šapovalova 1976, 157). As evidenced in Lesja Ukrajinka's translation of *Macbeth*, such work is best served by "up-to-date, colloquial" Ukrainian rather than a more bookish variety. It is not surprising then to find in her translation just a handful of bookish and dialectal forms that, by contrast, were liberally used by Kuliš and even Staryc′kyj, whose language was rooted in modern dialectal diversity.

Among several regional forms found in Lesja Ukrajinka's translation, one notices very rare southwestern Ukrainian words like *trivoha* "alarm" and *vbiraty* "to dress" (*Makbet*-L, 2, 11, Shakespeare, 1187) (compare *krivava rana* "gash" in Kuliš [*Makbet*-K/F, 3, Shakespeare, 1185]) or a few northern Ukrainian forms without the expected *ikavism* like *tabor* "camp" (*Makbet*-L, 2) next to *tabir* in Kuliš. In all other cases, the language of Lesja Ukrajinka's translation looks quite natural, thus demonstrating relatively homogeneous southeastern Ukrainian features. For instance, unlike the northern Ukrainian neuters ending in -*e* after long palatalized consonants as used consistently by Kuliš, she resorts to modern forms ending in -*a* (e.g., *nasinnja* "seeds," *žyttja* "life," *znattja* "knowledge," and even Kuliš's neologism *pryvyddja* "ghost" [ibid., 8, 9, 11; compare *Yov*, 1869, 72; Hrinč., 2:412]; the latter formation is also attested in Staryc′kyj's translation of *Hamlet*).

A "natural" genitive-accusative for animates is used by Lesja Ukrajinka in *byty svynej* (gen.-acc. pl.) "kill[ing] swine" (*Makbet*-L, 6, Shakespeare, 1185), while Kuliš in this case resorts to his usual, primarily southwestern Ukrainian nominative-accusative direct object of inactive entities (animals, children, etc.) in the plural after the transitives (*AUM*, 3, part 3, map 41): *dušyla svyni* (nom.-acc. pl.) "strangled swine" (*Makbet*-K, 4r) (compare the accusative in *pasty svynï* [*SP/NZ*, 77] in Kuliš and Puljuj's translation of the Bible).

In the morphology, deserving of attention is another "natural" feature (i.e., a regular plural [erstwhile dual] form used in the environment after the numerals *dva*, *try*, *čotyry* [Bevzenko 1978, 64]): *try vid′my* (*Makbet*-L, 1) as compared with the collective numeral in *troje vidjom* "three witches" in Kuliš (*Makbet*-K, 2r) in accordance with the "spirit" of vernacular Ukrainian (Smerečyns′kyj 1932, 107).

The vocabulary of Lesja Ukrajinka also looks fairly well balanced and dialectally homogeneous from the point of view of new literary Ukrainian. There are fewer stylistic variants in her translation as compared with the wide array of stylistically marked lexemes in the language of Kuliš, such as *žinka morjaka* (*Makbet*-L, 5) "a sailor's wife" (Shakespeare,

1185) or *staršyna* "captains" (*Makbet*-L, 3), compared to the colloquial derivatives *locmanyxa* and *het'many* in Kuliš (*Makbet*-K, 3r, 4r). In total, Lesja Ukrajinka's translation has only a handful of overtly stylistically marked lexemes, for example:

> *владарь* (a non-pleophonic word, most likely, of western Slavic origin) (*Makbet*-L, 3, 5; Žel., 1:110) next to *король* (Old Rusian) from *Karl* (Shevelov 1979, 97) and *владика* (Church Slavonic) in Kuliš's translation (*Makbet*-L, 3v, 7r) (*king* in the original [Shakespeare, 1185]);

> *злотий* (*Makbet*-L, 5), most likely a Polish borrowing, different from the old eastern Slavic non-pleophonic form *злото* "gold" (Shevelov 1979, 96) (*карбованець* in Kuliš [*Makbet*-L, 4r]);

> *віншувати* "to hail" (*Makbet*-L, 11, Shakespeare, 1187; Žel., 1:106) (Pol. *winszować* [Vytv., 327]);

> *преславний* (Church Slavonic) "most worthy" (*Makbet*-L, 11, Shakespeare, 1187), used also by Kuliš.

The overall impression created by Lesja Ukrajinka's translation is that of its contemporaneity and homogeneity. If compared to the translation of Kuliš, her translation seems to be more attuned to populist demands and the system of today's literary Ukrainian. Although based primarily on Southeast Ukrainian with a small admixture of Church Slavonicisms, her language was also open to Galician elements. Interestingly, such elements were introduced by Lesja Ukrajinka not so much in the high-style register but in daily vocabulary (Shevelov 1966, 100). The latter strategy was different from that chosen by Kuliš, who opted for Galician elements with an eye towards enriching abstract vocabulary. This is why the language of Kuliš's translation, combining, on the one hand, "radical phonetics" in spelling and stylistically unusual lexical collocations, on the other, may look somewhat clumsy as compared to the language of Lesja Ukrajinka:

Kuliš's Translation	Lesja Ukrajinka's Translation
А що ж? в непевности вона стояла, Мов два пловця, як шчепляцця й мішають Один одному в плаванні мистецькім. Безощадний Макдональд, що пороки Стовпились до нёго на бунтовництво, Засіг собі их островів західніх Підмоги в Кернів та у Кгаловкгласян. (*Makbet*-K, 2v)	Там обидва війська, Мов два плавці, що плинуть навперейми, А силою однакові. Там лютий Макдональд-бунтівник (такий він зроду, До нього все, що є лихого в світі, Зібралось), він з західних островів Зібрав до себе кернів, галловгласів. (*Makbet*-L, 2)

[Doubtful it stood, As two spent swimmers that do cling together And choke their art. The merciless Macdonald— Worthy to be a rebel, for to that The multiplying villainies of nature Do swarm upon him—from the Western Isles Of kerns and gallowglasses is suppli'd.] (Shakespeare, 1184–1185)

In sum, if assessed through the prism of the vernacular-based standard of modern Ukrainian, Kuliš's translation might appear incoherent and anachronistic. However, if evaluated from the point of view of hypothetical possibilities, Kuliš's *Makbet* exposes a parallel pathway for normalization and standardization, which literary Ukrainian could have taken in the second part of the nineteenth century.

"WE ARE ALL PEASANTS TODAY"

Panas Myrnyj (pseudonym of Panas Rudčenko, 1849–1920) was a prominent populist writer and normalizer of literary Ukrainian who, inspired by the work of Kuliš and Staryc´kyj, took his chance at translating

Shakespeare. He also translated the Song of Songs, although the quality of this paraphrase, permeated with highly regional vernacular forms, left much to be desired.

Panas Myrnyj tackled two of Shakespeare's plays, *Macbeth* and *King Lear*. As early as 1882, in one of his letters to Staryc´kyj, Panas Myrnyj (1971, 363) admitted that his first attempt to translate *Macbeth* was a complete disaster. He managed to translate Act 1, scenes 1, 2 and, partially, 3, and never returned to this translation afterward, discouraged by some insurmountable difficulties he faced at the very outset of the project. In the spirit of the populist *Weltanschauung*, he concluded disparagingly that

> however you translate Shakespeare, he sounds somewhat weird in our tongue; there is no real speech, not even a single human being. This is, I think, because he depicts a life unfamiliar to all of us; it is all about either kings or their courtiers while we are all peasants today . . . and under alien and unusual circumstance, all that seems alien. (ibid.)

What a chasm between, on the one hand, the *Kulturträgerism* of Kuliš prophesying the coming of a new messiah, Shakespeare, to deliver the unworthy Ukrainian people from their barbarism and, on the other, this homestead perception of the English playwright's legacy expressed in terms of local parochialism! It is no wonder that such a parochial vision of Shakespeare heavily affected Panas Myrnyj's translation, which appeared rustic when compared to the language of Kuliš and especially of Lesja Ukrajinka's translation, premised largely on the same populist foundations (Shevelov 1966, 100):

Panas Myrnyj's Translation	**Lesja Ukrajinka's Translation**
Сказать поправді— . . .	Кажу вам правду, що вони обидва,
Як хмара стріл і куль гудючих	Немов з подвійними набоями
Вони ударили на лави ворогів.	гармати,
Один Бог зна чого вони хотіли:	Отак вони подвійно вдарили на
Чі вмерти у гарячій вражій крові,	ворога завзято.

Kuliš's Translation	Shakespeare's Original
Чі нагадати знову всі страхи на Голгофі . . . Але я підтомивсь; заграли мої рани. (*Makbet*-M, 3)	Вони в крові скупатися хотіли, Чі нагадати людям про Голгофу, Запевне так . . . Але я млію: рани всі одкрились . . . . (*Makbet*-L, 5)
Коли по правді Казати вам, то се були гармати З двійним набоем: так вони | сипнули На ворога ударами двойними. Хиба б сказати, що вони хотіли Купатись у крівавих свіжих ранах, Чи ввіковічити нову Голгоθу,— Не знаю й сам . . . Та я ослаб; рятунку просять рани. (*Makbet*-K, 3r–3v)	[If I say sooth, I must report they were As cannons overcharg'd with double cracks; so they Doubly redoubled strokes upon the foe. Except they meant to bathe in reeking wounds, Or memorize another Golgotha, I cannot tell. But I am faint, my gashes cry for help.] (Shakespeare, 1185)

In 1895–1897, Panas Myrnyj worked assiduously on his translation of *King Lear*, which was based, as Šapovalova (1976, 106–109) convincingly demonstrated, on the 1893 prose Russian-language translation of Pavel Kanšin (1833–1893), who in his turn made use of an earlier prose translation of Nikolaj Ketčer (Nickolas Ketscher, 1809–1886). By general consensus, Ketčer's translation was better than the translation of Kanšin, who was criticized for his bookish and hackneyed style which obscured in some locations the original text of the tragedy (ibid.). Nevertheless, quite adamantly, Panas Myrnyj continued his translation of *King Lear*, supported by Vasyl' Horlenko. The latter ultimately praised his protégé's translation, which, to his mind, looked even better than that made by Kuliš. In his letter dated 28 May 1896, Horlenko wrote:

> The translation of Kuliš, as you will see, is not so natural and pure in its language as yours. He has many clumsy expressions

and words, and he plays with the Little Russian tongue too freely, albeit sometimes successfully and sometimes not. In addition, the reader is confused by his script, which seems somewhat prankish. He employs everywhere the *kh* to render the aspirated sound. He has translated *King Lear* and, as rumor has it, the whole of Shakespeare. He translated from the English with a full understanding of the spirit of the poet. But at the same time he employed the language too loosely. (Rudyns′ka 1928, 34)

One month later, in another letter to the same correspondent, trying to boost his morale, Horlenko continued criticizing the translation of Kuliš:

I am positive that, having familiarized yourself with the translations of Kuliš, you also share my opinion about their vain pretentiousness and the somewhat strange whims and language innovations that he introduces. All this makes his translations awkward and somewhat distracts the attention of the reader, since one has to get accustomed to so much new in both his language and orthography.... Your translation is quite plain, its language conveys the purity of the live common tongue, and this is why it is useful. (Rudyns′ka 1928, 36)

The most plausible explanation for this patently partisan critique is Horlenko's personal attitude toward Kuliš, who did not fall within the ambit of contemporary populist ideology. Horlenko was a devout populist whose views tended to limit the horizon of the revival of Ukrainian literature and language. In fact, Horlenko's aesthetic and literary predilections were reminiscent of Kostomarov's (1883) views on the homestead use of Ukrainian literature. Needless to say, in creating his translations, particularly of Shakespeare, Kuliš was fighting against this stance.

It is not surprising, therefore, that Horlenko preferred to extoll the purity and plainness of Panas Myrnyj's vernacular-based written Ukrainian over Kuliš's language. Being replete with unusual borrowings and derivations, Kuliš's language was at variance with the critic's vision of the monodialectal development of new literary Ukrainian. Quite in the vein of Horlenko's populist criticism, Panas Myrnyj deemed it necessary to add some scathing remarks about Kuliš's translation of *Othello*. According to Panas Myrnyj (1971, 433), despite his efforts to render this tragedy in an adequate manner, Kuliš ultimately failed to produce what he strove for—*Othello*'s flavor completely evaporated and the translator's language proved dry and stillborn.

One can wonder at this point what Panas Myrnyj accomplished in his translation of *King Lear* that compelled Šapovalova (1976, 112) to declare that, unlike the artificial language of Kuliš, his translation was "pure" and "very close to the spirit of the Ukrainian readership." Leaving aside the official Soviet constraints on Šapovalova's reasoning in 1976, it is possible to answer in one word: regionalism. To put it bluntly, the closeness of Panas Myrnyj's translation to the readership as well as the transparency and "purity" of its linguistic norms were rooted in its regional, southeastern dialectal idiom, which the writer had been cultivating all his life in the Poltava province. His idiom was premised exclusively on the language practice of the Poltava speakers of Southeast Ukrainian (Hrycenko 2007, 34–35). Thus the language of Panas Myrnyj's translation of *King Lear* was regionally exemplary since its puristic norms were anchored in Southeast Ukrainian. It is no wonder that the editors of Panas Myrnyj's translation made a minimum of corrections in its *Vorlage* before it went into press in 1970 (*Lir*, 1970).

What are those regional features that, unlike Kuliš's synthetic idiom, make *King Lear* familiar to the Poltava peasantry? I will list some of them following Hrycenko's (2007, 24–30) textual analysis of some of the protographs of Panas Myrnyj's prose works.

In the phonetics, there is the confusion of *e* and *y* as, for instance, in *podilyne* "divided" (n. sg.) (*Lir*-M, 2), the active use of the high-mid front vowel *y* in word-initial position as in *ynče* "differently" or *yde* (3 sg pres.) "to go" (ibid., 2, 10), and the introduction of *i* in place of other vowels (*mit'* [ibid., 10] instead of *myt'* "moment"). The last change is not attested in Kuliš's language. One should also mention palatalization of *r'* in the word-final position as in *hospodar'* "duke" (ibid., 3, 4) and the use of *y* in genitive singular neuters like *neoberežnosty* (gen. sg. n.) "sick[ness] in fortune" (ibid., 11, Shakespeare, 1144). Finally, there is no overt distinction between *h* and *g* in Panas Myrnyj's language. For instance, following the current practice of eastern Ukrainian literati, Panas Myrnyj did not mark the velar sound *g* in the spelling of western European geographical and personal names where Kuliš resorted to the digraph *kh*: *Burhundija*, *Halija*, *Hloster*, and *Rehana* (*Lir*-M, 1), compared to *Burkhundija*, *Khalija*, *Khloster*, and *Rekhana* (*Lir*-K, 1). There are, however, some most revealing cases of spelling in Kuliš that reflect his native, "non-southwestern" phonetics, uniting in one series of phonemic localization the phonemes *h*, *k*, and *x* but not *g* (Danylenko 2006c, 192), whence *Burhundy* (pl.) "population of Burgundy" and *Burhund* next to *Burkhund* "Duke of Burgundy" (*Lir*-K, 1v, 2v, 5r).

Assimilative changes are not rendered by Panas Myrnyj on the same scale as in Kuliš's phonetic orthography, such as in *beš* (< *bez*) *čuda* "without a miracle," *zvicci* (< *zvidci*) "from here," and *nat* (< *nad*) *toboju* "above you" (*Lir*-K, 8r, 9v, 10v). One of the most obvious examples is found in verb forms at the boundary with the reflexive particle -*sja* (e.g., *zdajetcja* [3 sg. pres.] "to seem" [*Lir*-M, 8] compared to *hodyccja* [3 sg. pres.] "[I find it] not fit" [*Lir*-K, 11r, Shakespeare, 1143]). Overall, unlike Kuliš's idiom, the regional features in Panas Myrnyj's phonetics and spelling are quite numerous. Unlike its earlier period of codification, showing many northern Ukrainian dialectal features (Matvijas 2008), translations made by Kuliš in the 1890s look more multidialectal and artificial; note a rare northern Ukrainian form, *šestyj* (*Lir*-K, 6v), in Kuliš compared to a southeastern (modern) Ukrainian form *šostyj* "sixth" in Panas Myrnyj (*Lir*-M, 6).

The morphological make-up of Panas Myrnyj's language demonstrates the same regional trend. Some features later became codified and are treated today as stylistic variants in modern Ukrainian. One should begin with the lexeme *ljude* "people" (*Lir*-M, 2), which was introduced into nineteenth-century language practice by Ševčenko (Tymošenko 1968, 152–153). Sporadically, Panas Myrnyj used a peculiar dative case form, *ljudim* (dat.) "people" (*Lir*-M, 8; Hrycenko 2007, 27), typical of Southeast Ukrainian (Matvijas 2006, 58). The neuter deverbatives in his language were modeled on the southeastern derivational pattern ending in -*nnja*/-*ttja*, as in *mennja* "name," *žyttja* "life" (*Lir*-M, 5), and even such a Church Slavonic form as *naroždennja* "birth" (ibid., 9); note the rare *koxanja* "love" without gemination (ibid., 2). Kuliš, instead, resorted to forms ending in *-nnje/-ttje* (e.g., *odriddje* "generation messes" [*Lir*-K, 5r, Shakespeare, 1141] with the southeastern Ukrainian prefix *od-*; compare the derogative Rus. *otrod'je* "spawn, seed"). Among the forms used today in poetic genres, one finds in Panas Myrnyj's language uncontracted forms of adjectives like *ostatnjuju* (acc. f.) "last" and *kraščeje* (n.) "[that is] better" (*Lir*-M, 7, 3).

Of particular interest are comparative formations of the type *radnišyj* (m.) "happier," and especially *molodčyj* (m.) "younger," *bahatčyj* (m.) "richer," and the superlative *najdorohšyj* (m.) "most expensive" (*Lir*-M, 2, 5, 6, 7), which are regularly attested in Panas Myrnyj's oeuvre (Hrycenko 2007, 27). Needless to say, all the aforementioned comparative and superlative forms were substituted for by other forms in the 1970 publication of Panas Myrnyj's translation, respectively *molodšyj*, *bahatšyj*, *najdorožčyj* (*Lir*-1970, 514, 523, 524). The latter forms were used by Kuliš (*Lir*-K, 2v, 3r, 4r), who conversely continued to employ bookish superlatives with *j* in the suffix *-ijš-* (Tymošenko 1971, 204) (e.g., *dostojnijšyj* "most worthy" and *najljubijšyj* "most beloved" [*Lir*-K, 7v, 8v]).

Most interesting, to be sure, is the vocabulary, including a peculiar dialectal form *ože*, liberally used by Panas Myrnyj in all his works; note also *odže* or *od že* (Hrycenko 2007, 27). This is a kind of identifying or emphatic particle whose semantics is sometimes very fuzzy as, for instance, in the following fragment:

Panas Myrnyj's Translation	Shakespeare's Original
У мене е ще й другий син— законний; старший від цего. *Оже* мое серце лежить до їх обох однаково. (*Lir*-M, 2)	[But I have a son, sir, by order of law, some year elder than this, who *yet* is no dearer in my account.] (Shakespeare, 1139)

However, the most striking feature of Panas Myrnyj's vocabulary is the recurrent use of diminutives belonging to different word classes (adjectives, adverbs, and nouns), which all "add an unnecessary coloring to the text of Shakespeare" (Šapovalova 1976, 112). Most of these diminutives seem to be out of place and, due to their dialectal origin, do not fit the lofty narrative of the tragedy. Suffice it to mention the following diminutives in the text of

Panas Myrnyj, which as "folkloric embellishment" do not have direct correspondences in the original: *harnen'ko* "well," *noven'ke* (n.) "new," *nedavnen'ko* "recently," *harazden'ko* "well," *durnisin'ko* "stupidly," and *pramisin'ko* "straight." Note also *serden'ko* "heart," *sestryčen'ko* "sister," *holovon'ka* "head," *baten'ko* and *taton'ko* "father," and many others (*Lir*-M, 2, 4, 5, 8, 9, 11, etc.). Unlike his early translations of the Bible, Kuliš employs diminutives in his translations of Shakespeare rather sparingly.

Panas Myrnyj indulges in vernacular and colloquial lexemes like *druzjaka* "friend," *bratuxa* "brother," *durosvit* "fool," *projdysvit*, *bydlo* and *kodlo* "villain" (*Lir*-M, 9, 10, 11, Shakespeare, 1144), *bazikaty* and *balakaty* "to talk" (*Lir*-M, 5, 10) or "to reverb no hollowness" in Shakespeare (1141), and many others. His language sometimes appears much too idiomatic (*izvyxnuvsja s pantelyku* "[Lear] is mad," *yz hluzdu zsunuvs'* "fell to folly" [*Lir*-M, 5, Shakespeare, 1141], and *ni pary z ust* "[on thy life] no more" [*Lir*-M, 5, Shakespeare, 1141]). In Panas Myrnyj one can find, nevertheless, interesting series of synonyms, which contain rare bookish forms like *korolevstvo ~ carstvo ~ vladarstvo* "kingdom" (*Lir*-M, 2, 3), *hospodar'* "Lord" ~ *vladyka ~ korol'* "king" (ibid., 3, 4), or *vladar'* "prince" (ibid., 6, Shakespeare, 1141), used also by Lesja Ukrajinka. Some of the forms have a wider, eastern Slavic folkloric connotation like *hospoda* "palace" (*Lir*-M, 2, Shakespeare, 1139), not attested in the dictionary of Jevhen Želexivs'kyj but found, instead, in the dictionary of Borys Hrinčenko (Hrinč., 1:359; Sr., 1:562–563). Note also *hornycja* "castle" (*Lir*-M, 8, Shakespeare 1143; Žel., 1:153) from ESl. *gorьnica* "large room" (Sr., 1:560). Strangely enough, Panas Myrnyj largely avoids ethnographic terms like *kozak* "Cossack" (*xata* "house" [*Lir*-M, 11]). They are also rarely attested in Kuliš's translation of *King Lear*, although one does find *kozače* "Cossack" (voc.) "sirrah" (*Lir*-K, 12r, Shakespeare, 1144).

As has been mentioned, the vocabulary of Kuliš, the translator, is much more diversified and multilayered. As evidence I would adduce some terms of address applied by Kuliš in his translation of *King Lear* (i.e., *knjaz'*, *korol'*, *car'*, and *monarx* "king" [*Lir*-K, 3r, 5v, 7r]), each one a borrowing into East Slavic. Unlike Kuliš's translations of the Bible, Church Slavonicisms are not numerous in his translation of *King Lear*, perhaps due partly to the secular contents of the tragedy (e.g., *vsuje* "in vain" [*Lir*-K, 6r, Shakespeare, 1141]). The lofty narrative is rendered, instead, with the help of Russian Church Slavonic and especially Russian lexemes, which are not found anywhere in Panas Myrnyj: *žyzn'* "life," *prežnja* (f.) "fore-vouch'd [affection]," *dobroditel'* "virtue" (*Lir*-K, 3v, 9r, 8r, Shakespeare, 1142), *predložyty* "to offer," *neobxodymost'* "divine thrusting" (*Lir*-K, 7r, 13r, Shakespeare, 1144), and *hrubyjan* "unmannerly [Kent]" (*Lir*-K, 5v, Shakespeare, 1141). The overseas coloring of the translation is highlighted through the use of Polish borrowings and Galician forms serving as "interlingual homophones"; consider *fortuna* (*Lir*-K, 13r) ~ "fortune" (Shakespeare, 1144), *katastrofa* (*Lir*-K, 13v) ~ "catastrophe" (Shakespeare, 1143), *vkontentuvaty* (*Lir*-K, 9v) ~ "to content" (Shakespeare, 1142), and *konspyracija* (*Lir*-K, 11v) ~ "conspiracy" (Shakespeare, 113).

As in his paraphrase of the Song of Songs, the language of Panas Myrnyj's translation of *King Lear* is dialectally homogeneous and conspicuously regional. Kuliš always tried to avoid these features in his language (Naxlik 2007, 2:383). Ideologically, all this brings Panas Myrnyj's translation closer to Jurij Fed'kovyč's vision of literary Ukrainian as intrinsically monodialectal and regional. The fact that modern Ukrainian is largely based on Southeast Ukrainian, which Panas Myrnyj emulated in his translation, is to some extent a historical coincidence (Danylenko 2008b). In a sense, neither Fed'kovyč nor Myrnyj, the translators, could offer a full-fledged pan-Ukrainian language program. A synthesizing mission was undertaken by other writers, especially Kuliš who, in his translations of Shakespeare in particular, was striving for a fusion of different dialectal and chronological elements into one language system.

ONE OR MULTIPLE HOMESTEADS?

One of the most prolific translators himself (M. Moskalenko 2006 5/6, 181–194), Ivan Franko was notoriously critical of Kuliš's translations of Shakespeare. Not surprisingly, while preparing them for publication, he introduced a lot of changes into the texts, especially *Hamlet*. Having learned about Franko's editorial intervention in Kuliš's translations, the widow of the writer pleaded with a Ukrainian composer, Mykola Lysenko (1842–1912), to forbid Franko from making any corrections in the translations of her late husband (Šapovalova 1976, 123–124). A staunch populist and an influential public figure in Russian-ruled Ukraine, Lysenko found himself in a delicate situation. In fact, it was he who, while Kuliš was still alive, organized a series of fundraising events for the publication of Kuliš's translations of Shakespeare and in a letter of 15 November 1894 asked Franko to undertake the editing and the writing of an introduction to each of the plays translated by Kuliš (Lysenko 1964, 244–245).

In his letter of 26 September 1899, while referring to the opinions of some Ukrainian writers, Lysenko asked Franko to make changes in the translations of Kuliš sparingly and only in those extreme cases that warranted editorial intrusion. Kuliš's works and his use of the Ukrainian language, he continued, were to be kept sacred for the sake of all Ukrainians. This is why Franko's emendations had to be based on his tactful understanding of the vernacular language used by Kuliš in his creative work (Bernac´ka 1993, 250). Agreeing with some changes made by Franko (e.g., *koroleva* instead of Kuliš's *korolycja*), Lysenko deemed it necessary to remind him of possible differences in the two regional varieties of Ukrainian (see Ohijenko 1927, 21–22). To give an example, he cited the word *vhonobyty*, which could mean "to respect, host" in Galicia and "to please" in Central Ukraine (Bernac´ka 1993, 251). But most importantly, Franko was not to refer anywhere in the introduction to actual editorial changes. Otherwise, Lysenko wrote, Kuliš's widow "will eat me alive since she gave me all the plays with one provision—not a single word or expression of her husband be changed" (ibid.).

Yet, although somewhat restrained, Franko's editorial work did not stand too still. Controversial as they might appear from the point of view of Kuliš's alternative language program, Franko's changes demonstrated not only his editorial skills but also his long-standing interest in the literary output of Shakespeare, an interest revived most likely during his editorial work on the translations of Kuliš. It is noteworthy that Franko was the first Ukrainian poet to translate Shakespeare's sonnets. From

1882 onward, he translated twelve sonnets, four of which were published during his lifetime and the rest posthumously in 1912; he also translated Mariana's song (Act 4, scene 1) in *Measure for Measure*, which was published in a footnote to the comedy in 1902 (M. Moskalenko 2006 5/6, 190; *Mira*, 74, 126, Shakespeare, 411). However, Shakespeare's plays remained beyond his creative capacity for a long period of time, if one leaves aside translations of very short excerpts from *King Lear* (1879) and *The Tempest* (1884) that were published together with the complete translation of *The Merchant of Venice* (1912) in 1956. Although dated 1912, the translation of the latter play was initiated as early as 1905, most likely as a result of his work on Kuliš's translations. The first two fragments were translated by Franko from German since the writer did not know English at all, which, as he lamented in one of his letters, hampered his efforts to probe the faithfulness of Staryc´kyj's translation of *Hamlet* (Franko 1956, 176–177). Only after the second half of the 1890s did he master English so that he became capable of translating Shakespeare from the original (Šapovalova 1976, 118).

There is a striking difference between the language of the two fragments, on the one hand, and the language of the translation of *The Merchant of Venice*, on the other. The first group of Franko's translations may be viewed as intrinsically regional, hence such dialectal features as the dative case form *ditjem* "children," the reduplicated demonstrative *toto* (preferred *inter alia* by Antin Kobyljans´kyj in his translation of the Gospels), adverbs like *vidsy* "from here" and *odoce* "up there" (*Lir*-F, 234–235), and words like *sylov* "force" (instr.) and the Church Slavonicism *otče* "father" (voc.) (*Tempest*-F, 237). Similar features are conspicuously absent in Franko's translation of *The Merchant of Venice* (*Merchant*-F). As a result, one can juxtapose the aforementioned two small translations of Franko with the translation of *King Lear* made by Panas Myrnyj rather than with Kuliš's translation. It is easy to notice that the regional forms in the following excerpts from Franko's and Panas Myrnyj's translations contrast with their more stylistically diversified counterparts in the parallel fragment from Kuliš's *King Lear*:

Franko's Translation

В *мні* та сама кров,
І щире серце каже *ми*, що також
Моя любов така, як і єї.
Лиш в тім моя *сильнійша*: всі утіхи,
Всі розкоши житя *нічо* для мене,
Моє єдине *щастє*—то любов
Для вас мій *отче і царю*!
(*Lir*-F, 235)

Panas Myrnyj's Translation

З сестрою ми одного роду,
Цініть же и мене, як и її цінили.
Палка була її та щира мова!
А все ж таки и я додам до неї:
Немає радощів найкращих у житті,
Як вас *кохать*. Одним отим коханням
Щаслива я й живу ним, милий *тату*! (*Lir*-M, 3)

Kuliš's Translation

С того ж *металу* я, що и сестриця:
Цініть мене по ній. Скажу *від* ерця,
Вона мов вийняна из *уст* у мене,
Як я люблю вас. Не сказала тілько,
Що я всіх инших радощів цураюсь,
Які ні є в найвишшій *сфері* чувства,
И тілько в мене щастя, щоб любити
Вас, дорогі *величество*! (*Lir*-K, 3r)

Shakespeare's Original

[I am made of that self metal as my sister,
And prize me at her worth. In my true heart
I find she names my very deed of love;
Only she comes too short, that I profess
Myself an enemy to all other joys
Which the most precious square of sense possesses,
And find I am alone felicitate
In your dear Highness' love.]
(Shakespeare, 1140)

Franko's translation of *The Merchant of Venice* looks different from his previous, less successful two attempts. Frist of all, in terms of its form, Franko retained prose and poetic parts, rendered adequately the iambic pentameter, maintained (with rare exceptions) an equal number of lines, and did not change anything in the content of the comedy. Linguistically, it was a true success, primarily for the normalizers preferring the southeastern vernacular model for literary Ukrainian. It is a pity that the translation appeared thirty-four years after the poet's death. Otherwise, it could have boosted the development of translation studies in Ukrainian, and in particular the creation of a canon of the "Ukrainian Shakespeare."

The language of this translation is dialectally homogeneous without the patent Galician elements or Polish loan forms that were commonplace in the local koiné. In fact, a similar homogeneity was typical of most of Franko's late literary works, especially those dealing with lofty narratives as in the poem *Moses* (Rusanivs'kyj 2001, 269). Thus, with the exception of several regional forms, the language of the translation of *The Merchant of Venice* looked sufficiently "distilled" to appeal primarily to Galician readers and even many Ukrainian speakers living in the Russian Empire. Among the most telling regionalisms are the following lexemes: *vidky* "whence," *dovh* "debt" (Žel., 1:98, 189), *mužčyna* "man" (Pol. *męščyzna*, Rus. *mužčina*), *procenty* (pl.) "percent" (Pol. *procenty*), *kopaty* "to kick" (Pol. *kopać*, ibid., 365), *xata* "house" next to *palata* (Church Slavonicism) and *kimnata* "room," *balačka* "talk," and *balakun* "talker" (*Merchant-*F, 253, 254, 255, 256, 257, 260, 262). Surprisingly, quite in the spirit of Kuliš and in compliance with the older eastern Slavic literary tradition, the translator employed a compound form *knjaz'-svatač*, literally "prince asking for a woman's hand." Oleksander Potebnja used the latter derivative type extensively in his translation of Homer's *Odyssey* (Danylenko 1999, 242–243).

Some morphological forms in Franko's translation, however, can be viewed as somewhat regional. First, they are not numerous and, second, they are also encountered in the language of some writers living in Dnieper Ukraine. Among those moderately regional forms one comes across the comparative suffix -*ijš*-, found in such comparative and superlative forms as *blyskučijšij* "more brilliant," *skorijše* "sooner," and *najharnijšyj* "best," compared to "fairer [than that word]" (*Merchant-*F, 252, 253, Shakespeare, 119). The -*ijš*- suffix made its way into Southeast Ukrainian, in particular into the language of Staryc'kyj and Kuliš. Yet the most radical regional form is the genitive plural ending -*yj* for masculines of the type *očyj* "eye" and *hrošyj* "money" (*Merchant-*F, 254, 255, 262);

this ending is attested in abundance in old Galician records and modern southwestern Ukrainian dialects (Kernyc′kyj 1967, 57).

Overall, the choice of linguistic devices was in no way incidental for Franko, whose language program was specifically designed to meet the demands of local Galician populists and readers. One should recall in this respect that his stance on the normalization of literary Ukrainian was controversial and, despite its leftist rhetoric, parochial. All this broke out during the 1891–1893 linguistic debate between Vasyl′ Čajčenko (Borys Hrinčenko), Ahatanhel Kryms′kyj, and other eastern Ukrainian populists, on the one hand, and Ivan Franko, Illja Kokorudz, Ivan Verxrats′kyj, and other western Ukrainian intellectuals, on the other (Shevelov 1966, 81–82). In his reply to Hrinčenko's polemical article attacking the numerous Polonisms, "Moskalisms" (Russianisms), provincialisms, and "Ruthenianisms" (Galician forms) in the written language (*jazyčije*) cultivated in Galicia and elsewhere (see Danylenko 2009c), Franko (1891a) discussed the historical reasons behind the dialectal diversity of the Ukrainian-speaking territories from 1772 onward—and the advantage of such a diversity. However, in his line of argumentation, Franko defended not only the multidialectal foundation of literary Ukrainian, which was positive, but also the possibility of a multidialectal variety of literary Ukrainian, a thesis that was fraught, according to Shevelov (1966, 63), with danger. In fact, Franko (1891a, 357) did not believe in the unity of literary Ukrainian, postponing this for the future, since "at the time being we do not have it yet and, due to the well-known, serious reasons, we cannot have it."

Shevelov (1966, 64) pointed out that in his language program, Franko removed from the agenda any plan for the unification of literary Ukrainian. As a result he opened a path to another type of parochialism, different from that of the "one eastern Ukrainian homestead" propounded by the bulk of eastern Ukrainian purists. As a matter of fact, Franko posited equal status for multiple homesteads, each having the right to develop independently in accordance with its internal laws and embracing ultimately a greater differentiation of southwestern Ukrainian dialects. Attractive as it might look, this scenario was not likely to bring the Ukrainian nation together in the linguistic or any other sense (Danylenko 2009d, 2015a).

It becomes clear, then, why Franko, influenced in his early creative period, in particular, by the local *jazyčije* (Cixoc′kyj 2006, 60–62, 236), proved so critical of the experiments of Kuliš in his translations of the Bible and Shakespeare. Kuliš's intention to create a language capable of uniting all Ukrainian speakers through the introduction of various dialectal and chronological elements in the system of new literary Ukrainian was, strictly speaking, alien to Franko. The latter was open to vernacular and other elements being used in one or even several regional standards, but with one major reservation: these standards should be minimally intermingled for now, whence the existence of the western Ukrainian (Galician) literary norm as opposed to that developed in Dnieper Ukraine. At first blush, it was, linguistically speaking, a democratic solution. In fact, however, such a solution was likely to lead to a political and societal impasse in the future (Shevelov 1966, 64).

Luckily this outcome was avoided, and the idea of one homestead vernacular ultimately prevailed in the creation of a new language standard based primarily on Southeast Ukrainian. Objectively speaking, this type of standard, although to a lesser extent, was also in the sights of Kuliš's normalization efforts. Yet his vision of a vernacular-based literary language was too refined and cosmopolitan to find its place in the new vernacular-based paradigm of literary Ukrainian. Still, it is precisely because of its cosmopolitanism that Kuliš's language program proved to be the most fitting one for rendering Shakespeare in nineteenth-century Ukrainian.

Conclusion

DETOURS OFFERED BUT NEVER TAKEN

In his numerous translations, Kuliš strove to achieve a twofold objective. First, from the early 1880s onward, pursuing the awakening of the Ukrainian people, he worked on the creation of a new translation tradition that would differ from the folkloric and burlesque trend cultivated by Petro Hulak-Artemovs´kyj, Leonid Hlibov, and other contemporary populist writers (Zerov 1967, 50–51; Dolžykova 2010, 20). While encompassing a wide range of authors and languages, his new translation approach was designed to expand the horizons of world literature for his compatriots, which would ultimately lead to a modern version of Ukrainian identity and nationality formation. Second, he strongly believed that first-rate translations could be created only with the help of a full-fledged literary language. This language should be furnished with a variety of styles, first and foremost the biblical high style and its secular variety, capable of rendering the books of both the Bible and classic world literature in Ukrainian.

Ideologically, translations of such works were aimed at the gradual acculturation of the Ukrainian people, evoking a universal vision of the world and suggesting strategies of identity politics that prefigured the modern interest in cultural and linguistic syncretism. This objective could be achieved, according to Kuliš, through translations of the Holy Scriptures and of masterpieces authored by Shakespeare. Not surprisingly, Kuliš worked on these translations until his last breath in 1897. Nevertheless, his attitude toward translations into Ukrainian was rather ambivalent at the outset of his literary career. As early as 1849, he maintained that writing original works was more important than translating somebody else's oeuvre, inasmuch as the public expected serious contributions from him as an author (Kuliš 2005, 296). But already in the late 1850s, he apparently modified his views and, at some point, came forward with the idea of eventually translating a wide array of English- and German-language works of literature. Such translations, he argued, would contribute to the formation of a true Ukrainian community premised on national ideals and ethnic aspirations (Kuliš to Galagan, 349, 354).

Still, nothing was definite in the 1850s and early 1860s since, as late as 1876 Kuliš believed that "[translations] wipe out the originality of the Ukrainian language, and literature therefore will not take a step forward" (Barvins′kyj 2004, 188). However, some ten years later, he concluded that in order to resist the influence of both Polish and Russian, "we must lead our Old Rusian [*staroruščyna*] through cultured languages as was done by New Rusian [*novoruščyna*]" (Naxlik 2007, 2:262). Translations from the cultured, that is, modern western European and liturgical, languages could in a sense strengthen Ukrainian, while elevating it to "scholarly status" with "civil esteem" and subsequently transforming it into a full-fledged literary language (Kuliš 1910, 570, 2005, 84).

The formation of written Ukrainian would be ultimately facilitated by various translations whose quality would reflect the appropriate level of normalization of this language. It becomes clear therefore that Kuliš's translation practice and its dynamics were changing in tandem with his linguistic views. The latter process was dependent on changes in his perception of the place of Ukrainian (vernacular), sandwiched historically between vernacular Polish and non-vernacular Russian (i.e., the "New Rusian language" stolen from the Ukrainians). Together with the problem of the dialectal foundation of future literary Ukrainian, the interrelations between Ukrainian, Polish, and Russian proved to be a stumbling block in debates, often full of acrimony, between Kuliš and Galician populists (Franko 1898).

The place of Ukrainian in its relation to Polish and Russian was discussed by Kuliš in his 1863 polemic article entitled "Dvi movi, knyžnja i narodnja" (Two Languages, the Bookish and the Vernacular), which did not go to press until 1914. Broadly speaking, his discussion can be reduced to the following several theses (Kuliš 1914, 26–28). To begin with, already in "Varangian times," there were two languages in the Ukrainian lands, one used by the aristocracy in the church and in court and the second utilized by the peasantry. During the "Lithuanian period," the local Rusian princes purportedly called in foreign teachers who helped them create a kind of "middle" plain language positioned between Church Slavonic and the Ukrainian vernacular. After their victory over Poland, the Ukrainians continued to employ the same two languages, although Ukrainian folklore became much more refined and sophisticated in terms of its language and poetic devices.

However, as soon as Ukraine was incorporated into the Muscovite state, the local bookish and scholastic language was transplanted into a Russian secular and spiritual milieu, where it gradually prevailed in the whole of society (Kuliš 1914, 27–28). In Ukraine, however, this "dead" language was further cultivated only at the monasteries and in the administration. Overall, having absorbed some Polish words and borrowed the Russian *akannje*, this type of bookish and scholastic language was not considered by the commoners as the language of Poland, Muscovy, or Ukraine. Yet this language gave rise to literary Russian, which, though re-introduced into Ukraine, was never viewed by either Russians or Ukrainians as their own tongue. The major competitor to vernacular Ukrainian, tempered in the times of the Old Rusian princes, was, as Kuliš argued, the Muscovite (Russian) language, which appropriated the legacy of Old Rusian (*ruščyna*) without offering anything in exchange (Kuliš 1910, 255–257).

Kuliš's interest in the state and status of vernacular Ukrainian, which, unlike the bookish language, had been struggling through many centuries, was well-grounded. At that time the writer was focused on the promotion of Ukrainian folklore and the vernacular devices that he planned to utilize in his own literary works. In a letter to Pëtr Pletnëv (1791–1866), the publisher of *Sovremennik* (The Contemporary), dated 20 March 1845, Kuliš wrote about his recent travels to Little Russia where he had recorded the local language, still unspoiled, as he maintained, in contrast to the old, aristocratic language, which had been conspicuously corrupted by the influence of western European cultured languages (Kuliš 2005, 50). In 1892 in his letter to Myxajlo Pavlyk, Kuliš once more returned to this topic, though using terms coined much later. He contended that Old Rusian in Dnieper Ukraine vanished under Russian rule, while in Galicia this language fell into oblivion during the Polish hegemony (Voznjak 1928a, 178).

Construed in the romantic spirit, this theory of Old Rusian looked controversial, especially in the context of the relationship of Ukrainian to the two neighboring languages, Polish and Russian. For example, in his 1864 letter to Leonid Hlibov, the author wrote that "half of the Polish lexicon is derived from our words" (Rytter 1992). At the same time, in the seventeenth and eighteenth centuries the Muscovite language also borrowed, supposedly, many Ukrainian words and grammatical forms (K-j 1924, 283–284; Cymbalistyj 1991). It was high time for the Ukrainians to take back what the Russians had borrowed and never returned, despite the fact that Aleksandr Puškin and other prominent Russian authors "managed our homestead" (Kuliš to Galagan, 349). This is why, as Kuliš pointed out, he translated Canto 1 of Lord Byron's *Childe Harold's Pilgrimage* into his mother tongue, as if there were only English and Ukrainian and no Russian language at all in the whole world (ibid.).

Nevertheless, the Russians developed a poor language (New Rusian, *novoruščyna*) that could hardly compete with Ukrainian (Old Rusian) or be used, for instance, in a versified translation of the Bible (Voznjak 1928a, 218). In his later years, having revised his historiosophic views, Kuliš completely changed his opinion of the historical context in which literary Russian (New Rusian) emerged. In his 13 May 1888 letter to his old friend Stepan Nis he claimed that, from time immemorial, the Ukrainians had been closer to Muscovite Rus´ than to Poland in terms of religion and language. Ultimately, it was the Poles who divided them and persecuted the Ukrainian Cossacks (Kuliš to Nos, 14). However, in spite of all these historical vicissitudes, the Ukrainian language retained its old literary tradition founded in the times of Old Rus´. To demonstrate this, in one of his letters to Myxajlo Pavlyk, Kuliš cited the use of patronymics in contemporary Ukrainian, a custom inherited by its speakers from the Old Rusian times (Voznjak 1928a, 198).

Yet, in the future, there was a chance to reconcile these two languages sharing the common legacy of Old Rus´. On the one hand, as Kuliš (2009, 2:323) wrote in his letter to a famous Russian thinker and writer, Sergej Aksakov (1791–1859), on 1 January 1856, the Russian language was likely to change under the influence of Nikolaj Gogol and other southern Russian writers. On the other hand, disillusioned by the burlesque idiom of Ivan

Kotljarevs′kyj, Ukrainian authors would search for more refined and polished forms, thus getting closer to literary Russian in the future. One or two talents would accomplish then a merger of the two languages. It would therefore be a mistake to label Ukrainian a dialect since Russian and Ukrainian were equal partners in striving for their merger (ibid., 323–324). Kuliš argued that, in his translations of the Psalms, Ševčenko took the first step, while his own *Čorna rada* (Black Council) followed suit in approaching Russian. His novel was written not in the language of the Ukrainian peasantry but in the language used by hetmans and the local aristocracy, whose education was comparable to a western European one: "That is almost Russian, biblical Russian, albeit with a Little Russian accent" (ibid., 323). At the same time this language did not deviate from Ukrainian since Ukrainians treated it as their mother tongue, whilst common Russians could easily understand the language of his novel (Kuliš 2005, 84).

In sum, while propagating a populist view of the Ukrainian language, Kuliš maintained that Ukrainian was a part of the all-Rusian legacy and that it had to develop in consonance with, not in opposition to, Russian (Luckyj 1983, 164). This stance was not unique in the cultural space of imperial Russia. Despite the existence of the project of the development of Ukrainian at that time, such a position was the most popular interpretation of the eastern Slavic languages in the second part of the nineteenth century (Symaniec 2012, 501–516, 571). It is worth mentioning, in this respect, the linguistic views of Oleksander Potebnja who, although a Ukrainophile, believed in the coexistence of literary Russian, the common standard for all the East Slavs, with the new literary Ukrainian in the making (Danylenko 2006c, 353).

In light of the diachronic perspective of Ukrainian as advocated by Kuliš, one wonders to what extent the whole theory of the distribution of Old and New Rusian can be sustained by the current distribution of Ukrainian dialects. One has to answer also which dialects might be taken as the basis of literary Ukrainian. Furthermore, what other (loan) elements could be allowed into the system of this language? In this respect, Kuliš held a unique position among all other normalizers, in that he tried to synthesize various dialectal elements in a new literary norm, whose foundation, however, remained solidly southeastern Ukrainian.

Kuliš homed in on his position on several occasions. One of the interesting *loci* is found in his 1864 letter to Leonid Hlibov:

> Nomys follows slavishly his local dialect, which is not advisable; otherwise we shall never bring together our torn, thoroughly distorted language. (K-j 1924, 284)

In the same letter, he gives a series of suggestions as to how to normalize certain linguistic forms:

> One has to retain the ending *-yty* in all the verbs inasmuch as this is how the largest and best part of Ukraine speaks, including Red Rus´ in a wide sense. We should assiduously support all the forms that are used over there and do not contradict the spirit of the language since, for the time being, the normalization of the language almost stands still in our lands, while in Galicia the younger generation and best minds work energetically on this. (K-j 1924, 283)

All in all, while giving credit to the language program(s) of the Galician and Transcarpathian Ukrainophiles, Kuliš proved to be more open to the introduction of multiple dialectal forms, which would help avoid parochialism in creating a new language standard.

His appraisal of the normalization and literary activities of his Galician and Transcarpathian compatriots changed drastically after a notorious misunderstanding with the young Galician populists, including Lev Lopatyns´kyj, Omeljan Partyc´kyj, and Natal´ Vaxnjanin in the 1870s (Voznjak 1928a, 166). The so-called "second letter" that Kuliš addressed to his Galician compatriots looked very interesting in this respect. Full of bitterness and somewhat sketchy in its argumentation, the letter offered in a succinct way the programmatic views of its author. Kuliš argued, for instance, that Galicia, while lagging behind the "Ukrainian poetic word," should not be focused on Ševčenko since "our Homer is not Ševčenko, but the people."

> Having emerged from the people and for its sake we advanced a small, yet completely independent literature, and with respect to it, we should not accept what you retain from the old times (etymology) or what you create in between etymology and

phonetics. When you stand up for your separate character, you show the narrowness of your tendency. We want to be read not only by Ukraine but also in Galicia, which we prove with the help of not Ševčenko alone, and you wish to write for your Galicia. ... They will and should read us in Galicia even if you did not accept anything from our taste; however, they will read you in Ukraine only when you adopt the Ukrainian taste.... (Franko 1898, 14)

There are two principal issues discussed in this excerpt. First, Kuliš was loyal to the idea of the primordial nature of the Ukrainian vernacular, which should be cultivated as a major literary language. Accordingly, neither Ševčenko nor some of the other figures of his caliber were the sole arbiters of a new literary standard, but rather the people themselves, in their speech practice and taste. And, second, not Galicia but Ukraine stood out as the pan-Ukrainian unifying center that had to be followed by the Galicians living in Austria-Hungary, who were still incapable of creating their own literature and language to compete with those engendered and cultivated in Dnieper Ukraine.

To put it schematically in linguistic terms, an exemplary literary language had to be vernacular at its core and based on Southeast Ukrainian. Were this language adopted by the Ukrainians of Austria-Hungary, then its norm might absorb some admixtures from Southwest Ukrainian and the Galician-Bukovynian koiné (including western European borrowings channeled through Polish). But such admixtures were not likely to change the structure of the southeastern literary norm, in particular its phonetic script (Franko 1898, 14). The latter had all the advantages over the etymological one used by Galician Russophiles or the combination of phonetic and etymological principles as offered in the first Galician school grammar of Myxajlo Osadca (1862) and in the grammar of the the Ukrainian language designed for elementary schools by Omeljan Partyc′kyj (1873) (Skurzewska 2007).

Kuliš applied the above conception in his original works as well as his biblical and secular translations. The use of borrowings and dialectal elements was not random in his works. Thus linguistic (vernacular) purity was still high in most of his literary works written in the 1840s.

Gradually, the period of linguistic purism gave way to what can be called a "synthetic period," which lasted from the 1880s until the death of the author in 1897 (Naxlik 2007, 2:386–387). During this second, synthetic period, Kuliš would not create new linguistic forms lest they were similar to the Russian equivalents. Also, he liberally introduced loan, archaic, and Church Slavonic forms that sometimes were of the same origin as their Russian counterparts, whence, perhaps, hasty accusations of Kuliš for using blatant Russianisms (Hordyns′kyj 1928, 64; Lazurs′kyj 1929, 30–32). In general, the issue of admixtures and borrowings in Ukrainian held center stage in the language program of Kuliš. In fact, the receptiveness of Ukrainian to loan forms became a signature feature of the language of Kuliš, who envisioned the future of Ukrainian as a synthetic (mixed) system comparable eventually to that of English, Italian, and other western European languages.

In a series of letters addressed to Stepan Nis in 1890, Kuliš defended the use of borrowings from western European languages. As a model for Ukrainian, he mentioned the borrowing process from Ancient Greek and Latin into the modern languages of Europe; one of them was modern English, heavily permeated with loan forms that did not, however, interfere with the ultimate transformation of English into one of the cultured languages (Kuliš to Nos, 19). In another letter to Nis, Kuliš raised again this topic and returned to the mixed nature of all major European languages quite in the spirit of Jan Niecisław Baudouin de Courtenay's thesis about the "mixed nature" of all human languages (Boduèn de Kurtene 1963). The Europeans, as Kuliš pointed out (Kuliš to Nos, 21), built their languages as well as their houses right on the ancient Greek and Roman ruins. Nobody would complain that the language of Dante was in fact stolen from the Romans, although at the very outset it was mere slang that Cicero would hardly have tolerated. Hence, while using the older marble and bricks, a house of Ukrainian could be erected, at least partly, independently.

Bookish and Church Slavonic forms were commonly used by Kuliš, depending on the cultural and linguistic context and the literary genre of a particular work. For example, in his translation of the New Testament in the 1870s, the author would choose a Church Slavonic form, even its Russianized version, rather than its Polish equivalent as sometimes was suggested by Puljuj. And indeed, Church Slavonic forms would fit naturally into the biblical translation, which as Kuliš admitted in 1870 was designed not so much for Galicia as for (Dnieper) Ukraine with its predominantly Orthodox readership (Studyns′kyj 1930, 4; Ohijenko 1927, 21–22). Obviously, Kuliš's ambivalent treatment of the Polish admixture in the Galician variety of Ukrainian was not accidental, being a consequence of his negative attitude toward the Poles and their culture (Shevelov 1966, 40–41).

Interestingly enough, Kuliš could tolerate some Polish forms appearing in harmony with the stylistic texture of a particular text. Some of them would remind him of the older Ukrainian (Ruthenian) forms of the sixteenth and seventeenth centuries, whose use would be appropriate in some contexts. Occasionally, some loan words, transferred by Poles from western European languages, could even appear indispensable. According to Kuliš, Polish borrowings, as appropriated and channeled through the Galician koiné into Southeast Ukrainian, represented other cultured languages and literatures that could serve as a model for a new literary standard of Ukrainian. Not surprisingly, in 1881, Kuliš asked Puljuj to help him find some Galician words and expressions for his translation of Shakespeare, which, as a result of the Ems Decree issued on 30 May 1876 by the Russian Tsar Alexander II, was prepared for publication in Galicia rather than in tsarist Russia (Studyns′kyj 1930, 283–284).

Overall, the adoption of Galician elements by Kuliš was selective and limited in some genres. In the Ukrainian Bible, for instance, one finds a few of them, both in the vocabulary and grammar. In his translations of Shakespeare, Galician forms were essentially Polish lexical transfers from the cultured languages, so indispensable for the coloring of the western European setting in Shakespeare's plays. There seem to be solid grounds for concurring with Shevelov (1966, 44–45), according to whom there were quite a few active Galician forms in the language of Kuliš. In other words, the Galician admixture was minimal in the language of this author. But chronologically speaking Kuliš was a pioneer in transferring Galician elements into a new vernacular standard in the making in Dnieper Ukraine. He was the first non-Galician writer to demonstrate that one could and had to use Galician elements in a literary language, even one based predominantly on Southeast Ukrainian. In the second part of the nineteenth century Kuliš's stance appeared even more radical, since the emergence of this new vernacular-based language hardly heralded a transgression from a bookish and purportedly dead language to another, vernacular standard. In the case of this language, one deals rather with a switch from the northern Ukrainian basis of the old literary tradition to a southeastern one of the vernacular standard, which had long flourished in particular genres, coexisting with the secular literary tradition of the *prostaja mova* (Danylenko 2008b, 70; Peredrijenko 1979). Speaking methodologically, Kuliš was a pioneering normalizer of written Ukrainian who "cleared away the rocks and stones" so Galician elements could make their way into a new literary Ukrainian premised largely on Southeast Ukrainian.

As evidenced by his translations, Kuliš's contribution to the normalization of literary Ukrainian proved matchless in the nineteenth century and beyond, even if compared with Ševčenko, viewed as the first writer to synthesize various genres and styles in vernacular Ukrainian. Yet Ševčenko's poetic idiom retained its intrinsic connection with the language of the Ukrainian peasantry. It was perhaps the major reason why the contemporary populist reader might treat his language as a kind of "authentic" and "natural" product, in contrast to the language of Kuliš that looked, especially in genres not explored by Ševčenko, unnatural because no "terminology of scholarly expressions" existed in his time (Lazurs′kyj 1929, 26). Interspersed with elements of different styles and registers, the language of Kuliš was truly synthetic and multilayered, thus impressing the readership with its alleged artificiality. This is why his "artificial" language either fascinated or repelled his contemporaries, while Ševčenko did not get this level of appreciation (Shevelov 1966, 45).

Among those who did not accept Kuliš's theory of Old Rusian and the corresponding archaizing trend in his choice of lofty vocabulary for the high style was the Ukrainian historian Mykola Kostomarov and the Galicia-based writer Ivan Franko. Although belonging to different generations of populists living in tsarist Russia and Austria-Hungary respectively and professing therefore different visions of Ukrainophilism, their judgments of Kuliš's vision of literary Ukrainian unexpectedly concurred. Both blamed Kuliš for supposedly disregarding the vernacular basis of Ukrainian and creating instead an artificial parlance barely acceptable in the two parts of Ukraine. In his notoriously unfavorable survey of Kuliš's literary activity, Kostomarov disavowed his former friend's capacity to be a leading normalizer of written Ukrainian. According to him (Kostomarov 1883, 224), the language of Kuliš's translations of Shakespeare would appear to Ukrainians living in the Russian Empire unnatural, artificial, tense, coined haphazardly, and devoid of any link with the plain idiom. Kostomarov's hypercriticism was provoked by his belief in cultural and linguistic differences between the two historical parts of Ukraine under Austro-Hungarian and Russian rule respectively. While the Ukrainian used in Galicia reached a high "degree of cultivation" (ibid.), Dnieper Ukraine, he insisted, was not yet ready to recognize the pioneering innovations of Kuliš, which the Galician reader could appreciate at least to some extent. By criticizing Kuliš's intent to create a "cultured language" for use in the two parts of Ukraine, Kostomarov expressed his total aversion to the integrative vision of Kuliš without breaking the confines of the "local homestead(s)" (see Danylenko 2009d).

Neither did Franko give credence to the pioneering role of Kuliš in the development of literary Ukrainian. The Galician critic offered the most vituperative attack on Kuliš's translations and on his language program in general (Zerov 1967, 49). It is worthwhile citing the following excerpt from Franko's introduction to the translation of Lord Byron's *Childe Harold's Pilgrimage* made by Kuliš:

> ... premised on a faulty understanding of the Ukrainian language, these translations cannot satisfy our taste (during the last years of his life, being deranged by his hatred of Cossacks, *hajdamaks*, and, in general, of the peasantry, Kuliš passed over vernacular Ukrainian and tried to create, specially for his translations, a certain "Old Rusian" language, that is, Ukrainian with purportedly archaic yet in fact Church Slavonic and Muscovite coloring). [This language] looks awkward, scholastic, naïve, and in fact poorly reminiscent of the faithful rendition of the original. ... As far as the lexicon is concerned, we are not speaking about it at

all—we left it without changes and believe that Kuliš developed his theory of "Old Rusian" to the hilt. It was not possible to follow this path any longer. (Franko 1905, v–vi)

In his invective, Franko lumped together linguistic and non-linguistic arguments, which were delivered impressionistically. Trying to get rid of the barbaric past of his people and revise Ukrainian history, Kuliš projected the same revisionist view onto the development of Ukrainian. In this he expressed what reason remained in romantic mythology, including the romantic interpretation of the vernacular basis of literary language. This mythology refused to die, especially as new injuries were being inflicted on the national psyche (Luckyj 1983, 160). An ostensibly positivist view of the Ukrainian language as offered by Franko remained in fact residually romantic and parochial. Eliminating the historical dimension, the critic was prepared to support a regional (dialectal) foundation of literary Ukrainian, which, being synchronic, could multiply in order to meet other "regional tastes." Apparently democratic, this solution, in reality, was not capable of advancing one pan-Ukrainian literary standard as implied by Kuliš in his theory of the Old Rusian foundation of Ukrainian.

Rejected on both banks of the Dnieper River, Kuliš was, nevertheless, a true unifier of the two parts of Ukraine. Unfortunately, his synthetic vision of literary Ukrainian was ultimately ousted by the ethnographic trend as determined by the principle of a monodialectal basis for its vernacular standard. That the latter principle got the upper hand in the competition over the southwestern and southeastern Ukrainian dialect foundations was not the decisive factor in the defeat of Kuliš's theory of Old Rusian in the nineteenth century (Danylenko 2008a). His was a completely alternative program that, being incompatible with the vernacular trends cultivated in Austrian- and Russian-ruled Ukraine, was doomed. Today one can only guess at the detours that literary Ukrainian would have made had Kuliš's language program prevailed.

Bibliography

PRIMARY SOURCES
(Abbreviations used in the text have been bolded and given first)

Antonij: Kuliš, Pantelejmon. 1901. *Uillijam Šekspir. Antonij i Kleopatra. Pereklad P. A. Kuliša.* With Introduction and Comments by Ivan Franko. Lviv: Naukove Tovarystvo imeni Ševčenka.

Apocrypha: Kohlenberger, John R., ed. 1997. *The Parallel Apocrypha.* New York and Oxford: Oxford University Press.

AUM: *Atlas ukrajins'koji movy.* 1984–2001. Vol. 1: *Polissja, serednja Naddniprjanščyna i sumižni zemli*; vol. 2: *Volyn', Naddniprjanščyna, Zakarpattja i sumižni zemli*; vol. 3: *Slobožanščyna, nyžnja Naddniprjanščyna, Pryčornomor'ja i sumižni zemli.* Kyiv: Naukova dumka.

Berynda: *Leksykon slovenoros'kyj Pamvy Beryndy.* 1961. Edited by Vasyl' Vasyl'ovyč Nimčuk. Facsimile reprint of 1627. Kyiv: Naukova dumka.

Biblija 1862: *Bíblija yly knýgy Svęščénnago pysanię vétxago y nóvago zavěta.* 1862. St. Petersburg: n.p.

Biblija 1907: *Byblija. Knigi svjaščennago pisanija Vetxago i Novago zavěta. Kanoničeskija. V russkom perevode s parallel'nymi mestami.* 1907. St. Petersburg: n.p.

Bil.-Nos.: Bilec'kyj-Nosenko, Pavlo. 1966. *Slovnyk ukrajins'koji movy.* Edited by Vasyl' Vasyl'ovyč Nimčuk. Kyiv: Naukova dumka.

Concordance: Ilnytzkyj, Oleh S. and George Hawrysch, eds. and comps. 2001. *A Concordance to the Poetic Works of Taras Shevchenko. Konkordancija poetyčnyx tvoriv Tarasa Ševčenka*, vols. 1–4. New York: Shevchenko Scientific Society; Toronto: CIUS Press.

ČR: Kuliš, P[antelejmon]. 1857. *Čorna rada, xronika 1663 roku.* St. Petersburg: n.p.

DMU: Humec'ka, Lukija Lukijanivna and Ivan Myxajlovyč Kernyc'kyj, eds. 1977–1978. *Slovnyk staroukrajins'koji movy*, vols. 1–2. Kyiv: Naukova dumka.

DUL: Hrynčyšyn, Dmytro et al., eds. 1994–2008–. *Slovnyk ukrajins′koji movy XVI–peršoji polovyny XVII st.*, vols. 1–14–. Lviv: Instytut ukrajinoznavstva im. I. Kryp'jakevyča NAN Ukrajiny.

EDU: Mel′nyčuk, Oleksandr Savyč et al., eds. 1982–2012–. *Etymolohičnyj slovnyk ukrajins′koji movy*, vols. 1–6–. Kyiv: Naukova dumka.

Enejida, Index: Vaščenko, Vasyl′ Semenovyč et al. 1955. *Leksyka "Enejidy" I. P. Kotljarevs′koho*. Kharkiv: Xarkivs′kyj deržavnyj universytet.

Fed′kovyč: Fed′kovyč, Jurij. 1902. *Dramatyčni pereklady Osypa Jurija Fed′kovyča*. Edited by Ivan Franko. Ukrajins′ko-rus′ka biblioteka, vol 3: *Pysannja Osypa Jurija Fed′kovyča*, part 2. Lviv: Naukove Tovarystvo imeni Ševčenka.

Franko to Drahomanov: Vakarčuk, Ivan et al., eds. 2006. *Lystuvannja Ivana Franka ta Myxajla Drahomanova*. Lviv: L′vivs′kyj nacional′nyj universytet imeni Ivana Franka.

Fraška: Fed′kovyč, Jurij. 1906. "Jak kozam rohy vypravljajut′. Fraška v I vidsloni̇̈. Vil′no za Šekspirovoju dramoju: Jak purjavyx uhovkujut′ napysav Ju. Fed′kovyč." In *Dramatyčni tvory Osypa Jurija Fed′kovyča z pervodrukiv i avtografiv*, edited by Oleksander Kolles, 411–453. Ukrajins′ko-rus′ka biblioteka, vol 3: *Pysannja Osypa Jurija Fed′kovyča*, part A. Lviv: Naukove Tovarystvo imeni Ševčenka.

Gospel: *The Gospel in Many Tongues: Specimens of 826 Languages in which The British and Foreign Society has Published or Circulated Some Portion of The Word of God*. 1954. London: The Bible House.

Grammatika: Pavlovskij, Aleksej Pavlovič [Oleksij Pavlovyč Pavlovs′kyj]. 1978. *Grammatika malorossijskogo narečija. St. Petersburg 1818. Pribavlenie k Grammatike malorossijskogo narečija. St. Petersburg 1822. Grammatici Ucraini*. Edited by Olexa Horbatsch [Oleksa Horbač]. Munich: Ukrajins′kyj Vil′nyj Universytet.

Halas: Kuliš, Pantelejmon. 1901. *Uillijam Šekspir. Bahac′ko halasu z nečevlja. Pereklad P. A. Kuliša*. With Introduction and Comments by Ivan Franko. Lviv: Ukrajins′ko-rus′ka vydavnyča spilka.

***Hamlet*-K**: Kuliš, Pantelejmon. n.d. *Hamlet. Pereklad z Šekspira*. Manuscript repository at the T. H. Ševčenko Institute of Ukrainian Literature of the National Academy of Sciences of Ukraine, Holding 18/37, 98 folios.

***Hamljet*-K/F**: Kuliš, Pantelejmon. 1899. *Uillijam Šekspir. Hamljet prync dans'kyj. Pereklad P. A. Kuliša*. With Introduction and Comments by Ivan Franko. Lviv: Ukrajins'ko-rus'ka vydavnyča spilka.

***Hamljet*-F/F**: Fed'kovyč, Jurij. 1902. *Hamljet*. In *Dramatyčni pereklady Osypa Jurija Fed'kovyča*, edited by Ivan Franko, 1–173. Ukrajins'ko-rus'ka biblioteka, vol 3: *Pysannja Osypa Jurija Fed'kovyča*, part 2. Lviv: Naukove Tovarystvo imeni Ševčenka.

***Hamlet*-S**: Staryc'kyj, Myxajlo. 1881. *Hamlet". Prync' Dans'kyj. Trahedija v" V dijax" V. Šekspira. Per. na ukrains'ku movu M. P. Staryc'kyj. Z" prylohoju muzyky M. Lysenka*. Kyiv: G. T. Korčak Novickij.

***Hamljet*-S**: Svij, Pavlo. 1865. *Hamljet", Dans'kyj Korolevyč"*. In *Nyva* 20 *sičnja* (2): 35–42; 10 *ljutoho* (4): 52–56; 20 *ljutoho* (5): 69–73; 10 *marta* (7): 101–104; 20 *marta* (8): 117–120; 30 *marta* (9): 132–138.

***Hemlet*-F**: Fed'kovyč, Jurij. n.d. *Hemlet Viljama Šekspira. Pereviv Ju. Fed'kovyč*. Manuscript repository at the T. H. Ševčenko Institute of Ukrainian Literature of the National Academy of Sciences of Ukraine, Holding 58/84, 62 folios.

Holosin'nja: Kuliš, Pantelejmon. 1897. *Starorus'kyj Pereklad S'vjatoho Pys'ma Staroho j Novoho Zapovidu perekladav že ëho Kuliš Olel'kovyč Pan'ko. Častyna druha. Holosin'n'*[sic]*nja j Pis'nja Pisen'*. Manuscript repository at the T. H. Ševčenko Institute of Ukrainian Literature of the National Academy of Sciences of Ukraine, Holding 18/22, folios 1r–19v.

Homer and Pot.: Potebnja, Aleksandr [Oleksander Potebnja]. 1905. *Otryvki iz perevoda Odissei*. In Aleksandr Potebnja, *Iz zapisok po russkoj slovesnosti*, 538–583. Kharkiv: M. Zil'berberg.

Horělka: "Raznovidnosti marcěpann" i hannuskovoj horělki." 1883. *Kievskaja starina* 7: 237–253, 637–651.

Hrinč.: Hrinčenko, Borys. 1924. *Slovar' ukrajins'koji movy. Ukrainsko-russkij slovar'*, 2 vols. Berlin: Ukrainske Slowo.

Hulak: Artemovs'kyj-Hulak, Petro. 1908. "Perespivy psalmiv." In *Tvory Ivana Kotljarevskoho, Petra Artemovskoho-Hulaka, Jevhenija Hrebinky*, 420–425. Rus'ka pys'mennist', vol. 1. Lviv: Naukove Tovarystvo imeni Ševčenka.

Hyjob: Kuliš, Pantelejmon. n.d. *Knyha Hyjoba*. Manuscript repository at the Myxajlo Kocjubyns'kyj Literary-Memorial Museum in Černihiv (Ukraine), No. A–4517, 67 folios (1324–1388).
Ioan: Kobyljans'kyj, Antin. 1881. *Pys'mo Svęte. Jevanhelije Ioana*. Lviv: A. I. Pik.
Iov: Aleksandrov, Volodymyr. 1877. *Knyha Iova na Malorus'ku movu pereložena prymïnęjučys' do Hrečeskoho, Latȳn'skoho, Pol'skoho, Jevrejskoho . . . Xar'kiv" roku božoho 1877*. Manuscript repository at the T. H. Ševčenko Institute of Ukrainian Literature of the National Academy of Sciences of Ukraine, Holding 22/87, 71 folios.
Kautzsch: Kautzsch, Emil. 1894. *Die heilige Schrift des Alten Testaments*. Freiburg im Breisgau: J. C. B. Mohr.
Kautzsch and Weizsäcker: Kautzsch, Emil and Carl Weizsäcker. 1911. *Textbibel des Alten und Neuen Testaments in Verbindung mit zahlreichen Fachgelehrten hearusgegeben von D. E. Kautzsch. Das Neue Testament in der Übersetzung von Carl Weizsäcker*. Tübingen: J. C. B. Mohr (P. Siebeck).
Knyha Tovyta: Aleksandrov, Volodymyr. 1881. *Knyha Tovyta. Pereložyv z Hreces'koho Dr". Med. Vlad. Aleksandrov". Xar'kiv" 1881 r.* Manuscript repository at the T. H. Ševčenko Institute of Ukrainian Literature of the National Academy of Sciences of Ukraine, Holding 22/89, 7 p. + 30 folios.
Kobzar': Ševčenko, Taras. 1861. "Kobzar'. XXXIV. Častyna poemy: Černycja Mar"jana." *Osnova* 9: 11–12.
Kor. and Slav.: *Peršyj rukopysnyj ukrajins'ko-latyns'kyj slovnyk Arsenija Korec'koho-Satanovs'koho ta Jepifanija Slavynec'koho*. 1968. Edited by Olexa Horbatsch [Oleksa Horbač]. Rome: Ukrajins'kyj Katolyc'kyj Univ. im. Sv. Klymentyja.
Kuliš to Biloborodov: Voznjak, Myxajlo, ed. 1929. "Pjat' lystiv P. Kuliša do Ol. Biloborodova." *Ukrajina. Naukovyj žurnal ukrajinoznavstva* (December): 88–92.
Kuliš to Galagan: "Častnaja perepiska G. P. Galagana. 3. Perepiska P. A. Kuliša (1856–1858 g.g.)." 1899. *Kievskaja starina* 66: 341–355.
Kuliš to Hatcuk: Savčenko, Fedir Jakovyč. 1929. "Spivrobitnyctvo P. Kuliša z Oleksoju Hatcukom. Lysty P. Kuliša do Oleksy Hatcuka

(1872–1874)." In *P. O. Kuliš (materijaly i rozvidky)*, part 1, edited by Kyrylo Studyns′kyj and Fedir Savčenko, 43–48, 49–72. Zbirnyk filolohičnoji sekciji Naukovoho Tovarystva imeni Ševčenka, vol. 22. Lviv: Naukove Tovarystvo imeni Ševčenka.

Kuliš to Kistjakovskij: "Pis′ma P. A. Kuliša k A. F. Kistjakovskomu." 1902. *Kievskaja starina* 2: 298–312; 3: 518–531; 4: 6–24.

Kuliš to Nos: "Iz pisem P. A. Kuliša k S. D. Nosu." 1899. *Kievskaja starina* 4: 8–31.

Kuliš to Tarnovskij: "Pis′ma P. A. Kuliša k V. V. Tarnovskomu-synu. 1857–1897." 1899. *Kievskaja starina* 1: 81–100.

Kuliš to Tymčenko: "Lystuvannja Pantelejmona Kuliša z Jevhenom Tymčenkom (1899–1895)." 1998. With Introduction and Comments by Stepan Zaxarkin. *Kyjivs′ka starovyna* 4: 94–108.

Kuliš to Veresaj: "Pis′ma k Ostapu Veresaju P. A. Kuliša i L. M. Žemčužnikova." 1904. *Kievskaja starina* 2: 212–228.

Kuliš to Xil′čevskij: "Pis′ma Kuliša k I. F. Xil′čevskomu." 1898. *Kievskaja starina* 1: 84–149.

Kuzela and Rud.: Kuzela, Zeno and Jaroslau Rudnyćkyj [Zenon Kuzelja and Jaroslav Rudnyc′kyj]. 1943. *Ukrainisch-Deutsches Wörterbuch*. Leipzig: Otto Harrassowitz.

Kvitka: Žovtobrjux, Myxajlo Andrijovyč, ed. 1978–1979. *Slovnyk movy tvoriv H. Kvitky-Osnov′janenka u tr′ox tomax*, vols. 1–3. Kharkiv: Xarkivs′kyj deržavnyj universytet.

Laur.: *Polnoe sobranie russkix letopisej*, vol. 1: *Lavrent′evskaja letopis′ i Suzdal′skaja letopis′ po akademičeskomu spisku*, 2nd ed. 1962. Moscow: Izd-vo vostočnoj literatury.

Lěč.: Potebnja, Aleksandr [Oleksander Potebnja]. 1890. "Malorusskie domašnie lečebniki XVIII v." *Kievskaja starina* 28: 91–94; *Supplement* 1: 1–32; 2: 33–48; 3: 49–59.

Leksykon″: *Suprasl′skij cerkovnoslavjano-pol′skij slovar′ 1722 g*. 1995. Edited by Jurij Andreevič Labyncev and Larisa Leonidovna Sčavinskaja. Minsk: Nacional′naja biblioteka Belarusi.

Lexicon: Miklosich, Franz von [Franjo Miklošič]. 1963. *Lexicon Palaeo-slovenico-Graeco-Latinum. Emendum auctum*. Facsimile reprint of 1862–1865. Darmstadt: Scientia Verlag Aalen.

Lir-F: Franko, Ivan. 1956. *Korol' Lir*. In *Literaturna spadščyna*, vol. 1: *Ivan Franko*, 234–235. Kyiv: Akademija nauk Ukrajins'koji RSR.
Lir-K: Kuliš, Pantelejmon. n.d. *Korol' Lyr*. In Pantelejmon Kuliš, *Šekspyrovy Tvory z Movy Brytans'koi Movoju Ukrains'koju poperekladav P. A. Kuliš. Tom druhyj. Korol' Lyr. Koryolan. Pryborkana Hostruxa*. Manuscript repository at the T. H. Ševčenko Institute of Ukrainian Literature of the National Academy of Sciences of Ukraine, Holding 18/39, 91+1 folios.
Lir-M: Myrnyj, Panas. 1897. *Korol' Lir. Pereklad z Šekspira*. Manuscript repository at the T. H. Ševčenko Institute of Ukrainian Literature of the National Academy of Sciences of Ukraine, Holding 5/232, 76 folios.
Lir-1970: Myrnyj, Panas. 1970. *Korol' Lir*. In Panas Myrnyj, *Zibrannja tvoriv u semy tomax*, vol. 6: *Dramatyčni tvory*, 511–682. Kyiv: Naukova dumka.
LLP: *Slovník jazyka staroslověnského. Lexicon linguae palaeoslovenicae*, vols. 1–4. 1958–1995. Prague: Československá akademie věd.
Luka-L: [Kobyljans'kyj, Antin]. 1874. *Evanhèlïe Lukì*. Lviv: A. Reichard.
Luka-U: [Kobyljans'kyj, Antin]. 1874. *Jevanhèlije Lukỳ*. Lviv: A. Reichard.
Lysenko: Lysenko, Panas Sylovyč. 1974. *Slovnyk polis'kyx hovoriv*. Kyiv: Naukova dumka.
Lystuvannja: Svjencic'kyj, Ilarion, ed. 1993. *Lystuvannja ukrajins'kyx slavistiv z Francem Miklošyčem*. Kyiv: Naukova dumka.
M-Synod: [Moračevs'kyj, Pylyp]. 1907. *Hospoda našoho Iysusa Xrysta Svjate Jevanhelije vid Matfeja, slavjans'koju j ukrajins'koju movoju*, 4th ed. Moscow: Synodal'na typohrafija.
Machek: Machek, Václav. 1957. *Etymologický slovník jazyka českého a slovenského*. Prague: Československé akademie věd.
Makbet-K: Kuliš, Pantelejmon. n.d. *Makbet*. In Pantelejmon Kuliš, *Šekspyrovy Tvory z Movy Brytans'koi Movoju Ukrains'koju poperekladav P. A. Kuliš. Tom četvertyj. Makbet. Antonij y Kleopatra. Mira za Miru*. Manuscript repository at the T. H. Ševčenko Institute of Ukrainian Literature of the National Academy of Sciences of Ukraine, Holding 18/40, 67 folios.

***Makbet*-K/F**: Kuliš, Pantelejmon. 1900. *Uillijam Šekspir. Makbet. Pereklad P. A. Kuliša.* With Introduction and Comments by Ivan Franko. Lviv: Naukove Tovarystvo imeni Ševčenka.

***Makbet*-M**: Myrnyj, Panas. n.d. *Makbet. Pereklad z Šekspira.* Manuscript repository at the T. H. Ševčenko Institute of Ukrainian Literature of the National Academy of Sciences of Ukraine, Holding 5/234, 23 folios.

***Makbet*-U**: Ukrajinka, Lesja. 1898. *Pereklad z Šekspira "Makbet."* Manuscript repository at the T. H. Ševčenko Institute of Ukrainian Literature of the National Academy of Sciences of Ukraine, Holding 2/903, 6 [11] folios.

***Merchant*-F**: Franko, Ivan. 1956. *Venec'kyj kupec'.* In *Literaturna spadščyna*, vol. 1: *Ivan Franko*, 238–333. Kyiv: Akademija nauk Ukrajins'koji RSR.

Mira: Kuliš, Pantelejmon. 1902. *Uillijam Šekspir. Mira za miru. Pereklad P. A. Kuliša.* With Introduction and Comments by Ivan Franko. Lviv: Ukrajins'ko-rus'ka vydavnyča spilka.

Molytovnyk: Puljuj, Ivan. 1997. *Zbirnyk prac'*, vol. 3: *Molytovnyk. Psaltyr*, 25–172. Kyiv: Rada.

Mosej: Kuliš, Pantelejmon. n.d. *S'vjate Pys'mo. Pjat' knyh Mosejëvyx.* Manuscript repository at the Myxajlo Kocjubyns'kyj Literary-Memorial Museum in Černihiv (Ukraine), No. A–4512/1–5, 497 folios.

Mosej, Biblija: Kuliš, Pantelejmon. n.d. *Pjat' knyh Mosejëvyx.* Manuscript repository at the Myxajlo Kocjubyns'kyj Literary-Memorial Museum in Černihiv (Ukraine), No. A–4513, 416 folios.

Narodni Pisni: "Narodni pisni." 1882. *Zorja* 22: 344–345.

Nekraševyč: Kistjakivs'ka, Natalja, ed. 1929. *Tvory Ivana Nekraševyča. Rozvidka j teksty.* Pam'jatky movy ta pys'menstva davn'oji Ukrajiny, vol. 2. Kyiv: VUAN.

Nomys: Nomys, Matvij. 1864. *Ukrains'ki prykazky, prysliv"ja y take ynše.* St. Petersburg: Tiblen i Kuliš.

NZ: Kuliš, Pantelejmon and Ivan Puljuj. 1887. *Svęte pys'mo Novoho Zavitu. Movoju rus'ko-ukrains'koju pereklaly vkupi P. A. Kuliš y Dr. Y. Puljuj.* Lviv: A. I. Pik.

Osnova: *Osnova. Južno-russkij literaturno-učenyj věstnik".* 1861–1862. St. Petersburg: n.p.

Otvět': [Kuliš, Pantelejmon]. 1861. "Otvet" Sovremennoj Lětopisi Russkago Věstnika." *Osnova* 2: 256–259.

Pentatevx: Kuliš, Pantelejmon. 1869. *Svjate Pys′mo abo vsja Byblyja Staroho y Novoho zavitu rus′ko-ukrains′koju movoju pereložena*. Lviv: Pravda.

PG 1556–1561: *Peresopnyc′ke Jevanhelije 1556–1561*. 2001. Facsimile reprint. Edited by Inna Petrivna Čepiha et al. Kyiv: Nacional′na Akademija nauk Ukrajiny, Nacional′na biblioteka Ukrajiny im. V. I. Vernads′koho.

Pipaš and Halas: Pipaš, Jurij and Borys Halas. 2005. *Materialy do slovnyka hucul′s′kyx hovirok*. Užhorod: Užhorods′kyj nacional′nyj universytet.

Pisn′, Navroc′kyj: Navroc′kyj, Oleksandr. n.d. *Pisn′ pisen′*. Manuscript repository at the T. H. Ševčenko Institute of Ukrainian Literature of the National Academy of Sciences of Ukraine, Holding 21/7, 24 folios.

Pisni: [Kuliš, Pantelejmon]. 1868. "Musijeva pisnja: Nad″ Červonym″ morem″. Peredsmertnja pisnja Musijeva." *Pravda* 42 (22 November): 498–501.

Pis′nja: Kuliš, Pantelejmon. 1897. *Starorus′kyj Pereklad S′vjatoho Pys′ma Staroho j Novoho Zapovidu perekladav že ëho Kuliš Olel′kovyč Pan′ko. Častyna druha. Holosin′ [n′]ja j Pis′nja Pisen′*. Manuscript repository at the T. H. Ševčenko Institute of Ukrainian Literature of the National Academy of Sciences of Ukraine, Holding 18/22, folios 20r–34v.

Pracht Bible: Fürst, Julius. 1874. *Illustrierte Pracht Bibel für Israeliten in dem masoretischen Text and neuer deutscher Übersetzung*. Leipzig: A. H. Payne.

Pryborkana hostruxa: Kuliš, Pantelejmon. 1900. *Uillijam Šekspir. Pryborkana hostruxa: komedija v 5 dijax z peredohroju. Pereklad P. A. Kuliša*. With Introduction and Comments by Ivan Franko. Lviv: Ukrajins′ko-rus′ka vydavnyča spilka.

Psal′ma 1: [Kuliš, Pantelejmon]. 1868. "Davydovi psal′my. Psal′ma I." *Pravda* 39 (22 October): 461.

Psal′ma 13: [Kuliš, Pantelejmon]. 1868. "Davydovi psal′my. Psal′ma XIII." *Pravda* 45 (15 December): 533.

Psal´ma 15: [Kuliš, Pantelejmon]. 1869. "Psal´ma XV." *Pravda* 1 (8 January): 6.

Psal´ma 16: Rataj, Pavlo [Pantelejmon Kuliš]. 1869. "Psal´ma XVI." *Pravda* 5 (8 February): 38.

***Psal´my,* Navroc´kyj**: Navroc´kyj, Oleksandr. n.d. *Knyha Psalmiv Proroka Davyda*. Manuscript repository at the T. H. Ševčenko Institute of Ukrainian Literature of the National Academy of Sciences of Ukraine, Holding 21/6, 181 folios.

Psalmy̆: Šaškevyč, Markijan. 1912. "Psalmy̆ Ruslanovy." In *Pysannja Markijana Šaškevyča*, edited by Myxajlo Voznjak, 69–70. Naukove Tovarystvo imeni Ševčenka, Zbirnyk fil´ologičnoji sekciji, vol. 14. Lviv: Naukove Tovarystvo imeni Ševčenka.

Psalom˝: "Z rukopysy 'Psaltyr´ perevedeny̆j svjašč. Pl. Dn.' (Psalom˝ 40)." 1855. *Zorja Halycka* 7 (16 February): 97.

Psalom˝ 20: Aleksandrov, Volodymyr. n.d. "Psalom˝ 20." Manuscript repository at the T. H. Ševčenko Institute of Ukrainian Literature of the National Academy of Sciences of Ukraine, Holding 22/37, 1 folio.

***Psaltyr,* Moračevs´kyj**: Moračevs´kyj, Pylyp. 1865. *Psaltyr na malorus´kij movi. Perelożyv P. Moračevs´kyj 1865 roku. h. Nižyn*. Institute of Manuscripts at the V. I. Vernads´kyj National Library of Ukraine, H 1/638, 30 folios.

***Psaltyr˝,* Moračevs´kyj**: *Psaltyr: pereklad novoju ukrajins´koju literaturnoju movoju P. S. Moračevs´koho (1865)*. 2015. Edited by Ljudmyla Anatolijivna Hnatenko and Vasyl´ Vasyl´ovyč Nimčuk. Pam'jatky ukrajins´koji movy XIX st., Serija kanoničnoji literatury. Kyiv: Nacional´na biblioteka Ukrajiny im. V. I. Vernads´koho.

***Psaltyr,* Rataj**: Kuliš, Pantelejmon. 1909. "Psaltyr abo Knyha xvaly Božoji. Perespiv ukrajins´kyj Pavla Rataja." In *Tvory Pantelejmona Kuliša*, vol. 3, 107–339. Rus´ka pys´mennist´, vol. VI, part 3. Lviv: Naukove Tovarystvo imeni Ševčenka.

***Psaltyr´,* Bačyn´skij**: Bačyn´skij, Aleksander. 1903. *Psaltyr´ v˝ jazy̆cě cerkovno-sloven´skôm˝ s˝ perevodom˝ na jazy̆k˝ narodno-ruskij O. Aleksandra Bačyn´skoho*. Lviv: Byblioteka bohoslovskaja.

Psaltyr´ 1862: *Psaltyr´ ili kniga xvalenij na rossijskom jazyke*. 1862. London: British and Foreign Bible Society.

***Psaltyr'* 1897**: Kuliš, Pantelejmon. 1897. *Psaltyr'. Knyha perva*. Manuscript repository at the Myxajlo Kocjubyns'kyj Literary-Memorial Museum in Černihiv (Ukraine), No. 4515, 48 folios.
PSP: "Po povodu izdanija Sv. Pisanija v ukrainskom perevode." 1904. *Kievskaja starina* 87: 54–65.
RD: *Rusalka Dněstrovaja. Ruthenische Volkslieder*. 1837. Buda: n.p.
Renan: *Le livre de Job traduit de l'hébreu avec une étude sur l'age et le caractère du poème par Ernest Renan*, 4th ed. 1882. Paris: Ancienne Maison Michel Lévy Prères.
Reuß: Reuß, Eduard. 1892–1894. *Das Alte Testament: übersetzt, eingeleitet und erläutert von D. Eduard Reuß*, vol. 1: *Algemeine Einleitung zur Bibel. Überblick der Geschichte der Israeliten. Die Geschichtsbücher*; vol. 2: *Die Propheten*; vol. 3: *Die heilige Geschichte und das Gesetz*; vol. 4: *Die Kirchenchronik von Jerusalem*; vol. 5: *Die hebraische Poesie*; vol. 6: *Religions- und Moralphilosophie der Hebräer*; vol. 7: *Die politische und polemische Litteratur der Hebräer*. Braunschweig: C. A. Schwetschke und Sohn.
Romeo: Kuliš, Pantelejmon. 1901. *Uillijam Šekspir. Romeo ta Džul'jeta. Pereklad P. A. Kuliša*. With Introduction and Comments by Ivan Franko. Lviv: Ukrajins'ko-rus'ka vydavnyča spilka.
Šaškevyč: Šaškevyč, Markijan. 1912. "Z jevanhelija sv. Mateja. Pereklad jevanhelija sv. Ivana." In *Pysannja Markijana Šaškevyča*, edited by Myxajlo Voznjak, 107–142. Naukove Tovarystvo imeni Ševčenka, Zbirnyk fil'ologičnoji sekciji, vol. 14. Lviv: Naukove Tovarystvo imeni Ševčenka.
Šaškevyč 1913: Šaškevyč, Markijan. 1913. "Pereklady jevanhelij." In *Tvory Markijana Šaškevyča i Jakova Holovac'koho*, 2nd ed., 128–132. Rus'ka pys'mennist', vol. III, part 1. Lviv: Naukove Tovarystvo imeni Ševčenka.
SEJP: Boryś, Wiesław. 2005. *Słownik etymologiczny języka polskiego*. Cracow: Wydawnictwo Literackie.
Šekspir: Kuliš, Pantelejmon. 1882. *Šekspyrovi tvory z movy brytans'koi movoju ukrains'koju poperekladav P. A. Kuliš*, vol. 1: *Otello. Troil ta Kressyda. Komedija pomylok*. Lviv: [Naukove] Tovarystvo imeni Ševčenka.

Šel´menko: Kvitka-Osnov'janenko, Hryhorij. 1830. *Šel´menko volostnoj pisar´*. Kharkiv: Universitetskaja Tipografija.

Shakespeare: Shakespeare, William. 1970. *The Complete Plays and Poems of William Shakespeare: A New Text Edited With Introduction and Notes By William Allan Neilson and Charles Jarvis Hill*. New York: Houghton Mifflin Company.

SK: *Svjaščennyja knigi Vetxago i novago Zavěta*. 1903. Vienna: Izd. Britanskago i Inostrannago Biblejskago Obščestva.

Sljusarčuk: "Sljusarčuk Oleksij." 1976. In *Encyklopedija ukrajinoznavstva*, vol. II/8, edited by Volodymyr Kubijovyč, 2913. Paris and New York: Shevchenko Scientific Society, Inc., Molode Zyttia Press.

Solomon: Myrnyj, Panas. n.d. *1. Solomonova pisnja nad pisnjamy. 2. Sučasna pisnja nad pisnjamy*. Manuscript repository at the T. H. Ševčenko Institute of Ukrainian Literature of the National Academy of Sciences of Ukraine, Holding 5/240, 241 (without pagination).

SP: *S´vjate Pys´mo Staroho i Novoho Zavitu movoju rus´ko-ukrajins´koju. Pereklad P. O. Kuliša, I. S. Levic´koho i Puljuja*. 1903. Translated by Pantelejmon Kuliš et al. Vienna: Vyd. Brytans´koho i Zahranyčn´oho Biblijnoho Tovarystva.

SP/NZ: *Novyj Zapovit*. 1903. In *S´vjate Pys´mo Staroho i Novoho Zavitu movoju rus´ko-ukrajins´koju. Pereklad P. O. Kuliša, I. S. Levic´koho i Puljuja*, translated by Pantelejmon Kuliš et al., 1–249. Vienna: Vyd. Brytans´koho i Zahranyčn´oho Biblijnoho Tovarystva.

SP, Ohijenko: *Biblija abo Knyhy Svjatoho Pys´ma Staroho j Novoho Zapovitu, iz movy davnjojevrejs´koji ta hrec´koji na ukrajins´ku nanovo perekladena*. 1988. Moscow: Moskovs´kyj Patryarxat.

SP, Xomenko: *Svjate Pys´mo Staroho ta Novoho Zavitu, povnyj pereklad, zdijsnenyj za oryginal´nymy jevrejs´kymy, aramijs´kymy ta hrec´kymy tekstamy*. N.p.: United Bible Societies.

Spivy̆: Aleksandrov, Volodymyr. 1882–1883. *Tyxomovni spivy̆ na svjati motivy̆. Pereviv˝z˝ Jevrejs´koho jazy̆ka Vl. Aleksandrov˝*. Manuscript repository at the T. H. Ševčenko Institute of Ukrainian Literature of the National Academy of Sciences of Ukraine, Holding 22/55, 38 folios (some parts of the manuscript without pagination).

Sr.: Sreznevskij, Izmail Ivanovič. 1893–1903. *Materialy dlja slovarja drevne-russkogo jazyka po pis'mennym pamjatnikam*; 1912. *Materialy dlja slovarja drevne-russkogo jazyka po pis'mennym pamjatnikam. Dopolnenija.* St. Petersburg: Tipografija Imperatorskoj Akademii nauk.

SŠ: Vaščenko, Vasyl' Semenovyč, ed. 1964. *Slovnyk movy Ševčenka*, vols. 1–2. Kyiv: Naukova dumka.

Svedenija: "Svedenija o četverojevangelii v perevode na malorusskij jazyk F. S. Moračevskogo." 1902. *Kievskaja starina* 78, no. 9: 93–99.

Tarkovyč: *Bíblija sýrěč' knýhy svjaščénnaho pysányja vétxaho y nóvaho zavěta*, vols. 1–5. 1804–1805. Buda: n.p.

Tempest-F: Franko, Ivan. 1956. *Burja.* In *Literaturna spadščyna*, vol. 1: *Ivan Franko*, 236–237. Kyiv: Akademija nauk Ukrajins'koji RSR.

Tovyt: Kuliš, Pantelejmon. 1909. "Tovytovi slovesa, perekazani starorusčynoju." In *Tvory Pantelejmona Kuliša*, vol. 3, 340–358. Rus'ka pys'mennist', vol. VI, part 3. Lviv: Naukove Tovarystvo imeni Ševčenka.

Tymč.: Tymčenko, Jevhen, ed. 1930–1932. *Istoryčnyj slovnyk ukrajins'koho jazyka*, vol. 1. Kyiv and Kharkiv: Deržavne Vydavnyctvo Ukrajiny.

Tymč. and Nimčuk: Tymčenko, Jevhen. 2003. *Materialy do slovnyka pysemnoji ta knyžnoji ukrajins'koji movy XV–XVIII st.*, vols. 1–2, edited by Vasyl' Vasyl'ovyč Nimčuk and Halyna Ivanivna Lysa. Kyiv and New York: Nacional'na Akademija nauk Ukrajiny, Ukrajins'ka Vil'na Akademija Nauk u SŠA.

UB: Kuliš, Pantelejmon. n.d. *Ustyxotvorena Byblyja: Knyha Nastan'nja S'vitu, Častyna Perva Knyhy Moyseëvoi Pervoi*. Manuscript repository at the Myxajlo Kocjubyns'kyj Literary-Memorial Museum in Černihiv (Ukraine), No. A–4540, 110 folios.

Umanec' and Spilka: Umanec', M. and A. Spilka. 1893. *Slovar' rosyjs'ko-ukrajins'kyj*. Lviv: [Naukove] Tovarystvo imeni Ševčenka.

VUI: Onatskyj, Euhen [Jevhen Onac'kyj]. 1977. *Vocabolario ucraino-italiano*. Romae: Editiones Universitatis Catholicae Ucrainorum S. Clementis Papae.

Vasmer: Vasmer, Max. 1953–1958. *Russisches etymologisches Wörterbuch*, vols. 1–3. Heidelberg: Carl Winter.

Vytv.: Rieger, Janusz, ed. 1997. *Slovnyk pol's'ko-cerkovnoslov'jans'ko-ukrajins'kyj Teodora Vytvyc'koho z polovyny XIX storiččja*. With

Introduction and Comments by Josyp Dzendzelivs'kyj. Warsaw: Semper.
Xil'čevskij, Nekrolog: Xil'čevskij, I. F. 1899. "Nekrolog." *Kievskaja starina* 2: 87.
Yov: Kuliš, Pantelejmon. 1868. *Yov.* Manuscript repository at the T. H. Ševčenko Institute of Ukrainian Literature of the National Academy of Sciences of Ukraine, Holding 18/166, 69 folios.
Yov, Pravda: Rataj, Pavlo [Pantelejmon Kuliš]. 1869. *Yov. Pravda* 6 (15 Februry): 41–45; 7 (22 February): 53–58; 8 (28 February): 65–70; 9 (8 March): 77–80; 10 (15 March): 85–89; 11 (22 March): 93–100.
Yov, 1869: [Kuliš, Pantelejmon]. 1869. *Yov, perespiv Pavla Rataja*. Lviv: Pravda.
Zinovijiv: Zinovijiv, Klymentij. 1971. *Virši. Prypovisty pospolyti*, edited by Inna Petrivna Čepiha and Viktorija Petrivna Kolosova. Kyiv: Naukova dumka.
Žel.: Želexovskyj, Jevhenyj [Jevhen Želexivs'kyj]. 1886. *Ruthenisch-Deutsches Wörterbuch*, vols. 1–2. Lviv: Szewczenko-Verein.

SECONDARY SOURCES

Ajzenštok, Ijeremija. 1928. "Peredmova." In *Kotljarevščyna*, edited by Ijeremija Ajzenštok, 5–121. Ukrajins'ki propileji, vol. 1. Kharkiv: Deržavne vydavnyctvo Ukrajiny.
Andriewsky, Olga. 2003. "The Russian-Ukrainian Discourse and the Failure of the 'Little Russian Solution,' 1782–1917." In *Culture, Nation, and Identity: The Ukrainian-Russian Encounter (1600–1945)*, edited by Andreas Kappeler et al., 182–214. Edmonton and Toronto: CIUS Press.
Aničěnka, Uladzimir Vasil'evič. 1969. *Belaruska-ukrainskija pis'mova-mounyja suvjazi*. Minsk: Navuka i tèxnika.
Antonovyč, Marko. 1969. "P. Kuliš v ocinci I. Nečuja-Levyc'koho." *Ukrajins'kyj istoryk* 4, no. 24: 38–46.
Arpolenko, Hanna. 2003. "P. Moračevs'kyj i peršyj povnyj pereklad Sv. Jevanhelija novoukrajins'koju movoju." *Volyn'-Žytomyrščyna* 10: 212–220.

Barvins'kyj, Oleksander. 2004. *Spomyny z moho žyttja*, parts 1–2. New York and Kyiv: Smoloskyp.
Batalden, Stephen K. 2013. *Russian Bible Wars: Modern Scriptural Translation and Cultural Authority*. Cambridge: Cambridge University Press.
Baudouin de Courtenay, Jan Niecisław Ignacy. 1925. "Kilka ogólników objektywnej i subjektywnej odrębności 'Ukrainy' pod względem językowym, plemiennym, narodowym i państwowym." In *Zapysky Naukovoho Tovarystva imeni Ševčenka*, vols. 141–143: *Juvilejnyj zbirnyk Naukovoho Tovarystva imeni Ševčenka v pjatdesjatylittja osnovannja. 1873–1923*, edited by Kyrylo Studyns'kyj, 1–19. Lviv: Naukove Tovarystvo imeni Ševčenka.
___. 1983. *Dzieła Wybrane*, vol. 6. Warsaw: Państwowe Wydawnictwo Naukowe.
Bernac'ka, Halyna. 1993. "Iz nevidomoho lystuvannja Mykoly Lysenka z Halyčanamy." In *Zapysky Naukovoho tovarystva imeni Ševčenka*, vol. 226: *Praci muzykoznavčoji komisiji*, edited by Oleh Kupčyns'kyj and Jurij Jasynovs'kyj, 245–264. Lviv: Naukove tovarystvo imeni Ševčenka.
Bevzenko, Stepan Pylypovyč et al. 1978. *Istorija ukrajins'koji movy. Morfolohija*. Kyiv: Nukova dumka.
___. 1997. "Formy vyjavu majbutnjoji diji v ukrajins'kyx dialektax." In *Ukrajins'kyj dialektolohičnyj zbirnyk*, vol. 3, edited by Pavlo Juxymovyč Hrycenko et al., 213–217. Kyiv: Dovira.
Bilenky, Serhiy. 2012. *Romantic Nationalism in Eastern Europe: Russian, Polish, and Ukrainian Political Imaginations*. Stanford: Standford University Press.
Bilodid, Ivan Kostjantynovyč, ed. 1969. *Sučasna ukrajins'ka literaturna mova. Vstup, fonetyka*. Kyiv: Naukova dumka.
Boduèn de Kurtene, Ivan Aleksandrovič [Jan Niecisław Ignacy Baudouin de Courtenay]. 1963. "O smešanom xaraktere vsex jazykov." In Ivan Aleksandrovič Boduèn de Kurtene, *Izbrannye trudy po obščemu jazykoznaniju*, vol. 2, edited by Sergei Grigor'evič Barxudarov, 363–366. Moscow: Izd-vo AN SSSR.
Boduen de Kurtene, Jan Njecislav Ignacy [Jan Niecisław Ignacy Baudouin de Courtenay]. 2002. "Dekil'ka zahal'nyx zavvah ščodo ob'jektyvnoji

ta sub'jektyvnoji orkemišnosti 'Ukrajiny' z movnoho, pleminnoho, nacional'noho j deržavnoho pohljadu," translated by Viktorija Piddubna. In *Zbirnyk Xarkivs'koho istoryko-filolohičnoho tovarystva*, vol. 9, edited by Serhii Vakulenko, 315–330. Kharkiv: Xarkivs'ke istoryko-filolohične tovarystvo.

Bulaxovs'kyj, Leonid Arsen'ovyč. 1977. *Vybrani praci v p'jaty tomax*, vol. 2: *Ukrajins'ka mova*. Kyiv: Naukova dumka.

Čaplenko, Vasyl'. 1955. *Ukrajins'ka literaturna mova, jiji vynyknennja i rozvytok*. New York: Ukrajins'kyj texničnyj instytut v N'ju-Jorku.

Cixoc'kyj, Ivan. 2006. *Mova prozy Ivana Franka (stytlistyčni novaciji)*. Lviv: Vydavnyčyj centr LNU imeni Ivana Franka.

Collins, John J. 2005. "The Judaism of the Book of Tobit." In *The Book of Tobit: Text, Tradition, Theology—Papers of the First International Conference on the Deuteronomical Books, Pápa, Hungary, 20–21 May, 2004*, edited by Géza G. Xeravits and József Zsengellér, 23–40. Leiden and Boston: Brill.

Čykalenko, Jevhen. 1955. *Spohady (1861–1907)*. New York: The Ukrainian Academy of Arts and Sciences.

Cymbalistyj, Petro. 1991. *Ukrainian Linguistic Elements in the Russian Language: 1680–1760*. London: University of London.

Danylenko, Andrii. 1999. "Šče raz pro vysokyj styl' u Potebnevim perekladi *"Odisseji."*" *Wiener slavistisches Jahrbuch* 45: 231–250.

___. 2001. "Deščo pro dijalektnu osnovu Ševčenkovoji movy." In *The Worlds of Taras Shevchenko*, vol. 2, edited by Larissa M. L. Z. Onyshkevych et al., 271–286. New York and Lviv: Ševčenko Scientific Society.

___. 2003a. *Predykaty, vidminky i diatezy v ukrajins'kij movi: istoryčnyj i typolohičnyj aspekty*. Kharkiv: Oko.

___. 2003b. "An Uneven Contest Between Ethnographism and Europeanism." *Journal of Ukrainian Studies* 28, no. 1: 89–103.

___. 2003c. "Misce ukrajins'koji movy v linhvistyčnyx pohljadax Oleksandra Potebni." In *Zapysky Naukovoho tovarystva imeni Ševčenka*, vol. 246, edited by Oleh Kupčyns'kyj, 300–320. Lviv: Naukove tovarystvo imeni Ševčenka.

___. 2005. "From *G to H* and Again to *G* in Ukrainian: Between the West European and Byzantine Tradition?" *Die Welt der Slaven* 50, no. 1: 33–56.

___. 2006a. "*Prostaja mova, Kitab*, and Polissian Standard." *Die Welt der Slaven* 51, no. 1: 80–115.

___. 2006b. "On the Name(s) of the *Prostaja mova* in the Polish-Lithuanian Commonwealth." *Studia Slavica Hungarica* 51, no. 1–2: 97–121.

___. 2006c. *Slavica et Islamica: Ukrainian in Context.* Munich: Otto Sagner.

___. 2007. "The Uniate *Catechism* of 1722: A Case of Regional Relapse from Script- to Language-Switching." *Slavia Orientalis* 56, no. 4: 543–557.

___. 2008a. "The Formation of New Standard Ukrainian: From the History of an Undeclared Contest Between Right- and Left-Bank Ukraine in the 18th Century." *Die Welt der Slaven* 53, no. 1: 82–115.

___. 2008b. "The New Ukrainian Standard Language (1798)—Between Tradition and Innovation." In *American Contributions to the 14th Congress of Slavists in Ohrid, Macedonia, 2008*, vol. 1: *Linguistics*, edited by Christina Y. Bethin, 59–74. Bloomington, IN: Slavica Publishers.

___. 2009a. "Myxajlo Lučkaj—A Dissident Forerunner of Literary Rusyn?" *The Slavonic and East European Review* 87, no. 2: 201–226.

___. 2009b. "'Xaj dufaje Srul' na pana': do istoriji stosunkiv I. Franka z P. Kulišem." In *Filolohični studiji*, edited by Lidija Andrijivna Lysyčenko et al., 354–363. Kharkiv: Xarkivs'kyj nacional'nyj pedahohičnyj universytet.

___. 2009c. "Between the Vernacular and Slaveno-Rusyn: The *Huklyvyj Chronicle* and the Eighteenth-Century Rusyn Literary Language." *Slavia Orientalis* 59, no. 1: 53–75.

___. 2009d. "Forward into the Past, or How to Particularize New Standard Ukrainian." *Slavic and East European Journal* 53, no. 3: 471–542.

___. 2010a. "The Holy Gospels in Vernacular Ukrainian: Antin Kobyljans'kyj (1874, 1877) vs. Pantelejmon Kuliš (1871)." *Die Welt der Slaven* 55, no. 1: 83–104.

___. 2010b. "The Ukrainian Bible and the Valuev Circular of 18 July 1863." *Acta Slavica Iaponica* 28, no. 1: 1–21.

___. 2010c. "Naskil'ky ukrajins'kyi syntetyčnyi majbutnij čas je syntetyčnym?" *Movoznavstvo* 4–5: 113–121.

___. 2011a. "Is There Any Inflectional Future in East Slavic? A Case of Ukrainian Against Romance Reopened." In *Grammaticalization in*

Slavic Languages, edited by Motoki Nomachi, 147–177. Sapporo: Slavic Research Center, Hokkaido University.

———. 2011b. "Mykola Khanenko: 'With a dispatch of seven cucumbers fresh . . .': A Case Study of Linguistic Mentality in the Eighteenth-Century Hetmanate." *Harvard Ukrainian Studies* 29, no. 1–4 (2007): *Ukrainian Philology and Linguistics in the Twenty-First Century*, edited by Michael S. Flier: 225–226.

———. 2012a. "Auxiliary Clitics in Southwest Ukrainian: Questions of Chronology, Areal Distribution, and Grammaticalization." *Journal of Slavic Linguistics* 20, no. 1: 3–34.

———. 2012b. "'Pyšy, jak movyš . . .,' abo čomu Pantelejmon Kuliš ne stav tvorcem sučasnoho ukrajins'koho pravopysu." *Movoznavstvo* 4: 37–54.

———. 2014a. "On the Relativization Strategies in East Slavic." In *Grammaticalization and Lexicalization in Slavic*, edited by Motoki Nomachi, Andrii Danylenko, and Piper Predrag, 183–204. Die Welt der Slaven Sammelbände. Sborniki, vol. 55. Munich: Otto Sagner.

———. 2014b. "Pro pol's'koho Šekspira P. Svjencic'koho ta manivci ukrajins'koji literaturnoji movy v Halyčyni v XIX st." In *Linhvistyčni studiji: na pošanu koryfeju* [Dorošenko Serhij Ivanovyč], edited by Lidija Andrijivna Lysyčenko et al., 304–308. Kharkiv: Xarkivs'kyj nacional'nyj pedahohičnyj universytet.

———. 2015a. "How Many Varieties of Standard Ukrainian Does One Need?" *Die Welt der Slaven* 60, no. 2: 223–247.

———. 2015b. "*Iazychie* and *Surzhyk*: Mixing Languages and Identities in the Ukrainian Borderlands." In *The Palgrave Handbook of Slavic Language, Identities and Borders*, edited by Tomasz Kamusella, Motoki Nomachi, and Catherine Gibson, 81–100. New York: Palgrave Macmillan.

———. 2015c. "The Chicken or the Egg? Onomatopoeic Particles and Verbs in Baltic and Slavic." In *Contemporary Approaches to Baltic Linguistics*, edited by Peter Arkadiev, Axel Holvoet, and Björn Wiemer, 524–542. Berlin and Boston: De Gruyter Mouton.

Dem'jančuk, Vasyl'. 1928. "Čy rumuns'koho poxodžennja formy pryjdučoho na -*mu*?" *Zapysky Istoryčno-Filolohičnoho Viddilu UVAN* 18: 313–317.

Dobrowsky [Dobrovský], Josef. 1822. *Institutiones linguae Slavicae dialecti veteris, quae quum apud Russos, Serbos aliosque ritus Graeci, tum apud Dalmatas glagolitas ritus Latini Slavos in libris sacris obtinet*. Vindobonae: n.p.

Dolžykova, Tetjana. 2001. "'U mojij duši oseljaje harmoniju Biblija' (pereklad Svjatoho Pys'ma P. Kuliša)." *Visnyk Luhans'koho deržavnoho pedahohičnoho universytetu imeni Tarasa Ševčenka. Filolohični nauky* 3, no. 35: 160–166.

___. 2004. "Movna osobystist' Pantelejmona Kuliša." Candidate of Sciences Dissertation, Institute of Ukrainian Language of the National Academy of Sciences of Ukraine, Kyiv.

___. 2010. "'Xočet'sja spivaty šče j po-ital'jans'ky, po-hrec'ky, po-latyns'ky...' (osoblyvosti movy perekladiv Pantelejmona Kuliša)." *Kul'tura slova* 72: 20–25.

Domanyc'kyj, Vasyl'. 1903. "Šekspirovskij fond i Rus'ko-ukrains'ka Vydavnyča Spilka." *Kievskaja starina* 40: 141–148.

Dorošenko, Volodymyr. 1918. *Pantelejmon Kuliš*. Kyiv and Leipzig: Ukrajins'ka nakladnja.

___. 1928. "Najnoviša literatura pro P. Kuliša." In *Zapysky Naukovoho Tovarystva im Ševčenka*, vol. 148: *V trydcjati rokovyny smerty Pantelejmona Kuliša*, edited by Kyrylo Studyns'kyj, 307–334. Lviv: Naukove Tovarystvo imeni Ševčenka.

Drahomanov, Myxajlo. 1894. *Lysty na Naddniprjans'ku Ukrainu*. Kolomyja: Myxajlo Bilous.

Dzjubyšyna-Mel'nyk, Natalja. 1998. "Ukrajins'ka *Biblija* 1903 roku v konteksti literaturnoji movy počatku XX stolittja." In *Człowiek—dzieło—sacrum*, edited by Stanisław Gajda and Helmut J. Sobeczko, 275–282. Opole: UO, Instytut Filologii Polskiej.

Esipova, V. A. 2014. "K voprosu ob istorii perevoda teksta Novogo Zaveta F. S. Moračevskogo: po materialam ORKP NB TGU." *Vestnik Tomskogo gosudarstvennogo universiteta* 384: 87–94.

Fedoruk, Oles´. 1998. "Kuliševyj pereklad Bibliji (počatok roboty: vybir koncepciji ta dejakyx pryncypiv)." In *Istorija relihij v Ukrajini. Materialy VIII mižnarodnoho kruhloho stolu (11–13 travnja 1998 roku)*, edited by Mykola Bandrivs´kyj et al., 278–281. Lviv: Lohos.

___. 2000a. "Nevidomyj lyst-spohad I. Nečuja-Levyc´koho pro P. Kuliša." In *Pantelejmon Kuliš. Materialy i doslidžennja*, edited by Mykola Hryhorovyč Žulyns´kyj, 277–296. Lviv and New York: M. P. Koc´.

___. 2000b. "Skonfiskovana brošura Pantelejmona Kuliša (sposterežennja nad tekstom [*Der Verwaltigung der Basilianer in Galizien durch Jesuiten*] i kontekstom)." In *Pantelejmon Kuliš. Materialy i doslidžennja*, edited by Mykola Hryhorovyč Žulyns´kyj, 185–212. Lviv and New York: M. P. Koc´.

___. 2000c. "Kulišeznavstvo za 1997–1998 rr." In *Pantelejmon Kuliš. Materialy i doslidžennja*, edited by Mykola Hryhorovyč Žulyns'kyj, 389–410. Lviv and New York: M. P. Koc´.

___. 2004. "Pantelejmon Kuliš: bibliohrafija literatury (1989–2002)." In *Vidkrytyj arxiv*, vol. 1, 453–573. Kyiv: Krytyka.

Fellerer, Jan. 2005. *Mehrsprachigkeit im galizischen Verwaltungswesen (1772–1914)*. Cologne, Weimer, and Vienna: Böhlau.

Flier, Michael S. 1987. "Morphophonemic Consequences of Phoneic Bifurcation: The Ukrainian Genitive Plural in -ÿj/-ej." In *Language, Literature, Linguistics: In Honor of Francis J. Whitfield on His Seventieth Birthday, March 25, 1986*, edited by Michael S. Flier and Simon Karlinsky, 40–57. Berkeley: Berkeley Slavic Specialties.

___. 1993. "Final Sonorant Clusters in East Slavic." In *Contributions to the Eleventh International Congress of Slavists, August– September 1993: Literature, Linguistics, Poetics*, edited by Robert A. Maguire and Alan Timberlake, 251–269. Columbus, IN: Slavica Publishers.

___. 1994. "Segmentation, Rank, and Natural Class." *Harvard Ukrainian Studies* 18, no. 1–2: *Ukrainian Philology and Linguistics*, edited by Michael S. Flier: 137–153.

Franko, Ivan. 1891a. "Hovorymo na vovka, skažimo za vovka." *Zorja* 18: 356–358.

___. 1891b. "Galicko-ruskij 'Savoir vivre.'" *Kievskaja starina* 10: 281–299.

___. 1898. "Miscellanea: Iz perepysky P. Kuliša z halyčanamy. 1870–1871 r." In *Zapysky Naukovoho Tovarystva imeni Ševčenka*, vol. 26, edited by Myxajlo Huševs'kyj, 6–16. Lviv: Naukove Tovarystvo imeni Ševčenka.

___. 1899. "Peredmova." In Pantelejmon Kuliš, *Uillijam Šekspir. Hamljet prync dans'kyj. Pereklad P. A. Kuliša*, with Introduction and Comments by Ivan Franko, iii–xxii. Lviv: Ukrajins'ko-rus'ka vydavnyča spilka.

___. 1900a. "Peredmova." In Pantelejmon Kuliš, *Uillijam Šekspir. Makbet. Pereklad P. A. Kuliša*, with Introduction and Comments by Ivan Franko, iii–xix. Lviv: Naukove Tovarystvo imeni Ševčenka.

___. 1900b. "Peredmova." In Pantelejmon Kuliš, *Uillijam Šekspir. Pryborkana hostruxa. Pereklad P. A. Kuliša*, with Introduction and Comments by Ivan Franko, iii–xv. Lviv: Ukrajins'ko-rus'ka vydavnyča spilka.

___. 1901. "Peredmova." In Pantelejmon Kuliš, *Uillijam Šekspir. Romeo ta Džul'jeta. Pereklad P. A. Kuliša*, with Introduction and Comments by Ivan Franko, iii–xv. Lviv: Ukrajins'ko-rus'ka vydavnyča spilka.

___. 1902. "Peredmova." In Jurij Fed'kovyč, *Dramatyčni pereklady Osypa Jurija Fed'kovyča*, edited by Ivan Franko, v-xiii. Ukrajins'ko-rus'ka biblioteka, vol 3: *Pysannja Osypa Jurija Fed'kovyča*, part 2. Lviv: Naukove Tovarystvo imeni Ševčenka.

___. 1905. "Peredmova." In Pantelejmon Kuliš, *Gordon Bajron. Čajl'd-Harol'dova mandrivka. Pereklav Panko Kuliš*, iii–vii. Lviv: Ukrajins'ko-rus'ka vydavnyča spilka.

___. 1910. *Narys istoriji ukrajins'ko-rus'koji literatury do 1890 r.* Lviv: Ukrajins'ko-rus'ka vydavnyča spilka.

___. 1955. "Myxajlo P. Staryc'kyj." In Ivan Franko, *Tvory v dvadcjaty tomax*, vol. 17, edited by Oleksandr Jevdokymovyč Kornijčuk et al., 303–345. Kyiv: Deržavne vydavnyctvo xudožn'oji literatury.

___. 1956. *Tvory v dvadcjaty tomax*, vol. 20, edited by Oleksandr Jevdokymovyč Kornijčuk et al. Kyiv: Deržavne vydavnyctvo xudožn'oji literatury.

___. 1982. "Poema pro sotvorennja svitu." In Ivan Franko, *Zibrannja tvoriv u p'jatdesjaty tomax*, vol. 35, edited by Jevhen Proxorovyč Kyryljuk et al., 266–320. Kyiv: Naukova dumka.

Fylypovyč, Pavlo. 1930. "Puškin v ukrajins′kij literaturi." In Pavlo Fylypovyč, ed., *A. Puškin. Vybrani tvory*, v–lx. Kharkiv and Kyiv: Knyhospilka.

Gaccuk, Mikola [Mykola Hatcuk]. 1862. "O pravopisanijax, zajavlennyx Ukrainskimi pisateljami s 1834 goda po 1861 g." *Osnova* 7: 1–23.

Gajda, Roman and Roman Pljacko. 1998. *Ivan Puljuj. 1845–1918. Žyttjepysno-bibliohrafičnyj narys*. Lviv: Naukove tovarystvo imeni Ševčenka.

Gervinus, Georg Gottfried. 1849–1852. *Shakespeare*, 4 vols. Leipzig: Wilhelm Engelmann.

Gillingham, S. E. 1994. *The Poems and Psalms of the Hebrew Bible*. Oxford: Oxford University Press.

Gorlenko, Vasilij [Vasyl′ Horlenko]. 1883. "Malorusskie izdanija 1882 goda." *Kievskaja starina* 6: 353–370.

Grabowicz, George G. 1981. "Three Perspectives on the Cossack Past: Gogol′, Ševčenko, Kuliš." *Harvard Ukrainian Studies* 5, no. 2: 171–194.

___. 1992. "Ukrainian-Russian Relations in the Ninteenth Century: A Formulation of the Problem." In *Ukraine and Russia in Their Historical Encounter*, edited by Peter J. Potichnyj et al., 214–244. Edmonton: CIUS Press.

Green, Jay P., ed. 2005. *The Interlinear Hebrew-Aramic Old Testament*, vol. 1: *The Interlinear Hebrew-Greek-English Bible*, 2nd ed. Peabody, MA: Hendrickson Publishers.

Haluščynskyj, T. 1925. "De ucrainis S. Scripturae versionibus." *Bohoslovija* 3, no. 1–4: 218–225, 309–319.

Hnatenko, Ljudmyla Anatolijivna and Tetjana Ivanivna Kotenko. 2007. "Pereklady Pylypa Moračevs′koho knyh Novoho Zavitu ta Psaltyrja ukrajins′koju movoju seredyny XIX st. (Oryhinaly ta spysky u knyhosxovyščax Rosiji ta Ukrajiny)." In *Rukopysna ta knyžkova spadščyna Ukrajiny*, vol. 12, edited by Ljubov Andrijivna Dubrovina et al., 154–177. Kyiv: Nacional′na biblioteka Ukrajiny imeni V. I. Vernads′koho.

Hnatjuk, Halyna Makarivna. 1982. *Dijeprykmetnyk u sučasnij ukrajins′kij movi*. Kyiv: Naukova dumka.

Hnatjuk, Lidija. 2010. *Movnyj fenomen Hryhorija Skovorody v konteksti staroukrajins′koji knyžnoji tradyciji*. Kyiv: Kyjivs′kyj universytet.
Holovac′kyj, Jakiv. 1850. "De ščo o dĕlovôm jazÿcĕ u nas na Rusi." *Zorja Halycka* 17 (15 February): 97–98.
Holovaščenko, S. I. 2006. "'Ukrajins′ka Psaltyr' M. O. Maksymovyča jak fenomen vitčyznjanoji biblejistyky: kil′ka zapytan′ do tekstu." In *Magisterium. Istoryko-filosofs′ki studiji*, vol. 23, edited by Vilen Serhijovyč Hors′kyj et al., 55–62. Kyiv: Kyjevo-Mohyljans′ka Akademija.
Hončaruk, Petro Stepanovyč. 2006. *Suspil′no-polityčni pohljady P. O. Kuliša*. Kyiv: DAKKKiM.
Horbač, Oleksa. 1988. "Movostyl′ novitnix perekladiv Sv. Pys′ma na ukrajins′ku narodnju movu 19–20 vv." In *Ukrajins′kyj Vil′nyj Universytet. Naukovi zapysky*, vol. 13: *Congressus series philologica*, edited by Olexa Horbatsch [Oleksa Horbač], 29–98. Munich: Ukrainian Free University.
Hordyns′kyj, Jaroslav. 1928. "Kuliševi pereklady dram Šekspira." In *Zapysky Naukovoho Tovarystva im Ševčenka*, vol. 148: *V trydcjati rokovyny smerty Pantelejmona Kuliša*, edited by Kyrylo Studyns′kyj, 55–164. Lviv: Naukove Tovarystvo imeni Ševčenka.
Hozenpud, Abram Akimovyč. 1947. *Poetyčnyj teatr*. Kyiv: Mystectvo.
Hruševs′kyj, Myxajlo. 1927. "Socijal′no-tradycijni vidnosyny Kuliševoji tvorčosty." *Ukrajina* 1–2: 9–38.
Hrycak, Jaroslav [Iaroslav Hrytsak]. 2006. *Prorok u svojij vitčyzni. Franko ta joho spil′nota (1856–1886)*. Kyiv: Krytyka.
Hrycenko, Pavlo. 2007. "Idiolekt i tekst." In *Linhvostylistyka: ob'jekt— styl′, meta—ocinka: Zbirnyk naukovyx prac′, prysvjačenyj 70-riččju vid dnja narodžennja prof. S. Ja. Jermolenko*, edited by Vitalij Hryhorovyč Skljarenko, 16–43. Kyiv: Instytut ukrajins′koji movy.
Hrytsak, Iaroslav [Jaroslav Hrycak]. 2003. "Ruslan, Bohdan, and Myron: Three Constructed Identities among Galician Ruthenians/Ukrainians, 1830–1914." In *Extending the Borders of Russian History: Essays in Honor of Alfred J. Rieber*, edited by Marsha Siefert, 97–112. Budapest and New York: CEU Press.

Humec′ka, Lukija Lukijanivna. 1958. *Narys slovotvorčoji systemy ukrajins′koji movy XIV–XV st.* Kyiv: Akademija nauk Ukrajins′koji RSR.

Husar, Olena. 1992. "Movni pytannja na storinkax žurnalu 'Osnova.'" *Kul′tura slova* 43: 6–12.

Jefimenko, P. 1862. "Po povodu zametki g. Levčenka 'O russinskoj terminologii.'" *Osnova* 8: 45–52.

Jefremov, Serhij. 1918. *Ivan Levyc′kyj Nečuj*. Kyiv and Leipzig: Ukrajins′ka nakladnja.

___. 1923. "Bez syntezu." *Zapysky Istoryčno-Filolohičnoho Viddilu VUAN* 4: 58–79.

___. 1924. *Istorija ukrajins′koho pys′menstva*, vols. 1–2, 4th rev. ed. Kyiv and Leipzig: Ukrajins′ka nakladnja.

Jermolenko, Svitlana. 2010. "Pantelejmon Kuliš v istoriji ukrajins′koji literaturnoji movy." *Kul′tura slova* 72: 6–15.

Jurkowski, Marian. 2001. "Ukraińskie przekłady *Biblii*." In *Varšavs′ki ukrajinoznavči zapysky*, vols. 11–12, edited by Stepan Kozak, 67–73. Warsaw: Varšavs′kyj universytet.

Jusyp-Jakymovyč, Julija. 2000. "Ivan Ohijenko pro rytmičnist′ movy." In *Xrystyjanstvo j ukrajins′ka mova. Materialy naukovoji konferenciji. Kyiv, 5–6 žovtnja 2000 roku*, edited by Vasyl′ Vasyl′ovyč Nimčuk, 412–419. Lviv: L′vivs′ka Bohoslovs′ka Akademija.

K-j, Iv. 1924. "Do žyttjepysu P. Kuliša." *Červonyj šljax* 17–18: 268–285.

Kautzsch, Emil. 1902. *Die Poesie und die poetischen Bücher des Alten Testaments*, 6th ed. Tübingen and Leipzig: J. C. B. Mohr.

Kernyc′kyj, Ivan Myxajlovyč. 1967. *Systema slovozminy v ukrajins′kij movi*. Kyiv: Naukova dumka.

Kobyljans′kyj, Bronyslav. 1928. "Hucul′s′kyj hovir i joho vidnošennja do hovoru Pokuttja." *Ukrajins′kyj dijaletolohičnyj zbirnyk* 1: 1–92.

Kočur, Hryhorij. 1968. "Šekspir na Ukraine." In *Masterstvo perevoda 1966*, no 5, edited by Kornej Ivanovič Čukovskij et al., 26–59. Moscow: Sovetskij pisatel′.

Komarov, Myxajlo. 1913. *Moračevs′kyj ta joho pereklad Sv. Jevanhelija na ukrajins′ku movu*. Odesa: Druk. Južno-russkogo O-va Peč. Dela.

Kostomarov, Nikolaj. 1882. "Zadači ukrainofil′stva." *Vestnik Evropy* 93, no. 1: 886–900.

___. 1883. "P. A. Kuliš i ego poslednjaja literaturnaja dejatel′nost′." *Kievskaja starina* 5: 221–234.

___. 1890. *Literaturnoe naslĕdie*. St. Petersburg: Tipografija M. M. Stasjuleviča.

Kotenko, Tetjana Ivanivna. 2013. "P. S. Moračevs′kyj jak doslidnyk ta perekladač ukrajins′koju movoju knyh Svjatoho Pys′ma v istoriohrafiji kincja XIX–počatku XX st." In *Rukopysna ta knyžkova spadščyna Ukrajiny*, vol. 17, edited by Ljubov Andrijivna Dubrovina et al., 79–88. Kyiv: Nacional′na biblioteka Ukrajiny imeni V. I. Vernads′koho.

Kovalenko, Oleksa. 1908. *Ukrajins′ka muza. Poetyčna antolohija*. Kyiv: Drukarnja Bars′koho.

Kryms′kyj, Ahatanhel. 1929. "Narys istoriji ukrajins′koho pravopysu do 1927 roku." *Zapysky Istoryčno-Filolohičnoho Viddilu UAN* 25: 175–186.

Kugel, James L. 1981. *The Idea of Biblical Poetry: Parallelism and Its History*. New Haven and London: Yale University Press.

Kuliš, Pantelejmon. 1843. *Ukrayna*. Kyiv: n.p.

___. 1856–1857. *Zapiski o Južnoj Rusi*, vols. 1–2. St. Petersburg: Aleksandr Jakobson.

___. 1857. *Hramátka*. St. Petersburg: n.p.

___. 1861. "Obzor ukrainskoj slovesnosti: 1) Klimentij, 2) Kotljarevskij." *Osnova* 1: 169–234, 235–262; "III. Artemovskij-Gulak." *Osnova* 3: 78–113; "IV. Gogol′, kak avtor povestej iz ukrainskoj žizni i istorii. Stat′ja pervaja." *Osnova* 4: 67–90; "Gogol′, kak avtor povestej iz ukrainskoj žizni i istorii. Stat′ja vtoraja." *Osnova* 5: 1–33; "V. Gogol′, kak avtor povestej iz ukrainskoj žizni i istorii. Stat′ja tret′ja." *Osnova* 9: 56–68; "VI. Gogol′, kak avtor povestej iz ukrainskoj žizni i istorii. Stat′ja četvertaja." *Osnova* 11–12: 1–11.

___. 1868. "Žyzn′ Kuliša." *Pravda* 43 (22 January): 32–34; 4 (30 January): 45–46; 7 (22 February): 79–80; 24 (30 June): 283–288.

___. 1874–1877. *Istorija vossoedinenija Rusi*, vols. 1–3. St. Petersburg: Obščestvennaja pol′za.

___. 1879. *Xutorskaja filosofija i udalennaja ot sveta poezija*. St. Petersburg: Obščestvennaja pol′za.

___. 1899. "Pis′mo P. A. Kuliša v Bukovinu, 1861 goda." *Kievskaja starina* 2: 3–4.

___. 1908. *Sočinenija i pis′ma P. A. Kuliša. Izdanie A. M. Kuliš*, vol. 1, edited by Ivan Kamanin. Kyiv: T. G. Mejnander.

___. 1909. *Tvory Pantelejmona Kuliša*, vol. 2. Rus′ka pys′mennist′, vol. VI, part 2; vol. 3. Rus′ka pys′mennist′, vol. VI, part 3; 1910, vol. 6. Rus′ka pys′mennist′, vol. VI, part 6. Lviv: Naukove Tovarystvo imeni Ševčenka.

___. 1914. "Dvi movi, knyžnja i narodnja." *Ukraina* 3: 22–34.

___. 1931. "Uljana Terentivna." In *Tvory Pantelejmona Kuliša*, vol. 6, edited by Oleksandr Doroškevyč, 137–231. Kharkiv and Kyiv: Literatura i mystectvo.

___. 2005. *Povne zibrannja tvoriv*, vol. 1: *Lysty. 1841–1850*; 2009, vol. 2: *Lysty. 1850–1856*. Kyiv: Krytyka.

Kumeda, Olena. 2010. "Leksyčni rehionalizmy v peršodrukax P. Kuliša." *Kul′tura slova* 72: 31–36.

Kurylo, Olena. 1960. *Uvahy do sučasnoji ukrajins′koji literaturnoji movy*, 5th ed. Toronto: Novi Dni.

Kyryljuk, Jevhen. 1929a. *Bibliohrafija prac′ P. O. Kuliša ta pysan′ pro n′oho*. Ukrajins′ka bibliohrafija, vol. 2. Kyiv: Vseukrajins′ka Akademija nauk, Bibliohrafična komisija.

___. 1929b. *Pantelejmon Kuliš*. Kharkiv and Kyiv: Deržavne vydavnyctvo Ukrajiny.

Kysilevs′kyj, Kost′. 1956. "Istorija ukrajins′koho pravopysnoho pytannja. Sproba syntezy." In *Zapysky Naukovoho Tovarystva imeni Ševčenka*, vol. 165, edited by Kost′ Kysilevs′kyj, 74–114. Zbirnyk Filologičnoji Sekciji, vol. 26. New York and Paris: Naukove Tovarystvo imeni Ševčenka.

Lazurs′kyj, Volodymyr. 1929. "Šekspir ukrajins′koju movoju." *Zapysky Odes′koho Naukovoho pry U. A. N. Tovarystva. Sekcija istoryčno-filolohična* 3: 22–38.

Lemke, Mixail. 1904. *Èpoxa cenzurnyx reform 1859–1865 godov*. St. Peterburg: M. V. Pirožkov.

Lesjuk, Mykola. 2003. "Istorija pravopysnoho pytannja v Halyčyni (II pol. XIX–XX st.)." *Visnyk Prykarpats′koho universytetu. Filolohija* 8: 34–38.

___. 2004. "Počatok azbučnoji vijny v Halyčyni." In *Šaškevyčiana. Zbirnyk naukovyx prac'*, vols. 5–6, edited by Jaroslav Isajevyč and Mykola Il'nyc'kyj, 41–56. Lviv and Winnipeg: Instytut ukrajinoznavstva im. I. Kryp'jakevyča NAN Ukrajiny, Ternopil's'kyj pedahohičnyj universytet im. V. Hnatjuka, Instytut-Zapovidnyk Markijana Šaškevyča u Vinnipezi.

Levyckij [Levyc'kyj], Ivan Emel'janovič. 1888. *Halycko-ruskaja bybliografija XIX-ho stolětija* . . . (1801–1886), vol. 1. Lviv: printed by author.

___. 1902. "Pohljad na rozvij nyzšoho y vysšoho škil'nyctva v Halyčyni v rr. 1772–1800, i rozvij rus'ko-narodnoho škil'nyctva v rr. 1801–1820." In *Materijaly do kul'turnoji istoriji Halyc'koji Rusy XVIII–XIX viku*, edited by Ivan Franko, 103–144. Zbirnyk istoryčno-fil'osofičnoji sekciji Naukovoho Tovarystva imeni Ševčenka, vol. 5. Lviv: Naukove Tovarystvo imeni Ševčenka.

Levyc'kyj, Jaroslav. 1924. "[Review of] Pantelejmon Kuliš. Tvory. Tom IV. Psaltyr. Biblioteka 'Ukr. Slova,' č. 37. Berlin. 1923, st. 264." *Bohoslovija* 2, no. 1–4: 240.

Lobodovskij, Mixail [Myxajlo Lobodovs'kyj]. 1897. "Tri dnja na xutore u Pantelejmona Kuliša i Aleksandry Mixajlovny (Hanny Barvinok) Kuliš." *Kievskaja starina* 57, no. 4: 163–176.

Lotoc'kyj, Oleksander. 1966. *Storinky mynuloho*, vol. 2. Reprint, Warsaw: Praci Ukrajins'koho Naukovoho Instytutu, 1934. N.p.: Naukovo-Bohoslovs'kyj Instytut Ukrajins'koji Pravoslavnoji Cerkvy v SŠA.

Lozyns'kyj, Josyp. 1850. "Perestoroha dlja perestereženyx." *Zorja Halycka* 20 (25 February): 119–120.

Lozyns'kyj, Myxajlo. 1917. *Myxajlo Pavlyk. Joho žyttje i dijal'nist'*. Vienna: Sojuz Vyzvolennja Ukrajiny.

Luckyj, George. 1983. *Panteleimon Kulish: A Sketch of His Life and Times*. New York: Columbia University Press.

___. 1988. "Kuliš, Panteleimon." In *Encyclopedia of Ukraine*, vol. 2: *G–K*, edited by Volodymyr Kubijovyč, 709–710. Toronto: University of Toronto Press.

Lučuk, Ol'ha. 1995. "Šekspir u lystax Pantelejmona Kuliša." In *Zapysky Naukovoho tovarystva imeni Ševčenka. Praci filolohičnoji sekciji*,

vol. 229, edited by Mykola Il'nyc'kyj and Oleh Kupčyns'kyj, 371–376. Lviv: Naukove tovarystvo imeni Ševčenka.
Lypa, Jurij. 1939. "Veletens'ke zavdannja. Svjate pys'mo ridnoju movoju." *Ridna mova* 2: 49–58.
Lysenko, Mykola Vitalijovyč. 1964. *Lysty,* edited by Ostap Lysenko. Kyiv: Mystectvo.
Macjuk, Halyna. 1996. "P. Kuliš i rozvytok literaturnoji movy v Halyčyni." In *Tretij Mižnarodnyj konhres ukrajinistiv. 26–29 serpnja 1996 r. Movoznavstvo*, edited by Serhii Vakulenko and Andrii Danylenko, 120–124. Kharkiv: Oko.
___. 2001. *Preskryptyvne movoznavstvo v Halyčyni (perša polovyna XIX st.)*. Lviv: L'vivs'kyj nacional'nyj universytet imeni Ivana Franka.
Magocsi, Paul Robert. 1984. "The Language Question in Nineteenth-Century Galicia." In *Aspects of the Slavic Language Question*, vol. 2: *East Slavic*, edited by Harvey Goldblatt and Ricardo Picchio, 49–64. New Haven: Yale Concilium on International and Area Studies.
___. 1987. *The Language Question among the Subcarpathian Rusyns*. Fairview, NJ: Carpatho-Rusyn Research Center.
Makar, M. F. 2006. "Značennja ta trudnošči stvorennja ukrajins'koho perekladu Svjatoho Pys'ma." *Zbirnyk naukovyx prac' Naukovo-doslidnoho instytutu ukrajinoznavstva* 8: 357–368.
Makovej, Osyp. 1903. "Try halyc'ki hramatyky. Dodatky." In *Zapysky Naukovoho Tovarystva imeni Ševčenka*, vol. 54, edited by Myxajlo Hruševs'kyj, 59–96. Lviv: Naukove Tovarystvo imeni Ševčenka.
Maksimovič, Mixail [Myxajlo Maksymovyč]. 1827. *Malorossijskija pěsni*. Moscow: Avgust Semen.
___. 1841. "O pravopisaniy malorossijskago jazÿka." *Kievljanin* 2: 153–180.
___. 1859. "Psalmy, pereložennye na ukrainskoe narečie." In *Ukrainec*, vol. 1, edited by Mixail Maksimovič [Myxajlo Maksymovyč], 1–41. Moscow: printed by author.
Maljuk, Myxajlo. 1993. "Pylyp Moračevs'kyj. Sproba portreta na tli zaboron ukrajins'koho slova." *Neopalyma kupyna* 1: 55–74.
___. 1995. "Jevanhelije u perekladi Pylypa Moračevs'koho." *Neopalyma kupyna* 1–2: 177–218.

Marčylo, Larysa Mykolajivna. 1997. "Z istoriji skladnyx form majbutn´oho času v ukrajins´kij movi." In *Systema i struktura sxidnoslov'jans'kyx mov*, edited Mykola Mykolajovyč Pylyns´kyj, 20–26. Kyiv: Ukrajins´kyj deržavnyj pedahohičnyj universytet im. M. P. Drahomanova.

Matvijas, Ivan Hryhorovyč. 1990. *Ukrajins´ka mova i jiji hovory*. Kyiv: Naukova dumka.

___. 1996. "Varianty ukrajins´koji literaturnoji movy v kinci XVIII i v XIX st." *Kul´tura slova* 48–49: 11–28.

___. 2005a. "Dialektna osnova konsonantyzmu v ukrajins´kij literaturnij movi." *Movoznavstvo* 2: 32–40.

___. 2005b. "Dialektna osnova slovotvoru v ukrajins´kij literaturnij movi." *Movoznavstvo* 5: 3–14.

___. 2006. "Dialektna osnova slovozminy v ukrajins´kij literaturnij movi." *Movoznavstvo* 5: 52–65.

___. 2007a. "Dialektna osnova syntaksysu v ukrajins´kij literaturnij movi." *Movoznavstvo* 1: 38–46.

___. 2007b. "Vidobražennja seredn´onaddniprjans´koho hovoru v movi tvoriv Nečuja-Levyc´koho." *Ukrajins´ka mova* 4: 33–41.

___. 2008. "Dialektna osnova movy v tvorax Pantelejmona Kuliša." *Ukrajins´ka mova* 1: 95–99.

Metlinskij, Amvrosij [Amvrosij Metlyns´kyj]. 1848. *Južnyj Russkyj Zbornyk"*. Kharkiv: n.p.

Miller, Alexei. 2003. *The Ukrainian Question: The Russian Empire and Nationalism in the Nineteenth Century*. Budapest and New York: CEU Press.

Minenko, Olesja Vasylivna. 2011. "Recepcija trahediji 'Makbet' u konteksti estetyčnyx pohljadiv ta perekladac´koji dijal´nosti Lesi Ukrajinky." *Visnyk Luhans´koho nacional´noho universytetu* 24, part 2: 168–174.

Moroz, Tetjana Vasylivna and Ljudmyla Oleksandrivna Tkač. 2006. "Do indyvidual´noji xarakterystyky perekladačiv Jevanhelija u zalučenni leksyčnyx džerel ukrajins´koji movy (Pylyp Moračevs´kyj, Pantelejmon Kuliš, Ivan Ohijenko)." *Naukovi zapysky NaUKMA* 60: *Filolohični nauky*: 22–36.

Moser, Mixael´ [Michael Moser]. 2004. "Movnyj svit L´vivs´koho 'Studium Ruthenicum.'" In *Současná ukrajinistika. Problémy jazyka, literatury a kultury. K 65. narozeninám prof. Josefa Anderše. Sborník článků. 2. Olomoucké symposium ukrajinistů 26.–28. srpna 2004*, 316–325. Acta Universitatis Palackianae Olomucensis. Facultas Philosophica. Philologica, vol. 82. Olomouc: Univerzita Palackého.

___. 2005. "Das Ukrainische im Gebrauch der griechisch-katholischen Kirche." In *Das Ukrainische als Kirchensprache*, edited by Michael Moser, 151–241. Vienna: Lit Verlag.

Moskalenko, Artem Ambrosijovyč. 1958. *Narys istorii ukrajins´koho alfavitu i pravopysu*. Odesa: Odes´kyj deržavnyj pedahohičnyj instytut.

___. 1968. "Pravopys avtohrafiv poezij Ševčenka." In *Zbirnyk prac´ p'jatnadcjatoji naukovoji ševčenkivs´koji konferenciji*, 163–172. Kyiv: Akademija nauk USSR.

Moskalenko, Myxajlo. 1993. "Narysy z istoriji ukrajins´koho perekladu." *Vsesvit* 9, no. 10: 113–120; 2006, 1, no. 2: 172–190; 3, no. 4: 154–171; 5, no. 6: 174–194; 7, no. 8: 192–206; 11, no. 12: 160–174.

Movčun, L. V. 1999. "Rehuljarna fonetyčna variatyvnist´ sliv ukrajins´koji movy z pohljadu movoznavciv XIX–poč. XX st." *Movoznavstvo* 2–3: 66–70.

Muromceva, Ol´ha Heorhijivna. 1985. *Rozvytok leksyky ukrajins´koji literaturnoji movy v druhij polovyni XIX–na počatku XX st.* Kharkiv: Xarkivs´kyj deržavnyj universytet.

Muromceva, Ol´ha Heorhijivna and Ihor Viktorovyč Muromcev. 1995. "P. Kuliš jak onovljuvač i tvorec´ ukrajins´koji literaturnoji movy." In *Pantelejmon Kuliš i ukrajins´ke nacional´ne vidrodžennja. Dopovidi ta povidomlennja naukovoji konferenciji, prysvjačenoji 175-m rokovynam vid dnja narodžennja pys´mennyka*, edited by Ihor Leonidovyč Myxajlyn, 11–17. Kharkiv: Xarkivs´kyj deržavnyj universytet.

Mykyta, Ivan and Pantelejmon Kuliš. 1868. "Zaprosyny do peredplaty." *Pravda* 46 (22 December): 541–542.

Mykytyn, Marija L´vivna. 2000. "Vidbyttja osoblyvostej narodnoho movlennja u tvorax P. Kuliša, nadrukovanyx na storinkax žurnalu 'Osnova.'" *Zapysky z ukrajins´koho movoznavstva* 9: 151–161.

Myrnyj, Panas. 1971. *Zibrannja tvoriv u semy tomax*, vol. 7: *Poezija, publicystyka, epistoljarij, lysty*. Kyiv: Naukova dumka.

Naumenko, Vladimir [Volodymyr Naumenko]. 1902. "F. S. Moračevskij i ego literaturnaja dejatelnost´." *Kievskaja starina* 79, no. 11: 171–186; 79, no. 12: 459–479.

Naxlik, Jevhen Kazymyrovyč. 2006. *Podružnje žyttja i pozašljubni romany Pantelejmona Kuliša*. Kyiv: Ukrajins´kyj pys´mennyk.

___. 2007. *Pantelejmon Kuliš. Osobystist´, pys´mennyk, myslytel´. Naukova monohrafija u dvox tomax*, vol. 1: *Žyttja Pantelejmona Kuliša*, vol. 2: *Svitohljad i tvorčist´ Pantelejmona Kuliša*. Kyiv: Ukrajins´kyj pys´mennyk.

Nazarova, Tetjana Viktorivna. 1972. "Rozvytok refleksiv *ě, *o, *e v ukrajins´kyx hovorax." *Movoznavstvo* 1: 13–27.

Nečuj [Nečuj-Levyc´kyj, Levic´kyj], Ivan. 1868. "Svitohljad" ukrajins´koho naroda." *Pravda* 35 (22 September): 415–417; 36 (30 September): 422–424; 37 (8 October): 436–438; 38 (15 October): 448–450; 39 (22 October): 459–461; 40 (30 October): 472–475; 41 (15 November), 484–486; 42 (22 November): 496–497; 43 (30 November): 507–508; 44 (8 December): 513–521; 45 (15 December), 531–533; 46 (22 December), 544–546.

___. 1869. "Dvi moskovky." *Pravda* 8 (22 February): 85–90; 9 (8 March): 97–100; 10/11 (15 March): 109–116; 12/13 (22 March): 133–141.

___. 1907. "S´ohočasna časopysna mova na Ukraini." *Ukraina* 1: 1–49, 183–237, 280–331.

___. 1912. *Kryve dzerkalo ukrains´koi movy*. Kyiv: I. I. Čokolov.

___. 1968. *Zibrannja tvoriv u desjaty tomax*, vol. 10, edited by Maksym Pavlovyč Komyšančenko. Kyiv: Naukova dumka.

Nikolaj M. [Pantelejmon Kuliš]. 1852. "Istorija Ul´jany Terent´evny." *Sovremennik* 8: 139–252.

Nimčuk, Vasyl´ Vasyl´ovyč. 1969. "Slovotvir pryjmennykiv u zakarpats´kyx hovirkax." In *Ukrajins´ka dialektna morfolohija*, edited by Fedot Troxymovyč Žylko et al., 71–81. Kyiv: Naukova dumka.

___. 1992. *Davn´orus´ka spadščyna v leksyci ukrajins´koji movy*. Kyiv: Naukova dumka.

___. 2001. "Ukrajins'ki dialektni pereklady Sv. Pys'ma." *Ukrajins'ke i slov'jans'ke movoznavstvo* 4: 383–389.

___. 2002. "Svjaščenoe Pisanie na ukrainskom jazyke." In *Rol' perevodov Biblii v stanovlenii i razvitii slavjanskix literaturnyx jazykov*, edited by Lev Nikolaevič Smirnov et al., 39–69. Moscow: Institut slavjanovedenija.

___. 2004. "Perednje slovo." In *Istorija ukrajins'koho pravopysu. XV–XX stolittja. Xrestomatija*, compiled by Vasyl' Vasyl'ovyč Nimčuk and Natalia Volodymyrivna Purjajeva, 5–26. Kyiv: Naukova dumka.

___. 2005. *Ukrajins'ki pereklady Svjatoho Pys'ma*. In *Das Ukrainische als Kirchensprache*, edited by Michael Moser, 15–64. Vienna: Lit Verlag.

Ohijenko, Ivan. 1927. *Metodolohija perekladu Svjatoho Pys'ma ta Bohoslužbovyx knyh na ukrajins'ku movu*. Warsaw: Drukarnja synodal'na.

___. 1930. *Ukrajins'ka literaturna mova XVI-ho st. i Krexivs'kyj Apostol 1560-x r.*, vols. 1–2. Studiji do ukrjins'koji hramatyky, vols. 7–8. Warsaw: Synodal'na drukarnja.

___. 1939a. "Vymova biblijnyx imen z *j* napočatku." *Ridna mova* 1: 3–5.

___. 1939b. "Rytmičnist' movy Sv. Pys'ma." *Ridna mova* 2: 57–62.

___. 1939c. "Najperše džerelo dlja vyvčennja ridnoji movy." *Ridna mova* 9: 352–360.

___. 1949 [1950]. *Istorija ukrajins'koji literaturnoji movy*. Winnipeg: Naša kul'tura.

Ohonovs'kyj, Omeljan. 1889. *Istorija literatury rus'koji*, part II/1; 1891, part III/1. Lviv: Naukove Tovarystvo imeni Ševčenka.

Osnovjanenko, Hryc'ko [Hryhorij Kvitka-Osnov'janenko]. 1887. *Ot toby y skarb. Povyst' Hryc'ka Osnovjanenka*, edited by Aleksandr Afanas'evič Potebnja. Kharkiv: Kaplan i Birjukov.

Ostaš, Ljubov. 2000. "Fonetyčna adaptacija cerkovno-xrystyjans'kyx vlasnyx osobovyx imen v ukrajins'kij movi XVII st.: počatkovi holosni." In *Xrystyjanstvo j ukrajins'ka mova. Materialy naukovoji konferenciji. Kyiv, 5–6 žovtnja 2000 roku*, edited by Vasyl' Vasyl'ovyč Nimčuk, 362–369. Lviv: L'vivs'ka Bohoslovs'ka Akademija.

Pan'kevyč, Ivan. 1922. "Tyšôvska *Aleksandrija* yz počatku XVIII v." *Naukovŷj Zbornyk Tovarystva "Prosvěta" v Užhorodě* 1: 6–108.
___. 1938. *Ukrajins'ki hovory Pidkarpats'koji Rusy i sumežnyx oblastej*. Prague: Orbis.
Partyc'kyj, Omeljan. 1868. "[Review of] Ivan Branik"." *Pryčyna tvorenija sja narěčej. Pravda* 20 (30 May): 239–240; 21 (8 June): 248–250.
[Partyc'kyj, Omeljan]. 1882. "L'vôvskŷ vŷdanja Pant. A. Kulěša. Davnijša dijal'nist' literaturna Kulěša ('Xutorna poezija' Kulěša)." *Zorja* 8: 120–123; "Klevety Kulěša na Ševčenka." *Zorja* 9: 135–136; "Jaki ideji rozšyraje Kulěš." *Zorja* 11: 169–170; "'Kijevskaja starina' o brošurax Kulěša." *Zorja* 12: 191–192; 13: 207–208; "L'vôvskŷ vŷdanja Pant. A. Kulěša (Krašanka rusynam y poljakam na velykden' 1882 roku ..." *Zorja* 17: 266–268; "L'vôvskŷ vŷdanja Pant. A. Kulěša (Šekspirovi tvory z movy brytans'koji movoju ukrajins'koju poperekladav P. A. Kuliš. Tom pervyj: Otello, Troil ta Kressyda, Komedija pomylok)." *Zorja* 21: 327–330.
Pavlyk, Myxajlo, ed. 1910. *Perepyska Myxajla Drahomanova z Melïtonom Bučyns'kym. 1871–1877*. Zbirnyk filjologičnoji sekciji Naukovoho Tovarystva imeni Ševčenka, vol. 13. Lviv: Naukove Tovarystvo imeni Ševčenka.
Pčilka, Olena. 1904. "Mixail Petrovič Starickij." *Kievskaja starina* 85: 400–449.
Peredrijenko, Vitalij Arkadijovyč. 1979. *Formuvannja ukrajins'koji literaturnoji movy XVIII st. na narodnij osnovi*. Kyiv: Naukova dumka.
Petrov, Nikolaj Ivanovič. 1884. *Očerki istorii ukrainskoj literatury XIX stoletija*. Kyiv: I. i A. Davidenko.
Petrov, Viktor. 1929. *Pantelejmon Kuliš u pjatdesjati roky. Žyttja. Ideolohija. Tvorčist'*. Zbirnyk Istoryko-Filolohičnoho Viddilu VUAN, vol. 88. Kyiv: Vseukrajins'ka Akademija Nauk.
Pivtorak, Hryhorij Petrovyč. 2000a. "Kulišivka." In *Ukrajins'ka mova. Encyklopedija*, edited by Vitalij Makarovyč Rusanivs'kyj and Oleksandr Onysymovyč Taranenko, 263. Kyiv: Vydavnyctvo "Ukrajins'ka encyklopedija" im. M. P. Bažana.

———. 2000b. "Pravopys." In *Ukrajins′ka mova. Encyklopedija*, edited by Vitalij Makarovyč Rusanivs′kyj and Oleksandr Onysymovyč Taranenko, 477–479. Kyiv: Vydavnyctvo "Ukrajins′ka encyklopedija" im. M. P. Bažana.

Pljušč, Pavlo Pavlovyč. 1971. *Istorija ukrajins′koji literaturnoji movy*. Kyiv: Vyšča škola.

Pokal′čuk, Volodymyr Feofanovyč. 1969. "Sposterežennja nad sufiksal′nym slovotvorennjam imennykiv u nadsarns′kyx hovirkax na Volyni." In *Ukrajins′ka dialektna morfolohija*, edited by Fedot Troxymovyč Žylko et al., 52–57. Kyiv: Naukova dumka.

Poljuha, Lev. 2004. "Pryncypy orfohrafiji Vuka Karadžyča ta pravopysna systema 'Rusalky Dnistrovoji.'" In *Šaškevyčiana. Zbirnyk naukovyx prac′*, *Šaškevyčiana. Zbirnyk naukovyx prac′*, vols. 5–6, edited by Jaroslav Isajevyč and Mykola Il′nyc′kyj, 80–84. Lviv and Winnipeg: Instytut ukrajinoznavstva im. I. Kryp'jakevyča NAN Ukrajiny, Ternopil′s′kyj pedahohičnyj universytet im. V. Hnatjuka, Instytut-Zapovidnyk Markijana Šaškevyča u Vinnipezi.

Pšepjurs′ka-Ovčarenko, Marija M. 1988. "Mova perekladu Novoho Zavitu P. Moračevs′koho." In *Ukrajins′kyj Vil′nyj Universytet. Naukovi zapysky*, vol. 13: *Congressus series philologica*, edited by Olexa Horbatsch [Oleksa Horbač], 203–248. Munich: Ukrainian Free University.

Puljuj, Ivan. 1871. *Lyst bez koverty jako odpovid′ Vpr. Krylošanynu Malynovs′komu na referat molytovnyka*. Vienna: Sommer.

———. 1905. *Novi i pereminni z′vizdy*, 3rd. ed. Vienna: Adolf Holzhausen.

Remy, Johannes. 2005. "The Ukrainian Alphabet as a Political Question in the Russian Empire Before 1876." *Ab Imperio* 2: 167–189.

———. 2007. "The Valuev Circular and Censorship of Ukrainian Publications in the Russian Empire (1836–1876): Intention and Practice." *Canadian Slavonic Papers / Revue canadienne des slavists* 49, no. 1–2: 87–110.

Revakovyč, Tyt. 1910. "Antin Kobyljans′kyj. Kil′ka zhadok." In *Zapysky Naukovoho Tovarystva imeni Ševčenka*, vol. 94, edited by Myxajlo Hruševs′kyj, 166–173. Lviv: Naukove Tovarystvo imeni Ševčenka.

Rozov, Volodymyr. 1928. *Ukrajins´ki hramoty*, vol. 1: *XIV v. i perša polovyna XV v.* Zbirnyk Istoryčno-Filolohičnoho Viddilu UAN, vol. 63. Kyiv: Ukrajins´ka Akademija Nauk.
Rudans´kyj, Stepan Vasyl´ovyč. 1908. "Psalom 136." In *Ukrajins´ka Muza. Poetyčna antologija*, edited by Oleksa Kovalenko, 299–300. Kyiv: Drukarnja Bars´koho.
Rudyns´ka, Jevhenija. 1928. *Lysty Vasylja Horlenka do Panasa Myrnoho*. Zbirnyk Istoryčno-Filolohičnoho Viddilu VUAN, vol. 60. Kyiv: Ukrajins´ka Akademija Nauk.
Rusanivs´kyj, Vitalij Makarovyč. 2001. *Istorija ukrajins´koji literaturnoji movy*. Kyiv: ArtEk.
___. 2002. *U slovi—vičnist´*. Kyiv: Naukova dumka.
Rusinko, Elaine. 2003. *Straddling Borders: Literature and Identity in Subcarpathian Rus´*. Toronto, Buffalo, and London: University of Toronto Press.
Rytter, Grażyna. 1992. *Wschodniosłowiańskie zapożyczenia leksykalne w polszczyźnie XVII wieku*. Łódź: Uniwersytet Łódzki.
Sabov, Evmenij. 1898. *Xristomatija cerkovno-slavjanskix i ugro-russkix literaturnyx pamjatnikov*... Ungvar: Kelet.
Samojlenko, Hryhorij Vasyl´ovyč. 1999. *Pylyp Moračevs´kyj—poet, dramaturh, perekladač*. Nižyn: Nauka-servis.
___. 2006. *Pylyp Semenovyč Moračevs´kyj (do 200-littja vid dnja narodžennja pedahoha i pys´mennyka)*. Nižyn: Lysenko M. M.
Šamraj, Hanna. 1929. "Xutorni plany Kuliša v 1870-x rokax." *Ukrajina* (October–November): 73–82.
Šapovalova, Marija Semenivna. 1976. *Šekspir v ukrajins´kij literaturi*. Lviv: Vyšča škola.
Saunders, David. 1993. "Mikhail Katkov and Mykola Kostomrov: A Note on Pëtr A. Valuev's Anti-Ukrainian Edict of 1863." *Harvard Ukrainian Studies* 17, no. 3–4: 365–377.
Scheludko [Šelud´ko], Dmytro. 1926. "Rumänische Elemente im Ukrainischen." *Balkan-Archiv* 2: 113–146.
Šelud´ko, Dmytro. 1931. "Nimec´ki elementy v ukrajins´kij movi." In *Zbirnyk komisiji dlja doslidžennja istoriji ukrajins´koji movy*, vol. 1,

edited by Ahatanhel Kryms′kyj et al., 1–60. Kyiv: Vseukrajins′ka Akademija Nauk.
Šenderovs′kyj, Vasyl′, ed. 1997. *Puljuj—Kuliš. Podvyžnyky naciji*. Kyiv: Rada.
Šenrok, Vladimir. 1901. "P. A. Kuliš (Biografičeskij očerk)." *Kievskaja starina* 72, no. 2: 153–179; 72, no. 3: 461–492; 73, no. 4: 126–152; 73, no. 5: 183–213; 73, no. 6: 344–382; 74, no. 7–8: 46–102; 74, no. 9: 304–330; 75, no. 10: 18–44.
Ševčenko, Taras. 1963–1964. *Povne zibrannja tvoriv u šesty tomax*, vols. 1–6. Edited by Mykola Hryhorovyč Žulyns′kyj et al. Kyiv: Akademija nauk URSR.
Ševel′ov, Jurij [George Y. Shevelov]. 1996. *Vnesok Halyčyny u formuvannja ukrajins′koji literaturnoji movy*. Ukrajinoznavča biblioteka NTŠ, vol. 7. Lviv and New York: Naukove tovarystvo imeni Ševčenka.
Shevelov, George Y. 1962. "The Year 1860 in Ševčenko's Work." In *Taras Ševčenko: 1814–1861. A Symposium*, edited by Volodymyr Mijakovs′kyj and George Y. Shevelov, 68–106. 's-Gravenhage: Mouton.
___. 1966. *Die ukrainische Schriftsprache 1798–1965*. Wiesbaden: Otto Harrassowitz.
___. 1969. "The Vicissitudes of a Syntactic Construction in Eastern Slavic (Impersonal sentences in *-no, -to* with the acc sg of object)." *Scando-Slavica* 15: 171–186.
___. 1979. *A Historical Phonology of the Ukrainian Language*. Heidelberg: Carl Winter.
___. 1989. *The Ukrainian Language in the First Half of the Twentieth Century (1900–1941): Its State and Status*. Cambridge, MA: Harvard Ukrainian Research Institute.
___. 1994. "Homer's Arbitration in a Ukrainian Linguistic Controversy: Aleksander Potebnja and Peter Niščyns′kyj." *Harvard Ukrainian Studies* 18, no. 1–2: *Ukrainian Philology and Linguistics*, edited by Michael S. Flier: 104–116.
Simovyč, Vasyl′. 1921. *Hramatyka ukrajins′koji movy dlja samonavčannja ta v dopomohu škil′nij nauci*. Kyiv and Leipzig: Ukrajins′ka nakladnja.
___. 1937. "Kuliševa mova j 'Kulišivka.'" *Žyttja i znannja* 2: 58–59.
___. 1981. *Ukrajins′ke movoznavstvo*, edited by George Y. Shevelov. Ottawa: The University of Ottawa Press.

Skljarenko, Vitalij Hryhorovyč. 2007. "Etymolohični rozvidky. 7. *Nevista.*" *Movoznavstvo* 3: 3–11.

Skurzewska, Agata. 2007. "Tradycja i innowacje w gramatyce języka ukraińskiego Omelana Partyckiego *Hramatyka jazyka ruskoho dlja vžytku v˝ školax˝ ljudovyx˝ v˝ Halyčyně.*" *Slavia Orientalis* 56, no. 4: 571–590.

Smerečyns′kyj, Serhij. 1932. *Narysy z ukrajins′koji syntaksy.* Kharkiv: Radjans′ka škola.

Solohub, Nadija. 2010. "'Čerez kraj iz sercja ridne slovo lljet′sja . . .' (pro movu poezij P. Kuliša)." *Kul′tura slova* 72: 15–20.

Sreznevskij, Vsevolod Izmailovič. 1902. "Oxrannaja opis′ rukopisnogo otdelenija biblioteki Imperatorskoj akademii nauk." *Izvestija Imperatorskoj akademii nauk* 16, no. 4: 089–094; 17, no. 5: 079–087; 1903, 18, no. 3: 01–019.

Staryc′kyj, Myxajlo Petrovyč. 1882. [Introduction]. In *Hamlet˝. Prync′ Dans′kyj. Trahedija v˝ V dijax˝ V. Šekspira. Per. na ukrains′ku movu M. P. Staryc′kyj. Z˝ prylohoju muzyky M. Lysenka*, translated by Myxajlo Petrovyč Staryc′kyj, i–v. Kyiv: G. T. Korčak Novickij.

Strixa, Maksym. 2006. *Ukrajins′kyj xudožnij pereklad: miž literaturoju i nacijetvorennjam.* Kyiv: Fakt.

Strumins′kyj, Bohdan. 1984. "The Language Question in the Ukrainian Lands Before the Nineteenth Century." In *Aspects of the Slavic Language Question*, vol. 2: *East Slavic*, edited by Harvey Goldblatt and Ricardo Picchio, 9–47. New Haven: Yale Concilium on International and Area Studies.

Studyns′kyj, Kyrylo. 1927. "Do istoriji zvjazkiv Kuliša z Halyčanamy v r. 1869–70." *Ukrajina* 1–2: 76–93.

———. 1928. "Slidamy Kuliša." In *Zapysky Naukovoho Tovarystva imeni Ševčenka*, vol. 148: *V trydcjati rokovyny smerty Pantelejmona Kuliša*, edited by Kyrylo Studyns′kyj, 241–306. Lviv: Naukove Tovarystvo imeni Ševčenka.

———, ed. 1930. *P. O. Kuliš (Materijaly i rozvidky)*, part 2. Zbirnyk filolohičnoji sekciji Naukovoho Tovarystva imeni Ševčenka, vol. 22, part 2. Lviv: Naukove Tovarystvo imeni Ševčenka.

Studyns′kyj, Kyrylo and Fedir Savčenko, eds. 1929. *P. O. Kuliš (materijaly i rozvidky)*, part 1. Zbirnyk filolohičnoji sekciji Naukovoho

Tovarystva imeni Ševčenka, vol. 22. Lviv: Naukove Tovarystvo imeni Ševčenka.

Sulyma, Mykola. 1924. "Najjaskraviši osoblyvosti frazy Ševčenkovoho 'Kobzarja.'" *Červonyj šljax* 10: 216–221.

Svěncyckij, Ilarion Sem´onovič [Ilarion Semenovyč Svjencic´kyj]. 1905. *Materialy po ystorii vozroždenija Karpatskoj Rusy*, vol. 1: *Snošenija Karpatskoj Rusy s˝ Rossijej v˝ 1-oj polovině XIX-ago věka.* Lviv: Stavropigijskij Institut˝.

___. 1993. "Peredmova." In *Lystuvannja ukrajins´kyx slavistiv z Francem Miklošyčem*, edited by Ilarion Semenovyč Svjencic´kyj, 10–58. Kyiv: Naukova dumka.

Symaniec, Virginie. 2012. *La construction idéologique slave orientale. Languages, races et nations dans la Russie du XIXe siècle.* Paris: Pétra.

Synjavs´kyj, Oleksa. 1925. "Deščo pro Ševčenkovu movu. (Sproba vyjasnyty dekotri sumnivni momenty Ševčenkovoji movy)." *Ukrajina* 1–2: 100–114.

Tarnawsky, Maxim. 2012. "Orthography, Copyright, and Legendary Anecdotes: The Story of Nečuj's Linguistic Peculiarities." In *Studien zur Sprache, Literatur und Kultur bei den Slaven. Gedenkschrift für George Y. Sevelov*, edited by Andrii Danylenko and Serhii Vakulenko, 295–308. Die Welt der Slaven Sammelbände. Sborniki, vol. 42. Munich: Otto Sagner.

___. 2015. *The All-Encompassing Eye of Ukraine: Ivan Nechui-Levyts´kyi's Realistic Prose.* Toronto, Buffalo, and London: University of Toronto Press.

Terex, Oleksandr. 1964. "Ukrajins´ka Šekspiriana." *Vsesvit* 4: 71–77.

Tichý, František. 1938. *Vývoj současného spisovného jazyka na Podkarpatské Rusi.* Prague: Orbis.

Timofeev, Konstantin. 1877. *Šekspir Gervinusa*, vols. 1–2. St. Peterburg: D. F. Fedorov.

Tkač, Ljudmyla. 2007. *Ukrajins´ka literaturna mova na Bukovyni v kinci XIX–na počatku XX stolittja*, part 2: *Džerela i sociokul´turni čynnyky rozvytku.* Černivci: Knyhy—XXI.

Tkač, Ljudmyla and Tetjana Moroz. 2003. "Ukrajins´ka narodnorozmovna leksyka u perekladax knyh Svjatoho Pys´ma, zdijsnenyx P. Kulišem, I. Puljujem, I. Ohijenkom (zistavlennja, spostereženija, mirkuvannja)." In *Biblija i kul'tura* 5, edited by Anatolij Jevhenovyč Njamcu, 280–293. Černivci: Ruta.

Tymčenko, Jevhen. 1928. *Akuzatyv v ukrajins'kij movi (z ukrajins'koji skladni)*. Zbirnyk Istoryko-Filolohičnoho Viddilu VUAN, vol. 67. Kyiv: Vseukrajins'ka Akademija Nauk.

Tymošenko, Petro Dmytrovyč. 1968. "Morfolohični rysy tvoriv Ševčenka (Imennyk)." In *Zbirnyk prac' pjatnadcjatoji naukovoji ševčenkivs'koji konferenciji*, 133–162. Kyiv: AN USSR.

———. 1969. "Morfolohični rysy tvoriv Ševčenka (Zajmennyk)." In *Zbirnyk prac' šistnadcjatoji naukovoji ševčenkivs'koji konferenciji*, 104–114. Kyiv: AN USSR.

———. 1971. "Morfolohični rysy tvoriv Ševčenka (Prykmetnykovi ta sporidneni z nymy zajmennykovi, dijeprykmetnykovi i čyslivnykovi formy)." In *Zbirnyk prac' visimnadcjatoji naukovoji ševčenkivs'koji konferenciji*, 195–212. Kyiv: AN USSR.

———. 1973. "Morfolohični rysy tvoriv Ševčenka (Infinityv)." In *Zbirnyk prac' dvadcjatoji naukovoji ševčenkivs'koji konferenciji*, 162–173. Kyiv: AN USSR.

———. 1979. "Morfolohični rysy tvoriv Ševčenka (Osobovi formy dijeslova)." In *Zbirnyk prac' dvadcjat' tret'oji naukovoji ševčenkivs'koji konferenciji*, 115–130. Kyiv: AN USSR.

Tymošyk, Halyna. 1998. "Orfohrafični normy perekladu Sv. Pys'ma P. Kuliša u tradicijax sučasnoho ukrajins'koho pravopysu." *Ukrajins'ka mova ta literatura* 38: 8.

———. 2000a. "Staroslov'janizmy u teksti perekladu Sv. Pys'ma P. Kuliša ta I. Puljuja." *Problemy slov'janoznavstva* 51: 243–244.

———. 2000b. "Iz sposterežen' nad movnymy osoblyvostjamy perekladiv Sv. Pys'ma." In *Šaškevyčiana. Zbirnyk naukovyx prac'*, vols. 3–4, edited by Jaroslav Isajevyč and Mykola Il'nyc'kyj, 100–107. Lviv and Winnipeg: Instytut ukrajinoznavstva im. I. Kryp'jakevyča NAN Ukrajiny, Prykarpats'kyj deržavnyj universytet im. V. Stefanyka, Drohobyts'kyj pedahohičnyj universytet im. I. Franka, Instytut-Zapovidnyk Markijana Šaškevyča u Vinnipezi.

Tymošyk, Mykola. 2006. "Cenzura ukrajins'koho drukovanoho slova jak čynnyk nyščennja ukrajinstva: do 130-riččja Ems'koho ukazu." *Ukrajins'ka mova* 3: 3–21.

Udvari, Ištvan. 1986. "Dannye o zakarpatsko-ukrainskoj oficial′no-delovoj pis′mennosti XVIII v." *Studia Slavica Hungarica* 32, no. 1–4: 63–100.

Ukrajinka, Lesja. 1956. *Tvory v p'jaty tomax*, vol. 5: *Lysty (1881–1913)*. Kyiv: Xudožnja literatura.

Urbutis, Vincas. 1969. "Dabartinės baltarusių kalbos lituanizmai." *Baltistica* 5: 43–68, 149–162.

Uškalov, Leonid. 2006. *Eseji pro ukrajins′ke baroko*. Kyiv: Fakt.

Uspenskij, Boris A. 2002. *Istorija russkogo literaturnogo jazyka (XI–XVII vv.)*, 3rd ed., corrected and revised. Moscow: Aspekt Press.

V. 1881. "[Review of] Svjate pys′mo Novoho Zavitu. Movoju rus′ko-ukrains′koju pereklaly vkupi P. A. Kuliš y dr. Y. Puljuj. Lviv. 1880." *Vestnik Evropy* 87, no. 1–2: 895–898.

Varčenko, I. O. 1954. "Refleksacija davn′oho *o* v lubens′kyx hovirkax." In *Poltavs′ko-kyjivs′kyj dialekt—osnova ukrajins′koji nacional′noji movy*, edited by Leonid Arsen′ovyč Bulaxovs′kyj et al., 49–67. Kyiv: AN Ukrajins′koji RSR.

Vasmer, Max. 1941. *Die Slaven in Griechenland*. Abhandlungen der Preußischen Akademie der Wissenschaften, Jahrgang 1941, Phil.-hist. Klasse, 12. Berlin: Verlag der Akademie der Wissenschaften.

Vaščenko, Vasyl′ Semenovyč. 1957. *Poltavs′ki hovory*. Kharkiv: Xarkivs′kyj deržavnyj universytet.

Vaxnjanin, Natal′. 1869. "Visti." *Pravda* 10 (15 March): 92.

Vaxnjanin, Natal′ and Pantelejmon Kuliš. 1869a. "Do čytateliv svjatoho pys′ma." *Pravda* 12 (30 March): 112.

___. 1869b. [Note]. *Pravda* 41 (8 February): 342.

Verxratskyj, Ivan. 1899. "Znadoby do piznannja uhorsko-ruskyx hovoriv." In *Zapysky Naukovoho Tovarystva imeni Ševčenka*, vol. 27, edited by Myxajlo Huševs′kyj, 1–68; vol. 28, edited by Myxajlo Huševs′kyj, 69–94; vol. 29, edited by Myxajlo Huševs′kyj, 95–200; vol. 30, edited by Myxajlo Huševs′kyj, 201–276. Lviv: Naukove Tovarystvo imeni Ševčenka.

___. 1901. "Znadoby do piznannja uhorsko-ruskyx hovoriv. Hovory z naholosom stalym." In *Zapysky Naukovoho Tovarystva imeni Ševčenka*, vol. 40, edited by Myxajlo Huševs′kyj, 1–113; vol. 44, edited by Myxajlo Huševs′kyj, 114–224; vol. 45, edited by Myxajlo Huševs′kyj, 225–280.

___. 1902. *Pro hovor halyc'kyx lemkiv.* Zbirnyk fil'ologičnoji sekciji Naukovoho Tovarystva imeni Ševčenka, vol. 5. Lviv: Naukove Tovarystvo imeni Ševčenka.

Vlasovs'kyj, Ivan. 1957. *Narys istoriji ukrajins'koji pravoslavnoji cerkvy*, vol. 3. New York and South Bound Brook: Ukrajins'ka Pravoslavna Cerkva v Z. D. A.

V. N. 1907. "[Review of] Hospoda Našoho Iysusa Xrysta Svjate Jevanhelije vid Matfeja." *Ukraina* 1: 106–113.

Vondrák, Wenzel [Václav]. 1924. *Vergleichende Slavische Grammatik*, vol. 1. Göttingen: Vandenhoeck & Ruprecht.

Voznjak, Myxajlo. 1911. *Halyc'ki hramatyky ukrajins'koji movy peršoji polovyny XIX st.* Lviv: Naukove Tovarystvo imeni Ševčenka.

___. 1928a. "Ostanni znosyny P. Kuliša z halyčanamy: (Z dodatkom joho lystuvannja z M. Pavlykom)." In *Zapysky Naukovoho Tovarystva imeni Ševčenka*, vol. 148: *V trydcjati rokovyny smerty Pantelejmona Kuliša*, edited by Kyrylo Studyns'kyj, 165–240. Lviv: Naukove Tovarystvo imeni Ševčenka.

___. 1928b. "Kuliš jak redaktor 'Pryčepy' Levyc'koho." In *Zapysky Naukovoho Tovarystva imeni Ševčenka*, vol. 148: *V trydcjati rokovyny smerty Pantelejmona Kuliša*, edited by Kyrylo Studyns'kyj, 1–54. Lviv: Naukove Tovarystvo imeni Ševčenka.

___, ed. 1930. "Gervinusiv 'Šekspir' v očax P. Kuliša." *Zbirnyk Zaxodoznavstva* 2: 168–176.

Vul'pius, Rikarda [Ricarda Vulpius]. 2005a. "Jazykovaja politika v Rossijskoj imperii i ukrainskij perevod Biblii (1860–1906)." *Ab Imperio* 2: 191–224.

___. 2005b. *Nationalisierung der Religion. Russifizierungspolitik und ukrainische Nationalbildung 1869–1920.* Forschungen zur osteuropäischen Geschichte, vol. 64. Wiebaden: Harrassowitz.

Vynnyk, Vasyl' Oleksijovyč et al. 1983. *Istorija ukrajins'koji movy. Leksyka i frazeolohija.* Kyiv: Naukova dumka.

Wingender, Monika. 2013. "Modell zur Beschreibung von Standardsprachentypen." In *Typen slavischer Standardsprachen. Theoretische, methodische und empirische Zugänge*, edited by Daniel Muller and Monika Wingender, 19–37. Wiesbaden: Harrassowitz.

Zakrevs'ka, Jaroslava, ed. 1997. *Hucul's'ki hovirky. Korotkyj slovnyk.* Lviv: Instytut ukrajinoznavstva im. I. Kryp'jakevyča NAN Ukrajiny.

Zales'kyj, Anton Mykolajovyč. 1969. "Častka *sja* u pivdenno-zaxidnyx hovorax ukrajins'koji movy." In *Ukrajins'ka dialektna morfolohija*, edited by Fedot Troxymovyč Žylko et al., 94–109. Kyiv: Naukova dumka.

Zaxarkin, Stepan. 1998. "Lystuvannja Pantelejmona Kuliša z Jevhenom Tymčenkom (1894–1895)." *Kyjivs'ka starovyna* 4: 94–108.

Zelens'ka, Ljudmyla. 2000. "Kataloh rukopysiv P. O. Kuliša ta lystiv do n'oho u zibranni Černihivs'koho muzeju-zapovidnyka M. M. Kocjubyns'koho." In *Pantelejmon Kuliš. Materialy i doslidžennja*, edited by Mykola Hryhorovyč Žulyns'kyj, 353–386. Lviv and New York: M. P. Koc'.

___. 2001. "Lysty Ivana Puljuja do Hanny Barvinok." In *Hanna Barvinok. Zbirnyk do 170-riččja vid dnja narodžennja*, edited by Vasyl' Šenderovs'kyj, 294–367. Kyiv: Rada.

Zerov, Mykola. 1960. *Nove ukrajins'ke pys'menstvo. Istoryčnyj narys*, part 1. Munich: Instytut literatury.

___. 1967. *Do džerel. Istoryčno-literaturni ta krytyčni stattji.* State College, PA: Žyttja i Škola.

Žiteckij, Pavel. 1900. *Eneida Kotljarevskogo i drevnejšij spisok eë v svjazi s obzorom malorusskoj literatury XVIII veka.* Kyiv: Izdatel'stvo žurnala "Kievskaja starina."

___. 1905. "O perevodax evangelija na malorusskij jazyk." *Izvestija Otdelenija russkogo jazyka i slovesnosti* 10, no. 3–4: 1–65.

Žovtobrjux, Myxajlo Andrijovyč et al. 1979. *Istorija ukrajins'koji movy. Fonetyka.* Kyiv: Naukova dumka.

Žulyns'kyj, Mykola Hryhorovyč, ed. 2000. *Pantelejmon Kuliš. Materialy i doslidžennja.* Lviv and New York: M. P. Koc'.

Žulyns'kyj, Mykola Hryhorovyč and Jevhen Kazymyrovyč Naxlik. 1995. "Kuliš, Pantelejmon Oleksandrovyč." In *Ukrajins'ka literaturna encyklopedija*, vol. 3, edited by Myxajlo Pavlovyč Zjabljuk, 95–98. Kyiv: Vydavnyctvo "Ukrajins'ka encyklopedija" im. M. P. Bažana.

Žylko, Fedot Troxymovyč. 1966. *Narysy z dialektolohiji ukrajins'koji movy.* Kyiv: Radjans'ka škola.

Indices

GEOGRAPHICAL AND PERSONAL NAMES

Note: names of the authors whose writings have been excerpted are not, with some exceptions, included in the index

A
Aksakov, Ivan, 49
Aksakov, Sergej, 377
Aleksandrov, Volodymyr, 21, 27–31, 34–36, 60–61, 64–65, 90, 152, 163–164, 169–172, 196, 275–276
Austria-Hungary, xii, xvi–xvii, xix, xxi, 49, 58, 91, 129, 132, 154, 331, 380, 383–384
Austro-Hungarian Empire, see Austria-Hungary
Austrian-ruled Ukraine, see Galicia

B
Bačyn′skij, Aleksander, 23, 84, 132, 133, 135–140, 270
Bačyns′kyj, Andrij, Bishop, 84, 125, 129n2, 137
Balašenko, Myxajlo, 154
Barvinok, Hanna, see Bilozers′ka-Kuliš, Oleksandra
Barvins′kyj, Oleksander, 39, 46, 51, 63, 107, 143, 181, 188, 231–232, 282–285, 289, 375
Baudouin de Courtenay, Jan Niecisław, 66–67, 381
Bednars′kyj, Karol′, 283
Belarus′, 67n6
Belej, Ivan, 287
Biloborodov, Oleksij, 5, 52, 154–155, 172–174, 253–254, 257, 265, 278
Bilozers′ka-Kuliš, Oleksandra, 153, 228
Bilozers′kyj, Ivan, 51
Bilozers′kyj, Vasyl′, 67n6, 174, 228
Borec′kyj, Jov, xxi
Borovykovs′kyj, Levko, 228, 277

Branik, Ivan, 37–38
Bučyns′kyj, Meliton, 37, 53, 58, 181
Bukovyna, xx–xxi, 95–96, 107–108, 117, 120, 124–125, 138, 140–141, 151–152, 161–162, 187, 201, 210, 240, 277, 320, 326, 330, 337
Byron, George Gordon, xii, 157, 223, 281, 321, 338, 342, 356, 377, 384
Byzantium, 233

C
Čajčenko, Vasyl′, 372
Catherine II, xi, 280
Central Ukraine, see Dnieper Ukraine
Černivci, 37, 140n6, 149n10
Corneille, Pierre, 7
Cossack Ukraine, see Hetmanate
Cromwell, Oliver, 286

D
Dante, 281, 356, 381
Deržavin, Gavrila, 13, 18, 19
Dnieper Ukraine, xi, xii, xvi, xvii, xx, 31, 34, 38, 44, 46–48, 55, 58, 59, 60, 65, 67, 79, 82, 83, 90, 95, 96, 101, 103, 108, 109, 112, 113, 120, 126, 131, 145, 148n9, 152, 163, 179, 180, 185, 187, 201, 214n6, 215, 216, 227, 231, 239, 262, 269, 276, 278, 291, 295, 297, 311, 312, 313, 315, 320–322, 334, 335, 337, 338, 368, 371, 373, 376, 380, 382, 384, 385, 401
Dobrovský, Josef, 105, 118
Dolgorukov, Vasilij, 56
Domanyc′kyj, Vasyl′, 291

Drahomanov, Myxajlo, 62, 140, 154, 156, 181, 266, 320–321, 355
Drozdov, Mixail, see Filaret, Metropolitan of Moscow
Dykovs'kyj, Myxajlo, 195

F

Fed'kovyč, Jurij Osyp, xvii, 140, 148, 308, 314 320–326, 330–331, 336, 367
Filaret, Metropolitan of Moscow, 13n3
Fogarašij, Ivan, 117–118
Franko, Ivan, xvii, 46–48, 53–54, 63n4, 93–97, 112, 117, 150, 193–196, 202, 204, 219, 266, 282–283, 287–288, 290–292, 300–304, 306, 309, 311, 314, 315–322, 324–326, 331, 330–337, 339–340, 343, 345, 351, 367–373, 375, 380, 383–385
Fürst, Julius, 233
Fylypovyč, Pavlo, 344

G

Galagan, Hryhorij, 281–282, 375, 377
Galicia, xvi–xvii, xx, 37, 39, 41, 44, 46–47, 51, 53–54, 60, 62–63, 65, 80–81, 85n9, 92, 95–97, 101, 107–152, 161, 163, 179, 186–187, 189, 193n3, 201, 211, 221–223, 227, 229, 231, 233, 235, 237, 250, 262, 270, 277, 282, 284, 293, 296–297, 306, 320, 324, 326, 330, 335, 337, 344, 368, 372, 376, 379–380, 382–383
Gervinus, Georg Gottfried, 286–288, 311
Goethe, Wolfgang Johann von, xii, 157, 223, 281
Gogol, Nikolaj, xxiii, 62, 377
Golovnin, Aleksandr, 56, 57
Grand Duchy of Lithuania, xx
Grigorij, Archbishop of Kaluga, 69

H

Habsburg Empire, see Austria-Hungary
Halip, Teodot, 140
Harasevyč, Myxajlo, 124
Hatcuk, Mykola, 228
Hatcuk, Oleksa, 4, 184
Heine, Heinrich, 157, 223, 338
Hetmanate, xxi, 9, 68, 125, 214, 309–310
Hnylevyč, Hryhorij, 37
Hohol', Mykola, see Gogol, Nikolaj

Holovac'kyj, Jakiv, 48, 109n1, 117, 221
Homer, 22, 106, 164, 202n4, 216, 272–273, 281, 285, 298, 306, 356, 371, 379
Horlenko, Vasyl', 341, 344, 361–363
Hrebinka, Leonid, 82, 207, 277
Hrečulevyč, Vasyl', 3
Hrinčenko, Borys, 23, 62, 79, 87, 106, 112, 167, 171, 179–180, 184, 187, 190, 215, 219–220, 227, 230, 260, 263, 282, 326, 328, 334, 341, 366, 372
Hryhorij, Archimandrite, 152
Hulak-Artemovs'kyj, Petro, 6–13, 18, 28–29, 35, 207, 275, 277, 354, 374

J

Jefremov, Serhii, 6, 8, 46, 63n4, 65n5, 91, 161–162, 210
Jireček, Josef, 140
Joseph II, 124
Juzefovyč, Myxajlo, 281

K

Kamanin, Ivan, 224
Karadžić, Vuk, 231
Katkov, Mixail, 49, 57
Kautzsch, 174, 242, 251, 253, 256–258
Ketčer, Nikolaj, 281, 290, 361
Kistjakivs'kyj, Oleksander, 4, 49, 66
Kmicykevyč, Volodymyr, 282
Kobyljans'kyj, Antin, 85n9, 95, 102, 139, 140, 140n6, 141, 142, 143, 144, 145, 146, 148, 148n9, 149, 149n10, 150, 151, 152, 270, 277, 317, 318, 369
Kocjubyns'kyj, Myxajlo, viii, 155, 271n9
Kokorudz, Illja, 372
Kolomyja, 37, 95, 139, 156
Konys'kyj, Oleksander, 154, 282
Korš, Fëdor, 70, 89
Kosač, Larysa, see Ukrajinka, Lesja
Kostomarov, Mykola, xvii, 57, 228, 295, 383
Kotljarevs'kyj, Ivan, xv, 8, 33, 36, 79, 86, 119, 164, 207, 216, 218, 229, 239, 275, 277, 313, 378
Koval'skyj, Vasyl', 125
Kropyvnyc'kyj, Marko, 314
Kryms'kyj, Ahatanhel, 59, 225n7, 227, 372
Kurylo, Olena, 59, 309
Kvitka-Osnov'janenko, Hryhorij, 8–9, 21, 84–85, 97, 119, 164, 207, 216,

219–220, 225–226, 225n7, 248, 307, 342
Kyivan Rus', xxii, 46, 298, 312

L

Left-Bank Ukraine, see Dnieper Ukraine
Lermontov, Mixail, 60n2, 338
Levic'kyj, Ivan, see Nečuj-Levyc'kyj, Ivan
Levyc'kyj, Josyf, 140n7
Levyc'kyj, Parfenij, 70, 75, 89
Lindheim, Ralph, xiii
Lobodovs'kyj (Loboda), Myxajlo, 62–65, 71, 72, 101–108, 152, 161, 188, 196, 299
Lodij, Petro, 124
Lopatyns'kyj, Lev, 379
Lozyns'kyj, Josyf, 140, 140n7
Lučkaj, Myxajlo, 117, 138
Lviv, ix, xii, 4–5, 41, 43, 49, 52, 64, 70n7, 84, 124–126, 132, 149n10, 157, 180, 250–251, 261, 282, 284–285, 289–291, 293, 301, 315, 321, 337
Lysenko, Mykola, 368

M

Maksymovyč, Myxajlo, 6, 13–16, 28–29, 31, 35, 62, 207, 222, 237, 275
Malynovs'kyj, Myxajlo, 41, 127
Mandel'štam, Leon, 27
Metlyns'kyj, Amvrosij, 164, 222, 228, 239, 277
Mickiewicz, Adam, 60n2, 338, 356
Miklošič, Franjo, see Miklosich, Franz
Miklosich, Franz, 37, 38, 40, 42, 49–50, 86, 140, 221
Millard, Edward, 37, 38, 50, 177
Millard, Henry, 177
Moračevs'kyj, Pylyp, 21, 24, 31, 53–56, 62n3, 65–75, 77–93, 96, 97, 99–100, 102, 104–108, 152, 153, 159, 200, 216, 219, 235, 249, 275
Mordovcev, Daniil, 339
Mordovec', Danylo, see Mordovcev, Daniil
Mukačeve, 125
Muscovy, xxi, 376
Mykyta, Ivan, 203
Myrnyj, Panas, 58, 82, 92, 119, 167, 169, 184, 247, 268–270, 314, 337, 345–346, 348, 359–367, 369–370

Mytkevyč, Mykola, see Grigorij, Archbishop of Kaluga

N

Naumburg, 50–51, 154
Naumovyč, Ivan, 37, 95, 139
Navroc'kyj, Oleksander, 21–26, 28, 35, 36, 89, 90, 152, 169, 196, 275, 276
Nečuj, Ivan, see Nečuj-Levyc'kyj, Ivan
Nečuj-Levyc'kyj, Ivan, xvii, 59, 78, 82, 85, 86, 91–96, 98, 121, 131, 145–147, 161, 162, 176, 177, 179, 180–193, 202, 209, 210, 237, 242–249, 272, 302, 335, 337, 345, 347, 348
Nekraševyč, Ivan, 119, 164, 241, 301
Nekrasov, Nikolaj, 338
Nikitenko, Aleksandr, 68
Nis, Stepan, 40, 155, 173, 207, 210, 377, 381

O

Ohijenko, Ivan, 23–24, 87, 158, 192, 202, 235, 252–253, 278
Ohonovs'kyj, Omeljan, 42, 124
Orlaj, Ivan, 117
Osadca, Myxajlo, 41, 222, 380

P

Padura, Tymko, 168
Partyc'kyj, Omeljan, 38, 64, 222, 293, 379–380
Pavlovs'kyj, Oleksij, 229, 236, 239
Pavlovyč, Andrij, 124
Pavlyk, Myxajlo, 47–48, 154, 156–158, 173, 181, 249–251, 267, 320, 376–377
Pčilka, Olena, 343
Peter the Great, 280
Petrov, Nikolaj, 340
Petruševyč, Antin, 37
Pletnëv, Pëtr, 376
Počajiv, 129n2, 151
Polish-Lithuanian Commonwealth, xx
Polissja, 104, 205–206, 335
Poltava, 84, 89, 92, 119, 188, 204, 282, 363
Potebnja, Oleksander, 85, 106, 169, 202n4, 211, 215–216, 225–226, 272–273, 297–298, 306, 352, 371, 378
Puškin, Aleksandr, 63n4, 126, 377

R
Racine, Jean, 7
Renan, Ernest, 255
Reuß, Eduard, 4n1, 157, 175, 251, 265
Right-Bank Ukraine, see Galicia
Rudans'kyj, Stepan, 10n2
Rudčenko, Ivan, 37, 58
Rudčenko, Panas, see Myrnyj, Panas
Russian Empire, xxi, 32, 46, 64, 67n6, 153, 185, 222, 224, 309, 338, 371, 384
Russian-ruled Ukraine, see Dnieper Ukraine
Rustaveli, Šota, 22

S
Sapieha, Adam, 63
Šaškevyč, Markijan, 85n9, 95, 109–115, 117–126, 137–140, 146–149, 151, 223, 231, 270, 277
Šaxmatov, Aleksej, 70, 89
Ščepkin, Myxajlo, 207
Schiller, Friedrich, 157, 281–282
Scott, Walter, 281
Sembratovyč, Josyf, 41
Sembratovyč, Sylvester, 43
Šeptyc'kyj, Varlaam, 125
Ševčenko, Taras, xi, xiv, xvi, 5–6, 9–11, 14, 16, 19–21, 24, 26, 36, 80, 82–83, 85, 103–104, 119, 126, 141, 164, 184, 186, 207, 209, 215–217, 225–227, 250, 260, 270, 275–277, 280–281, 302–303, 306, 309, 343, 347, 364, 378–380, 383
Shakespeare, William, xii–xiii, xv–xvi, xviii–xix, xxii, 44, 64, 106, 131, 223, 281–289, 293–294, 299
Siedlce, 180
Simovyč, Vasyl', 59, 140, 232
Skovoroda, Hryhorij, 20, 48
Sljusarčuk, Oleksij (Oleksa), 93n11, 132n4, 179
Sloboda Ukraine, xvi, xxi, 9, 84, 125, 161, 166, 169, 205, 214, 219, 239, 342
Smerečyns'kyj, Serhij, 59, 309
Smotryc'kyj, Meletij, xvi
Sreznevskij, Izmail, 62, 68, 73n8
Sreznevskij, Vsevolod, 73, 99
Staryc'kyj, Myxajlo, 23, 292, 298, 314, 337–357, 359, 360, 369, 371
Stebnyc'kyj, Petro, 246

Subcarpathian Rus', see Transcarpathia
Suškevyč, Kornylo, 52
Suvorov, Aleksandr, 18
Svij, Pavlo, see Svjencic' kyj, Pavlyn
Svjencic'kyj, Pavlyn, 67n6, 301, 314–315

T
Tarkovyč, Hryhorij, 123, 124, 129
Tarnovs'kyj, Jr., Vasyl', 50, 180, 278, 290
Timofeev, Konstantin, 286–288
Timoféevič, Semion, 119
Transcarpathia, xx–xxi, 55, 95–96, 107, 110, 117–118, 120, 124–125, 130, 138, 151–152, 187, 200–201, 205–206, 302, 336–337, 345, 379
Tuptalo, Dymitrij, 21
Tymčenko, Jevhen, 59, 67n6, 174, 282, 309

U
Ukrajinka, Lesja, 82, 119, 314, 337, 354–360, 366
Užhorod, 125

V
Vahylevyč, Ivan, 117, 164
Valuev, Pëtr, 55–57
Vasylijevyč, Myxajlo, 152
Vaxnjanin, Natal', 37, 203, 233
Veresaj, Ostap, 45
Verxrats'kyj, Ivan, 84, 372
Vienna, 37–38, 40–42, 49, 52, 61, 63, 88, 117, 125, 131, 138, 155, 184, 280
Vitte, Sergej, 70
Vjazemskij, Pëtr, 13n3
Voljan, Vasyl', 125, 127
Vostokov, Aleksandr, 68
Voznjak, Myxajlo, 109

X
Xarkiv, 60n2, 61, 62, 65, 79, 204, 222
Xmel'nyc'kyj, Bohdan, 286
Xomenko-Pljuta, Ivan, 23, 158, 192, 202, 278
Xyl'čevs'kyj, Ivan, 4, 50, 85, 265

Z
Zalens'kij (Załęski), Apolinarij, 154
Zerov, Mykola, 8, 343

SUBJECTS, NAMES OF PERIODICALS, TITLES OF LITERARY WORKS AND TRANSLATIONS

a > *'e*, 110
accusative case: independent accusative of time, 170, 171
accusative-genitive direct object, 105, 348, 357
"Adagio pensieroso," 355
adjective: long (non-contracted) form, 104, 160
agentive phrase, see passive constructions
akannje, 376
all-Russian language, 296, 297, 311
alternation *o, e : i*, 25n4, 167, 302
alternation *u- : v-*, 79, 101, 103, 122, 145, 242–243, 308–309
anaptyxis, 25n4, 264, 316
apheresis, 104, 160, 264, 309, 335
Apocrypha, 153, 158, 177, 185, 253
Apokalypsys˝ čy odkrovennje svjatoho apostola Yvana Bohoslova, 73n8
apostrophe, 187
assimilation of obstruents, 34, 82, 168, 335
assimilative palatalization, 34, 142, 143
auxiliary clitics: clause-second (Wackernagel's) position, 323; conditional auxiliaries, 324–325; future auxiliaries, 165, 209–212, 323, 324, 347; preterit auxiliaries, 103, 108, 110, 124, 130, 137, 147, 150, 212, 304, 317, 325; verb-adjacent position, 210, 323–324
auxiliary verbs, 99, 122, 170, 212, 247, 304, 348

Barbareum, 124–125
Bible: "analytic" order, 175; Czech Bible, 196; Elizabeth Bible, 129, 131, 195; French Bible, 67, 196; Hebrew, 34, 249, 252, 265, 275; Judeo-German Bible, 196; German Bible, 4n1, 50, 185; Italian Bible of 1903, 196; Poetic Books, 174, 176, 275; "poetic" order, 175; Rusian Bible, 38, 188; Ukrainian Bible, 109, 153, 173, 178, 184–185, 193, 204–205, 243–244, 249, 251, 264, 275–276, 278, 283, 382; versified Bible, 40, 173, 176, 270–274, 277, 335
biblical style, see high style
bilingualism, xvi, 108, 283, 336
British and Foreign Bible Society, 37, 43–44, 50, 52, 64, 86, 93, 129, 132, 141, 153, 158, 173, 177, 185–186, 189, 195, 265
Bukovyna dialects, 162
Byblija syrič˝ Knyhy Svjatoho Pysanija. 1.Staroho Zapovitu, 61

Cari, 174
Carpatho-Rusyn, 117, 138
Central Dnieper dialects, 44, 55, 65, 121, 145, 168, 200, 207, 214n6, 217, 267, 345–346
Charitable Society of the Publication of Useful and Cheap Books, 69
Childe Harold's Pilgrimage, 281, 377, 384
Church Slavonic, xvi, xx, 6, 11, 19, 21, 32, 33, 36, 39, 41, 43, 44, 45, 55, 77, 82, 88, 90, 94, 95, 96, 98, 99, 100, 110, 111, 117, 118, 119, 120, 122, 124, 125, 129n2, 132, 135, 138, 139, 144, 148, 150–152, 159, 182, 201, 235, 246, 250, 276, 277, 376: East Slavic recension, 47; Russian recension, 152, 167, 171, 276, 277; Ukrainian (Meletian) recension, xvi, 200; "vernacular Church Slavonic," 138–139
Church Slavonicisms, xvi, 6–7, 12–13, 19–21, 24, 26, 29–31, 36, 44, 47, 71, 83–84, 87, 90, 102, 111–112, 118, 121, 125, 131, 133, 135–136, 139, 148, 150–152, 160, 162–164, 170, 172, 179, 194–195, 199–202, 204, 218–219, 221, 246, 264, 267, 269, 272–273, 304–305, 307–308, 312, 358, 366
čn > šn, 160
colloquialisms, 218, 326, 330
Common East Slavic, 250, 298
comparative degrees, 161, 212, 365, 371
Čorna rada, xv, 235, 244, 303, 334–335, 378

Cossackophilism, 298
Cossacks, 20, 39, 83, 189, 229, 262, 280, 285, 292, 377, 384
Cymbelin, 290

Das Alte Testament: übersetzt, eingeleitet und erläutert von D. Eduard Reuß, 4n1
Deuterocanonical books, see Apocrypha
Dijanyja svjatyx″ apostoliv″ pysannyi svjatym″ apostolom″ y jevanhelystom″ Lukoju, 73n8
diminutives, 8–9, 13, 23–24, 105, 113, 160, 171, 299, 307, 352, 354, 365–366
Dniester dialects, 102, 130, 137, 139, 140, 142, 162, 187, 240, 317, 334, 335, 341
Do čumaka, abo vojna janhlo-xrancuzo-turec′ka u 1853 y 54 rokaxi, 65n5
Dvi moskovky, 181
"Dvi movi, knyžnja i narodnja," 375
Dzvin, 231, 281, 285

-*e* ending, 26, 162, 184, 207–208, 246, 263, 303, 317, 346, 357
-*ej* ending, 161, 170, 170n2
Ems decree of 1876, 58–59, 225, 266, 338, 382
Enejida, xv, 8, 33, 79, 84, 86–87, 164, 216, 261, 218, 313
-*enk(o)* suffix, 202
euphony, 10n2, 79, 103, 122, 145, 243, 308–309
-*ex* ending, 170n2
Ezekyjel′, 174

future tense: analytic forms, 160, 169, 210–211, 323, 347; synthetic forms in -*mu*, 209–211, 160, 169, 209, 210, 212, 323, 324, 325, 347

Galician-Bukovynian dialects, 207
Galician-Bukovynian koiné, 16, 215, 313, 316, 325, 327–331, 334–335, 371, 380, 382
Galicianisms, see western Ukrainian regionalisms
"Gamlet v postolax," 340
gemination of consonants by assimilation of *j*, 26, 59, 122, 207, 238, 272, 303, 309, 364, 365

genitive-accusative direct object, 105, 357
genitive-partitive case, 348
Grammatica Slavo-Ruthena, 117
Great Russian language, see Russian language
Great Russianiasms, see Russianisms
Greek Catholic Church, 54, 65, 124, 129, 132–133, 233

Habakuka, 174
Hajdamaks, 281, 292, 384
Hakhkheja, 174
halyčanščyna, 48
Hamlet, 281, 290–292, 301, 308, 315–316, 319n1, 320–326, 331–357, 367, 369
Hamljet, 281, 292, 301–303, 306, 315, 317–319, 321–322, 324–331, 336, 351
Hamljet″. Dans′kyj korolevyč, 315
Hebrew, 4, 18, 21–24, 27, 30, 32, 34, 40, 60n2, 61, 66–67, 129, 166, 174–176, 183, 191–196, 221, 249–253, 257, 261–262, 265, 270, 272, 274–275
Hemlet Viljama Šekspira, 323–324, 330, 336
high style, 4, 7, 13, 18, 40, 58, 60, 172, 184, 220, 249, 273, 306, 383: biblical variety, xviii, 17, 96, 270, 278, 305, 313; secular variety, xviii, 304–305, 311–314, 374
Hiob, 4n1, 257
Holos na holos dlja Halyčyny, 140n6
Holosin′nja, 250, 261–264
Holosin′nja j Pis′nja Pisen′, 157
Holy Scriptures, see Bible
Holy Synod, 53, 56, 66, 68–70, 89, 152, 153, 177, 185
"Homer i Šekspir," 285
Hoseja, 174
Hramatka, 5–6, 10, 235
Hramatyka jazÿka ruskoho, 293
Hucul dialects, 102, 118, 140, 142, 144, 162, 167, 205, 210, 302, 320–325, 327–329
Hyjob, 4n1, 254–255, 258
Hÿob, 174

i < *o, e* see ikavism
ikavism, 23, 25n4, 80, 112, 119, 197, 204, 243, 302, 345, 357
Iliad, 22

Illustrierte Pracht Bibel für Israeliten in dem masoretischen Text and neuer deutscher Übersetzung, 233
impersonal constructions, 81, 99, 122, 148, 165, 170, 208, 246–247, 348
Ioana, 174
Ioel', 174
Iosuja Nunenko, 174
Istorija vossoedinenija Rusi, xi, 3, 280
-ivn(a) suffix, 202
-ix ending, 29, 169, 264, 346

j > *l'*, 206
Jak kozam rohy vypravljajut', 320
jazyčije, xx, 127, 140n6, 148n9, 200, 277–278, 312, 372–373
Judaism, 158
Južnyj Russkyj Zbornyk", 222

kh digraph, 268–269, 301, 362, 364
Kievskaja starina, 62, 291
Knyha Iova na Malorus'ku movu pereložena, 166
Knyha Psal'miv Proroka Davyda, 22
Knyha Tovytova, na malorus'ku movu pereložena s" tekstu hrečes'koho, 163
Kobzar, 5, 34, 82, 209
kolomyjka, 158, 190, 276
kotljarevščyna, 36, 65n5
Krašanka rusynam i poljakam na Velykden' 1882 roku, xii, 63, 156
Kulišisms, 21–24, 26, 276
Kul'tura slova, xiv

l' "light," 214
Le livre de Job, 256
Lečebnik, 215
Leksikon" slavenorosskij y ymen" tl"kovanije, 86, 111, 215, 216
Leksykon" syrěč" slovesnyk" slavenskij, 215
Lemkian dialects, 84, 130, 137, 206, 328–329, 336
Leo XIII, Pope, 64
Lexicon palaeoslovenico-graeco-latinum, 42
linguistic debates, 93, 372
linguistic parochialism, 42, 360, 372, 379
literary Ukrainian: Carpatho-Rusyn, 117, 138, 141; Central Dnieper variety, 44, 55, 65, 121, 145, 168, 200, 207, 214n6,

217, 267, 345–346; Europeanizing trend, xv; Galician variety, 45, 48, 113, 125, 317, 323, 382; "Galician vogue," 91, 95, 131, 186; monodialectal, 93, 354, 362, 367, 385; multidialectal, 146, 334, 364, 372; regional varieties, 43, 102, 185, 201, 368; vernacular-based, xv, xx, 10, 77, 90, 159, 166, 201, 228, 242, 245, 275–276, 297, 311, 330–331, 359, 362, 373, 383
Little Russian, xvi, xxi, 3, 16, 32, 34, 41, 56, 60, 68–69, 71, 84, 88, 103, 163, 166, 222, 230, 248, 296–299, 338, 362, 378
Little Russianisms, 125, 311, 363, 371
Luna, 342
"Lyst bez koverty jako odpovid' Vpr. Krylošanynu Malynovs'komu na referat molytovnyka," 42

"Mahomet i Xadyza," xii, 224–225
Makbet, 359
Malejaxyj, 174
Malorusko-nimeckyj slovar, 34, 142, 186, 211, 229
"Marija," 19
"Marusja Bohuslavka," 224
Middle Ukrainian, xx, xxiii, 84, 88, 98–99, 136, 147, 162, 199, 204–206, 216–217, 220, 233–234, 239, 241–243, 246, 248, 298, 301–302, 309, 329, 334, 337, 341
Mixail Čarnyšenko, ili Malorossija vosem'desjat let nazad, xi
Molytovnyk dlja rus'koho narodu, 42, 44, 55, 61, 88n10
Molytvoslov" y korotka nauka o xrystijans'ko-katolyckój věrě, 41–42, 44, 88n10, 127
"Moskalisms," see Russianisms
moskovščyna, 107
Muscovite language, see Russian language

Na temy movy, 59
Nahum, 174
Narod, 79, 156, 197, 243
Narys istoriji ukrajins'ko-rus'koji literatury do 1890 r., 93
Ne xody, Hrycju, 60n2
"Neofity," 19

"new g," 301
New Testament, 5, 24, 38, 43–44, 49–50, 52, 54–56, 58, 60–62, 64–69, 71, 82, 85, 88n10, 90–91, 95, 104, 113, 132, 139, 140n7, 145, 149n10, 152–153, 155, 172, 177, 183–184, 186, 188–189, 193n3, 204, 210–211, 216, 221, 234, 249–250, 262, 265, 277–278, 296, 317, 341, 381
neutralization: of place and manner, 70, 228–229, 240–241, 300–301; of voicing, 25, 168, 241, 261, 264
nimeščyna, 107
-no, *-to* predicative forms, see impersonal constructions
nominative-accusative direct object, 105, 357
non-pleophonic forms, 30, 162, 195, 358
normalization of literary Ukrainian: archaization, 77, 83, 96–102, 121, 158–159, 162, 188, 196, 200, 303–305; vernacularization, 36, 84, 96, 100, 102–108, 122, 125, 159, 163, 166, 233, 326
North Ukrainian, 81, 104, 122, 161–162, 164, 206, 301, 335, 346, 353
northern dialects, see North Ukrainian
novorus'ka mova, see *novoruščyna*
novoruščyna, xxi, 251, 375, 377

Obadyja, 174
obščerusskij jazyk, see all-Russian language
Odyssey, 22, 86, 106, 202n4, 216, 272–273, 298, 306, 352, 371
Old Rusian, xvi, xxi–xxii, 47, 88, 159–160, 179, 218, 233, 248, 250–251, 265, 285, 292, 310, 344, 354, 358, 375–377, 383–385
Old Testament: Amos, 174; Apocalypse, 173; Chronicles, 175, 185, 241, 246, 272; Daniel, 175, 185, 273; Ecclesiastes, 175, 177, 267, 270; Esther, 175, 185, 273; Exodus, 61, 173, 190–191, 216, 271; Genesis, 61, 191, 233, 271; Habakkuk, 174–175; Haggai, 174–175; Hosea, 174–175; Job, 4, 23, 50, 58, 61, 145, 156–172, 174–176, 190, 236, 248, 251, 253–262, 270, 272, 275–276; Joel, 174; Jonah, 174–175; Joshua, 174–175; Judges, 174–175; Isaiah, 19, 174–175, 190; Kings 174; Lamentations, 157, 174–176, 250, 253, 261–265, 272–273, 277; Malachi, 174; Moses, 4, 17, 47, 94, 155, 158, 160, 173, 184, 189, 190–191, 194, 233, 265, 271, 371; Nahum, 174–175; Nehemiah, 175, 185, 272; Obadiah, 174–176; Pentateuch, 4, 37, 47, 58, 61, 66, 174–175, 179, 191, 220, 241, 253, 303; Proverbs, 174–176, 185, 190, 270; Psalms, 3–6, 14, 17, 19, 27, 33, 37, 50, 61, 126, 132, 158, 175–176, 182, 184–185, 197; Samuel, 174–175; Song of Songs, 265–270; Tobit, 61, 156–172, 175, 177, 185, 249, 276; Zechariah, 174–175
Orthography; etymological, 38, 43, 141, 185, 236; *jarÿžka*, 224; *kotljarivka*, 223–224; *kulišivka*, 54, 144–145, 185, 211, 221, 223, 226–227, 230, 232, 235–237, 242, 273, 295; *kulišôvka*, 41–42; *latinica*, 140–141; *maksymovyčivka*, 132, 222–224; phonetic, xvi, xxiii, 37, 41–42, 47, 53–54, 79–80, 82–84, 91, 93, 95–96, 98, 103–104, 117–118, 141–145, 159–160, 167, 185, 187, 189, 204, 215, 220– 233, 235–237, 241–244, 261, 268, 270, 295, 299–300, 323, 325, 333, 335, 345, 363–364, 380; "radical phonetics," 34, 143, 230, 239, 264, 268, 273, 346, 358
Osnova, 49, 60n2, 228–229, 238–239, 282
-ovi, *-evi* dative case ending, 26, 165, 169
-ovi, *-evi* locative case ending, 169

"P. Kuliš pro svoju spravu z Poljakamy," 156
paratactic constructions, 105, 273
passive constructions, 81, 97–98, 100, 111, 122, 147
Pentatevx, see *Pentatevx Musijevyj*
Pentatevx Musijevyj, 4–5, 37, 58, 61, 85, 95

Pieśni białorusko-polskie z powiatu Sokólskiego, gubernii Grodzieńskiej, 67n6
Pjat' knyh Mosejëvyx, 155
Pjatoknyžže, 174
Plejada, 355
pleophonic forms, 96, 126, 199, 216, 295
pluperfect tense, 213, 245, 347
Podolja dialects, 137, 187, 204, 206–207, 341
Pokuttja dialects, 102, 140, 210
"Pokuttja-Dniester-Hucul" dialect, 102, 140
Polish language, 43–45, 47–48, 67, 111–113, 118, 125–126, 139, 142–143, 147–150, 152, 155, 161, 163, 166–167, 170, 182, 197, 200, 209, 214–216, 220, 236, 246–247, 249, 260, 265, 276–278, 294, 297, 302, 304, 306, 312–313, 316–318, 320, 325–330, 336–337, 341, 344, 348, 353–354, 358, 367, 371, 375–378, 380, 382
Polissian dialects, 82, 103, 164, 186, 208, 240–241, 264, 268, 300, 336, 345, 347, 353
Polonisms, 26, 44, 86, 125, 133, 151, 260, 277, 372
pol'ščyzna, see Polish language
Poltava dialects, 65n5, 84, 89, 119, 188, 204, 208, 282, 363
populists, xi, xvii, xxi, 22, 53, 59, 65, 83, 90, 94–96, 126, 152, 181, 183, 223, 265, 280, 282, 289, 311–312, 331, 335, 372, 375, 379, 383
Pravda, 4–5, 22, 37–38, 42, 46, 49, 86, 157–158, 161, 167, 180–181, 197, 203, 223, 233, 236, 255, 266, 282
Pozyčena kobza, 157, 231
Pro vojnu z Francuzom, 85n9
prostaja mova, xvi, xx–xxiii, 81, 88, 96, 110, 117, 119, 121, 124, 152, 195, 201, 214, 220, 240, 278, 372, 383
Prosvita Society, 5, 16, 35, 43, 158
prothesis, 5n1, 235, 303 336
"Pryčepa," 86, 181, 209–210, 243, 245
Pryčyna tvorenija sja narěčej, 38

Pryručnȳj slovar' polsko-sloven'skij y narodno-ruskij, 215
Prysmyrena kaverznycja, 283
Psalter, 4–5, 10, 13n3, 20, 27, 29, 31–32, 34, 61, 70n4, 132, 139, 175–176, 250, 253, 262, 275, 277
Psaltyr, see *Psaltyr abo knyha xvaly Božoji*
Psaltyr abo knyha xvaly Božoji, 5, 14, 23
Psaltyr" na malorossyjskim" jazyci, 73n8
Psaltyr' v" jazȳčě cerkovno-sloven'skôm" s" perevodom" na jazȳk" narodno-ruskij, 132, 215
Psaltyrja rozšyrena v" dusě xrystijan'skoj molytvȳ y cerkovnoho bohoslužen ja, 93n11
Psal'ma 15, 4, 15, 34–35
Psal'ma 16, 4, 22, 30
purists, 372

"radical phonetics," see orthography
regionalisms, 9, 131, 139, 200, 220, 249, 318, 371
relative clause: resumption, 209, 304 ; relative pronouns, 9, 137, 201, 208, 304; absolute relativizer, 118, 169, 200, 208, 304
rumunščyna, 107
Rusalka Dněstrovaja, 126, 142, 231
Ruska čytanka dlja nyžšoji hymnaziȳ, 125
Rus'ka pys'mennist', 109n1
Rus'ka trijcja, 109, 117, 126
Rus'ko uhors'ka ili madęrska hrammatika, 117
Russian Bible Society, 129n3
Russian Church Slavonicisms, 164, 170, 345, 367
Russian language, xvii, xix, xxi, xxii, 16, 18, 27, 43, 53, 59n1, 63, 65n5, 67, 85, 88, 94, 95, 107, 117, 125, 129, 152, 161, 167, 171, 209, 214n6, 221, 226, 227, 232, 242, 248, 251, 277, 278, 281, 286, 296, 311, 312, 343, 348, 361, 375, 376–378
Russian Old Believers, 41, 42
Russianisms, 121, 125, 151, 164, 172, 214, 220, 260, 263, 267, 299, 305–308, 311–312, 372, 381

Russophiles, 37, 94–96, 127, 139, 141, 152, 200, 221–223, 233, 335, 380
Rusyns, xii, xxi, 39, 51, 55, 62n3, 63, 125, 141, 156
ruščyna, 107, 376
Ruthenian, see *prostaja mova*
Ruthenianisms, 372

Samuel', 174
sandhi positions, 25, 204, 243
scriptural translation, see translation of the Bible
-ščyn(a) suffix, 107
secular style, see high style
Ševčenko Scientific Society, ix, 52, 67n6, 141, 284
Shakespeare's plays: *Antony and Cleopatra*, 291; *The Comedy of Errors*, 290–291, 313; *Coriolanus*, 282, 291, 355; *Cymbeline*, 290; *Hamlet*, 281, 290–292, 301, 308, 315–316, 319n1, 320–326, 331–357, 367, 369; *Julius Caesar*, 291; *King Lear*, 282–283, 291, 355–356, 360–363, 366–367, 369; *Macbeth*, 291, 308, 315, 320–321, 325, 355–356, 360; *Measure for Measure*, 291, 369; *The Merchant of Venice*, 290, 369–371; *Much Ado About Nothing*, 291; *Othello*, 290–291, 296, 298, 306, 309, 355, 363; *Richard III*, 320, 355; *Romeo and Juliette*, 320; *The Taming of the Shrew*, 282–283, 291, 320–321; *The Tempest*, 369; *Troilus and Cressida*, 290–291, 305, 307
slavenorosskij iazyk", see Church Slavonic
Sloboda dialects, 29, 84, 269, 346
Slovar' malorossijskaho jazȳka po poltavskomu narečiju, 65n5
Slovar' malorossijskaho, ili juho-vostočnorusskaho jazyka, 88, 248
Slovar' ukrainskaho jazyka, 79, 112, 184, 187, 230, 326, 327, 334, 341, 366
Slovo, 13n3, 140n6
Slovo na slovo do Redaktora "Slova," 140n6
S'ohočasna časopysna mova na Ukraini, 91

Southeast Ukrainian, 32, 79–80, 82, 88, 94, 96, 102–103, 119, 122, 131, 137, 145–146, 164–165, 187, 197, 207, 210, 229–230, 270, 273, 275, 277, 299, 306, 308, 326, 331, 334–335, 345–347, 350, 358, 363–364, 367, 371, 373, 380, 382–383
southeastern dialects, see Southeast Ukrainian
Southwest Ukrainian, 97, 130, 170, 179, 197, 199, 204, 207, 214–215, 218, 229, 246, 326, 329, 337, 350, 380
southwestern dialects, see Southwest Ukrainian
Sovremennik, 376
spelling, see orthography
staroruščyna, xxi, 47, 159, 344, 354, 375
Studium Ruthenum, 124, 138
Sud'di, 174
Svit, 287
Svitohljad' ukrajins'koho naroda, 245
Svjate Pys'mo, abo vsja Byblyja staroho y novoho Zavitu, rus'ko-ukrajins'koju movoju pereložena, 5, 85
Svjate Pys'mo Novoho Zavitu, 52; *Pys'mo Novoho Zavitu movoju rus'ko-ukrains'koju pereklaly vkupi P.A.Kuliš y dr.Y.Puljuj*, 52

Taras Bul'ba, 62
tautological expressions, 262
The Igor' Tale, 217
Tovytovi slovesa, 61, 156–159, 161, 163, 170, 249, 276
transitional dialects, 162, 207, 270, 303
translation of the Bible: paraphrase, 4–6, 10n2, 18: poetic, 40, 157, 173, 220, 221, 249, 272; prose, 17, 51, 156, 160, 173–174, 177, 179, 192, 213, 219–221, 257, 263–264, 268, 270, 317, 321, 361; scholarly, xxii–xxiii, 40, 42, 49, 86, 131, 193, 204, 255, 292, 375, 383; Synodal, 75–78, 80–82; versified, 270–274
transliteration, xxiii, 4n1
Tȳxomovni spivȳ na svjati motivȳ, 27, 61

-*uč*- suffix, 97
Ukrainian language, xiv, xix, xxi, xxiii, 5, 13, 21, 32, 49, 55, 60, 62, 64, 66, 67n6, 70n7, 79, 90, 93n11, 107, 120, 158, 184, 186, 203, 215, 222, 230, 282–283, 300, 310, 330–331, 339–342, 354, 356, 367–368, 375, 377–378, 380, 384–385
"Ukrainian Shakespeare," 290, 300, 302–304, 306, 313–314
Ukrainophilism, 46, 156, 341, 383
ukrainščina, see Ukrainian language
-*ušč*- suffix, 6, 349

Valuev Circular of 1863, 58–59, 68, 180, 338
Venec'kyj kupec', 290
verb serialization, 262
Vergewaltigung der Basilianer in Galizien durch Jesuiten, 64
Věstnyk", 125
Volhynian dialects, 110, 206, 347
"Vsjakomu horodu nrav" y prava," 20
Vteky, 216
vulgarisms, see Russianisms
Vyl'hel'm Tel', 282

West Ukrainian, 166, 168, 187, 216, 219
western Ukrainian regionalisms, 23, 78, 102, 139, 146, 200, 205, 220, 316
written Ukrainian, see literary Ukrainian

Xarkiv Historical and Philological Society, 67n6
Xarkiv Romanticists, 28, 44, 65
Xliborob, 156
Xutorjanka, 266–267, 277
Xutorna poezija, 281, 284–285
Xutorni nedoharky, 224
Xutorskaja filosofija, 266

-*yj* ending, 170, 170n2, 371
Yov, 4, 145, 157–158, 161, 167–171, 220, 236, 251, 255, 257, 261, 276, 357

x^w counter-etymological, 78, 80, 84–85, 159, 235, 303
Z davn'oho zšytku, 338
Za Neman' idu, 60n2
Zapiski o Južnoj Rusi, 227, 235
Zaxaryja, 174
Zorja, 64, 126, 282, 293

WORD-FORMS

Note: some word-forms cited as random examples are not included

English
brothel, 351
catastrophe, 367
conspiracy, 367
content, 313, 367, 370
fortune, 338, 352, 363, 367
friends, 257, 315, 352
illusion, 334, 351
king, 71, 136, 141, 247, 310, 326, 358, 366
passion, 351
sir, 150, 313, 352, 365
welcome, 352

Church-Slavonic
а҆́зъ 123, 134, 136
бл҃гослове́нїе 12
бл҃же́нъ 133
болѣ́зни 134
врадꙋ 12
бра́тїи 12
бы́сть 99
бы́ти 99
вкꙋ́пѣ 12, 123
внидо́сте 123
во́нъ 100
врагѡ́въ 143
врази 134
вѣ́чныи 123
гд҃ь 12, 133, 134
гд҃и 134
добро̀ 12
дꙋшꙋ 134
е҆го̀ 99, 133, 134, 136
е҆си̂ 134
е҆́смь 136
е҆́сть 123
жа́ти 123
живи́тъ 134
живо́тъ 12, 123
жи́ти 12
жнѧ́и 123
ꙃлаѧ 134
и҆́мѧ 134
и҆сцѣли 134
красно̀ 12
ле́въ 135
ло́же 134
ло́но 99
лю́тъ 133
мѧ̀ 134, 135
мѵ́ро 12
нады 136
нѣгѡ̀ 136
ни́ща 133
пло́дъ 123
погребо́ша 99
поми́лꙋи 134
разꙋмѣва́ю 133
рꙋ́ки 134
сі҆ѡ́номъ 136
скꙋ́менъ 135
сло́во 123
согрѣши́хъ 134
со́ль 100
сохрани́тъ 134
сходѧ́щаѧ 12
сходѧ́щее 12
сѣѧи 123
то́чїю 100
трꙋди́шасѧ 123
трꙋдъ 123
оу҆бо́га 133
оу҆́мре 99
оу҆́мрети 99
ѡ҆бита́ю 135
ѡ҆ме́ты 12
ѡ҆соли́тсѧ 100
ѿ 136
ца́рь 136
чл҃вѣ́ки 100
ꙗ҆́кѡ 12, 123, 134, 135

German
Ablösung, 328
Befleckung, 327
Erde, 258, 259
Fluch, 257
Hiob, 5, 257
los, 327
ruthenisch, xxi, 124
Schandfleck, 327
Strolch, 330
Traktament, 318
Welle, 243

Greek
Ἰωσήφ, 235
καράβιον, 303
φᾶρος, 306

Latvian
kluôns, 119

Lithuanian
klúonas, 119

Polish
błąkać, 328
cynamon, 215
dufać, 327
dworzanin, 218
fala, 243
fantazować, 329
frasunek, 330
fraszka, 320
gadać, 130
gaduła, 130
godło, 121, 327
kmieć, 217
konwencjonalny, 318
kopać, 371
kralka, 326

który, 304

loz, 327
luz, 327
łatoszyć, 328
łotoszyć, 328

męščyzna, 371
mizerny, 260

natchnienie, 294
oznajmującу, 320

potęga, 318
pugilares, 318

skaza, 327
skupowanie, 318
śpiżowy, 329

twarz, 329

ulica, 336
uprzejmość, 294

winszować, 358

zabójstwo, 349
zamiar, 349
zmaza, 327
żądanie, 349

Ukrainian Cyrillic script

благословеньня, 11
благочестивихъ, 15
блаженъ, 28, 31
блаженний, 198
блудить, 319
божкар, 326
божкодайкати, 326
божкородіти, 326
божницû, 144
борзо, 326
борше, 148

варводѣти, 149
вдаюцьця, 258
величество, 370
вивождати, 271
видима, 194
выкурованый, 149
високий, 11
від, 29, 98, 114, 115, 264, 365, 370
відъ, 18, 319
віншувати, 358
вконтентуваньня, 313

владарь, 358
водовъ, 144
вороги, 127, 134, 263
востоціх, 272
вповав, 149
вподобав, 115

Галілеї, 143
Галілеѣ, 143
гараздъ, 31, 294
гармѣдеръ, 149
глаголючи, 74, 114, 115
го, 127, 128, 147, 322
голота, 149
Господень, 33, 271
Господь, 11, 30, 32, 127, 128, 133, 134, 190–192, 198, 226, 254, 271
грішні, 198
громадянського, 178
гроно, 268
грудіх, 264, 268
грудях, 268
гумно, 115
гуртом, 127

Ґалілеї, 143
ґотло, 327

датокъ, 127
дворовикъ, 350
димидіти, 327
діськи, 327
добровоннє, 11
дознаку, 327
докупи, 263
долів, 143
дорогиі, 11
дуфати, 327

Ермонськиі, 11
ехидних, 258
ехидства, 258

єдинородный, 148
єднородный, 148

жданьнє, 271
жидôвска, 144
журби, 127

забресклити, 327
закон, 33, 74, 76, 98
законі, 31, 198
зоружжя, 350

збавлю, 7
здавання, 350
здуфалий, 327
земнородним, 11
зла, 15, 258
злиднями, 263
злотий, 358
злото, 358
злюзувати, 327
злюка, 319, 333
змаза, 327
знуджений, 263
зôправды, 143, 148

ізбавлю, 7
Іоанъ, 115, 148
ид, 114
Йоан, 114, 115
Йордан, 115
Йуда, 263

камѣнныхъ, 144
карбованець, 358
кораблярня, 350
Креститель, 114
клевети, 15
королевство, 149
которогомъ, 115
кохать, 370
краля, 326
кревна, 149
креститисѧ, 115
крещеніє, 114
кличущого, 114

левчук, 135
левчукъ, 135
лихва, 128
личкуватися, 350
лоточити, 328
лудка, 149

марні, 127
маючій, 146
металу, 370
мете, 324
меть, 324
миро, 11
мовлячи, 114
моцар, 149
муки, 7

нев, 147
невгасающимъ, 115

невпорядкована, 194
него, 74, 114, 115, 136, 145, 150, 272, 359
нêмъ, 144
непіт, 328
неплоднов, 147
непороченъ, 15
непота, 328
неприкаянный, 319
нечестивиі, 32
нечестивіі, 198

облазунок, 328
овощу, 115
ôвцû, 144
огонь, 115
од, 7, 11, 77, 98, 128, 258, 435
одежу, 11, 114
ôдки, 148, 150
ôдси, 148
оже, 365
озбройний, 350
ознаймуюющ ий, 319
окаяньні, 264
олива, 178
омети, 11
отацьке, 263
отото, 146
офіра, 149

пада, 11
Пан, 150
певнякъ, 350
пелька, 258
перемотатись, 328
періже, 328
першішний, 328
печали, 7, 271
пітьма, 194
пленичитись, 328
плоди, 33
плôдъ, 143
повсталъемъ, 128
погибає, 198
подуфалість, 328
покаяньє, 115
поночі, 258
постать, 350
потребѣ, 127
поховали, 99
похоронили, 99
поясниці, 114
правдиво, 148
празникувати, 128

премного, 164
преславний, 190, 358
претці, 328
преціньь, 328
прибічник, 350
привиддя, 350
привидок, 350
привіддя, 350
пригарна, 268
придворець, 350
приміром, 11
принади, 271
прихороший, 269
причілє, 350
причілля, 350
причіпок, 351
приятель, 128
просатарь, 328
проява, 329, 350
пустошня, 194
пуща, 148
пючій, 150

раваш, 329
ратує, 127
рече, 115, 194
ризи, 11
родичка, 149
рость, 15

самарати, 329
святиі, 11
сильнійша, 370
Сионі, 15
Сионськиі, 11
сновидати, 263
сокотити, 324, 329
сокотитиму, 324
споломъ, 127
статкомъ, 128
сфантазоватіти, 329
сціленийй, 149

тварь, 329
тварям, 11
творить, 198, 258
темритись, 351
темрява, 194, 254
тиму, 330
тогді, 271, 319
тото, 146

убій, 330
убійник, 330
ув, 115
уповає, 7

фрасунек, 330

хлопакъ, 149
хороба, 149

царство, 74–76, 114, 149
царю, 370

через, 98, 287
черпало, 150
човен, 149, 306
чоловік, 127, 143, 198, 271

шаблёваний, 351
шараньча, 114
штроль, 330
щирий, 128

Roman script
Abraham, 47, 183
Abrajam, 183
Adam, 234
aktjer, 348
alkannje, 303
apel′, 316, 320
Aron′, 234

babuvaty, 218
baby, 106
bačjat′, 103
bačyvo, 220
bahac′ko, 205
bahactvo, 303
bahatyj, 99, 205
bahatyr, 99
bajdužist′, 342
balačka, 371
balakaty, 366
balakun, 371
barytysja, 164
batečko, 105
baten′ko, 105, 366
bat′ko, 78, 105, 165, 348
bazikaty, 366
bedra, 119
benket, 163, 171, 248
bezvidnyj, 167
bezzakonije, 20
bezzakonnja, 26
bezzakonnje, 26, 200
bidolašnyj, 160
Bih, 316

Indices 441

bilaja, 304
bilja, 29
bišenstvo, 306
bižjat'-utekajut', 262
blaha, 6, 272
blahaja, 20, 30
blahannja, 24
blaho, 6, 24
blahodat', 151
blahodatnï, 13
blahodijstvo, 29
blahosloven, 162, 213
blahoslovennja, 12, 24
blahosloven'nje, 162
blahoslovenje, 318
blahyj, 24, 94, 189
blazen', 87, 88
blaznyty, 87, 88
blažen, 31, 130, 131
blažen˝, 27, 33, 131
blaženni, 80, 81
blažennyj, 24, 84, 87, 199
bludnyci, 72
bodjaky, 219
Bohom, 25
bohomillja, 165
bolest', 100, 151
bolězn', 136
bovvan, 247
brama, 247, 294
bramy, 197, 201
branka, 262
brašno, 163
bratïky, 9
bratuxa, 366
bratymu, 210
brexnesvidkuj, 72
brona, 294
brotel', 351
budivlja, 216
budovano, 122
Burhundija, 364
Burkhundija, 364
busurmens'kyj, 165
buty, 209–211

car, 9, 71, 326, 366
carstvamy, 264
carstvo, 366
cej, 186, 207, 244, 304
cerkvu, 122
cmulyty, 308
cyc'ky, 71
cymbaly, 10

cynamon˝, 215
čambul, 188, 262
čari, 295
čarŷ, 295
čeljad', 171, 218
čeljadija, 218
čelověk˝, 130
čelověku, 27
čerevyka, 112
čerez, 98, 99, 111, 147, 246
černec'-lukavec', 352
čertohy, 24
červonijšyj, 346
čestyvost, 302
čolověk, 111
čolovik, 199
čolovik˝, 27, 227
čolovikovbyvec', 72
čom, 219
čudesa, 101
čuliste, 110
čvan'ko, 8
čvannyj, 8
čynite, 104
čystijšyj, 346

dali, 161
darovaty, 130
datok˝, 130
davaty, 35
Dažboh, 326
derevo, 96, 199, 272
deriv, 302
desnyca, 30
desnycja, 163
detyna, 316
dijament, 243
dilajuči, 200
dobro, 6
dobroditel', 305, 367
dobrovonnje, 10
dokolě, 6
dokoli, 6, 20
dolen'ka, 160
dolhoterpelyvyj, 20
domovyna, 165
dorohyi, 10
dosih, 295
dosjah˝, 295
doškuljaty, 8
dovh, 371
dovhoterpelyvyj, 20
dožu, 295

drevo, 20, 24, 29, 96, 179, 199, 272, 299
druzjaka, 366
dubravyna, 217
dubrovyna, 217
duka, 217
dufaje, 94
durosvit, 366
dušehubec', 72
dušohubstvo, 349, 353
dvijči, 346
dvijčy, 346
dvorjanyn, 218, 310
dytyna, 316
dyvno-čudno, 352
dyxannje, 303, 349
džerelo, 349

Ermons'kyi, 10
esy, 30
Evfrat, 233
exydnyj, 260
exydstvo, 260
exydztvo, 305

farysej, 84, 85, 87
fikha, 268
fit', 84
fit'fit'katy, 84
fol'guvaty, 302
forbje, 85
fortuna, 293, 367
fortupljas, 86
furažka, 85
fyhovyna, 269
fylja, 243, 303
fylystiji, 184
fylystymci, 183
fylystymljany, 183

Galileï, 143

hadaje, 130
haduje, 130
Halija, 364
halyčanščyna, 48
Hamljet˝, 316
hamor, 112
harjučyj, 26
harna, 106, 304
harnen'ko, 366
Havrylo, 65, 71
hde, 334
Hemmorenko, 202
het'man, 120, 122, 217, 248, 309, 358

hillja, 25n4
hlaholaty, 87, 101, 121, 151, 196, 216
hlaholjučyj, 97
hlas", 29
Hloster, 364
hlum, 92
hlynyšče, 106
ho, 110, 130, 323
hod, 171, 204
hodyni, 304
holodneča, 106
homonity, 172
honŷtel´, 29
hordota, 344
Horijenko, 202
horjačka, 112
hornycja, 366
horod, 20, 87, 217
hospoda, 78, 86, 216, 267, 366
Hospoden´, 33
hospodnjaja, 113
hosudarstvo, 349
hovirka, 112
hovoryty, 24, 120, 216
hovorytymeš, 210
hręduščij, 146, 151
hrib, 197
hrjaduščyj, 97, 213, 305
hrjanyčnyj, 345
hromadjans´kyj, 178
hrono, 269
hroši, 35
hrošyj, 372
hrudix, 264, 269, 346
hrudïx", 169
hulycja, 232, 268, 303, 336
hvaryv, 117
Hyjob, 5n1, 254, 255, 258
hynuty-pohybaty, 25

id, 118, 160, 187, 205, 206, 302
idol, 247
iljuzija, 334
Iosyp, 234
isty-požyraty, 25
istynno, 78, 87
istyno, 78, 87
iudej, 71
iudejskij, 71
Izrail´, 94

izvidsi, 103

jaduščyj-pyjuščyj, 160
Jakho, 301
Jafet, 235, 243
jasuvaty, 23, 163, 293
jasnyty, 106
jasyr, 262
jasyty, 23, 106
jati, 209, 211
Jaxvet, 235
jazyk, 263, 296
jazŷk ", 124, 132
jedinorodnŷj, 111
jedynorodnyj, 96
jehypci, 183
Jehypta, 92
jehyptiji, 184
jehyptjany, 183, 184
Jerusalym, 10n2
jest´, 82, 97
jesy, 71, 97, 101, 147, 151, 160, 162, 209, 212, 237, 245, 304
Josyf, 234, 235
Josyp, 235
Judyna, 262
julycja, 232, 268
juxta, 294,
Jysus, 267, 267n8

kadylo, 213
karabel´, 303
karablyk, 303
katastrofa, 367
kaznačej, 164
kaže, 97
kelep, 351
k´ernyčyna, 146
khaleri, 301
Khalija, 364
khaljantnŷj, 294
khal´ony, 301
Khloster, 364
khondol´er, 301
khraty, 268
khrona, 268
khvaltom, 301
kiš, 310
klanętymessja, 211
klanjaty, meš, sja, 211
Kljavdij, 315
klunja, 119, 121

klyčuščoho, 118
klymatura, 333
kmet, 217
knjaz´, 122, 217, 273, 366, 371
knyžnyk, 84
kobylycja, 267
kodlo, 121, 366
komonnyk, 218, 273
konspyracija, 367
korablyk", 303
korali, 267
korenja, 92
korol´, 326, 366
koroleva, 351, 368
korolevstvo, 366
korolycja, 351, 368
koryca, 215
korycja, 215
kostoida, 294
kotoryj, 126
kotryj, 9, 81, 148, 200, 209, 304
koxve, 85
kozak, 310, 366
koždyj, 136
krad´koma, 164
kralev, 323
kramnycja, 267
kraščeje, 365
Krestytel´, 119
krivavyj, 302, 316, 345
krovy, 111
krynycja, 146, 199
kryvo, 72
kryži, 248
kurvy, 71
kusok, 90
kuzyn, 351
kyjanci, 183
kyjany, 183

lampa, 214, 215
lampada, 215
lazjuščyj, 213
ledačyi, 24
letjučyj, 272
levčuk, 23, 171
levčuk", 137
levenja, 23, 171
levyk, 23
ližko, 99, 248, 267
ljampa, 214, 215, 336

Indices 443

ljubočyns´tvovat´, 78, 86
ljubodějstvovat´, 86
ljubyj, 92
ljude, 6, 24, 105, 184, 199, 218, 246, 263, 364
ljudej, 105, 111
ljudix˝, 165
ljud´my, 100, 224
ljudohubec´, 72
ljuds´kyi, 24
ljut˝, 131
ljutȳj, 131, 135
locmanyxa, 358
lono, 99, 101
ḷos, 142
lukavyj, 260
lycar´, 217
lyce, 29, 31, 258, 305
lycjari, 217
lyk, 305
lynuty, 25
lyška, 16
lys´tje, 34
lyxodij, 72
lyxosliv'je, 344
lyxva, 16, 25, 35, 130, 137
lyxvov´, 130
lyxvov˝, 130

majdan, 164
majdani, 166
makhnyfyka, 301
mara, 353
maslyčnyj, 179
maslyna, 179
Matvij, 58
maty-meš, 160
maxaje, 347, 353
mennja, 164, 364
merši, 161
meršij, 161
meškaje, 137
meškajučij, 137
mid, 197, 204
mini, 29, 165, 186, 205, 237, 303
mirkuvaty, 199
mja, 110, 130
Mojsej, 94
molodycja, 106, 219
molyš, sja, 93
molyssja, 93, 186
molyššja, 93

monarx, 366
mord˝, 318
moskovščyna, 107
motorno, 353
movbȳ, 136
movčky, 262
movljaty, 25
movyty, 120
mu, 137, 210, 323, 324
muky, 24
mury, 24
Musij, 47, 94, 233
mužčyna, 371
mužes´kyj, 205
muz´kyj, 205
mužs´kyj, 205
myni, 186, 303, 323, 346, 347
myzernyj, 260
mzda, 16

nadežna, 306
nadolužyty, 189
naj, 112, 113, 137
najbil´šov˝, 317
najdorohšyj, 365
najmyčka, 8
najmyt, 8
namet, 171, 178, 179, 218
nanjaty, 9
nan´myčka, 9
nan´myt, 9
narid, 113, 197, 204
narod, 79, 197, 243, 145
narodu, 92
naroda, 92
narody, 104
narodnjaja, 24
naruha, 92
nasinnja, 246, 357
nasinnje, 207, 208, 246
naslědętь, 84
nas´lid´dje, 263, 272
naslidjat´, 84
naslidovaty, 84
naxyl´nist´, 189
nebesax˝, 21, 137
nebesax, 200
nebesy, 9
nebo, 87
neboha, 8
nečestyvi, 199
nečestyvyi, 31

nedijnis´t´, 344
neduha, 100
Neho, 80, 94, 97
neho, 111, 119, 121, 145, 151
neju, 300
nemovljatočko, 105
neobašnyj, 160
neporočen˝, 16
nepotrebnyci, 72
nev, 323
nevěsta, 111
nevmiraky, 267
nevsypučyj, 245
nevsypuščyj, 245
nimeščyna, 107
norvec´kyj, 323
norvedz´kyj, 323
Norveg, 302
Norvega, 335
Norvegčyk˝, 316
norveh, 345
noven´ke, 366
novonastannju, 72
nozi, 267
nuždočka, 8, 13
nyn´ki, 318, 351
nyškom, 25

obereha, 59n1
obid, 171
obikradenyj, 20
'biznanyj, 160
oblyččja, 26, 208
oblyk, 172
obmanjuje, 136
obrjaščete, 101
obuv'ja, 89, 112, 219
obuvje, 112, 219
obvynuvatar, 107
očax, 212
occe, 241
occja, 239, 241
očiju, 212, 264
očix, 346
očix˝, 165, 169
očortity, 294
očyj, 372
očyx˝, 29
'd, 243, 264, 309
od, 78, 80, 91, 97–99, 111, 119, 141, 145, 147, 165, 244, 302, 365

od", 29, 346
Odam, 234
'dcurajsja, 309
'ddaty, 160
odeža, 121
oditny, 80
odjahnyt', 104
odno, 104
'dnoho, 104
odpovid', 42, 346
odrečessja, 93
odrid'dje, 272
okradenyj, 20
okrome, 219
oliva, 179
oltar', 87
olyva, 179
omety, 10
opec'ky, 308
Oron, 233, 234
orudarstvo, 107
oružnyj, 353
oryginal, 316
osavulï, 82
oselja, 25, 107
osuda, 59n1
ošukannje, 309
otamannja, 208, 294
otamany, 248, 262
Otec', 78, 87
otrod'je, 365
ottakol'ki, 352
ovoči, 197, 200
ovošč, 121, 200
Ovram, 47, 233, 234
ovšem", 318
ozbrojnyj, 353
oz'de, 301
oznajmujuščyj, 317, 320

pakybŷtiy, 72
paljučyj, 26
panekhyryk, 301
pane-prynce, 352
pani, 8
panna, 262
pan'skyj, 8
panstvo, 349
parus, 306
pasty, 105, 357
paterycja, 339
partreta, 348
pasija, 351
pečal', 8, 29, 131, 264

pečatanne, 207
pečatatŷmu, 210
pekel'nyj, 88n10
pekol'nyj, 88n10
pel'ka, 197, 260, 261
penjatymeš, 306
pered, 25, 110, 117, 212, 264, 300
peredo, 25, 204, 243, 300
perepolyrovuvatŷmu, 210
perestup, 309
peretopyv, 182
perevaže, 82
perevažyt', 82
peršišnov, 323
pidmoha, 25
pido, 25, 80
pidojšly, 80
pidpora, 25
pidsonni, 337
pidsonnju, 337
pijaty, 317
pijšov, 92
pip, 71
pit'ma, 112, 195
plačušča, 111
pleskaty, 308
plid, 23
plidne, 272
plod", 29, 33, 121
plodjušči, 97
plodove, 29
plodovyte, 272
plut, 306
plutovstvo, 306
počeznuty, 168, 199
podilyne, 363
podružžja, 160
podyvyssja, 145, 168
pohodoju, 317
pojasnyci, 107, 121
pokažite, 104
poklykujučyj, 97
polapky, 260, 261
Pol'onij, 316
polova, 119, 201
pol'ščyzna, 48
pomeršyj, 200
ponapovaty, 105
poperek, 248
poperekŷ, 107
popoisty, 219
porohy, 247
pôrvaty, 137

porxvyru, 84
posažene, 29
poslavšyj, 97, 146
posluhač, 218
posmïšešče, 167
pos'mišyšče, 167
posmixovyšče, 167
posol'stvo, 326
pospišnost', 333, 336
postat', 353
postel', 131, 136
postoly, 339
poštyvo, 345
posylano, 348
potala, 217, 261
potuha, 23, 172, 318
potuha-syla, 25
potuhi, 316
povkydaty, 101
povverhaty, 101
povynen, 304
povynen", 78, 82
pozajak, 246
pozčeznut', 168
pozŷr, 107
požyva, 248
pravaja, 22
praveden, 162
pravednyj, 209n5
pravcja, 22, 30, 163, 220
pravyty, 35
praznykuvaty, 131
predmit, 302
preispodnij, 305
preljubodijstvovat', 78, 86
premnoho, 264
premudra, 24
premudrost', 167
premudryj, 24, 260, 267
prespidnę, 167
prespodnycja, 167
preyspodnja, 167
preyspodnŷj, 305
prijty, 92
pris'bamy, 323
pročane, 263
procent, 35
procentuvaty, 35
prokljat, 213, 304
prokljatyj, 256
prology, 335
proloh, 302, 345
prolokhy, 335
prol'og, 302, 316

promovlja, 347, 353
promovljaje, 347, 353
propovědujušče
proreče, 29
prorok, 101, 102
prorokuvannja, 165
prosju, 169, 268, 269
prošu, 103n12, 268
prosvitnist', 189
provynnost', 313
prozirlyvost', 313
prutko, 240
pryčyna, 248
pryharna, 270
pryhoda, 8
pryhody, 309
pryjatel', 131
pryjmaty, 35
pryključénnja, 309
pryključka, 248
pryljubnist', 189
pryncju, 346
pryviddja, 353
pryvyddja, 172, 357
pryvydky, 172, 219, 220
pryxorošyj, 270
psity, 308
pugilares", 318
put', 30
pyr, 163
pys'mennyk, 87

rab, 101, 171, 217
rabstvo, 263
radnišyj, 346, 365
radyj, 346
ranen'ko-rano, 25
ratuje, 130
reče, 5n1, 29, 94, 97, 121,
    150, 163, 194–196,
    202, 216
rečenec', 247
reměnec, 112
ricci, 239
robe, 29, 165
robotnyk", 167
robotnyky, 171
rodjuščyj, 97
Rodrikho, 301
rozlehlïst', 167
rozmynat'cja, 229
rozpirka, 302
rozxristana, 345
ruci, 267

rukopysanne, 207
rukopys'mo, 165
rumunščyna, 107
Rusalym, 10n2
ruščyna, 107, 376
Ruxva, 58
rycar', 217
rŷkajučyj, 135
ryzy, 10
rŷzy, 120

sčastę, 168
scenka, 352
se, 186, 207, 244, 303
sedity, 160, 205
sej, 186, 207, 303
serden'ko, 352, 366
sestryčen'ko, 366
sim, 170
sïm, 171
s'kaly, 113
skarb, 167, 168
skarbivnyčyj, 164
skelja, 168
skorb', 136
skotyna, 219
skupovanje, 318
skynija, 179
skynja, 179
slaven, 213, 245
slovesa, 163, 179
slučaj, 349
slučajem, 349
smijessja, 232
smutok", 136
snaha, 131
sobornyj, 178
sokotyty, 324
sovsim", 29
spasajuščyj, 200
spasenie, 29
spasennja, 29
spasennŷj, 111
spasïn'nja, 8
spokušaty, 87
spokušuvaty, 87
spolom", 130
spor", 167
spovytuxa, 219
sprava, 24
Srul', 94
ssučyx", 135
ssuščyx", 135
staren'ki, 161

starodavni, 78
starorusy, 47
staros'vickyj, 87
statek, 130
stehna, 107
stežka, 199
stohnanie, 26
stohnanje, 137
stôl'cy, 136
storoža, 306
strava, 248
straž, 306
strebuvaty, 189
streljajuči, 244
stužajuščïy, 6
stydno, 306
sud'ba, 172
suddi, 24
Sud'di, 174
suložnycja, 273
sulycja, 273
sumni, 81
superečka, 151
supokoja, 130
sut', 135
světlyčka, 113
svidčennja, 92, 179
svidčennje, 26, 146
s'vidkuvannje, 92
svidoctvo, 92
svitlyci, 171
svjaščennyk, 71
s'vjato, 104
svjatyi, 10
svŷnej, 105
svyni, 357
svyta, 93
Syons'kyi, 10
syplec'cja, 34
Syrašenko, 267
sxovysko, 197
syžu, 103n12

šaran'ča, 119
šater, 218
šater", 171
šatro, 29
sčastje, 318
sčatkŷ, 240
ščo, 9, 71, 81, 118, 130, 137,
    142, 148, 169, 200,
    201, 206, 208, 209,
    212, 222, 244, 304, 308
ščodennyj, 42

ščynyccja, 301
ščyroho, 247, 268
šeljah, 86
škarb, 167, 168
škelę, 167
šljatysja, 201
šljaxu, 25
šmatok, 90
šolomje, 217
štraxv, 86
štučnist′, 189
štučnyc′kyj, 189
štukars′kyj, 189
šuhaty, 25
švydko, 353
šyrjav, 195
šytyi, 10

tabir, 357
tabor, 357
tamečky, 23
tamen′ky, 24, 105
temnycju, 81
tepera, 351, 352
teperen′ki, 105
teperišnov, 323
teperky, 318
teren, 219
terzaty, 163
tijatr, 347, 349
tiji, 10n2
tisnjava, 23
tja, 110, 261, 323
tjažkiji, 10n2
tjažkyi, 24
t′ma-t′mušča, 25
tobě, 110
tohdi, 272, 334
topnějučij, 137
toročyty, 308
tovarystvo, 267
trepet, 151
tretjačka, 220
tretjak, 220
trivoha, 316, 357
troje, 357
trud, 124
tryjdcjat′, 206
tuta, 351
tutky, 318
tverdïst′, 167
tverža, 22
tvorjaščij, 20
tvorjaščyj, 24

tyxi, 80
tyxost′, 302
tyxyi, 80

ubohi, 80, 102
ubohyi, 80
ubyvač, 220
udjahanka, 93
udovov, 323
ukrajinščyna, 107
ukupi, 13
ulycja, 232, 336
umyraty, 303
urjadnyky, 107
ušax, 212, 304
usix, 145
usta, 84, 87, 197, 245, 260
ušu, 212, 304
utroba, 264
uv, 122, 242, 304
uves′, 103, 104
uvijty, 103
uz, 206
uzhranyččja, 208

važennyj, 263
vbozi, 102
vbyto, 247, 348
vegetujuščoho, 317
vel′moža, 248
vel′my, 293
velykee, 24
verba, 216, 299
verbon′ka, 299
verbycja, 299
vertrohrad, 305
verxovodnyk, 120
veselost′, 167, 171
ves′koje, 119
vhonobljaty, 308
vhonobyty, 368
viči, 212
viččju, 212, 264
vid, 91, 97, 98, 104, 117,
    119, 121, 122, 145,
    147, 151, 244, 302, 346
vid″, 165
vidduxopelyty, 308
vidhet′katy, 107
vidky, 371
vidradošči, 163
viky, 13, 199
vino, 101
viščuny, 334
vistjanec′, 171

vistovci, 334
vïstovỹj, 171
vitrylo, 306
Vittenberg, 326
Vittenberh, 345
Vitynhrad, 326
vkontentuvannja, 313
vkontentuvaty, 367
vkupě, 13
vkupci, 9
vkynuto, 81
vladar′, 366
vladarstvo, 366
vladyka, 305, 366
vlast′, 100
vlyznuty, 308
vmiraty, 204
vodỹ, 29
voenščyna, 313
vojny, 25, 334, 336
volik, 295
volocjuha, 218
volossje, 303
v′na, 323
v′no, 323
vontpyty, 318
vorotar, 247
voskresennje, 101
voskresnuty, 151
voskresyty, 101
vosxvalyty, 24
vovk, 118
vozdaty, 131
vozdux, 348, 349
voz′mite, 302
vozstavyty, 131
vozviščatel′, 162
vozxodyty, 206
vp″jat′, 164
vpokij, 308
vpovaje, 94
vprejmost′, 294
vpryvyleëvanyx, 308
vrěšti, 101
vsen′ka, 318
vsue, 24
vsuje, 366
vtišatcja, 82
vtïšjat′, sja, 82
vuhillja, 25n4
vuhollja, 25n4
vulycja, 232
vverženъ, 81
vves′, 103, 145, 308

Indices 447

vvičlyvost´, 302
vvijdete, 79
vvixodyty, 308
vyd, 107
vydjuščyj, 160, 213
vydovyna, 220
vydumky, 182
vydženje, 318
vyhadky, 182
vynarnja, 267
vynuvatel´, 107
vyšni, 24, 171
vysokist´, 24, 167
vysokyi, 10, 24
vytannje, 145
Vyttenberkh, 326
vyvoždaty, 272
vzjatok″, 16

xarč, 248
xata, 78, 86, 87, 216, 366, 371
xit´, 349, 353
xljaby, 101
xlopci, 171
xlopčyk, 105
xlop'jatko, 105
xlopotá, 171
Xlorencija, 85
xolm, 217, 278
xoromẏ, 171
xotinnę, 169
xovm, 217, 268
xrancuz″, 85
Xrat, 233
xreščennje, 58, 122
xrestytys´, 121
xudoba, 219
xuten´ko, 105
xutko, 353
xvalij, 341
Xvaraon, 85
xvarysei, 80
xvarysejska, 84
Xvedor, 86
xvyhove, 235
xvylja, 303
xvylozoxvyja, 86
xyžyna, 112

yg, 236
yk, 206, 236
yljuzija, 351

yl´ljuc´cja, 264
ynče, 363
ys, 240, 268, 300
yskustvo, 305, 349
yssunuv, 309
ystočnyk″, 349
Ysus, 58, 150
Ysus″, 79
yz, 300, 366
yzdrihnetcja, 229
yzijšov″, 79
yzmyloserdysja, 309

zabijstvo, 349, 353
zabiraty, 204
zadljatys´, 308
zablyščyt´, 126
zajistysja, 219
zajmanščyna, 106
zakavyka, 339
zakovulok, 263
zaky, 219
zalẏčkovuvan´nja, 72
zamir, 349
zamješkaje, 137
zapevne, 78, 87
zapomoha, 23
zapopasty, 197
zaprymitju, 189
zaslona, 25
zastupa, 25
zaturkaty, 308
zavahonity, 106
zavdovžky, 219
zavita, 92
zavitu, 92
zavstydajut´, sia, 136
zavšyršky, 219
zbavyty, 8
zdoroven´ky, 352
zdorovlja, 206
zdrihnutysja, 302
zeliznyj, 197, 316
zemlï, 111
zemlja, 170, 205, 208, 258
zemly, 111
zemniji, 104
zillja, 207
zima, 270
ziždav, 204
zkaraty, 25
zkepkuvaty, 25
zlamaty, 78

zlapano, 122
zlebedyte, 120
zlïščyj, 92
zliy, 113
zljuka, 319
zljušči, 6
zločynec´, 72
zloreččja, 22
zloričyty, 22
zlorika, 22, 33, 199
zlorikyj, 22, 33
zlorob, 72
zlyi, 6
zmahannje, 151
zminja, 29
zmučenẏj, 136
znadlyvyj, 339
znattja, 208, 357
znattje, 207
znaxodju, 103
znaxodžu, 103
zo, 204, 209, 317
zoždav, 204
zperšu, 168
spimnuty, 197
zuzdrity, 219
zvada, 113
zvidtilja, 80
z´vir, 237
Zyjons´ka, 262
zymlja, 205

žadannja, 353
žaha, 349, 353
žakovyna, 219
žena, 96, 111, 160
žertivnja, 87
žeruščyj, 213
žinka, 96,141
žoludok″, 136
žona, 160, 353
žurba, 29, 130
žyd, 71
žydivs´kyj, 71
žyhačka, 112
žytel´, 9
žyttja, 357, 364
žyttje, 104, 146, 303, 317
žyty, 211, 339
žyvota, 30
žyvuščyj, 24
žyzn´, 131, 305, 367
žžyrajut´, 240